Global Navigation for Pilots

2nd Edition

International Flight Techniques and Procedures

Dale De Remer, Ph.D.
Donald W. McLean

Aviation Supplies & Academics, Inc.
Newcastle, Washington

*Global Navigation for Pilots: International Flight
Techniques and Procedures*
Second Edition

Aviation Supplies & Academics, Inc.
7005 132nd Place SE
Newcastle, Washington 98059-3153

Cover photo of Falconjet 900 © Russell Munson

Printed in the United States of America

09   08   07   06   05   9   8   7   6   5   4   3   2

ISBN 1-56027-312-7
ASA-GNP-2

Library of Congress Catalog Card Number: 94-210279

Photography and other illustration credits: cover—Russell Munson, photo; Mayumi Thompson, map/photo illustration; p. xvii – xviii—UND Aerospace Department, W.D. Van Wormer; p. 1—Depts. of U.S. Army and Navy, *Air Navigation*, 1972; p. 48—D. De Remer; p. 54—American Avionics; pp. 57–58—De Remer; pp. 80 – 85—material reprinted with permission Jeppesen Sanderson; p. 100*ff*—"Dataplan" material in Ch. 6 reprinted with permission Jeppesen Sanderson; pp. 107, 112, 116—material reprinted with permission Official Airline Guides; p. 182—A. Bernabeo; pp. 192 – 195—material from WMO Publ. No. 782 reprinted with permission World Meteorological Organization; p. 277—De Remer; p. 315—De Remer.

Contents

3: Maps and Charts   25

12: LORAN-C   217

13: Global Positioning System   227

About the Authors

Dale De Remer was raised in Southern California and received his Bachelor of Science degree from California State Polytechnic University. While completing his Master of Science and Ph.D. at Utah State University, flying became a part of everyday life. During his career, he has served as corporate pilot, agricultural pilot and chief pilot for his own and other companies, while logging over 20,000 hours total time in general aviation aircraft of many types. He holds ATP, CFI-A, CFI-H, CFI-I, and MEI licenses with single- and multi-engine land and sea, rotorcraft-helicopter and instrument ratings. He has over seventeen years experience teaching aviation at the university level.

Dale De Remer is presently teaching as Professor of Aviation at the Center for Aerospace Sciences, University of North Dakota. For several years, he has taught advanced wilderness seaplane pilot courses to pilots from many states and several foreign countries, which take students far north into the Canadian boreal forest and arctic tundra waters, and as far south as Central America. He is Central Northwest Field Director for the Seaplane Pilots Association.

Dale De Remer is also the author of the well-known *Water Flying Concepts*, a text on wilderness water flying; *Aircraft Systems for Pilots*, published by Jeppesen and Co., Inc; *Human Factors and Crew Resource Management for Flight Instructors*, published by Eastern Dakota Publishers (Grand Forks, N.D.); and *Seaplane Operations — Basic and Advanced Techniques for Seaplanes, Amphibians and Flying Boats From Around the World*, new in 1998 and available from the author (http://www.aero.und.edu/~deremer).

Donald McLean began his aviation career at the University of North Dakota in 1969. He received his Bachelor of Science degree with a major in Aviation Administration in 1971. After acquiring several years of experience as a flight instructor and charter pilot, he joined the U.S. Navy, becoming a naval aviator. His duty with the Navy allowed him to obtain a Master's degree in Business Management, a DC-9 type rating, and to serve as an advanced jet flight instructor. In 1980, he was employed as a pilot with Eastern Airlines. He was serving as a DC-9 Captain when Eastern ceased operation in 1991. Don is currently a Captain for the airlines. He holds ATP, CFI, CFI-I, MEI, Seaplane, Turbojet Flight Engineer and DC-9 type rating.

Acknowledgments

The authors gratefully acknowledge the contributions of the many students who have passed through the International and Long Range Navigation, and Global Navigation classes at the University of North Dakota. Many of your research papers and other contributions helped in the compilation of this book. Our thanks to AOPA and several people at Jeppesen, ICAO and NBAA for their assistance. Our special salute to Captain W. VanWormer for his assistance with current materials and the Foreword. He and the many pilots who fly oceanic and other international routes every day, and the controllers who facilitate those many passages, are the big contributors to this very special career field.

Mr. Fred Remer, meteorologist at Weather Mod, Inc., Fargo ND, and Dr. Mike Poellot, meteorologist at the Center for Aerospace Sciences, University of North Dakota, wrote and revised most of Chapter 10 just because they wanted to. Our thanks to them, because they are very busy men.

Everyone should know that we, the authors, encourage and welcome any and all corrections and additions from any who care to make them, in order that this book written for pilots who are learning, will continue to improve and be updated by pilots who are doing and teaching the art and science of international flight.

Dr. Alberto Bernabeo of the University of Bologna, Italy, and an ATP who is type-rated in several aircraft, wrote most of the chapter on European operations (Chapter 9) — our thanks to him for his wisdom about flying in Europe.

Foreword

This book is the result of Dr. De Remer's several years of teaching an international procedures course at the University of North Dakota, during which time I enjoyed numerous discussions with him about how and what to teach in such a course, and lectured to his students on many occasions. Up until now there has been no single, all-inclusive book devoted to international and oceanic operations. Of the airlines flying internationally, each has worked up its own system of training courses for its pilots and dispatchers. Except for a few training courses for general aviation and ab-initio training, there have been no books devoted to the subject. So this text is a welcome addition to fill this important gap in the dissemination of aviation knowledge.

This text presents the background needed by pilots to learn the oceanic system. The book also gives listings of many original sources of information to allow even deeper study.

Oceanic operation with today's equipment, from the light single-engine aircraft up through the B-747, is safe and efficient. In all cases, however, the system and the hazards must be well understood. All of the procedures described in this book are the result of input from present day users of the system. I am sure the reader will be ready to continue learning the system in the air if the basics, as presented in these chapters, are understood. We who do it every day, will be listening for your call on 131.8, if you ever need a "relay".

W. D. Van Wormer, Captain, B-747

Author's note: Captain Van Wormer's piloting achievements are an inspiration for young pilots everywhere. Here are his ratings:

ATP DC-9, B-727, B-767, B-757, L-1011; B-747 Part 121 Check Airman, Domestic & International; ETOPS: Simulator DC-9, B-727; All Seats B-767, L-1011, B-747; Commercial ASES, Glider, Balloon; CFI, Airplane, Instrument, glider, renewals; Designated Examiner, Airplane—all ratings through ATP; Airframe and Powerplant with Inspection Authorization; NWS: Certified Weather Observer.

1: Introduction and International Regulations

Introduction to Global Navigation

Global navigation, to be defined, must be broken down into its two parts. **Navigation** comes from two Latin words *navis,* meaning ship, and *agere,* meaning to direct or move or "manage the movement of." So navigation is defined as the process of directing or managing the movement of a craft from one place to another. A craft is any object requiring direction from one place to another, usually a sea craft, a land craft or an aircraft. Unlike surface navigation, air navigation involves movement above the surface of the earth, within or just above the atmosphere. **Global** denotes operations over the entire earth, giving the connotation of long-range flight navigation.

Air navigation, then, can be defined as the process of determining the geographical position and maintaining the desired direction of the aircraft in order to manage the movement of the aircraft along the desired route toward the intended destination.

Earlier Days of Navigation

Early explorers were aided by the invention of the **astrolabe** (Figure 1-1), which will with reasonable accuracy determine latitude by measuring the altitude of the sun in the sky at local apparent noon, or the altitude of Polaris (the North Star) at night; and the **Nocturnal** (Figure 1-2), which will give a close approximation of the time. (These processes are explained in more detail in Chapter 17.) But it was not

Figure 1-1. The astrolabe

until the 1700s that an accurate chronometer (clock) made possible the determination of longitude, and the **sextant** or octant (instruments which more accurately measure the altitude of a celestial body) made it possible for navigators to accurately—within a mile or two—fix their position on the surface of the earth (**celestial navigation**), even when far from land.

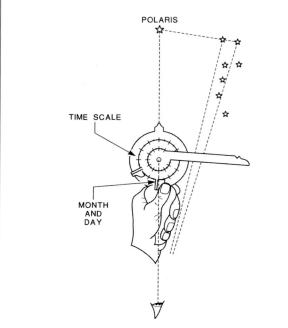

The Nocturnal, an ancient navigational instrument believed to have been invented in the sixteenth century. By sighting the pole-star (Polaris) through the center hole, and moving the long arm until it was parallel with the pointers of the Big Dipper, the hour in sidereal time could be read from a 24-hour scale on the opposite side of the instrument. By means of the small arm above the thumb, which could be set to the month and day, using tables prepared for the purpose, the sidereal time of observation was converted into solar time with an accuracy of about 15 minutes. Since the Nocturnal could fix the approximate hour of midnight, latitude could be found as with observation of the sun at noon.

Some Nocturnals were extremely complex but not terribly accurate. Because of this, and the development of the chronometer and sextant, they were not used as navigational instruments after about 1700.

Figure 1-2. The Nocturnal

The Science and Art of Navigation

Navigation is considered both an art and a science. Science is involved in the development of instruments and methods of navigation as well as in the computations involved. The skillful use of navigational instruments and the interpretation of available data may be considered an art. This combination has led some to refer to navigation as a "scientific art."

As instruments and other navigational aids have become more complicated, an increasing proportion of their *development* has been shifted from practicing navigators to navigational scientists. These navigational scientists draw together the application of principles from such sciences as astronomy, cartography, electronics, geodesy, mathematics, meteorology, oceanography, and physics. Such applications help to explain navigational phenomena and aid in developing improvements in speed, accuracy, or routine actions, to perfect the "scientific art" of navigation.

Early navigators largely practiced the science of navigation; that is, they gathered data and used it to solve the navigation problem in a more or less mechanical manner. It is not until after many hours of flying that air navigators of more recent times began to realize that the navigator's total role involves an integration based on judgment. Navigators build accuracy and reliability into their performance by applying judgment based upon experience.

The Arrangement and Use of This Book

Pilots who must navigate over long distances must be able to plan flights covering all eventualities. In flight, they must be able to evaluate the progress of the aircraft, determine the accuracy of the navigation systems in use, plan for the remainder of the flight, and quickly deal with unexpected route changes. High speed flight demands that they have the ability to anticipate changes in flight conditions, think ahead of the aircraft, and make correct decisions very quickly on the basis of anticipated changes. Many navigation methods and systems are available to the pilot for use in long-range navigation. Some of them, such as dead reckoning and pilotage (which is covered in Chapter 5), are relatively simple. Others, such as INS and GPS (Chapters 11 and 13) are very complex but are simplified by modern, powerful computers. All systems require the pilot/navigator to understand the errors and limitations of the systems in use (Chapter 16), the basics of charts (Chapter 3) and navigation instruments (Chapter 4) in order to skillfully practice the "art" of navigation.

Getting there is a big part of the task, which requires a sound understanding of international procedures (Chapters 8 and 9) and knowledge of international weather data presentations (Chapter 10).

Time is a vital ingredient in any form of navigation, so it is discussed in detail in Chapter 15.

An adjective is widely used with the word "navigation" to indicate the type or primary method being used, such as dead reckoning navigation, pressure pattern navigation or inertial navigation.

Global is one of those adjectives which, when used with navigation, indicates the ability or capability to manage movement (navigate) to anywhere on Earth. This process of managing travel to various parts of the globe must recognize that international boundaries are crossed, people of different cultures and languages are encountered and must be interacted with, and air and ground operating regulations must be known and complied with. Preflight planning, therefore, plays a very major role in the successful execution of an international flight (Chapters 6 and 7).

This book is for the pilot who wants to know more about making international flights, in order that such flights may be properly planned for and executed. It takes the reader from the basic knowledge of air navigation expected of an instrument-rated private pilot onward, well into the subjects necessary to understand the methods and systems used to accomplish flight over longer distances and across international borders.

In the pages ahead, the reader should be alert for **bold words**, as they are special words that should be part of the knowledgeable pilot's vocabulary. The reader will find that the bold word will soon be defined, or has already been defined. The bold word will be found in the index, which is a good place to determine if the word is used elsewhere in the book.

The term *figures* is used for all diagrams, photographs, and tables. Figures are numbered as follows: *chapter number- figure number* (within the chapter). For example, *Figure 12- 4* is the fourth figure in Chapter 12.

Some chapters have study questions at the end. It is suggested that these be used to further solidify the reader's understanding gained in that chapter.

The glossary follows the last chapter. It contains some of the terminology a pilot familiar with long-range navigation and international operations should know. For terms not found in the glossary, search the index, as they are probably defined on the page(s) indicated by the index.

Please note that this glossary is broken into two parts. The first part covers terminology necessary to the art and science of navigation. The second part is terminology necessary to international operations.

Have a good flight!

Sources of Navigational Information

In addition to this text, several other sources provide partial references to all methods and techniques of navigation. Some of these are:

- US Navy Oceanographic Office, *Air Navigation*, HO Pub 216. This is a general reference book for air navigators.

- US Navy Oceanographic Office, *American Practical Navigator*, Bowditch, HO Pub 9. An epitome of navigation, this text provides a compendium of navigational material. Although designed primarily for the marine navigator, it has valuable application for the air navigator.

- United States Naval Institute, *Navigation and Piloting*, Dutton. This is a teaching text for the elements of marine navigation.

- Air Training Command, *Navigation for Pilot Training*, ATCP 51-16. This manual explains the basic principles and procedures of air navigation used by pilots.

- USAF, Air Training Command, *The Navigator*, USAFRP 50-3, published three times per year by ATC. This magazine contains a variety of articles from worldwide sources that relate to navigation and which advance new and different means for accomplishing techniques of navigation.

The following United States Observatory and U.S. Navy Oceanographic Office publications are also available for use:

- *Air Almanac*

- *American Ephemeris and Nautical Almanac*

- HO Pub 9 (Part 11), *Useful Tables for the American Practical Navigator*

- HO Pub 211, *Dead Reckoning Altitude and Azimuth Tables*

- HO Pub 249, *Sight Reduction Tables for Air Navigation*

The Department of Defense (DOD) Catalog of Aeronautical Charts and Flight Publications, published by the Defense Mapping Agency (DMA), contains information on the basis of issue of aeronautical charts.

The following publications from Jeppesen-Sanderson, Inc. will be of considerable value to the international navigator: airway manuals, including low and high altitude route charts, terminal charts, and J-Aid information, for Canada, Mexico, Latin America, South America, Caribbean, Pacific Basin, Australia, Far East, Hawaii, Europe, Mediterranean, Atlantic, Eastern Europe, Africa, China, and the Middle East. Jeppesen's products and services catalog gives more details.

Additional sources of planning material are given in the flight planning chapter (Chapter 6).

A Historical Background of International Air Law

The Question of Sovereignty in Airspace

Two principal theories of national sovereignty of airspace have existed since the early days among international jurists. One side believed that the air was free and therefore individual states (nations) have no authority over it, either in time of peace or in time of war, except when necessary for self preservation. The other side believed that individual states have the right of sovereignty over the airspace over their soil. This group held that aircraft flying only a few miles over the land would be in a position to observe, photograph, and otherwise obtain data that might be used to disadvantage the country overflown.

Airspace sovereignty law evolution started within just a few years of the Wright Brothers' first flight.

The Paris Convention 1919

The International Air Navigation Code is usually referred to as the **Paris Convention of 1919**. The International Commission for Air Navigation drew up a list of the principles to govern the drafting of the convention that included the following:

1. The recognition of the **principle of the full and absolute sovereignty** of each state over the air above its territories and territorial waters, carrying with it the right to deny entry and regulate foreign flights and to otherwise impose jurisdiction over the air above its territories and territorial waters.

2. The recognition of the desirability of the greatest freedom of international air navigation subject to the principle of sovereignty, insofar as this freedom was consistent with the security of the state and with the enforcement of reasonable regulations relative to the admission and operation of aircraft of the imposing state.

3. The recognition that the admission and treatment of the imposing aircraft of the contracting state was to be governed by the recognition of the principle of the absence of all discrimination on grounds of nationality.

4. The recognition of the principle that every aircraft must possess the nationality of the contracting state only and that every aircraft must be entered upon the register of the contracting state whose nationality it possesses.

The following provisions were recognized as desirable from an international point of view to ensure the safe conduct of air navigation:

1. The requirement of a compulsory certificate of airworthiness and licenses for wireless equipment, at least of aircraft used for commercial purposes; mutual recognition of these certificates and licenses by the contracting states.

2. The requirement of compulsory licenses for pilots and other personnel in charge of aircraft; mutual recognition of these licenses by the contracting states.

3. International rules of the air, including international rules for signals, lights, and the prevention of collisions; regulations for landing and for procedures on the ground.

Among the principles adopted to guide the convention were the following:

1. Special treatment for the military, naval, and state aircraft when they are in government service.

2. The right to transit without landing for international traffic between two points outside of the territory of a contracting state, subject to the right of the state transversed to reserve to itself its own commercial traffic and to compel landing of any aircraft flying over it by means of appropriate signals.

3. The right of use, by the aircraft of all contracting states, of all public airports, on the principle that charges for landing facilities should be imposed without discrimination on the grounds of nationality.

4. The principle of mutual indemnity between the contracting states to cover damage done in another state.

5. The necessity of a permanent international aeronautical commission.

6. The obligation of each contracting state to give effect to the provisions of the convention by its domestic legislation.

7. The principle that the convention does not affect the rights and duties of belligerents or neutrals in time of war.

The rules and regulations incorporated in the International Convention for Air Navigation were adopted by the principal European nations. The 34 articles covered the reservation of the sovereignty of airspace by the contracting nations; each nation's registry of aircraft; the issuance of certificates of airworthiness and competence by each contracting nation; the flight of aircraft across foreign territory; international aircraft navigation rules; prohibition of the transportation of arms, explosives, and photographic equipment by aircraft; and the establishment and maintenance of a permanent commission for air navigation.

The Havana Convention 1928

At the fifth Pan-American Conference in 1923, an Intra-American Commercial Aviation Commission was appointed to draft a code of laws and regulations, the adoption of which was recommended to all the American nations. These rules dealt with commercial aviation, the determination of air routes, the establishment of special customs procedures for aviation, the determination of adequate landing policies, and recommendations with respect to the establishment of landing facilities.

The Commercial Aviation Commission met in May 1927 and prepared a draft of the code, which was revised by the director-general of the Union and submitted to the sixth Pan-American Conference, which met at Havana in 1928. The Havana Convention included most of the basic tenets established by the Paris Convention. The draft was adopted, with some minor modifications, and signed by representatives of the 29 states of the Pan-American Union.

Worldwide International Law

With the expansion of commercial aviation after World War I, the need became obvious for drafting an international code of regulations linking the continents, to govern commercial aviation. Commercial aviation, like all other means of transportation, involves many difficult legal problems, including the rights and duties of shippers and carriers and the questions of carrier liability. These questions were handled at the outset by applying the laws of the several nations, but the lack of uniformity among the commercial laws of different countries constituted a formidable obstacle to international commerce and transportation by air. In response to this need, several important international organizations sponsored movements seeking the international codification of commercial aviation law.

The first organized need for the promotion of an international conference to draft a code of private international aviation law was recognized publicly by the International Chamber of Commerce. In its conferences in 1923 and 1925, a resolution was adopted calling the attention of the public to the need for the establishment of a uniform code of international control over private and commercial air navigation.

The Warsaw Convention 1929

This convention for the unification of certain rules relating to international transportation by air applies to any international transportation of persons, baggage, or merchandise by aircraft for compensation. It is commonly called the **Warsaw Convention of 1929**. The United States has been a party to it since 1934.

This convention defined international transportation as any transportation between two points in different contracting countries, irrespective of an interruption of the transportation or trans-shipment, and as any transportation between two points in the territory of one state when a stop is made in another country or countries en route.

The Warsaw Convention provided that an air carrier was liable for damages sustained by (1) death or injury to passengers; (2) destruction, loss, or damage to baggage or goods; or (3) loss resulting from delay in the transportation of passengers, baggage, or merchandise.

Signed on October 12, 1929, the Warsaw Convention has become one of the most important documents in international commercial air transportation. The convention was amended on September 28, 1955, at The Hague, Netherlands, where a diplomatic conference was held primarily to discuss the *limit* of liability.

A diplomatic conference, held in Guatemala City in 1971, adopted a far-reaching revision of the provisions of the Warsaw Convention and The Hague Protocol. Among other things, the Guatemala City Protocol provided for absolute liability (no proof of negligence) on the part of the air carrier, and an unbreakable limit of the carrier's liability of a maximum amount of $100,000 per person.

The Chicago Conference 1944

World War II had a tremendous impact on the technical development of air transportation. A vast network of passenger and freight carriage was set up, but there were many problems, both political and technical, for which solutions had to be found for the benefit and support of a world at peace. There was the question of commercial rights. What arrangements would be made for airlines of one country to fly into and through the territories of another? There were other concerns with regard to the legal and economic conflicts that might come with peacetime flying across international borders, such as how to maintain existing air navigation facilities, many of which were in sparsely settled areas.

The difficulty of carrying on specific negotiation for each new route was one of many reasons the United States and some other nations were anxious for the ratification of international law for civil aviation. In early 1944, the United States government issued invitations to the International Conference on Civil Aviation, often called the **Chicago Conference**. Representatives of 52 nations assembled in Chicago in November 1944. Although invited, the Soviet Union did not send representatives to the conference.

The preamble of this conference stated that the purpose of the document was to foster development of international civil aviation "in a safe and orderly manner" and to establish international air transport service on the basis of equality of opportunity and sound and economical operation. The first of the 96 articles of the conference made the usual grant to each state of complete and exclusive sovereignty over the airspace above its territory. The right of transit over the contracting sites and the right to land in a foreign state is made available to aircraft on nonscheduled flights, while scheduled services must secure prior authorization. Each state was granted the right to reserve to its own airline aviation traffic exclusively within its own borders.

The conference established the application of customs regulations and national traffic rules to aircraft in international flight, bound the states to take effective measures to prevent the spread of disease by air, and granted to each nation the right of reasonable search of arriving and departing aircraft. Among the measures provided to facilitate air navigation were rules for avoiding delays in "immigration, quarantine, customs, and clearance." Aircraft in transit and their normal supplies of fuel and oil were made safe from seizures on patent claims. Each state undertook "so far as it may find practicable" to adopt such standard procedures on airport control, radio services, navigational facilities, use of signals, publication of maps, and similar matters as it was contemplated would be recommended under the terms of the conference.

The conference specified that an aircraft engaged in international flight must carry certain documents, including certificates of registration and airworthiness, licenses for crew members, a logbook, and passenger or cargo manifests. The carriage of munitions was prohibited, and it was specified that a state might restrict the carriage of other articles but that these regulations should be applied uniformly to the aircraft of all states.

The contracting states were required to undertake to secure the highest degree of uniformity in complying with international standards and practices, as might from time to time seem appropriate, with respect to the following:

1. Communications systems and air navigation aid, including ground marking
2. Characteristics of airports and landing areas
3. Rules of the air and air traffic control practices
4. Licensing of operating and mechanical personnel
5. Airworthiness of aircraft
6. Registration and identification of aircraft
7. Collection and exchange of meteorological information
8. Logbooks
9. Aeronautical maps and charts
10. Customs and immigration procedures
11. Aircraft in distress and investigation of accidents, and other matters concerning the safety, regularity, and efficiency of air navigation.

The History of ICAO

The Chicago Conference in 1944 established the **International Civil Aviation Organization (ICAO)**, composed of "an Assembly, a Council, and such other bodies as may be necessary" to foster the planning and development of international air transport in accordance with certain enumerated principles. Permanently headquartered in Montreal, Quebec, Canada, ICAO is charged with administration of the articles under the conference. In 1947, ICAO became a specialized agency of the United Nations.

The ICAO Assembly is composed of one representative from each contracting state. At its annual meetings, it may deal with any matter within the scope of the organization not specifically assigned to the Council. There were 157 member states as of December 1986.

The Council members, composed of 33 contracting states, are elected by the Assembly for three year terms. The Council is charged with the establishment of an air transport committee and an air navigation commission, with the collection and publication of information on international air services, the reporting of infractions of the conference, and the adoption of international standards and practices to be designated as annexes to the conference.

The Chicago Conference of 1944 specifically stated that it superseded Havana and Paris conventions. It also provided that all existing aeronautical agreements and those subsequently contracted should be registered with the Council of ICAO and that those that are inconsistent with the terms of the convention should be abrogated.

Disputes may be settled by reference to the Permanent Court of International Justice or a special arbitration tribunal. Enforcement of the conference is founded on the power to suspend an airline from international operation or to deprive a state of its voting power. The conference does not deprive a state of its freedom of action in the event of war.

The Chicago Conference provided two other significant documents: the International Air Services Transit Agreement, which became known as the **Two Freedoms Agreement**, and the International Air Transport Agreement, or the **Five Freedoms Agreement**.

The Two Freedoms Agreement provided that each contracting state grant the other contracting states the following freedoms of the air with respect to scheduled international air services: (1) the privilege of flying across its territory without landing, and (2) the privilege of landing for non-traffic purposes. The International Air Transport Agreement (Five Freedoms Agreement) also included (3) the privilege of putting down passengers, mail, and cargo taken on, in the territory of the state whose nationality the aircraft possesses; (4) the privilege of picking up passengers, mail, and cargo destined for the territory of the state whose nationality the aircraft possesses; (5) the privilege of picking up passengers, mail, and cargo destined for the territory of an other contracting state; and the privilege of putting down passengers, mail, and cargo coming from any such territory.

These latter freedoms would have in effect eliminated the need for special negotiations in the conduct of international air transportation. Unfortunately, the Five Freedoms Agreement did not receive support from the representatives. The United States was among the original signers of the Five Freedoms document, but the State Department subsequently gave notice of the United States' withdrawal. The Two Freedoms Agreement, on the other hand, received fairly wide acceptance by various nations.

The Bermuda Agreement 1946

Although a number of countries were willing to conclude bilateral arrangements with the United States based on the Chicago format, there were fundamental differences of opinion between some of the countries represented at the Chicago Conference as to how international air transportation should be developed. The United States and certain other countries favored a relatively liberal approach to the problem, without any arbitrary restrictions or predetermined formulas on capacity of aircraft, number of frequencies, carriage of so-called fifth-freedom traffic, and fixing of rates. Another group of countries, led by the United Kingdom (U.K.), was not prepared to go this far and wanted these matters regulated to such an extent that, in the opinion of the United States and other countries, the full development of air transportation would be hampered.

However, as the airlines of the United States, United Kingdom, and other countries became better prepared to offer services to each other's territories, it became obvious that these fundamental differences in air policy should be reconciled. Accordingly, representatives of the United States and the United Kingdom met at Bermuda in 1946 and negotiated a bilateral understanding that is generally known as the **Bermuda Agreement**.

In addition to incorporating the Chicago standard clauses, the Bermuda Agreement provided that disputes that could not be settled through bilateral consultation were to be referred to ICAO for an advisory opinion and also that the agreement should be revised to conform with any subsequent multilateral air pact that might be subscribed to by both countries.

The Bermuda Agreement also included a number of collateral understandings on the operation and development of air transportation services between the two countries. No arbitrary restrictions were placed on capacity, number of frequencies, or fifth-freedom traffic, but it was stipulated that the airline of one country would not treat the airline of the other unfairly.

ICAO—The Organization Described

The Assembly

The Assembly is composed of 152 member states who meet once every 3 years in order to discuss matters of importance and elect member states to the Council.

The Council

Thirty-three states are members for three years, whose representatives work full-time in the headquarters of ICAO in Montreal, Quebec, Canada. Their job is to establish international standards for recommendation to member states and the world. It is the principal executive body of ICAO. Under the council and reporting directly to it are the following:

Council Committees

Air Transport

Joint Support

Finance

Unlawful Interference

Other miscellaneous

Air Navigation Commission (15 Aeronautical Specialists)—
a. Air Navigation Conference
b. Divisional Meetings

Under the Council and reporting directly to it is the Secretariat, the main functional organization that does the day-to-day operations of ICAO.

The Secretariat

Headed by the Secretary General, the Secretariat is divided up into bureaus as follows:

Air Transport Bureau

Technical Assistance

Air Navigation

Legal Bureau

Administration

These bureaus contain the workers from member states who accomplish the tasks specified by the Council. The Secretariat has regional offices in the following locations:

Dakar, Senegal (Western Africa)

Bangkok, Thailand (Asia and Pacific)

Nairobi, Kenya (Eastern Africa)

Paris, France (European and North Atlantic)

Cairo, Egypt (Middle East)

Mexico City, Mexico North and Central America, Caribbean)

Lima, Peru (South America)

ICAO Rules

Implementation of ICAO rules is "voluntary"; however, when a member state joins ICAO, it agrees to support ICAO worldwide. To be ousted from ICAO means air commerce to that country would likely stop, which would be a powerful blow. With only minor exceptions, all members comply with the rules. Domestic rules are gradually being modified to conform with international (ICAO) standards. There are exceptions, but they are minor in nature and are published.

The rules pertaining to Aeronautics are published as "Annexes" to the basic ICAO document. The annexes are organized as follows:

Annex 1 .... Personnel Licensing

Annex 2 .... Rules of the Air

Annex 3 .... Meteorology Service for International Air Navigation

Annex 4 .... Aeronautical Charts

Annex 5 .... Units of Measurement, Air-Ground Communications

Annex 6 .... Operation of Aircraft

Annex 7 .... Aircraft Nationality and Registration Markings

Annex 8 .... Airworthiness

Annex 9 .... Facilitation (the efficient movement of
 air traffic between countries)

Annex 10 ...... Aeronautical Telecommunications

Annex 11 .... Air Traffic Services

Annex 12 ...... Search and Rescue

Annex 13 ...... Aircraft Accident Investigation

Annex 14 ...... Aerodromes

Annex 15 ...... Aeronautical Information

Annex 16 ...... Aircraft Noise

Annex 17 ...... Security

Annex 18 ...... Hazardous Cargo

All of the ICAO information may be accessed on the Internet at http://www.cam.net/~icao.

Signals

Signals that are ICAO-approved for situations of distress and interception include:

Distress and Urgency Signals. To signal a grave or immediate danger, requiring immediate assistance, the following methods may be used:

- an SOS signal in Morse code . . . – – – . . .
- the word **MAYDAY** used in radio calls
- red glowing rockets or shells, fired one at a time
- red parachute flare

To signal a situation where the aircraft is having difficulties, but no immediate assistance is necessary, the following methods may be used:

- repeated switching on and off of landing lights
- repeated switching on and off of navigation lights

If the situation is more urgent, the following signals can be added:

- a signal made consisting of the group XXX.
- the words PAN PAN PAN used. (PAN is pronounced *"pawn"*).

Interception of Civil Aircraft. When the interception of an aircraft is necessary, ICAO has a set of procedures in place to standardize how this is done. Interception is to be a last resort, and it is to be used only to identify aircraft, or possibly to provide navigation assistance.

The interception should take place in three phases, as described in the **IFIM (International Flight Information Manual)**. Pilots flying internationally should be familiar with international interception procedures and signals.

The Safe Transport of Dangerous Goods by Air

Every pilot flying internationally must keep in mind the international rules concerning the safe transport of dangerous goods by air. ICAO Annex 18 contains the general rules about how dangerous goods should be packed and transported and the responsibilities of various parties involved with their transportation. Keep in mind that each country has its own regulations on the subject, which will be similar if they are an ICAO member, but any differences should first be explored.

Definitions

consignment. A single grouping of dangerous goods that are delivered to one party at one particular time.

dangerous goods. Items which are capable of causing significant health, safety, or property hazards when transported by air.

incompatible. A characteristic of some dangerous goods. When substances are incompatible, it means that when they are mixed they are more dangerous than either of the ingredients by themselves, producing dangerous heat, gas, or a poisonous or corrosive substance.

overpack. An enclosure over a package or packages to form one unit to handle.

UN number. A four-digit number assigned by the United Nations to a particular chemical.

Transporting Dangerous Goods

The standards to which States are expected to comply are the ICAO Technical Instructions for the Safe Transport of Dangerous Goods by Air. Domestic flights are expected to conform to the same requirements. Exceptions include substances carried on an aircraft that are required to be on board according to the airworthiness certificate or regulations, and substances for personal use by the passengers.

ICAO Identifying Codes

Aircraft Nationality and Registration Marks

When registering an aircraft, ICAO states that the nationality mark should come before the registration mark. (For a table of registration marks and their associated countries, *see* Figures 1-3 and 1-4.)

Registration marks should be painted or otherwise permanently affixed. They should be on the wings of the aircraft, 50 cm high. They should also be on the fuselage or vertical tail, and be 30 cm high. If these requirements are not met, then some other easy means of identification should be included. The letters, and dimensions of the letters are also given in ICAO Annex 7, which further states that the aircraft should have a registration certificate, and an identification plate. Both items should contain the registration number of the aircraft.

International Airport Identifiers

Airports are identified with a four-letter ICAO code, consisting of a one- or two-letter country identifier and a three- or two-letter airport identifier. Not all airports in a given country have international four-letter identifiers, but those that are considered important do. The country identifiers are listed in Figure 1-5 (on Pages 13 and 14).

Country	Mark	Area Code	UTC
Afghanistan	YA		+3.5
Algeria	7T	213	
Angola	D2		
Antigua and Barbuda	V2		−4
Argentina	LQ, LV	54	−3
Armenia	EK		
Australia	VH	61	+11
Austria	OE	43	+1
Bahamas	C6		−5
Bahrain	A9C	973	+3
Bangladesh	S2	880	
Barbados	8P		−4
Belgium	OO	32	+1
Belize	V3	501	−6
Benin	TY		
Bhutan	A5		
Bolivia	CP	591	−4
Botswana	A2		+2
Brazil	PP, PT	55	−3
Brunei Darussalam	V8		+8
Bulgaria	LZ	359	+2
Burkina Faso	XT		
Burundi	9U		
Cambodia	XU		+7
Cameroon	TJ		
Canada	C, CF	1	−4 to −8
Cape Verde	D4		−2
Central African Republic	TL		−1
Chad	TT		−1
Chile	CC	56	−3
China	B	86	+8
Colombia	HK	57	−5
Comoros	no mark		
Congo	TN		+1
Cook Islands	no mark		−0.5
Costa Rica	TI	506	−6
Cote d'Ivoire	TU	225	+0
Cuba	CU		−5
Cyprus	5B	357	+2
Czechoslovakia	OK	42	+1
Democratic People's Republic of Korea	P	82	+9
Denmark	OY	45	+1
Djibouti	J2		
Dominica	J7		
Dominican Republic	HI		−5
Ecuador	HC	593	−5
Egypt	SU	20	+2
El Salvador	YS	503	−6
Equatorial Guinea	3C		+1
Ethiopia	ET	251	+3
Federal States of Micronesia	no mark	689	+9
Fiji	DQ	679	+12
Finland	OH	358	+2
France	F	33	+1
Gabon	TR		+1
Gambia	C5		+1
Germany, Federal Republic of	D	49	+1
Ghana	9G		+0
Greece	SX	30	+2
Grenada	J3		−4
Guatemala	TG	502	−6
Guinea	3X		+0
Guyana	8R	592	−3
Haiti	HH	509	−5
Honduras	HR	504	−6
Hungary	HA	36	+1
Iceland	TF	354	+0
India	VT	91	+5.5
Indonesia	PK	62	+7
Iran	EP	98	+3.5
Iraq	YI	964	+3
Ireland	EI, EJ	353	+0
Israel	4X	972	+2
Italy	I	39	+1

Figure 1-3. Aircraft nationality and common marks—by country

Country	Mark	Area Code	UTC
Jamaica	6Y		−5
Japan	JA	81	+9
Jordan	JY	962	+2
Kenya	5Y	254	+3
Korea, Republic of	HL	82	+9
Kuwait	9K	965	+3
Laos	RDPL		+7
Lebanon	OD		+2
Lesotho	7P		
Liberia	EL	231	+0
Libyan Arab Jamahiriya	5A	218	+2
Liechtenstein	HB plus nat'l emblem	41	+1
Luxembourg	LX	352	+1
Madagascar	5R		+3
Malawi	7QY		
Malaysia	9M	60	+7.5
Maldives	8Q	960	+5
Mali	TZ		+0
Malta	9H	356	+1
Marshall Islands	no mark		+1
Mauritania	5T	230	+0
Mauritius	3B		
Mexico	XA, XB, XC	52	−6
Micronesia	no mark		+9
Monaco	3A	33	+1
Mongolia	no mark		+8
Morocco	CN	212	+0
Mozambique	C9		+2
Myanmar	XY, XZ		
Nauru	C2		
Nepal	9N		+5.5
Netherlands	PH	31	+1
Netherlands Antilles	PJ		
New Zealand	ZK, ZL, ZM	64	+12
Nicaragua	YN	505	−6
Niger	5U		+1
Nigeria	5N	234	+1
Norway	LN	47	+1
Oman	A4O		+4
Pakistan	AP	92	+5
Panama	HP	507	−5
Papua New Guinea	P2	675	+10
Paraguay	ZP	595	−3
Peru	OB	51	−5
Philippines	RP	63	+8
Poland	SP	48	+1
Portugal	CR, CS	351	+0
Qatar	A7	974	+3
Republic of Korea	HL	82	+9
Romania	YR	40	+2
Rwanda	9XR		+2

Country	Mark	Area Code	UTC
Saint Kitts and Nevis	V4		−4
Saint Lucia	J6		−4
Saint Vincent and the Grenadines	J8		−4
Samoa	5W		−11
San Marino	no mark	39	+1
Sao Tome and Principe	S9		+0
Saudi Arabia	HZ	966	+3
Senegal	6V, 6W	221	+0
Seychelles	S7		+4
Sierra Leone	9L		+0
Singapore	9V	65	+8
Solomon Islands	H4		+11
Somalia	6O		+3
South Africa	ZS, ZT, ZU	27	+2
Spain	EC	34	+1
Sri Lanka	4R	94	+5.5
Sudan	ST		+2
Suriname	PZ	597	−3.5
Swaziland	3D		+2
Sweden	SE	46	+1
Switzerland	HB plus nat'l emblem	41	+1
Syrian Arab Republic	YK		+3
Thailand	HS	66	+7
Taiwan		886	+4
Togo	5V		+0
Tonga	A3		
Trinidad and Tobago	9Y		−4
Tunisia	TS	216	+1
Turkey	TC	90	+2
Uganda	5X	256	+3
United Arab Emirates	A6	971	+4
United Kingdom	G	44	+0
United Kingdom Colonies and Protectorates	VP, VQ		
United Republic of Tanzania	5H	255	+3
United States	N	1	−5 to −8
Uruguay	CX	598	−3
Vanuatu	YJ		
Venezuela	YV	58	−4
Vietnam	XV		+8
Yemen	7O	967	+3
Yugoslavia	YU	38	+1
Zaire	9Q	243	+1
Zambia	9J	260	+2
Zimbabwe	Z	263	+2

Notes: 1. Multiply the UTC by 15 to get the approximate longitude of the country ("−" = Western and "+" = Eastern hemispheres).
2. Add values in UTC column to UTC time to get local time.

Figure 1-3. Aircraft nationality and common marks—by country *(continued)*

Mark	Country	Mark	Country	Mark	Country
AP	Pakistan	LZ	Bulgaria	YA	Afghanistan
A2	Botswana	N	United States	YI	Iraq
A3	Tonga	OB	Peru	YJ	Vanuatu
A5	Bhutan	OD	Lebanon	YK	Syrian Arab Republic
A6	United Arab Emirates	OE	Austria	YN	Nicaragua
A7	Qatar	OH	Finland	YR	Romania
A9C	Bahrain	OK	Czechoslovakia	YS	El Salvador
A4O	Oman	OO	Belgium	YU	Yugoslavia
B	China	OY	Denmark	YV	Venezuela
C, CF	Canada	P	Democratic People's Republic of Korea	Z	Zimbabwe
CC	Chile	PH	Netherlands	ZK, ZL, ZM	New Zealand
CN	Morocco	PJ	Netherlands Antilles	ZP	Paraguay
CP	Bolivia	PK	Indonesia, West Irian	ZS, ZT, ZU	South Africa
CR, CS	Portugal	PP, PT	Brazil	3A	Monaco
CU	Cuba	PZ	Suriname	3B	Mauritius
CX	Uruguay	P2	Papua New Guinea	3C	Equatorial Guinea
C2	Nauru	P4	Aruba	3D	Swaziland
C5	Gambia	RDPL	Laos	3X	Guinea
C6	Bahamas	RP	Philippines	4R	Sri Lanka
C9	Mozambique	SE	Sweden	4X	Israel
D	Germany, Federal Republic	SP	Poland	5A	Libyan Arab Jamahiriya
DQ	Fiji	ST	Sudan	5B	Cyprus
D2	Angola	SU	Egypt	5H	United Republic Tanzania
D4	Cape Verde	SX	Greece	5N	Nigeria
EC	Spain	S2	Bangladesh	5R	Madagascar
EI, EJ	Ireland	S7	Seychelles	5T	Mauritania
EL	Liberia	S9	Sao Tome and Principe	5U	Niger
EP	Iran	TC	Turkey	5V	Togo
ET	Ethiopia	TF	Iceland	5W	Samoa
F	France	TG	Guatemala	5X	Uganda
G	United Kingdom	TI	Costa Rica	5Y	Kenya
HA	Hungary	TJ	Cameroon	6O	Somalia
HB	Switzerland	TL	Central African Republic	6V, 6W	Senegal
HC	Ecuador	TN	Congo	6Y	Jamaica
HH	Haiti	TR	Gabon	7O	Yemen
HI	Dominican Republic	TS	Tunisia	7P	Lesotho
HK	Colombia	TT	Chad	7QY	Malawi
HL	Republic of Korea	TU	Cote d'Ivoire	7T	Algeria
HP	Panama	TY	Benin	8P	Barbados
HR	Honduras	TZ	Mali	8Q	Maldives
HS	Thailand	VH	Australia	8R	Guyana
HZ	Saudi Arabia	VL	Laos	9G	Ghana
H4	Solomon Islands	VP, VQ	United Kingdom Colonies and Protectorates	9H	Malta
I	Italy	VT	India	9J	Zambia
JA	Japan	V2	Antigua and Barbuda	9K	Kuwait
JY	Jordan	V3	Belize	9L	Sierra Leone
J2	Djibouti	V4	Saint Kitts and Nevis	9M	Malaysia
J3	Grenada	V8	Brunei Darussalam	9N	Nepal
J6	Saint Lucia	XA, XB, XC	Mexico	9Q	Zaire
J7	Dominica	XT	Burkina Faso	9U	Burundi
J8	Saint Vincent and the Grenadines	XU	Cambodia	9V	Singapore
LN	Norway	XV	Vietnam	9XR	Rwanda
LQ, LV	Argentina	XY, XZ	Myanmar	9Y	Trinidad and Tobago
LX	Luxembourg				

Figure 1-4. Aircraft nationality and common marks—by mark

ICAO Code	Country	ICAO Code	Country	ICAO Code	Country
AB	Australia	FO	Gabon	MB	Caicos Islands/Turks Islands
AD	Australia	FP	Sao Tome and Principe	MD	Dominican Republic
AG	Solomon Islands	FQ	Mozambique	MG	Guatemala
AM	Australia	FS	Seychelles	MH	Honduras
AN	Nauru (South Pacific)	FT	Chad/N'Djameno	MK	Jamaica
AP	Australia	FV	Zimbabwe	MM	Mexico
AS	Australia	FW	Malawi	MN	Nicaragua
AY	Papua/New Guinea	FX	Lesotho	MP	Panama
A1	Antartica (Aus/NZ)	FZ	Zaire	MR	Costa Rica
BG	Greenland	F1	Antarctica (Afr.)	MS	El Salvador
BI	Iceland	GA	Mali	MT	Haiti
CF	Miquelon Island/St.Pierre Island (Canada)	HA	Ethiopia	MU	Cuba
CY	Canada	HB	Burundi	MW	Cayman Islands
DA	Algeria	HC	Somalia	MY	Bahamas
DB	Benin	HE	Egypt	MZ	Belize
DF	Burkina Faso	HF	Djibouti	NC	Cook Islands
DG	Accra/Ghana	HK	Kenya/Nairobi	NF	Fiji Islands/Tonga
DI	Ivory Coast	HL	Libya	NG	Kiribati/Tuvalu (S. Pacific)
DN	Nigeria	HR	Rwanda	NI	Niue (S. Pacific)
DR	Niamey/Niger	HS	Sudan	NL	Futuna Islands/Wallis Islands
DT	Tunisia	HT	Tanzania	NS	American Samoa/Western Samoa
DX	Togo	HU	Uganda	NT	French Polynesia/Society Islands/Tuamotu Islands
EB	Belgium	K1	USA; Idaho, Montana, Oregon, Washington, Wyoming	NV	Vanuatu
ED	Germany	K2	USA; Arizona, California, Colorado, Nevada, New Mexico, Utah	NW	New Caledonia
EF	Finland	K3	USA; Iowa, Kansas, Minnesota, Missouri, Nebraska, North Dakota, South Dakota	NZ	New Zealand
EG	Shanwick Oceanic/ United Kingdom	K4	USA; Houston Oceanic Control Area, Arkansas, Louisiana, Oklahoma, Texas	OA	Afghanistan
EH	Netherlands	K5	USA; Illinois, Indiana, Kentucky, Michigan, Ohio, Wisconsin	OB	Bahrain
EI	Ireland	K6	USA; New York Oceanic	OE	Jedda/Saudi Arabia
EK	Denmark/Faroe Islands	LA	Albania	OI	Iran
EL	Luxembourg	LB	Bulgaria	OJ	Jordan
EN	Norway	LC	Cyprus/Republic of North Cyprus	OK	Kuwait
EP	Poland	LE	Spain	OL	Lebanon
ES	Sweden	LF	France	OM	United Arab Emirates
ET	Germany	LG	Greece	OO	Oman
FA	Bophuthastwana/Ciskei/ Johannesburg/Namibia South African Republic/ Southwest Africa/ Transkei/Venda	LH	Hungary	OP	Pakistan
FB	Botswana	LI	Italy	OR	Iraq
FC	Brazzaville/Congo	LK	Czechoslovakia	OS	Syria
FD	Swaziland	LL	Israel/Jerusalem	OT	Qatar
FE	Central African Republic	LM	Malta	OY	Yemen Arab Republic
FG	Equatorial Guinea	LO	Austria	P	Oakland OCTA
FH	Acension/St. Helena	LP	Azores/Madeira Island/Portugal/ Santa Maria Oceanic	PA	Alaska
FI	Mauritius	LR	Romania	PC	Kiribati
FJ	British Indian Ocean Tr/Chagos Archipelago	LS	Switzerland	PG	Guam/Mariana Islands
FK	Cameroon	LT	Turkey	PH	Hawaii
FL	Zambia	LX	Gibralter	PJ	Johnston Atoll
FM	Antanarivo/Cormors/ Madagascar/Mayotte Island/ Reunion	LY	Yugoslavia	PK	Marshall Islands
FN	Angola			PL	Kiribati
				PM	Midway Island
				PT	Caroline Islands/Micronesia/ Palau
				PW	Wake Island
				RC	Taiwan
				RJ	Japan

Figure 1-5. ICAO identifiers for international airports

ICAO Code	Country	ICAO Code	Country	ICAO Code	Country
RK	Korea	TK	St. Kitts/Nevis Island	WA	Indonesia
RO	Japan	TL	St. Lucia	WB	Brunei/Malaysia
RP	Philippines	TN	Aruba/Netherland Antilles	WI	Indonesia
SA	Argentina	TQ	Anguilla	WM	Malaysia
SB	Brazil	TR	Montserrat Island	WP	Indonesia
SC	Chile/Easter Island	TT	Tobago Island/Trinidad	WR	Indonesia
SE	Ecuador	TU	British Virgin Islands	WS	Singapore
SF	Falkland Island	TV	St Vincent	ZB	China, Peoples Republic of
SG	Paraguay	TX	Bermuda	ZG	China, Peoples Republic of
SK	Colombia/San Andres	VA	India	ZH	China, Peoples Republic of
SL	Bolivia	VC	Sri Lanka	ZK	Korea, Democratic Peoples Republic of
SM	Suriname	VD	Kampuchea		
SO	French Guiana	VE	India	ZL	China, Peoples Republic of
SP	Peru	VG	Bangladesh	ZM	Mongolia
SU	Uruguay	VH	Hong Kong	ZP	China, Peoples Republic of
				ZS	China, Peoples Republic of
SV	Venezeula	VI	India	ZU	China, Peoples Republic of
SY	Guyana	VL	Laos	ZW	China, Peoples Republic of
S1	Antarctica (Argentina, Chile)	VM	Macau	ZY	China, Peoples Republic of
TA	Antigua	VN	Nepal		
TB	Barbados	VO	India		
TD	Dominica	VQ	Bhutan		
TF	Guadeloupe/Martinique	VR	Maldives		
TG	Grenada	VT	Thailand		
TI	Virgin Islands	VV	Vietnam		
TJ	Puerto Rico	VY	Myanmar		

Figure 1-5. ICAO identifiers for international airports *(continued)*

Country	Mark	Country	Mark
Azerbaijan	4K	Republic of Moldova	ER
Belarus	EW	Russian Federation	RA
Bosnia and Herzegovina	T9	San Marino	T7
Brazil	PR, PU	Slovakia	OM
Croatia	9A	Slovenia	S5
Democratic Republic of the Congo	9Q	Tajikistan	EY
Eritrea	E3	Turkmenistan	EZ
Estonia	ES	Uzbekistan	UK
Georgia	4L	United Kingdom Colonies and Protectorates	
Guinea-Bissau	J5	Anguilla	VP-A
Kyrgyzstan	EX	Bermuda	VP-B
Latvia	YL	Cayman Islands	VP-C
Lithuania	LY	Falkland Islands (Malvinas)	VP-F
Macedonia (former Yugoslav Republic of)	Z3	Gibralter	VP-G
Marshall Islands	V7	Virgin Islands	VP-L
Micronesia (Federated States of)	V6	Montserrat	VP-M
Mongolia	JU	St. Helena/Ascension	VP-H
Namibia	V5	Turks and Caicos	VQ

Figure 1-6. Addendum to Figure 1-3 aircraft nationality and common marks

2: Earth Reference Systems

Location

"We are not lost… we're here… it's where we're going that's lost!"

Most pilots have experienced the undesirable feeling of not knowing exactly where they are and also the good feeling of re-establishing their position. Knowing and expressing where the aircraft is at any given time is done in reference to a point on the earth's surface. This point may be either real (an airport, a town, a navaid) or imaginary (intersection of a line of latitude and longitude, or VOR radial and DME distance). For most of us, our first reference point was the airport from which we departed, and for most of us, we concentrated so heavily on the mechanics of flying the airplane that we lost track of where the airport was. We had to rely on our instructor to help us find the airport. Remember?

In order to locate ourselves and to describe the location, reference systems are used to respond to the question: where are you? "I'm in room 206." "I'm at the corner of 5th and Main streets." "I'm in the garage." These are all examples of reference systems that are used daily. There are many reference systems that can be used by navigators, but only two are in general use by modern air navigators. These two systems are called FRD and latitude/longitude. In addition, there is a *concept* that is used by all navigators. First, let's take a look at that concept, which involves the **LOP** and the **fix**.

LOP and Fix

A **line of position (LOP)** is a line containing all possible geographic positions of the observer at a given instant of time. If I told you that I was on Main street, you would know that I was somewhere on a line as defined by Main street. Other examples of lines of position: the aircraft's position is on the 335° radial of the VOR, or on the 335° bearing from the NDB, or on the center line of the LOC.

Additionally, the line of position doesn't have to be a straight line. It can be a curved line such as on the 7 mile DME arc (actually, DME provides a hemispherical LOP), or an irregular line such as over the west coastline. One LOP only partially defines a position. Two intersecting LOPs are required to define a position or establish a **fix**. Examples of a fix defined by two intersecting LOPs are: 5th and Main streets; the 335° radial of the VOR at 7 DME (remember, a **radial** is an imaginary line drawn *from* the VOR); over the coastline (an irregular LOP) 10 miles south of the Golden Gate Bridge (an arc LOP).

The term "fix" describes a geographic position which can be defined by intersecting LOPs, latitude/longitude (actually two LOPs), the location of a navaid, a well known geographical feature, etc.

FRD

FRD is an acronym for Fix/Radial/Distance. It defines two LOPs, and thus a geographical position (fix). A distance and direction from a known geographical position defines the location of the aircraft.

Examples are:

TVF / 094 / 14 .... VOR / radial / distance

CKN / 176 / 24 .... NDB or airport (co-located in this case) / radial (*see Note* below) / distance.

The above examples of FRDs would be acceptable as departure points, destinations, or enroute fixes when filing flight plans, provided the fix used in the FRD is defined in the NAS (National Airspace System computer).

Note: When studying VOR and NDB navigation, we learned that the term *radial* applied to VOR navigation and NDBs (ADF navigation stations) always used the term *bearing*, never *radial*. In the case of the FRD, however, *radial* refers to a magnetic direction from any fix. Perhaps it is time to pause and review the direction terms a pilot-navigator uses.

Direction

Terms of Direction

Direction is the position of one point in space relative to another without reference to the distance between them. The time-honored nautical *point system* (22.5°/point) for specifying a direction (north, north-north-west, northwest, west-northwest, west, etc. or, in saltier terms: "steer two points west o' north") is not sufficiently accurate for modern navigation, but it provided the beginning of the compass rose direction system based on dividing the horizon into 360°. One of the two points in space, the reference point, is the direction to the true North Pole (000°) and the true South Pole (180°), giving a compass rose aligned to provide *true* direction (*see* Figure 2-1). If the compass rose is aligned with the magnetic north and south poles, *magnetic* direction values are provided. It is necessary for the navigator to always specify which system is in use.

Since determination of direction is one of the most important aspects of the navigator's work, the various terms of direction should be clearly understood.

Azimuth is the true direction to a point in space. Usually, the point in space is a celestial body (star, sun, moon or planet).

Bearing is the horizontal direction of one terrestrial point from another. As illustrated in Figure 2-2,

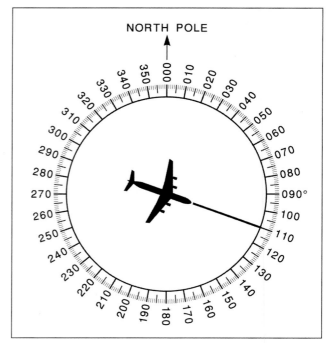

Figure 2-1. Compass rose, aligned to give true direction

the direction of the island from the aircraft is marked by the line of sight (a **visual bearing**). Bearings are usually expressed in terms of (1) true north (**true bearing**), (2) magnetic north (**magnetic bearing**), or (3) the direction clockwise from the nose of the aircraft (**rel-**

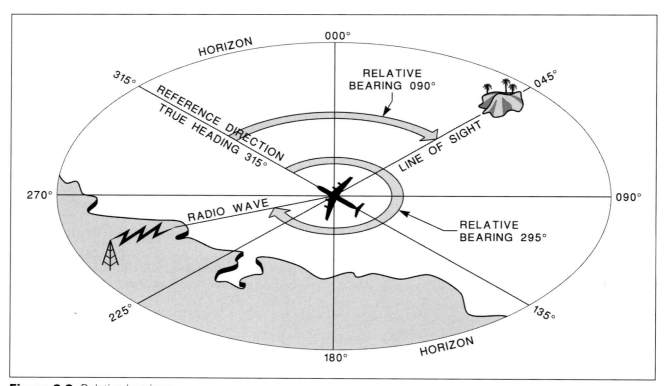

Figure 2-2. Relative bearings

ative bearing). In Figure 2-2, the island is located on a visual relative bearing from the aircraft of 090° or a true bearing of 315° + 090° = 405° − 360° = 045°. (Remember from your study of ADF navigation that MH + RB = MB). Likewise, in the diagram, the radio station bears 295° relative from the aircraft. What is the radio station's true bearing from the aircraft?

Course is the intended horizontal direction of travel. Remember to specify true or magnetic.

Heading is the horizontal direction in which an aircraft is pointed—the orientation of the longitudinal axis of the aircraft, with respect to true or magnetic north.

Radial is the bearing from a VOR station to the aircraft. Expressed as magnetic direction except for a few VOR stations that are located at very high latitudes. A notable variation is the use of the term when defining an FRD.

Track is the actual horizontal direction of travel made by the aircraft.

A complete explanation of these terms and their use in navigation is given in the glossary.

Great Circle and Rhumb Line Direction

The *direction* of the **great circle route** (Figure 2-3) makes an angle of about 50° with the meridian of New York, about 90° with the meridian of Iceland, and a still greater angle with the meridian of London. In other words, the direction of the great circle with respect to true north is constantly changing as progress is made along the route, and is different at every point along the great circle. Flying such a route requires constant change of direction and therefore would be more difficult to fly than a rhumb line course defined below. The great circle route is more desirable because it is the shortest route between two points on a spheroid such as the earth.

The exception to the above would be a flight tracking true north or south, since meridians (lines of constant longitude) are great circles, and no change of true course is necessary to fly along a meridian. Obviously, the more east-west a great circle route lies, the more true heading change is necessary to maintain the great circle route.

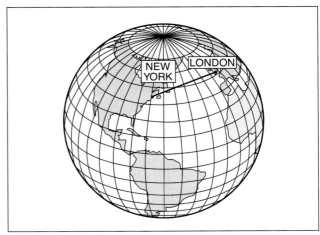

Figure 2-3. The Great Circle Route crosses meridians at different angles.

A line which makes the same angle with each meridian (except a true north or true south line) is called a **rhumb line**. An aircraft holding a constant true heading (that has an easterly or westerly component) is flying a rhumb line. The rhumb line path results in a greater distance traveled. If continued, a rhumb line spirals toward one of the poles in a constant true direction, but theoretically never reaches the pole. The spiral formed is called a **loxodrome** or loxodromic curve, as shown in Figure 2-4.

Distance

Distance is the spatial separation between two points. It is measured by the length of a line joining the two points, expressed in units of length such as kilometers, statute miles, nautical miles, etc. Distance measured between two points on a plane surface is a relatively simple matter. However, distance between two points on a sphere such as the earth involves the length of arcs and the use of spherical trigonometry. In order to simplify calculations, air navigation sometimes utilizes the assumption that the earth is a plane surface. To do so requires that the navigator accept the error associated with this assumption. When navigating long distances, this error becomes too large to be acceptable. The fact that the earth is nearly a sphere must be acknowledged in order to achieve accuracy.

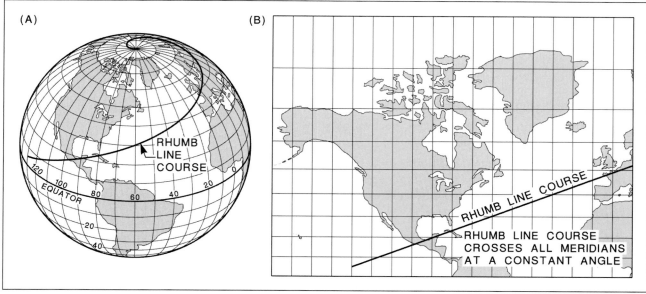

Figure 2-4. The rhumb line (or loxodrome) crosses all meridians at the same angle.

In air navigation, the most common unit of measuring distances is the **nautical mile**. For most practical navigational purposes, all of the following units are used interchangeably as being equivalent to one nautical mile:

- 6,076.1 feet (nautical mile)
- 6,087.08 feet — one minute of arc on the earth's equator (geographic mile)
- One minute of arc of a great circle on a sphere having the same area as that of the earth
- One minute of arc of latitude — that is, one minute of arc along a **meridian** (a line of longitude)

Conversion of statute miles to nautical miles can be accomplished by using the ratio of 76 statute miles to 66 nautical miles, or roughly 7 to 6, or 1.15:1.

Closely related to the concept of distance is **speed**, the rate of change of position, or distance/time. It is customary to use the terms **knots** for "nautical miles per hour," and MPH for statute miles per hour. For example, 150 nautical miles/hour is 150 knots, or 172.7 MPH. It is incorrect to use the term "150 knots/hour" unless referring to acceleration.

Latitude and Longitude

Since **latitude** and **longitude** and **great** and **small circles** are terms specific to spheres like the earth, a little background knowledge about the earth's size and shape is important.

Size and Shape of the Earth

For many navigational purposes, the earth is assumed to be a perfect sphere, although in reality it is not quite perfect. Inspection of the earth's crust reveals that there is a height variation of approximately 12 miles from the top of the tallest mountain to the bottom of the deepest point in the ocean. Smaller variations in the surface (valleys, mountains, oceans, etc.) cause an irregular appearance.

Measured at the equator, the earth is approximately 6,887.91 nautical miles in diameter, while the polar diameter is approximately 6,864.57 NM. This difference expresses the **ellipticity** of the earth. Sometimes, this is expressed as a ratio of the difference between polar and equatorial diameters to the equatorial diameter:

Ellipticity = (6,887.91 − 6,864.57)/6,887.91 = 1:295

Since the equatorial diameter exceeds the polar diameter by only 1 part in 295, the earth is very nearly spherical. A symmetrical body having the same dimensions as the earth, but with a smooth surface, is called an **oblate spheroid**.

In Figure 2-5, the points Pn, E, Ps, and W represent points on the surface of the earth. Points Pn and Ps represent the aids of rotation. As viewed from space at the perspective of this figure, points on the visible surface move from left to right or west to east. If the earth were to be viewed looking down on the north pole, the earth would appear to be rotating counterclockwise at the rate of 15.04° per hour or 360.96° per 24-hour day.

The **equator** (the circumference W-E) is defined as an *imaginary circle on the surface of the earth, equidistant from the north and south poles, whose plane passes through the center of the earth and is perpendicular to the axis of rotation.*

Great and Small Circles

A **great circle** is a circle on the surface of a sphere whose center and radius are those of the sphere itself. It is the largest circle that can be drawn on the sphere. It is the intersection with the surface of the earth, of any plane which passes through the center of the earth.

Understanding the concept of the great circle is important to any navigator because the arc of a great circle is the shortest distance and most direct route between any two points on the surface of a sphere, just as a straight line is on a plane surface.

Circles on the surface of a sphere other than great circles are called **small circles**. Great and small circles are shown in Figure 2-6.

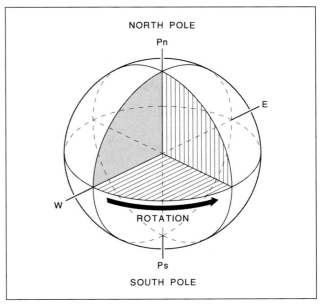

Figure 2-5. A representation of the earth showing rotation, spin axes, and equator

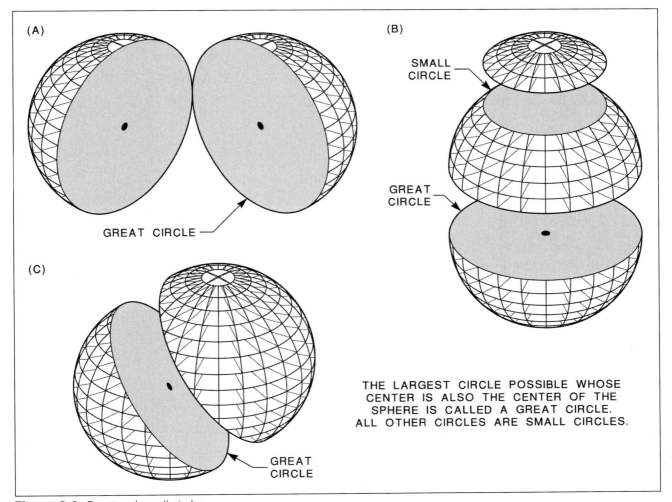

THE LARGEST CIRCLE POSSIBLE WHOSE CENTER IS ALSO THE CENTER OF THE SPHERE IS CALLED A GREAT CIRCLE. ALL OTHER CIRCLES ARE SMALL CIRCLES.

Figure 2-6. Great and small circles

Latitude and Longitude as a Reference System

This is the geographical reference system most commonly used for spherical surfaces. Air and marine navigators, particularly those working with long distances, utilize this system to a great extent. All long distance navigation systems (LORAN, GPS, INS, etc.) utilize the latitude/longitude system.

Once a day, the earth rotates on its north-south axis which is terminated by the north and south geographic poles. The imaginary line of the **equator** is constructed along the surface of our sphere, midway between the poles, creating a great circle. If one were able to journey to the exact center of the earth and there set up a surveyor's transit to measure the angle between a sight to the north or south pole and a sight to any point on the equator, the angle (Pn-C-Q or Ps-C-Q of Figure 2-7) would be found to be 90°. Arbitrarily, let us call the equator, which is the only possible great circle lying directly east-west, the reference for east-west lying lines of position, and assign it a value of zero degrees.

Now, after sighting from the center of the earth (C) to the equator (Q), imagine changing the angle of the sight 30° toward the north pole and having the surveyor's helper pound stakes wherever the line of the sight intersected the earth's surface. The stakes would mark the 30° north parallel (M-M'). It is labeled such because it is located in the northern hemisphere and is separated from the equator (the reference point) by 30° of arc (Q-M).

It is apparent from Figure 2-7 that the lines of **latitude** are labeled based on the degrees of angle or arc, north or south of the equator, and that these lines are circles (when viewed from a perspective above the north pole). Except for the equator, they are small circles because they do not fit the definition of a great circle. They are all parallel to each other when viewed from the perspective of Figure 2-7, hence they are called **parallels**.

It should now be apparent that line N-N' (in Figure 2-7) describes the 45° south parallel. All points on this line are at latitude 45° south. The north pole is at latitude 90° north and the south pole is 90° south. Thus, any point on the surface of the earth may be assigned a value of latitude, which is a line of position (LOP) running E-W, parallel to the equator. The point requires another LOP (longitude) to properly define its location (fix) on the surface of the sphere.

Half of a great circle, which is a line drawn on the earth's surface from pole to pole, is called a **meridian**.

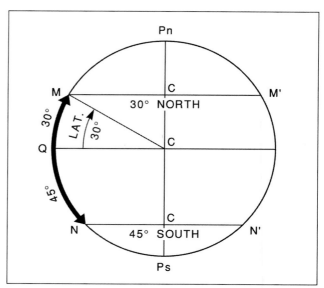

Figure 2-7. Latitude of M is angle QCM or arc QM.

If a meridian is drawn from the north pole, through a point on the grounds of the royal observatory near Greenwich, England, to the south pole (remember, the plane within this semicircular line must pass through the center of the earth), the **Prime Meridian** is the result, which is given the value of 0° of longitude. The other half of this great circle, occurring half-way around a 360° circle, has a value of 180° of longitude and is the meridian called the **International Date Line**. (*See* Figures 2-8 and 2-9).

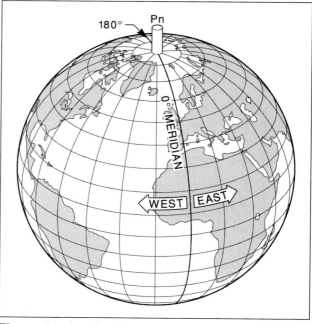

Figure 2-8. Longitude is measured east and west of the Greenwich Meridian.

Longitude is the angular distance along the arc from the Prime Meridian or Greenwich Meridian to the location of the point. This defines a second LOP which runs N-S through the point. All lines of longitude (meridians) are great circles.

Values of latitude range from 0° to 90° north and 0° to 90° south. Values of longitude range from 0° to 180° east and west. When expressing latitude and longitude, latitude values are *always* given first. A degree may be broken down into its smaller parts: *minutes* and *seconds*. There are 60 seconds per minute and 60 minutes per degree. One minute of latitude (measured N-S along any meridian) is equal to one nautical mile. One minute of longitude (measured E-W along lines of latitude) is equal to one nautical mile *only at the equator*.

It is apparent that meridians get closer together as they approach the poles, so the distance between minutes of longitude decreases as latitude increases. Nautical miles per minute of longitude = 1 x Cosine of the latitude. For example: at 50° north, one minute of longitude = 1 x Cos 50° = .643 NM.

Various formats for reporting lat./lon. are in use today, including degrees, minutes and seconds (ddd:mm:ss); degrees, minutes and decimal fractions of minutes (ddd:mm.m) or (ddd:mm.mm). Converting from one to the other is not difficult, recalling that 60s = 1 NM, so 6s = .1 NM. For example, 35°12'18" converts to 35°12.3'.

In addition, the computers in our navigation equipment today are not standardized with respect to lat./lon. input format. For example, the input format for the example in the paragraph above could be 3512.3, 35.12.3, 3512.30, 35.12.30, or 35123 or 351230, if the value was for latitude. Longitude values are slightly more complex as there is one more digit. Some computers require the input to be preceded by a zero if the value of longitude is less than 100°, and some computers do not require this. For example, the longitude 94°30 minutes west is input into the DUAT system as 9430 when filing a flight plan. It is input into the FAA (flight service station) computer as 09430. The values north and west (lat./lon.) are not required as they are assumed for US flight plans because all areas within the US are north latitudes and west longitudes. I often use a LORAN in which the same value is entered as 094.30.00 (west is assumed by the computer but can be changed during input).

The need for standardization is obvious, but it simply doesn't exist; therefore, there is a tremendous need to *exercise extreme caution when values are input into any*

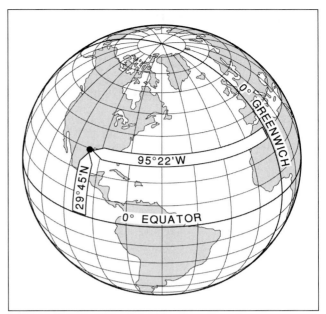

Figure 2-9. Latitude is measured north and south from the equator. Longitude is measured east and west from the Prime Meridian.

navigation computer. Will standardization occur? A pessimist would say that we need only take a look at the CDI instruments manufactured by King and Narco, the "big two" general aviation avionics manufacturers, during the past thirty years to find that standardization is not likely. (One manufacturer's unit reads the value at the top and the reciprocal at the bottom, while the other's is reversed.)

A Change in the Geodetic Referencing System

On October 15, 1992, the horizontal geodetic referencing system used in all charts and chart products published by the National Oceanic and Atmospheric Administration (NOAA)/National Ocean Service (NOS) changed from the North American Datum of 1927 (NAD27) to the North American Datum of 1983 (NAD83). Pilots should become familiar with this congressionally-mandated change because it affects the latitude and longitude coordinates of almost all points identified in the National Airspace System. The coordinates have changed by zero to 16 seconds (of latitude and longitude).

In the United States, latitude and longitude are based on a network of geodetic control points established and maintained by the National Geodetic Survey (Department of Commerce). Control point coordinates are determined mathematically based on a reference point. The NAD27 used a reference point in Kansas for the lower 48 states (conterminous U.S.), Canada, and Alaska. Technological advances of Global Positioning Systems (GPS) and other systems now allow satellite systems to pinpoint much more accurately geographic locations by referencing the center of the earth. NAD83 is based on the center of the earth and geodetically ties Puerto Rico and Hawaii to North America.

The greatest coordinate shifts are in Alaska and Hawaii where latitude has been moved by as much as 1,200 feet and longitude by up to 950 feet. In the conterminous U.S., the maximum changes were approximately 165 feet in latitude and 345 feet in longitude. Magnetic variation will be altered so minutely the aviation community need not be concerned.

The shift is not significant enough to change the latitude and longitude grid on Sectional Charts or WACs, but it could change the grid on the TACs, Helicopter Charts, and Sectional Insets, and most certainly will affect Airport Diagram Charts. All coordinates in the Digital Aeronautical Chart Supplement, Airport/Facility Directory, Pacific and Alaska Chart Supplements, on enroute navigation charts and all digital products sold by NOS or FM have been affected.

User questions relating to NOS charts and chart products should be directed to 1-800-626-3677.

Summary

All of the information in this chapter is considered basic and necessary to the knowledge base of the pilot/navigator, so the reader should not consider this summary section as the "bottom line, all that's needed to know" part of the chapter. In fact, the reader should use the study questions at the end of this chapter in an effort to solidify the principles above into a position of familiarity.

If a globe has the circles of latitude and longitude drawn upon it according to the principles described, and the latitude and longitude of a certain point have been determined by observation, this point can be located on the globe in its proper position. In this way, a globe can be formed that resembles a small scale copy of the spherical earth (see Figure 2-9). Thus, a small scale reproduction of the surface above which the pilot navigates is produced, to allow the pilot to gain the perspective needed to understand the navigational concepts and be able to predict what the surface that is about to be flown over should look like.

This brings us to the subject of maps and charts, which need to be understood in order to be able to fully utilize this major navigator's aid at a high level of sophistication. However, before going on to the study of maps and charts in Chapter 3, go through the study questions in order to fully understand the concepts presented in this chapter.

Study Questions

1. Find a globe of the earth. Note how the lines of latitude and longitude are placed. Find and list the latitude and longitude of ten major cities in the world, including one near the equator, one each nearest the south and north poles.

2. Set up a table with four columns labeled: city; lat./lon. from globe; airport lat./lon. from IFIM (International Flight Information Manual), ICAO airport identifier. From the globe, find the latitude and longitude of the following cities. Then, using the IFIM, list the airport lat./lon. and four-letter identifier for the city. Compare the two lat./lon. values. Are they close? Write a short conclusion about what you have learned from these efforts.

   a. Lisbon

   b. Tokyo

   c. Yellowknife (Canada)

   d. Moscow

   e. Cairo

   f. Georgetown (How many can you find?)

3. Show how you solved the following: how far is

   a. 46°34'12"N/096°12.0'W from 48°10'00"N/096°12.0'W?

   b. 12°16'18"N/94°30'W from 10°08'12"S/094°30'W?

   c. 00°00'/80°20'W from 00°00'/160°20'E? (Determine values for both short and long path.)

   d. 46°30'N/93°00'W from 46°30'N/94°56'W?

4. Define:

   a. LOP

   b. fix

   c. radial

   d. FRD

   e. nautical compass point

   f. bearing

   g. azimuth

   h. course

   i. track

   j. heading

   k. knot

   l. oblate spheroid

   m. equator

   n. great circle

   o. latitude

   p. longitude

3: Maps and Charts

Charts vs. Maps

A **chart** is a representation in miniature, on a plane surface, of a portion of the earth's surface. In a chart, emphasis is on conformality (which is discussed in the "projection" section of this chapter) and on topographical and geographical features, rather than on items of interest to the intended user. A **map** is most concerned with items of interest to the intended user (such as roads on a road map), and has less accuracy with respect to conformality. It is correct to say that we use a road *map*, but pilots use an aeronautical *chart*. It is considered improper to use the term *map* when referring to a *chart*.

A **projection** can be defined as *a systematic construction of lines on a plane surface to represent the parallels of latitude and the meridians of longitude of the earth or a section of the earth.*

Charts and Projections

There are several basic terms and ideas, relative to charts and projections, that the reader should be familiar with prior to discussing the various projections used in the creation of aeronautical charts.

- A map or chart is a small-scale representation on a plane surface of the spherical surface of the earth or some portion of it.

- A chart projection is a method for systematically representing the meridians and parallels of the earth on a plane surface.

- The chart projection forms the basic structure on which a chart is built and determines the fundamental characteristics of the finished chart.

- There are many difficulties which must be resolved when representing a portion of the surface of a sphere upon a plane. Two of these are **distortion** and **perspective**.

Distortion cannot be entirely avoided, but it can be controlled and systematized to some extent in the drawing of a chart. If a chart is drawn for a particular purpose, it can be drawn in such a way as to minimize the type of distortion which is most detrimental to the purpose. Surfaces that can be spread out in a plane without stretching or tearing such as a cone or cylinder are called **developable surfaces**, and those like the sphere or spheroid that cannot be formed into a plane are called **nondevelopable surfaces** (*see* Figure 3-1).

The problem of creating a projection lies in developing a method for transferring the meridians and parallels to the chart in a manner that will, as much as possible, preserve certain desired characteristics nearly distortion-free.

The two methods of projection used are called *mathematical* and *perspective*. The perspective method consists of geometrically projecting a coordinate system based on the earth-sphere from a given point directly onto a developable surface. The properties and appearance of the resultant map depends upon two factors: the type of developable surface, and the position of the point of projection.

The mathematical projection is derived analytically to provide certain properties or characteristics which cannot be arrived at geometrically. Some of the choices available for selecting projections which best accommodate these properties and characteristics are discussed in the next section.

Choice of Projection

The ideal chart projection portrays the features of the earth in their true relationship to each other; that is, directions would be true, and distances would be represented at a constant scale over the entire chart. This would result in equality of area and true shape throughout the chart.

Such a relationship can only be represented on a globe. It is impossible to preserve, on a flat chart, constant scale and true direction in all directions at all points, nor can both relative size and shape of the geo-

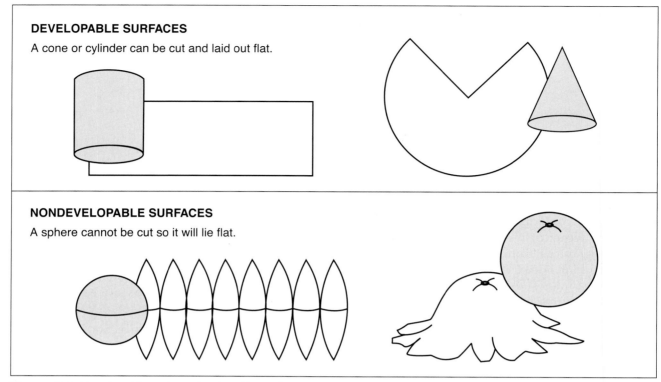

DEVELOPABLE SURFACES
A cone or cylinder can be cut and laid out flat.

NONDEVELOPABLE SURFACES
A sphere cannot be cut so it will lie flat.

Figure 3-1. Developable and nondevelopable surfaces

graphic features be accurately portrayed throughout the chart. The characteristics most commonly desired in a chart projection are:

- Conformality
- Constant Scale
- Equal area
- Great circles as straight lines
- Rhumb lines as straight lines
- True azimuth
- Geographic position easily located

Of the many projection characteristics, **conformality** is the most important for air navigation charts. The limitations imposed by selection of this characteristic, with the resulting loss of other desirable but inharmonious qualities, are offset by the advantages of conformality. For any projection to be *conformal*, three conditions must be satisfied:

1. The scale at any given point on the projection must be independent of azimuth. In other words, from any one point, the scale must be equal and uniform in all directions. This does not imply, however, that the scale about two different points at different latitudes will be equal. It means, simply, that the scale at any given single point will, for a short distance, be equal in all directions.

2. The outline of areas on the chart must conform in shape to the feature being portrayed. This condition applies only to relatively small areas; large land masses must necessarily reflect any distortion inherent in the projection.

3. Since the meridians and parallels of Earth intersect at right angles, the longitude and latitude lines on all conformal projections must also be perpendicular. This characteristic facilitates the plotting of points by geographic coordinates.

The property of **constant scale** throughout the entire chart is highly desirable but impossible to obtain, as it would require that the scale be the same at all points and in all directions throughout the chart. This is simply not possible when converting a spherical shape to a planar shape. This quality can be maintained for short distances in some projections, such as the Lambert Conformal, for use by navigators.

These charts are designed to maintain a constant ratio of **equal area** throughout, although original shapes may be distorted beyond recognition. Equal area charts are of little value to the navigator, since an equal area chart cannot be conformal. They are, however, often used for statistical purposes.

The **rhumb line** and the **great circle** are the two curves that a navigator might wish to have represented on a map as **straight lines**. The only projection which shows all rhumb lines as straight lines is the Mercator. The only projection which shows all great circles as straight lines is the gnomonic projection. However, the gnomonic is not a conformal projection and cannot be used directly for obtaining direction or distance. No conformal chart will represent all great circles as straight lines.

It would be extremely desirable to have a projection which showed directions or azimuths as true throughout the chart. **True azimuth** would be particularly important to the navigator, who must determine from the chart the heading to be flown. There is no chart projection that will represent true great circle direction along a straight line from all points to all other points.

The geographic latitudes and longitudes of places should be easily taken from or plotted on the chart when the latitudes and longitudes are known.

Classification of Projections

Chart projections may be classified in many ways. In this text, the various projections are divided into three classes according to the type of developable surface to which the projections are related. These classes are **azimuthal**, **cylindrical**, and **conical**.

Azimuthal Projections

Azimuthal or zenithal projections are ones in which points on the earth are transferred directly to a plane tangent to the earth. Depending on the positioning of the plane and the point of projection, various geometric projections may be derived. If the origin of the projecting rays (the point of projection) is the center of the sphere, a **gnomonic** projection results. If it is located on the surface of the earth opposite the point of the tangent plane, the projection is a **stereographic**. If the origin is at *infinity*, an **orthographic** projection results. Figure 3-2 shows these various points of projection.

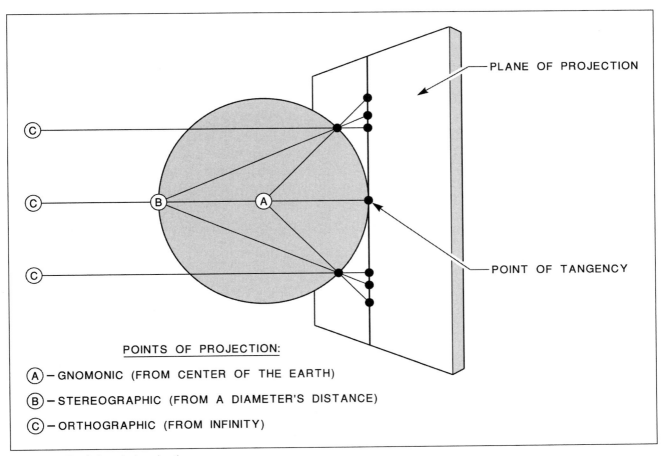

Figure 3-2. Azimuthal projections

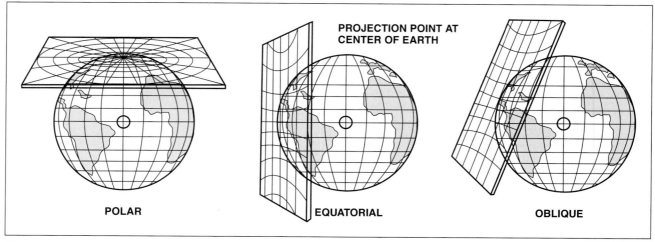

Figure 3-3. Gnomonic projections

Gnomonic Projections

All gnomonic projections are direct perspective projections. Since the plane of every great circle cuts through the center of the sphere, the point of projection is in the plane of every great circle. This property is the most important and useful characteristic of the gnomonic projection. Each and every great circle is represented by a straight line on the projection.

A complete hemisphere cannot be projected onto this plane because points 90° from the center of the chart project lines parallel to the plane of projection. Because the gnomonic is nonconformal, shapes or land masses are distorted, and measured angles are not true. At only one point, the center of the projection, are the azimuths of lines true. At this point, the projection is said to be azimuthal.

Gnomonic projections are classified according to the point of tangency of the plane of projection. A gno-

monic projection is **polar gnomonic** when the point of tangency is one of the poles, **equatorial gnomonic** when the point of tangency is at the equator and any selected meridian, and **oblique gnomonic** when the point of tangency is at any point other than one of the poles or the equator (Figure 3-3).

Stereographic Projection

The stereographic projection is a perspective-conformal projection of the sphere. The term **oblique stereographic** is applied to any stereographic projection where the center of the projection is positioned at any point other than the geographic poles or the equator. If the center is coincident with one of the poles, the projection is called **polar stereographic**. If the center lies on the equator, the prime circle is a meridian, which gives the name **meridian stereographic** or **equatorial stereographic**. The illustration in Figure 3-4 shows the

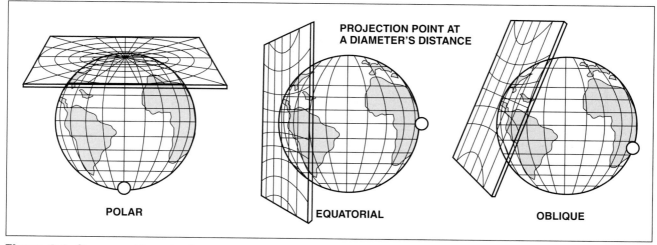

Figure 3-4. Stereographic projections

three stereographic projections. Since the horizon stereographic and the meridian stereographic are not used in navigation, they are not discussed in this text.

Orthographic Projection

As discussed above, the point of projection is located at an infinite distance from the plane of the chart. If the plane is tangent to the earth at the equator, the parallels appear as straight lines and the meridians as elliptical curves, except for the meridian through the point of tangency, which is a straight line. The illustration in Figure 3-5 shows an **equatorial orthographic** projection. Its principal use in navigation is in the field of navigational astronomy, where it is useful for illustrating celestial coordinates, since the view of the Moon, the Sun, and other celestial bodies from the earth is essentially orthographic.

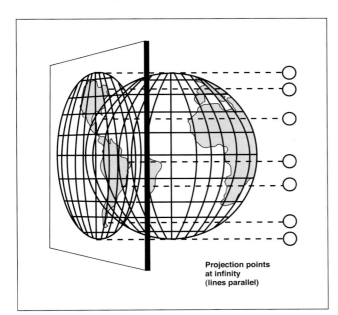

Figure 3-5. Equatorial orthographic projection

Azimuthal Equidistant Projection

This projection is neither perspective, equal area, nor conformal. It is called azimuthal equidistant because straight lines radiating from the center represent great circles as true azimuths, and distances along these lines are true to scale. The entire surface of the sphere is mapped in a circle, the diameter being equal to the circumference of the Earth at reduced scale. With respect to the entire Earth, the perimeter of the circle represents the points diametrically opposite the center of the projection. The appearance of the curves representing the parallels and meridians depends upon the point se-

lected as the center of the projection, and may be described in terms of three general classifications:

1. If the center is one of the poles, the meridians are represented as straight lines radiating from it, with the convergence factor equal to unity, and the parallels are represented as equally spaced concentric circles. (Convergence factor is defined below, under "Conic Projections.")

2. If the center is on the equator, the meridian of the center point and its antimeridian, on the other side of the sphere, form a diameter of the circle (shown as a vertical line) and the equator is also a diameter perpendicular to it. One-fourth of the Earth's surface is mapped in each of the quadrants of the circle determined by these two lines.

3. If the center is any other point, only the central meridian (and its antimeridian) form a straight-line diameter. All other lines are curved (*see* Figure 3-6).

The property of true distance and azimuth from the central point makes this projection useful in aeronautics and radio engineering. For example, if an important airport is selected for the point of tangency, the great circle distances and courses from that point to any other positions on the earth are quickly and accurately determined. Similarly, for communications work at a fixed point (point of tangency), the path of an incoming signal whose direction of arrival has been deter-

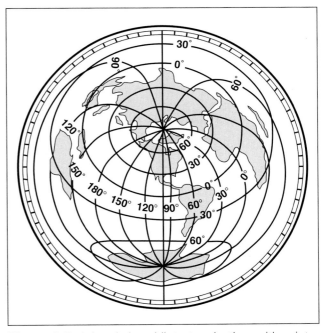

Figure 3-6. Azimuthal equidistant projection, with point of tangency latitude 40°N, longitude 100°W

mined is at once apparent, as is the direction in which to train a directional antenna for desired results.

Cylindrical Projections

The only cylindrical projection used for navigation is the **Mercator**, named after its originator, Gerhard Mercator, who first devised this type of chart in the year 1569. The Mercator is the only projection ever constructed that is conformal and at the same time displays the rhumb line as a straight line. It is used for navigation, for nearly all atlases (a word coined by Mercator), and for many wall maps.

Imagine a cylinder tangent to the equator, with the source of projection at the center of the earth. It would appear much like the illustration in Figure 3-7, with the meridians as straight lines and the parallels as unequally spaced circles around the cylinder. It is obvi-

ous from the illustration that those parts of the terrestrial surface close to the poles could not be projected unless the cylinder was tremendously long, and the poles could not be projected at all.

On the Earth, the parallels of latitude are perpendicular to the meridians, forming circles of progressively smaller diameters as the latitude increases. On the cylinder, the parallels of latitude are shown perpendicular to the projected meridians but, since the diameter of a cylinder is the same at any point along the longitudinal axis, the projected parallels are all the same length. If the cylinder is cut along a vertical line (a meridian) and spread flat, the meridians appear as equal-spaced, vertical lines, and the parallels as horizontal lines.

The cylinder may be tangent at some great circle other than the equator, forming other types of cylindrical projections. If the cylinder is tangent at some meridian, it is a **transverse cylindrical projection** and, if it is tangent at any point other than the equator or a meridian, it is called an **oblique cylindrical projection**. The patterns of latitude and longitude appear quite different on these projections, since the line of tangency and the equator no longer coincide.

Mercator Projection

The Mercator projection is a conformal, nonperspective projection; it is constructed by means of a mathematical transformation and cannot be obtained directly by graphical means. The distinguishing feature of the Mercator projection among cylindrical projections is that at any latitude the ratio of expansion of both meridians and parallels is the same, thus preserving the relationship existing on the earth. This expansion is equal to the secant of the latitude, with a small correction for the ellipticity of the earth. Since expansion is the same in all directions and since all directions, and all angles are correctly represented, the projection is conformal. Rhumb lines appear as straight lines, and their directions can be measured directly on the chart. Distance can also be measured directly, but not by a single distance scale on the entire chart, unless the spread of latitude is small. Great circles appear as curved lines, concave to the equator, or convex to the nearest pole. The shapes of small areas are very nearly correct, but are of increased size unless they are near the equator as shown in Figure 3-8.

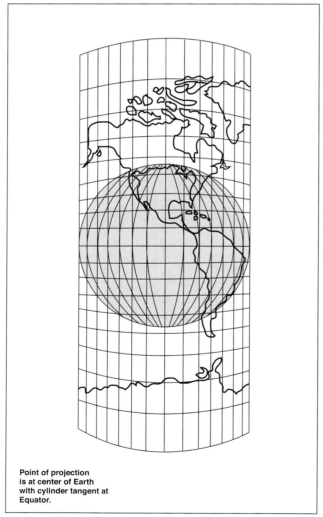

Point of projection
is at center of Earth
with cylinder tangent at
Equator.

Figure 3-7. Cylindrical projection

The Mercator projection has the following disadvantages:

- Difficulty of measuring large distances accurately.
- Conversion angle must be applied to great circle bearing before plotting.
- The chart is useless in polar regions above 80°N or below 80°S since the poles cannot be shown.

Transverse Mercator

The transverse or inverse Mercator is a conformal map designed for areas not covered by the equatorial Mercator. With the **transverse Mercator**, the property of straight meridians and parallels is lost, and the rhumb line is no longer represented by a straight line. The parallels and meridians become complex curves and, with geographic reference, the transverse Mercator is difficult to use as a plotting chart.

The transverse Mercator, though often considered analogous to a projection onto a cylinder, is in reality a nonperspective projection that is constructed mathematically. However, this analogy (illustrated in Figure 3-9), does permit the reader to visualize that the transverse Mercator will show scale correctly along the central meridian which forms the great circle of tangency. In effect, the cylinder has been turned 90° from its position for the ordinary Mercator, and some meridian, called the central meridian, becomes the tangential great circle. One series of USAF charts that uses this type of projection places the cylinder tangent to the 90°E – 90°W longitude.

These projections use a fictitious **graticule** similar to, but offset from, the familiar network of meridians and parallels. The tangent great circle is the fictitious equator. Ninety degrees from it are two fictitious poles. A group of great circles through these poles and perpendicular to the tangent constitutes the fictitious meridians, while a series of lines parallel to the plane of the tangent great circle forms the fictitious parallels.

On these projections, the fictitious graticule appears as the geographical one ordinarily appearing on the equatorial Mercator. That is, the fictitious meridians and parallels are straight lines perpendicular to each other. The actual meridians and parallels appear as curved lines, except for the line of tangency. Geographical coordinates are usually expressed in terms of the conventional graticule. A straight line on the transverse Mercator projection makes the same angle with all fictitious meridians, but not with the terrestrial meridians. It is, therefore, a fictitious rhumb line.

The appearance of a transverse Mercator using the 90°E – 90°W meridian as a reference or fictitious equator is shown in Figure 3-9. The dotted lines are the lines of the fictitious projection. The N-S meridian through the center is the fictitious equator, and all other original meridians are now curves concave to the N-S meridian, with the original parallels now being curves concave to the nearer pole.

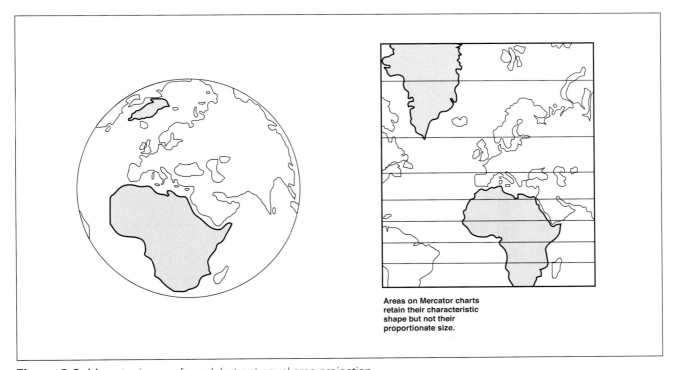

Areas on Mercator charts retain their characteristic shape but not their proportionate size.

Figure 3-8. Mercator is a conformal, but not equal area projection.

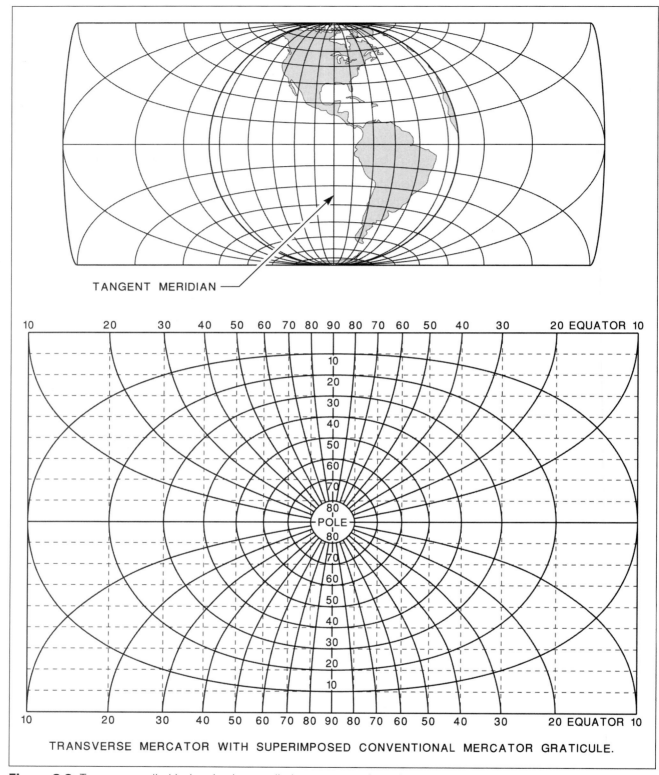

TANGENT MERIDIAN ──

TRANSVERSE MERCATOR WITH SUPERIMPOSED CONVENTIONAL MERCATOR GRATICULE.

Figure 3-9. Transverse cylindrical projection—cylinder tangent at the poles

Oblique Mercator

The cylindrical projection in which the cylinder is tangent at a great circle other than the equator or a meridian is called an **oblique Mercator** (Figure 3-10). One can see that as a sphere fits into a cylinder, it makes no difference how it is turned. The fit, or line of tangency, can be any great circle. Thus, the oblique Mercator projection is unique in that it is prepared and used for special purposes. This projection is used principally to depict an area in the near vicinity of an oblique great circle, such as along the great circle route between two important centers that are a relatively great distance apart (Figure 3-11).

Consider a flight between Seattle and Tokyo. The shortest distance is naturally the great circle distance, and is therefore the route to fly. Plotting the great circle on a Mercator, one finds that it takes the form of a high arching curve (toward the nearest pole), as shown. Since the scale on a Mercator changes with latitude, there will be a considerable scale change when one considers the latitude band that this great circle route covers.

If the navigator were only concerned with the great circle route and a small band of latitude (such as 5°) on either side, the best chart to use would be the oblique Mercator. With the cylinder made tangential along the great circle joining Seattle and Tokyo, the resultant graticule would enjoy most of the good properties found near the equator on a conventional Mercator.

Advantages

The oblique Mercator projection has several desirable properties. The projection is conformal. The x-axis is a great circle course at true scale. The projection can be constructed using any desired great circle as the x-axis. The scale is equal to the secant of the angular distance from the x-axis. Therefore, near the x-axis, the scale change is slight. This makes the projection almost ideal for strip charts of great circle flights.

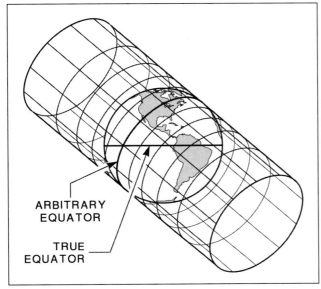

Figure 3-10. Oblique Mercator projection

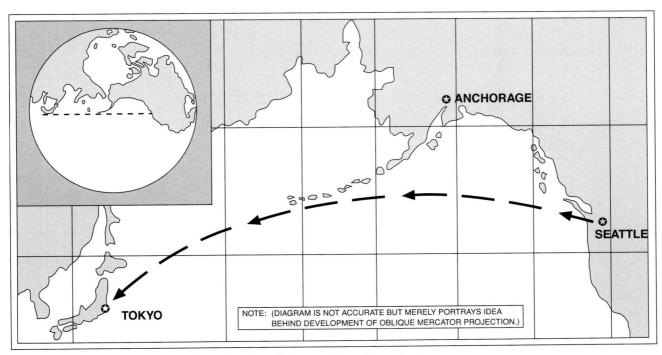

NOTE: (DIAGRAM IS NOT ACCURATE BUT MERELY PORTRAYS IDEA BEHIND DEVELOPMENT OF OBLIQUE MERCATOR PROJECTION.)

Figure 3-11. Great Circle Route, from Seattle to Tokyo, on Mercator projection

Limitations

The projection also has many disadvantages. Rhumb lines are curved lines; therefore, except as mentioned above, the chart is of little use to the navigator. Scale expansion and area distortion in the region of the oblique pole are the same as that of the standard Mercator in the region of the pole. Radio bearings cannot be plotted directly on the chart. All meridians and parallels are curved lines. A separate projection must be computed and constructed for each required great circle course.

Conic Projections

There are two classes of **conic projections**. The first is a simple conic projection constructed by placing the apex of the cone over some part of the earth (usually the pole) with the cone tangent to a parallel called the **standard parallel** and projecting the graticule of the reduced earth onto the cone as shown in Figure 3-12. The chart is obtained by cutting the cone along some meridian and unrolling it to form a flat surface.

Notice in Figure 3-13 the characteristic gap that appears when the cone is unrolled. The second type of conic projection is a **secant cone**, which cuts through the earth at two **standard parallels** as shown in Figure 3-14.

Probably the chart projection that pilots are most familiar with, because they use the sectional and WAC charts from the time they begin to learn to fly, is the

Lambert conformal projection. It is a secant conic projection in which the meridians are straight lines which meet at a common point beyond the limits of the chart; the parallels are concentric circles, the center of each being the point of intersection of the meridians. Meridians and parallels intersect at right angles. Angles formed by any two lines or curves on the Earth's surface are correctly represented.

This projection may be developed by either the graphic or mathematical method. It employs a secant cone intersecting the spheroid at two parallels of lati-

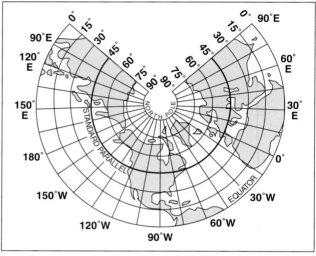

Figure 3-13. Appearance of a simple conic projection of the northern hemisphere, when laid out in a plane

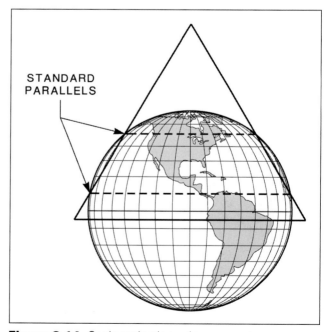

Figure 3-12. A simple conic projection

Figure 3-14. Conic projection using a secant cone

tude, called the **standard parallels**, of the area to be represented. The standard parallels are represented at exact scale. Between these parallels, the scale factor is less than unity and, beyond them, greater than unity. For equal distribution of scale error (within and beyond the standard parallels), the standard parallels are selected at one sixth and five sixths of the total length of the segment of the central meridian represented. The development of the Lambert conformal conic projection is shown by Figure 3-15.

Following are some additional terms appropriate to this important projection. The **geodesic** is a curved line always concave toward the midparallel, except in the case of a meridian line where, by definition, it is a straight line. This word is derived from the term **geodesy**, *the science of measuring the size and shape of the earth.*

The **loxodrome** is a curved line concave toward the poles (with exception of a true north-south line), which crosses each meridian at the same angle to true north or south, and is also called a **rhumb line** (*see* Figure 2-4 on Page 18).

The chief use of the Lambert conformal conic projection is in mapping areas of small latitudinal width but great longitudinal extent. No projection can be both conformal and equal area; but by limiting latitudinal width, scale error is decreased to the extent that the projection gives very nearly an equal area representation, in addition to giving the inherent quality of conformality. This makes the projection very useful for aeronautical charts.

Advantages

Some of the chief advantages of the Lambert conformal conic projection are as listed below.

- Conformality.

- Great circles are approximated by straight lines (actually, slightly concave toward the midparallel).

- For areas of small latitudinal width, scale is nearly constant. For example, the U.S. may be charted with standard parallels at 33°N and 45°N with a scale error of only 2.5% for southern Florida. The maximum scale error between 30.5°N and 47.5°N is only one-half of 1%.

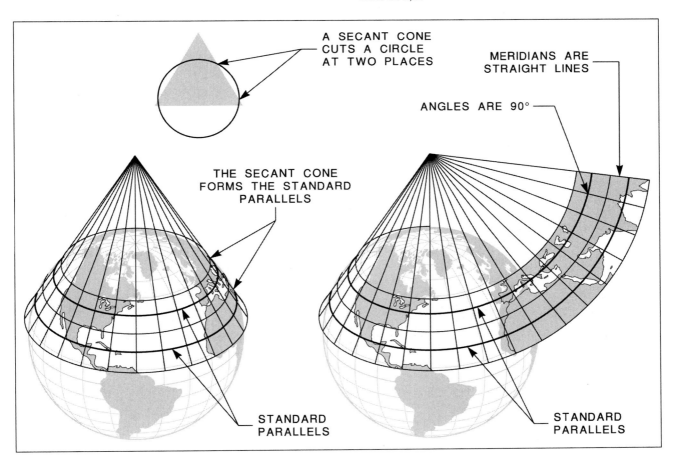

Figure 3-15. Lambert conformal conic projection

- Positions are easily plotted and read in terms of latitude and longitude.

- Construction is relatively simple.

- The two standard parallels give this projection two lines along which elements are represented true to shape and scale, with minimum error elsewhere on the chart.

- Distance is measured with good accuracy. For example, the distance from Pittsburgh to Istanbul is 5,277 nautical miles; distance as measured by the graphic scale on a Lambert projection (standard parallels 36°N and 54°N) without application of the scale factor is 5,258 nautical miles—an error of less than four-tenths of 1%.

Limitations

Some of the chief limitations of the Lambert Conformal conic projection are as listed below.

- Rhumb lines are curved lines which cannot be plotted accurately.

- Great circles are curved lines concave toward the midparallel.

- Maximum scale error increases as latitudinal width increases.

- Parallels are curved lines (arcs of concentric circles).

- Continuous conformality ceases at the junction of two bands, even though each is conformal. If both have the same scale along their standard parallels, the common parallel (the junction) will have a different radius for each band; therefore, they will not join perfectly.

Constant of the Cone

Most conic charts have the constant of the cone (**convergence factor**—see below) computed and listed on the chart as shown in Figure 3-16.

Convergence Angle

The convergence angle is the actual angle on a chart formed by the intersection of the Greenwich meridian and some other meridian; the pole serves as the vertex of the angle. Convergence angles, like longitudes, are measured east and west from the Greenwich meridian.

Convergence Factor

A chart's convergence factor is a decimal number that expresses the ratio between meridional convergence as it actually exists on the Earth and as it is portrayed on the chart. When the convergence angle equals the number of the selected meridian, the chart convergence factor is 1.0. When the convergence angle is less than the number of the selected meridian, the chart convergence factor is proportionately less than 1.0.

The subpolar projection illustrated in Figure 3-17 portrays the standard parallels, 37°N and 65°N. It presents 360° of the Earth's surface on 283° of paper. Therefore, the chart has a convergence factor (CF) of 0.785 (283° divided by 360° equals 0.785). Meridian 90°W forms a west convergence angle (CA) of 71° with the Greenwich meridian. This is expressed as a formula:

CF x longitude = CA

.785 x 90°W = 71° west CA

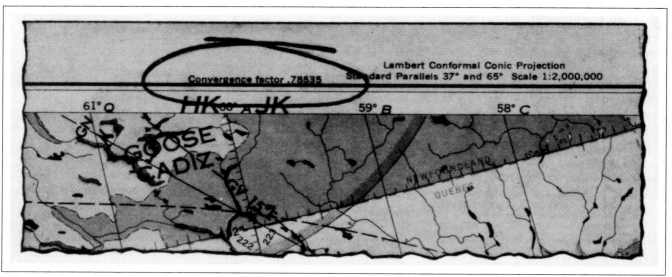

Figure 3-16. Convergence factor on a Jet Navigation (JN) Chart

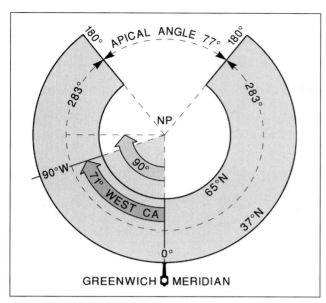

Figure 3-17. Lambert conformal chart, showing a convergence factor of 0.785

A chart's convergence factor is easily approximated on subpolar charts by:

1. Drawing a straight line which covers 10 lines of longitude.

2. Measuring the true course at each end of the line, noting the difference between them, and dividing the difference by 10.

3. The quotient represents the chart's convergence factor.

Because of its projection, the meridians on a transverse Mercator chart do not coincide with the meridians on the earth. As a result, the meridians appear as curved lines on the chart.

Figures 3-18, 3-19, and 3-20 (on Pages 38 – 40) list characteristics of cylindrical, conical, and azimuthal projections. They are presented as a review of the material covered so far concerning projections.

Aeronautical Charts

An aeronautical chart is a pictorial representation of a portion of the Earth's surface upon which lines and symbols in a variety of colors represent features and/or details that can be seen on the Earth's surface. In addition to ground image, many additional symbols and notes are added to indicate navigational aids and data necessary for air navigation. Properly used, a chart is a vital adjunct to navigation; improperly used, it may even prove a hazard. Without it, modern navi-

gation would never have reached its present state of development. Because of their great importance, the navigator must be thoroughly familiar with the wide variety of aeronautical charts and understand their many uses.

Aeronautical charts are produced on many different types of projections. Recall from the first page of this chapter that a **projection** can be defined as *a systematic construction of lines on a plane surface to represent the parallels of latitude and the meridians of longitude of the earth or a section of the earth.* These projections may range from the equatorial Mercator for a LORAN chart to the transverse Mercator for the polar region. Since the demand for variety in charts is so great and since the properties of the projections vary greatly, there is no one projection that will satisfy all the needs of contemporary air navigation. The projection that answers nearly all the navigator's needs is the Lambert conformal, and it is the one most widely used for aeronautical charts.

Aeronautical charts, in their full range of projections, give worldwide coverage. Some single projections used for a single series of charts will cover nearly all the Earth. An aeronautical chart of some projection and scale can be obtained for any portion of the Earth. The accuracy of the information displayed on these charts will vary but, generally speaking, worldwide aeronautical charts in use today are very accurate representations of the Earth's surface.

Scale

Obviously, charts are much smaller than the area which they represent. The ratio between any given unit of length on a chart and the true distance it represents on the Earth is the **scale** of the chart. The scale may be relatively uniform over the whole chart, or it may vary greatly from one part of the chart to another. Charts are made to various scales for different purposes. If a chart is to show the whole world and yet not be too large, it must be drawn to small scale. If a chart is to show much detail, it must be drawn to a large scale; then it shows a smaller area than does a chart of the same size drawn to a small scale. Remember, large area, small scale; small area, large scale.

The scale of a chart may be given by a simple statement, such as "1 inch equals 10 miles." This, of course, means that a distance of 10 miles on the earth's surface is shown 1 inch long on the chart. On aeronautical charts, the scale is indicated in one of two ways: **representative fraction** or **graphic scale**.

Continued on Page 41

		Mercator	Transverse Mercator
Characteristics of the Projection	Conformality	Conformal	Conformal
	Distance Scale	Variable (measure at Mid-Latitude)	Nearly Constant (near Meridian of true scale)
	Distortion of Shapes and Areas	Increases Away From Equator	Increases Away From Tangent Meridian
	Angle Between Parallels and Meridians	90° Angle	90° Angle
	Appearance of Parallels	Parallel Straight Lines Unequally Spaced	Curves Concave Toward Nearest Pole
	Appearance of Meridians	Parallel Straight Lines Equally Spaced	Complex Curves Concave Toward Central Meridian
	Appearance of Projection		
	Graphic Illustration		
Production	Method of Production	Mathematical	Mathematical
	Origin of Projectors	From Center of Sphere (for illustration only)	From Center of Sphere (for illustration only)
	Point of Tangency	Equator	Great Circle Through the Poles
Appearance of Lines on Charts	Straight Line Crosses Meridians	Constant Angle (Rhumb line)	Variable Angle (approximates Great Circle)
	Great Circle	Curved Line (except Equator and Meridians)	Approximated by Straight Line
	Rhumb Line	Straight Line	Curved Line
	Navigational Uses	Dead Reckoning and Celestial (suitable for all types)	Grid Navigation in Polar Areas

Figure 3-18. Cylindrical projections

		Lambert Conformal	**Azimuthal Equidistant**
Characteristics of the Projection	Conformality	Conformal	Not Conformal
	Distance Scale	Nearly Constant	Correct Scale at All Azimuths From Center Only
	Distortion of Shapes and Areas	Very Little	Increases Away From Center
	Angle Between Parallels and Meridians	90° Angle	Variable Angle
	Appearance of Parallels	Arcs of Concentric Circles Nearly Equally Spaced	Curved Lines Unequally Spaced
	Appearance of Meridians	Straight Lines Converging at the Pole	Curved Lines Converging at the Pole
	Appearance of Projection		
	Graphic Illustration		
Production	Method of Production	Mathematical	Mathematical
	Origin of Projectors	From Center of Sphere (for illustration only)	Not Projected
	Point of Tangency	Two Standard Parallels	None
Appearance of Lines on Charts	Straight Line Crosses Meridians	Variable Angle (Approximates Great Circle)	Variable Angle
	Great Circle	Approximated by Straight Line	Any Straight Line Radiating From Center of Projection
	Rhumb Line	Curved Line	Curved Line
	Navigational Uses	Pilotage and Radio (suitable for all types)	Aeronautics/Radio Engineering and Celestial Map

Figure 3-19. Conic Projections

		Polar Stereographic	Polar Gnomonic
Characteristics of the Projection	Conformality	Conformal	Not Conformal
	Distance Scale	Nearly Constant Except on Small Scale Charts	Variable
	Distortion of Shapes and Areas	Increases Away From Pole	Increases Away From Pole
	Angle Between Parallels and Meridians	90° Angle	90° Angle
	Appearance of Parallels	Concentric Circles Unequally Spaced	Concentric Circles Unequally Spaced
	Appearance of Meridians	Straight Lines Radiating From the Pole	Straight Lines Radiating From the Pole
	Appearance of Projection		
	Graphic Illustration		
Production	Method of Production	Graphic or Mathematical	Graphic or Mathematical
	Origin of Projectors	From Opposite Pole	From Center of Sphere
	Point of Tangency	Pole	Pole
Appearance of Lines on Charts	Straight Line Crosses Meridians	Variable Angle (approximates Great Circle)	Variable Angle (Great Circle)
	Great Circle	Approximated by Straight Line	Straight Line
	Rhumb Line	Curved Line	Curved Line
	Navigational Uses	All Types of Polar Navigation	Great Circle Navigation and Planning

Figure 3-20. Azimuth projections

Representative Fraction

The scale may be given as a representative fraction, such as 1:500,000 or 1/500,000. This means that one of any unit on the chart represents 500,000 of the same unit on the earth. For example, 1" on the chart represents 500,000" on the earth. A representative fraction can be converted into a statement of miles to the inch. Thus, if the scale is 1:1,000,000, 1 inch on the chart stands for 1,000,000 inches or 1,000,000 divided by (6,080 x 12) equaling about 13.7 nautical miles. Similarly, if the scale is 1:500,000, 1" on the chart represents about 6.85 NM. Thus, the larger the denominator of the representative fraction, the smaller the scale.

Graphic Scale

The graphic scale may be shown by a graduated line. It is usually printed along the border of a chart. Take a measurement on the chart and compare it with the graphic scale of miles. The number of miles that the measurement represents on the earth may be read directly from the graphic scale on the chart.

The distance between parallels of latitude also provides a convenient scale for distance measurement. As shown in Figure 3-21, 1° of latitude always equals 60 nautical miles and 1 minute of latitude equals 1 nautical mile.

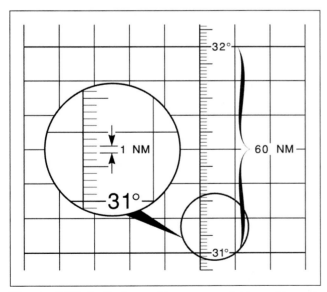

Figure 3-21. Latitude provides a convenient graphic scale.

DOD Aeronautical Charts and Flight Information Publications

The following publications are available to pilots and navigators in numerous locations where aeronautical charts are sold or where flight planning takes place. A valuable aid to selecting appropriate charts is the DOD Catalog of Aeronautical Charts and Flight Information Publications. This catalog provides information on the latest aeronautical cartographic products produced and distributed by the Defense Mapping Agency Aerospace Center (DMAAC) and the Defense Mapping Agency Hydrographic Center (DMAHC). A brief description of each series or type of chart listed in this catalog is presented in Chapter 6.

Types of Charts

Aeronautical charts are differentiated on a functional basis by the type of information they contain. These charts are grouped into three major types: general purpose, special purpose, and plotting. The name of the chart is a reasonable indication of its intended use. Thus, a LORAN-C plotting chart has information needed by the navigator in order to use LORAN-C time difference LOPs, as a navigation aid; a Minimal Flight Planning Chart is primarily used in minimal flight planning techniques; and a Jet Navigation (JN) Chart has properties that make it adaptable to the speed, altitude, and instrumentation of jet aircraft. In addition to giving different types of information, charts vary according to the amount of information displayed. Charts designed to facilitate the planning of long distance flight carry less detail than those required for navigation en route. Local charts present great detail.

Standard Symbols

Chart symbols are used for easy identification of information portrayed on aeronautical charts. While these symbols may vary slightly between different projections, the amount of variance is slight and once the basic symbol is understood, different versions of it are easy to identify. A **chart legend** is the key which explains the meaning of the relief, culture, hydrography, vegetation, and aeronautical symbols (Figure 3-22).

Relief (Hipsography)

Chart relief shows the physical features related to the differences in elevation of land surface. These include features such as mountains, hills, plateaus, plains, depressions, etc. Standard symbols and shading techniques are used in relief portrayal on charts; these include contours, spot elevations, variations in tint, and shading to represent shadows.

Contour Lines

A **contour line** is a line connecting points of equal elevation. Figure 3-23 shows the relationship between contour lines and terrain. Notice that on steep slopes the contours are close together, and on gentle slopes they are farther apart. The interval of the contour lines usually depends upon the scale of the chart and the terrain depicted.

In the illustration, the **contour interval** is 1,000 feet. **Depression contours** are regular contour lines with spurs or ticks added on the downslope side. **Spot elevations** are the height of a particular point of terrain above an established datum, usually sea level. The relief indicating by contours is further emphasized on charts by a system of **gradient tints**. Different color tints are used to designate areas within certain elevation ranges.

Perhaps the most obvious portrayal of relief is supplied by graduated **shading** applied to the southeastern side of elevated terrain and the northwestern side of depressions. This shading simulates the shadows cast by elevated features, lending a sharply defined, three-dimensional effect.

All structural developments appearing on the terrain are known as **cultural features**. Three main factors govern the amount of detail given to cultural features: the scale of the chart, the use of the chart, and the geographical area covered. Populated places,

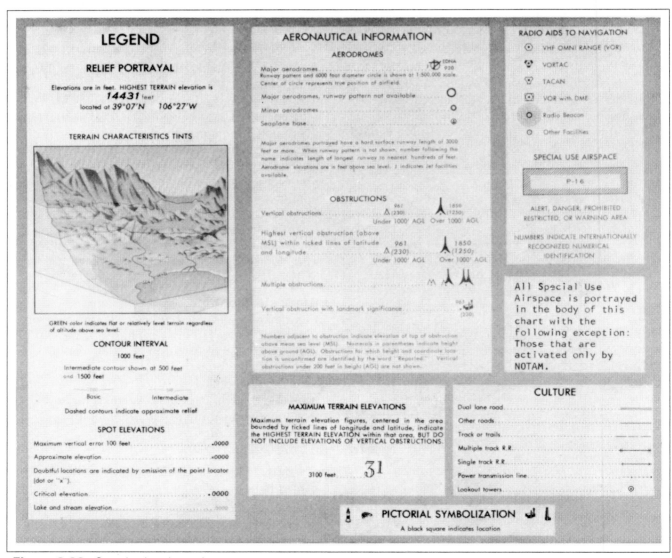

Figure 3-22. Sample chart legend

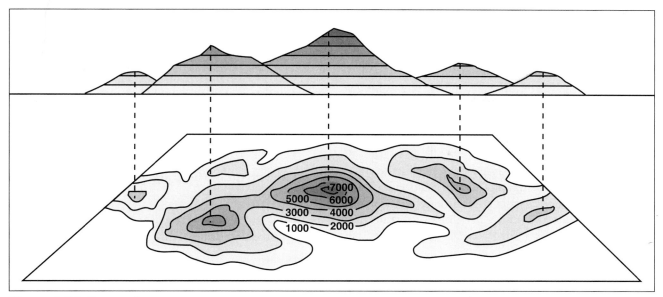

Figure 3-23. Contour lines

roads, railroads, installations, dams, bridges, and mines are some of the many kinds of cultural features portrayed on aeronautical charts. The true representative size and shape of larger cities and towns are shown. Standardized coded symbols and type sizes are used to represent smaller population centers. Some symbols denoting cultural features are usually keyed in a chart legend. However, some charts use pictorial symbols which are self-explanatory and require no further description in the legend.

Hydrography
In this category, aeronautical charts portray oceans, coastlines, lakes, rivers, streams, swamps, reefs, and numerous other hydrographic features. Open water may be portrayed by tinting, by **vignetting** (shading that fades gradually), or may be left blank.

Vegetation
Vegetation is not shown on most small scale charts. Forests and wooded areas in certain parts of the world are portrayed on some medium scale charts. On some large scale charts, park areas, orchards, hedgerows, and vineyards are shown. Portrayal may be by solid tint, vignette, or supplemented vignette.

Aeronautical Information
In the aeronautical category, coded chart symbols denote airfields, radio aids to navigation, commercial broadcasting stations, Air Defense Identification Zones (ADIZ), compulsory corridors, restricted airspace,

warning notes, lines of magnetic variation, and items of special navigational interest. Some aeronautical information is subject to frequent change. For economy of production, charts are retained in stock for various periods of time. So as not to provide the chart user with aeronautical information that is rapidly out of date, only the more stable types of information are printed on navigation charts.

Aeronautical data subject to frequent change is provided to the user by the DOD Flight Information Publications (FLIP) documents. Consult the DOD Flight Information Publications, Chart Updating Manual (CHUM), and Notices to Airmen (NOTAMs) for the most current information.

Jeppesen Sanderson
The Jeppesen company has been a well-known source of flight information for pilots for more than fifty years. Worldwide coverage of IFR en route and approach charts as well as flight procedure information are available from Jeppesen by writing or calling 55 Inverness Dr. East, Englewood, CO 80112-5498; Telephone (303) 799-9090. Besides coverage for the conterminous United States, coverage is available for international flights to all parts of the world. This coverage is discussed in more detail in Chapter 6.

Governments

The governments of many countries produce charts and flight information specific to their areas. Charts and flight information for Canada are available from the AOPA, numerous chart stores and pilot's catalogs, or can be ordered from: Canada Map Office, Department of Energy, Mines and Resources; 130 Bently Road, Ottawa, Ontario, K1A OE9; Telephone (613) 952-7000 or 1-800-465-6277.

The Canadian VFR Navigation Chart is the same scale and general format as the U.S. Sectional Chart, but is superior with respect to feature detail, enabling pilotage navigation over vast regions of terrain that have only natural features.

Study Questions

1. What is the difference between a map and a chart?

2. What is a chart projection?

3. What are the three characteristics of conformality?

4. How do rhumb lines and great circles differ?

5. Make up a study chart of the different projections and their attributes, disadvantages and uses.

6. Define:
   a. standard parallel
   b. Prime meridian
   c. geodesic
   d. loxodrome

7. Where does one find the distance scale on a chart that shows latitude and longitude?

4: Basic Navigation Instruments

Introduction

Instruments mechanically measure physical quantities or properties with varying degrees of accuracy. Much of a navigator's work consists of applying corrections to the indications of various instruments and interpreting the results. Therefore, navigators must be familiar with the capabilities and limitations of the instruments available to them.

An air navigator obtains the following flight information from basic instruments:

- **Direction**
- Altitude
- Temperature
- Airspeed
- **Drift**
- **Ground speed**

In this chapter, some of the basic instruments that indicate direction, ground speed, and drift are discussed. The more complex instruments which make accurate, long distance navigation possible are discussed in later chapters.

Why are we concerned with the basic instruments and techniques covered in this and the next chapter? There are two reasons:

1. Because the pilot/navigator must have developed the understanding and skills necessary to use the basic techniques of navigation well enough to "carry on" with confidence over long distances if the more sophisticated systems fail.

2. Because the pilot/navigator must have developed the basic skills in order to be able to judge the quality of navigation performed by the sophisticated systems of today and tomorrow. Otherwise, that pilot/navigator is destined to forever wander the skies, totally dependent on a complex "black box" to take the aircraft to its destination. This would not fit the meaning of the term "pilot-in-command."

Direction

Basic Instruments

The pilot/navigator must have a fundamental background in navigation to ensure accurate positioning of the aircraft. Dead reckoning procedures aided by basic instruments give a foundation that helps solve the four basic problems of navigation, which are also the **four dimensions of navigation: position** of the aircraft, **direction** to destination, **distance** traveled and remaining, and **time** of arrival. It is possible, using only basic instruments such as the compass, airspeed meter, driftmeter and clock, to navigate directly to any place in the world with considerable accuracy. In fact, practice has shown the accuracy to be as good as VOR navigation. As discussed in later chapters, various fixing aids such as pilotage, celestial, radar, LORAN, etc., can greatly improve the accuracy of basic DR procedures.

Earth's Magnetic Field

The main method of obtaining the directional information needed to navigate uses the Earth's magnetic lines of force. A compass system uses a device that detects and converts the energy from these lines of force to a directional indicator reading. The magnetic compass operates independently of the aircraft electrical systems. The later-developed flux gate and flux valve compass systems require electrical power to convert these lines of force to an indication of aircraft heading.

The Earth has some of the properties of a bar magnet. However, its magnetic poles are located approximately 1,300 nautical miles from the geographic poles, and the two magnetic poles are not located exactly opposite each other as on a straight bar. The north magnetic pole is located approximately at latitude 73°N and longitude 100°W. The south magnetic pole is located at latitude 68°S and longitude 144°E, on Antarctica. To further complicate matters, the magnetic poles move around continuously—not enough to be a big problem, but enough that aeronautical charts must be periodically updated to give the correction needed to compensate for this difference in pole location with time.

The Earth's magnetic poles, like those of any magnet, can be considered to be connected by a number of lines of force. These lines result from the magnetic field which envelops the Earth. They are considered to be emanating from the south magnetic pole and terminating at the north magnetic pole, as illustrated in Figure 4-1.

The force of the Earth's magnetic field can be divided into two components: the vertical and the horizontal. The relative intensity of these two components varies so that, at the magnetic poles, the vertical component is at maximum strength and the horizontal component is minimum. At approximately the midpoint between the poles, the horizontal component is at maximum strength and the vertical component is minimum.

Only the horizontal component is useful as a directive force for a magnetic compass. Therefore, a magnetic compass loses its usefulness in an area of weak horizontal force, such as the area around the magnetic poles (in the high latitudes). The vertical component causes the end of the sensing needle nearer to the magnetic pole to tip as the pole is approached. This departure from the horizontal is called magnetic dip.

Compasses

A **compass** may be defined as an instrument which indicates direction over the Earth's surface with reference to a known datum. Various types of compasses have been developed, each of which is distinguished by the particular datum used as the reference from which direction is measured. Two basic types of compasses are in current use.

The **magnetic compass** uses the lines of force of the Earth's magnetic field as a primary reference. Even though the Earth's field is usually distorted by the pressure of other local magnetic fields, it is the most widely used directional reference.

The **gyrocompass** uses as its datum an arbitrary fixed point in space determined by the initial alignment of the gyroscope axis. Compasses of this type are widely used today.

Magnetic Compass

In order to fly from one location to another, we must have some form of instrument that will maintain a constant directional relationship as we fly. We have been using just such a device since the 12th century. The **magnetic compass** indicates direction in the horizontal plane with reference to the horizontal component of the Earth's magnetic field. This field is made

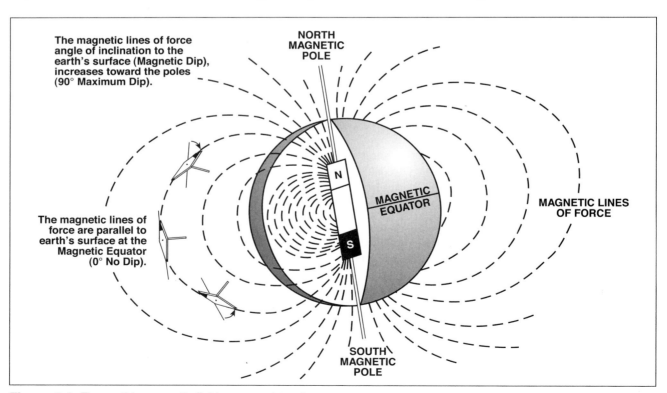

Figure 4-1. The earth's magnetic field compared to a bar magnet

up of the Earth's magnetic field in combination with other magnetic fields in the vicinity of the compass. These secondary magnetic fields are caused by the presence of ferromagnetic objects near the compass, electromagnetic fields generated by electrical and electronic equipment in the aircraft and, if the aircraft is on the ground, iron rebar in the concrete, or metal buildings, etc.

But within the last couple of decades such great strides have been made in the development of navigational systems that the magnetic compass is no longer the most used navigational instrument, and has been relegated to a standby position in most aircraft. This has caused a navigational paradox, because of the tremendous importance of this basic navigation instrument.

Magnetic compasses may be divided into three categories:

1. The direct-indicating magnetic compass.

2. The remote-indicating, gyro-stabilized magnetic compass.

3. The magnetic heading output from the computer of a flight management system gets the magnetic direction information directly from a gyro-stabilized flux gate instrument, which measures the direction of the Earth's magnetic field (as in item 2 above). Or, the computer may be generating an indication of magnetic direction, artificially based on location and earth-spin-rate information from something like an RLG INS system (see Chapter 11).

Direct Indicating Magnetic Compass

Basically, the magnetic compass is a magnetized rod, pivoted at its middle, with a compass rose attached and **lubber line** (reference) aligned with the aircraft's longitudinal axis. The standard aircraft compass (affectionately referred to as the *whiskey compass*) is basically a freely suspended permanent magnet, functioning near the surface of the Earth which will always align itself with the earth's lines of flux linking the two magnetic poles. Because of this alignment, navigation should be simple; but there are problems with alignment that must be understood before we can reliably use a magnetic compass for navigation.

Since all charts are laid out according to the geographic poles, and the magnetic compass points to the magnetic poles, an error called **variation** exists. To simplify the correction for this error, aeronautical charts are marked with lines of equal variation, called **isogonic lines**. Anywhere along an isogonic line, there is a constant angle between the magnetic and geographic north poles. The variation error is the same on any heading flown, and is determined only by position on or near the surface of the Earth.

Another error inherent in magnetic compasses is called **deviation**, which is an error caused by the magnetic fields in the aircraft mixing and interfering with those of the Earth. A magnetic field surrounds any wire carrying electricity, and almost all of the steel parts of an aircraft and the engine contain some magnetism. Magnetos, alternators, and generators have strong magnets in them, and these may be so close to the compass that they influence it.

Aircraft compasses are equipped with two or more small **compensator magnets** in the housing (Figures 4-2 and 4-3). They may be adjusted to cancel the effect of all of the local magnetic fields in the aircraft. Any uncorrected error caused by this local magnetism is called the **deviation error**. This error is different for each heading flown, but it does not change with the geographic location of the aircraft. The pilot or an A&P technician must compensate for deviation errors by performing a procedure called **swinging the compass** (see "Compass Compensation," below). After the error has been minimized, a dated chart called a **deviation card** (Figure 4-2A), is made of the error that remains. This chart is mounted in a holder mounted on the compass bracket, or on the instrument panel adjacent to the compass, so the pilot will be able to apply the correction in flight.

The compass is a magnificent instrument. It is simple, with few moving parts. There is only one moving part in the case of the "whisky compass" or standard aircraft compass. Older models utilized alcohol as the internal fluid (hence the name, "whiskey compass"). Now, odorless (don't you believe it) kerosene is used with additives that keep it clear. The fluid dampens the oscillations of the compass card, lubricates the bearing the card rotates on, and decreases the loading on this bearing by floating the compass card to some extent. Therefore, it is important that sufficient fluid is in the compass. If a bubble of air can be seen in the compass window, the rubber diaphragm (which allows for expansion and contraction due to temperature and pressure) should be replaced and fluid added.

The main body of the compass is a cast aluminum housing, and one end is covered with a glass lens. Across this lens is a vertical reference mark called a **lubber line**. Inside the housing and riding on a steel pivot in a jeweled post is a small brass float surrounded by a graduated dial, which is part of a cone. Around the full 360° of the dial are 36 marks, representing tens of degrees. Above every third mark is either a one- or two-digit number representing the number of degrees with the last zero left off. Zero is the same as 360°, and is north. Nine is east, or 90°, 18 is south (180°), and 27 is 270°, or west. Usually, two small bar-type permanent magnets are soldered to the bottom of the float, aligned with the zero and 18 marks, north and south. A rubber expansion diaphragm or bellows is mounted inside the housing. A set of compensator magnets is located in a slot in the housing outside of the compass bowl, and a small instrument lamp screws into the front of the housing and shines inside the bowl to illuminate the lubber line and the numbers on the card (*see* Figures 4-2 and 4-3).

Compass Compensation

When it is first installed, or any time equipment is added or removed (such as a new radio in the panel), or any time the pilot suspects compass inaccuracy, the magnetic compass should be swung and a new deviation card made up. It is recommended that this be done at least once a year. A check of deviation cards in aircraft on any given airport usually shows that most

Floating magnet-type magnetic compass showing compensating magnet adjusting screws below and light bulb keeper housing above the window

Figure 4-2. Magnetic compass

N2125Z	Magnetic Compass Deviation Radios On										4/27/97
FOR N	030	060	E	120	150	S	210	240	W	300	330
FLY 355	022	054	090	129	159	185	212	235	270	300	328

N2125Z	Magnetic Compass Deviation Radios Off										
FOR N	030	060	E	120	150	S	210	240	W	300	330
FLY 358	025	056	092	126	156	182	109	236	268	296	328

ADF Relative Bearing Correction											
FOR N	030	060	E	120	150	S	210	240	W	300	330
FLY 002	036	068	090	122	152	195	217	249	268	292	319

Figure 4-2A. A deviation card

cards are very old. There is no reason for this, when it is so easy to swing an aircraft compass.

An aircraft compass should not be swung on the ground, except as a first approximation, as many errors will exist there. Reinforcing iron in the concrete on the ramp, iron and steel in nearby vehicles, airplanes, and buildings are all capable of creating compass errors. The greatest error is produced by the fact that the magnetic field from the generator or alternator is not present unless the engine is running up to speed. Try this, the next time you do a runup: with the aircraft on a constant heading and with engine idling, note the compass reading. Then increase RPM until the alternator or generator is showing an output. Note the compass reading. The compass is actually a pretty good alternator/generator output indicator, at least on some single-engine aircraft, isn't it?

Pilots should know how much effect on the compass there will be if the alternator quits (and in which direction), in case such a failure should occur on a critical leg going cross-country.

Therefore, swing the compass while airborne. Besides, it's a great excuse to go flying. Getting bored on a long, smooth cross-country? Swing the compass— it will only add a few minutes to the trip time.

If flying over an agricultural area, using section lines works very well. Fence lines and roads are constructed on section lines in many areas. Section lines are oriented to true north. First, determine the magnetic direction the section lines are running. If you have forgotten how to apply the old "East is least and West is best" rule, look at a VOR rose on an aeronautical chart. The chart is laid out on the basis of true direction. The VOR north arrow is pointing to magnetic north. In an area of easterly variation, the VOR north indicator will be pointing east of true north. A straight edge, placed over the VOR station on the chart and aligned true north-south (parallel with a meridian), will tell the magnetic direction of the north-south section line and make it clear how the magnetic variation must be applied.

Fly over and along the section line. Line-up the center line of the aircraft with the section line, and set the directional gyro to the MAGNETIC direction of the section line. For example, if the magnetic variation is 7° East, the north section line is pointing 353° magnetic, if variation is 7° West, the section line is pointing 007° magnetic.

If there are not section lines in the area, use the runway center line of the nearest paved airport. The tower will be happy to provide the runway magnetic heading to the nearest degree. If the field is not controlled, ask the airport manager for the precise runway heading before going aloft. Then, fly down the runway in a low pass, align the aircraft center line with the runway center line and set the gyrocompass.

With the gyrocompass set, its readings become the FOR numbers in the deviation card, and the magnetic compass readings are the FLY values. While holding a

360° heading on the gyro, read the magnetic compass. If it reads 003°, the first entry on the deviation card should read: FOR 360 (degrees), FLY 003 (degrees). Repeat this process every 30°, then check the gyrocompass against the section line. Your deviation card can now be made up. Be sure to include the date and conditions (radios on, etc.) on the card. It might be well to repeat the calibration process in the opposite direction to be sure that the same numbers are displayed on the compass. If they aren't, then there was an error in the process or the compass is "hanging up" a little bit.

There should not be deviations greater than 10° on any noted heading. If there is, then the compass compensating magnets should be adjusted, as described below.

Adjusting the compensator magnets may not be necessary, if not more than 10° difference between the FOR and FLY values are found. If the error is more than 10°, adjusting the compensator magnets may help reduce error to bring it within accepted values. Adjusting the compensator magnets may first be done on the ground or it may be done in flight.

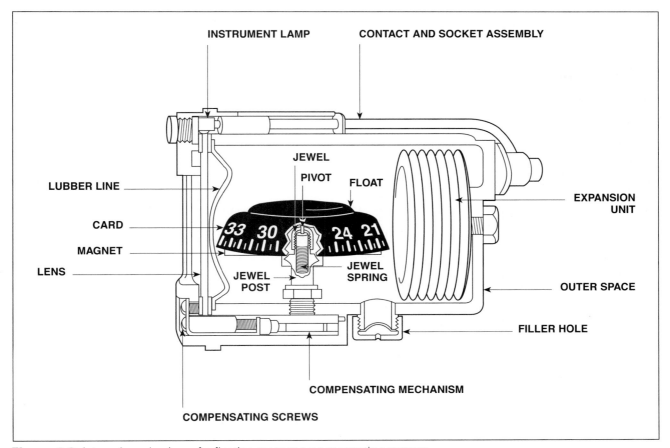

Figure 4-3. Internal mechanism of a floating magnet-type magnetic compass

Most of the larger airports have a compass rose laid out, usually on one of the least used taxi strips as far from electrical interference as possible, and at a location where a technician may be undisturbed while swinging the compass. The rose is laid out according to magnetic directions and is usually marked with a line every 30°. If there is no compass rose available, one can be laid out using an accurate compass or, better yet, a surveyor's transit, the sun, and a computer or set of Sun's true bearing tables. However, it is easier to make the adjustment while doing an airborne check.

Prepare the aircraft by removing any material from the instrument panel area and glove box that could possibly interfere with the compass. Be sure that all of the normally installed instruments and radio equipment are in place and are properly functioning. Adjust the compensator magnets until the dot on the screw head is aligned with the dot on the instrument case. Align the aircraft headed magnetic north.

Adjust the N-S compensator screw with a nonmagnetic screwdriver until the compass reads north (0). Now, turn the aircraft until it is aligned with magnetic east. Adjust the E-W screw until the compass reads east (9). Continue by turning the aircraft south and adjust the N-S screw to remove one-half of the south heading error. This will throw the north heading off, but the total north-south error should be divided equally between the two headings. Complete the adjustment by turning the aircraft west (27), and adjust the E-W screw to remove one-half of the west error. Then, swing the compass again, as described above, to develop the new deviation card.

When the compass is swung to your satisfaction, fill out the calibration card and date it. Make a proper logbook entry in the airframe log, with date, pilot's name, license number and description of the task completed.

Vertical Card Compasses

Vertical card compasses have come on the scene recently and are enjoying quite a bit of success. They have a stronger sensing magnet, and therefore work quite well at higher latitudes. I have used mine to 65° North latitude, and it was going strong while most of the whisky compasses I have flown in the North become useless in light turbulence north of 50° North, and then become totally useless "north of sixty." They just turn slowly around and around.

Vertical card compasses don't exhibit "northerly turning error" and acceleration error like a fluid compass, but they are roll, pitch and yaw sensitive.

With respect to vertical card compasses: Do not panel mount them, as they are sensitive to vibration and need to be mounted quite loosely. If it is necessary to mount one near the panel support bars that are found on many seaplanes or near other ferrous structures or radios, the external compensating magnets are also needed as the internal compensating magnets will not be sufficient to produce good results. Some people have not had good luck adjusting out large deviations in their vertical card compasses. It is absolutely imperative that the manufacturer's instructions be followed exactly during the adjustment process, as it is easy to align the compensating magnets in such a way that they are fighting each other, canceling their corrective abilities.

A quick check of the compass before a critical leg is a good idea. There are good directional indicators everywhere. If there are no section lines or paved runways, use the direction of a line drawn between two prominent points on the chart, such as two islands 10 to 15 miles apart in a lake. While flying over one island, align the aircraft's center line with the distant island and set the gyrocompass. Then check the compass' indication against the gyro reading, when headed in the general direction of the critical leg that is yet to be flown.

As mentioned before, the standard aircraft compass isn't much good in the far north or south. There, the lines of magnetic force point down into the earth, so the horizontal component of that force is small, making for poor direction-sensing capability of the parallel magnet ("whiskey") compass.

In the far north or south, pilots don't rely on the magnetic compass at all. They use their gyrocompass set to the runway heading at the beginning of the flight and compensate for its known errors en route, by using an astrocompass, or a shadow-pin pelorus and computer, (*see* Figures 4-12 and 4-13 on Page 57) or simply by applying corrections for the gyrocompass' known errors and hoping that precession errors, which are not totally predictable, remain small.

Magnetic Compass Errors
Magnetic Variation

It has been stated that the earth's magnetic poles are joined by irregular curves called magnetic meridians. The angle formed at any point between the magnetic meridian and the geographic meridian is called the **magnetic variation**. Variation is listed on charts as east or west. When variation is east, magnetic north is east of true north. Similarly, when variation is west, magnetic north is west of true north (Figure 4-4). Lines connecting points having the same magnetic variation are called **isogonic lines** (Figure 4-5). Lines connecting points having zero magnetic variation are called **agonic lines**. Magnetic variation is an error which must be corrected if a compass indication is to be converted to true direction.

Magnetic Deviation

Another error which the navigator is concerned with is caused by nearby magnetic influences, such as those related to magnetic material in the structure of the aircraft and its electrical systems. These magnetic forces deflect a compass needle from its normal alignment. The amount of such deflection is called **deviation** which, like variation, is labeled east or west as the north-seeking end of the compass is deflected east or west of magnetic north, respectively.

The correction for variation and deviation is usually expressed as a plus or minus value, and is computed as a correction to true heading. If variation or deviation is east, the sign of the correction is minus, and if west, the sign is plus. Hence, the old saying from aviation lore "east is least and west is best" helps us remember how to make the correction.

Aircraft headings are expressed in various ways, according to the basic reference for the heading. If the

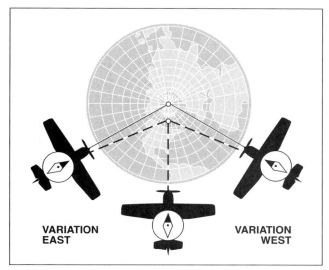

Figure 4-4. Variation is the angle between true north and magnetic north.

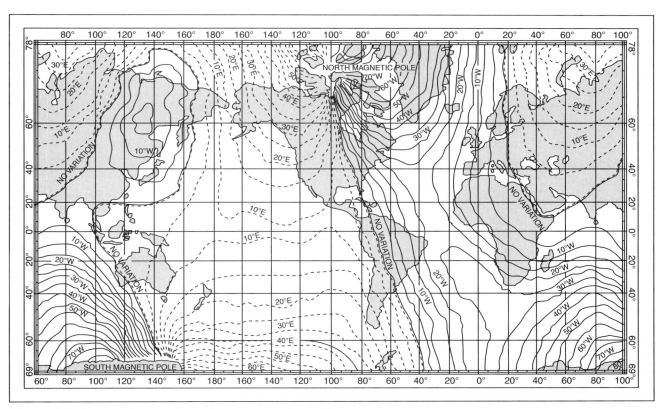

Figure 4-5. Isogonic lines are lines of equal magnetic variation.

heading is measured in relation to geographical north, it is a **true heading**. If the heading is in reference to magnetic north, it is a **magnetic heading**, and if it is in reference to the compass lubber line, it is a **compass heading**. *Compass heading differs from true heading by the amount of variation and deviation encountered. Magnetic heading varies from true heading by the amount of variation.*

Magnetic Dip

Discussed above in the section on the Earth's magnetic field, magnetic dip causes all compasses that sense the Earth's magnetic field to become less accurate in flight at high latitudes (above 50°), and to fail completely in higher latitudes. This makes navigation in high latitudes much more difficult and requires the pilot/navigator to utilize special techniques while flying there. Usually, the gyrocompass is set using runway heading as a reference, or sighting the longitudinal axis of the aircraft along geographical features (lake edge to lake edge, etc.) of which the pilot knows the true or magnetic bearing, or aligning the aircraft's longitudinal axis with the sun, with the sun's true bearing known to the navigator from one of several sources (a small computer, or a publication of the sun's true bearing, such as the Canadian government publication TP 784). At high latitudes, magnetic values are rarely used as they can't be sensed. Even the VORs there (in the Northern Domestic Airspace of Canada, for example) are aligned to true north, which makes navigation a bit easier as there is no need to convert back and forth from true to magnetic.

The Remote Indicating Magnetic Compass

Pilots who operate aircraft equipped with a **slaved gyrocompass** system, or a panel-mounted indicator instrument giving magnetic heading information, should be aware that somewhere in the aircraft is a magnetic-field sensing device, which provides electronic output of direction information to the panel indicator or slaved gyrocompass. The sensing device is located in a wing or the tail cone in order to locate it as far as possible from magnetic fields generated within the aircraft itself. The system requires a source of electric power and may have to be switched on by the pilot in order to function.

The **flux gate** or **flux valve** is the heart of the system, sensing the direction of the Earth's magnetic field (lines of flux). If this unit is not kept level, the lines of flux enter at odd angles (depending on the angle of

bank or pitch). This weakens the directional input, decreasing compass accuracy. The more sophisticated of these units incorporate a vertical-seeking gyro to maintain the sensing unit in a level attitude regardless of the attitude of the aircraft; these are called **gyro flux-gate compasses**. If the system is without a gyro (either a vertical-seeking gyro or a slaved gyrocompass), the pilot may not expect accurate readings unless the aircraft is level.

Like all magnetic compasses, the flux-gate system loses its ability to sense direction when operating in far northerly or southerly latitudes, due to the angle that the magnetic lines of flux take as they dip into the earth. Typically, pilots shut off the slaving feature of their gyrocompass when operating in the far north or south.

The **flux gate** is a special three-section transformer which develops a signal whose characteristics are determined by the position of the unit with respect to the Earth's magnetic field. The flux-gate element consists of three highly permeable cores arranged in the form of an equilateral triangle, with a primary and secondary winding on each core.

Operation of a **flux valve** is very similar to the flux gate, but construction is a little different. Instead of the three equilaterally spaced coils of the flux-gate, the **flux-valve spider** is constructed with three legs spaced 120° apart with the primary winding around a core in the center.

Gyroscopes as Directional Indicators

The characteristics possessed by a small spinning gyroscope have not only intrigued us by their seemingly odd behavior, but they have made possible the flight of aircraft without reference to a visible horizon.

In 1851, the French physicist Leon Focault devised a small wheel with a heavy outside rim that, when spun at a high speed, demonstrated the strange characteristic of remaining rigid in the plane in which it was spinning. He deduced that because the wheel remained rigid in space, it could show the rotation of the Earth. Because of this he named the device the **gyroscope**, a name that translated from the Greek means "to view the earth's rotation."

A spinning gyroscope possesses two characteristics we use in aircraft instrumentation. The first of these is **rigidity in space**. Let's assume that a gyro were positioned as shown in Figure 4-6, having no friction in its bearings, but with a power source to keep it spinning. If we could view it from the United States, at noon we would see the tail of the arrow. By the time the earth

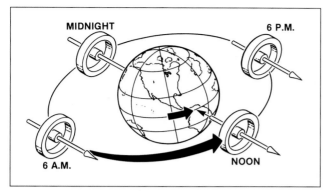

Figure 4-6. Rigidity in space causes a spinning gyroscope to remain in one position as the earth rotates.

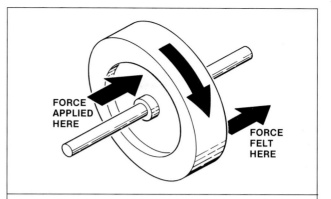

The precessive characteristic of a gyroscope causes a force applied to a spinning wheel to be felt 90° to the point of application, in the direction of the wheel's rotation.

Figure 4-7. Precession

rotated 90°, at 6:00 p.m., we would see the side of the wheel with the arrow pointing to the right. At midnight, we would again be in line with the arrow, only this time it would be pointing at us. By 6:00 a.m., we would again see the side of the wheel. Now, however, the arrow would be pointing to the left. This characteristic makes the gyroscope valuable to us as a stable reference for determining both the attitude and the direction of the aircraft carrying the gyro.

In the description of directional gyros, it is mentioned that there must be no friction in the bearings. The reason for this lies in the second characteristic of the gyro: **precession**.

If a force is applied perpendicular to the spin-plane of a spinning gyroscope, its effect will be felt not at the point of application, but at a point 90° from the point of application in the direction of rotation of the wheel. If a gyro is spinning in the plane shown in Figure 4-7, and a force is applied to the top of the wheel, it will not topple over as a static body would; it will rotate about its vertical axis. This rotation is called the precession of the gyro. If one of the bearings which supports the gyro shaft has friction, it will produce a force that will cause precession. Precession is a much stronger force than rigidity in space.

Precession is not desirable because it produces errors in directional and attitude gyros, but it is a useful force in erection of attitude gyros and in rate gyros, because the amount of precession is related to the amount of force that caused it. **Rate gyros** are used to measure the rate of rotation of the aircraft about one or more of its axes. Most aircraft have either a turn and slip indicator or a turn coordinator, both of which use precession as the actuating force.

The most commonly used magnetic compass is quite adequate for visual flight when it is only

occasionally referred to, but since it oscillates back and forth so much in turbulence, reads incorrectly during turns and is unreliable at high latitudes, it is less than satisfactory as a heading indicator when flying on instruments.

Remember that one of the two primary characteristics of a gyroscope is its ability to remain rigid in space. If a freely spinning gyroscope is set to align with the Earth's magnetic field, this gyro can be used to visualize heading, and since this gyro does not oscillate or hang up in a bank or pitch, it can be used as a heading indicator for instrument flight.

The Directional Gyro (DG) or Gyroscopic Heading Indicator

This instrument has no north-seeking tendency, so it must be set to agree with the magnetic compass. Early directional gyros called **horizontal card gyrocompasses** resembled the magnetic compass with the gyro rotor suspended in a double gimbals, and its spin axis in a horizontal plane inside the calibrated scale (Figure 4-8). The rotor was spun by a jet of air impacting on buckets cut into the rotor periphery. Pushing in on the caging knob on the front of the instrument leveled the rotor and locked the gimbals. The knob could then be turned to rotate the entire mechanism and bring the desired heading opposite the reference mark, or lubber line. Pulling the knob out unlocked the gimbals so the rotor could remain rigid in space. As the aircraft turned about the gyro, the pilot had a reference between the heading of the aircraft and the Earth's magnetic field.

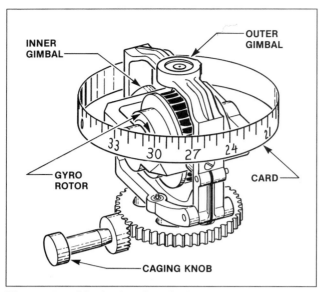

Figure 4-8. Mechanism for a horizontal card directional gyro

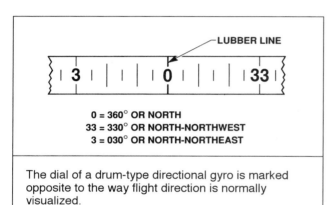

0 = 360° OR NORTH
33 = 330° OR NORTH-NORTHWEST
3 = 030° OR NORTH-NORTHEAST

The dial of a drum-type directional gyro is marked opposite to the way flight direction is normally visualized.

Figure 4-9. Dial of a drum-type directional gyro

Notice the card, as the dial is called, of the directional gyro in Figure 4-9. When the pilot is flying on a heading of 0°, or north, and wants to turn left to a heading of 330°, they see the number 33 (for 330°) to the right of the zero mark, but they must turn left to bring the 33 under the lubber line. This is no major problem to the thousands of pilots who learned to fly instruments using the floating magnet compass and the horizontal drum-type directional gyro, but to new instrument pilots it did create a problem. This was easily solved, however, by the **vertical card directional gyro** as shown in Figure 4-10.

Instead of a simple lubber line in front of the card, this instrument has a symbol of an airplane on its face in front of the dial, with its nose pointing straight up, representing straight ahead. The circular dial is con-

Figure 4-10. Vertical card directional gyro

nected to the gyro mechanism, so it remains rigid in space, and as the airplane turns about it, the dial rotates. The knob in the lower left-hand corner of the instrument may be pushed in to cage the instrument. This locks the gimbals so the pilot can turn the mechanism to get the indication on the dial under the nose of the symbolic airplane, which corresponds to the heading shown on the magnetic compass. When the knob is released, a spring pushes it back out and disengages it. The rotor support of these instruments is such that the gyro will not reach its stops during any flight maneuver, and therefore there is no need to cage the gyro. The bearings are of such high quality that friction is minimized and precession is not as big a problem as it is on older instruments. This type of directional gyro, like the older type, must be set to agree with the magnetic compass, and it too must be periodically checked to be sure that it has not drifted out of agreement with the compass. If it has, the knob may be pushed in and the dial reset.

The modern directional gyro, like the gyro horizon, has been combined with other instruments to make it the versatile flight instrument found in more sophisticated aircraft today. One of the most useful combinations has been that of **slaving** the gyro to a magnetic compass. A flux gate, or flux valve, picks up an induced voltage from the Earth's magnetic field and after processing it, directs it to a slaving torque motor in the instrument. This motor rotates the dial until the airplane's magnetic heading is under the nose of the symbolic airplane on the face of the instrument. This slaving gives the directional gyro all of the advantages of a magnetic compass, without its most disturbing faults. These faults will be discussed further in the section below on gyrocompass errors.

In the more exotic direction-indicating instruments, the slaved directional gyro is combined with radio navigation systems so it will display information from the VOR, ADF, or RNAV system, as well as from the glide slope. These instruments are called the horizontal situation indicator (HSI) and radio magnetic indicator (RMI).

Gyrocompass Errors

There are three errors associated with the non-slaved gyrocompass, two of which are totally predictable and one which is not predictable (**precession**). Often, the sum of the three errors (total error) is erroneously referred to as precession.

Drift, sometimes called **apparent precession**, is caused by the fact that the Earth is turning but the gyro wheel remains rigid in space. This error increases as one goes from the equator (zero drift error) to the true north or south pole where the error is slightly more than 15° per hour.

To help understand this, let's park an airplane on the ice at the true north pole, facing an igloo that is there. The engine is running, so there is suction to drive the gyros. The brakes are set and the airplane is tied down. We would be correct in setting the gyrocompass to 180° because no matter what direction we are headed, we are headed south, correct?

As every hour passes, the gyrocompass will show that the aircraft has turned left about 15°, even though it is still tied down and pointed at the igloo. The gyrocompass is correct: the Earth has turned under the aircraft. Had the aircraft been airborne over the north pole, flying a south heading, it would be pointed at the same point in space that it was an hour ago, but it would be flying a path over the ground in a southwesterly direction. If the aircraft flew for 24 hours by the gyrocompass' south heading, it would cross every line of longitude!

If you are having a little problem with this discussion, it is time to find a globe of the earth. Start the globe turning — counterclockwise as viewed from the north pole, correct? Now launch your imaginary flight from the north pole, headed south (in any direction). Note that the path over the ground is a spiral which crosses every meridian of longitude as the globe completes one revolution.

Please keep in mind that this is a theoretical discussion aimed only at understanding gyro drift, and that I said "flying over the north pole." During this imaginary flight, keep the airplane at or very near the north pole for the 24 hours of the flight.

Now let's get practical for awhile. It is obvious that flying in the extreme north requires some special techniques and applications, which are dealt with in the section below on using the gyrocompass in high latitudes. The following discussion of gyrocompass errors has application for all pilots.

Gyro drift is a predictable error which the pilot can compensate for. Here is how its value is calculated. Gyro drift H of a *stationary* airplane can be found with the use of the formula:

15.04 x Sine of the latitude = H degrees per hour

For example, at 30° and 60° north latitude, the drift of a stationary gyro would be:

15.04 x Sin 30° = 7.52° per hour

15.04 x Sin 60° = 13.02° per hour

Gyro Drift in Flight

In order to have zero drift, the gyro would have to remain stationary with respect to space rather than move with the surface of the earth. At the equator, a point on the surface of the Earth is moving at a speed of 900 knots (as viewed from space), so the speed of a point on the earth at any latitude can be found by:

900 x Cosine of the latitude = knots

For example, at 30° north, the surface of the earth is moving at a speed of:

900 x Cos 30° = 780 knots

If an aircraft departed a point on the earth at 30° north latitude and flew west at 780 knots, from space it would appear that it was remaining stationary and the Earth was turning under it at a speed of 780 knots. Since the aircraft would be stationary with respect to space, the gyrocompass would have zero drift error.

At 60° north, the aircraft would only have to fly west at a speed of:

900 x Cos 60° = 450 knots

in order to remain stationary with respect to space, and have zero gyro drift error. Now we know that a flight to the west will reduce gyro drift error and a flight to the east will increase it, over the stationary drift value. We can now compute the amount of drift of our gyrocompass while moving in flight in any direction.

On a flight to the north or south, drift H will be:

15.04 x Sin of the average latitude = H

For example, if we fly from 49° north to 51° north, the average latitude is 50° north, so drift will be:

15.04 x Sin 50° = 11.520 (decrease)/Hr

To correct the gyro drift on this trip, the pilot will need to add about 11.52/4 = 3° every 15 minutes.

If the flight is to the east or west, gyro drift will be H (the stationary drift rate) minus (westerly) or plus (easterly) the drift rate due to aircraft speed.

The drift value for aircraft speed easterly or westerly can be determined by the following reasoning: since the Earth's speed J at 50° north is 578.5 knots and the stationary (zero speed) drift rate H is 11.52° per hour, the drift rate will be zero if the aircraft flew west at J; it would be H if the aircraft was parked; and twice H if the aircraft flew east at J.

At 100 knots, drift due to east or west movement would be:

{east or west movement per hour (knots)/J} x H = K

and total drift, D, for flight in any direction is:

westerly: H minus K = D, and

easterly: H plus K = D

Our gyrocompass should be corrected by adding the amount of the drift D each hour, or better yet, add one-fourth of D every 15 minutes. If drift values are large (greater than 12°/hour) corrections are made more often, and adjusted so that the aircraft *averages* the correct heading.

To help the reader-pilot get a feel for the values of drift, Figure 4-11 shows values of drift for various latitudes for flights to the north, south, east and west, at 100 knots. Flights to other points of the compass are easy to estimate. Just use the average latitude (actually, at these speeds, latitude of any point on the flight is

close enough). For the east-west speed component, use the number of nautical miles you will go to the east or west in one hour as the entry value.

Remember, as we fly north, gyro drift error increases to a maximum of 15° per hour at the pole. Flying east increases and flying west decreases the error. Drift is a predictable gyro error and can be corrected by adding (in the northern hemisphere) the proper correction to the gyrocompass every 15 minutes.

The Other Predictable Gyrocompass Error

When flying by gyrocompass, the pilot should understand all of the errors inherent in the instrument that lead a pilot astray. The three major errors of the gyrocompass are *drift*, (or apparent precession), changes in *magnetic variation*, and *precession*. The first two are predictable; precession is not.

Changes in **magnetic variation** encountered en route will affect the magnetic compass reading, but not the gyrocompass. Therefore, the magnetic compass and the gyrocompass will disagree by the amount of the change in magnetic variation. If the gyrocompass is not corrected, it will show an error with respect to the magnetic compass. In the north, large changes in magnetic variation occur in relatively short distances. This is one of the reasons why, in the far north, all navigation is done with respect to true north.

A pilot using magnetic headings should remember that the gyrocompass and magnetic compass will disagree by the amount of any change in magnetic variation. For example, on a trip from Grand Forks, ND (7°E) to Duluth, MN (2°E), magnetic variation changes by 5°. For this example flight, let's assume the gyrocompass has no other errors. Departing GFK, we establish a heading of 112° magnetic. Both magnetic and gyro compasses are reading 112°. The gyro is not reset during the trip. If we steer by the magnetic compass, the gyrocompass will be reading 107° when we get near Duluth.

So it can be said that the gyrocompass has developed an error of -5°, over whatever period of time the flight took. To be correct, we must add 5° to the gyrocompass. This is another "apparent" error—the gyro wasn't really wrong; it was reading correctly with respect to space, but we wanted direction with respect to magnetic north.

FLIGHT DIRECTION AT 100 KNOTS			
LATTITUDE DEGREES	N. OR S.	WEST	EAST
30	7.52	6.5	8.5
40	9.67	8.3	11.1
50	11.52	9.5	13.5
60	13.02	10.1	15.9
70	14.1	9.5	18.7

Figure 4-11. Drift values

The Unpredictable Gyrocompass Error

Precession, it is called. It is caused by forces applied to the axis of the gyro wheel. These forces are due to small amounts of friction in the gimbal bearings that support the gyro wheel. While the gyro wheel attempts to remain rigid in its orientation in space, the aircraft is rolling, pitching and yawing. This causes the gimbal bearings to move with every aircraft movement. Since these bearings are not perfectly frictionless, the aircraft's movements apply small forces to the axis of the gyro wheel, causing it to precess from its original orientation. This translates to changes in the aircraft's indicated heading—an error.

Precession error increases if:

1. There is an increase in the aircraft's movements (turbulence, pilot-induced attitude changes).

2. Gimbal bearings are worn or contaminated with oil, tars, nicotine, etc. (including body and machine oils, and other residues from smoking, all of which end up as contaminants in air (vacuum)-driven gyros).

Precession error (not total error) should be less than 3° in 15 minutes. Pilots should be alert for indications of poor gyro health, such as increasing precession error, short spin-down time, vibration, and noise from the gyro after engine shutdown.

Using the Gyrocompass in the North

In the far north, where there are no section lines and the magnetic compass is unreliable, other means are used to periodically reset the gyrocompass.

Occasionally, terrain features of known alignment (from plotting on a sectional chart) can be used. Another old standby for this purpose is the **astrocompass** (Figure 4-12). With inputs of time (Local Hour Angle), approximate latitude and declination, and alignment of the instrument so that sunlight casts a shadow in the sighting tray, true north can be read from the instrument and the gyrocompass corrected.

The astrocompass is somewhat cumbersome to use in a small airplane but is ideal for use in larger aircraft, especially those fitted with a sighting dome, where the astrocompass can be properly mounted.

With the advent of the small, programmable microcomputer, the **shadow pin pelorus** has become a useful instrument to keep the gyrocompass set properly. It is far simpler than the astrocompass to use, and takes up far less space in the aircraft. It consists of a compass rose of 3 to 5 inches in diameter with an upright pin in the center of the rose. It is mounted level

Figure 4-12. The astrocompass, when aligned with the sun, indicates true heading.

on the sun shield on top of the instrument panel in front of the pilot. Sunlight, falling on the pin, casts a shadow on the compass rose. If the sun's azimuth from the aircraft is known (sun's true bearing), the reciprocal of that number is the true direction from the sun to the aircraft. In the example of Figure 4-13, the sun's azimuth is 261°, so the direction from the sun (the direction the sun's shadow falls) is 081° true. Knowing this, the pilot rotates the compass rose of the pelorus until the shadow falls on 81°. The compass rose now indicates true direction. The pilot can read the true heading of the aircraft at the lubber line (line indicating

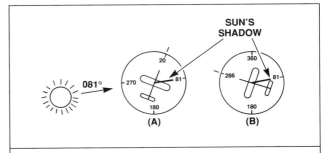

Use of the pelorus. In this example, the sun's azimuth is 261° true, so the sun's shadow will be 081°. The pilot rotates the compass rose until the shadow falls on 81°, and reads the aircraft's true heading of 020° for airplane A, and 286° for airplane B.

Figure 4-13. Shadow pin pelorus

alignment with the longitudinal axis of the aircraft), and reset the gyrocompass accordingly.

The difficult task of computing the sun's azimuth is made easy by the use of a small microcomputer. A software program will provide the sun's azimuth given date, time, latitude and longitude. Some modern navigation receivers will also provide the pilot with the sun's true or magnetic bearing (*see* Figure 4-14). As long as the sun is shining, gyrocompass error can be easily corrected.

Sometimes the crew must rely on their knowledge of many navigation systems in order to devise a means of "carrying on" with accurate movement across the earth when the aircraft's navigation systems fail. Figure 4-15 shows one solution to how to "carry on" while flying across featureless terrain in the far north where the magnetic compass is useless and when the vacuum pump has failed, rendering the gyrocompass useless. In this situation, all heading information was lost. Thinking quickly, before the aircraft wandered away from the heading that had been working and the gyrocompass spun down, the pilot grabbed a handy

Figure 4-15. Using the sun's shadow

chart pin and stuck it in the upholstery to take advantage of the sun's shadow across the headphone plug. The shadow falling across the pin was used to steer accurately for the next 50 minutes until the coastline came into view.

Track

The direction the aircraft is pointed (heading) is not necessarily going to coincide with the direction the aircraft travels (**track**). The difference between these two directions is referred to as the **drift angle**. If the drift angle is known and the aircraft's heading is known accurately, track can be determined.

With modern-day flight, track over the ground is usually established by using electronic navaids. But if the pilot/navigator is not familiar with the principles of the driftmeter and able to utilize the technique, even without the instrument itself he or she is destined to forever wander about the skies, totally dependent on the electronic navaid with no hope of being able to judge whether or not an accurate track is being flown. For this reason, the reader is encouraged to study the principles in the following section carefully and understand the section in the next chapter (*see* Page 66 "Precise Determination of Track") which describe how the pilot/navigator can function as a driftmeter without having one aboard.

Driftmeter

Most methods of wind determination depend on the knowledge of the **drift angle**, the angle between heading and track. When the Earth's surface (land or sea) is visible, this angle can be measured directly with an instrument found on some older aircraft, known as a **driftmeter**.

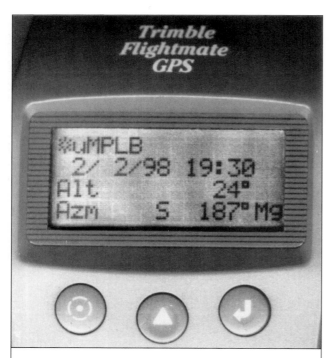

This hand-held GPS in "sun" mode provides the sun's true or magnetic bearing at any time of day/year from any location on earth. It shows here that on February 2nd, 1998, at exactly 19:30 UTC at location MPLB (a user waypoint in northern Minnesota), the sun's bearing was 187° magnetic and was 24° above the horizon.

Figure 4-14. Hand-held GPS provides the sun's true bearing.

The principle of the driftmeter is very simple. Suppose that the ground is observed through a hole in the floor of the aircraft. As the aircraft flies along its track, objects on the ground appear to move across the hole in the direction exactly opposite to the track.

Thus, in Figure 4-16, if the aircraft track is in the direction of line BA, a house appears to move across the hole from A to B. Suppose now that a wire is stretched across the hole parallel to the longitudinal axis of the aircraft. This wire YX represents the true heading of the aircraft. Since BA is the track and YX is the true heading, the drift angle is the angle AOX. The driftmeter measures this angle AOX. A simple driftmeter might be built as shown in Figure 4-17. A glass plate, which may be rotated by means of the handle on the right, is placed over a hole in the floor of the aircraft. On the glass, parallel drift lines are drawn. The drift lines, together with the two or three cross lines (timing lines) usually present in a driftmeter, are called the **reticle**. The center drift line extends to the edge of the plate as a pointer. On the floor ahead of the hole is a drift scale which shows the position of the drift lines relative to the longitudinal axis of the aircraft. Thus, when the pointer is on 0°, the drift lines are parallel to the longitudinal axis; and when the pointer is on 10°R, the drift lines make a 10° angle to the right of the axis.

To use this simple driftmeter, turn the glass plate so that objects on the ground move across the hole parallel to the drift lines. Then, the drift lines are parallel to the track of the aircraft. Read the drift scale opposite the pointer. If the pointer indicates 15°L, the aircraft is drifting 15° to the left. Therefore, if the true heading is 090°, the track is 075°.

On every driftmeter, the drift scale is marked with the words "right" and "left" or with the letters "R" and "L." These words always refer to the drift and not to the drift correction. Normally, driftmeters have a plus and minus sign on the scale. These give the sign of the drift correction (which is discussed in the next chapter, under "Precise Determination of Track"). Most driftmeters have the capability to measure ground speed when used with a stopwatch and a radar altimeter by timing passing targets.

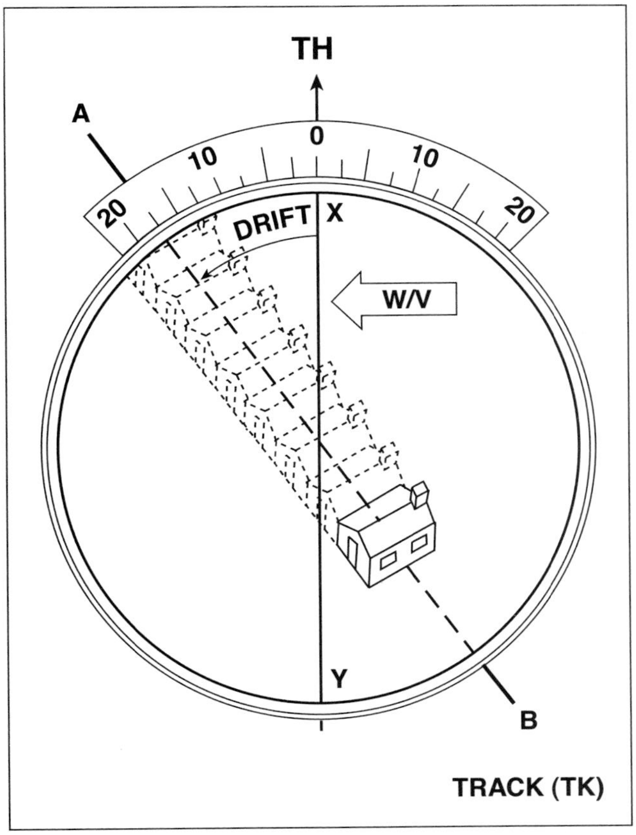

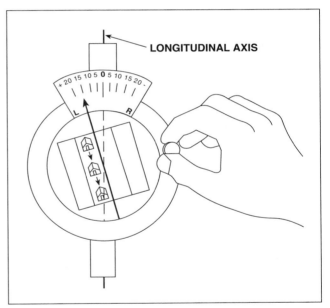

Figure 4-17. Read drift on scale opposite pointer.

Figure 4-16. Principle of a driftmeter

Study Questions

1. Explain:

   Variation.

   Isogonic line.

   Deviation.

2. What are the four dimensions of navigation?

3. What is an isogonic line? An agonic line?

4. Describe how a pilot "swings the compass."

5. What are the three errors of a gyrocompass?

6. Which of the errors in #5. are predictable?

7. Describe the components, and their functions, of a slaved gyro. Why does a slaved gyro need to have a switch that allows the pilot to shut off the slaving feature?

5: Basic Navigation Techniques

Introduction

Now that the basic instruments available to the navigator have been discussed, it is time to review the mechanics of dead reckoning procedures. These Include precision dead reckoning: precisely determining track and ground speed. Plotting on various chart projections, pilotage, and determining wind effect solutions are also discussed in this chapter.

Using basic skills in dead reckoning procedures, a pilot/navigator can predict aircraft position in the event more reliable navigation equipment is unavailable or not operative.

Understanding and practicing the skills needed to use these techniques will greatly improve the pilot/navigator's ability to monitor and evaluate the performance of today's sophisticated navigation systems. Therefore, a good foundation in the basic skills of dead reckoning and **pilotage** (flight from one recognizable landmark to another) is imperative for the pilot/navigator.

Dead Reckoning Navigation

Are you prepared to fall back to the art and skill of compass and clock, if your electronic aids fail? Are you so skilled at the art of using the compass and clock that you intuitively know when the electronic aids are lying to you? If not, what is your defense against false information from electronic aids?

It is generally agreed that the compass is a pilot's primary navigation tool. But when it comes to specifying the second most valuable such device in the cockpit, there is often some difference of opinion.

New pilots generally favor the VOR receiver, or the LORAN, or the GPS. But those with more experience vote for the clock. After all, when a fuse blows or the left-right needle behaves like a metronome gone berserk, or the warning flags come on, or worse—there is no warning, a pilot must resort to basics. The reliable compass and clock become the primary weapons in a battle of wits against the elements. The compass

indicates where the aircraft is and has been going, and the clock tells how far. Without either of these allies, a pilot can get lost, very fast, especially when above clouds or over terrain where checkpoints are confusingly few and far apart (featureless terrain).

Compass-and-clock, or dead-reckoning navigation, however, is slowly becoming a lost art as increasingly more reliance is placed on electronic guidance. Although no one can deny that VOR navigation simplified cockpit workloads many years ago and LORAN and GPS have furthered that end, pilots must somehow avoid becoming too complacent.

Some, for example, don't keep track of their forward progress while navigating along a radial or course. They simply wait for the TO-FROM flag to drop or the LORAN to tell them they have arrived at the way point, which may provide the first positive fix since passing the previous station. But shouldn't a pilot always know his position relative to the nearest airport?

Dead reckoning (DR navigation) is a relatively painless procedure that can and should be combined with radio navigation, so that the pilot is aware of the aircraft's approximate position at all times. According to popular definition, **dead reckoning** is short for "deduced reckoning," or as the old-timers used to say, "you're dead if you don't reckon right." In truth, however, the term originated with maritime navigation and refers to *reckoning or reasoning one's position relative to something stationary or dead in the water.* Simply stated, DR navigation is a method of predicting en route progress based on the direction of flight and the estimated ground speed since the last known position.

Unfortunately, the mere mention of DR often makes pilots uncomfortable with memories of FAA written examinations, wind triangles, and E-6B problems. But DR doesn't have to be laborious. Consider, for example, one pilot, an ATP who flies his Aerostar all over North and South America without the aid of LORAN or GPS. He has so simplified his dead reckoning procedures that he feels they are not only fun to use, but frequently result in reduced flight time, because he is not confined to the often dog-legged dictates of Victor airways. Also, he claims he is more relaxed holding a constant heading than reacting to the semaphore-like movements of a VOR needle.

Prior to a VFR flight, this pilot simply uses a yardstick and a VFR planning chart (JN charts outside the U.S.) to plot a direct course between the departure and destination airports (assuming that intervening terrain and other restrictions do not pose a threat to safety or legality).

He then uses the forecasted winds aloft together with Figures 5-1 and 5-2 (the rule-of-sixty, which is explained later in this chapter under "Precision Tracking," easily replaces Figure 5-2) to determine the true heading and ground speed. Assume, for example, that the measured true course is 040° and the winds aloft are expected to be from 010° at 40 knots. In other words, the wind will be blowing from 30° to the left of the nose. Using Figure 5-1, he determines that this is equivalent to a 35-knot headwind component and a 20-knot, left crosswind component.

Since the planned true airspeed is 220 knots, he expects the en route ground speed to be 185 knots (220 − 35 = 185) (Figure 5-1). Next he consults Figure 5-2 and determines that a 20-knot, left crosswind component combines with 220 knots of airspeed to require a 5° (left) wind correction angle. Therefore the true heading for the proposed flight is 040° less 5°, or 035°.

End of problem…without having to plot a wind triangle!

If more than one wind condition is to be encountered en route, they may be arithmetically averaged with reasonable accuracy if wind directions don't vary by more than 90° and wind speeds are within 15 knots of each other. For example, assume that the winds aloft for each of three flight segments along the direct route are forecast to be 080° at 15 knots, 100° at 30 knots and 150° at 30 knots. The average wind direction is (080° + 100° + 150°) ÷ 3 = 110°. Similarly, the average wind speed is 25 knots. However, this technique should not be used when maximum accuracy is required (such as on a long, overwater flight).

En route, the pilot keeps track of his progress visually, or uses elapsed time and estimated ground speed to plot a "DR position." Often, he doesn't turn on the dual VOR receivers until within range of the destination—if at all. When necessary, he applies a mid-course correction to compensate for an errant wind forecast.

Dead reckoning works, and it's reasonably accurate. Ask the man who pioneered the 2,000-mile, Newfoundland-to-Ireland route in 1927 as well as the thousands of pilots who have flown in his wake—with little more than a compass and a clock. Lindberg was luckier than is generally realized, however. According to John P.V. Heinmuller, one of the official FAA observ-

		Angle Between Wind Direction and True Course									
		0°	10°	20°	30°	40°	50°	60°	70°	80°	90°
Wind Speed	10	10 / 0	10 / 2	9 / 3	9 / 5	8 / 6	6 / 8	5 / 9	3 / 9	2 / 10	0 / 10
	20	20 / 0	20 / 3	19 / 7	17 / 10	15 / 13	13 / 15	10 / 17	7 / 19	3 / 20	0 / 20
	30	30 / 0	30 / 5	28 / 10	26 / 15	23 / 19	19 / 23	15 / 26	10 / 28	5 / 30	0 / 30
	40	40 / 0	39 / 7	38 / 14	35 / 20	31 / 26	26 / 31	20 / 35	14 / 38	7 / 39	0 / 40
	50	50 / 0	49 / 9	47 / 17	43 / 25	38 / 32	32 / 38	25 / 43	17 / 47	9 / 49	0 / 50
	60	60 / 0	59 / 10	56 / 21	52 / 30	46 / 39	39 / 46	30 / 52	21 / 56	10 / 59	0 / 60
	70	70 / 0	69 / 12	66 / 24	61 / 35	54 / 45	45 / 54	35 / 61	24 / 66	12 / 69	0 / 70

The upper-left number in each square represents a headwind or tailwind component, depending on whether the wind is coming from ahead or behind.

The lower-right number is the value of the the left or right crosswind component.

Figure 5-1. Headwind/tailwind and crosswind components for various wind velocities

	True Airspeed								
	80	100	120	140	160	180	200	220	240
5	4°	3°	2°	2°	2°	2°	1°	1°	1°
10	7°	6°	5°	4°	4°	3°	3°	3°	2°
15	11°	9°	7°	6°	5°	5°	4°	4°	4°
20	14°	12°	10°	8°	7°	6°	6°	5°	5°
25	18°	14°	12°	10°	9°	8°	7°	7°	6°
30	22°	17°	14°	12°	11°	10°	9°	8°	7°
35	26°	20°	17°	14°	13°	11°	10°	9°	8°
40	30°	24°	19°	17°	15°	13°	12°	10°	10°
45	34°	27°	22°	19°	16°	14°	13°	12°	11°
50	39°	30°	25°	21°	18°	16°	14°	13°	12°

Crab angle necessary to compensate for a given crosswind component, when flying at a given airspeed.

Crosswind Component (leftmost column label)

Caution: Valid for any units of speed as long as wind velocities and airspeeds are both in the same unit.

Figure 5-2

ers for the New York-to-Paris flight, a freak wind condition existed over the North Atlantic on May 20-22, 1927. The pressure patterns were arranged in such a way that the net drift acting upon the Spirit of St. Louis was zero, the first time this had ever been recorded by weather experts.

If an aircraft maintains its predicted ground speed and track, then a positive fix obtained at any time during the flight will agree with the aircraft position as determined by DR methods. More likely, however, an actual fix (using radio or pilotage / or both) will disagree with the DR position. Usually this is because one or more variables have been appraised incorrectly. In other words, there is an element of uncertainty surrounding every fix determined purely by dead reckoning.

A statistical analysis of DR data shows that 90% of the time, the maximum dead reckoning error (per hour of flight) is 20 miles plus 1% of the estimated distance flown during that hour.

Groundspeed loss due to crabbing into the wind when flying at a given true airspeed (Valid for knots or mph. Refer to caution note under Figure 5-2.)

True Airspeed	Wind Correction Angle (CRAB)				
	10°	15°	20°	25°	30°
80	−1	−3	−5	−7	−11
100	−2	−3	−6	−9	−13
120	−2	−4	−7	−11	−16
140	−2	−5	−8	−13	−19
160	−2	−5	−10	−15	−21
180	−3	−6	−11	−17	−24
200	−3	−7	−12	−19	−27
220	−3	−7	−13	−21	−29
240	−4	−8	−14	−22	−32

Figure 5-3

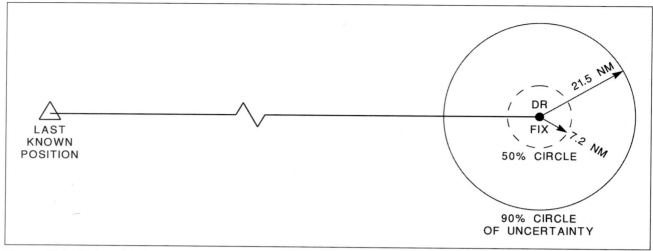

Figure 5-4. Circles of 90% and 50% confidence based only on DR for a 1-hour flight in a 150-knot aircraft

Figure 5-4, for example, shows where the pilot of a 150-knot aircraft has computed his position to be at the end of one hour. The radius of the circle of uncertainty is therefore equal to 20 nautical miles (NM) + 1%, which equals 21.5 NM. In other words, there is a 90% probability that the pilot is actually within 21.5 NM of where he thinks he is. It also can be shown that 50% of the time the aircraft is located within a circle with only one-third the radius of the larger circle. In this case, the pilot has a 50-50 chance of being within 7.2 NM of the DR position.

One way to reduce the size of the circle of uncertainty is to make sure the compass deviation card is accurate. The FAA doesn't require a periodic compass swing, but pilots would be wise to perform this check at least annually. Deviation errors can change significantly over a period of time and with changes in equipment in the aircraft.

Also, pilots should make it a habit to glance at the compass whenever lining up on a runway of known magnetic direction. Remember, however, that the runway number usually represents the magnetic direction rounded off to the nearest 5°. Some runway numbers disagree by more than 10° with the actual magnetic directions. Tucson's Runway 11L, for example, has a magnetic direction of 122°.

None of this should be interpreted as an argument against radio navigation, in favor of DR. But it is nice to know that there is an alternate, reliable way to get from one place to another when VOR is unavailable and pilotage is difficult. All that is required is some common-sense reasoning and occasional practice. The idea is to be aware of the wind and its effects and to maintain a running score of flight progress, either on a flight log or by making marks on the chart and labeling each position (estimated or actual) with the time of passage.

The Running Fix

Not only can DR be used to compute progress along a radial, it can also be used in conjunction with VOR or pilotage to arrive at a **"running fix."**

Consider the pilot flying from A to B in Figure 5-5. He's not necessarily lost, but it has been a while since the last positive fix. He's also having trouble correlating contour lines and other features on the chart with those on the ground. At 1:00 p.m., the aircraft crosses a railroad track, an excellent line of position (LOP). But one LOP does not establish a fix. Eighteen minutes later, the pilot is within range of a VOR station and determines that he is on the 230° radial. Again, the pilot has a single LOP, not enough to establish position—or is it?

A fix can be obtained by advancing the 1:00 p.m. LOP (the railroad tracks) toward the second LOP (the radial). This is accomplished by first estimating the distance flown since crossing the first LOP. Assume, for example, that the estimated ground speed of the aircraft in Figure 5-5 is 150 knots. In 18 minutes, therefore, the distance flown is about 45 NM. The first LOP is then advanced (parallel to itself) 45 NM in the direction of the estimated track being flown. The point where the advanced LOP intersects the VOR radial (the second LOP) is the fix for 1:18 p.m. and shows the aircraft to be north of course.

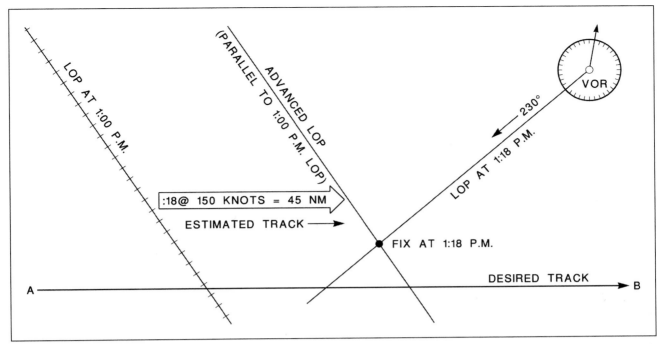

Figure 5-5. The running fix

A running fix can be obtained using any two LOPs as long as they cross at a reasonably oblique angle. They may be highways, rivers, or even a pair of VOR radials crossed at deferent times.

The Single LOP Approach

Another combination of DR and VOR navigation is called the "single-LOP approach." This technique can be life-saving and is illustrated in Figure 5-6 (on Page 66).

For example, a pilot is endeavoring to fly a true course of 090° toward the Tufluk Airport which is on the 170° radial of a VORTAC (far to the north of course). The pilot estimated arrival over the airport would be at 2:55 p.m. Unfortunately, he has been unable to obtain a reliable and recent fix and isn't sure that he's on course. So, what should he do if, upon intercepting the 170° radial, the airport cannot be found? Should the pilot fly north or south along the radial to find the destination? Since he is running low on fuel, he can't afford to turn in the wrong direction.

Dead reckoning (or common sense) navigation offers a logical solution. About 30-45 minutes prior to ETA, the pilot should make a sufficiently large turn and purposefully intercept the radial north of the airport (or south; in this example, north may give better VOR reception).

When the 170° radial is finally intercepted, the pilot knows with reasonable confidence which way to turn. By turning off course intentionally, he eliminates the likelihood of turning, searching, and wasting fuel in the wrong direction. This procedure is also known as the **landfall intercept**, used by mariners before invention of the chronometer (and thus, before longitude could be accurately determined). This procedure doesn't require that the destination be on a VOR radial. The airport could be situated on a river, shoreline, highway, railroad, or anything else that is easily identifiable and is approximately perpendicular to the true course. Nor does the single LOP approach have to be reserved for locating a destination. It can be used with equal effectiveness to find a needed enroute checkpoint.

DR teaches another valuable lesson—how to avoid a mid-air collision.

In pre-radar days, one of the techniques a fighter aircraft could use to intercept another airplane required that the two aircraft lie on a "line of constant bearing." In other words, the direction of one aircraft from the other must remain constant (as long as each aircraft maintains a constant heading and airspeed). The same is true of two aircraft on collision courses. Visually, this means that if an aircraft remains fixed at a specific point on the windshield and at the same altitude, expect an encounter of the wrong kind. To avoid such an

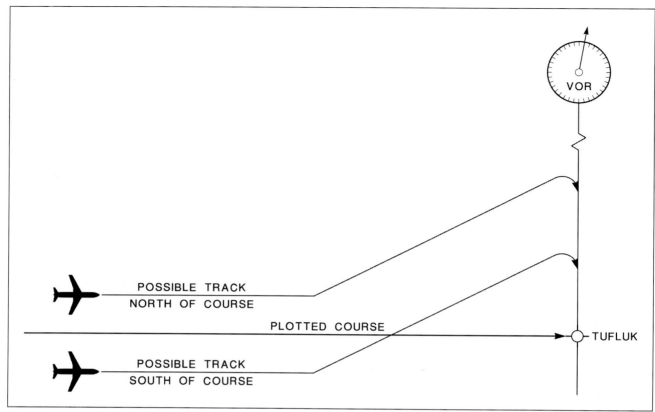

Figure 5-6. Example of the single LOP approach

unpleasantry, change heading so that the "bogie" appears to move across the windshield. When this happens, the two aircraft are not maintaining a constant bearing from one another and an "intercept" is impossible.

DR offers much to the pilot willing to expend a little extra effort, and it won't take long to learn that DR really stands for Darned Reliable. The pilot/navigator who becomes skilled in the use of DR will also learn that the big three in navigation aren't Collins, King, and Narco; they're rate (speed), time, and distance.

Precision Dead Reckoning

Precise Determination of Track Without Avionics

Many years ago, I rode in the right seat of an old seaplane, flying across the featureless terrain in the Northwest Territories. It was a 1935 Stinson Gullwing, and it had no navigation radios of any kind. Looking out on the thousands of little lakes that dotted the landscape, I wondered how the pilot was navigating and

how he would be able to find the one little lake that was to be our destination, still over an hour away.

When asked, the pilot said, "We are tracking 142°, right on course."

"How do you know that?" was my next question.

"That's easy," he responded, "I know my compass is accurate because I calibrated (swung) it recently. Right now it is reading 135°. Looking out over the nose, there is a bush coming directly at us, and that bush is 7° to the right of where the aircraft is pointed. Therefore, we are drifting to the right, tracking 7° more than the compass says our heading is, so 135° + 7° is 142°."

"How do you know that angle is 7°?" I wanted to know.

"Well," he said, "I used to have a protractor I carried on my glareshield to help me judge angles in front of the airplane but, with practice, I got good at judging angles and don't need it anymore. If I'm in doubt about the angle, I can point the aircraft at that bush and read the compass—it will read 142°. In another 15 minutes we should be over Bracken Lake, which is such an odd shape you can't miss it. Then we will know how many degrees we are off course."

I said, "OK, now I see how you knew your track so precisely. It's really quite simple now that you've explained it—you have figured out how to be your own **driftmeter**! I am intrigued by how it is you will know how many degrees you are off course when you get to Lake Bracken, but first let me ask you one more question about driftmeters: With a driftmeter, ground speed can be determined—can you also do that without the driftmeter?"

Precise Determination of Ground Speed Without Avionics

"Sure," the old pilot said, "it is especially easy when flying a floatplane, but I've also done it in big, fast landplanes with quite good accuracy—within 3 or 4% when compared to a sophisticated plane's GPS readout. Just like the driftmeter, I measure the time in seconds it takes for a bush or lake shoreline to pass from a sighting even with the bow of the float, to a point on the float even with the sixth pumpout plug, which just happens to be a 90° angle as viewed out my window. The seconds go on the inside (time) scale of my E6-B and height above ground in feet goes on the outside (distance) scale. The ground speed (knots) is read on the outside scale opposite the driftmeter K factor on the inside scale. For a 90° sighting angle, the K factor is 118. The K factor can be found for any angle by backing into the problem with the actual ground speed known by flying a measured course. So, with no fancy, sophisticated gismos, I can 'dead reckon' long distances very accurately over featureless terrain that just won't allow pilotage techniques. Over courses of 80-100 miles, I expect to be within one minute of my time estimate and ½-mile cross track distance. With one or two pilotage sightings like Lake Bracken up there along the way, the DR accuracy is about the same as can be done with the fancy avionics."

"That *is* impressive," I said, "but now, what about the off-course angle—is that Lake Bracken there?"

"Yes, and it looks like we are about one mile off course," the old pilot commented, "I am holding the determined course and track very precisely, in other words, doing DR navigation only, rather than just flying to a point I can see, so that the off-course angle can be determined, even though it puts the lake slightly off to our left. One mile off course in thirty miles is equivalent to a 2° error, according to the **rule-of-sixty**, which says *if the adjacent side of any right triangle is 60 units long, the opposite side will be equal in units to the angle in degrees.* So, if we are one mile off in thirty miles, that's equal to two miles in sixty, which makes the angle be 2°. Therefore, a heading correction of 2° left should cause us to parallel the intended course and 4° left should get us back on the intended course in another 15 miles, eh?"

"Remember, though, that the rule-of-sixty only works well up to about 25°. There are dozens of uses for the rule-of-sixty for pilots."

So much for that cockpit conversation that took place many years ago in the land of the midnight sun. I hope it provides as much food for thought for those who read this as it did for me. Any pilot who understands the above basics and practices with them will be well equipped to judge whether or not the sophisticated navigation device(s) in use are working well or leading the aircraft astray. Chapter 16 also deals with errors and limitations of sophisticated navigation systems, and should help improve the knowledge base and judgment needed to continually monitor and judge the performance of these systems.

Doppler

Since people first flew, they have searched for ways to determine aircraft ground speed and drift angle without aid from the ground. Various models of the driftmeter provided a partial answer to the problem. Their use consumed a great deal of the navigator's time, and they could not be used over smooth water or when weather obscured the surface. **Doppler Radar** provides the navigator with continuous, instantaneous, accurate readings of ground speed and drift angle in all weather conditions, both over land and over water, although very smooth water for considerable distances is also a problem for this system. It does this automatically with equipment of practical size and weight and its operation makes use of the Doppler effect.

Doppler Effect

The **Doppler effect** was discovered in 1842 by Christian Johann Doppler. This effect, simply stated, is that transmitted energy undergoes an *apparent* shift in frequency as the distance between the transmitter and receiver decreases or increases. It is this frequency shift which makes possible the instantaneous sensing and measuring of ground speed and drift angle by Doppler radar.

The Doppler effect applies to all wave motion including electromagnetic, light, and sound. The effect on sound waves can be observed by listening to the whistle of a passing train. As the train approaches, its whistle, as heard by a stationary observer, has a fairly steady pitch; that is, higher than the true pitch. As the train passes, the pitch drops quickly to a frequency below the true pitch and remains at approximately the lower value as the train moves away from the observer.

This principle is utilized in **Doppler (side-looking) radar** in that the frequency of the transmitted pulse appears to change when received back as a reflected signal. The amount of frequency change is proportional to the speed of the reflecting object, relative to the speed of the aircraft. Three or four beams are directed at 90-120° from each other. The frequency shifts from each are directed into a computer which determines forward velocity and sideward velocity (drift) over the ground. Drift is then resolved around true heading to produce ground track.

Explanation of Terms

Several terms have been mentioned in earlier portions of this text. The definitions of these terms should now be reviewed before the mechanics of chart work are learned.

True course (TC) is the *intended* horizontal direction of travel over the surface of the earth, expressed as an angle measured clockwise from true north (000°) through 360°.

Course line is the horizontal component of the *intended* path of the aircraft comprising both direction and magnitude or distance.

Track (Tr) is the horizontal component of the *actual* path of the aircraft over the surface of the earth. Track may, but very seldom does, coincide with the true course or intended path of the aircraft. The difference between the two is caused by the inability to predict perfectly all in-flight conditions.

True heading (TH) is the horizontal direction in which an aircraft is pointed. More precisely, it is the angle measured clockwise from true north through 360° to the longitudinal axis of the aircraft. The difference between **track** and **true heading** is caused by wind and is called **drift**.

Ground speed (GS) is the speed of the aircraft over the ground. It may be expressed in nautical miles, statute miles, or kilometers per hour, but nautical miles per hour (knots) is most commonly used.

True airspeed (TAS) is the rate of motion of an aircraft relative to the air mass surrounding it. Since the air mass is usually in motion in relation to the ground, airspeed and ground speed seldom are the same.

Dead reckoning position (DR Position) is a point in relation to the Earth established by keeping an accurate account of time, ground speed, and track since the last known position. It may also be defined as the position obtained by applying wind effect to the true heading and true airspeed of the aircraft.

A **Fix** is an accurate position determined by one of the aids to DR, often occurring at the intersection of two LOPs.

Most probable position (MPP) is a position determined with partial reference to a DR position and partial reference to a fixing aid.

Plotting

Chart work should be an accurate and graphic picture of the progress of the aircraft from departure to destination; with or without the log, it should serve as a complete record of the flight. Thus, it also follows that the navigator should be familiar with and use standard symbols and labels, even if self-developed, on charts.

Plotting on charts used for **pilotage** (flying from one recognizable landmark to another), or a combination of pilotage and DR is vitally important. The most important aid to pilotage navigation is a line scribed on the chart which represents the intended ground track. The track line should be marked with distance-remaining-to-way point, or to destination tics in order to assist the pilot/navigator with judging distances and gaining a perspective of the size of natural features. During the flight, there is *always* a point noted on the chart, close behind the aircraft, where time was noted and where the pilot/navigator knew for certain that the aircraft was over that point. Those times are usually noted on the chart and underlined to differentiate them from an *estimated* time, which *always* appears on the chart in front of the aircraft, without underline (or some other method of differentiation devised by the user).

Before starting any plot, note the **scale**, **projection** of the chart, and check the **date** to be certain that the chart is current.

Plotting Procedure, Mercator Chart

A great many charts and plotting sheets are printed on the Mercator projection.

The latitude scale (measured N-S) is used to represent nautical miles. The longitude scale should never be used to measure distance. Some charts carry a linear scale in the margin, and, where present, it indicates that the same scale may be used anywhere on the chart. Some charts provide a scale in the margin that is latitude variable; that is, the scale changes with latitude.

Plotting Positions

On most Mercator charts, the spacing between meridians and parallels is widely spaced, necessitating the use of dividers. There are several methods by which positions can be plotted on Mercator charts. One method is illustrated in Figure 5-7 (Page 70). Place the straight edge of the plotter in a vertical position, at the desired longitude. Set the dividers to the desired number of minutes of latitude. Hold one point against the straight edge on the parallel of latitude corresponding to the whole degree of latitude given. Let the other point also rest against the straight edge and lightly prick the chart. This marks the desired position. In measuring the latitude and longitude of a position already plotted, reverse the procedure.

Plotting and Measuring Courses

Plot departure and destination on the chart, as shown in Figure 5-8 (Page 71), Step 1. Step 2 is to draw the course line between the two points. If they are close together, the straight edge of the plotter can be used. If they are far apart, two plotters can be used together, or a longer straightedge can be used. If none of these methods is adequate, fold the edge of the charts so that the fold connects the departure and destination points, and make a series of pencil marks along the edge. A plotter or straightedge can then be used to connect the points where the chart is unfolded.

After the course line has been plotted, the next step is to determine its direction. Place the points of the dividers or a pencil anywhere along the line to be measured (Step 3). Place the plotter against the dividers (Step 4). Slide the plotter until the center hole is over any meridian, as shown in Step 5. Read TC on the protractor at the meridian (Step 6). Make a mental estimate of the approximate direction of the line when reading the protractor to avoid obtaining a reciprocal heading.

Plotting Course From Given Position

A course from a given position can be plotted quickly in the following manner: Place the point of a pencil on the position and slide the plotter along this point, rotating it as necessary, until the center hole and the figure on the protractor representing the desired direction are lined up with the same meridian. Hold the plotter in place and draw the line along the straight edge (Figure 5-9 Page 72).

Measuring Distance

One of the disadvantages of the Mercator chart is the lack of a constant scale. If the two points between which the distance is to be measured are approximately in a north-south direction and the total distance between them can be spanned, the distance can be measured on the latitude scale opposite the midpoint. However, the total distance between any two points that do not lie approximately north or south of each other should not be spanned unless the distance is short.

In the measurement of long distances, select a mid-latitude lying approximately halfway between the latitudes of the two points. By using dividers set to a convenient, reasonably short distance, such as 60 NM picked off at the mid-latitude scale, you may determine an approximate distance by marking off units along the line to be measured as shown in Figure 5-10 (Page 72). The scale at the mid-latitude is accurate enough if the course line does not cover more than 5° of latitude (somewhat less in high latitudes). If the course line exceeds this amount or if it crosses the equator, divide it into two or more legs and measure the length of each leg with the scale of its own mid-latitude.

Plotting Procedures, Lambert Conformal and Gnomonic Charts

Plotting Positions

On a Lambert conformal chart, the meridians are not parallel as on a Mercator chart. Therefore, plotting a position by the method described under Mercator charts may not be accurate. On small scale charts, or where there is marked convergence, the plotter should intersect two graduated parallels of latitude at the desired longitude, rather than parallel to the meridian. Then, mark off the desired latitude with dividers. On a large scale chart, the meridians are so nearly parallel that this precaution is unnecessary.

Continued on Page 72

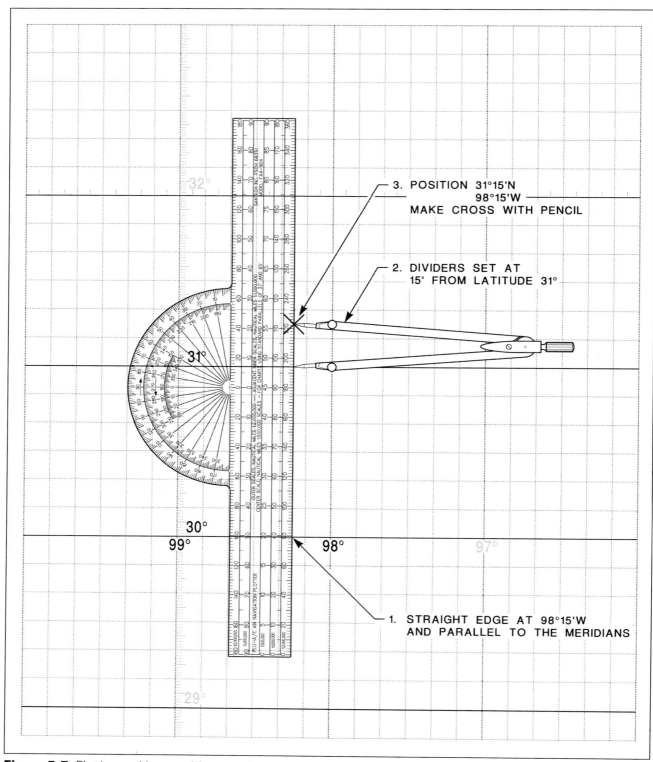

Figure 5-7. Plotting position on a Mercator chart

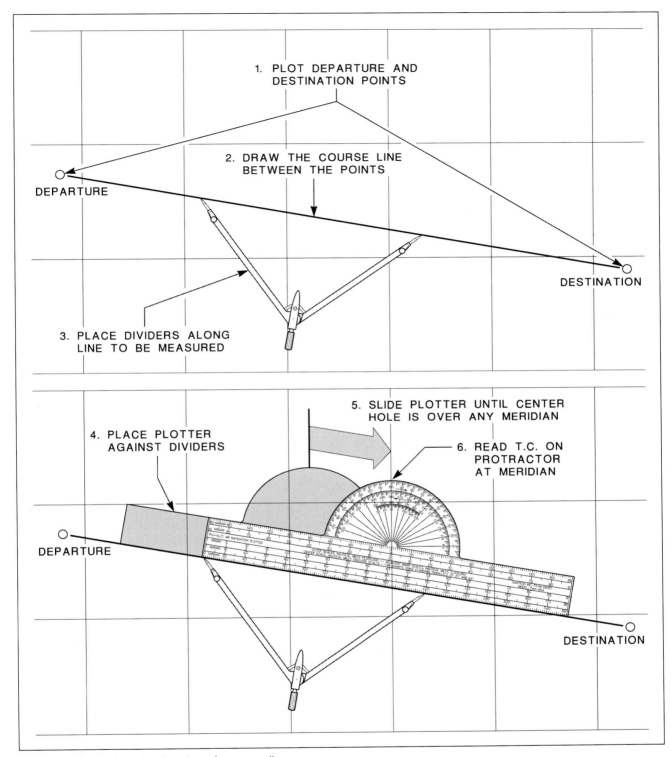

1. PLOT DEPARTURE AND
   DESTINATION POINTS

2. DRAW THE COURSE LINE
   BETWEEN THE POINTS

DEPARTURE

DESTINATION

3. PLACE DIVIDERS ALONG
   LINE TO BE MEASURED

4. PLACE PLOTTER
   AGAINST DIVIDERS

5. SLIDE PLOTTER UNTIL CENTER
   HOLE IS OVER ANY MERIDIAN

6. READ T.C. ON
   PROTRACTOR
   AT MERIDIAN

DEPARTURE

DESTINATION

Figure 5-8. Reading the direction of a course line

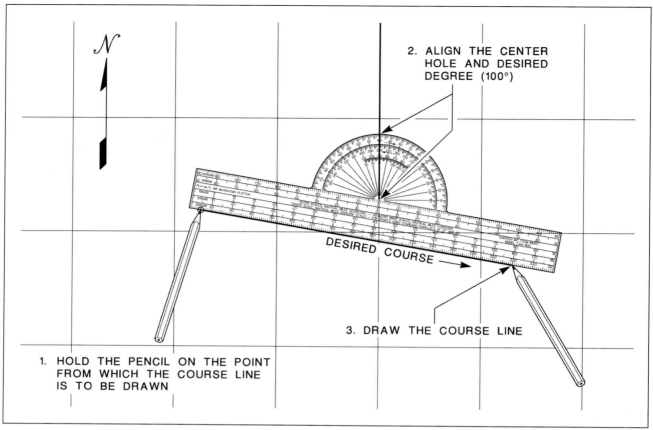

Figure 5-9. Plotting course from given position

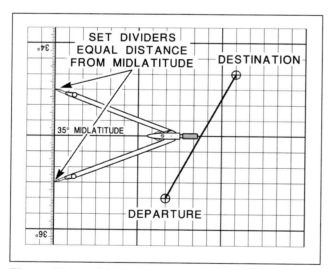

Figure 5-10. Mid-latitude scale

Continued from Page 69

The scale on all parts of a Lambert conformal chart is essentially constant. Therefore, it is not absolutely necessary to pick off minutes of latitude near any particular parallel except in the most precise work.

Plotting and Measuring Courses

Any straight line plotted on a Lambert conformal chart is approximately an arc of a great circle. In long distance flights, this feature is advantageous since the great circle course line can be plotted as easily as a rhumb line on a Mercator chart.

However, for shorter distances where the difference between the great circle and rhumb line is negligible, the rhumb line is more desirable because a constant heading can be held. For such distances, the approximate direction of the rhumb line course can be found by measuring the great circle course at midmeridian as shown in Figure 5-11. In this case, the track is not quite the same as that indicated by the course line drawn on the chart, since the actual track (a rhumb line) appears as a curve convex to the equator on a

Lambert conformal chart, while the course line (approximately a great circle) appears as a straight line. Near mid-meridian, the two have approximately the same direction (except for very long distances) along an oblique course line as indicated in Figure 5-12.

For long distances involving great circle courses, it is not feasible to change heading continually, as is necessary when exactly following a great circle. It is customary to divide the great circle into a series of legs,

each covering about 5° of longitude. The direction of the rhumb line connecting the ends of each leg is found at its mid-meridian.

Measuring Distance

As previously stated, the scale on a Lambert conformal chart is practically constant, making it possible to use any part of a meridian graduated in minutes of latitude to measure nautical miles.

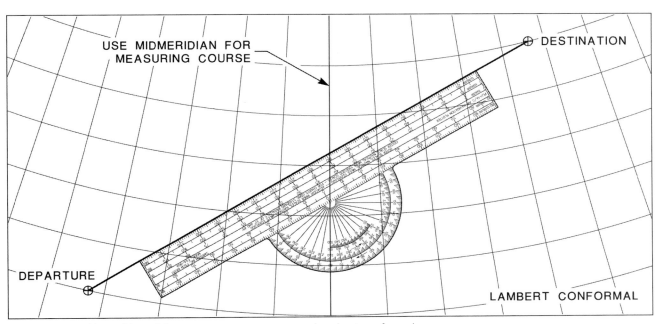

Figure 5-11. Use mid-meridian to measure course on a Lambert conformal.

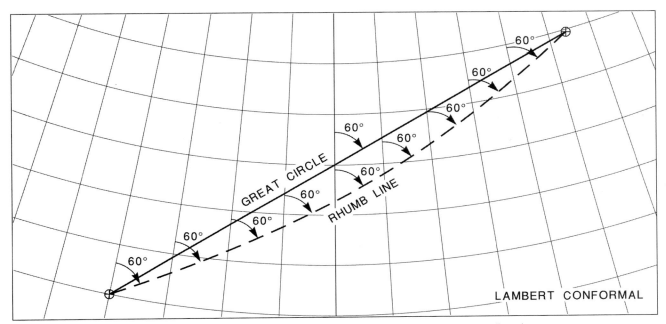

Figure 5-12. At mid-meridian, rhumb line and Great Circle have approximately the same direction.

Plotting on a Gnomonic Chart

Gnomonic charts are used mainly for planning great circle routes. Since any straight line on a gnomonic chart is an arc of a great circle, a straight line drawn from the point of departure to destination will give a great circle route. Once obtained, this great circle route is transferred to a Mercator chart by breaking the route into segments as shown in Figure 5-13.

Plotting Hints

The following suggestions should prove helpful in developing good plotting procedures:

- Measure all directions and distances carefully. Check and double-check all measurements, computations, and positions.

- Avoid plotting unnecessary lines. If a line serves no purpose, erase it.

- Keep plotting equipment in good working order. If the plotter is broken, replace it. Keep sharp points on dividers. Use a sharp-pointed, soft pencil and an eraser that will not smudge.

- Draw light lines at first, as they may have to be erased. When the line has been checked and proven to be correct, then darken it if desired.

- Label lines and points immediately after they are drawn. Use standard labels and symbols. Letter the labels legibly. Be neat and exact.

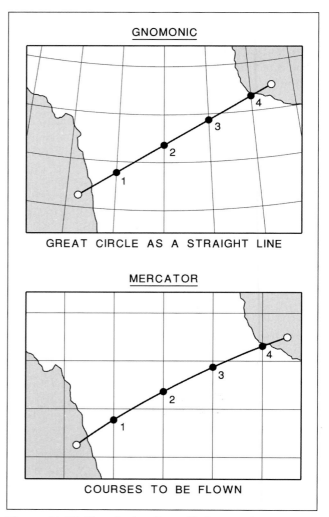

Figure 5-13. Transferring Great Circle route from gnomonic to Mercator chart

6: International Trip Planning and Preparation

International flight planning is more complex than planning for a domestic flight because of the additional need for information. Besides the need for additional charts and flight information, each country may have slightly different rules-of-the-air.

International airspace flight has special requirements. Add to this the need to, before and upon arrival, comply with the entry requirements, pay for fuel and services in a currency foreign to the crew, accomplish a meteorological briefing and file a flight plan (both of which will be in a different format), and comply with local requirements while on the ground.

Only very good preflight planning will simplify the above complexities to a level which can be tolerated. Whether international flights are accomplished often or seldom, preflight planning must start weeks and even months before starting the flight. As with any task, some of the preparation can be accomplished well in advance—in anticipation that such a trip might happen someday (passports for all crew members is just one of many examples).

More preparation occurs as soon as a foreign destination is chosen. Preparation can be categorized into (1) readiness or **advance preparation**, and (2) specific trip preparation (**route specific**). Preparation can also be categorized by type, such as:

1. the aircraft
2. the crew
3. the passengers
4. acquisition and study of flight information and regulations
5. route planning
6. flight planning
7. en route and destination arrangements
8. special equipment acquisition, weather briefing and flight plan filing.

There is a lot to do! How can everything be remembered? A **checklist** is absolutely required.

The Checklist

The checklist is where planning begins. The checklist is the result of planning. And the checklist is the only known way to be sure that *all* of the planning and preparation is accomplished before departure. Figure 6-1, shown on the next two pages, is a most comprehensive international flight planning checklist. It is a composite of many checklists, yet it is not complete. Rather, it is offered here as a basic checklist upon which one can build, modify and improve to fit the needs of the particular airplane, crew and trip. Take a moment now to look it over, to get an idea of what is involved in the preparation for an international flight.

Checklists may be arranged in different ways; this one is categorized by type. Route-specific items are asterisked in the figure to distinguish them from advance-preparation items.

Planning Resources

The resources needed for international flight planning increase with the distance and with the number of countries involved with the flight. The following discussion covers most of the major sources of this information.

Planning the flight often starts with reference to the **IFIM (the International Flight Information Manual)**. This document is produced by the U.S. DOT-FAA Air Traffic Procedures Service. Similar documents are produced by other countries, such as the CAP 555 from the U.K.

The IFIM is a bountiful resource of information about visas and passports, national security, north Atlantic routes, and the entry airports and requirements for each country in the world. It is available from the U.S. GPO, but may be accessed at the nearest federal depository library. If a community library is not a federal depository library, they will know where the nearest one is located. For ordering information for either of the documents discussed here, *see* Figure 6-13 on Page 88.

DOCUMENTATION

Aircrew

1. Current in international operations and regulations
2. Adequate rest — pilot's discretion*
3. Trip itinerary* — include stops along the way
4. Passenger manifest* — including full names, citizenship, dates of birth, current addresses, next of kin, any drugs properly labeled and documented
5. List of U.S. embassy locations
6. FAA Airmen's Certificates
   a. Pilot's license
   b. Current medical certificate
7. FCC radiotelephone license
8. Current passports (county clerk)
9. Visas or tourist cards* (information on acquisition provided by the IFIM or professional planning service)
10. Second form of identification with photo (besides passport)
11. Proof of citizenship
    a. Birth certificate
    b. Naturalization papers
    c. Social security card
12. Immunization records
13. Traveler's checks
14. Credit cards
    a. Internationally accepted
    b. Recommendation from professional planner
15. Currency for every country*
16. Customs forms
    a. U.S. Customs Form 178
    b. General declaration
    c. List of hours of customs operations
    d. List of inspections required
    e. Copy of "U.S. Customs Guide for Private Flyers"
17. Current charts*
    a. Enroute charts, approach charts (obtain through Jeppesen, NOS or DMA)
       i. High altitude enroute charts
       ii. Approach charts
    b. Current flight and entry regulations of country
18. All luggage properly marked
19. IBAC aircrew cards
20. List of emergency phone numbers
    a. Police
    b. Lawyers
    c. Next of kin

Aircraft

1. Airworthiness certificate
2. Registration (Note: Aircraft may not fly internationally with a temporary registration or a copy — must be the original)
3. Radio license (FCC — check expiration date and be sure HF radio frequencies are permitted)
4. Current aircraft operations manual with weight and balance
5. Minimum equipment list (FAA)
6. Metric conversion tables (with pre-converted aircraft size and weights)
7. Airframe and engine logs
8. Certificates proving insurance coverage (from insurance company)*
9. Aircraft maintenance manuals
10. Import papers for aircraft of foreign manufacture
11. Liquor sealing device(s)
12. ETP/Wet footprint calculations*
13. Foreign meteorology reference book*
14. HF radio telephone operating manual and documentation
15. Copy of IFIM/AIP
16. Battery (age and time since deep cycle)*
17. Emergency quick reference guide* (tailored to suit needs of the trip planned)
18. Checklists
19. Notarized letter of authorization to use aircraft if borrowed, leased, or rented
20. 12" Registration marks and external ID plate are needed if ADIZ is penetrated

Passengers

1. List of passengers and any known illness or medication*
2. Copy of trip itinerary*
3. Passenger manifest*
4. Passports
5. Visas or tourist cards*
6. Immunization records
7. Internationally accepted credit cards
8. Traveler's checks
9. Currency for each country*
10. Camera
11. List of U.S. embassy locations*
12. Any drugs properly labeled and documented*
13. List of emergency phone numbers
14. Luggage and personal possessions properly labeled with U.S. customs certificates of importation if of foreign manufacture

OPERATIONS

Permits

1. Overflight and landing*
2. File ICAO flight plan
   a. Write ADCUS in remarks section before crossing international airspace
3. Export license
4. Minimum navigation performance specifications for route (found in IFIM "Aircraft's certification for MNPS operation")
5. Airspace authorization*

Services

1. Customs/Pratique
   a. Requirements, hours of operation and emergency procedures*
   b. Inspections required* (know what they are)
   c. Complete CF178 for U.S. airport of arrival
   d. Customs Form 6059-B for items to be transported from abroad
   e. Appointment made with custom officials with adequate notice given*

Figure 6-1. An international flight checklist

2. Ground
  a. Security* (make prior arrangements for hangar space or guard if necessary)
  b. If hangar not available, arrange preheat, covers, EPU, device, battery removal, heat storage for battery*
  c. Handling agent
3. ASOs and FBOs*
4. Fuel*
  a. Sufficient fuel at each stop
  b. Credit cards accepted
  c. Prist (premixed)
  d. Oxygen, hydraulic fluid, other fluids
  e. Catering
5. Maintenance*
  a. Availability of airframe, powerplant, and electronics technicians (get list of approved service locations from a/c manufacturer)
  b. Acquisition of parts (source)
6. Financial
  a. Credit cards accepted
  b. Currency (for each country)*
  c. Letter of credit*
    i. Bank
    ii. Handlers
    iii. Fuelers

COMMUNICATIONS EQUIPMENT*

1. Communication equipment check before departure
2. VHF (check operation on all frequencies)
3. HF (check operation)
4. Headphones (check operation)
  a. Spare headphone
5. Microphones (check operation)
  a. Spare push-to-talk switch
6. SELCAL frequency
7. Portable ELT
8. Agreements (ARINC and BERNA contracts)

NAVIGATION EQUIPMENT*

1. Navigation equipment check to specifications before departure
2. GPS (check status of satellites)
3. LORAN (check suitability of use for route planned and check for planned outages)

PUBLICATIONS

Flight Deck*

1. Jeppesen orientation charts
2. Jeppesen high altitude enroute charts
3. Jeppesen approach charts
4. Flight management system update
5. NAT track message
6. AIP for selected countries
7. International Flight Information Manual (IFIM)
8. International NOTAMs
9. Current weather
10. Information from tourist agency regarding facilities

FACILITATION AIDS

1. U.S. Department of State, Office of Aviation
2. U.S. Customs Service

3. Foreign Countries Custom Service
4. U.S. Embassy in Country of Destination
5. FAA Office of International Aviation
6. FAA Office of Security

SURVIVAL EQUIPMENT* — (as a minimum, must meet 14 CFR 91.509)

1. Emergency locator transmitter
2. 1 Life jacket for each occupant
3. Life raft sufficient to accommodate all persons on board
4. Area survival kit with manual and contents
5. Medical kit
6. List of companies that can supply proper equipment
  a. Sporty's Pilot Shop
     Clermont County Airport
     Batavia OH 45103-9747
  b. Aerofusion of Maine
     Bangor Int'l Airport (207) 945-3561
  c. Cabela's
     812 13th Ave.
     Sidney NE 69162 (308) 254-5505
7. Halon 1211 fire extinguisher
8. Signal pistol kit
9. Firefly rescue light/strobes
10. Survival booklet
11. Tents for passengers and crew
12. Dye marker
13. Knife
14. Whistle
15. Signal mirror
16. Hole plugs
17. Bail bucket and sponge
18. Water purification tablets
19. Signal sheet (conspicuity panel)
20. Compass
21. Sealed matches
22. Winter sleeping bags
23. Stove and supply of fuel
24. Mosquito netting
25. Insect repellent
26. Food (carbohydrates at least 10,000 calories per person)

OTHER CONSIDERATIONS

1. Aircraft locks (check operation)
2. Spare keys (three sets)
3. Ground transportation*
4. Catering*
5. Tourist information crew briefings* (culture, customs, food, points of interest, history, etc.)
6. Sic sacs
7. List of international service providers
8. Hotel reservations*
9. IBAC feedback cards
10. Survival/safety briefing cards for PAX

*Denotes route-specific items, but many of the sources for these items may be contacted and/or arranged during advance preparation.

Figure 6-1. An international flight checklist *(continued)*

DOD Aeronautical Charts and Flight Information Publications

The following publications are available to pilot/navigators in numerous locations where aeronautical charts are sold or where flight planning takes place. A valuable aid to selecting appropriate charts is the DOD Catalog of Aeronautical Charts and Flight Information Publications. This catalog provides information on the latest aeronautical cartographic products produced and distributed by the Defense Mapping Agency Aerospace Center (DMAAC) and the Defense Mapping Agency Hydrographic Center (DMAHC). A brief description of each series or type of chart listed in this catalog is presented with the appropriate index or listing. The DOD Catalog is divided into the following sections:

Section I, *General Information.* The overall purpose of this section is to acquaint users with the information in the catalog. It also provides basic information on projections and a variety of other basic cartographic data.

Section II, *Requisitioning and Distribution Procedures — General Procedures.* A detailed description of procedures to follow in normal requisitioning of charts and publications. This section contains samples of requisitioning forms and charts depicting areas of distribution, and defines responsibilities for issuance and procurement of charts and publications.

Section III, *Flight Information Publications (FLIP).* These publications consist of the textual and graphic information required to plan and conduct an IFR flight. The FLIP is separated into three basic categories corresponding to phases of flight, as follows:

Planning. Complete description of (1) Flight Information Publication Planning Document, which includes: Planning Data and Procedures; Military Training Routes, United States; International Rules and Procedures and Regulations, (2) FLIP Planning Charts, and (3) Foreign Clearance Guide.

En route. A complete listing of DOD enroute charts and supplements covering United States, Alaska, Canada and North Atlantic, Caribbean and South America, Europe and North Africa, Africa and Southwest Asia, Australia, New Zealand, Antarctica, the Pacific and Southeast Asia. TACAN facility chart coverage of Alaska is also included.

Terminal. Describes the DOD publications which contain approved low and high altitude instrument approach procedures and aerodrome sketches. It should be noted that FLIP is the official publication medium for terminal information for use by the U.S. Armed Forces. As such, it does not contain all terminal instrument procedures available within the area of coverage; contents are determined by military requirements. A FLIP area of coverage chart for the Pacific, Australasia and Antarctica area is shown in Figure 6-2.

Section IV, *Navigational Charts.* This section contains a general description of the scale, code, projection, size, purpose, cartographic style, and information shown on navigational charts. They are grouped in three categories: general purpose, special purpose, and plotting charts.

Section V, *General Planning.* This section contains a general description of the scale, code, projection, size, purpose, style, and information shown on all charts used for planning references and wall displays.

Section VI, *Special Purpose.* This section outlines all requisitioning procedures for the special purpose charts along with a brief description of their purpose.

Aeronautical Chart Currency and Updating Information

DOD Bulletin Digest

This document is published semiannually in both classified and unclassified versions. It provides a complete cumulative listing of current chart editions available for distribution to users. Information available in these documents (within each chart series) is the chart number, current edition, and date of edition.

DOD Bulletin

This document is published monthly in both classified and unclassified versions. It provides a listing of the availability of new aeronautical charts, new editions of previously published charts, discontinued charts, miscellaneous ICAO and FAA publications and amendments, requisitioning information, and charts scheduled for completion. This document supplements the Bulletin Digest.

DOD Chart Updating Manual (CHUM)

This document is published monthly in both classified and unclassified versions. It lists, for each current chart edition, corrections and additions which could affect flying safety. The additions and corrections listed for the appropriate charts should be checked and the applicable ones annotated on the charts.

Jeppesen Sanderson

Worldwide coverage of IFR en route and approach charts as well as flight procedure information is available from Jeppesen. (*See* address and telephone information on Page 88) Besides coverage for the conterminous United States, Airway Manual coverage is available for the entire world, as shown in Figures

6-3 through 6-9 (on Pages 80 – 85). These services are documented in the Jeppesen Products and Services Catalog.

The **Airway Manual** contains enroute IFR charts, Area Charts, Terminal Charts and an Information Section which gives detailed information regarding chart and enroute NOTAMs, radio aids, meteorology, appropriate tables and codes, ATC rules and requirements, entry requirements, airport and terminal directory and emergency information.

Trip kits are available that contain all the above information, but for a specific route. VFR charts and plotting charts are also available.

Continued on Page 86

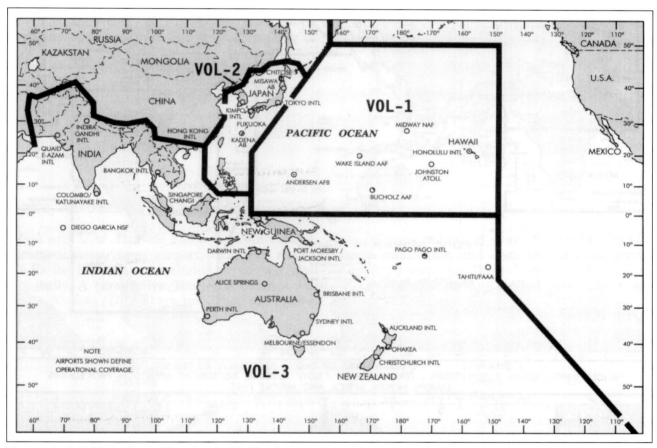

Figure 6-2. FLIP Coverage Chart for the Pacific, Australasia, and Antarctica

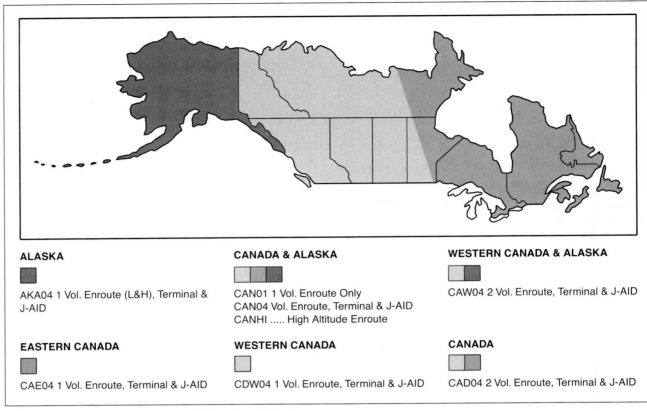

ALASKA

AKA04 1 Vol. Enroute (L&H), Terminal & J-AID

CANADA & ALASKA

CAN01 1 Vol. Enroute Only
CAN04 Vol. Enroute, Terminal & J-AID
CANHI ..... High Altitude Enroute

WESTERN CANADA & ALASKA

CAW04 2 Vol. Enroute, Terminal & J-AID

EASTERN CANADA

CAE04 1 Vol. Enroute, Terminal & J-AID

WESTERN CANADA

CDW04 1 Vol. Enroute, Terminal & J-AID

CANADA

CAD04 2 Vol. Enroute, Terminal & J-AID

Figure 6-3. Jeppesen coverage of Canada and Alaska

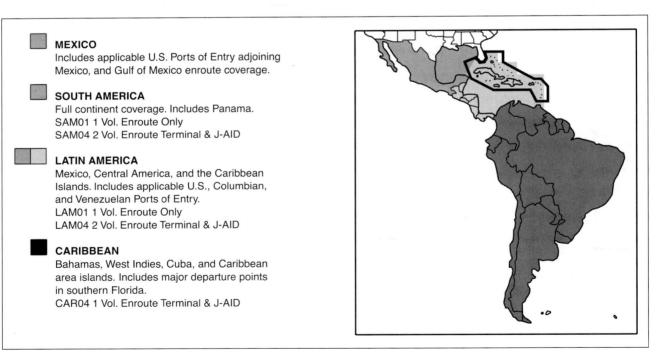

MEXICO
Includes applicable U.S. Ports of Entry adjoining Mexico, and Gulf of Mexico enroute coverage.

SOUTH AMERICA
Full continent coverage. Includes Panama.
SAM01 1 Vol. Enroute Only
SAM04 2 Vol. Enroute Terminal & J-AID

LATIN AMERICA
Mexico, Central America, and the Caribbean Islands. Includes applicable U.S., Columbian, and Venezuelan Ports of Entry.
LAM01 1 Vol. Enroute Only
LAM04 2 Vol. Enroute Terminal & J-AID

CARIBBEAN
Bahamas, West Indies, Cuba, and Caribbean area islands. Includes major departure points in southern Florida.
CAR04 1 Vol. Enroute Terminal & J-AID

Figure 6-4. Jeppesen coverage of Mexico, Central and South America, and the Caribbean

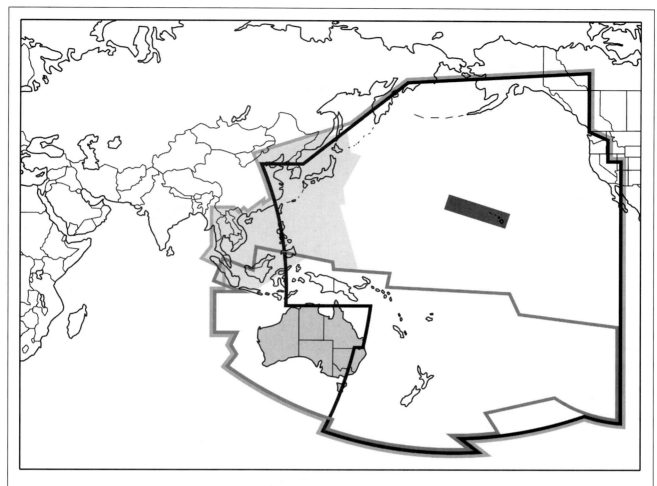

Terminal charts for the services below contain both civilian and military airports. Low Altitude and High Altitude or combination High/Low Altitude Enroute Charts are included. J-AID information is also included.

PACIFIC OCEAN

Enroute information and terminal charts for major airports in Hawaii, Japan, Korea and the Philippines. Includes Terminal Charts for all Pacific Island airports. Supplements Australasia and Far East services for crossing the North and South Pacific.

PACIFIC BASIN

Combination of Pacific Ocean, Far East and Australasia coverages.
PBN01 1 Vol. Enroute Only
PBN04 3 Vol. Enroute Terminal & J-AID

AUSTRALASIA

Enroute information and Terminal Charts for major airports in Australia, New Zealand, New Guinea, Fiji Islands, Indonesia, Singapore and Malaysia.
AUS04 2 Vol. Enroute Terminal & J-AID

AUSTRALIA

Enroute information and Terminal Charts for all airports on the continent.
ASD04 2 Vol. Enroute Terminal & J-AID

FAR EAST

Includes Japan, Korea, Hong Kong, Taiwan, Philippines, Southeast Asia, Singapore, Malaysia and Indonesia.
FES04 2 Vol. Enroute Terminal & J-AID

HAWAII

HAW04 1 Vol. Enroute Terminal & J-AID

Figure 6-5. Jeppesen coverage of the Pacific Basin

STANDARD SERVICES for these geographic areas, where applicable, include:
Enroute Charts – Low or combination High/Low Altitude. High Altitude Charts are available where indicated.
Area Charts – High Density areas.
Terminal Charts – SIDs, STARs, Instrument Approach Procedures, airport layouts (includes military airports).
Text Pages – Introduction, Chart NOTAMs, Enroute, Radio Aids, Meteorology, Tables and Codes, Air Traffic Control, Entry Requirements, Emergency, Airport Directory and Terminal.

SPECIAL USE SERVICES
Resource – Enroute and Reference Guides for Europe-Mediterranean.
Metric – Available for China and Eastern Europe-USSR.

SPECIAL USE CHARTS
Atlantic Orientation Charts, Route planning, and over-ocean enroute navigation between major transatlantic terminals.

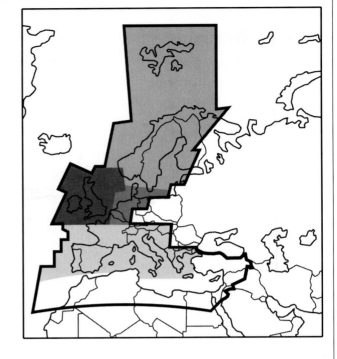

EUROPE
Albania, Austria, Belgium, British Isles, Denmark, Finland, France, Germany, Greece, Italy, Luxembourg, Madeira, Malta, Netherlands, Norway, Portugal, Spain, Sweden, Switzerland, Yugoslavia. Flight operations above FL200 in Europe also require Europe-Mediterranean High Altitude.
EUR04 5 Vol. Enroute, Terminal & Test Pages

EUROPE-MEDITERRANEAN
Europe plus Algeria, Canary Islands, Cypress, Egypt, Israel, Jordan, Lebanon, Libya, Morocco, Syria, Tunisia and Turkey. Flight operations above FL200 also require Europe-Mediterranean High Altitude.
ERM04 5 Vol. Enroute, Terminal & Test Pages

EUROPE-MEDITERRANEAN REFERENCE GUIDE
Ideal for planning and preflight purposes. Contains Flight Planning Chart and general information sections: Introduction, Radio Aids, Meteorology, Tables and Codes, Air Traffic Control, Entry Requirements, Emergency and Airport Directory.
ERMJD 1 Vol.

EUROPE-MEDITERRANEAN ENROUTE GUIDE
Ideal for second pilot or navigator. Contains Flight Planning Chart, Enroute and Terminal Area Charts, Chart NOTAMs and Chart Legend.
ERM01 1 Vol.

EUROPE-MEDITERRANEAN HIGH ALTITUDE
High Altitude Enroute Charts for European and Mediterranean upper airspace. Required for flight operations above FL200 within Europe.
ERMHI 1 Vol. High Altitude Enroute.

UNITED KINGDOM-IRELAND
United Kingdom, Ireland, Channel Islands, Faroes, Continental Europe to Amsterdam, Brussels and Northern France to Paris. Flight operations above FL200 also require Europe-Mediterranean High Altitude.
UKI04 2 Vol. Enroute, Terminal & Text Pages

NORTHERN EUROPE
Belgium, British Isles, Denmark, Finland, France as far south as Paris, Germany as far south as Munich, Luxembourg. Netherlands, Norway, Sweden. Flight operations above FL200 also require Europe-Mediterranean High Altitude.
NOR04 3 Vol. Enroute, Terminal & Test Pages

CENTRAL EUROPE
Europe *excluding* Finland, Norway and Sweden. Flight operations above FL200 also require Europe-Mediterranean High Altitude.
CEN04 4 Vol. Enroute, Terminal & Text Pages

Figure 6-6. Jeppesen coverage of Europe and the Mediterranean

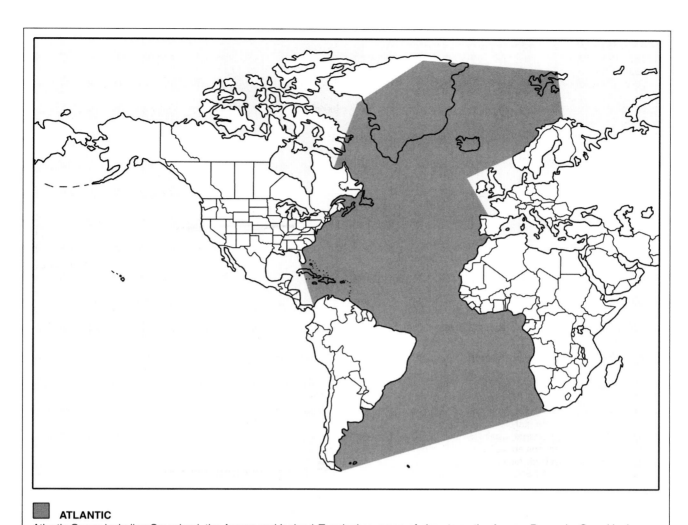

■ **ATLANTIC**
Atlantic Ocean including Greenland, the Azores and Iceland. Terminal coverage of airports on the Azores, Bermuda, Cape Verde, Greenland and Iceland. Meteorlogy and Radio Aids data. New Polar High Altitude Enroute Chart included. ATL does not include Terminal Charts for Eastern or Western seaboard locations, nor the Canary, Caribbean and Madeira Islands.
ATLSM 1 Vol. Enroute, Terminal & Test Pages

Figure 6-7. Jeppesen coverage of the Atlantic

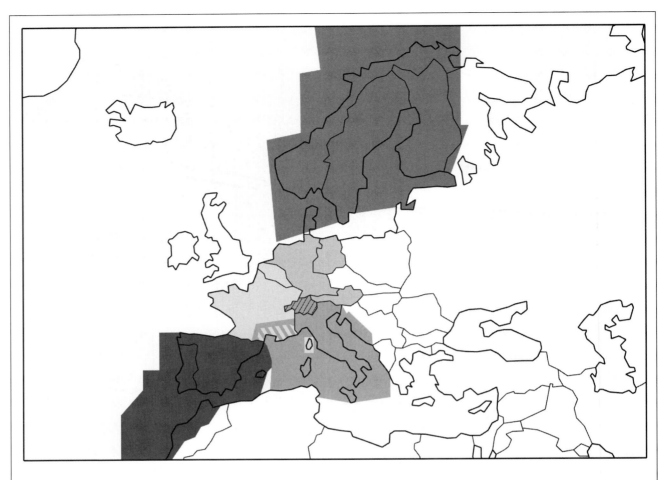

ITALY

Corfu, France (southern coast), Italy, Malta, Tunis, Yugoslavia (western coast). Flight operations above FL200 also require Europe-Mediterranean High Altitude.
ITA04 1 Vol. Enroute, Terminal & Text Pages

GERMANY

Austria, Germany, Netherlands, Switzerland. Flight operations above FL200 also require Europe-Mediterranean High Altitude.
GER04 1 Vol. Enroute, Terminal & Text Pages

NORTH SEA

A manual designed especially for IFR operations in the North Sea area. Contains enroute, general information, and terminal charts for airports in coastal areas of Belgium, Denmark, Faroes, France, Germany, Netherlands, Norway, Sweden, and United Kingdom.
NSE04 1 Vol.

SCANDINAVIA

Denmark, Finland, Norway, Sweden.
SCA04 1 Vol. Enroute, Terminal & Text Pages

FRANCE

Belgium, France, Luxembourg, Switzerland, Channel Islands. Flight operations above FL200 also require Europe-Mediterranean High Altitude.
FRA04 2 Vol. Enroute, Terminal & Text Pages

SPAIN

Canary and Madeira Islands, Gibraltar, Morocco (western coast), Portugal, Spain. Flight operations above FL200 also require Europe-Mediterranean High Altitude.
SPA04 1 Vol. Enroute, Terminal & Text Pages

Figure 6-8. Jeppesen coverage of portions of Europe

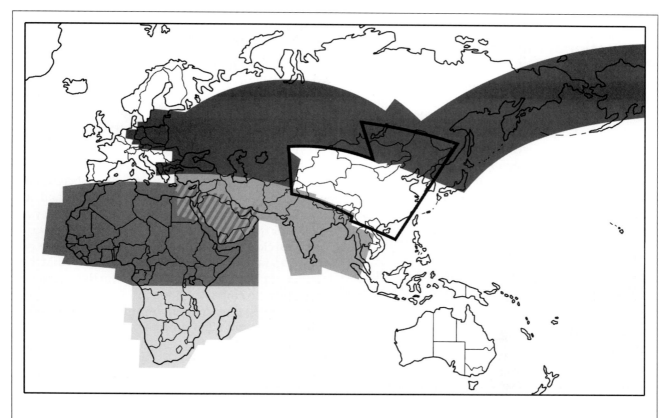

EASTERN EUROPE-USSR

Area of Coverage: Bulgaria, Czechoslovakia, Hungary, Poland, Romania, and USSR (covers the Trans-Siberian Routes to Tokyo and the ATS Routes between the eastern part of USSR and Alaska).
EEU04 1 Vol. Enroute, Terminal & Text Pages
EEUM4 1 Vol. Metric Edition

SOUTHERN AFRICA

Southern Africa (south of 11° S), Madagascar, Mauritius, Reunion.
SAF04 1 Vol. Enroute, Terminal & Text Pages

CHINA

China (P.D.R.) International Routes and Airports, Korea (P.D.R.). Also available in metric edition.
CHI04 1 Vol. Enroute Terminal & Text Pages
CHIM4 1 Vol. Metric Edition

AFRICA

Africa (complete continent), Cape Verde, Madagascar, Mauritius, Reunion, Saudi Arabia (west coast), Seychelles, Yemen.
AFR04 2 Vol. Enroute, Terminal & Text Pages
AFRHI 1 Vol. High Altitude Enroute (North/South oriented)

MIDDLE EAST/SOUTH ASIA

Afghanistan, Bahrain, Bangladesh, Myanmar, Cyprus, Egypt, India, Iran, Iraq, Israel, Jordan, Kuwait, Lebanon, Nepal, Oman, Pakistan, Qatar, Saudi Arabia, Sri Lanka, Syria, Thailand (Bangkok), Turkey, U.A.E., Yemen.
MES04 2 Vol. Enroute, Terminal & Text Pages

Figure 6-9. Jeppesen coverage of Eastern Europe, USSR, China, Middle East, Southern Asia, and Africa

Planning Services

International Planning Service Providers

Several organizations offer services which pull together much of the international flight planning information. Figure 6-10 is an outline of the basic services offered by most planning services providers. Some provide additional services. Figure 6-11 is at least a partial list of organizations which provide such planning services. An example of **IFPS (International Flight Planning Services)** will be found near the end of this chapter.

Computer Access Services

Figure 6-12 is a partial list of resources for international planning that can be accessed by computer/modem.

Additional Resources

Figure 6-13A (*see* Pages 88 – 89) contains a partial listing of other resources. Important to the planning process is learning how to use these resources effectively, well before the planning for a specific trip begins. They should be studied and their value to the planning process noted before serious flight planning begins.

Preliminary Planning

With the above documentation, pilots or a flight department should be able to evaluate their equipment and the transportation needs of the organization they serve, and in conference with management, reach a decision about what type of international travel will and will not be done. Then, and only then, can serious planning begin, in order to establish a readiness level which will allow the aircraft and crew to smoothly transport passengers and cargo in international operations.

Preliminary planning is done in order to maintain a certain level of readiness of crew and aircraft, without a specific destination in mind. Look over the checklist (Figure 6-1) and list all of the items that can be done in preparation for international flight without knowing a specific destination. Sit down with your flight support group and brainstorm in order to add to the checklist—this should produce a good **preliminary planning checklist**.

International Flight Planning—the Concept

International flight is a three-part process. First, get to the first international border or the ocean. Second, cross the ocean or overfly (including fuel stops in) the intermediate foreign countries. Third, get to where landing is planned in the destination country.

Possibly the most difficult part of this process starts with arrival at the destination. I have often felt that the most difficult part of international flying begins after getting on the ground. Unfamiliar language and customs, combined with the natural human tendency not to like or trust someone who is "different" or wearing unusual clothes, adds to the stress. Crew members and passengers should remain aware at all times that their actions are having an effect on those in their presence. Sometimes a smile and a request for assistance is far more effective than an attempt to bully one's way through an unfamiliar process.

Continued on Page 91

1. Computer-generated Flight Plans
2. Overflight/Landing Permits
3. Weather Services
4. Flight Plan filing
5. Arrangements for Ground Services
   Ground Transportation
   Ground Handling/Hangaring
   Fuel, Maintenance
   Hotel Accommodations
   Credit Arrangements
   Aircraft/Personnel Security
   Customs, Immigration
   Catering
6. Arrangements for Communication Services
7. Special Services
   Military Facilities Licenses
   Special Export Licenses
   Visa Assistance
   Charter Aircraft
   HF Radio Networking (worldwide)
   State Department Advisories
   ATC Flow Control Advisories
   High Density Airport reservation slots
   Landing and Overflight Permits
   ICAO Crew ID Cards
8. Flight Following
9. Tourist Information Crew Briefings
10. Monthly Statements by Tail Number

Figure 6-10. Services provided by international service providers

Air Routing International

2925 Briarpark
Suite 610
Houston TX 77042
713-977-1020
800-231-5787
FAX: 713-787-8716

AOPA International Flight Planning

Membership Services Dept.
421 Aviation Way
Frederick MD 21701
301-695-2000
800-872-2672

(Verbal briefings on international flights with emphasis on North and South America, Caribbean and North Atlantic. International packets available to members for North Atlantic, Alaska, Mexico, Central and South America, Caribbean, Bahamas, Canada, and limited information for the Pacific. Jeppesen, NOS, and DOD charts available.)

BaseOps International

333 Cyprus Run, Ste. 200
Houston TX 77094
281-556-2400
800-333-3563
FAX: 281-556-2500

Jeppesen Dataplan, Inc.

121 Albright Way
Los Gatos CA 95030
Attn: International Flight Service
408-866-7613
800-538-7526
FAX: 408-866-5648

Dispatch Services, Inc.

P.O. Box 592036
Miami International Airport
Miami FL 33159
305-526-5307

CompuFlight, Inc.

48 Harbour Park Drive
Port Washington NY 11050
516-625-0202
FAX: 516-625-0202

Universal Weather & Aviation

P.O. Box 12632
Houston TX 77017
800-231-5600

Island Air

Owen Roberts Int'l Airport
General Aviation Terminal
P.O. Box 1991
Grand Cayman BWI
809-949-7786
FAX: 809-949-7786

(Cuban Overflight Permits only)

Figure 6-11. International service providers

CompuServe Information Service

5000 Arlington Centre Blvd.
P.O. Box 20212
Columbus OH 43220   *A variety of pilot access*
Tel: 614-457-0802   *services, including Wx*
800-848-8199   *from EMI Aerocorp.*

EMI Aerocorp, Inc.

7 North Brentwood Blvd.
St. Louis MO 63105   *See CompuServe*
Tel: 314-727-9600

Global Weather Dynamics, Inc.

2400 Garden Rd.
Monterey CA 93940   *Worldwide Wx and*
Tel: 408-649-4500   *communication services.*
800-538-9507

Pan Am Weather Systems

6300 34th Ave. S.
Minneapolis Int'l Airport   *Offers on-site computers*
Minneapolis MN 55450   *and software for accessing*
Tel: 612-727-1084   *many Wx formats.*
888-726-2649

Weather Network

568 Manzanita Ave. Ste. #1 *Primarily Wx for U.S. and*
Chico CA 95928   *Canada, can provide*
Tel: 530-893-0308   *worldwide Wx.*
FAX: 530-893-4517

WSI Corporation

4 Federal St.   *Full range of pilot services*
Billerica MA 01821   *for all types of users.*
Tel: 508-670-5000

Figure 6-12. Computer access services

Air Distance Manual
International Aeradio Limited (IAL)
Aeradio House
Hayes Road, Southall
Middlesex UB2 5NJ England

Airport Directory
(IBAC Update)
• European airport directory
International Business Aircraft Association
(Europe)
Gagelstraat 6A
5611 BH Eindohoven
The Netherlands

DOD Flight Information Publications (FLIP)
• DOD En route and Area Charts
• DOD En route Supplements
• DOD Terminal Instrument
Approach Procedures
DMA Office of Distribution Services
Attention: DOCS
Washington DC 20315
202-227-2816

Flight International Airport Guide (IPC)
Transport Press Limited
Quadrant House
The Quadrant
Sutton, Surrey SM2 5AS England

Health Information for International Travel
U.S. Department of Health and
Human Services
(Public Health Service)
Center for Disease Control
Atlanta GA 33033

IBAC Update
See NBAA

International Civil Aviation Organization (ICAO)
Documents
• Various Annex publications
• DOC 7910 Location indicators
(four-letter identifiers)
• DOC 5858 Designators
(operator designators)
International Civil Aviation Organization
Attn: Document Sales Unit
1000 Sherbrooke Street West
Suite 400
Montreal, Quebec
Canada H3A 2R2
515-286-6304

International Flight Information Manual
Superintendent of Documents
Government Printing Office
Washington DC 20402
202-783-3238

International Notices to Airmen (bi-weekly)
Superintendent of Documents
Government Printing Office
Washington DC 20402
202-783-3238

Jane's Airports and Handling Agents
115 5th Avenue
New York NY 10003

Jeppesen Airway Manual Service
55 Inverness Drive East
Englewood CO 80112-5498
800-525-7379

Key Officers of Foreign Service Posts
(Pub No 7877)
Superintendent of Documents
Government Printing Office
Washington DC 20402

The McAlpine Directory
(European FBO directory)
McAlpine Aviation Limited
Luton International Airport
Luton, Beds LU2 9NT England

NBAA
The National Business Aircraft Association
1200 18th Street NW
Washington DC 20036-2598
202-783-9000

Membership required for most services, and
access to IBAC services, which is worthwhile if
you travel internationally often. Published
IBAC update, which became part of the
Maintenance and Operations Bulletin. This
useful data will soon be published separately
again by NBAA. NBAA's "Oceanic Flying —
Operations and Procedures Manual" is an
excellent resource (see Figure 6-13B).

NoPac Operations Manual
U.S. Department of Transportation
Subsequent Distribution Unit, M-494.3
Washington DC 20590

Figure 6-13A. Other international planning resources

North Atlantic MNPS Airspace Ops Manual
Civil Aviation Authority
Greenville House
37 Gratton Road
Cheltenham, England
*(Also available through FAA,
Washington DC)*

Oceanic Flying — Operations & Procedures
1992
NBAA

Official Airline Guide
OAG Publications
Dept M563
2000 Clearwater Drive
Oak Brook IL 60521

Official Hotel and Resort Guide
Murdoch Magazines
500 Plaza Drive
Secaucus NJ 07090
201-902-2000

**Overseas Non-scheduled Flight
    Clearances Guide**
CAP 555
Civil Aviation Authority, Rm 166,
Control Tower Bldg.
London Heathrow Airport
Middlesex, TW6 1JJ, England

(Similar to the IFIM but with more detail about
fuel availability, acceptable methods of pay-
ment, current agent list, etc.)

Pan Am World Guide
(Encyclopedia of practical information on
countries, people, politics, etc.)
Pan Am World Airways, Inc.
Sales Promotions Dept.
P.O. Box 476
Boston MA 02102

Quarantinable Diseases
U.S. Dept. of Health and Human Services
Center for Disease Control
Atlanta GA 33033

Security Guidelines Handbook
(Available to service subscribers)
Jeppesen DataPlan, Inc.
121 Albright Way
Los Gatos CA 95030

Swiss Air NOTAM Service
(Complements and expands NOTAM summary
and IFIM weekly)
Swiss Air
Attn: Route Documents
OFLR
8058 Zurich, Switzerland

U.S. Customs Guide for Private Flyers
Dept. of the Treasury
U.S. Customs Service
Washington DC 20229

Winds on World Air Routes
DOC #W3412
(Statistical en route winds aloft)
Boeing Commercial Airplane Company
P.O. Box 3707
Mail Stop 02-62
Attn: Software Sales
Seattle WA 98124
206-342-2649

Figure 6-13A. Other international planning resources *(continued)*

International Section VI

REGION GENERAL

Ms. Maria Lohlein, Assistant Manager for Training for the MIA/AIFSS, who was also a speaker at the NBAA International Operators Conference, has recently announced the publication of their latest *Miami AIFSS, Letter to Airmen*. It is available along with international services and other information pertinent to Caribbean and Bahamian operations by writing to, FAA/AIFSS, 14301 SW 128 Street, Miami, FL 33186. For information call 305-233-2600.

Assuming all goes according to plan, this will be the last time the International Section will be included in the MOB.

In response to members requests, beginning with the next issue, all international feedback and any relevant articles will be published in the new *International Operations Bulletin* or *IOB*. As in the past, your support will be required to make it a useful document and of course your feedback will also go into the NBAA Electronic Bulletin Board (202) 331-7968.

The IOB will be a quarterly publication mailed together with the MOB. Any suggestion you may have can be sent in on a feedback card or placed on the Bulletin Board.

REGION   NAM

Customs Arcanum—Know, Then Go

On page six of NBAA's *US Custom's Guide '92*, it thoroughly explains how to put "ADCUS" (**AD**vise **CUS**toms) in the "Remarks" block of your flight plan. It then states that "it is the ultimate responsibility of the pilot to insure that Customs is properly notified" followed by a threat of "penalty action."

What does it really mean? You, as the pilot in command, are responsible for notifying US Customs of your need for their services. If for any reason they don't get the message, you, as pilot in command, are still responsible. If any authority, foreign or domestic, private or bureaucratic, fails to forward your message, you are responsible and will be the recipient of "penalty action"—up to $5000 the first time (see page 85 of the *Guide*).

What to do? You call US Customs, talk with them directly, and document the request with badge numbers, time, numbers, and date. Their phone numbers can be found beginning on page 24 of the *Guide*. Those coming from south of the CONUS may call 305-536-6591 (in Miami) or 714-351-6674 (in Riverside) up to 23 hours in advance.

More information can be found in the *Guide* which was sent earlier this year and handed out to all attendees at the International Operators Committee annual conference. Additional copies can be procured from NBAA.

REGION II   CAR

BAHAMAS   Nassau (MYNN)   5/92

For several months this winter, Nassau Flight Services (via BaseOps) handled three or more turnarounds for us per week. Despite the fact that Nassau can be accomplished without handlers, we found NFS to be worthwhile. Baggage was handled without the usual hordes of porters who usually hang around for tips and grudgingly do very little. High marks to Nassau Flight Services for offering consistently good service even though we constantly threw surprises their way. Well done. For information call: 305-776-7900, ask for R.R.

DOMINICAN REPUBLIC   Santo Domingo (MDSD)   4/92

Airline Service Company (via BaseOps) handles flights to most Dominican airports although some require prior arrangement. Movement is through the main terminal which seems to present no undue complication. For information call: 305-776-7900, ask for R.R.

MEXICO   Acapulco (MMAA)   5/92

Aviacion Ejecutivo (via BaseOps) provides more impressive service with each successive trip. Alberto presides over most operations and has attained a high standard of service in response to Mexico's increasingly demanding corporate operators as well as we "Nortes." Through this effort Aviacion Ejecutivo wins our designation as one of the up and coming FBO's in the Americas. For information call: 305-776-7900, ask for R.R.

MEXICO   Cancun (MMUN)   2/92

Vidal of Servicios Aereos Internacional arranged for his agent to handle us through TAESA in Cancun. Remote parking and basic services should be expected. For information call: 305-776-7900, ask for R.R.

MEXICO   Hermosillo (MMHO)   7/92

Fuel may be purchased with cash, UVAir or AirFuel. The hotel Araiza Inn in very good. Good luck with catering! Not much English is spoken here. The local handler does an excellent job! The security is accurate. Temperatures here are very hot; this is the desert. For information call: 717-986-7391, ask for T.H.

MEXICO   Mexico City (MMMX)   2/92

Servicios Aereos Internacional (via BaseOps) performed wonderfully. The manager, Vidal, is very familiar with the corporate aviation routines and yet willing and able to address any individual requirements. Customs and Immigration was accomplished at the TAESA (a Mexican operator chartering Lears to Boeings). For information call: 305-776-7900, ask for R.R.

VENEZUELA   Caracas—Maiquetia (SVMI)   5/92

Ramrey International (via BaseOps) gets enough demanding clientele to keep it up to scratch. They functioned well in importing parts for unscheduled maintenance. One irritating moment occurred during a late night arrival that required a transfer from the G/A ramp to the taxi stand at the main terminal. It's too far to walk and the arrival agent transferred us in his car. Before I could find a tip, he said, "Funny as it seems, I'm also a taxi driver. That'll be $10.00." I thought it was deadpan humor but he was serious. The more things change, the more they stay the same. For information call: 305-776-7900, ask for R.R.

REGION III   SAM

ARGENTINA   Buenos Aires (SAEZ)   7/92

UVAir's handlers were very good. Domingo Barbusci is the agent. Initial landing fees and taxes are very high—$2500, but that is good for a month at any airport in Argentina. Fluency in Spanish or an interpreter is necessary, especially at SAVV and SACO where we landed. The new hotel in Cordoba is the Panorama. It is modern and very nice. For information call: 901-345-5840, ask for N.D.

ARGENTINA   Buenos Aires (SAEZ)   5/92

American Airlines was selected against advice of our handlers because of our passenger's previous experience. American did an acceptable job of handling although after discussions with, and rescue by, Southeast Aviation (via BaseOps). We will likely change handlers for the next trip. For information call: 305-776-7900, ask for R.R.

Figure 6-13B. A page from NBAA's MOB of 8-31-92

Continued from Page 86

What to Expect Upon Arrival

One of the best sources of information on what to expect upon arrival is the document that once was called the IBAC Update, which was incorporated (in about 1988) into the NBAA's MOB (Maintenance and Operations Bulletin). In this publication will be found recent experiences of aircrews on the ground at locations all over the world, with their recommendations and advice on how to avoid difficult situations at certain locations. Figure 6-13B is an example from the MOB (which heralds the new *International Operations Bulletin*, and shows notices from aircrews about their recent experiences).

It would be well for the crew to become familiar with the cultural customs of the people who will be encountered upon arrival. Some good resources for this are given at the end of this chapter.

The International Flight Plan

Flight plans are required for all flights into international and foreign airspace. The standard flight plan form is the FAA Form 7233-4, available at most U.S. FSS's. Flight plans must be transmitted to and should be received by ATC authorities in each ATC region in order to be entered into the ATC system at least two hours prior to aircraft entry, unless otherwise stated in the various country requirements. It is extremely important that when filing flight plans in countries outside the U.S., the pilot should inquire as to where and when the subsequent transmission of flight plan information (to pertinent en route and destination points) will take place. This is further assurance that the above requirements will be met.

The flight plan serves both the purpose of providing advance notice of foreign airspace penetration, and of providing effective ATC procedures. For some foreign states, the flight plan is the only advance notice required; for others, it serves as a check against previously granted permission to enter national airspace. See aircraft entry requirements for the individual countries and time limitations for advance flight plan filing in the **International Flight Information Manual** (IFIM).

Acceptance of a flight plan and the issuance of a flight clearance by a foreign ATC unit does not constitute official approval for airspace penetration, if prior permission for airspace penetration is required from the civil aviation authorities and such permission has not been previously secured. Airspace violations arising in these instances are pursued and in-flight interception may result.

It is particularly important in the case of flights outside of U.S. airspace that pilots leave a complete itinerary and time schedule of the flight with someone directly concerned, and to keep that person advised of the flight's progress. The pilot should inform this person prior to departing, that if serious doubt arises as to the safety of the flight, an FAA FSS or the nearest U.S. Foreign Service Post (Embassy and Consular Office), as appropriate, should be contacted. Upon receipt of information from any source that an aircraft of U.S. registry or an aircraft with U.S. citizens aboard is in distress or missing while on a journey in or over foreign territory or foreign territorial waters, all available information should be passed to the nearest U.S. Foreign Service Post, as well as the search and rescue facilities and services in that area.

The sections below, "General" and "Itemized Instructions for Flight Plan Completion," are a description of the content of items to be completed on an international flight plan form. Follow along with this description in the example of the international flight plan form shown in Figure 6-14 (Page 92). The FAA complies with much of the ICAO format, except it does not accept cruising speed / level in metric terms (see the differences to ICAO Doc. 4444 in the U.S. **AIP**[1]).

Note: Use the instructions in a *current issue* of the IFIM or other up-to-date source for the completion of an actual ICAO format flight plan, as the information given for example below may no longer be current. After you study the complexities of the ICAO flight plan format shown below, the need should become apparent to complete most parts of the flight plan for each leg of the flight *during the planning phase* of the flight. Many pilots complete ICAO format flight plan blank forms for each flight before starting the trip, so that little time is lost at the actual time of filing.

---

[1] The term "AIP" indicates Air Information Publication, which is what most countries call the publication that in the U.S. is called the "AIM" (Aeronautical Information Manual). Therefore, "U.S. AIP" is international terminology referring to the AIM.

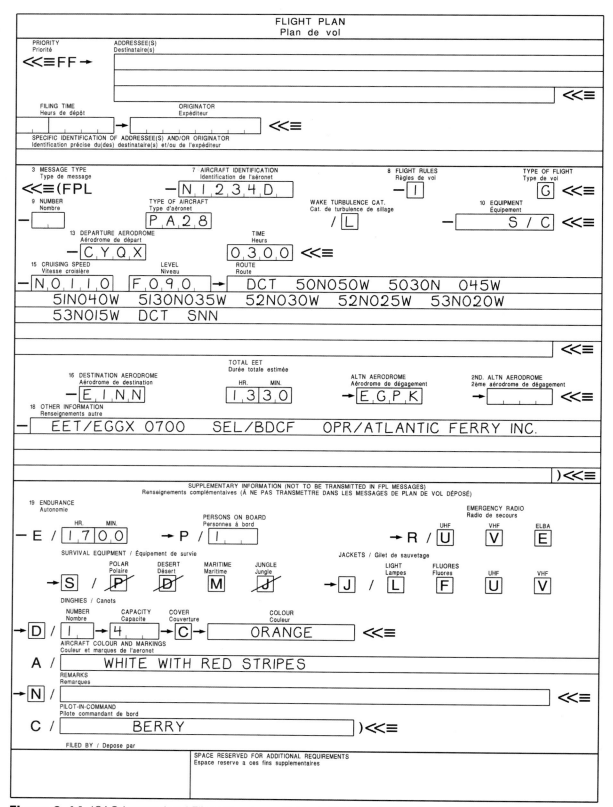

Figure 6-14. ICAO International Flight Plan form. (A blank ICAO Flight Plan form for photocopying purposes is included in the Appendix, Page 344.)

General Instructions

1. Use block capitals when completing each item.

2. *Adhere closely* to the prescribed formats and manner of specifying data.

3. Insert all clock times in four figures, UTC.

4. Insert all estimated elapsed times in four figures (hours and minutes).

5. Shaded area preceding item 3 is to be completed by ATS and COM services.

6. Complete Items 7 to 18 as indicated below.

7. Complete also item 19 as indicated below to facilitate alerting of SAR (search and rescue) services.

Note: Item numbers on the form are not consecutive, as they correspond to the field type numbers in ATIS messages. (Text in **bold italics** below indicates an entry to be made in a field on the form.)

Itemized Instructions for Flight Plan Completion

Item 7: Aircraft Identification

AIRCRAFT IDENTIFICATION, max. 7 characters.

Insert one of the following types of aircraft identification (not to exceed seven characters):

The registration marking of the aircraft (e.g., EIAKO, 4XBCD, N2567GA) when,

1. (in radio-telephony) the call sign to be used by the aircraft will consist of this identification alone (e.g., OOTEK), or will be preceded by the ICAO telephony designator for the aircraft operating agency (e.g., SABENA OOTEK);

2. the aircraft is not equipped with radio; or the ICAO designator for the aircraft operating agency followed by the flight number (e.g., KLM 511, NGA 123, JTR 25), when in radio-telephony the call sign to be used by the aircraft will consist of the ICAO telephony designator for the operating agency followed by the flight number (e.g., KLM 111, NIGERIA 213, HERBIE 25); or the call sign determined by the military authorities, if this will be used to identify the aircraft in radio-telephony during flight.

Item 8: Flight Rules and Type of Flight

FLIGHT RULES, 1 or 2 characters.

Insert one of the following letters to denote the category of flight rules with which the pilot intends to comply:

I .... if IFR

V .... if VFR

Y .... if IFR first

Z .... if VFR first, and *specify* in Item 15 the point or points where the change of flight rules is planned.

TYPE OF FLIGHT

Insert one of the following letters to denote the type of flight:

S .... if scheduled air transport

N ...... if nonscheduled air transport

G ...... if general aviation

M ...... if military

X .... if other than any of the defined categories above.

Item 9: Number and Type of Aircraft and Wake Turbulence Data

NUMBER OF AIRCRAFT, 1 OR 2 characters.

Insert the number of aircraft, if more than one.

TYPE OF AIRCRAFT, 2 to 4 characters.

Insert the appropriate designator, as specified in ICAO Document #8643, "Aircraft Type Designators." Or, if no such designator has been assigned, or in case of formation flights comprising more than one type, *insert ZZZZ,* and *specify* in Item 18 the (numbers and) type(s) of aircraft preceded by the letters TYP.

WAKE TURBULENCE CATEGORY, 1 character.

Insert an oblique stroke (/) followed by the appropriate letter below, to indicate the wake turbulence category of the aircraft:

H ...... HEAVY, an aircraft type with a maximum certificated takeoff mass of 136,000 kg (300,000 lbs) or more.

M ...... MEDIUM, an aircraft type with a maximum certificated takeoff mass of less than 136,000 kg (300,000 lbs) but more than 7,000 kg (15,500 lbs).

L .... LIGHT, an aircraft type with a maximum certificated takeoff mass of 7,000 kg (15,500 lbs) or less.

Item 10: Equipment

RADIO COMMUNICATION, NAVIGATION AND APPROACH AID
EQUIPMENT

Insert one letter as follows:

N ......if no COM/NAV approach aid equipment
for the route to be flown is carried, or the
equipment is unserviceable.

S ....if standard COM/NAV approach aid equipment for the route to be flown is carried. (*See*
Note 1, below.)

And/or insert one or more of the following letters to
indicate which COM/NAV approach aid equipment
is available and serviceable:

A ......LORAN A

B ....(not allocated)

C.......LORAN C

D ......DME

E ....Decca

F ....ADF

G ......(not allocated)

H ......HF RTF

I ....Inertial Navigation

J ....(not allocated)

K.......(not allocated)

L ....ILS

M ......Omega

O ......VOR

P ....Doppler

Q ......(not allocated)

R ....RNAV route equipment

T ....TACAN

U ......UHF RTF

V ....VHF RTF

W .....RVSM approved aircraft (*see* Note 3, below)

X ....MNPS approved aircraft

Z ....Other equipment carried (*see* Note 2, below)

Note 1: Standard equipment is considered to be
VHF, RTF, ADF, VOR, and ILS, unless another combination is prescribed by the appropriate ATS authority.

Note 2: If the letter Z is used, *specify* in Item 18 the
other equipment carried, preceded by COM/ and/or
NAV/, as appropriate.

Note 3: RVSM approved aircraft should also indicate X, if flight is in MNPS airspace.

SSR EQUIPMENT (transponder)

Insert one of the following to describe the serviceable
SSR equipment being carried:

N ......None

O ......Transponder (no coding)

2 ....Transponder (2 digits—64 codes, Mode A)

4 ....Transponder (4 digits—4096 codes, Mode A
but no Mode C)

C.......Transponder (4 digits—4096 codes, Modes
A and C)

Item 13: Departure Aerodrome and Time

DEPARTURE AERODROME, 4 characters.

Insert the ICAO four-letter location indicator of the
aerodrome of departure; if no location indicator has
been assigned, *insert* ZZZZ and *specify* in Item 18 the
name of the aerodrome, preceded by DEP/. Or, if the
flight plan is received from an aircraft in flight, *insert*
AFIL and *specify* in Item 18, the ICAO four-letter location indicator of the location of the ATS unit from
which supplementary flight plan data can be obtained,
preceded by DEP.

TIME, 4 characters

Then, *without a space* in between, *insert* for a flight
plan submitted before departure, the estimated off-
block time; or, for a flight plan received from an
aircraft in flight, the actual or estimated time over the
first point of the route to which the flight plan applies.

Item 15: Route

Insert the first CRUISING SPEED and the first CRUISING
LEVEL as shown below, *without a space between them*.
Then, following the arrow, *insert* the ROUTE description
as shown below.

CRUISING SPEED, max. 5 characters.

Insert the true airspeed for the first or the whole
cruising portion of the flight, in terms of kilometers per
hour expressed as K followed by 4 figures (e.g., K0830),
or knots, expressed as N followed by 4 figures (e.g.,
N0285), or the Mach number to the nearest hundredths
of unit Mach preceded by the letter M (e.g., M082).

CRUISING LEVEL, max. 5 characters.

Insert the planned cruising level for the first or the whole portion of the route to be flown, in terms of:

1. Flight level expressed as F followed by 3 figures (e.g., F085, F330); or

2. Altitude in hundreds of feet expressed as A followed by 3 figures (e.g., A045, A100); or

3. Standard metric level in tens of meters, expressed as S followed by 4 figures (e.g., S1130); or

4. Altitude in tens of meters expressed as M followed by 4 figures (e.g., M0840).

5. When so prescribed by the appropriate ATC authorities or, for VFR flights where the flight is not planned to be flown at a specific cruising level, the letters VFR.

ROUTE, including changes of speed, level or flight rules.

Flights along designated ATS routes:

Insert, if the aerodrome of departure is located on the ATS route, the designator of the first ATS route; or, if the aerodrome of departure is not on the ATS route, the letters DCT followed by the point of joining the first ATS route, followed by the designator of the ATS route.

Then, insert each point at which either a change of speed or level, a change of route, and/or a change of flight rules is planned, *followed in each case* by the designator of the next ATS route segment, even if the same as the previous one, *or* by DCT, if the flight to the next point will be outside a designated route (unless both points are defined by geographical coordinates or by bearing and distance).

Flights outside designated ATS routes:

Insert points, normally not more than 30 minutes flying time or 200 NM apart, including each point at which a change of speed or level, a change of track, or a change of flight rules is planned.

Alternately, when required by appropriate ATS authority(ies), *define* the track of flights operating predominantly in an east-west direction between 70°N and 70°S, by reference to significant points formed by the intersections of half or whole degrees of latitude, with meridians spaced at intervals of 10° of longitude. For flights operating in areas outside those latitudes, the tracks shall be defined by significant points formed by the intersection of parallels of latitude, with meridians normally spaced at 20° of longitude. The distance between significant points shall, as much as possible, not exceed one hour's flight time. Additional significant points shall be established as deemed necessary.

For flights operating predominantly in a north-south direction, define tracks by reference to significant points formed by the intersection of whole degrees of longitude, with specified parallels of latitude that are spaced at 5°.

Insert DCT between successive points unless both points are defined by geographical coordinates or by bearing and distance.

Use only the conventions in (1) through (5) below and *separate* each sub-item by a *space*:

1. ATS Route, 2 to 7 characters: The coded designator assigned to the route or route segment including, where appropriate, the coded designator assigned to the standard departure or arrival route (e.g., BCNI, BI, RI 4, UB 10, KODAP2A).

2. Significant Point, 2 to 11 characters: The coded designator (2 to 5 characters) assigned to the point (e.g., LN, MAY, HADDY); or, if no coded designator has been assigned, one of the following ways:

   a. Degrees only (7 characters): 2 figures describing latitude in degrees, followed by N (North) or S (South), followed by 3 figures describing longitude in degrees, followed by E (East) or W (West). Make up the correct number of figures, where necessary, by insertion of zeros (e.g., 46N078W).

   b. Degrees and minutes (11 characters): 4 figures describing latitude in degrees and tens and units of minutes followed by N or S, followed by 5 figures describing longitude in degrees and tens and units of minutes, followed by E or W. Insert zeros, where necessary (e.g., 4620N07805W).

   c. Bearing and distance from a navigation aid: The identification of the navigation aid (normally a VOR), in the form of 2 or 3 characters; then the bearing from the aid in the form of 3 figures giving degrees magnetic; then the distance from the aid in the form of 3 figures expressing nautical miles. Make up the correct number of figures, where necessary, by insertion of zeros (e.g., a point of 180° magnetic at a distance of 40 NM from VOR "DUB" should be expressed as DUB 180040).

3. Change of Speed or Level, max. 21 characters: The point at which a change of speed (5% TAS, or 0.01 Mach or more) or a change of level is planned, expressed exactly as in (2) above, followed by an oblique stroke (/) and both the cruising speed and the cruising level, expressed exactly as shown above *without a space between them,* even when only one of these quantities will be changed.

Examples:

LN / N0284A045

MAY / N0305F280

HADDY / N0420F330

4602N07805W / N0S00F350

46N078W / M082F330

DUB 1 80040 / N0350M0840

4. Change of Flight Rules, max. 3 characters: The point at which the change of flight rules is planned, expressed exactly as in (2) or (3) above as appropriate, *followed by a space* and one of the following:

VFR if from IFR to VFR

IFR if from VFR to IFR

Examples:

LN VFR

LN / N0284 A050 IFR

5. Cruise Climb, max. 28 characters: The letter "C" followed by a oblique stroke (/), then the point at which cruise climb is planned to start expressed exactly as in (2) above, followed by an oblique stroke. *Then,* the speed to be maintained during cruise climb expressed exactly as above (under "Cruising Speed"), followed by the two levels defining the layer to be occupied during cruise climb, each level expressed exactly as above (under "Cruising Level"); or, the level above which cruise is planned followed by the letters "PLUS," *without a space* between them.

Examples:

C / 48N050W / M082F290F350

C / 48N050W / M082F290PLUS

C / 52N050W / M220F580F620

Item 16: Destination Aerodrome and Total Estimated Elapsed Time, Alternate Aerodrome(s)

DESTINATION AERODROME AND TOTAL ESTIMATED ELAPSED TIME, 8 characters.

Insert the ICAO four-letter location indicator of the aerodrome of destination followed ***without a space*** by the total estimated elapsed time. Or, if no location indicator has been assigned to the aerodrome of destination, *insert* ZZZ followed, ***without a space*** by the estimated time of arrival, and *specify* in Item 18 the name of the aerodrome preceded by DEST / .

Note: For a flight plan received from an aircraft in flight, the total estimated elapsed time is the estimated time from the first point of the route to which the flight plan applies.

ALTERNATE AERODROME(S), 4 characters.

Insert the ICAO four-letter location indicator(s) of not more than two alternate aerodromes, ***separated by a space.*** Or, if no location indicator has been assigned to the alternate aerodrome, *insert* ZZZZ and *specify* in Item 18 the name of the aerodrome preceded by ALTN.

Item 18: Other (Control) Information
Insert:

0 (zero) if no other information; or, any other necessary information in the preferred sequence shown below, in the form of the appropriate indicator followed by a slant (/) and the information to be recorded:

EET /   These are significant points or FIR boundary designators, and accumulated estimated elapsed times to such points or FIR boundaries, when so prescribed on the basis of regional air navigation agreements, or by the appropriate ATS authority (e.g., EET / CAP 0745 XYZ0830 EET / EINN0204 RIF /). The route details to the revised destination aerodrome, followed by the aerodrome's ICAO four-letter location indicator. The revised route is subject to reclearance in flight (e.g., RIF / DTA HEC KLAX RIF / ESP G94 CLA APPK RIF / LEMD).

REG /   The registration markings of the aircraft, if different from the aircraft identification in Item 7.

SEL /   The SELCAL Code, if so prescribed by the appropriate ATS authority.

OPR /   Name of the operator, if not obvious from the aircraft identification in Item 7.

STS/ Reason for special handling by ATS (e.g., hospital aircraft), one engine inoperative (e.g., STS/HOSP, STS/ONE ENG INOP).

TYP/ Type(s) of aircraft, preceded if necessary by number of aircraft, if ZZZZ is inserted in Item 9.

PER/ Aircraft performance data, if so prescribed by the appropriate ATS authority.

COM/ Significant data related to communication equipment, as required by the appropriate ATS authority (e.g., COM/UHF only).

NAV/ Significant data related to navigation equipment, as required by the appropriate ATS authority (e.g., NAV/INS).

DEP/ Name of aerodrome of departure, if ZZZZ is inserted in Item 13, or the ICAO four-letter location indicator of the location of the ATS unit from which supplementary flight plan data can be obtained, if AFIL is inserted in Item 13.

EET/ Significant points or FIR boundary designators and accumulated estimated elapsed times to such points or FIR boundaries, when so prescribed on the basis of regional air navigation agreements. or by the appropriate ATS authority (e.g., EET/CAP 0745 XYZ0830 EET/EINN0204). *Note:* When the estimated times refer to geographical coordinates, use only the latitude or longitude, as appropriate, to identify the points (e.g.,

  EET/60N/1540   SSN/1613 50N/1648 etc.,
  or,
  EET/10W/1025   20W/1105 30W/1145 etc.)

DEST/ Name of destination, if ZZZZ is inserted in Item 16.

ALTN/ Name of alternate aerodrome(s), if ZZZZ is inserted in Item 16.

RMK/ Any other plain language remarks, when required by the appropriate ATS authority or deemed necessary.

Item 19: Supplementary Information

ENDURANCE

After E/... *Insert* a 4-figure group giving the fuel endurance in hours and minutes.

PERSONS ONBOARD

After P/... *Insert* the total number of persons (passengers + crew) onboard. Insert TBN ("to be notified") if the total number of persons is not known at the time of filing.

EMERGENCY AND SURVIVAL EQUIPMENT

R/(Radio). *Cross out* U if UHF on frequency 243.0 MHz is not available. *Cross out* V if VHF on frequency 121.5 MHz is not available. *Cross out* E if emergency locator beacon — aircraft (ELBA) is not available.

S/(Survival Equipment). *Cross out* all indicators if survival equipment is not carried. *Cross out* P if polar survival equipment is not carried. *Cross out* D if desert survival equipment is not carried. *Cross out* M if maritime survival equipment is not carried. *Cross out* J if jungle survival equipment is not carried. List which is not carried.

J/(Jackets). *Cross out* all indicators if life jackets are not carried. *Cross out* L if life jackets are not equipped with lights. *Cross out* F if life jackets are not equipped with fluorescent. *Cross out* U or V, or both as in R/ above, to indicate radio capability of jackets, if any.

Frequency. *Insert* RDO/ followed by transmitting/receiving frequencies of any life jacket radios carried.

D/ (Dinghies) (Number). *Cross out* indicators D and C if no dinghies are carried, or *insert* number of dinghies carried; and under (Cover), *cross out* indicator C if dinghies are not covered.

Color. *Insert* color of dinghies, if carried.

Number. *Insert* number of dinghies carried.

Total. *Insert* total capacity, in persons, Capacity of all dinghies carried.

Other Equipment. Indicate after RMK/ any other survival equipment carried, and any other remarks regarding emergency and survival equipment.

A/(Aircraft Color and Markings). *Insert* color of aircraft and significant markings.

N/(Remarks). *Cross out* indicator N if no remarks, or indicate any other survival equipment carried and any other remarks regarding survival equipment.

C/(Pilot). *Insert* name of pilot-in-command.

Filed by. *Insert* the name of the unit, agency or person filing the flight plan.

Completing the Flight Planning Process

Armed with the knowledge from the above pages and from the documents listed in those pages, the flight crew should be ready to complete the flight planning process. There is a lot to do: however, as with any complex task, broken down into its parts the task becomes simpler and easier to do. Remember how long it took you to plan the first and second student cross country flights? How long would such a flight take to plan now? Any complex task can be done much quicker with a little practice. I haven't met a pilot yet who didn't enjoy the planning process (although I have met some who didn't exactly enjoy the flight because they didn't plan properly).

Getting current weather information, arranging for facilities and services, permits, etc., requires efforts beyond those needed for flights within national airspace. Therefore, that process should be started as soon as the flight route is determined.

Some of the process should be started even before the route is determined, such as acquiring charts and other necessary publications, and international credit cards, for example. Sources for these are listed earlier in this chapter. The checklist developed by the flight crew from brainstorming, the customized checklist early in this chapter are tasks that can both be broken down and arranged in a proper chronological order. (A weather source must be arranged for long before the actual weather is needed, for example.)

Even after the flight log is developed and permits requested, the planning job is finished for the pilot/planner who is operating at a high level of planning sophistication, only after additional planning for contingencies is accomplished (*see* Chapter 7).

International Flight Planning Services (IFPS)

There is a good way to circumvent much of the work involved in actually acquiring planning information and making arrangements. Utilize a planning service, many of which are listed in the resources section earlier in this chapter. There are several good organizations that offer these services. The **Jeppesen Dataplan** is one that is described below. The authors are not specifically recommending this IFPS, but rather are offering this information as an example.

Jeppesen Dataplan IFS (International Flight Services) has responded to our request for flight planning services for an imaginary flight in a Challenger 601, operating at Mach .80 with 600 pounds of payload from White Plains, New York to London, Budapest, Paris, Shannon and return. As shown in Figures 6-15 through 6-23 (starting on Page 100), arrangements have been made for crew transportation and hotel reservations, slot times, discount fuel and acceptable international Cartels (credit cards) for fuel purchase, overfly permits, ground service and agents, as well as flight planning and flight logs. Furthermore, arrangements are made for the flight crew to receive appropriate weather briefings at stops along the way and to have communications services with later billing, on an as-needed basis. These figures are provided to show what a packaged IFS product might look like (courtesy of Jeppesen Dataplan).

Figure 6-15 (Page 100) shows the Jeppesen Dataplan IFS Itinerary, Handling & Communications summary.

Figure 6-16A is flight planning information for the White Plains to Gander leg. (Jeppesen Dataplan also furnishes a complete flight log printout, but that is not shown here.) Figure 6-16B is Gander ground handling information.

Figure 6-17A is flight planning information for the Gander to Heathrow leg. Figure 6-17B shows the pertinent Atlantic high-level significant weather prognostics chart. Figure 6-17C is the Heathrow ground handling information. Figure 6-17D is the hotel request and confirmation for the London stop. Figure 6-17E is a basic data sheet for the U.K. from the Official Airline Guide Travel Planner, which is useful for crew and passenger briefing.

Figure 6-18A is the Heathrow to Budapest flight plan information. Figure 6-18B is proof of the Hungary landing permit. Figure 6-18C is Budapest ground handling information. Figure 6-18D is the Budapest hotel confirmation. Figure 6-18E is travel data for Hungary, courtesy of OAG and furnished by Jeppesen Dataplan.

Figure 6-19A is the Budapest to Paris flight plan information. Figure 6-19B is the Paris ground handling information, and Figure 6-19C is the Paris hotel confirmation. Figure 6-19D is travel data for France, courtesy of OAG.

Figure 6-20A is the Paris to Shannon flight plan information. Figure 6-20B is the Shannon ground handling information.

For the trip back across the Atlantic, Figure 6-21A is the Shannon to White Plains flight plan information. Figure 6-21B is the pertinent Atlantic high level significant weather prognostics chart.

Also included in the IFS package is a company Newsfax (Figure 6-22), and a procedures sheet for using Berna Radio (provides HF communications services for operational messages) as shown in Figure 6-23.

Readings about International Culture and Customs

It has often been said, "International flight problems usually begin after the airplane is on the ground." Usually, problems are amplified because a crew has no knowledge of the culture and customs of the people they must deal with. Therefore, it is strongly recommended that the crew complete their flight planning with some study of the culture and customs of the countries they will descend upon. Doing so almost guarantees a more satisfying visit! It is a good idea to make the materials you study available to your passengers, too. *See* the Appendix for a list of recommended readings.

JEPPESEN DATAPLAN
International Flight Services

121 Albright Way
Los Gatos, California 95030

800-358-6468 ARINC: PAOYRXH
408-866-7611 SITA : PAOJD7X
AFTN:KSFOXLDI

Date: March 3, 1992
Company: ABC Industries

Itinerary-Handling-Communications

Page No. 1
Pilot: J. Sanderson
Aircraft Type: CL601
Reg. N321R

Date	Time	City	Ident	Requirements	Agent	Communication
12 Mar	lv 1300z	White Plains	KHPN	Flt. Plan & Wx		
12 Mar 12 Mar	ar 1500z lv 1600z	Gander Gander	CYQX CYQX	Ground Handling Customs Fuel Flt. Plan & Wx Catering	Agent: Phone: AFTN: Fuel: Fees:	Century Aviation VHF:122.95 709-256-2929 CYQXHAIX Irving Oil/MultiService Card Invoiced
12 Mar 14 Mar	ar 2020z lv 0800z	Heathrow Heathrow	EGLL EGLL	Slot Times Ground handling Customs Fuel Flt. Plan & Wx Crew Trpt. Hotac: 3 Sgls.	Agent: Phone: SITA: Fuel: Fees: Hotel:	Fields Aviation VHF: 130.6 011-44-81-7592141 LHROPFP Fields/MultiService Card Invoiced InterContinental-London Addr: 1 Hamilton Place Ph: 011-44-71-409-3131
14 Mar 15 Mar	ar 1000z lv 0800z	Budapest Budapest	LHBP LHBP	Landing Permit Gound Handling Customs Fuel Flt. Plan & Wx Crew Trpt Hotac: 3 Sgls.	Agent: Phone: AFTN: Fuel: Fees: Hotel:	G.A.C. Budapest VHF: 130.9 011-361-157-6292 LHBPYDYV Malev/World Fuel Card Invoiced Duna InterContinental Addr: Apaczai Csene Janos 4 Ph: 011-361-117-5122
15 Mar 17 Mar	ar 0945z lv 0800z	Paris Paris	LFPB LFPB	Ground Handling Customs Fuel Flt. Plan & Wx Crew Trpt Hotac: 3 Sgls.	Agent: Phone: Telex: Fuel: Fees:	Computed Air Services VHF: 121.3 011-331-4934-6677 842-600679 BP via TransAir/MultiService Invoiced Hotel: Marriott Prince de Galles Addr: 33 Avenue George V Ph: 011-331-4723-5511
17 Mar 17 Mar	ar 0930z lv 1030z	Shannon Shannon	EINN EINN	Ground Handling Customs Fuel Flt. Plan & Wx Catering	Agent: Phone: SITA: Fuel: Fees:	Shannon Repair Service VHF:131.5 011-353-61-61544 SNNXREI Esso/MultiService Invoiced
17 Mar	ar 1700z	White Plains	KHPN	Customs		

Figure 6-15. The Jeppesen Dataplan IFS Itinerary, Handling and Communications summary

```
02      POD   KHPN
03      POA   CYQX
06      ROUTE
07      HOLD, ALTERNATE/DIST   CYJT
08      ETD 1300Z
09      PROFILE I
10      A/C   TYPE/REGN   C601/N321R
11      CRZ   MODE  M8   0
12      PRFM  INDEX  F
13      OPERATIONAL WT   24685
14      PAYLOAD 600
16      POD OR POA FUEL  D15000
17      RESERVE 2000
18      CLIMB FUEL, TIME, DIST BIAS
19      DESCENT FUEL, TIME, DIST BIAS

PLAN 9621                      KHPN     TO      CYQX    C601    M80/F    IFR 03/12/92
NONSTOP        COMPUTED   1807Z   FOR     ETD     1300Z      PROGS    141200Z LBS

               FUEL       TIME    DIST    ARRIVE  TAKEOFF    LAND     AV PLD   OPNLWT

POA   CYQX     004412     01/57   0943    1457Z   040285     035873   000600   024685
ALT   CYJT     001249     00/31   0159    1528Z
HLD            000000     00/00
RES            009339     05/26
TOT            015000     07/54

KHPN           VECTOR     GREKI.  .ENE    J573    CM         J500     CYQX
WIND           P067               MXSH    5/EBONY
FL        370
```

Figure 6-16A. Flight planning information for the White Plains to Gander leg

Gander Ground Handling Confirmation

```
QU SFOYRXH
.CYQXHAIX  150100
FF  KSFOXLDI
1501100 CYQXHAIX

ATTN: JEPPESEN DATAPLAN
REF: ABC INDUSTRIES // N321R // ETA CYQX  12 MAR  1500 UTC

WE CONFIRM ALL SERVICES FOR THIS FLIGHT AS STATED IN YOUR 181828.

WARMEST REGARDS,
S. WINTERS
CENTURY AVIATION GANDER
```

Gander Ground Handling Request

```
QU  PAOYRXH
.PAOYRXH  181828 PAOYRXH
FF  CYQXHAIX    KSFOXLDI
181828 KSFOXLDI

ATTN:  CENTURY AVIATION
FROM:  JEPPESEN DATAPLAN

REQUEST GROUND HANDLING ON BEHALF OF ABC INDUSTRIES,
121 ALBRIGHT WAY, LOS GATOS, CALIFORNIA, 95030 USA
OPERATING ACFT TYPE CL601 REG N321R
CAPTAIN J. SANDERSON PLUS 2 CREW AND 5 PAX

ETD    KHPN    12 MAR    1300Z
ETA    CYQX    12 MAR    1500Z
ETD    CYQX    12 MAR    1600Z
ETA    EGLL    12 MAR    2020Z

SERVICES REQUIRED:
A.  GROUND HANDLING
B.  FUEL—IRVING OIL/CHARGED TO MULTISERVICE CARD.
C.  CUSTOMS ASSISTANCE AS REQUIRED.
D.  FLIGHT PLAN WILL BE SENT TO YOUR OFFICE 4 HOURS PRIOR TO DEPARTURE. PLEASE FILE ON BEHALF
    OF CAPTAIN.
E.  PLEASE SEND ARR/DEP MESSAGES TO KSFOXLDI.
F.  CATERING—PLEASE PREPARE 1 SEAFOOD TRAY FOR 7.

PLEASE INVOICE JEPPESEN DATAPLAN FOR ALL GROUND HANDLING AND LANDING FEES. PLEASE ACKNOWLEDGE
RECEIPT OF THIS MESSAGE AND CONFIRM GROUND HANDLING TO KSFOXLDI.

REGARDS,
CONNIE HIGGINBOTHAM
JEPPESEN DATAPLAN/INTERNATIONAL FLIGHT SERVICES
```

Figure 6-16B. Gander ground handling information

```
02    POD   CYQX/CYQX
03    POA   RGLL/EGLL
06    ROUTE J
07    HOLD, ALTERNATE/DIST  EGGW
08    ETD 1610
09    PROFILE I
10    A/C  TYPE/REGN  C601/N321R
11    CRZ  MODE  M80
12    PRFM  INDEX  F
13    OPERATIONAL  WT  24685
14    PAYLOAD 600
16    POD OR POA FUEL D16685
17    RESERVE 2000
18    CLIMB FUEL, TIME, DIST BIAS
19    DESCENT FUEL, TIME, DIST BIAS

PLAN 9648CYQX  TO  EGLL  C601              M80/F   IFR     03/12/92
NONSTOP   COMPUTED   2037Z   FOR   ETD   1610Z     PROGS   241200Z   LBS

              FUEL    TIME    DIST   ARRIVE    TAKEOFF    LAND    AV PLD    OPNLWT
POA EGLL      009239  04/08   2062   2018Z     041970    032731  000600    024685
ALT EGGW      000407  00/06   0024   2024Z
HLD           000000  00/00
RES           007039  04/21
TOT           016685  08/35

CYQX      5050   5140   5230   5220   5215   UN522   CRK   UB10   STU   UG1   MALBY
MALBY    OCK1A    EGLL
WIND     P059MXSH     3/5050
FL     370/5215   410

ETP    CYQX/EGLL   01/48   0928NM   M033/PO31   BURN   0047   N51576W030432
```

Figure 6-17A. Flight planning information for the Gander to Heathrow leg

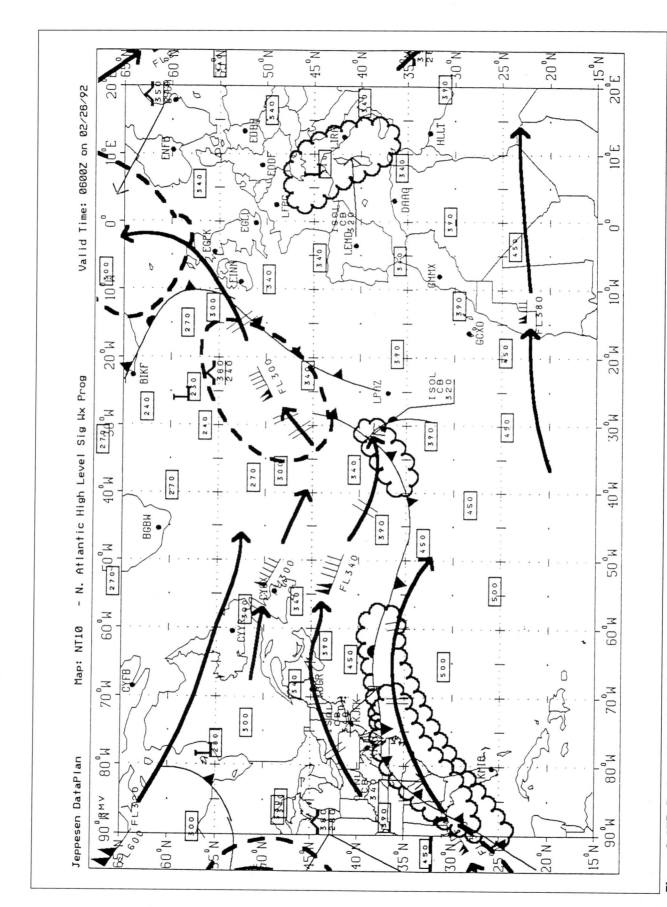

Global Navigation for Pilots

Figure 6-17B. Pertinent high-altitude significant weather prognostics chart

```
QU PAOJD7X
.LHROPFP  123541

ATTN:  C. HIGGINBOTHAM

///  REF  :  ABC INDUSTRIES—CL601-N321R ///
PER YOUR 130834 MESSAGE, WE ACKNOWLEDGE ALL SERVICES AND CONFIRM SLOTS PER YOUR SCHEDULE.

RGRDS,
L. OLIVIER—FIELDS HEATHROW
```

```
FROM:  P1024:   09:24:45
QU  LHROPFP  PAOJD7X
.PAOJD7X  130834  PAOJD7X

ATTN:  FIELDS AVIATION
FROM:  JEPPESEN DATAPLAN

REQUEST GROUND HANDLING ON BEHALF OF ABC INDUSTRIES,
121 ALBRIGHT WAY, LOS GATOS, CALIFORNIA, 95030 USA
OPERATING ACFT TYPE CL601   REG  N321R
CAPTAIN J. SANDERSON PLUS 2 CREW AND 5 PAX

ETD   CYQX   12  MAR   1600Z
ETA   EGLL   12  MAR   2020Z
ETD   EGLL   14  MAR   0800Z
ETA   LHBP   14  MAR   1000Z

SERVICES REQUIRED:
A.  ARRIVAL/DEPARTURE SLOTS
B.  GROUND HANDLING
C.  FUEL—FIELDs AVIATION/CHARGED TO MULTISERVICE CARD.
D.  CUSTOMS ASSISTANCE AS REQUIRED.
E.  TRANSPORT—PLEASE ARANGE FOR 1 CAR W/DRIVER TO TAKE CREW TO/FROM THE LONDON INTERCONTINEN-
    TAL.
F.  FLIGHT PLAN WILL BE SENT TO YOUR OFFICE 4 HOURS PRIOR TO DEPARTURE. PLEASE FILE ON BEHALF
    OF CAPTAIN.
G.  PLEASE SEND ARR/DEP MESSAGES TO PAOJD7X

PLEASE INVOICE JEPPESEN DATAPLAN FOR ALL GROUND HANDLING AND LANDING FEES. PLEASE ACKNOWLEDGE
RECEIPT OF THIS MESSAGE AND CONFIRM GROUND HANDLING TO PAOJD7X.

REGARDS,
CONNIE HIGGINBOTHAM
JEPPESEN DATAPLAN/INTERNATIONAL FLIGHT SERVICES
```

Figure 6-17C. Heathrow ground handling information

London Hotel Confirmation

```
RX-DDD
184787 JEPPESEN UT
INTLON
TO  : C. HIGGINBOTHAM
REF : MSSR. J SANDERSON

WE ARE PLEASED TO ACKNOWLEDGE YOUR RESERVATIONS FOR:
03 SWB ARR 12 MAR DEP 14 MAR
OUR CREW 50% DISCOUNT RATE IS 80 POUNDS/NIGHT.

THANK YOU FOR CHOOSING THE INTERCONTINENTAL,
M. DAVIDSON—RESERVATIONS
LONDON INTERCONTINENTAL HOTEL
```

London Hotel Request

```
TRT
184787 JEPPESEN UT
85187354
87354 INTLON

ATTN:   LONDON INTERCONTINENTAL
        RESERVATIONS MANAGER
FROM:   JEPPESEN DATAPLAN
        121 ALBRIGHT WAY
        LOS GATOS, CALIFORNIA 95030 USA

WE REQUEST HOTAC FOR OUR CREW MEMBERS AS FOLLOWS:

03 SWB TO BE HELD UNDER THE NAME: J. SANDERSON

CREW WILL BE ARRIVING 12 MAR AND DEPARTING 14 MAR SO ROOMS WILL BE REQUIRED FOR 2 NIGHTS.
PLEASE GUARANTEE ROOMS FOR LATE ARRIVAL

REQUEST YOU PLEASE EXTEND CREW DISCOUNT IF AVAILABLE.

PLEASE ACKNOWLEDGE RECEIPT OF THIS MESSAGE TO TELEX 184787
CONFIRMING RESERVATIONS AND ADVISING APPLICABLE ROOM RATE.

THANK YOU FOR YOUR ASSISTANCE IN THIS MATTER.

KINDEST REGARDS,
CONNIE HIGGINBOTHAM
INTERNATIONAL FLIGHT SERVICES
```

Figure 6-17D. Hotel request and confirmation for the London stop

UNITED KINGDOM
Includes England, Scotland, Wales and Northern Ireland
THE BASICS

For Documentary Requirements, Currency Conversion Rates and the International Standard Time Chart, refer to the General Travel Information Section.

DOCUMENTARY REQUIREMENTS

U.S. CITIZENS: Passport—Required. **Visa**—Not required for stays of 6 months or less. **Other**—Sufficient funds, ticket to leave and necessary documents for onward travel. **Vaccination Certificates**—None required unless coming from an infected area.

CANADIAN CITIZENS: Same as for U.S. Citizens.

CONSULATE OFFICES IN NORTH AMERICA
CANADA

HIGH COMMISSION:
Ottawa, ON K1P 5K7, 80 Elgin St. TEL: 613/237-1530. TLX: 0533318. FAX: 613/237-7980. Immigration/Visa Information: 613/237-2008. Passport Information: 613/237-1303.

CONSULATE GENERAL:
Edmonton, AB T5J 1S6, 1404-10025 Jasper Ave. TEL: 403/428-0375.
Montreal, PQ H3B 3A7, 1155 University St., Ste. 901. TEL: 514/866-5863.
Toronto, ON M5G 2G2, 777 Bay St., Ste. 1910, (College Park). TEL: 416/593-1290.
Vancouver, BC V6E 3V6, 1111 Melville St., Ste. 800. TEL: 604/683-4421.

UNITED STATES

EMBASSY:
Washington, DC 20008, 3100 Massachusetts Ave., NW. TEL: 202/462-1340. TLX: 211427, 216760. FAX: 202/898-4255.

CONSULATE GENERAL:
Atlanta, GA 30303, 245 Peachtree Center Ave. TEL: 404/524-5856.
Chicago, IL 60602, 33 N. Dearborn St. TEL: 312/346-1810.
Houston, TX 77002, 1100 Milam Bldg., Ste. 2260. TEL: 713/659-6270.
Los Angeles, CA 90010, 3701 Wilshire Blvd. TEL: 213/385-7381.
New York, NY 10022, 845 Third Ave. TEL: 212/745-0200.
San Francisco, CA 94104, 1 Sansome St. TEL: 415/981-3030.

UNITED STATES CHAMBER OF COMMERCE OFFICE

MAIN OFFICE:
London, England, W1Y 2EB, 75 Brook St. TEL: 71/493-0381. TLX: 23675.

UNITED STATES FOREIGN SERVICE OFFICES

EMBASSY:
London, England, 24/31 Grosvenor Sq., W1A 1AE. TEL: 71/499-9000. TLX: 266777. FAX: 71/409-1637.

CONSULATE GENERAL:
Belfast, Northern Ireland, Queen's House, 14 Queen St., BT1 6EQ. TEL: 232/328239. TLX: 747512.
Edinburgh, Scotland, 3 Regent Ter. EH7 5BW. TEL: 31/556-8315.

CLIMATE

Britain

Average		Jan	Feb	Mar	Apr	May	June	July	Aug	Sept	Oct	Nov	Dec
Low	(F)	35°	35°	37°	40°	45°	51°	55°	54°	51°	44°	39°	36°
	(C)	2°	2°	3°	4°	7°	11°	13°	12°	11°	7°	4°	2°
High	(F)	44°	45°	51°	56°	63°	69°	73°	72°	67°	58°	49°	45°
	(C)	7°	7°	11°	13°	17°	21°	23°	22°	19°	14°	9°	7°
Rainfall	(in)	2	2	1	2	2	2	2	2	2	2	3	2
	(mm)	51	51	25	51	51	51	51	51	51	51	76	51

COMMUNICATIONS

When dialing direct to the United Kingdom, dial the proper International Access Code + **44** (Country Code) + City Code (see individual city listings) + Local Number. The International Access Code if calling from the U.S. is **011**.

Audible Sounds: Ringing - two short tones followed by a pause. Repeated more rapidly than the U.S. ringing tone. Busy Signal - similar to the U.S. busy tone but faster. All Circuits Busy Signal - a rapid series of high-low tones. Number Not In Use - a high-pitched continuous tone.

When transmitting telex messages from the U.S., the code **851** for the United Kingdom must precede the telex number.

CURRENCY

Pound 1 = 100 pence. Coins: 1p, 2p, 5p, 10p, 20p, 50p and £1. Two of the old silver coins are still in circulation - 2s.(two shillings) the exact equivalent of the new 10p coins; 1s.(one shilling) the exact equivalent of the new 5p coins. Bills: 5, 10, 20 and 50.

ELECTRIC CURRENT

Electrical appliances run on 240 volt, AC, 50 cycles. Variations between 200 and 250 volt may still be found. Notices are generally displayed in the few areas where DC is still used. A plug adapter is necessary for electrical equipment.

LANGUAGE

English, Gaelic and Welsh

TAXES/TIPPING

Airport Taxes: Departure taxes are not collected of passengers at the airport.
Tipping: In most instances, hotel and restaurant service charges are included in the bill. However, if not included, it is customary to divide 10-15% of the bill among the staff who have given good service. Gratuities for porters, 50P per bag; taxi drivers, 10-15% of fare.

TIME

Banking Hours: England: 9:00 AM-3:00 PM (Mon-Fri). Wales: 9:00 AM-3:00 PM (Mon-Fri). Scotland: 9:30 AM-12:30 PM, 1:30-3:30 PM (Mon-Wed); 9:30 AM- 12:30 PM, 1:30-3:30 PM, 4:30-6:00 PM (Thur); 9:30 AM-3:30 PM (Fri). Northern Ireland: 10:00 AM-3:30 PM (Mon-Fri)
Business Hours: 9:00 AM-5:00 PM
Shopping Hours: 9:00 AM-5:30 PM. Most towns have an early closing day once a week.

TOBACCO/LIQUOR

Import Allowances
Tobacco: 2 cartons of cigarettes or 100 cigars or 1 lb. 1½ oz. of tobacco.
Liquor: 2 litres of still table wine plus 1 litre liquor or 2 litres of fortified or sparkling wine or a further 2 litres of still table wine.
Above applies for travelers 17 years of age or older.

PUBLIC HOLIDAYS & CALENDAR OF EVENTS

January
1-31   Japanese Festival, **Belfast**
1   New Year's Day (Public Holiday)
2   Bank Holiday (Public Holiday), **Scotland** only
2-5   Intl. Holiday & Travel Fair, **Birmingham**
2-12   Intl. Boat Show, **London**
11-14   Crufts Dog Show, **Birmingham**
16-19   Antiques Fair, **London**

February
5-9   Scottish Boat, Caravan, Camping & Leisure Show, **Glasgow**
8-29   Jorvik Viking Festival, **York**
10-15   Ulster Motor Show, **Belfast**
15-23   Boat, Caravan & Leisure Show, **Birmingham**

March
10-12   Horse Racing, **Cheltenham**
10-21   Chelsea Antiques Fair, **London**
13-Apr. 5   Daily Mail Ideal Home Exhibition, **London**
17   St. Patrick's Day Celebrations, **Northern Ireland** only
20-Nov. 3   Cathedral's 900th Anniversary Celebrations, **Durham**

April
Thru Jan. '93   Shakespeare Theatre Season, **Stratford-Upon-Avon**
1-10   Intl. Folk Festival, **Edinburgh**
1-18   Intl. Festival of Science & Technology, **Edinburgh**
9-15   British Intl. Antiques Fair, **Birmingham**
15-22   Intl. Youth Music Festival, **Harrogate**
17   Good Friday (Public Holiday)
17-20   Intl. Motor Rally, **Belfast**
17-21   Intl. Canoe Race, **Devizes to London**
20   Easter Monday (Public Holiday)
23-25   Spring Flower Show, **Harrogate**
30-May 3   Westminster Antiques Fair, **London**

May
Thru Sept.   Open Air Theatre Season, **London**
1-23   Mayfest '92, **Glasgow**
1-Oct. 4   Garden Festival, **Ebbw Vale, Wales**
1-Oct. 10   Theatre Festival Season, **Pitlochry**
4   May Day (Public Holiday)
4   Marathon, **London**
7-17   Harpers' Festival, **Belfast**
20-22   Royal Ulster Agricultural Society's Annual Show & Industrial Exhibition, **Belfast**
22-June 7   Intl. Festival, **Bath**
25   Spring Bank Holiday (Public Holiday)
25-June 6   English Riviera Dance Festival, **Torquay**

June
10-20   Grosvenor House Antiques Fair, **London**
12-28   Festival of Music & the Arts, **Aldeburgh**
13-July 5   Festival & Mystery Plays, **York**
18-21   Royal Intl. Horse Show, **Birmingham**
19-21   Folk Festival, **Beverley**
20-July 4   Music Festival, **Bournemouth**
26-27   World Championship Irish Motocross Grand Prix, **Killinchy**

August
12-16   Grand Regatta Columbus 92-Quincentenary, **Liverpool**
        Transatlantic race beginning in Genoa (Italy) and Lisbon (Portugal) ports to Cadiz and Canary Islands, followed by Atlantic crossing to San Juan, to U.S.A. ports, and then return race to Liverpool.

TOURIST BOARD OFFICES

British Tourist Authority:
London SW1, British Travel Centre, 12 Regent St. TEL: 71/730-3400.
North America (Information for United Kingdom)
Atlanta, GA 30339, 2580 Cumberland Pkwy., Ste. 470. TEL: 404/432-9635. FAX: 404/432-9641.
Chicago, IL 60611, 625 N. Michigan Ave., Ste. 1510. TEL: 312/787-0490. FAX: 312/787-7746.
Los Angeles, CA 90071, World Trade Center, 350 S. Figueroa St., Ste. 450. TEL: 213/628-3525. TLX: 46695. FAX: 213/687-6621.
New York, NY 10019, 40 W. 57th St., 3rd Fl., Ste. 320. TEL: 212/581-4700. TLX: 237798. FAX: 212/265-0649.
Toronto, ON M5R 3N3, 94 Cumberland St., Ste. 600. TEL: 416/925-6326. FAX: 416/961-2175.
Europe
Amsterdam, Netherlands 1054 ES, Stadhouderskade 2., Aurora Gebouw 5th Fl. TEL: 20/685-50-51.
Brussels, Belgium 1050, 306 Avenue Louise. TEL: 2/646-35-10.
Copenhagen K, Denmark DK 1116, Montergade 3. TEL: 33-12-07-93. FAX: 33-14-01-36.
Dublin, Ireland 2, 123 Lower Baggot St. TEL: 1/614-188.FAX: 1/618536.
Frankfurt, Fed. Rep. of Germany 6000, Taunusstr. 52-60. TEL: 69/2380711. TLX: 4185209. FAX: 69/2380717.

Figure 6-17E. Basic data sheet for the U.K., from the *Official Airline Guide Travel Planner, European Edition,* which is useful for crew and passenger briefing.

```
                                                        Heathrow-Budapest Flight Plan

02   POD  EGLL
03   POA  LHBP
06   ROUTE J
07   HOLD, ALTERNATE/DIST  LOWW
08   ETD 0800
09   PROFILE I
10   A/D  TYPE/REGN  C601/N321R
11   CRZ  MODE  M80
12   PRFM  INDEX  F
13   OPERATIONAL WT  24685
14   PAYLOAD 600
16   POD OR POA FUEL D15000
17   RESERVE 2000
18   CLIMB FUEL, TIME, DIST BIAS
19   DESCENT FUEL, TIME, DIST BIAS

PLAN 9672EGLL  TO LHBP  C601         M80/F   IFR    03/12/92
NONSTOP   COMPUTED   2041Z   FOR   ETD   0800ZZ     PROGS   241200Z   LBS

           FUEL     TIME    DIST    ARRIVE   TAKEOFF   LAND     AV PLD    OPNLWT
POA LHBP   004352   01/56   0864    0956Z    040285    035933   000600    024685
ALT LOWW   000913   00/21   0115    1017Z
HLD        000000   00/00
RES        009735   05/37
TOT        01500    07/54

EGLL  DVR2F  DVR  UG1   FFM   UA19   OKG   UA17   BNO   UA4   DUN   STAR   LHBP
WIND  P030MXSH   2/BNO
FL   370
```

Figure 6-18A. Heathrow to Budapest flight information

```
                                                    Hungary Landing Permit
QU PAOYRXH
.LHBPYEYX 134529
FF  KSFOXLDI

TO:     JEPPESEN DATAPLAN
FROM:   HUNGARIAN CIVIL AVIATION

LANDING PERMISSION GRANTED FOR ABC INDUSTRIES-N321R
ETA LHBP 3.14.1000Z  /  ETD LHBP 3.15.0800Z WITH PERMIT
D.A.C. # 1267739
M. DIERHZNY  /  CIVIL AIR


                                                    Hungary Landing Request
QU PAOYRXH
.PAOYRXH  124672  PAOYRXH
FF LHAAYAYX LHBPYEYX KSFOXLDI
124672 KSFOXLDI

ATTN:  HUNGARY CIVIL AVIATION
FROM:  JEPPESEN DATAPLAN

RESPECTFULLY REQUEST PERMISSION ON BEHALF OF ABC INDUSTRIES,
121 ALBRIGHT WAY, LOS GATOS, CALIFORNIA 95030 USA
TO LAND FERIHEGY/BUDAPEST ON A PRIVATE, NON-COMMERCIAL FLIGHT
OPERATING ACFT TYPE CL601  REG N321R
CAPTAIN J. SANDERSON PLUS 2 CREW AND 5 PAX

ETD   EGLL   14   MAR   0800Z
ETA   LHBP   14   MAR   1000Z
ETD   LHBP   15   MAR   0800Z
ETA   LFPB   15   MAR   0945Z

REQUIRED INFORMATION:
1.  CAPT. J. SANDERSON—6//18/1947—PP#E49608587
2.  CONTACT: MR. FRANZ SMIERTOV—BUDAPEST AVIATION COUNCIL
3.  PASSENGERS: ALL U.S. CITIZENS

PLEASE ACKNOWLEDGE RECEIPT OF THIS MESSAGE AND CONFIRM LANDING
PERMISSION TO KSFOXLDI.

REGARDS,
CONNIE HIGGINBOTHAM
JEPPESEN DATAPLAN/INTERNATIONAL FLIGHT SERVICES
```

Figure 6-18B. Proof of the Hungary landing permit

Budapest Ground Handling Confirmation

```
QN PAOJD7X BUDHKVX
.BUDHKVX 046752
ATTN:  JEPPESEN DATAPLAN
WE CONFIRM YOUR HANDLING AND REFUELING REQUEST FOR THE FOLLOWING
FLIGHT: ABC IND. N321R ON 14-15.03.92
ALL REQUESTED SERVICES CONFIRMED.
Z.Z.GABOR—G.A.C. BUDAPEST
```

Budapest Ground Handling Request

```
FROM:  P1024:     10:20:02
QN BUDHKVX PAOJD7X
.PAOJD7X 092352 PAOJD7X

ATTN:  G.A.C. BUDAPEST
FROM:  JEPPESEN DATAPLAN
REQUEST GROUND HANDLING ON BEHALF OF ABC INDUSTRIES,
121 ALBRIGHT WAY, LOS GATOS, CALIFORNIA, 95030 USA
OPERATING ACFT TYPE CL601   REG N321R
CAPTAIN J. SANDERSON PLUS 2 CREW AND 5 PAX

ETD  EGLL  14  MAR  0800Z
ETA  LHBP  14  MAR  1000Z
ETD  LHBP  15  MAR  0800Z
ETA  LFPB  15  MAR  0945Z

SERVICES REQUIRED:
A.  GROUND HANDLING
B.  FUEL—MALEV/CHARGED TO MULTISERVICE CARD.
C.  ENGLISH SPEAKING CUSTOMS ESCORT.
D.  TRANSPORT—PLEASE ARANGE FOR 1 CAR W/DRIVER TO TAKE CREW TO/FROM THE DUNA INTERCONTINENTAL.
E.  FLIGHT PLAN WILL BE SENT TO YOUR OFFICE 4 HOURS PRIOR TO DEPARTURE. PLEASE FILE ON BEHALF
    OF CAPTAIN.
F.  PLEASE SEND ARR/DEP MESSAGES TO KSFOXLDI.

PLEASE INVOICE JEPPESEN DATAPLAN FOR ALL GROUND HANDLING AND LANDING FEES. PLEASE ACKNOWLEDGE
RECEIPT OF THIS MESSAGE AND CONFIRM GROUND HANDLING TO KSFOXLDI.

REGARDS,
CONNIE HIGGINBOTHAM
JEPPESEN DATAPLAN/INTERNATIONAL FLIGHT SERVICES
```

Figure 6-18C. Budapest ground handling information

```
                                                   Budapest Hotel Confirmation
RX-DDD
184787 JEPPESEN UT
DUNA
ATTN: C. HIGGINBOTHAM
REF : RESERVATIONS. J SANDERSON

WE ARE PLEASED TO ACKNOWLEDGE YOUR RESERVATIONS FOR:
     03 SWB ARR 14 MAR DEP 15 MAR
AT THE RATE OF 120 USD PER NIGHT.

REGARDS,
D. CIAVIK/RESERVATIONS
DUNA INTERCONTINENTAL HOTEL

                                                        Budapest Hotel Request
TRT
184787 JEPPESEN UT
86129843
29843 DUNA

ATTN:   DUNA INTERCONTINENTAL—BUDAPEST
        RESERVATIONS MANAGER
FROM:   JEPPESEN DATAPLAN
        121 ALBRIGHT WAY
        LOS GATOS, CALIFORNIA 95030 USA

WE REQUEST HOTAC FOR OUR CREW MEMBERS AS FOLLOWS:

03 SWB TO BE HELD UNDER THE NAME: J. SANDERSON

CREW WILL BE ARRIVING 14 MAR AND DEPARTING 15 MAR SO ROOMS WILL BE REQUIRED FOR 1 NIGHT. PLEASE
GUARANTEE ROOMS FOR LATE ARRIVAL

REQUEST YOU PLEASE EXTEND CREW DISCOUNT IF AVAILABLE.

PLEASE ACKNOWLEDGE RECEIPT OF THIS MESSAGE TO TELEX 184787
CONFIRMING RESERVATIONS AND ADVISING APPLICABLE ROOM RATE.

THANK YOU FOR YOUR ASSISTANCE IN THIS MATTER.

KINDEST REGARDS,
CONNIE HIGGINBOTHAM
INTERNATIONAL FLIGHT SERVICES
```

Figure 6-18D. Budapest hotel confirmation

THE BASICS

COMMUNICATIONS

When dialing direct to Hungary, dial the proper International Access Code + **36** (Country Code) + City Code (see individual city listings) + Local Number. The International Access Code if calling from the U.S. is **011**.

Audible Sounds: Ringing - similar to the U.S. ringing tone. Busy Signal - similar to the U.S. busy tone but faster.

When transmitting telex messages from the U.S., the code **861** for Hungary must precede the telex number.

CURRENCY

The Hungarian unit of currency is the Forint. 1 Ft. equals 100 Fillers. Coins: 1, 2, 5, 10 and 20 Forints, 10, 20 and 50 Filler coins. Bills: 5, 10, 20, 50, 100, 500 and 1,000 Forints.

ELECTRIC CURRENT

Electric appliances run on 220 volt, 50 cycles. A plug adapter is necessary for electrical equipment.

LANGUAGE

Hungarian

TAXES/TIPPING

Airport Taxes: Departure taxes are not collected of passengers at the airport.
Tipping: Hotel and restaurant service charges are included in the bill, however, in restaurants it is recommended to tip 10-15% of the net bill. It is also appropriate to tip taxi drivers and hotel staff based on the service.

TIME

Banking Hours: 8:30 AM-3:00 PM (Mon-Fri)
Business Hours: 8:30 AM-5:00 PM
Shopping Hours: Food Stores:7:00 AM-6:00/8:00 PM. Shops: 10:00 AM-6:00 PM (Mon-Fri); 10:00 AM-2:00 PM (Sat)

TOBACCO/LIQUOR

Import Allowances
Tobacco: 1 carton of cigarettes for travelers 18 years of age or older.
Liquor: 1 quart of liquor for travelers 16 years of age or older.

PUBLIC HOLIDAYS & CALENDAR OF EVENTS

January
1   New Year's Day (Public Holiday)

April
4   Liberation Day (Public Holiday)
20   Easter Monday (Public Holiday)

May
1   May Day (Public Holiday)

TOURIST BOARD OFFICES

Ibusz Hungarian Travel Bureau:
Budapest, Ferenciek Tere 5, 1053 Budapest. TEL: 1/117-9997. FAX: 1/117-7723.
North America
Fort Lee, NJ 07024, One Parker Plaza, Ste. 1104. TEL: 201/592-8585. FAX: 201/592-8736.
Europe
Belgrade, Yugoslavia 11000, Strahinjica Bana 47. TEL: 623-826.
Berlin, Fed. Rep of Germany, Karl Liebknecht St. 9. TEL: 212-35-59.
Brussels, Belgium 1040, 6 Rue de Luxembourg. TEL: 511-4-85.
Frankfurt, Fed. Rep. of Germany 6000, Baseler St. 46-48. TEL: 252-018.
London, England W1R 9TG, Conduit St. TEL: 71/493-0263.
Madrid, Spain 8, Juan Alvarez Mendizabel No. 1 111, Piso 6. TEL: 241-25-44.
Moscow, U.S.S.R., ul. Gorkogo 26/1. TEL: 299-8010.
Paris, France 75002, Rue de Quatre Septembre 27. TEL: 742-5025.
Prague, Czechoslovakia 11000, Praha, ul. Kaprova 5. TEL: 22-40-08.
Rome, Italy 00185, Via V.E. Orlando 75. TEL: 485-871.
Sofia, Bulgaria 6, ul. G. Dimitrov 44. TEL: 89-21-36.
Stockholm, Sweden 10326, Beridarebanan 1. TEL: 20-40-40.
Vienna, Austria A-1010, Krugerstrasse 4. TEL: 1/52-92-60.
Warsaw, Poland 00517, ul. Marszalkowska 80. TEL: 25-99-15.
Pacific Asia
Tokyo, Japan 106, Togensha Bldg., 3rd Fl., 12-10 Roppongi 4-chome, Minato-Ku. TEL: 3/3404-80-89.

DESTINATIONS AND ACCOMMODATIONS

Hotel Listings: The Hungarian Government has established ratings for hotels. These rating classifications appear in parenthesis within the individual hotel listings. A decode of the classifications follows:

★★★★★ = Luxury
★★★★ = Upper First Class
★★★ = First Class
★★ = Tourist
★ = Economy

All room rates presented are for guideline purposes only and should be confirmed directly with the hotels or their Sales Representatives. In some instances, service charges and/or taxes may be included in the room rate range.

Figure 6-18E. Travel data for Hungary, courtesy of OAG and furnished by Jeppesen Dataplan

Budapest-Paris Flight Plan

```
02   POD  LHBP
03   POA  LFPB
06   ROUTE J
07   HOLD, ALTERNATE/DIST  LFPG
08   ETD 0800
09   PROFILE I
10   A/C  TYPE/REGN  C601/N321R
11   CRZ  MODE  M80
12   PRFM  INDEX  F
13   OPERATIONAL  WT  24685
14   PAYLOAD 600
16   POD OR POA FUEL D14500
17   RESERVE 2000
18   CLIMB FUEL, TIME, DIST BIAS
19   DESCENT FUEL, TIME, DIST BIAS

PLAN 9708        LHBP TO  LFPB  C601                M80/F   IFR    03/12/92
NONSTOP   COMPUTED   2045Z   FOR   ETD    0800Z      PROGS   241200Z   LBS

               FUEL    TIME    DIST   ARRIVE   TAKEOFF   LAND     AV PLD    OPNLWT
POA LFPB       003979  01/47   0726   0947Z    039785    035806   000600    024685
ALT LFPG       000325  00/03   0005   0950Z
HLD            000000  00/00
RES            010196  05/49
TOT            014500  07/39

LHBP   SID   TORNO  G1   GYR   UG104  SNU   UG4   RLP   STAR   LFPBSTAR    LHBP
WIND   M021    MXSH    2/SNU
FL   310/GYR   350/SNU   390
```

Figure 6-19A. Budapest to Paris flight plan information

```
QU PAOJD7X
.LBGCACR 101005 CAS OPS LBG / MAR92

ATTN:  CONNIE HIGGINBOTHAM
FROM C.A.S / LE TERMINAL PARIS LBG
REF/RQST HDG CL601 / REG N321R
 WE CFM GROUND HANDLING AS FOLLOWS:
   AA/FULL ASSISTANCE
   BB/BP VIA TRANSAIR ON MULTISERVICE CREDIT CARD OK
   CC/IN HOUSE CUSTOMS IN LE TERMINAL
   DD/A CAR WITH ENGLISH SPEAKING DRIVER WILL BE PROVIDED FROM THE M.L.G. COMPANY.
   EE/WE WILL FILE FLIGHT PLAN FOR CAPT.
   FF/ALL MESSAGES TO PAOJD7X

THKS FOR YOUR COOP. BRGDS / J.C. KILLY / C.A.S. OPS
```

```
FROM:  P1024: 10:53:56
QU LBGCACR PAOJD7X
.PAOJD7X 1000026 PAOJD7X

ATTN:  COMPUTED AIR SERVICES
FROM:  JEPPESEN DATAPLAN

REQUEST GROUND HANDLING ON BEHALF OF ABC INDUSTRIES,
121 ALBRIGHT WAY, LOS GATOS, CALIFORNIA, 95030 USA
OPERATING ACFT TYPE CL601   REG N321R
CAPTAIN J. SANDERSON PLUS 2 CREW AND 5 PAX

ETD  LHBP  15  MAR   0800Z
ETA  LFPB  15  MAR   0945Z
ETD  LFPB  16  MAR   0800Z
ETA  EINN  16  MAR   0930Z

SERVICES REQUIRED:
A.  GROUND HANDLING
B.  FUEL—BP VIA TRANSAIR/CHARGED TO MULTISERVICE CARD.
C.  ENGLISH SPEAKING CUSTOMS ESCORT.
D.  TRANSPORT—PLEASE ARANGE FOR 1 CAR W/DRIVER TO TAKE CREW TO/FROM THE
    MARIOTT PRINCE DE GALLES.
E.  FLIGHT PLAN WILL BE SENT TO YOUR OFFICE 4 HOURS PRIOR TO DEPARTURE. PLEASE FILE ON BEHALF
    OF CAPTAIN.
F.  PLEASE SEND ARR/DEP MESSAGES TO PAOJD7X.

PLEASE INVOICE JEPPESEN DATAPLAN FOR ALL GROUND HANDLING AND LANDING FEES. PLEASE ACKNOWLEDGE
RECEIPT OF THIS MESSAGE AND CONFIRM GROUND HANDLING TO PAOJD7X.

REGARDS,
CONNIE HIGGINBOTHAM
JEPPESEN DATAPLAN/INTERNATIONAL FLIGHT SERVICES
```

Figure 6-19B. Paris ground handling information

Paris Hotel Confirmation

```
RX-DDD
184787 JEPPESEN UT
MARDG
ATTN: JEPPESEN DATAPLAN—C. HIGGINBOTHAM
REF : MSSR. J SANDERSON

WE ARE PLEASED TO ACKNOWLEDGE YOUR RESERVATIONS FOR:
03 SWB .ARR 15 MAR DEP 17 MAR
OUR CREW 40% DISCOUNT RATE IS 1100FF / NIGHT.

BEST WISHES,
MARCEL / RESERVATIONS DEPART.
LE MARRIOTT PRINCE DE GALLES
```

Paris Hotel Request

```
TRT
184787 JEPPESEN UT
842280627
124382 MARDG

ATTN:   MARRIOTT PRINCE DE GALLES
        RESERVATIONS MANAGER
FROM:   JEPPESEN DATAPLAN
        121 ALBRIGHT WAY
        LOS GATOS, CALIFORNIA 95030

WE REQUEST HOTAC FOR OUR CREW MEMBERS AS FOLLOWS:

03 SWB TO BE HELD UNDER THE NAME: J. SANDERSON

CREW WILL BE ARRIVING 15 MAR AND DEPARTING 17 MAR SO ROOMS WILL BE REQUIRED FOR 2 NIGHTS.
PLEASE GUARANTEE ROOMS FOR LATE ARRIVAL

REQUEST YOU PLEASE EXTEND CREW DISCOUNT IF AVAILABLE.

PLEASE ACKNOWLEDGE RECEIPT OF THIS MESSAGE TO TELEX 184787
CONFIRMING RESERVATIONS AND ADVISING APPLICABLE ROOM RATE.

THANK YOU FOR YOUR ASSISTANCE IN THIS MATTER.

KINDEST REGARDS,
CONNIE HIGGINBOTHAM
INTERNATIONAL FLIGHT SERVICES
```

Figure 6-19C. Paris hotel confirmation

YLAKOLI   **EDC 73**
NEAREST AIR SERVICE THROUGH JOENSUU, JOE, 97 KM/60 MI NE.
ADDITIONAL THROUGH KUOPIO, KUO, 209 KM/130 MI NE.

YLIVIESKA   **EDC 83**
NEAREST AIR SERVICE THROUGH KOKKOLA, KOK, 80 KM/50 MI NE. RAIL: FINNISH STATE.
ADDITIONAL THROUGH OULU, OUL, 113 KM/70 MI SW. RAIL: FINNISH STATE.

○—✈HOTEL/MOTEL (City Centre and other)
KAENPESA HOTEL   ✕♦
  LINTUTIE 1   PN: 84100
                    $96-123ⓒ   L-390-500ⓒ   ④
  TEL: 83/423611   FAX: 423622

FRANCE
THE BASICS

For Documentary Requirements, Currency Conversion Rates and the International Standard Time Chart, refer to the General Travel Information Section.

DOCUMENTARY REQUIREMENTS

U.S. CITIZENS: Passport—Required. **Visa**—Not required for stays of 3 months or less, except for on duty airline personnel, persons traveling on diplomatic or official passports, and students on study programs. **Other**—Sufficient funds, ticket to leave and necessary documents for onward travel. **Vaccination Certificates**— None required unless coming from an infected area.

CANADIAN CITIZENS: Same as for U.S. citizens.

CONSULATE OFFICES IN NORTH AMERICA

CANADA

EMBASSY:
Ottawa, ON K1M 2C9, 42 Sussex Dr. TEL: 613/232-1795.

CONSULATE GENERAL:
Edmonton, AB T5J 3L8, Highfield Pl., 10010-106 St., Ste. 300. TEL: 403/428-0232.
Moncton, NB E1C 8P6, 250 Lutz St., Box 1109. TEL: 506/857-4191.
Montreal, PQ H5A 1A7, 2 Elysee, Pl. Bonaventure, Box 177. TEL: 514/878-4381, Ext. 70/71/72.
Quebec, PQ G1S 3C3, 1110 Ave. Laurentides. TEL: 418/688-0430.
Toronto, ON M5S 1N5, 130 Bloor St. W; Ste. 400. TEL: 416/925-8041; Visa Info. 416/925-8233.
Vancouver, BC V6Z 1H9, 736 Granville St., Ste. 1201. TEL: 604/681-4345; Visa Info. 604/681-2301.

UNITED STATES

EMBASSY:
Washington, DC 20007-2170, 4101 Reservoir Rd., NW. TEL: 202/944-6000. (Consular section: 202/944-6195).

CONSULATE GENERAL:
Atlanta, GA 30303, 285 Peachtree Center Ave., Ste. 2800. TEL: 404/522-4226. TLX: 212646.
Boston, MA 02116, 3 Commonwealth Ave. TEL: 617/266-1680. TLX: 940985. **Note:** Visas issued **only**, at 20 Park Plaza. TEL: 617/482-3650.
Chicago, IL 60611, 737 N. Michigan Ave., Ste. 2020, (Olympia Center). TEL: 312/787-5359/85. TLX: 190229.
Honolulu, HI 96813, 2 Waterfront Plaza, Ste. 300, 500 Ala Moana Blvd., TEL: 808/599-4458. TLX: 7238129.
Houston, TX 77019, 2727 Allen Pky., Ste. 976. TEL: 713/528-2181. TLX: 825078.
Los Angeles, CA 90024, 10990 Wilshire Blvd., Ste. 300. (Beverly Hills). TEL: 213/653-3120. TLX: 6831406.
Miami, FL 33131, One Biscayne Tower, 2 S. Biscayne Blvd., 17th Fl., TEL: 305/372-9799/9541. TLX: 587399.
New Orleans, LA 70115, 3305 St. Charles Ave. TEL: 504/897-6381/82. TLX: 587399.
New York, NY 10019, 934 Fifth Ave. TEL: 212/606-3600/80.
San Francisco, CA 94108, 540 Bush St. TEL: 415/397-4330.
San Juan, PR 00918, Mercantil Plaza, Ponce de Leon Ave., Ste. 720., Stop 27 1/2, Hato Rey. TEL: 809/753-1700/01. TLX: 325432.

UNITED STATES CHAMBER OF COMMERCE OFFICE

MAIN OFFICE:
Paris 75008, 21 Ave. George V. TEL: 1/47-23-80-26.

UNITED STATES FOREIGN SERVICE OFFICES

EMBASSY:
Paris, 2 Avenue Gabriel, 75382 Paris Cedex 08. TEL: 1/42-96-12-02 or 42-61-80-75. TLX: 650221. FAX: 1/42-66-97-83.

CONSULATE GENERAL:
Bordeaux, 22 Cours du Marechal Foch, 33080 Bordeaux Cedex, TEL: 56-52-65-95. TLX: 540918. FAX: 56-51-60-42.
Lyon, 7 Quai General Sarrail, 69454 Lyon Cedex 3. TEL: 78-24-68-49. TLX: 380597.
Marseille, 12 Blvd. Paul Peytral, 13286 Marseille Cedex. TEL: 91-54-92-00. TLX: 430597. FAX: 91-55-09-47.
Strasbourg, 15 Ave. D'Alsace, 67082 Strasbourg Cedex. TEL: 88-35-31-04. TLX: 870907.

CLIMATE

Marseille

Average		Jan	Feb	Mar	Apr	May	June	July	Aug	Sept	Oct	Nov	Dec
Low	(F)	38°	37°	38°	41°	46°	52°	58°	61°	61°	57°	50°	43°
	(C)	3°	3°	3°	5°	8°	11°	14°	16°	16°	14°	10°	6°
High	(F)	53°	52°	55°	59°	65°	72°	78°	83°	82°	76°	67°	59°
	(C)	12°	11°	13°	15°	18°	22°	26°	28°	28°	24°	19°	15°
Rainfall	(in)	2	2	2	2	2	1	1	1	3	4	3	2
	(mm)	51	51	51	51	51	25	25	25	76	102	76	51

Paris

Average		Jan	Feb	Mar	Apr	May	June	July	Aug	Sept	Oct	Nov	Dec
Low	(F)	32°	33°	36°	41°	47°	52°	55°	55°	50°	44°	38°	33°
	(C)	0°	1°	2°	5°	8°	11°	13°	13°	10°	7°	3°	1°
High	(F)	42°	45°	52°	60°	67°	72°	76°	75°	69°	59°	49°	43°
	(C)	6°	7°	11°	16°	19°	23°	24°	24°	21°	15°	9°	6°
Rainfall	(in)	2	1	2	2	2	2	2	2	2	2	2	2
	(mm)	51	51	51	51	51	51	51	51	51	51	51	51

COMMUNICATIONS

When dialing direct to France, dial the proper International Access Code + **33** (Country Code) + City Code (see individual city listings) + Local Number. The International Access Code if calling from the U.S. is **011.** NOTE: With the exception of Paris and its suburbs, City Codes (EDC's) for most cities in France are now included within individual local phone numbers.

Audible Sounds: Ringing - similar to the U.S. ringing tone but longer. Busy Signal - similar to the U.S. busy tone but faster. This tone also indicates that all circuits are busy. Transit Signal - a rapidly repeated tone. It is heard while the connection is being established through the French network.

When transmitting telex messages from the U.S., the code **842** for France must precede the telex number.

CURRENCY

100 Centimes equals 1 Franc. Coins: 5, 10 and 50 Centimes: 1, 5 and 10 Francs. Bills: 20, 50, 100, 200 and 500 Francs.

ELECTRIC CURRENT

Electrical appliances run on 220-230 volt, 50 cycles. Some areas may still run on 110-115 volt. A plug adapter and voltage transformer are necessary.

LANGUAGE

French

TAXES/TIPPING

Airport Taxes: Departure taxes are not collected of passengers at the airport. For transportation taxes which may apply, refer to the Local Taxes section of the OAG Desktop Flight Guide-Worldwide Edition.

Tipping: In most instances, restaurant service charges are included in the bill. However, if not included, 15% of net bill is appropriate. In addition, it is customary to tip as follows: chambermaid, 10 FF a day; porter, 5-10 FF per bag; cloakroom attendants in theatres and restaurants, 5 FF per item; if personally served by the wine waiter, 10 FF; washroom attendant, 2 FF; theatre usherettes, 2 FF per person; hairdressers, 10% of net bill; group guides, 5 FF per person; and taxi drivers, 10-15% if metered fare.

TIME

Banking Hours: 9:00 AM-4:30 PM (Mon-Fri) Closed midday on days preceding public holidays.
Business Hours: 9:00 AM-Noon, 2:00-6:00 PM (Mon-Fri); 9:00 AM-Noon (Sat)
Shopping Hours: Department Stores: 9:00 AM-6:30 PM (Tue-Sat). Fashion Boutiques and Shops: 10:00 AM-Noon, 2:00-6:30 PM (Tue-Sat).

TOBACCO/LIQUOR

Import Allowances
Tobacco: 2 cartons of cigarettes or 125 cigars or 1 lb. of tobacco for travelers 18 years of age or older.
Liquor: 1 bottle of liquor and 3 bottles of wine (per family) for travelers 17 years of age or older.

PUBLIC HOLIDAYS & CALENDAR OF EVENTS

January
1   New Year's Day (Public Holiday)
10-14   Intl. Jewelry Exhibition, **Paris**
19-23   Intl. Record Music Publishing & Video Music Market, **Cannes**
20-27   3rd Intl. Museum & Exhibitions Fair, **Paris**
24-26   Intl. Cartoon Festival, **Angouleme**
31-Feb. 4   Intl. Ladies Ready-to-Wear Clothing Exhibition, **Paris**

February
1-4   Intl. Sporting & Leisure Equipment Exhibition, **Paris**
6-8   3rd Annual Top Resa, **Paris**
8-23   XVIth Olympic Winter Games, **Albertville and Savoie**
The XVI Olympic Winter Games will feature 13 events: Biathlon, Bobsleigh, Nordic Combined, Curling, Ice Hockey, Figure Skating, Speed Skating, Short Track, Freestyle Skiing, Ski Jumping, Alpine Skiing, Cross Country Skiing and Speed Skiing.

Albertville will host the opening and closing ceremonies, and the skating events. Other Olympic sites in the Savoie region are Val D'Isere, Les Saisies, Tignes, Les Arcs, La Plagne, Pralognan-La Vanoise, Les Menuires/Val Thorens, Courchevel and Meribel.

Reservations for accommodations should be made as far in advance as possible. For hotel information, refer to the Hotel/Motel listings for Aix-Les-Bains, Annecy, Belley, Briancon, Chambery, Chamrousse, Chamonix-Mont-Blanc, Cluses, Combloux, Courchevel, Divonne-Les-Bains, Evian, Faverges, Get, Grenoble, Le Corbier, Les Get, Les 2 Alpes, Megeve, Meribel, Moutiers, Sallanches, Thonon, Val D'Isere, Valloire, Val Thorens, Villard De Lans, and in Switzerland, see Geneva.

Information for accommodations can also be obtained through Maison de Savoie, c/o Maison des Jeux Olympiques, 11 Rue Pargoud, 73200 Albertville, France. Tel. 79-45-92-92 FAX: 79-49-39-52, and Maison de

Savoie, 31 Avenue de L'Opera, 75001 Paris, France. Tel. 1/42-61-74-73. Ticket sales in the United States have been authorized by the Albertville Olympic Organizing Committee (COJO '92) through Olson-Travelworld, Ltd., Olympic Division, P.O. Box 10066, Manhattan Beach, CA 90266. Phone and Fax ticket orders cannot be accepted. For information, call (800) 874-1992.

For further information regarding the Olympic Games, contact the French Tourist Office.

Figure 6-19D. Travel data for France, courtesy of OAG

```
                                                      Paris-Shannon Flight Plan
02   POD  LFPB
03   POA  EINN
06   ROUTE J
07   HOLD, ALTERNATE/DIST  EIDW
08   ETD 0800
09   PROFILE I
10   A/C  TYPE/REGN  C601/N321R
11   CRZ  MODE  M80
12   PRFM  INDEX  F
13   OPERATIONAL  WT  24685
14   PAYLOAD 600
16   POD OR POA FUEL D13500
17   RESERVE 2000
18   CLIMB FUEL, TIME, DIST BIAS
19   DESCENT FUEL, TIME, DIST BIAS

PLAN 9755       LFPB   TO  EINN  C601              M80/F   IFR    03/12/92
NONSTOP   COMPUTED   2048Z   FOR   ETD    0800Z     PROGS   241200Z   LBS

               FUEL    TIME    DIST    ARRIVE    TAKEOFF    LAND    AV PLD    OPNLWT
POA EINN       002874  01/18   0527    0918Z     038785     035911  000600    024685
ALT EIDW       000789  00/17   0106    0935Z
HLD            000000  00/00
RES            009837  05/39
TOT            013500  07/15

LFPB   ABB6C   ABB  UA20   BIG   UA30  CPT   UG1   EINN
WIND   M15      MXSH   2/STU
FL   390
```

Figure 6-20A. Paris to Shannon flight plan information

Shannon Ground Handling Confirmation

```
QU PAOJD7X
.SNNXREI 234152

TO JEPPESEN DATAPLAN
REFERENCE YOUR 245715 MESSAGE, WE CONFIRM HANDLING
FOR BC INDUSTRIES/N321R/J. SANDERSON
17 MAR 0930Z–17 MAR 1030Z
ALL SERVICES REQUIRED ARE CONFIRMED.

REGARDS//J. JOYCE//SHANNON REPAIR SERVICE
```

Shannon Ground Handling Request

```
FROM:   P1024:      8:53:32
QU SNNXREI PAOJD7X
.PAOJD7X  24571  PAOJD7X

ATTN:  SHANNON REPAIR SERVICE
FROM:  JEPPESEN DATAPLAN

REQUEST GROUND HANDLING ON BEHALF OF ABC INDUSTRIES,
121 ALBRIGHT WAY, LOS GATOS, CALIFORNIA, 95030 USA
OPERATING ACFT TYPE CL601   REG N321R
CAPTAIN J. SANDERSON PLUS 2 CREW AND 5 PAX

ETD  LFPB  17  MAR  0800Z
ETA  EINN  17  MAR  0930Z
ETD  EINN  17  MAR  1030Z
ETA  KHPN  17  MAR  1810Z

SERVICES REQUIRED:
A.  GROUND HANDLING
B.  FUEL–ESSO/CHARGED TO MULTISERVICE CARD.
C.  CUSTOMS ASSISTANCE AS REQUIRED.
D.  FLIGHT PLAN WILL BE SENT TO YOUR OFFICE 4 HOURS PRIOR TO DEPARTURE. PLEASE FILE ON BEHALF
    OF CAPTAIN.
E.  PLEASE SEND ARR/DEP MESSAGES TO PAOJD7X.
F.  CATERING–1 TRAY OF SMOKED SALMON AND 1 TRAY OF FRESH FRUIT FOR 7.

PLEASE INVOICE JEPPESEN DATAPLAN FOR ALL GROUND HANDLING AND LANDING FEES. PLEASE ACKNOWLEDGE
RECEIPT OF THIS MESSAGE AND CONFIRM GROUND HANDLING TO PAOJD7X.

REGARDS,
CONNIE HIGGINBOTHAM
JEPPESEN DATAPLAN/INTERNATIONAL FLIGHT SERVICES
```

Figure 6-20B. Shannon ground handling information

```
02    POD  EINN/EINN
03    POA  KHPN/KHPN
06    ROUTE J
07    HOLD, ALTERNATE/DIST  KTEB
08    ETD 1030
09    PROFILE I
10    A/C  TYPE/REGN  C601/N321R
11    CRZ  MODE  M80
12    PRFM  INDEX  F
13    OPERATIONAL  WT  24685
14    PAYLOAD 600
16    POD OR POA FUEL D16685
17    RESERVE 2000
18    CLIMB FUEL, TIME, DIST BIAS
19    DESCENT FUEL, TIME, DIST BIAS

PLAN 9794        EINN TO  KHPN  C601              M80/F   IFR     03/12/92
NONSTOP    COMPUTED   2053Z   FOR   ETD   1030Z      PROGS   241200Z    LBS

              FUEL    TIME    DIST    ARRIVE    TAKEOFF    LAND     AV PLD    OPNLWT
POA KHPN     014204  06/34   2760     1704Z     041970   027766   000600   024685
ALT KTEB     000308  00/06   0021     1710Z
HLD          000000  00/00
RES          002173  01/33
TOT          016685  08/13

BB6C . . 5415 . . 5620 . . 5830 . . 5840 . . 5650 . . OYSTR . . ATS
KLAMM . . YNA . . YGP . . HUL . . BGR   J581 PUT . . KHPN
WIND   M30   MXSH 5/5620
FL   350/5840    390
ETP  EINN/KHPN  03/24  1476NM   P027/M017   BURN  0083  N55510W050246
```

Figure 6-21A. Shannon to White Plains flight plan information

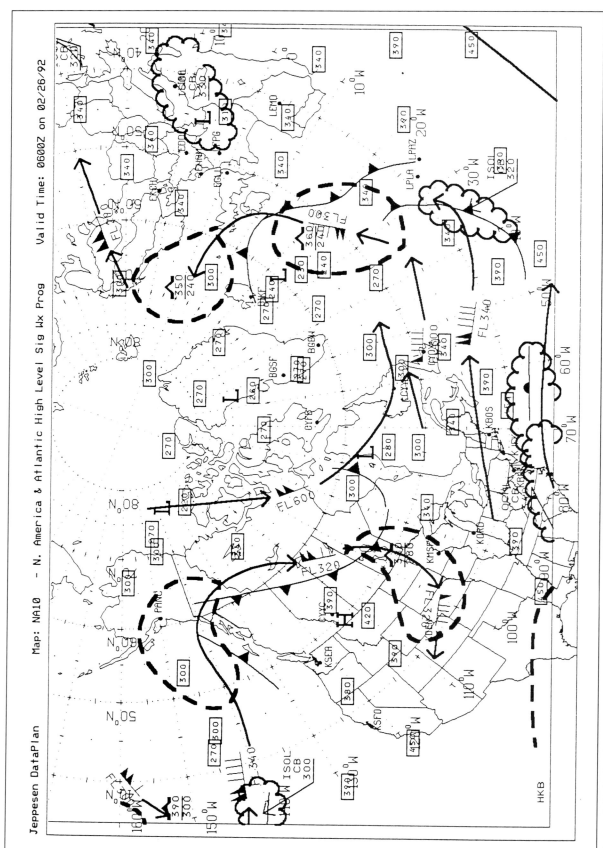

Figure 6-21B. Pertinent Atlantic high-level significant weather prognostics chart

Jeppesen DataPlan's

NEWSFAX

July 1992   *Updates from International Flight Services*

WELCOME TO "*NEWSFAX*"

We'd like to welcome you to our first issue of Jeppesen DataPlan's "*NEWSFAX*," distributed by the International Flight Services Department. It's our intent with *NEWSFAX* to keep you up-to-date on late-breaking International News pertinent to private aircraft flights. Also, we'll be bringing you items on new or enhanced services available at Jeppesen DataPlan and any newsworthy items of aviation interest. *NEWSFAX* will be distributed monthly. Your comments and feedback are always appreciated. We hope you enjoy this first edition of *NEWSFAX*.

WHO IS IFS?

The International Services Department at Jeppesen DataPlan consists of individuals with very diverse backgrounds, bringing to this service an abundance of talent and experience. Connie Higginbotham, Supervisor, has 8 years of IFS related experience, with an additional 10 years of airline operations experience. Nancy Schnetz has 3 years experience with DataPlan and speaks fluent German. Sharon Ellison has 4 years experience, along with Private Flight Attendant Service and FBO work. Sharon is also well versed in French. Kate Ha, our newest member, recently graduated from San Jose State University with an Aviation Degree. Kate speaks fluent Korean and Spanish. On call to the department are Gustav Maldonado, also a recent graduate from SJSU, and Tim Murphy. Gustav speaks fluent Spanish and Portuguese. All these individuals are ready, able and willing to assist you with your flight planning needs utilizing their aviation experience and talent.

NEWSFAX FLASH:

PAKISTAN OVERFLY

Jeppesen's agent is now able to obtain overflys of Pakistan! This will save time AND $$$ as past procedure has required all aircraft to stop in Karachi to pay the overflight fees.

LONDON LUTON CUSTOMS

Effective June 30th, Customs at Luton Airport has changed the procedures for clearing private aircraft. PAX and crew will no longer have to go through the normal customs channels as long as certain criteria are met. Contact IFS for details!

LONDON HEATHROW - BUSINESS AVIATION

Heathrow now has a business aviation terminal with customs and immigration facilities available. This will save passengers and crew time since you will now be able to avoid the main terminals.

NEW GROUND HANDLERS

Since our goal is to find you the best Ground Handlers available, some changes have been made at the following locations -

Dusseldorf - Executive Flight Services: Good new handler with whom we have full credit arrangements.
Stansted - Avitat: New FBO facility with in-house Jeppesen access software and personnel trained on JAS.
Turkey - Gozen: Recommended for all of your stops in Turkey
Prague - Czech Air Handling: Full handling facility, credit with IFS available.

STATE DEPARTMENT BRIEFS

The State Department has issued new warnings and advisories for the following countries: Azerbaijan, Bolivia, Colombia, Ethiopia, India, Kenya, Libya, Nigeria, Pakistan, Papua New Guinea, Tajikistan, Yemen, Albania, Bangladesh, Central African Republic, Cyprus, Malawi, Tanzania, Thailand, Ukraine, Germany, Madagascar, and Saudi Arabia. Call IFS if you would like copies.

CUSTOMER FEEDBACK

Customer feedback is important to us! Starting next month we will be sending a Jeppesen feedback form along with your invoice. We would appreciate any information you can give us on our service or the service you receive from our Ground Handling Agents. See details in your next monthly invoice!

CORPORATE TRAVEL SERVICES

You're already aware of the flight services Jeppesen offers to corporate pilots and flight crews. Now we've extended our travel services beyond the cockpit to include the cabin, handling every aspect of travel, domestically or internationally, for your corporate executives and other personnel as well as for your flight crew. It's the best of both worlds in corporate travel!

COMING SOON!

Look for new products and services coming soon: SRS Phase II, and International NOTAMS from Jeppesen Sanderson. Contact Customer Service for details.

121 Albright Way, Los Gatos, CA 95030
(800) 358-6468

Figure 6-22. Jeppesen DataPlan company Newsfax

Procedures for Using Berna-Radio

This direct communication facility is at the User's disposal 24 hours a day. The Berna-Radio Ground Station operates in the shortwave band 3010 KHZ to 23285 KHZ.

Equipment Required

1. The aircraft must be equipped with a SSB (Single Sideband) HF transceiver, an automatic tuner and appropriate antenna.
2. The minimum recommended transmitter power should be approximately 100 watts which will provide adequate transmission under good radio conditions.
3. The aircraft should be equipped with SELCAL equipment if ground to air call-backs are expected.

Note: SELCAL equipment is not required if only transmitting via Berna-Radio.

Use of Frequencies

To ensure optimum propagation for HF communications, Berna-Radio has assigned (8) frequencies from which a choice is made depending on the following conditions:
A. Ground to aircraft distance.
B. The time of day.
C. The season.

Current Frequency List

3,010	KHZ -	Night frequency on request.
4,654	KHZ -	Night and short range frequency.
6,643	KHZ -	Preferred night frequency.
10,069	KHZ -	Frequency for general use within European area (24 hours). Worldwide range during night.
13,205	KHZ -	Frequency (24 hours) for general use.
18,023	KHZ -	Long Range frequency between 0600Z and 2200Z.
21,988	KHZ -	Preferred frequency, for Middle East and Africa between 0500Z and 2000Z.
23, 285	KHZ -	Long range frequency between 0600Z and 2000Z.

Calling Procedure

Select the appropriate frequency on your HF Transceiver and Transmit the following information:
1. Name of facility being called. . ."Berna-Radio"
2. Give your aircraft full registration and SELCAL.
3. State your position and the frequency you are receiving on, and
4. The word. . . "Over".
5. Wait for Berna-Radio to acknowledge your initial contact.
6. State whether you want a phone or SITA message sent:
   Telephone — Phone messages to Lockheed DataPlan should be sent to 408-866-7611 California U.S.A.
   SITA — SITA messages should be addressed to: PAOYRXH
7. Inform the Berna-Radio operator that billing will be made to Lockheed DataPlan's billing account.
8. Transmit your message when contact with Berna-Radio is established.

SELCAL

Aircraft equipped with SELCAL facilities can be called up selectively from the ground. SELCAL watch is established by setting the HF equipment to the "AM" mode on a suitable frequency agreed with the Berna-Radio operator.

Notice to Airmen

Pilots should be aware that radio contact may be difficult or impossible from certain geographical positions at certain times.

If difficulties arise, try the next higher or lower frequency.

For the best choice of the particular frequency, consult the quarterly distributed frequency forecast of Berna-Radio.

Figure 6-23. Procedures sheet for using Berna-Radio

7: Trans-Oceanic and Trans-Wilderness Planning

Pilots planning actual flights must realize that the information contained in this text may go out of date. It was deemed necessary to present this information in order to provide sufficient examples for learning purposes; however, changes occur often. Pilot's *must* consult current relevant AIPs, charts, facilities directories and Notices to Airmen (NOTAMs) when planning actual flights.

Flight Planning for the North Atlantic

Crossing the Atlantic ocean provides a good case-in-point for the need to engage the planning processes. Route planning starts first with an analysis of the range and altitude capability of the aircraft. If the aircraft is capable of non-stop flight to Europe, probably **MNPS airspace** (altitudes from FL285 to FL420) across the Atlantic will be utilized; in which case the routing, once the **coast-out point** is reached, will be very specific.

The **coast-out point** and **coast-in point** are the places where the aircraft enters and leaves oceanic control airspace. Usually, VHF communications and VHF navigation reception is available at this point, so LRNS positions can be confirmed there or with VHF (VOR/DME).

The flight crew would do well to review the **North Atlantic MNPS Airspace Operations Manual**, which outlines the special requirements and approvals needed for the aircraft in this area. Some of the specifics covered in the manual are discussed later in this chapter.

If the aircraft's range is limited, as is the case with the majority of general aviation aircraft, the only option may be a route through Canada, Greenland and Iceland to reach Europe. In this case, the planner should use the **North American Route Structure**, a series of preferred routes grouped according to direction and coastal fix that will simplify flight planning and streamline ATC clearances. They are named by the letters "NA" followed by a number, and can be found in the AIM or Jepp manuals. For example: NA11 goes from Boston along J573, until it changes to Canadian HL (high level) 573 to Sydney, then HL577 to Gander. This route would be specified in a clearance request as BOS NA11 CYQX (Gander).

Before proceeding further with actual route planning, the planner should first become familiar with the MNPS Ops Manual mentioned above, and the NAIGOM (**North Atlantic International General Aviation Operations Manual**). Some of this manual is reproduced in following paragraphs, in order to help the reader become thoroughly familiar with the requirements of oceanic flight.

NAIGOM Excerpts

This manual was developed by the North Atlantic Systems Planning Group (NATSPG), to assist International General Aviation (IGA) pilots in flight planning and operations across the North Atlantic. It is not, however, intended to be a detailed listing of procedures or air regulations of the various states that provide air traffic service in the North Atlantic region, and does not in any way replace the information contained in various national Aeronautical Information Publications (AIPs). Pilots *must* consult relevant AIPs and Notices to Airmen (NOTAMs) when planning the flight and prior to departure. ICAO Annex # 1 provides information on obtaining regulatory publications that may be of assistance.

Flights by light general aviation aircraft across the North Atlantic have increased dramatically over the years. Unfortunately, there has also been a corresponding increase in the number of general aviation fatalities and lost aircraft. Because of the harsh climate, lack of ground-based radio and navigation aids, as well as the immense distances involved, a trans-Atlantic flight is a serious undertaking. While IGA flights constitute a relatively small percentage of the overall North Atlantic traffic, they account for the majority of search and rescue operations and expenses. The information contained in this manual is intended to help the IGA plot complete a safe and enjoyable flight.

Within the NAT Region there are both civil and military air traffic operations. The civil operations include supersonic commercial flights, a significant volume of subsonic commercial traffic, as well as an increasing number of IGA aircraft. In addition to routine trans-Atlantic military air traffic, at least twice annually large-scale, joint force military operations are conducted. These exercises may restrict, if not eliminate entirely, access by general aviation aircraft to large portions of North Atlantic airspace.

The North Atlantic (NAT) Region comprises the following **Flight Information Regions** (FIRs):

Bodo Oceanic

Gander Oceanic

New York Oceanic

Reykjavik

Santa Maria Oceanic

Shanwick Oceanic

Sondrestrom

Description of North Atlantic Airspace

The portion of the North Atlantic airspace covered in the NAIGOM manual, along with the associated Flight Information Regions, is depicted in Figure 7-1. Because NAIGOM is primarily designed for the IGA pilot, it is primarily that airspace located north of 350 north latitude and below 28,000 feet MSL (outside of MNPS airspace).

Most of the airspace involved in Oceanic FIRs is high-seas airspace within which the International Civil Aviation Organization (ICAO) Council has resolved that rules relating to flight and operation of aircraft apply without exception. The majority of the airspace is also controlled airspace, and instrument flight rules apply to all flights in oceanic airspace when at or above FL060 (6,000 feet MSL) or 2,000 feet (600 m) above ground level, even when not operating in instrument meteorological conditions (IMC). These controlled airspaces include:

1. The New York Oceanic, Gander Oceanic, Shanwick Oceanic, Santa Maria Oceanic and Reykjavik FIRs; and

2. The Bodo Oceanic FIR, when operating more than 100 NM seaward from the shoreline; and

3. Sondrestrom FIR, when operating outside the shoreline of Greenland; and

4. Reykjavik FIR, when operating in the Oceanic Sector, or in the Domestic Sector at or above FL200.

Equipment Requirements

On October 10, 1997, Canada changed many aspects of its air regulations. Until that time, Canadian Air Regulation 540 (CAR 540) specified requirements that had to be met before crews flying single-engine airplanes could depart Canada to cross any portion of the North Atlantic. Although CAR 540 is defunct, the discussion of it has been retained in this chapter (*see the sidebars on* Pages 127 – 129) because most of it just makes good sense.

Now, the appropriate Canadian regulation is **CARs Part 602.39** (*see the sidebar on* Page 126). Basically, the requirement to land at Moncton, New Brunswick, has been removed; however, from several eastern Canada airports, Canada is still conducting random ramp checks of aircraft about to launch across the North Atlantic. Such a ramp check will determine if the aircraft and crew is in compliance with CARs Part 602 (the pertinent regulation is 602.39), and with the NAIGOM.

Very little has changed from the information in the "CARs 540" box below (Pages 127 – 129), except the fuel requirement has been reduced to a 10% reserve (beyond IFR reserve). For some aircraft, the original 3-hour reserve was very close to the new 10% reserve. GPS is now okay, but if you are ramp-checked, the GPS may have to be one that is IFR-certified. Emergency equipment required is now that required by the NAIGOM (October, 1996, Pages 12 – 13). To a large extent, the discretion of the operator determines how extensive is the survival gear carried on board. Items listed in the NAIGOM, including an appropriate survival handbook, are considered minimum.

Again, the requirements of CAR 540 make a lot of sense, with some small exceptions. The Atlantic region manager of general aviation for Transport Canada is a good resource for questions. The telephone number there is 506-851-7131, and the mailing address is P.O. Box 42, Moncton, NB E1C 8K6.

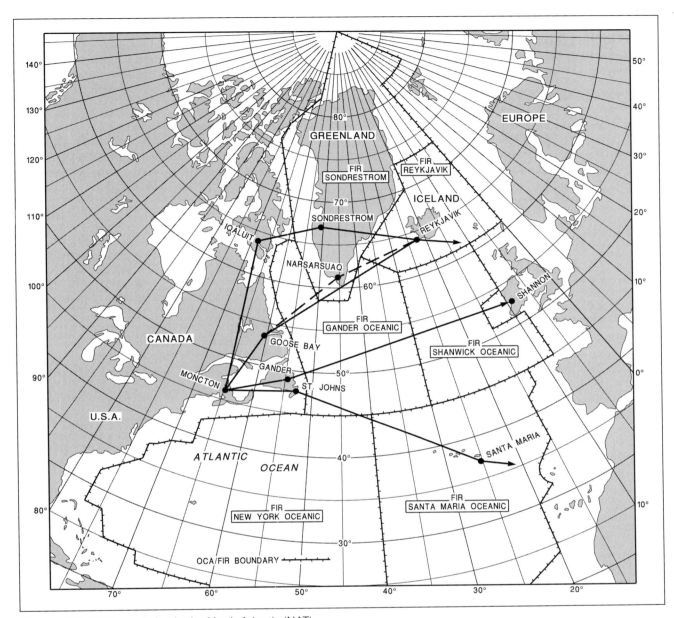

Figure 7-1. FIR boundaries in the North Atlantic (NAT)

Canadian Air Regulation 602.39 – 605.38 (current law)

No pilot-in-command of a single-engined aircraft, or of a multi-engined aircraft that would be unable to maintain flight in the event of the failure of any engine, shall commence a flight that will leave Canadian Domestic Airspace and enter airspace over the high seas unless:

   a. The pilot-in-command holds a pilot licence endorsed with an instrument rating;

   b. The aircraft is equipped with —

     (i) the equipment referred to in Section 605.18,

     (ii) a high frequency radio capable of transmitting and receiving on a minimum of two appropriate international air-ground general purpose frequencies, and

     (iii) hypothermia protection for each person on board; and

   c. The aircraft carries sufficient fuel to meet the requirements of Section 602.88 and, in addition, carries contingency fuel equal to at least 10 percent of the fuel required pursuant to Section 602.88 to complete the flight to the aerodrome of destination.

Section 605.18 *Instrument Flight*

No person shall conduct a take-off in a power-driven aircraft for the purpose of IFR flight unless it is equipped with:

   a. When it is operated by day, the equipment required pursuant to paragraphs 605.16(1)(a) to (h);

   b. When it is operated by night, the equipment required pursuant to paragraphs 605.16(1)(a) to (k);

   c. An attitude indicator;

   d. A vertical speed indicator;

   e. An outside air temperature gauge;

   f. A means of preventing malfunction caused by icing for each airspeed indicating system;

   g. A power failure warning device or vacuum in-dicator that shows the power available to gyro-scopic instruments from each power source;

   h. An alternative source of static pressure for the altimeter, airspeed indicator and vertical speed indicator;

   i. Sufficient radiocommunication equipment to permit the pilot to conduct two-way communications on the appropriate frequency; and

   j. Sufficient radio navigation equipment to permit the pilot, in the event of the failure at any stage of the flight of any item of that equipment, including any associated flight instrument display —

     (i) to proceed to the destination aerodrome or proceed to another aerodrome that is suitable for landing, and

     (ii) where the aircraft is operated in IMC, to complete an instrument approach and, if necessary, conduct a missed approach procedure.

Section 602.88 *Fuel Requirements*

   1. This Section does not apply in respect of any glider, balloon or ultra-light aeroplane.

   2. No pilot-in-command of an aircraft shall commence a flight or, during flight, change the destination aerodrome set out in the flight plan or flight itinerary, unless the aircraft carries sufficient fuel to ensure compliance with subsections 3. to 5.

   3. An aircraft operated in VFR flight shall carry an amount of fuel that is sufficient to allow the aircraft:

   a. In the case of an aircraft other than a helicopter,

     (i) when operated during the day, to fly to the destination aerodrome and then to fly for a period of 30 minutes at normal cruising speed, or

     (ii) when operated at night, to fly to the destination aerodrome and then to fly for a period of 45 minutes at normal cruising speed; or

   b. In the case of a helicopter, to fly to the destination aerodrome and then to fly for a period of 20 minutes at normal cruising speed.

   4. An aircraft operated in IFR flight shall carry an amount of fuel that is sufficient to allow the aircraft:

   a. In the case of a propeller-driven aeroplane,

     (i) where an alternate aerodrome is specified in the flight plan or flight itinerary, to fly to and execute an approach and a missed approach at the destination aerodrome, to fly to and land at the alternate aerodrome and then to fly for a period of 45 minutes, or

     (ii) where an alternate aerodrome is not specified in the flight plan or flight itinerary, to fly to and execute an approach and a missed approach at the destination aerodrome and then to fly for a period of 45 minutes; or

   b. In the case of a turbo-jet-powered aeroplane or a helicopter,

     (i) where an alternate aerodrome is specified in the flight plan or flight itinerary, to fly to and execute an approach and a missed approach at the destination aerodrome, to fly to and land at the alternate aerodrome and then to fly for a period of 30 minutes, or

     (ii) where an alternate aerodrome is not specified in the flight plan or flight itinerary, to fly to and execute an approach and a missed approach at the destination aerodrome and then to fly for a period of 30 minutes.

   5. Every aircraft shall carry an amount of fuel that is sufficient to provide for

   a. Taxiing and foreseeable delays prior to take-off;

   b. Meteorological conditions;

   c. Foreseeable air traffic routings and traffic delays;

   d. Landing at a suitable aerodrome in the event of loss of cabin pressurization or, in the case of a multi-engined aircraft, failure of any engine, at the most critical point during the flight; and

   e. Any other foreseeable conditions that could delay the landing of the aircraft.

Canadian Air Regulation 540 (superseded — *see* text)

The equipment, documents, and qualifications specified in this chapter were formerly required for trans-Atlantic flight. The items listed were required by Transport Canada Air Regulation 540 for all flights beginning their trans-Atlantic flights from Canada. Since most eastbound trans-Atlantic flights by light aircraft will commence their oceanic crossing from Canada, this equipment was mandatory. Denmark/Greenland and Iceland also require all the equipment mandated by Regulation 540. Remember, these Canadian requirements were there to ensure that trans-Atlantic flight ends as planned, and not as another "lost in the North Atlantic" statistic. Sections of the now defunct Air Regulation 540 applying specifically to authorization, pilot qualifications, required documents, survival and emergency equipment, communication and navigation equipment, etc., follow.

The legislation states:

"Except as authorized by the Minister, no person shall commence, in any single-engine aircraft or in any multi-engine aircraft that is unable to maintain flight in the event of a failure of its critical engine, a flight that is intended to be a transoceanic flight.

"Multi-engine aircraft able to maintain flight after failure of the critical engine are not subject to Canadian inspection. However, the requirements and especially the fuel reserves are equally applicable. The Canadian requirements now reflect the thinking of all NAT ICAO Provider States who are working on establishing joint requirements for all IGA light aircraft.

"To obtain authorization to commence a trans-Atlantic flight from Canada, the pilot-in-command of a single-engine aircraft shall land at Moncton Airport, New Brunswick, where the necessary authorization will be granted provided the appropriate officers of the Department are satisfied that certain conditions have been met.

At least forty-eight (48) hours prior to landing at Moncton Airport, the pilot-in-command shall inform the Regional Manager Aviation Licensing, P.O. Box 42, Moncton, N.B. telephone number: (506) 851-7131, fax number: (506) 851-7206, of the intended transoceanic flight stating the date and time the inspection is requested, the aircraft type, nationality and registration marking, and the pilot's name and address."

Inspections are also possible at the other regional offices in Montreal, Toronto, Winnipeg, Edmonton, and Vancouver. However, the pilot must contact Moncton to coordinate the details.

Inspection Requirements for Aircraft Specified in Air Regulation CAR 540

Fuel Reserves

The only routes authorized will be those which will provide a minimum of three hours fuel reserve at destination considering usable fuel, an appropriate flight manual fuel consumption and TAS, and a ZERO wind component.

Navigation Log

The examining officer will want to see a complete nav log for the ocean crossing showing 5° longitude checkpoints, tracks, variation, distances, etc., all ready for the forecast enroute wind. Emphasis should be placed on dead reckoning navigation techniques.

Pilot Qualifications

The Pilot-in-Command shall:

1. Hold a valid pilot license and a valid instrument rating;
2. Satisfy an examining officer as to his knowledge of the meteorological, communications, air traffic control, search-and-rescue facilities and procedures over the route to be flown; and
3. Satisfy an examining officer as to his knowledge of the radio and other navigational aids to be used on the flight and as to his ability to navigate using these aids.

Aircraft Documents

1. Certificate of Registration from the state of registry (permanent, temporary, or provisional);
2. Certificate of Airworthiness, flight permit, or Special Airworthiness Certificate;
3. Certification and special conditions issued by the state of registry to allow overgross weight operation if applicable;
4. Certification issued by the state of registry for fuel tank modification (e.g., FAA Form 337);
5. Revised weight and balance report, in the case of aircraft modified to carry extra fuel.

continued

CAR 540 *continued* (superseded — *see* text)

Caution: An Export Certificate of Airworthiness does not constitute authority to operate an aircraft. It must be accompanied by one of the authorities in **2.** above. Be sure to have all the applicable documents before embarking on the trip. Moncton has no authority to issue them, and it may take considerable time and expense to obtain them from the state of registry by FAX or mail.

Note: All aircraft entering Canada or transiting through Canada on transoceanic flights, which are operating with restricted Certificates of Airworthiness or flight permits, must be issued with Canadian validations of these flight authorities before entering Canada. Canadian validations will be issued upon receipt of a copy of a valid U.S. or foreign flight authority, and information relating to the dates and routing for the flight. This procedure does not apply to aircraft operating with unrestricted Certificates of Airworthiness.

Sea Survival Equipment

Aircraft shall carry the following:

1. A readily accessible watertight immersion suit including undergarments which provide thermal protection for each occupant;

2. A readily accessible life-jacket complete with light, for each occupant;

3. A readily accessible Type W water-actuated, self-buoyant, water resistant ELT;

4. A readily accessible life raft sufficient to accommodate all persons on board the aircraft, fitted with:

   - water, or a means of desalting or distilling salt water, sufficient to provide at least one pint of water per person;
   - a water bag;
   - water purification tablets;
   - food that is in the form of carbohydrate, has a caloric value of at least 500 calories per person, and is not subject to deterioration by heat or cold;
   - flares (at least three per raft);
   - hole plugs, a bail bucket and sponge, a signal mirror;
   - a whistle, a knife, a survival-at-sea manual;
   - waterproof flash lights (minimum two per raft);
   - first aid kit containing eye ointment, burn ointment, compresses, bandages, methylate and sea sick pills; and
   - a dye marker.

5. The water and food may be stored and carried in appropriate containers separate from the rafts if the containers can be readily and quickly attached to the raft.

Polar Survival Equipment

In addition to the items listed on the Sea Survival Equipment list, aircraft shall carry the following for flights over Labrador, and or any flight routing north of Prins Christian Sund over Greenland:

1. A signaling sheet (minimum 1 x 1 m) in a reflecting color;

2. A compass;

3. Winter sleeping bags sufficient in quantity to accommodate all persons carried;

4. Matches in waterproof covers;

5. A ball of string;

6. A stove and supply of fuel or a self-contained means of providing heat for cooking and the accompanying mess-tins;

7. A snow saw;

8. Candles or some other self-contained means of providing heat with a burning time of about 2 hours per person — the minimum to be carried shall not be less than 40 hours of burning time;

9. Personal clothing suitable for the climatic conditions along the route to be overflown;

10. A suitable instruction manual; and

11. Mosquito netting and insect repellent.

Aircraft Instruments and Equipment

Aircraft must be equipped with the following instruments and equipment in serviceable condition:

1. An airspeed indicator and heated pitot head;

2. A sensitive pressure altimeter;

3. A direct reading magnetic compass that has been swung within the preceding thirty (30) days with the aircraft in the same configuration as for the intended transoceanic flight;

4. A gyroscopic direction indicator or a gyromagnetic compass;

5. A turn and bank indicator;

CAR 540 *continued* (superseded — *see* text)

6. A gyroscopic bank and pitch indicator;

7. A rate of climb and descent indicator;

8. An outside air temperature gauge;

9. Unless another timepiece is available, a reliable timepiece with a sweep-second hand;

10. If there is a probability of encountering icing conditions along the route to be flown, deicing or anti-icing equipment for the engine, propeller and airframe, and

11. If the flight is to be made at night:
   - navigation lights;
   - two landing lights or a single landing light having two separately energized filaments;
   - illumination for all instruments that are essential for the safe operation of the aircraft, and
   - an electric flashlight at each flight crew member's station.

Note 1: All equipment and cargo carried in the cabin shall be secured to prevent shifting in flight and placed as to not block or restrict the exits.

Note 2: Consider carrying portable oxygen equipment. It would be useful when trying to avoid icing, and for additional height over the Greenland ice cap.

Communications Equipment

High Frequency Radio

In the Oceanic CTA/FIRs, VHF coverage is not sufficient to ensure continuous two-way communications with ground stations. Although relay through other aircraft is possible, it is not guaranteed. Therefore, HF radio is mandatory for each aircraft crossing the Atlantic. The only exception is for aircraft flying at FL250 or above on routes crossing Greenland.

Very High Frequency Radio

VHF radios shall include 121.5 MHz capability. A listening watch should be maintained on 121.5 MHz unless communications on another frequency prevents this. 121.5 MHz is not authorized for routine use; 131.8 MHz should be used for air-to-air communications.

Navigation Equipment

Each aircraft shall be equipped with the following navigation equipment in order to navigate in accordance with the flight plan and any Air Traffic Control clearance. Translated to the North Atlantic routes, this means the following avionics is required:

Iqaluit (CFYB) to Greenland: Two independent ADF receivers with BFO / CW capability. Portable ADF no longer accepted.

Goose Bay to Narsarsuaq: Two independent ADF receivers with BFO / CW capability.

Goose Bay to Reykjavik via Prins Christian Sund: Two independent ADF receivers as above, or, one ADF set and one LORAN C set. Danish CAA strongly recommends two ADF sets because of poor LORAN C reception around Greenland.

Gander to Shannon: One LORAN C set and one ADF set.

St. John's to Santa Maria: One LORAN C set and one ADF set. Note that LORAN C reception ends short of the Azores.

Note: Recent reports indicate that one (1) ADF and one (1) GPS are acceptable for all routes.

Maps and Charts

Each aircraft shall carry *current* aeronautical charts, aerodrome data, and IFR letdown plates covering the area over which the aircraft might be flown. This includes en route and departure diversions as well as destination alternates. Whether planning to file VFR or IFR, there is always the potential for IMC conditions in the NAT region; therefore, pilots must carry IFR publications.

Aircraft landing at Narsarsuaq shall carry either the BGBW Visual Approach Chart depicting the fjord approach, or a topographical chart of large enough scale to permit map-reading up the fjord.

Operational Considerations in Sparsely Settled Areas

Experience has shown that there is a tendency for pilots who are not familiar with the problems of navigating and the potential dangers of operating in the sparsely settled areas of Canada, Denmark, Iceland, and Scotland, to underestimate the difficulties involved.

Some pilots assume that operating in these areas is no different than operating in the more populated areas. This can lead to a lack of proper planning and preparation which can result in the pilot-in-command exposing himself, his crew, his passengers, and his aircraft to unnecessary risks. This, in turn, can lead to considerable strain being placed on the limited local resources at stop-over or destination airports. Lengthy and expensive searches have resulted which, with careful planning and preparation, could have been avoided. *In some cases, it has resulted in unnecessary loss of life.*

The fact is that in sparsely settled areas, aircraft operations require special considerations. Radio aids to navigation, weather information, fuel supplies, aircraft servicing facilities, accommodations, and food are usually limited and often nonexistent.

In addition to Regulation 540 requirements concerning pilot qualifications and experience, the NAIGOM recommends:

1. The pilot have flight experience with significant cross country, night, and instrument time.

2. The pilot have experience in the use of the same navigational equipment to be used to cross the Atlantic.

3. The pilot have experience in the same type aircraft to be flown across the Atlantic.

Most states in the NAT region provide pilot training in both general and commercial aviation. Flying schools are available for instruction leading to private, instrument or commercial pilot licensing.

North Atlantic Route Planning

For those aircraft which are subject to inspection, Canada, Denmark, and Iceland will only authorize routes which will provide a minimum fuel reserve of 10% in excess of the IFR reserve. While other states don't have this fuel requirement, it is still considered a good "rule of practice" to have fuel on board, *beyond* that required for the flight, equal to 400 NM for fast aircraft and three hours for slow aircraft. Consider-

ations must include usable fuel, true air speed (TAS), a zero wind component, and an appropriate fuel consumption flight log. Additional concerns include the importance of accurate weight and balance calculations, as well as the appropriate trim configuration.

Freezing levels at or near the surface can be expected at any time of year over the NAT region. The dangers of airframe and/or engine icing must always be taken into account, so be prepared to wait for favorable conditions.

Commonly Flown Routes (Preferred Routes)

The most frequently flown NAT routes from Canada are as follows (*see* Figure 7-1 on Page 125, or a North Atlantic Plotting Chart):

1. Iqaluit, Sondrestrom, FW28, Kulusuk, 65N/30W, X-ray, Keflavik, 61N/12.34W, Stornoway, Prestwick.

2. Iqaluit, Godthaab, FW47, Kulusuk, 65N/30W, X-ray, Keflavik, 61N/ 12.34W, Stornoway, Prestwick.

3. Goose Bay, Loach, 59N/50W, SI-Narsarsuaq, 62N/40W, 63N/30W, Uniform, Keflavik, 61N/12.34W, Stornoway, Prestwick.

4. Goose Bay, Loach, 58N/50W, OZN, 61N/40W, 63N/30W, Uniform, Keflavik, 61N/12.34W, Stornoway, Prestwick.

5. Gander, 54.14N/50W, OZN, 61N/40W, 63N/30W, Uniform, Keflavik, 61N/12.34W, Stornoway, Prestwick.

6. Gander, 50N/50W, 52N/40W, 53N/30W, 53N/20W, 53N/15W, UN530, Shannon.

7. St. John's, G/C Flores, Santa Maria.

It is extremely unlikely that a flight can be conducted across the Atlantic and remain in visual meteorological conditions (VMC) for the entire flight. VFR flight in this airspace deprives the pilot of the flexibility of using the altitudes above FL055 (5,500 feet). The higher altitudes may enable a smoother flight, free of precipitation, icing or turbulence.

ICAO flight plans must be filed for flights operating in the North Atlantic Region. At or above FL060, an IFR flight plan must be filed. Detailed instructions for completion of the ICAO flight plan are found in the ICAO Document 4444 Appendix 2, the AIP Canada RAC 3.16, as well as similar publications printed in other countries; also, an example of an ICAO Flight Plan was completed in the previous chapter.

Prospective transoceanic fliers should carefully review the ICAO flight plan instructions as they are quite different from domestic Canadian/U.S. flight plan formats. International flight service stations can provide assistance in filing an ICAO flight plan.

All generally eastbound or westbound aircraft in the NAT Region must plan the flight so that specified tenth degrees of longitude (60°W, 50°W, 40°W, 30°W, etc.) as applicable, are crossed at whole degrees of latitude. Generally northbound or southbound aircraft must plan the flight so that specified parallels of latitude spaced at 5° intervals (65°, 60°N, 55°N, 50°N, etc.) are crossed at whole degrees of longitude.

Pre-Flight Planning

Plan the flight using current aeronautical charts, the latest edition of pertinent flight supplements, and Class 1/Class 2 NOTAMs. The pilot must become familiar with the nature of the terrain over which the flight is to be conducted. If the pilot is not familiar with the area, the aviation authority officials at appropriate local aviation field offices should be consulted before departure. These officials, as well as local pilots and operators, can provide a great deal of useful advice, especially on the ever-changing supply situation, the location and condition of possible emergency landing strips, potential hazards, and enroute weather conditions. Pre-flight planning must ensure the availability of fuel, food, and services required at intermediate stops and at the destination.

The majority of military activity takes place in the NAT below MNPS altitudes. Military exercise particulars will be published in a NOTAM/International NOTAM, and should be reviewed during the preflight briefing.

Planning the trans-Atlantic flight for the summertime will allow the aircraft to take advantage of the most favorable conditions. Not only are the ground (and water) temperatures less menacing, but the amount of available daylight is considerably greater.

Depth perception is poor at night. North of 60° North Latitude, which includes the most common trans-Atlantic routes flown by light aircraft, there are only about four hours of daylight during December. To this is added an additional complication: VFR flights at night are prohibited in Iceland and Greenland. When all this is combined with the increased possibility of

storms during the winter, it is easy to understand why it is recommended that flights should plan to utilize the better conditions that exist along those routes during the summer.

Carriage of Arms

A rifle may be carried subject to a valid permit being issued from the appropriate provincial and territorial authorities to have such weapons aboard. Under *no* circumstances will permission be granted for the carriage of small arms or automatic weapons.

Physiological Factors

It's a long flight across the Atlantic in a small aircraft, and it's physically demanding. The planner will want to make some provisions to eat, drink, and take care of all necessary bodily functions (we don't know of any delicate way to discuss this). Desperately needing a rest room, WC, toilet facilities, or whatever you choose to call them has been the foundation for countless comedy routines. But if one suddenly discovers a failure to plan for this inevitable need, it won't be funny at the time (although it may be later).

Navigation

Navigation in the North Atlantic, or in any oceanic area for that matter, is considerably more difficult than over land. There are no landmarks, and ICAO standard navigational aids (VOR/NDB), are few and far between. The aircraft should be equipped with some type of Long Range Navigation System (LRNS) equipment for such a flight. LORAN C, a popular type of area navigation in many parts of the world, is *not* reliable in all areas of the North Atlantic because of poor ground wave signal coverage in some areas. This statement contradicts some maps depicting LORAN C ground wave coverage, but experience demonstrates that LORAN C should *not* be used as a sole means of area navigation in the North Atlantic. The use of a self-contained navigation system (INS/IRS), or GPS navigation system is recommended.

On the Northern routes, it is important to note the pronounced magnetic variation—up to approximately 45°. When performing turns or accelerations, the **dip effect** causes the compass to turn more slowly than most pilots are used to in the lower latitudes. Moreover, many magnetic compasses will not function adequately at high latitudes.

Route Concerns

There are a few VOR/NDB routes in the North Atlantic. These routes are sometimes known as **Blue Spruce routes** and are depicted on navigation charts from Jeppesen and other sources. Other than the Blue Spruce routes, there is little navaid coverage at the low altitudes in the NAT. Figures 7-2 and 7-3 on the following pages depict VHF radio coverage at 10,000 and 20,000 feet. These figures are calculated based on theoretical coverage; actual coverage may be considerably less than that shown, and these charts should by no means be used for navigational purposes.

Since the coverage is so limited, *it is strongly recommended that the aircraft have an HF transceiver* (required for IFR flight—IFR clearances are required for flight above FL060 in the NAT airspace). Radio equipment should be tested prior to departure. For VHF equipment, this is best done by calling the tower or ATC on the proper frequency for a ground radio check. HF equipment shall be tested by calling the nearest Aeronautical Radio or Flight Service Station for a ground radio check. If a contact cannot be made on the initial test frequency, try others. If no contact can be made, have the equipment checked. Do not leave the ground until everything is working satisfactorily.

Pilots should be aware that on most occasions when they communicate with Oceanic Air Traffic Control Centers on HF, and on rare occasions VHF, they do not talk directly to controllers. Radio Communication staff, i.e., Aeronautical Radio Inc. (ARINC) or an international flight service station (IFSS), relay incoming messages and may not always be co-located with an ATCC. For example, Shanwick Radio is in the Republic of Ireland, while Shanwick Control is based at Prestwick, Scotland. Also, it is important to mention that controller workload on low-level IGA flights is usually high, so expect a short delay to your request for a change of flight level, route, etc.

Although HF coverage exists throughout the NAT, there are a few associated problems. Depending on atmospheric conditions, it can be relatively noisy with the signal fading in and out. Sometimes several attempts are required to successfully transmit or receive a single message. Additionally, sunspot activity can completely disrupt HF communications for considerable periods of time, varying from a few minutes to several hours. Notices are published whenever disruptive sunspot activity is expected. Pilots may be able to relay VHF or UHF communications through other aircraft operating in the NAT. 131.8 MHz should be used for air-to-air communications. Pilots should not plan

to use other aircraft as the primary means of communication. There is no guarantee there will be another aircraft within range when you need it. Consider this an emergency procedure and plan accordingly.

VHF radios for North Atlantic crossings shall include 121.5 MHz capability. A listening watch should be maintained on this frequency unless communications on another frequency prevents it. 121.5 MHz is not authorized for routine use.

Radar Coverage and SAR in the NAT

Radar coverage in the NAT region is very limited. As in most oceanic areas, there is a lot of airspace and no place to put a radar site. The majority of radar sites that do cover portions of the NAT are secondary radar equipped only. Unlike primary radar, secondary radar can only "see" aircraft that have an operating transponder. It cannot "paint" a target based on a radar echo from the aircraft's skin.

It is important to note that many search and rescue (**SAR**) missions occur within radar coverage. In any emergency situation (lost, out of fuel, engine failure, etc.), the chances of survival are vastly increased if the distressed aircraft is able to be radar-identified and SAR services can be radar vectored directly to the correct position, thus saving precious time. The importance of an operable transponder cannot be over-emphasized.

Air traffic services authorities must receive position information on all aircraft within their jurisdiction at least once per hour. If these hourly reports are not received, SAR procedures are initiated. Pilots should request advisories or assistance at the earliest indication that something may be wrong. Most search and rescue facilities and international air carriers monitor VHF 121.5 continuously. SAR aircraft are generally equipped with homing devices sensitive to VHF 121.5 MHz. Aircraft unable to reach any facility, may attempt contact with other aircraft on 131.8 MHz or 121.5 MHz. Most international carriers are also able to receive Emergency Locator Transmitter (ELTs).

SAR satellites are able to receive both VHF radio and ELT transmitters if continuously activated. The position drawn from the satellite may be as much as 20 km (12 NM) in error and 30 minutes old, but any position is better than none at all.

At many locations throughout the North Atlantic, neither search and rescue personnel nor equipment is available on a 24-hour basis. The primary SAR asset is

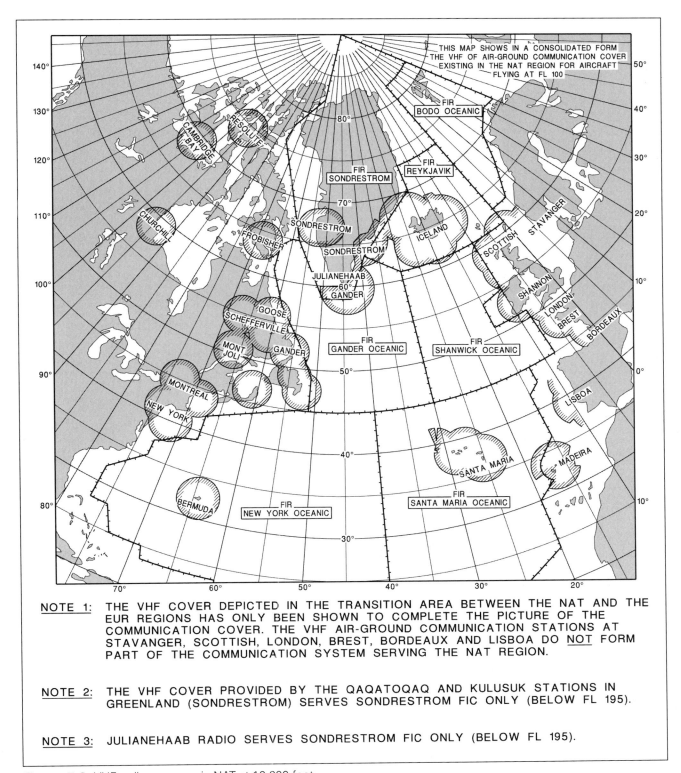

THIS MAP SHOWS IN A CONSOLIDATED FORM
THE VHF OF AIR-GROUND COMMUNICATION COVER
EXISTING IN THE NAT REGION FOR AIRCRAFT
FLYING AT FL 100

NOTE 1: THE VHF COVER DEPICTED IN THE TRANSITION AREA BETWEEN THE NAT AND THE
EUR REGIONS HAS ONLY BEEN SHOWN TO COMPLETE THE PICTURE OF THE
COMMUNICATION COVER. THE VHF AIR-GROUND COMMUNICATION STATIONS AT
STAVANGER, SCOTTISH, LONDON, BREST, BORDEAUX AND LISBOA DO NOT FORM
PART OF THE COMMUNICATION SYSTEM SERVING THE NAT REGION.

NOTE 2: THE VHF COVER PROVIDED BY THE QAQATOQAQ AND KULUSUK STATIONS IN
GREENLAND (SONDRESTROM) SERVES SONDRESTROM FIC ONLY (BELOW FL 195).

NOTE 3: JULIANEHAAB RADIO SERVES SONDRESTROM FIC ONLY (BELOW FL 195).

Figure 7-2. VHF radio coverage in NAT at 10,000 feet

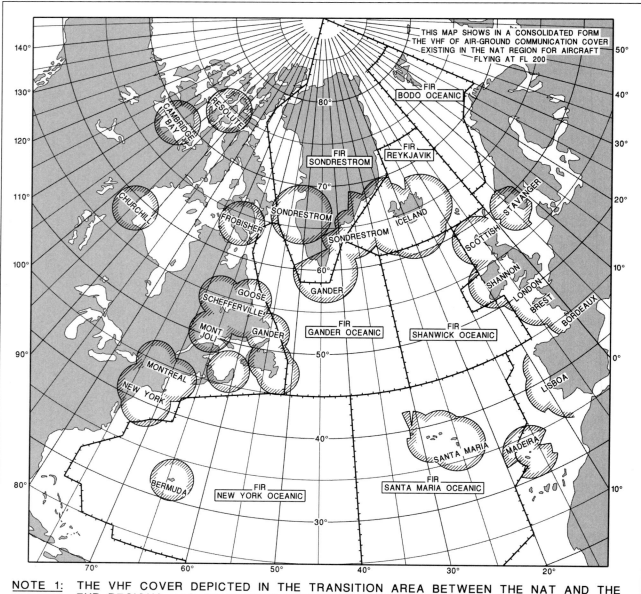

THIS MAP SHOWS IN A CONSOLIDATED FORM
THE VHF OF AIR-GROUND COMMUNICATION COVER
EXISTING IN THE NAT REGION FOR AIRCRAFT
FLYING AT FL 200

NOTE 1: THE VHF COVER DEPICTED IN THE TRANSITION AREA BETWEEN THE NAT AND THE
EUR REGIONS HAS ONLY BEEN SHOWN TO COMPLETE THE PICTURE OF THE
COMMUNICATION COVER. THE VHF AIR-GROUND COMMUNICATION STATIONS AT
STAVANGER, SCOTTISH, LONDON, BREST, BORDEAUX AND LISBOA DO NOT FORM
PART OF THE COMMUNICATION SYSTEM SERVING THE NAT REGION.

NOTE 2: THE VHF COVER PROVIDED BY THE QAQATOQAQ AND KULUSUK STATIONS IN
GREENLAND (SONDRESTROM) SERVES SONDRESTROM FIC ONLY (BELOW FL 195).

Figure 7-3. VHF radio coverage in NAT at 20,000 feet

often civilian aircraft chartered from private companies at great expense. These aircraft and their crews are frequently exposed to dangers which could have been avoided simply by better preparation on the part of IGA pilots. The main reasons for alerts, searches, and fatalities in the NAT are most often poor planning, poor navigation, insufficient fuel, and the lack of knowledge of flying in the northern NAT region.

It is important to note that some states may hold an individual liable for the costs of **SAR** actions should a pilot be found to be in breach of current regulations.

Should worst come to worst and it becomes necessary to put down in the North Atlantic, all the pre-flight planning, all the survival equipment carried is of little use if those aboard cannot survive long enough to allow SAR forces to recover live bodies. If planners of NAT flights remember nothing else, they should remember **the first two principles of survival: protection and location**. In the NAT Region at any time of year, the weather is the enemy and a person's survival time, once wetted, is measured in seconds and minutes, so protective garments should be worn at all times. It is much too late to be climbing into clothing while presiding over an engine that is refusing to cooperate, and at the same time trying to contact a friendly 747 to explain the nature of the emergency. Immersion suits are required and are of no value unless worn by occupants of light aircraft while crossing the water.

With excellent satellite coverage of the region, location is no problem if the ELT works. But who is going to recover you? In general terms, helicopters operate out to a maximum of 300 NM from base without air to air refueling and the latter is a very scarce enhancement. Long-range specialist SAR aircraft could localize your ELT, but their time on task in the area, on low-level visual search (should that be necessary) is only in the order of two to three hours. It is fairly obvious that a 24-hour search would take eight airframes and a visual search for a single life raft, even with a comparatively good datum, is a "needle-in-a-hay-stack" problem. So guard the ELT with your life; it could be your only salvation. There should be a second, portable, waterproof ELT packed with the water survival gear.

Preflight, In-Flight and Emergency Checklists

A thorough pilot will make every attempt to avoid in-flight problems prior to departure. Experience has shown that the best way to do this is to utilize a pre-planned general checklist for pre-flight preparation, inspection and in-flight contingencies.

Be prepared for systems failure. Know what to do in advance. Always pre-plan a way out of as many situations as can be thought of, then practice them involving all members of the crew. If a borderline decision has to be made, take the safest course of action. Don't exceed your own or the aircraft's limitations. Face the fact that if anything, including weather, equipment, or your health, is not up to par—*don't go*.

Position survival gear so that it is readily available, but clear of controls, then practice its removal from the aircraft under simulated emergency conditions until all are satisfied with their roles. The best survival techniques include thorough planning, knowledge of the route, and reliable weather information. There is almost no room for error in transoceanic flight, so plan accordingly, then re-check.

Allow sufficient time for a thorough briefing, planning, and administrative details before each leg. Try to put the airplane to bed ready to go, avoiding the possibility of last-minute mistakes.

Pre-Flight Preparation

The following checklist, cross-referenced to text appearing in the NAIGOM, will assist planning during the preparation stages of an oceanic flight. However, it is not intended that this checklist address all aspects of oceanic flight preparation.

_____ Have you obtained all the current departure, en route arrival and topographical charts for your entire route of flight and your alternate? *(NAIGOM Pages 10, 13 and 30)*

_____ Do you have an instrument rating and have you recently flown IFR? *(Page 9)*

_____ What long range navaids are you planning to use? When did you last practice long range navigation? *(Page 17)*

_____ What can you expect in terms of available daylight in Iceland? *(Page 7)*

Continued

_____ Has your aircraft been thoroughly inspected by a licensed mechanic for suitability for a long, over-water crossing? Do you have the necessary aircraft documents? *(Page 9)*

_____ If your flight will transit Canadian airspace, and chances are good that it will, do you have the suggested Sea / Polar Survival equipment necessary to adhere to Canadian Air Regulation 540 / 602 – 605? *(Page 9)*

_____ What is the proper format to be used when filing an oceanic flight plan? *(Page 13)*

_____ Are you aware of the proper procedures to be used in obtaining an oceanic clearance? *(Page 16)*

_____ What do you know of hypothermia? How can it be prevented? *(Page 24)*

_____ What can you expect in terms of VHF radio coverage in the NAT Region? *(Page 19)*

_____ Do you know what to include in a position report? When should a revised estimate be forwarded to ATC? *(Page 19)*

_____ Are you fully briefed on what to expect in the way of Search and Rescue services? Do you understand the importance of an operable ELT? *(Page 24)*

_____ Have you obtained the relevant meteorological information for your flight? *(Pages 3 and 4)*

_____ Have you checked current NOTAMs with special regard to the status of radio navigation aids and airport restrictions? *(Pages 13 and 30)*

_____ Have you prepared a proper international preflight inspection, operational, and emergency checklist?

This completes the presentation of material dealt with in the North Atlantic International General Aviation Operations Manual. The NAIGOM contains more specifics than are listed here, thus is considered recommended reading for anyone planning an ocean crossing.

ETOPS

Pilots joke about ETOPS being an acronym for "engines turning or pilots (passengers) swimming," but in reality, ETOPS means "Extended Range (Time) Operation with Two-Engine Airplanes", dealing with operations over the water. For many years, 14 CFR Part 121 (transport category) operations over large expanses of water required more than two engines. With the advent of very dependable turbine engines, the rules were changed in 1985 to allow operations within one hour of an adequate airport. If a carrier could show high engine reliability, authority to operate 75 to 120 minutes from an adequate alternate airport could be applied for. More recently, it has become possible to secure permission to operate a two-engine aircraft out to 180 minutes from an alternate.

While this rule applies only to Part 121 operations, the *concept* is important to all pilots of multi-engine airplanes flying oceanic or sparsely settled area routes. Crews monitor the availability status of alternates continuously, in order to know where to go if the aircraft's range decreases due to mechanical, pressurization, medical or other situations which require the aircraft to land short of its destination.

Interested readers will find more information on the specifics of ETOPS (EROPS in Canada) in the following documentation: FAA AC 120-42, AC 120-42A, 14 CFR Parts 21.3, 25.901, 25.903, 25.1309, 33.19, 33.75, 121.161, 121.197, 121.373, 121.565, and 121.703.

North Atlantic MNPS Airspace

14 CFR (FARs) Part 91.705, Part 91 Appendix C, and similar sections in Parts 135 and 121 define the **North Atlantic Minimum Navigation Performance Standards Airspace** and state the fact that this airspace is only available to aircraft and crews that are qualified, equipped, and specially licensed to use it. General aviation operators may consult FAA AC 91-49 for details of aircraft authorization approval for MNPS operations.

MNPS airspace is that volume of airspace between FL280 and FL420[1] extending between latitude 27° North and the North Pole, bounded in the east by the eastern boundaries of Control Areas Santa Maria Oceanic, Shanwick Oceanic, and Reykjavik Oceanic and in the west by the western boundary of Reykjavik Oce-

---

[1]Until April 1997, these altitudes were FL275 and FL400.

anic Control Area, the western boundary of Gander OCA and the western boundary of New York Oceanic Control Area, excluding the areas west of 60° West and south of 38° 30 minutes North (*see* Figure 7-4).

Planning for Operation in the MNPSA

Much of the following discussion can be found covered in more detail in the current edition of the North Atlantic MNPS Airspace Operations Manual, available from the U.S. DOT (USGPO). Some of the material below is excerpted from that document.

The Organized Track System

As a result of passenger demands, time zone differences and airport noise restrictions, much of the North Atlantic air traffic contributes to one of two flows; a westbound flow departing Europe in the morning, and an eastbound flow departing North America in the evening. The effect of these flows is to concentrate most of the traffic unidirectionally, with peak westbound traffic operating between 1130Z and 1900Z, and peak eastbound traffic between 0100Z and 0800Z at 30° West.

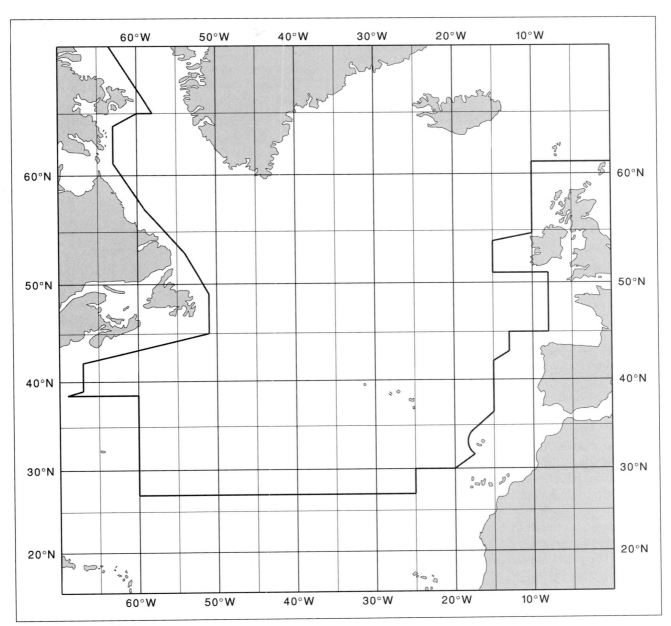

Figure 7-4. MNPS airspace

Because of the constraints of large horizontal separation criteria (60 NM laterally and 10-15 minutes longitudinally) and a limited, *economical* height band (FL310-390) the airspace is very congested at peak hours. In order to provide the best service to the bulk of the traffic, a system of **organized tracks** is constructed every 12 hours to accommodate as many aircraft as possible on or close to their minimum cost paths.

At jet levels, all the NAT Region is controlled airspace in which IFR applies at all times; however, in many areas airspace utilization can be and is improved by the strategic use of so-called "opposite direction" flight levels — i.e. FL350, 390 eastbound and FL330, 370 westbound during peak flow periods. The application of **Mach Number Technique** (*see* Page 145) permits further utilization improvement in the longitudinal plane and helps to facilitate enroute step-climbs.

The variability of the weather system would in any case necessitate reconstruction of the organized track system at frequent intervals. Furthermore, because of the energetic nature of weather systems, including jet streams, eastbound and westbound minimum time paths are seldom identical. It is therefore necessary to create a different organized track system every 12 hours.

Organized Track System (OTS) Construction

After determination of basic minimum time tracks, with due consideration to airlines' preferred tracks and taking into account airspace restrictions such as Danger Areas and military airspace reservations, the organized track system is constructed by the appropriate Oceanic Area Control Center (OAC). The nighttime OTS is constructed by Gander OAC, and the day-time by Shanwick OAC (Prestwick), each taking into account tracks which New York, Reykjavik and/or Santa Maria OACs may require in their Oceanic Control Areas (OCAs). In each case OAC planners consult each other, coordinate as necessary with adjacent OACs and domestic ATC agencies to ensure that the proposed system is viable for lateral and vertical separation criteria. They also take into account the anticipated requirements of opposite direction traffic and ensure that sufficient track/flight level profiles are provided to satisfy anticipated traffic demand. The impact on domestic route structures and the serviceability of transition area radar and navaids are checked before the system is finalized.

The agreed organized track system is then promulgated as the NAT Track Message via the AFTN (teletype network) to all interested addressees. A typical time of publication of the daytime OTS is 0100Z, and the night-time OTS is 1300Z. Examples of both systems showing track and flight level availability are shown in Figures 7-5 and 7-6, with the tracks plotted in Figures 7-7 and 7-8.

The NAT Track Message

This message gives full details of the coordinates of the organized tracks as well as the flight levels expected to be in use on each track. In most cases, there are also details of domestic entry and exit routings associated with individual tracks, and the portion of airspace within which the Datum Line Technique (discussed on Page 146) is applicable. In the daytime system, the track most northerly at its point of origin is designated Track "A" (Alpha) and the next most northerly Track "B" (Bravo), etc.

For the nighttime system, the most southerly track at its point of origin is designated Track "Z" (Zulu) and the next most southerly "Y", etc. The hours of validity of the two organized track systems are normally as follows:

Daytime OTS 1130Z – 1900Z at 30°W

Nighttime OTS 0100Z – 0800Z at 30°W

Changes to these times can be negotiated between Gander and Shanwick OACs; however, in all cases the hours of validity are specified in the NAT Track Message for each system.

Correct interpretation of the track message by airline dispatchers and aircrews is essential to both economy of operation and in minimizing the possibility of misunderstanding leading to the use of incorrect track coordinates. Oceanic airspace outside the published OTS is available, subject to separation criteria and NOTAM restrictions, for use by random operations. It is usually possible for ATC to clear aircraft to join or leave an outer track of the OTS without difficulty. If an operator wishes to file partly or wholly outside the OTS, knowledge of separation criteria, the forecast upper wind situation and correct interpretation of the NAT Track Message will assist in judging the feasibility of the planned route.

When anticipated volume of traffic does not warrant publication of all available flight levels on a particular track, ATC will publish only those levels required to meet traffic demand. The fact that a specific flight level is not published for a particular track does not necessarily mean that it cannot be made available if requested.

OTS Changeover Periods

In order to ensure a smooth transition from night to day track system and vice-versa, a period of several hours is interposed between the termination of one system and the commencement of the next.

Eastbound traffic crossing 30°W between 0930Z and 1029Z in MNPS airspace should file random flight plans at eastbound FLs (290, 330, 370). Where the flight will conflict with the daytime (westbound) OTS, the route should follow the daytime structure from 30°W. However, such traffic may plan to join the outer track of the daytime structure at any point.

Westbound traffic crossing 30°W between 2300Z and 2359Z in MNPS airspace should file random flight plans at westbound FLs (280, 310, 350, 390). Where the flight will conflict with the night-time (eastbound) OTS, the route should follow the night-time structure from 30°W. However, such traffic may plan to join the outer track of the night-time structure at any point.

Flights against the Peak Flow

Eastbound traffic crossing 30°W at 1030Z or later, and westbound traffic crossing 30°W at 0000Z or later should plan to avoid the organized track system and the Datum Line level.

Continued on Page 142

```
         NAT TRACKS FL 310/370 INCLUSIVE
         APRIL 25/1130Z TO APRIL 25/1900Z

  A  57/10 58/20 59/30 58/40 56/50 SCROD YYR
         WEST LVLS 310 330 350 370
         EAST LVLS NIL
         EUR RTS WEST 2
         EUR RTS EAST NIL
         NAR NA222 NA230

  B  56/10 57/20 58/30 57/40 55/50 OYSTR KLAMM
         WEST LVLS 310 330 350 370
         EAST LVLS NIL
         EUR RTS WEST 2
         EUR RTS EAST NIL
         NAR NA202 NA204

  C  55/10 56/20 57/30 56/40 54/50 CARPE REDBY
         WEST LVLS 310 330 350 370
         EAST LVLS NIL
         EUR RTS WEST 2
         EUR RTS EAST NIL
         NAR NA180 NA182

  D  54/15 55/20 56/30 55/40 53/50 YAY
         WEST LVLS 310 330 350 370
         EAST LVLS NIL
         EUR RTS WEST 2 VIA ACKIL
         EUR RTS EAST NIL
         NAR NA160 NA166

  E  53/15 54/20 55/30 54/40 52/50 DOTTY
         WEST LVLS 310 330 350 370
         EAST LVLS NIL
         EUR RTS WEST 2 VIA SNN
  R      EUR RTS EAST NIL
         NAR NA152 NA154

         NOTE  1 DATUM TRACK ALPHA**
               2 R99 IN EFFECT FOR EUR/CAR
                 TRAFFIC##
```

**see "Datum Line Technique", Page 146
\#\#*see* item #5, "Caribbean area", Page 145

Figure 7-5. Westbound NAT Track message

```
         NAT TRACKS FL 330/390 INCLUSIVE
         APRIL 25/0100Z TO APRIL 25/0800Z

  V  YSG 51/50 52/40 53/30 54/20 54/15 ACKIL
         WEST LVLS NIL
         EAST LVLS 330 350 370 390
         EUR RTS WEST NIL
         EUR RTS EAST NIL
         NAR NA141 NA149

  W  YQX 50/5U 51/40 52/30 53/20 53/15 SNN
         WEST LVLS NIL
         EAST LVLS 330 350 370 390
         EUR RTS WEST NIL
         EUR RTS EAST NIL
         NAR NA125 NA127 NA131

  X  VYSTA 49/50 50/40 51/30 52/20 52/15 CRK
         WEST LVLS NIL
         EAST LVLS 330 350 370 390
         EUR RTS WEST NIL
         EUR RTS EAST NIL
         NAR NA105 NA107 NAIII

  Y  YYT 48/50 49/40 50/30 51/20 51/15 TIVLI
         WEST LVLS NIL
         EAST LVLS 330 350 370 390
         EUR RTS WEST NIL
         EUR RTS EAST NIL
         NAR NA83 NA89 NA93

  Z  COLOR 47/50 48/40 49/30 50/20 50/08 LND
         WEST LVLS NIL
         EAST LVLS 330 350 370 390
         EUR RTS WEST NIL
         EUR RTS EAST NIL
         NAR NA41 NA51 NA53

         NOTE  1 DATUM TRACK VICTOR**
               2 R99 IN EFFECT FOR EUR/CAR
                 TRAFFIC##
```

**see "Datum Line Technique", Page 146
\#\#*see* item #5, "Caribbean area", Page 145

Figure 7-6. Eastbound NAT Track message

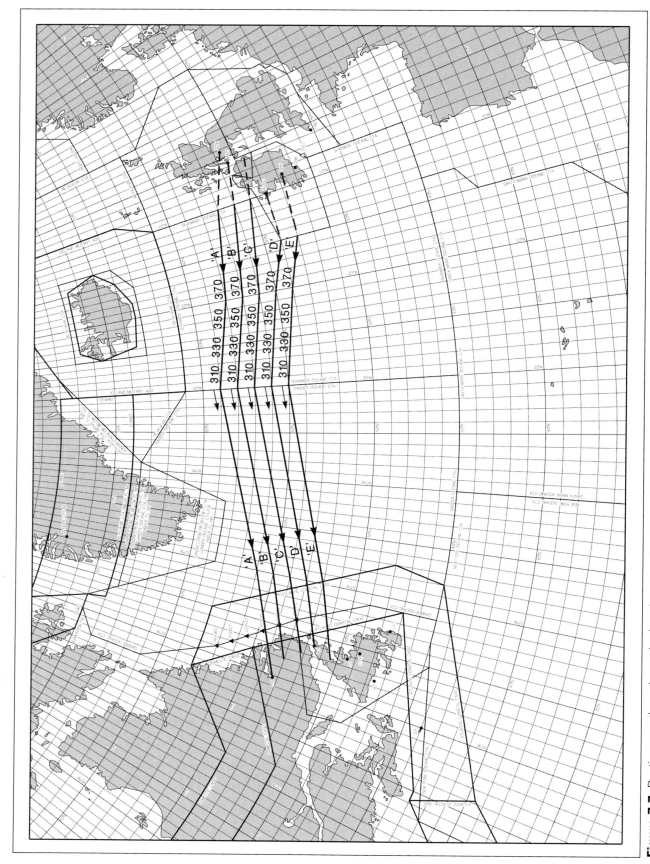

Figure 7-7. Daytime westbound organized track system (*see* Figure 7-5)

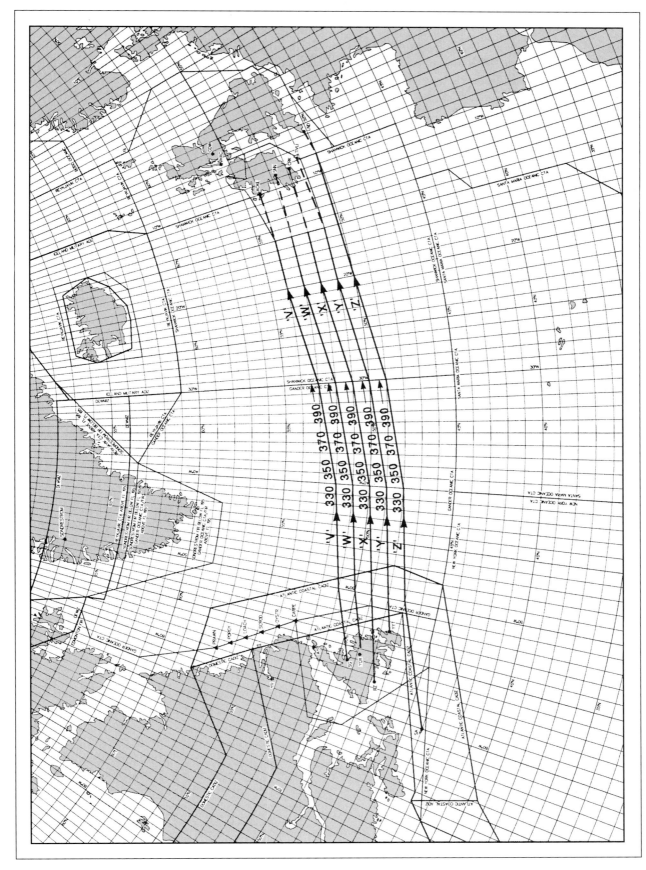

Figure 7-8. Nighttime eastbound organized track system *(see Figure 7-6)*

The Polar Track Structure (PTS)

Like most other NAT traffic flows, traffic on the Europe to Alaska axis is predominantly unidirectional; in the Reykjavik CTA the westbound peak is between 1200Z – 1800Z, and the eastbound peak is between 0001Z – 0600Z. In order to facilitate the flow of this traffic during peak periods and avoid a multiplicity of random routes, a Polar Track Structure (PTS) consisting of 20 fixed tracks has been established (*see* Figure 7-9).

Although not mandatory, flights planning operations on the Europe Alaska axis at FL 310 – 390 inclusive during peak periods are strongly recommended to submit flight plans in accordance with one of the promulgated PTS tracks.

Abbreviated Clearances

An abbreviated clearance may be used when clearing an aircraft to follow one of the polar tracks throughout its flight within the Reykjavik CTA. When an abbreviated clearance is issued, it shall include:

1. The cleared track specified by the track code number;

2. The cleared flight level(s);

3. The cleared Mach Number.

Upon receipt of an abbreviated clearance, the pilot shall read back the contents of the clearance message, and in addition, the full details of the track specified by the code number.

Abbreviated Position Reports

When operating on the PTS within the Reykjavik CTA, position reports may be abbreviated by replacing the normal latitude coordinate with the word "Polar" followed by the track code number; e.g., "Position Japanair 422 Polar 320W/1537 (longitude/time) estimating Polar 340W/1620 next Polar 3 LT (Alert NDB)."

Unless otherwise required by air traffic services, a position report shall be made at the significant points listed for the relevant PTS track.

Further information on PTS procedures, track coordinates, etc., is contained in AIP Iceland, and/or Icelandic NOTAMs.

Other Routes and Route Structures Within or Adjacent to NAT MNPS Airspace

The organized track system and the polar track structure are the most significant route structures within the NAT MNPS airspace, but there are other routes and route structures within and adjacent to the MNPS airspace, the knowledge of which completes the picture of upper airspace organization in the NAT Region and immediately adjacent areas.

Other routes within NAT MNPS airspace, which are illustrated in Figure 7-10 (Page 144), are as follows:

1. **Upper air routes** established to facilitate the traffic flow between Europe and the Caribbean (R99, G61, UB47) or Miami (A699, A700) areas;

2. Special **short range nav routes** between North Eastern Canada and Europe via Greenland and Iceland, between Ireland/United Kingdom and Spain, and between the Azores and the Portuguese mainland for aircraft equipped with normal short range navigation equipment (VOR, DME, ADF) and at least one approved fully operational long-range navigation system;

3. Special routes of short stage lengths where aircraft equipped with normal short-range navigation equipment can meet the MNPS track-keeping criteria (G3 and G11).

Route Structures Adjacent to MNPS Airspace

1. The **SST route structure** (also illustrated in Figure 7-10) comprises three fixed tracks: "SM" westbound; "SN" and "SO" eastbound. SST flights on these tracks normally operate well above MNPS airspace (FL500+); the exception is in the event of a delayed supersonic acceleration or emergency descent. Standard separation is applied in the first case, and emergency descent contingency procedures take into account the possible existence of organized track system traffic operating below the SST tracks.

2. **U.K. westbound domestic Recommended Route Structure** (RRS) consists of recommended routes through the U.K. FIR from European departure areas to oceanic entry points. The routes are listed in the U.K. AIP, grouped into three structures numbered 1, 2, and 3. The structure of routes to be used is dependent on the alignment of the organized track system, and anticipated traffic density and is published as part of the westbound NAT Track Message for each track under the heading "EUR

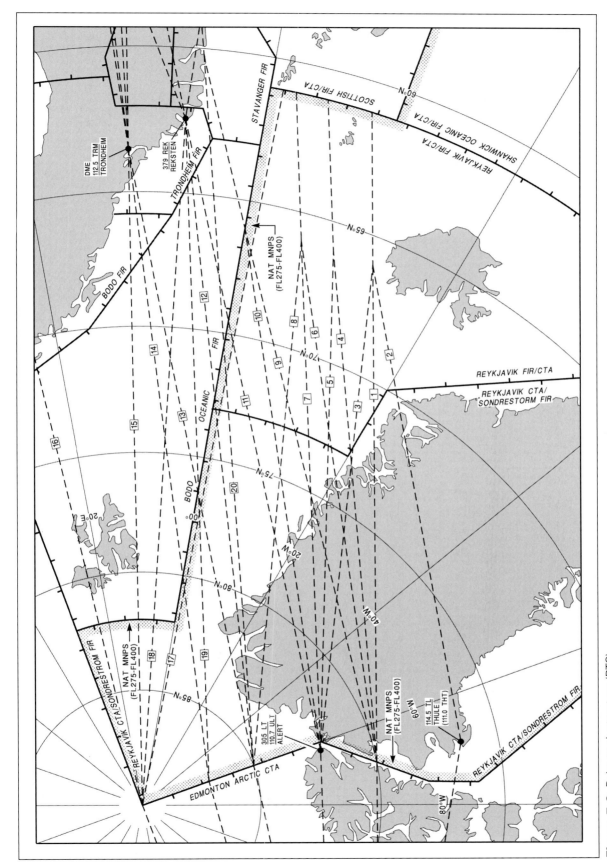

Figure 7-9. Polar track structure (PTS)

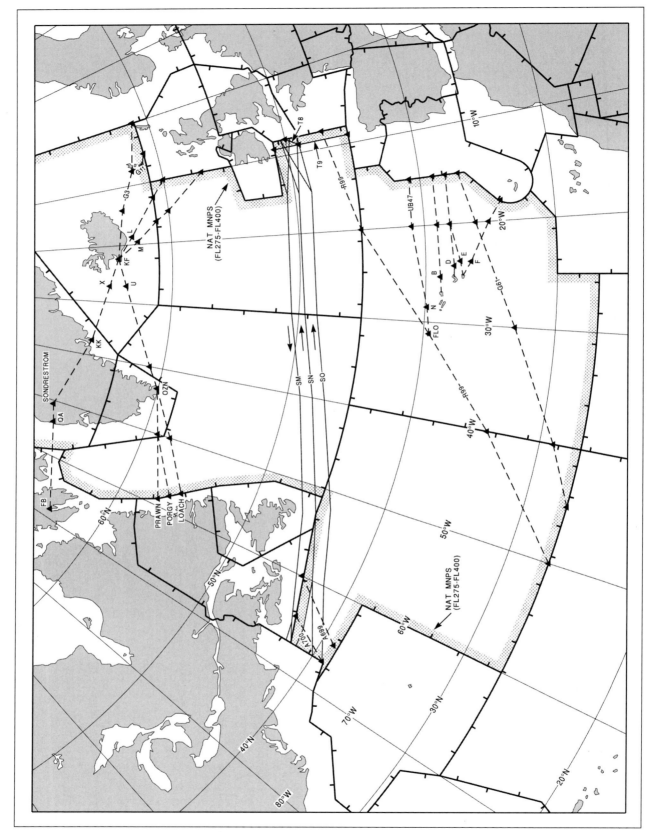

Figure 7-10. Other routes and structures within and above NAT MNPS airspace

RTS WEST." For example "EUR RTS WEST 3" under track "E" means that Structure three is in operation for traffic planning on that track.

3. **North American routes** (NARS) consist of a numbered series of predetermined routes which form a link between oceanic track exit and entry points, and the North American domestic airspace route structure in both directions. Specific route numbers related to each track exit/entry point are published in the NAT Track Message under the heading "NAR." For example, "NAR NA 20, NA 24" under track "B" means, after the exit point of Track "B," flights may flight plan on NA 20 or NA 24, depending on their destination. Full details of the routings procedures, etc., can be found in U. S. and Canadian AIPs.

4. **Canadian Northern and Arctic Track Systems are** found north of the North American routes and consist of two track systems: the Northern Track System which links with NAT random route traffic operating between Europe and western North America (Los Angeles, San Francisco, etc.), and an Arctic Route System which interfaces with the Polar Track Structure for traffic between Europe and Alaska. Both systems are established within Canadian MNPS airspace, procedures for which, together with full details of the track systems, can be found in the appropriate Canadian AIP. (Some of the rules for Canadian MNPS airspace such as vertical dimensions differ from those in NAT MNPS airspace.)

5. **Routes between North America and the Caribbean area:** In the New York Oceanic Control Area to the west of 60°W, there is an extensive network of routes linking points in the United States and Canada with Bermuda, the Bahamas and the Caribbean area. Details of these routes and associated procedures are contained in the United States AIPs.

Application of Mach Number Technique

The term **Mach Number Technique** describes a technique whereby subsonic turbojet aircraft operating successively along suitable routes are cleared by ATC to maintain appropriate Mach Numbers for a relevant portion of the enroute phase of their flight.

The principal objective of the use of Mach Number Technique is to achieve improved utilization of the airspace on long route segments where ATC has no means, other than position reports, of ensuring that the longitudinal separation between successive aircraft is not reduced below the established minimum. Practical experience has shown that when two or more turbojet aircraft operating along the same route at the same flight level maintain the same Mach Number, they are more likely to maintain a constant time interval between each other than when using other methods. This is due to the fact that the aircraft concerned are normally subject to approximately the same wind and air temperature conditions and minor variations in speed. While this might increase or decrease the spacing between them, those differences tend to be neutralized over long periods of flight.

The Mach Number Technique is based on the True Mach Number. The ATC clearance must include the assigned Mach Number, which is to be maintained. It is therefore necessary that information on the desired Mach Number be included in the flight plan by pilots intending to operate turbojet aircraft in NAT oceanic airspace. The normal requirement for ATC to calculate estimated times for significant points along track still remains. This is necessary for both the provision of longitudinal separation between aircraft and for coordination with adjacent ATC units.

The prescribed longitudinal separation between successive aircraft flying at the same flight level must be provided over the entry point for a particular track or tracks. Intervention by ATC thereafter should normally only be necessary if an aircraft is required to change its Mach Number due to conflicting traffic or change in flight level.

In the application of Mach Number Technique, particularly in the 10-minute longitudinal separation environment, it is imperative that pilots adhere strictly to their assigned Mach Numbers unless a specific reclearance is obtained from the appropriate ATC unit. If an immediate temporary change in the Mach Number is essential (e.g., due to turbulence), ATC must be notified as soon as possible.

After leaving oceanic airspace, pilots must maintain their assigned Mach Number in domestic controlled airspace to the final position contained in the oceanic clearance, unless the appropriate ATC unit authorizes a change.

The initial oceanic clearance will specify a Mach Number which pilots must adhere to. However, as the aircraft weight reduces, it may be more fuel efficient to adjust the Mach Number. ATC approval of requests for change in cruise Mach Number will be given if traffic conditions permit.

Application of Datum Line Technique

Datum Line Technique is a method used in the NAT Region to assist, at the flight planning stage, by delineating in advance a block of airspace in which flight level(s) not appropriate to the direction of flight can be used. This is done to accommodate a peak flow of aircraft operating on random routes. Within the confines of the Gander and Shanwick OCAs, the Datum Line, as specified in the appropriate NAT Track Message, defines the southern limit of the airspace within which the following procedures apply:

1. During daytime OTS, FL330 is released for random routing of westbound aircraft on and north of the published Datum Line.

2. During nighttime OTS, FL350 is released for random routing of eastbound aircraft on and north of the published Datum Line.

Aircraft Minimum Navigational Capability

It is implicit in the concept of MNPSA that all operations within the airspace, whether they are by Public Transport or General Aviation aircraft, achieve the highest standards of navigation performance accuracy.

Thus all flights within the NAT MNPSA must have the approval of either the State of Registry of the aircraft, or the State of Registry of the Operator. Such approvals encompass all aspects of the expected navigation performance accuracy of the aircraft, including the navigation equipment carried, installation and maintenance procedures, and crew navigation procedures and training. These matters are addressed in NAT Doc.001.T13.5N/S, "Guidance and Information Material concerning Air Navigation in the North Atlantic Region" which is prepared by the European Office of ICAO, Paris.

The content of this document is provided to assist States of Registry, and also Operators, Owners and Planning Staff who are responsible for obtaining MNPS approvals for their aircraft. *However, the ultimate responsibility for checking that a flight has the necessary approval for NAT MNPS operations rests with the Pilot-in-Command.* In most cases, this check is a matter of simple routine; but pilots of special charter flights, private flights, ferry and delivery flights are advised to pay particular attention to this matter. Routine monitoring of NAT traffic regularly reveals examples of non-approved flights from within these user groups. All such instances are prejudicial to the safety of the MNPS

concept and are referred to the relevant State Authorities for further action.

There are two navigational requirements for aircraft planning to operate in the MNPSA. One refers to the navigation performance which should be achieved, in terms of accuracy. The second refers to the need to carry stand-by equipment with comparable performance characteristics (ICAO Annex 6 Parts 1 and 2). Thus, in order to justify consideration for State approval for future unrestricted operation in the MNPSA, an aircraft will be required to be equipped as follows:

1. *Two* fully serviceable Long Range Navigation Systems (LRNS's). A LRNS may be one of the following:

    a. One Inertial Navigation System (INS)

    b. One GPS

    c. One Flight Management Computer System (FCMS) with inputs from one or more Inertial Reference Systems (IRS), or GPS, or both.

2. It is highly desirable and probably essential that the navigation system employed for the provision of steering guidance is capable of being coupled to the auto-pilot.

Notes:

1. LORAN C equipment with an integral navigation computer has an acceptable performance accuracy but use of this equipment would entail an operational restriction to routes on which unambiguous ground wave coverage is available.

2. Installations of Doppler radar and computer, plus one other LRNS cannot be recommended for future approvals for unrestricted operations.

3. An FMCS, with inputs from one or more IRS/GPS, constitutes one LRNS for NAT MNPS purposes.

Some aircraft carry triplex equipment (3 x LRNS's) and hence, if one system fails even before takeoff, the two basic requirements for MNPSA operations may still be unaffected and the flight can proceed normally.

Reduced Vertical Separation Minimum Airspace (RVSM)

As specified in 14 CFR Part 91, Appendix G, **Reduced Vertical Separation Minimum (RVSM) Airspace** is that which has been designated, by international agreement, as airspace in which air traffic control (ATC) separates aircraft by a minimum of 1,000 feet vertically between FL290 and FL410 (inclusive). Typically, this airspace is designated in areas of very high density traffic.

In order to operate in RVSM airspace, an operator must acquire RVSM operating certification by showing that the aircraft is equipped and capable of maintaining altitude within certain altitude limits, and that the crew is properly trained to fly the aircraft to meet the specifications. Specifications and procedures are shown in Appendix G. There is help available to simplify the process of certification. The FAA offers a step-by-step video on how to achieve compliance, and a number of independent service providers are available to help complete the process for the operator.

RVSM is in effect over the North Atlantic in selected airspace. It is anticipated that, by the year 2000, RVSM will be in effect in all the North Atlantic airspace between FL290 and FL410. It is likely that other airspace will be designated RVSM as the need arises, as that airspace becomes limiting due to high traffic, notably areas of Europe and North America, and over the North Pacific.

Flight Planning for the North Pacific

The North Pacific has many similarities to North Atlantic flight, but some differences, too. Figure 7-11 shows the vast expanse (it is about 2,600 NM from Los Angeles to Hawaii), and the ATC boundaries of the North Pacific Oceanic area.

North Pacific Oceanic Route Structure

Composite Route System

To facilitate the movement of air traffic along the organized route system between Anchorage and Tokyo, composite lateral/vertical separation is authorized at and above FL280, composed of 5 ATS Routes: R-220, R-580, A-550, R-591, and G-344. Composite lateral/

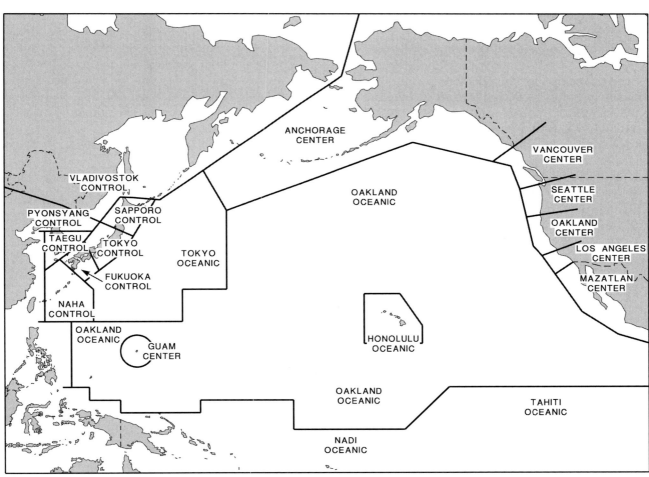

Figure 7-11. Limits and names of air traffic control units for the North Pacific and Orient

vertical separation is achieved in this mostly non-radar environment by management of route and altitude assignments.

Direction of flight and altitudes normally assigned in the **Composite Route System** are as follows:

R-220 one-way westbound: FL290, 310, 330, 350, 370, 410 and 430.

R-580 one-way westbound: FL280, 300, 320, 340, 360, 380, 400 and 420.

A-590 one-way eastbound: FL290, 310, 330, 350, 370, 390, 410 and 430.

R-591 one-way eastbound: FL280, 300, 320, 340, 360, 380, 400 and 420.

G-344 one-way eastbound: FL290, 310, 330, 350, 370, 390, 410 and 430.

As outlined in the Jeppesen Pacific Ocean H/L Altitude Enroute Charts (P 1 & 2), and Narita Flight Dispatch Bulletin 87-08, R-580 and A-590 may be used under certain circumstances as bidirectional routes. A-590 may be used for westbound aircraft crossing the Tokyo/Anchorage FIR between 2300Z and 0500Z at or above FL350. Check with ATC if a clearance is issued on a one-way route the wrong way. There are times when this is OK. Additionally, there are two tracks south of the composite structure, A-227 and R-339, which may be available at anytime with ATC approval. Just south of route R-339 is an area designated as the **Free Flow Boundary area**. Flight within this area is approved along the track as designated daily by ATC NOTAMs. A flexible track system similar to the North Atlantic's organized track system is in place just below the present NOPAC (north Pacific) routes.

Transition Routes within the Tokyo FIR, **Oceanic Transition Routes** (OTRs) and, in one case, a Victor route, have been established for aircraft transitioning to or from the NOPAC Composite Route System. Within the Oakland and Anchorage FIRs, certain ATS routes are used for the same purpose. They are as follows: B-327, G-469, A-342, G-215 and R-451.

Separation Standards

The Composite Route System allows application of a combination of 50 NM lateral and 1,000 feet vertical separation between aircraft on immediately adjacent routes. Aircraft on the same route are separated by a minimum of 2,000 feet vertically or 20 minutes longitudinally. The latter maybe reduced to 10 minutes or less when the Mach Number Technique is applied.

Preferred Routes

Anchorage ARTCC will periodically issue International NOTAMs specifying the preferential routes to be flown within the Anchorage FIR. Flights filed contrary to these NOTAMs may expect reroutes, sequencing delays, or severe altitude restrictions for crossing or opposite direction traffic.

Special Reporting Procedures

1. All aircraft operating on Routes R-220, R-580, R-591 and G-344 shall, in addition to other position determination methods, cross check their position over reporting points abeam Shemya VORTAC (109.0 MHz, DME-27, ident SYA). The radial/DME distances are as follows:

   a. For NEEVA on R-220: SYA 328R/135 DME

   b. For ONADE on R-580: SYA 328R/068 DME

   c. For AMMOE on R-59 1: SYA 148R/050 DME

   d. For CHIPT on G-344: SYA 148R/100 DME

2. In addition to normal position reporting procedures, when making progress reports, pilots shall provide this cross-check in terms of the DME distance when crossing the specified radial. For example: "Position, Clipper 1, CHIPT, Shemya 148 radial, 100 DME, 1708, FL350 estimating CAMBO 1818, next CUDDA."

Anchorage/Tokyo/Khabarovsk Communications

Direct voice communications between Anchorage ARTCC, Tokyo ACC and Khabarovsk ACC allows coordination between these facilities to assist civil aircraft in emergency situations. These situations include:

1. Aircraft mechanical problems requiring immediate landing.

2. Unlawful seizure of aircraft.

3. Loss of communication.

4. Unidentified aircraft in Russian airspace.

5. Possible entry of aircraft into Russian airspace.

Procedures

Peak Traffic Constraints

Peak Traffic Periods are:

Eastbound—1000Z to 1900Z

Westbound—2300Z to 0600Z

Due to traffic volume, flights desiring to operate contrary to the peak traffic flow can expect to be rerouted or assigned less than optimum flight If feasible, users planning to operate in the NOPAC Composite System at airspeeds below Mach 0.78 should use other than the peak hours for their flights.

In-Flight Contingencies

1. If an aircraft experiences navigational difficulties, it is essential that the pilot inform ATC as soon as the condition is apparent, so that appropriate action can be taken, as necessary, to prevent conflict with other aircraft.

2. If an aircraft is unable to continue flight in accordance with its air traffic control clearance, a revised clearance shall, whenever possible, be obtained prior to initiating any action, using the radio telephone distress or urgent signals as appropriate.

3. If prior clearance cannot be obtained, an air traffic control clearance shall be obtained at the earliest possible time; and, in the meantime, the aircraft shall broadcast its position (including the ATS route designator) and intentions on 121.5 at suitable intervals until air traffic control clearance is received.

   Note: In such circumstances, communication with certain stations on VHF may also be practicable, i.e., ADAK Approach on 134.1, Shemya Tower on 126.2, Anchorage Center on 118.5 at Cold Bay, 124.4 at Dutch Harbor, 119.1 or 127.8 at St. Paul Island, 119.1 or 132.1 at Shemya, or 126.4 at Adak.

4. If unable to comply with the provisions of paragraph 2. above, the aircraft should leave its assigned route by turning 90° to the right or left, whenever this is possible. The direction of the turn should be determined by the position of the aircraft relative to the route system, i.e. whether the aircraft is outside, at the edge of, or within the system, the levels allocated to adjacent routes, and other known traffic, if appropriate.

   Note: Aircraft operating on ATS route R-220 under these circumstances should, if possible, avoid turning northward to leave the route due to its proximity to the boundary between Anchorage/Tokyo and the USSR FIRs.

5. An aircraft able to maintain its assigned altitude should, nevertheless, climb or descend 500 feet while acquiring and maintaining in either direction, a track laterally separated by 25 NM from its assigned route.

6. An aircraft not able to maintain its assigned altitude should start its descent while turning to acquire and maintain in either direction a track laterally separated by 25 NM from its assigned route. For subsequent level flight, a level should be selected which differs by 500 feet from those normally used.

Tokyo-Honolulu Flexible Track System

The Flexible Track System (FTS) is permanently established between the Orient and Hawaii in order to achieve a more efficient use of airspace. Traffic shall operate within the system on the designated Flex Track Routes (FTR).

1. **Geographical boundary:** The airspace within which the FTRs will be established is as charted.

2. **Time Frame:** Effective daily.

   Within Tokyo FIR: 1200Z – 1700Z

   Within Oakland FIR: 1300Z – 1900Z

3. **Usable Flight Levels:** All IFR flight levels at or above FL290.

4. **Preparation of the FTRs:** Preparation of the geographical coordinates of the selected FTRs will be made at or before 0400Z daily by Japan Air Lines for Tokyo ACC, Oakland ARTCC and Honolulu CERAP. The FTS will comprise one or two routes. When two routes (primary and secondary) are used, they will be separated by at least 100 NM laterally within the airspace between the Tokyo and Honolulu gateways. The north route will be designated as the North FTR and the south route as the South FTR. The North FTR will normally terminate at THOMA Int and the South FTR at CANON Int. One route will be used when active military airspace prevents the use of two. This single route will terminate at SILVA Int.

5. **Notification of the FTRs:** Notification of the geographical coordinates of the selected FTR will be transmitted by NOTAM at approximately 0500Z daily by Tokyo ACC.

6. Flight Planning:

a. Eastbound traffic departing from or traversing Central West Japan proper and crossing longitude between 1200Z – 1500Z should flight plan as follows: For destination of Honolulu,

  i. Via the North FTR, South FTR or single FTR as described in the daily NOTAM;

  ii. Via a gateway and route laterally separated by at least 100 NM from the FTRs until at least 170°W; and

  iii. Domestic routing after THOMA, CANON or SILVA Ints. is normally via SOK BOOKE HNL.

Note: Operators are to file North FTR or South FTR in the remarks section of their flight plan, identifying which route has been selected.

b. The FTR between gateway fixes must be filed by geographical coordinates for computer acceptance.

c. Eastbound traffic from other locations may file to join or leave the FTR at the gateway fixes or at any even 10° of longitude along the routes.

d. Westbound traffic departing from Hawaii during the period the FTS is in effect should flight plan via a gateway fix at least 100 NM south of CANON Int (when a single FTR is used; via a route at least 100 NM south of SILVA Int.) then via a route separated 100 NM laterally from the FTR to the Tokyo gateway fixes.

Note 1: Gateway THOMA Int is not available for westbound flight planning.

Note 2: Westbound flights may elect to file gateway CANON Int or a gateway fix less than 100 NM from CANON Int but should expect to be assigned a flight below FL290 until a 100 NM lateral separation is established from the FTR.

e. Westbound flights departing from other locations while the FTS is in effect should flight plan via a route separated by at least 100 NM from the FTRs.

7. Clearances:

a. When requesting the departure clearance, a pilot having flight planned via an FTR, when two routes are in effect, should suffix the words "North FTR" or "South FTR."

b. The controller will clear the flight using the words "North FTR" or "South FTR" as appropriate.

c. The controller may clear the flight on the alternate FTR when the requested FTR is saturated.

8. Position Reporting: Position reports on the routes between gateway fixes shall be made using geographical coordinates.

Position Reports Over Oakland FIR/CTA Boundary

All aircraft are required to forward boundary position reports to Oakland ARTCC upon entering the Oakland Oceanic CTA, whether or not the boundary fix was filed in the flight plan. Aircraft leaving the Oakland FIR and entering uncontrolled airspace shall forward the time over the boundary outbound.

Mach Number Procedures

For oceanic departures, Mach speed and flight level should be specified in the flight plan in one of the following ways:

Preferred method: Mach number and flight level immediately preceding the initial domestic portion of the route of flight. Example of Field 15 of ICAO Flight Plan for Honolulu to San Francisco:

  M084F340 MOLOKAI 3 CLUTS R-465 CLUKK/ N0494F360 OSI

Alternate method: True airspeed and flight level in field 15, and Mach number in the remarks section 18 of ICAO Flight Plan. Example of Field 15 and Field 18 of ICAO Flight Plan for Honolulu to San Francisco:

  N0480F340 MOLOKAI 3 CLUTS R-465 CLUKK/ N0490F360 OSI

  M084 REG / NI23XX SEL / ABCD EET / KZAK0043 KZAK0415

Oceanic Position Reporting Procedures

Position Reports

1. When operating on a fixed or NOTAM'd route, report and estimate the designated reporting points using the specified names of such points or coordinates as specified in the NOTAM.

2. When operating on a random route,

  a. Flights whose tracks are predominantly east and west shall report over each 5° or 10° (10° will be used if the speed of the aircraft is such that 10° will be traversed within 80 minutes or less) meridian longitude extending east and west from 180°.

b. Flights whose tracks are predominantly north and south shall report over each 5° or 10° (10° if traversed within 80 minutes) parallel of latitude extending north and south of the equator.

3. ATC may require specific flights to report more frequently than each 5° for aircraft with slow ground speeds.

4. Position reports shall be transmitted at the time of crossing the designated reporting point or as soon thereafter as possible.

Position Report Contents

Position reports shall comprise information on present position, estimated next position, and ensuing position in sequence as indicated below. Forward planned flight level change information while in the Oakland FIR.

1. Present position—Information shall include:

   a. The word "position"

   b. Aircraft identification

   c. Reporting point name, or if not named:

       i. Latitude (4 digits)

       ii. Longitude (5 digits)

   d. Time over reporting point (4 digits UTC)

   e. Altitude (flight level)

2. Estimated next position:

   a. Reporting point name, or if not named, latitude and longitude (as in 1.c. i. and ii. above)

   b. Estimated time over next position (4 digits UTC).

3. Ensuing Position:

   a. Name only of the next succeeding reporting point whether compulsory or not, or if not named, latitude and longitude (as in 1.c. i. and ii. above).

4. Pre-planning Flight Levels: Within the Oakland FIR, pilots should forward the time requesting the next subsequent cardinal flight level.

Exceptions to Position Reports

1. Within Oakland FIR, no 5° report need be made that would fall within 100 NM of Guam. Aircraft cleared via terminal area routes report compulsory reporting fixes. Other aircraft report 100 NM from Nimitz VORTAC. Where other island destinations within the Oakland FIR are not more than 1° latitude/longitude from a 5° fixed line reporting

point, the ETA and arrival report may be substituted in lieu of the adjacent fixed-line report.

2. To the east of the Hawaiian Islands, it will not be necessary to report the 155°W position if position will be reported at the entry/exit fixes at the Honolulu Domestic/Oceanic boundary. To the west of Honolulu, 160°W need not be reported.

Automated Mutual Assistance Vessel Rescue System

The Automated Mutual Assistance Vessel Rescue (AMVER) is an International Maritime Mutual Assistance Program. It provides Rescue Coordination Centers Surpics (surface pictures) of vessels' present DR positions as well as their predicted positions, speed, search and rescue capabilities. The system can provide the above information for any specific area.

Precautionary Surpics

If an aircraft declares an emergency on an overwater flight, the Rescue Coordination Center will produce a precautionary AMVER Surpic which will provide the predicted location of ships which may be of assistance, should ditching become necessary. This message will also indicate the search and rescue capabilities of the ships in the area indicated. These Surpics may be a circle of specific radius centered on a precise point, a polygon described by latitude and longitude limits, or a path along any rhumb line or great circle course. The time for the Surpic may be the present, or any specific time in the future.

U.S. Coast Guard Assistance Procedures— Ditching Aircraft

U.S. Coast Guard ships at sea maintain a radio-telephone watch on 121.5 and 243.0 MHz, if equipped, a radio-telephone watch on 500 kHz, the international maritime emergency frequency, and provide beacon signals for aircraft on 410 kHz. They will provide ditching assistance by providing black smoke to aid the aircraft in sighting the ship, provide information on weather, wind direction and velocity, and sea conditions, and they will lay a foam path along the selected ditching heading. When aircraft is in sight, they will set course parallel to the selected ditching heading. If not in communication with the aircraft and unable to obtain ditching heading, they will set a course parallel to main swell system and into the wind, if any.

Finishing the Planning Job

Even after the flight log is developed and permits requested, the planning job isn't finished for the pilot/planner who is operating at a high level of planning sophistication. Some additional planning is in order: planning and training for contingencies.

Equipment for survival in the ocean and wilderness should be acquired based upon the type of terrain the flight will pass over. Desert, jungle, boreal forest, and arctic survival equipment needs are very different. The equipment is of little use unless the survivors know how to deploy and use it, so training becomes very important. In a ditching scenario with a specific aircraft, training to decrease time to deploy water survival gear will often open the flight crews eyes as to how the baggage areas should be arranged.

Planning for in-flight contingencies is also best done well before the flight. Below are two important tools for that task that are used on every trans-oceanic flight.

ETP and the Wet Footprint

The ETP (Equal Time Point)

This is a useful tool for decision-making on extended overwater or over-wilderness flights. It provides a quick indication of which way to go in the event of onboard problems which change aircraft performance (particularly **specific range**—miles flown per pound of fuel used).

The ETP represents a geographic position along the route where the time needed to fly to destination equals the time needed to return to point of origin. For example, a medical emergency occurring before reaching the ETP requires a return. If the emergency occurs after the ETP, proceeding to the destination will get the victim to medical assistance quickest (assuming the level of services is not a factor).

There are several different ETPs that can be calculated for a flight, one for each situation that changes aircraft performance. Some examples are:

- Medical emergency (normal performance)
- Loss of pressurization (utilizes driftdown and performance at 12,000 feet ASL)
- Loss of engine (utilizes single engine performance)
- Airframe icing (often a 10% fuel penalty is assumed).

The formula to calculate ETP (assuming no change of winds or aircraft performance along the route), is:

$$ETP = (D \times GSret)/(GSret + GSfwd)$$

where:

D	=	total distance for the flight
Gsret	=	ground speed from the ETP back to the origin
Gsfwd	=	ground speed from the ETP to the destination
ETP	=	distance from departure airport to the ETP

With an 1,800 NM leg, a TAS of 395 knots at FL350, using 1,650 pounds per hour with an average wind factor of +50 knots, the ETP is 786 NM from the origin airport, at which point it is 02:17 to go either way. This value should be calculated and noted for reference during the flight.

The ETP calculation should be calculated for the scenario of an engine loss, which would produce a driftdown to a lower altitude, with about the same fuel burn but a lower speed. For example, on one engine at FL180 if the speed is 280 knots and burn is 1,620 lbs/hr, with a wind factor of +30 knots, the ETP changes to 804 NM. So, single engine ETP should also be computed and noted. Loss of pressurization will require descent to 12,000 feet, and in the example aircraft, would move the ETP out to 864 NM.

If there is a wind shift en route, the ETP problem becomes a bit more complex. One way to solve the original problem, with a wind shift to -40 knot wind factor at 60% of the way through the trip, for example, is to diagram the situation (*see* Figure 7-12). A glance would indicate that logic puts the ETP on the origin side of the wind change point. Flight time is found by dividing distance by ground speed, so:

$$\frac{\text{Distance to return}}{\text{GS to return}} = \frac{\text{Distance to continue}}{\text{GS to continue}}$$

distance to return (all at 345 kts) = x,

distance to continue = 1080 – x at 445 kts + 720 NM at 350 kts, so

$$\frac{x}{345 \text{ kts}} = \frac{1080 - x}{445 \text{ kts}} + \frac{720}{350 \text{ kts}}$$

An algebraic solution for x indicates the ETP is about 871.5 NM from the origin airport, and just over 2.5 hours from origin and destination airports. Another good way to solve this sort of problem is to set it up on a computer spreadsheet.

Wet Footprint

ETP is also a useful tool in the calculation of another important concept, the **wet footprint**. This is the amount of time on either side of the ETP during which, if specific range is degraded for any reason, the airplane will have to ditch (it can't make the origin or destination airports, or any suitable airport, with the fuel remaining on board).

In the lost-engine situation discussed above, the aircraft had to descend to FL180 and proceed at 280 knots with about the same fuel flow. This produced nearly a 30% decrease in ability to convert fuel to miles! If full fuel in the above example aircraft will be adequate for 1,800 NM plus 30 minutes holding or time to alternate at 5,000 feet, the crossing (4.04 hours at 1,650 pph) plus holding will use up the 7,600 pounds of fuel on board.

If the engine loss occurred at the worst time (at the ETP), the aircraft has already burned about 3,000 pounds getting to the ETP, with just over 4,600 pounds remaining. Just to get to the destination, 3.2 hours at 1,620 pph, or about 5,200 is needed, leaving a shortage of 600 pounds! The wet footprint exists for $^{600}/_{1620}$ x 60, or 22 long minutes on either side of the ETP. A 44-minute wet footprint means the crew has to sit there for 44 minutes, way out there in the middle of nowhere, knowing that, if one engine quits, the best they can hope for is a terrifying swim.

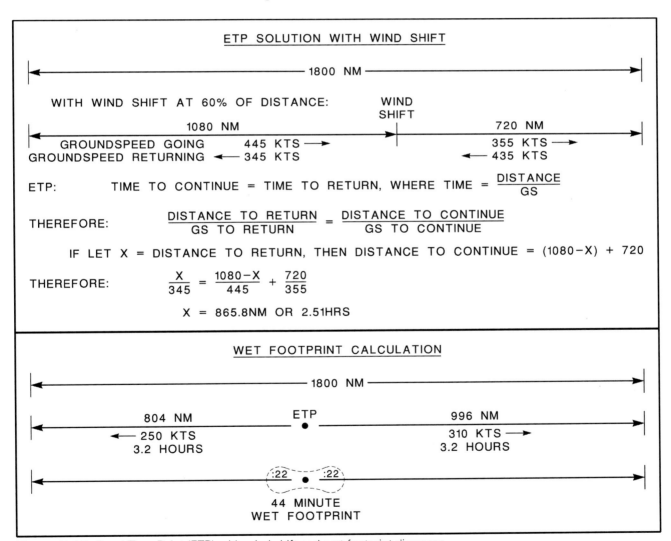

Figure 7-12. Equal Time Point (ETP) with wind shift and wet footprint diagrams

I would not be comfortable being aboard a flight that had a wet footprint greater than zero. I would consider myself far safer in a single-engine airplane (with the same type of engine) flying across water out of gliding distance of land for the same number of minutes as the wet footprint of a multi-engine airplane. The chances of one engine failure in the multi is greater by the number of engines. To say it another way: flying across an ocean or wilderness wet footprint in a multi is like flying across a distance equivalent to the wet footprint in a single but, in the case of the multi, with a greatly increased chance of engine failure.

So, the ETP and wet footprint calculations should be done for conditions that would reduce range, such as engine failure, pressurization failure, etc. If a wet footprint exists, calculations should be done considering a diversion to enroute alternates (examples on the North Atlantic crossing might be Stephenville, Newfoundland; Keflavik, Iceland, Santa Maria, etc.). In flight, however, the crew must continuously monitor the VOLMETs to be sure the planned alternate is indeed available.

8: International Flight Operations

Operational Considerations for International Flight

Cabotage

Cabotage was originally a marine shipping term from the Portuguese *cabo*, meaning coast or the French *cabotier*, meaning *one who trades along the coast*. For modern aviation, it has come to refer to the rights of **states** (nations) to regulate the air traffic within their territories. Pilots of international flights should remember the several possibilities that exist for states to regulate the cabotage rights, which include: the right to overfly, the right to land for servicing only, the right to land to discharge nonpaying passengers or cargo, the right to carry nonpaying passengers or cargo from one point to another within the foreign state, the right to carry nonpaying passengers or cargo from a point within the foreign state to a destination outside of the state.

Generally, carrying paying passengers or cargo is more restricted and requires permits. About the only "right" that is universally available is the right to land to avoid loss of life or property. The rest of the cabotage rights are permitted in some states and not permitted in others. In some cases, "passengers" are differentiated based on their citizenship or even their place of residence (Canada, for example, operates this way). So, it may or may not be legal for an aircraft registered in country A to carry nonpaying passengers of country B between two points in country B, even if the carriage is done for free.

In another example, Mexico's "cabotage laws" state (among other things): "Aircraft must operate and leave Mexico with the same persons and crew as are listed on the GHC-001 form." In other words, the aircraft must enter and leave the country with the same persons on board. In the case of Mexico, enforcement of these regulations is done by the local airport manager who is a government employee. Sometimes, matters of this nature can be negotiated if the crew speaks the language and is familiar with the negotiating process.

Pilots flying internationally should keep in mind the matter of cabotage, and should alert their passengers, The time to advise the passengers about prevailing cabotage rules is before a passenger invites a citizen of the country being visited to ride along, not after.

Other Entry Requirements

The cabotage and other regulations pertaining to entry should be examined in the IFIM or in Jeppesen's J-Aid for the country of interest, and complied with. Air regulations, **disinsection** (spraying to kill insects on board before arrival), airports of entry and times available for entry, firearms, radio transmitters (even a hand-held CB radio), alcohol, tobacco and certainly, drugs on board, are some of the items that can become major problems for the crew entering or leaving a country. **Pratique** is a term used to describe the process of entry into another country.

The Nine "Fs" of International Flight

It is simply not possible to read information about everything one experiences on an international flight, but a lecture given by Mr. Roger Tilbury, atmospherics research test pilot, to the International and Long Range Navigation class at the University of North Dakota did a fine job of enumerating many of the non-textbook aspects of long-range international flight, by the example of the nine "Fs." They are listed below.

1. **Fear**—When out over the North Atlantic, looking down at icebergs as it gets dark, knowing you are at least two hours from another human being, and knowing that the time of useful consciousness, should you have to ditch and get wet, is less than 30 seconds in that black, nearly frozen water below, it is only normal to feel fear. Fear is debilitating. It is nearly impossible to think clearly or rationally while experiencing fear, and that is when you need it the most.

   Adding to the fear, much of it subconscious (so the crew doesn't recognize it), is the knowledge that there may be the need for an approach, at night, into a foreign (*see #6 below*), unknown location that requires the crew to "get it right the first time"—especially with fatigue (#2, below) as a player in the scenario. For example, the approach into Akureyri, Iceland (*see* Figure 8-1) calls for "threading the needle" down a fjord with mountains as high as 5,000 feet along the edges of the "groove" that must be flown, with a 36° left turn at a critical time!

2. **Fatigue**—Long hours of preparation, plus: long hours of flight, interruption of the normal body rhythms, sleeping fitfully in a strange bed in a strange place with strange sounds, and the knowledge that tomorrow you have to fly across the North Atlantic to strange places—all of this just about guarantees that, in the morning, you will not be well rested when you meet the airplane on the ramp. Fatigue greatly diminishes the brain's ability to think and our ability to perform complex tasks. Judgment, sensitivity and situational awareness is impaired. How "up-to-the-challenges" will you be, while flying internationally?

3. **Fuel**—As we learned in the last chapter, crossing the North Atlantic via Canada, Greenland or Iceland required fuel reserves of 3 hours, or in faster aircraft, 400 miles. Crossing from the U.S. directly to Europe or flying other oceanic routes doesn't. What are your minimums? What if there is an engine failure? Loss of pressurization? Leaky fuel gasket? Failure of a fuel transfer pump? Stronger than forecast headwinds? Deterioration of weather at destination? All of these are worries related to fuel, and are best combated by superior pre-planning, including formulation of alternative plans for such contigencies.

4. **Food**—Food and water from foreign places can be incapacitating. It is best to see to it that, as much as possible, each member of the flight crew eats different foods from different sources for the eight hours before that long flight, so as to lessen the chance that all of the crew will become incapacitated.

5. **Finger Trouble**—Many of the problems that flight crews create for themselves in modern aircraft are related to what pilots call "finger trouble": pressing the wrong buttons, incorrectly programming a navigation system or FMS. There are procedures designed to find this kind of error before it becomes a big problem, yet many crises still occur because of finger trouble and improper procedures.

6. **Foreign**—Wilderness, wasteland, arctic survival equipment, pack-ice fields are all foreign to us and exposure to them—just looking at them and knowing one is surrounded by them—causes psychological changes in most of us that decrease our ability to function. Managing a flight along a route that is well known to the flight crew is always much easier. A flight to a place with strange sounding names, weird approaches (flying up a fjord), different procedures (altimeter settings in millibars or hectopascals instead of inches of mercury, for example), all increase pilot workload and stress.

7. **Foreigners** (individuals from different or unknown cultures)—Just understanding a clearance or the weather given (supposedly) in English in places as close as the Bahamas or Quebec, by peoples who may not take as seriously the matter of proper phraseology, increases pilot stress. One never knows quite what to expect from different and unknown cultures.

8. **Fallacies**—Misconceptions, developed from the thought that "I've done it this way correctly for many years, so it must be OK to do it here and now" or "I didn't research to see if it is done differently in this country because the way I've done it has always been right." This is fairly good rationalization from a pilot who asked for takeoff clearance, and got it, with one-quarter mile visibility. He did it many times at home—it was legal there.

   But why didn't the controller withhold the takeoff clearance? Well, it turns out that one-half mile is required for all operations in that country and it wasn't the controller's responsibility to keep the pilot from breaking the law—his responsibility was to keep the pilot from hitting another airplane in his airspace. See the difference in logic? Neither logic system is wrong—just different. It is the traveller's responsibility to be on guard for this and, "when in Rome, do as the Romans do." *How does one know what the rules are?* First, know (and carry on board a copy of) ICAO Annex 6, International Rules of the Air, available from ICAO or found in the Jeppesen J-Aid, and learn the "differences from ICAO Rules" for the country of interest, found in the IFIM or the Jeppesen J-Aid.

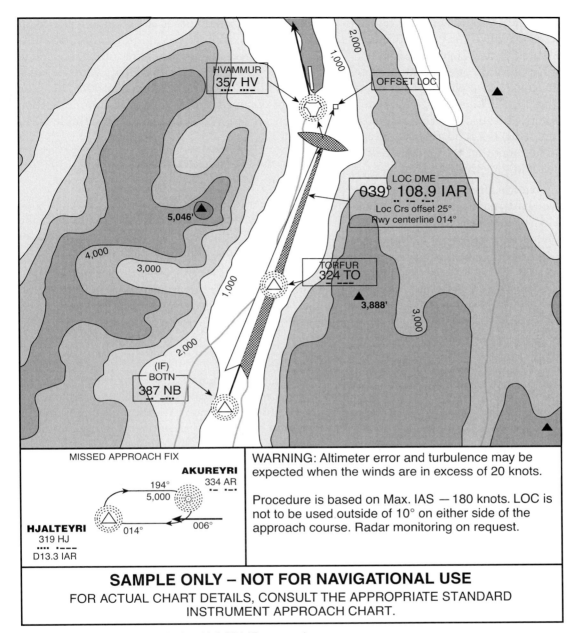

MISSED APPROACH FIX

AKUREYRI
334 AR

194°
5,000

HVAMMUR
357 HV

OFFSET LOC

LOC DME
039° 108.9 IAR
Loc Crs offset 25°
Rwy centerline 014°

5,046'

4,000

3,000

1,000

TORFUR
324 TO

3,888'

3,000

2,000

(IF)
BOTN
387 NB

HJALTEYRI
319 HJ
D13.3 IAR

014°   006°

WARNING: Altimeter error and turbulence may be
expected when the winds are in excess of 20 knots.

Procedure is based on Max. IAS — 180 knots. LOC is
not to be used outside of 10° on either side of the
approach course. Radar monitoring on request.

SAMPLE ONLY – NOT FOR NAVIGATIONAL USE
FOR ACTUAL CHART DETAILS, CONSULT THE APPROPRIATE STANDARD
INSTRUMENT APPROACH CHART.

Figure 8-1. The Akureyri, Iceland LOCDME approach

9. **Flummoxed**—This was a new word for my vo-cabulary. Perhaps it will be for yours. It means confused, disoriented. Because of many of the "Fs" listed above, it happens too often on long, inter-national flights. How to deal with it? Turn it into "the pilot's friend." Learn to recognize the symp-toms your symptoms, because if you can recognize it in its early stages, that is a good, first step in risk management. One must first recognize a risk in order to be able to do something about it.

Being flummoxed is often associated with the discovery that you have made a mistake. Often, the flummoxed feeling precedes detection of a specific problem (and therefore is a good early warning).

Example: if the ADF needle is not pointing where you think it should be, there is trouble in the cockpit and something needs to be done about it. The above is a much better situation (being flummoxed and recognizing it) than a similar situ-ation where the pilot doesn't recognize that the ADF needle is pointing the wrong way. See the difference? Learn to recognize that "flummoxed feeling"!

North Atlantic Operational Considerations

The following is excerpted largely from the NAIGOM publication. A current edition of this document should be reviewed carefully by flight crews before flight across the North Atlantic.

Clearances

All flights planned at or above FL060 in oceanic con-trol areas are required to obtain an IFR clearance prior to leaving FL055. Additionally, all operations in the Sondrestrom and Reykjavik FIRs above FL195 must be on IFR flight plans. It is important to note that the air-space over Southern Greenland (south of 63°30'N) above FL195 is controlled by Gander OCA. Therefore, clearance is required from Gander OCA prior to de-scent into the Sondrestrom FIR below FL195 in this airspace. Clearance can be obtained from Gander IFSS, or if unable, from Sondrestrom.

When operating on an IFR clearance, any change of altitude or true airspeed greater than 5% requires re-clearance from ATC. Clearances for VFR climb or de-scent will not be granted.

Pilots are strongly urged to obtain a clearance, or as a minimum, receive traffic information from the ATS[1] unit responsible for the area of operation, and to follow the procedures specified in appropriate AIPs. Where possible, clearance to enter controlled airspace should be obtained prior to takeoff, as communication problems are often encountered at low altitudes.

Obtaining a Clearance

Canada
Oceanic clearances for eastbound IGA NAT flights, departing from eastern Canada, are obtained from the control tower or the flight service station at the aero-drome of departure prior to departure.

Eastbound IGA NAT over-flights obtain their oceanic clearance directly from Gander ACC, Moncton ACC, Montreal ACC, or through a flight service sta-tion, depending on the route of flight.

United Kingdom
At some airports situated close to oceanic boundaries, the oceanic clearance can be obtained before departure (e.g., Prestwick, Shannon). Westbound aircraft operat-ing within the U.K. FIR should request oceanic clear-ance from Shanwick Oceanic on VHF at least 30 minutes before point of entry. Aircraft unable to get clearance on VHF should request clearance on NARTEL HF (North Atlantic Enroute HF Network). Aircraft unable to contact Shanwick, as detailed above, should request the ATC authority for the airspace in which they are operating to relay their request for oce-anic clearance to Shanwick. Flights planned to enter the Reykjavik OCA from the Scottish FIR east of 10°W, should request oceanic clearance from the appropriate Scottish domestic sector.

United States
Prior to entering oceanic airspace, pilots must receive a specific oceanic clearance detailing the oceanic entry point, route, landfall (or oceanic exit point), and air-ways to destination. This clearance should be issued by the ATC unit responsible for providing air traffic service in the airspace abutting the oceanic area. If you should not receive an oceanic clearance upon ap-proaching the oceanic entry fix, *request one.*

---

[1] Aeronautical Telecommunications Station (*See* Glossary, Page 338)

Oceanic Clearances

Pilots should request oceanic clearances from the appropriate ATS authority as early as possible. Although the clearances are obtained prior to reaching the oceanic boundary/entry fix, they are only applicable from that point. Follow the procedures and timeframe established for clearance requests in the appropriate AIPs.

Methods of obtaining oceanic clearances include:

- use of VHF clearance delivery frequencies when in coverage area;
- use of HF to the OAC through the appropriate aeradio station (if possible, at least 30 minutes before boundary/entry fix estimate); request through domestic or other ATC agencies.

Note: A reminder—at some airports situated close to oceanic boundaries the oceanic clearance can be obtained before departure (e.g., Prestwick, Shannon).

An **abbreviated clearance** is only issued by air traffic services when clearing an aircraft to fly along the whole length of an organized track or along a Polar track within Reykjavik OCA. In all other circumstances, full details of the cleared track are specified in the clearance message. When an abbreviated clearance is issued it includes:

- cleared track specified by track and code letter or Polar track and number;
- cleared flight level;
- cleared Mach number;
- if the aircraft is designated to report Met (weather) information en route, the phrase "Send MET Reports."

Procedures exist for abbreviated **readback** of westbound clearances issued by Shanwick on VHF. If the pilot is cleared on the original track as requested and the details of that track are confirmed by listening to the Shanwick Track Broadcast Frequency, the readback of the routing element of the clearance may refer only to the track code letter. Otherwise, the pilot *must* read back the contents of the clearance message and full details of the track specified. If in any doubt, the pilot should request a detailed description of the route from the ATC unit.

Oceanic clearances for flights intending to operate within the NAT region and subsequently enter the EUR or NAM regions are strategic clearances intended to provide a safe separation for each flight from oceanic entry to track termination point. Should a pilot receive a clearance on a track other than originally

flight-planned, special caution should be exercised to ensure that the coordinates of the assigned track and the associated landfall and domestic routings are fully understood and correctly inserted into the automated navigation system, with appropriate cross checks. In all cases where an enroute reclearance is requested by a pilot, the pilot should ensure that the revised ATC clearance includes the new routings from the exit from oceanic airspace to the first landfall point or coastal fix. If at the time given a clearance or reclearance, the pilot has any doubt about it, the pilot should check the details with the ATC unit relaying the clearance/reclearance.

Oceanic clearances for random flights intending to operate within the NAT region and subsequently enter regions other than NAM or EUR are similar to domestic ATC clearances in that clearances are to destination, on the assumption that coordination will be effected ahead of the aircraft's passage. In this case, the flight profile is subject to change en route prior to hand over from one center to another, dependent on traffic conditions in the adjacent area. As such, center/center coordination is sometimes carried out well in advance, there is a possibility that upon entry into the next FIR a more economical profile may be available than envisaged at the time of coordination.

For westbound flights intending to operate in the Shanwick OCA after obtaining and reading back the clearance, the pilot should monitor the forward estimate for oceanic entry. If this changes, the pilot should pass a revised estimate to ATC. As planned longitudinal spacing by Shanwick OACC is based solely on boundary estimates, failure to adhere to this ETA amendment procedure may result in a reclearance to less economical track/flight level for the complete crossing. In most other OACCs, planned longitudinal spacing is based on fixes or by radar, making accuracy of estimates less critical.

If the oceanic clearance the pilot is given in flight differs from the route originally requested, it then becomes the pilot's responsibility to obtain the necessary domestic route clearance in order to ensure compliance with the oceanic clearance when they enter oceanic airspace.

The pilot should appreciate that irrespective of the flight plan filed, the great majority of clearances given to individual aircraft are at a specific flight level, and that in such cases no level changes should be made without prior ATC clearance.

For current information on oceanic clearances, reference Jeppesen Enroute Chart AT (H/L) 1, Panel 4. For current information concerning Pacific operations, reference Jeppesen Enroute Chart P (H/L) 3-4, front panel.

Airborne Oceanic Clearance Call Format

The crew calls:

Oceanic Clearance Delivery

Gander

Shanwick

Iceland

(Etc.)

Stating, upon initial call:

1. Flight Number
2. ETA for the Entry Point
3. Requested FLT LVL
4. Requested Mach

Clearance is then read by OCA Delivery. Readback must be in detail: Route, Altitude, Mach, and any restrictions.

Some Common Restrictions are:

1. Meter time for entry point, for flow control
2. Altitude / Speed / Routing — which is *not* the aircraft's present domestic airspace clearance. Since the aircraft must arrive at the oceanic entry point at altitude and at Mach number, the crew must coordinate a matching clearance, and be cleared to do so by the domestic airspace controlling agency, before entering oceanic airspace.

For example: Leaving Lisbon with a clearance limit of N42 W20 via the Atlantico 4N SID (*see* Figure 8-2). Once airborne, FL240 is assigned. Aricia RBN is a good point for an accuracy check. The oceanic clearances should be requested as soon as possible (available only from Santa Maria on HF). Santa Maria will say "[aircraft number], cleared to [landfall fix] via [route — often a lat/lon every 10° of longitude], altitude, FL370 by the oceanic boundary, Mach [number]." It is the pilot's responsibility to coordinate with Lisbon (pre-oceanic airspace) to reach FL370 by the oceanic boundary (and adjust speed to assigned Mach if this speed is different than filed or cleared).

Notes:

1. The oceanic boundary is at 15 west, not 20 west; 20 west was the clearance limit given by Lisbon ATC. In this case, Lisbon domestic is able to clear some distance into oceanic airspace due to a letter of agreement between Lisbon and Santa Maria. It is the flight crew's responsibility to arrive at oceanic airspace enter point (15W) at the altitude and speed given in the oceanic clearance, but the aircraft may not deviate from the domestic clearance. The flight crew must request and receive an amended clearance from Lisbon domestic in order to be able to meet the oceanic clearance requirements.

2. One other procedure is a good idea while still on the ground at Lisbon: Due to the uncertainties of HF radio and the need to establish the correct HF frequency for communications with Santa Maria (usable HF frequencies vary with distance, time of day, season, etc.), it would be well to call Santa Maria on HF for a "radio check" or a "SELCAL check" (give Santa Maria your SELCAL ID so they can "ring" you at any time). Then the crew is fairly certain they can reach Santa Maria on HF after airborne, when they know an accurate oceanic entry estimate and the oceanic clearance can be requested.

ATC System Loop Errors

By definition, an **ATC system loop error** is any error caused by a misunderstanding between the pilot and the controller regarding the assigned flight level, Mach number, or route to be followed. Such errors can arise by incorrect interpretation of the NAT Track Message by dispatchers or pilots, errors in coordination between ATC centers, or misinterpretation of oceanic clearances or reclearances by pilots. Complete readback of routing and altitudes after clearances are received is vital in order to minimize such errors.

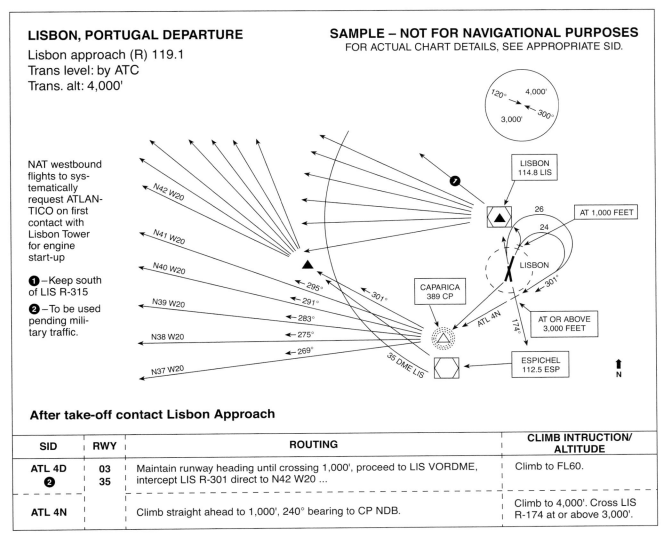

LISBON, PORTUGAL DEPARTURE

Lisbon approach (R) 119.1
Trans level: by ATC
Trans. alt: 4,000'

NAT westbound flights to systematically request ATLAN-TICO on first contact with Lisbon Tower for engine start-up

❶–Keep south of LIS R-315

❷–To be used pending military traffic.

LISBON 114.8 LIS

AT 1,000 FEET

LISBON

CAPARICA 389 CP

AT OR ABOVE 3,000 FEET

ESPICHEL 112.5 ESP

After take-off contact Lisbon Approach

SID	RWY	ROUTING	CLIMB INTRUCTION/ ALTITUDE
ATL 4D ❷	03 35	Maintain runway heading until crossing 1,000', proceed to LIS VORDME, intercept LIS R-301 direct to N42 W20 ...	Climb to FL60.
ATL 4N		Climb straight ahead to 1,000', 240° bearing to CP NDB.	Climb to 4,000'. Cross LIS R-174 at or above 3,000'.

Figure 8-2. Lisbon Standard Instrument Departure

Position Reporting Procedures

Time and Place of Position Reports

Unless otherwise required by air traffic services, position reports from flights on routes which are not defined by designated reporting points should be made at the significant points listed in the flight plan.

Air traffic services may require any flight operating in a north-south direction to report its position at any intermediate parallel of latitude when deemed necessary.

In requiring aircraft to report their position at intermediate points, ATS are guided by the requirement to have positional information at approximately hourly intervals, and also by the need to cater for varying types of aircraft and varying traffic and MET conditions. Position information should be based on the best obtainable navigational fix.

Position Report Prefix

The prefix "POSITION" should be used when passing NAT position reports to ground aeradio stations either on the initial call, or prior to the text of the message.

Contents of Position Reports

For flying outside the Polar Track Structure and domestic ATS route network, position should be expressed in terms of latitude and longitude except when flying over oceanic "fish points" or other named reporting points. For flights whose tracks are predominantly east or west, latitude should be expressed in degrees and minutes, longitude in degrees only. For flights whose tracks are predominantly north or south, latitude should be expressed in degrees only, longitude in degrees and minutes. All times should be expressed in four digits giving both the hour and the minutes when making position reports in the NAT region.

Position report format can be found on AT (H/L) 1 chart, panel 8, or the P (H/L) 3 and 4 chart.

Pilots must realize that the requirement to report next position allows ATC to closely monitor the progress of flights and more time to intervene and correct possible deviations.

Next Position and Time Over

"Next position" should normally be expressed as the significant point at which the aircraft is next required to report position.

If the estimated time for the next positions is found to be in error by three minutes or more, a revised estimate should be transmitted to the ATC unit concerned as soon as possible.

Next Subsequent Position

The name or coordinates of the ensuing significant point following "the next position and estimated time over" should be given when making position reports in the NAT Region and when reporting over the last domestic reporting point prior to entry into oceanic airspace.

This requirement allows ATC to closely monitor the progress of flights related to their assigned track and domestic routing and more time to correct possible deviations.

Examples:

"Position Swissair 110 52 North 20 West 1020 FL350 Estimate 52 North 30 West 1102 Next 51 North 40 West."

"Position Lufthansa 440 Springdale 0342 FL370 Estimate 51 North 50 West 0410 Next 52 North 40 West."

Unless otherwise authorized by ATC, predominantly north/south NAT flights shall make position reports on the appropriate frequencies at each significant point listed in the flight plan. Eastbound and westbound flights are required to report at every 10° of longitude. Position reports are to be forwarded to air traffic control at least at approximately hourly intervals. However, in the event of low ground speed, a position report may be required every 5° of longitude.

When making position reports, all times are to be expressed in UTC, giving both the hour and minutes. A position report example follows:

"Position N1234D 53 North 25 West 1237, Flight Level 090, Estimate 53 North 20 West 1356, Next 53 North 15 West."

Transmission of Position Reports

Position reports made by aircraft operating within an oceanic control area at a distance of 60 NM or less from the common boundary with an adjacent oceanic control area (including aircraft operating on track thorough successive points on each boundary), should also be made to the area control center serving the adjacent control area. (In practice this only requires an addition to the address such as "Shanwick copy Iceland" if both have a common frequency; "Shanwick relay to Santa Maria," if other station is not on common frequency.)

Make all position reports, as detailed above, and report any problems to Air Traffic Control agencies as soon as possible. It is also good policy to report fuel remaining in hours and minutes when relaying position or other relevant flight information.

Meteorological Reports

From among the aircraft intending to operate on the organized track system, OACs designate those which shall be required to report routine meteorological observations at each prescribed reporting point. See AT (H/L) 1 chart, panel 8 for more information on meteorological reports.

In-Flight Contingencies

Do not deviate from the current flight plan unless approval from the appropriate air traffic control unit has been requested and obtained or unless an emergency situation arises which necessitates immediate action. After such emergency authority is exercised, the appropriate air traffic services unit must be notified of the action taken and that the action has been taken under emergency authority.

If difficulties are encountered, report immediately on the appropriate VHF/HF frequency or on VHF 121.5. Don't delay in this call as it could take SAR (search and rescue) forces up to four hours to reach your position.

Remember that commercial airline traffic over the North Atlantic is heavy. Do not hesitate to enlist the assistance of these aircraft in relaying a position or discussing a problem. The VHF frequency 131.8 MHz is for exclusive use as an air-to-air communications channel over the Atlantic, 128.95 MHz in the eastern Pacific, and 130.55 MHz in the Caribbean oceanic areas when out of ground VHF range. The moral support alone may be enough to settle nerves and return your thought processes to normal.

The weather at the destination should be well above IFR minimums and forecast to remain so or improve. After 10 to 14 hours at altitude, the pilot's ability to handle marginal weather conditions may be in serious doubt. Therefore, a pilot's personal weather minimums may need to be well above the published minimums. Alternate airports should be chosen with the same care.

International Air Traffic Control Phraseology

ICAO member states may use all or part of the Standards and Recommended Practices (SARPS) regarding air traffic control phraseology. The United States does not use all of the SARPS. Therefore, some phraseology used in most ICAO member countries varies somewhat from what we are accustomed to hearing in the U.S.

ICAO Phraseology and Requirements

Following is a review of a few ICAO phraseologies and requirements.

- The use of the words "clear," "cleared," and "clearance" is restricted to takeoff/landing clearances, approach clearances and instructions, and ATC route clearances.

- The following items shall always be read back: ATC route clearances; all clearances to enter, land on, takeoff on, cross and backtrack on the runway in use; other clearances or instructions that include conditional clearances; and runway in use, altimeter settings, SSR (transponder) codes, level instructions and, if required, transition levels.

- In many member states, clearance must be received to start engine(s) before doing so.

- After a pilot advises "ready to taxi," the response may be "N1234W taxi to holding point, Runway 28," This instruction is *not* approval to taxi onto the runway.

- The word "takeoff" is restricted to the actual takeoff clearance or its cancellation (e.g., "N1234W, cleared for takeoff" or "N1234W cancel, I say again, cancel takeoff"). In all other cases it is referred to as "Departure" (e.g., "N1234W are you ready for (immediate) departure?"). To stop a takeoff in emergency conditions, the phraseology "N1234W stop immediately" is used twice. For pilots to request takeoff clearance, use the phraseology "N1234W, ready for departure."

- If takeoff clearance cannot be given, you may be instructed to "Line up," or "Line up runway (number)." In these two cases the aircraft may taxi onto the runway and must wait for takeoff clearance.

- You may also be given a "conditional" instruction or "conditional" clearance which will contain the call sign, the condition, and the clearance or instruction. For example, "N1234W after L-1011 on short final, line up." The pilot should read back the conditional instruction and after the landing L-1011 passed, line up on the runway and wait for takeoff clearance.

- An aircraft will be "cleared to land," and after landing but still on the runway, may be instructed to "expedite vacating" or given instructions which way to turn to "vacate" the runway. When off the runway, use the phrase "N1234W, runway vacated."

Standardization

Standardization of ATC phraseology is a continuing process. Pilots may encounter some minor variations, especially when new procedures are implemented. The readback of ATC clearances is an important part of enhancing communications and improving safety. If any doubt exists, the pilot should verify the clearance with Air Traffic Control.

MNPSA Operational Considerations

Much of the following discussion can be found covered in more detail in the current edition of the North Atlantic MNPS Airspace Operations Manual, available from **IATA**[2] or the CAA, London. Much of the following discussion is excerpted from that document.

ATC Flight Plans

General Requirements

Operators are encouraged to flight plan as follows:

1. In accordance with the OTS; or

2. A route to join or leave an outer track of the OTS; or

3. A random route to remain clear of the OTS.

Note: Nothing in the paragraph above prevents operators from flight planning across the OTS. However, they should be aware that while ATC will make every effort to clear random traffic across the OTS at published levels, re-routes or changes in flight level may be necessary during peak OTS traffic periods.

Outside the hours of validity of the OTS and the changeover periods (*see* Chapter 7, Pages 138 – 139), operators are encouraged to flight plan a random route at flight levels appropriate to the direction of flight. If necessary and in all cases of doubt, dispatchers should seek the advice of the appropriate Oceanic Center on the best procedure to adopt.

The correct completion of the flight plan is extremely important as errors can lead to delay in data processing and subsequent clearance of the flights concerned.

Flight plans for flights departing from points in other regions, and those entering the NAT Region without intermediate stops, should be submitted as far in advance of departure as possible.

If (and only if) the flight is planned to operate along the whole length of one of the organized tracks as detailed in the North Atlantic Track Message, the intended organized track should be defined in Item 15 of the flight plan using the abbreviation "NAT" followed by the code letter assigned to the track.

Flights wishing to join or leave an organized track at some intermediate point are considered to be random route aircraft, and full track details must be specified in the flight plan. The track letter should not be used to abbreviate any portion of the route in these circumstances.

The requested Mach number and flight level at the commencement point of the organized track should be specified at either the last domestic reporting point prior to ocean entry, or the organized track commencement point. Each point at which a change of Mach number or flight level is requested must be specified as geographical coordinates in latitude or longitude, followed in each case by the abbreviation "NAT" and the code letter assigned to the track.

For flights operating along the whole length of one of the organized tracks, estimates are only required for the commencement point of the track.

For flights planning on random route segments at or south of 70°N, the requested Mach number and flight level should be specified at either the last domestic reporting point prior to ocean entry or the oceanic control area boundary.

The route of the flight should be specified in terms of the following significant points:

1. The last domestic reporting point prior to oceanic entry point;

2. The oceanic control area boundary entry point;

3. Significant points formed from the intersection of half or whole degrees of latitude with meridians spaced at intervals of 10° of longitude from the Greenwich Meridian to 70°W;

4. The oceanic control area boundary exit point;

5. The first domestic reporting point after ocean exit.

Each point at which a change of Mach number or flight level is requested must be specified and followed in each case by the next route segment expressed as geographical coordinates in latitude and longitude.

Estimates are required for all significant points listed in 1, 3 and 5 above. Estimates may also be required for points listed in 2 and 4.

Note: FIR boundary estimates are only required in flight plans for flights operating through Shanwick, Santa Maria and New York FIRs. Details in the MNPSA Operations Manual should be noted and complied with before filing.

---

[2] International Air Transport Association (*see* Glossary, Page 340)

Operation of Transponders

Unless otherwise directed by ATC, pilots of aircraft equipped with SSR transponders flying in NAT flight information regions shall operate transponders continuously in Mode A Code 2000, except that the last assigned code shall be retained for a period of 30 minutes after entry into NAT airspace.

Note: This procedure does not affect the use of the special purpose codes (7500, 7600 and 7700) in cases of unlawful interference, radio failure, interception or emergency.

Special Procedures for In-Flight Contingencies

The following procedures are from the MNPSA Ops Manual and are intended for guidance only. Although all possible contingencies cannot be covered, they provide for such cases as inability to maintain assigned level due to weather, aircraft performance, or pressurization failure. They are applicable primarily when rapid descent, turnback, or both are required. The pilot's judgment shall determine the sequence of actions taken, with regard to the specific circumstances.

General Procedures

If an aircraft is unable to continue flight in accordance with its air traffic control clearance, a revised clearance shall whenever possible be obtained prior to initiating any action, using the radio telephony distress (Mayday) or urgent (pan) signal, as appropriate.

If prior clearance cannot be obtained, an air traffic control clearance shall be obtained at the earliest possible time and, in the meantime, the aircraft shall broadcast its position (including the ATS route designator or the track code as appropriate) and intentions on 121.5 MHz at frequent intervals until air traffic control clearance is received.

Special Procedures
Initial Action

If unable to comply with the above provisions, the aircraft should leave its assigned route or track by turning 90° to the right or left whenever this is possible. The direction of the turn should be determined by the position of the aircraft relative to any organized route or track system (e.g., whether the aircraft is outside, at the edge of, or within the system), the levels allocated to adjacent routes or tracks, and if appropriate, terrain clearance.

Subsequent Action

An aircraft able to maintain its assigned level should:

1. if above FL290, climb or descend 1,000 feet;
2. if below FL290, climb or descend 500 feet;
3. if at FL290, climb 1,000 feet or descend 500 feet, while acquiring and maintaining in either direction a track laterally separated by 30 NM from its assigned route or track.

An aircraft not able to maintain its assigned level should start its descent while turning to acquire in either direction a track laterally separated by 30 NM from its assigned route or track. For subsequent level flight, a level should be selected which differs from those normally used by 1,000 feet if above FL290, or by 500 feet if below FL290.

Procedures for Loss of Navigational Capability

The following guidance is offered to those aircraft with only two operational LRNS's:

1. **One system fails before takeoff.**
   The pilot should consider:

   a. Delaying departure if timely repair is possible;

   b. Planning on the special routes which have been recommended for use by aircraft suffering partial loss of navigation capability. (The routes are listed in the MNPSA Ops Manual.) Subject to the following conditions:

   - sufficient navigation capability remains to meet the MNPS (Minimum Navigational Performance Standards), and the requirements in Annex 6 Part I Chapter 7 can be met by relying on short range navaids;

   - a revised flight plan is filed with the appropriate ATS unit;

   - an appropriate ATC clearance is obtained.

   c. Obtaining a clearance above or below MNPS airspace.

2. **One system fails before the oceanic boundary is reached.**
   The pilot will have to consider:

   a. Landing at a suitable aerodrome before the boundary, or returning to the aerodrome of departure.

b. Diverting by the special routes indicated in 1.b. above, subject to the same conditions.

c. Obtaining a reclearance above or below MNPS airspace.

3. **One system fails after the OCA boundary is crossed.**

Once the aircraft has entered oceanic airspace, the pilot should normally continue to operate the aircraft in accordance with the oceanic clearance already received, appreciating that the reliability of his total navigation system has been significantly reduced.

a. The pilot should, however:

- Assess the prevailing circumstances (e.g., performance of the second system, remaining portion of the flight in MNPS airspace, etc.);

- Prepare a proposal to ATC with respect to prevailing circumstances (e.g., request above or below MNPS airspace, turnback, obtain clearance to the special routes, etc.);

- Advise and consult with ATC as to the most suitable action;

- Obtain appropriate clearance prior to any deviation from oceanic clearance;

b. When the flight continues in accordance with its original clearance (especially if the distance ahead within MNPS airspace is considerable), the pilot should begin a special monitoring program:

- To take special care in the operation of the remaining system, taking into account that the routine method of error checking is no longer available; and

- To check the main and standby compass systems against the available information.

c. To check the performance record of the remaining equipment, and if doubt arises regarding the performance and/or reliability, the pilot should consider:

- attempting visual sighting of other aircraft or their contrails which may provide a track indication;

- calling the appropriate OAC to obtain information on aircraft adjacent to the pilot's estimated position; and/or calling on VHF to establish contact with such aircraft (preferably same track/level), obtaining from them information which could be useful (drift, magnetic heading, wind details).

4. **The remaining system fails after entering MNPS airspace** (or the remaining system gives an indication of degradation of performance, or neither system fails completely but the system indications diverge widely and the defective system cannot be determined).

a. The pilot should:

- notify ATC;

- make best use of procedures specified above relating to attempting visual sightings and establishing contact on VHF with adjacent aircraft for useful information;

- keep a special look-out for possible conflicting aircraft, and make maximum possible use of exterior lights;

b. If no instructions are received from ATC within a reasonable period consider:

- climbing or descending 500 feet if below FL290;

- climbing or descending 1,000 feet if above FL290;

- climbing 1,000 feet or descending 500 feet if at FL290;

- broadcasting action on 121.5 MHz;

- and advising ATC as soon as possible.

5. **Complete failure of FMCS**

A characteristic of the Flight Management Computer System is that the computer element might fail, and thus deprive the aircraft of steering guidance and the indication of position relative to Cleared Track, but the raw outputs of the IRS/OSS (Lat/Lon; Drift and Ground speed) would be left unimpaired. A typical drill to minimize the effects of a total flight management computer failure is suggested below. It requires the carriage of a suitable plotting chart (Note the AERAD Charts NAT 1 and 2 at 1:8.5 Million scale; the Jeppesen Charts AT (H/L) 1 and 2 at 1:9.6 Million; and the Jeppesen North/Mid Atlantic INS Plotting Chart (1:8.75 Million) are considered suitable for this purpose.)

a. Draw the cleared route on charts, extract mean true tracks between waypoints (Note: this could be done before flight).

b. Use the IRS/OSS outputs to adjust heading to maintain mean track and to calculate ETAS.

c. At interval of not more than 15 minutes plot position (Lat/Lon) on chart and adjust heading to regain track.

Note: Where large wind changes cause frequent fluctuations in track and ground speed, the aircraft position should be plotted more frequently.

Managing Errors

Procedures to manage errors should be utilized throughout the flight. Error management is discussed in detail in Chapter 16.

Conducting the Flight in the MNPSA

Leaving the Ramp

If INS systems are to be utilized for the flight, the aircraft must not be moved prior to the NAV mode being initiated, otherwise inertial navigation systems must be realigned. In this event, the aircraft should be relocated where it will not block the gate position or otherwise interfere with airport traffic while the realignment is being carried out.

After leaving the ramp, INS ground speeds should be checked (a significantly erroneous reading may indicate a faulty or less reliable unit). A check should be made on the malfunction codes while the aircraft is stopped, but after it has taxied at least part of the way to the takeoff position, any significant ground speed indications while stationary may indicate a faulty unit such as a tilted platform. GPS speed and direction indications should be checked unless such equipment is inhibited from providing a speed indication until the aircraft is airborne. GPS present position coordinates should be checked before takeoff as well.

While on Airways

If the initial part of the flight is conducted along airways, the airways facilities should be used as the primary navigational aids and the aircraft navigation systems monitored, in order to ascertain which system is giving the most accurate performance.

ATC Oceanic Clearance

Where practicable, two flight crewmembers should listen to and record every ATC clearance and both agree that the recording is correct. Any doubt should be resolved by requesting clarification from ATC.

If the ATC Oceanic Clearance is identical to the flight-planned track, it should be drawn on the plotting chart and verified by the other pilot.

If the aircraft is cleared by ATC on a different track from that flight-planned, it is strongly recommended that a new **master document** be prepared showing the details of the cleared track. Overwriting of the existing flight plan can cause difficulties in reading the waypoint numbers and the new coordinates. For this purpose, a pro-forma should be carried with the flight documents. One flight crewmember should extract track and distance data from the appropriate reference source and this should be checked by another crewmember. If necessary, a new plotting chart may be used on which to draw the new track. The new document(s) should be used for the oceanic crossing. If the subsequent airways section of the flight corresponds to that contained in the original flight plan, it should be possible to revert to the original **master document** at the appropriate point.

Experience suggests that when ATC issues a reclearance involving re-routing and new waypoints, there is a consequent increase in the risk of errors being made. Therefore, this situation should be treated virtually as the start of a new flight, and the procedures employed with respect to copying the ATC reclearance, amending the **master document**, loading and checking waypoints, extracting and verifying flight plan information, tracks and distances, etc., and the preparation of a new chart should be identical to the procedures employed at the beginning of a flight.

Strict adherence to the above procedures should minimize this risk. However, cockpit management should be such that one pilot is designated to be responsible for flying the aircraft while the amendments to the cockpit documentation and the reprogramming of the navigation systems are being carried out by the other crewmembers.

Approaching the Ocean

In the event of significant impairment of navigational capability, it should be understood by all concerned that the aircraft should not enter the MNPSA if it is no longer able to meet the navigational requirements.

Prior to entering the oceanic area, the aircraft's position should be checked as accurately as possible by means of external navigational aids, in order to ascertain the preferred aircraft navigation system to be used for the ocean crossing. This may perhaps necessitate DME/DME, DME/VOR checks at which stage navigation system errors can be determined by comparison of displayed and actual position. There are other means of carrying out such a check (e.g., flying directly over a VOR or NDB). In the event of a significant discrepancy (e.g., greater than 6 NM), the question of whether the affected navigation system should be updated may be given cautious consideration. Updating is not normally recommended where the discrepancy is less than 6 NM. If it is decided to update the system, the proper procedures should be carried out in accordance with a prepared checklist. The duration of the flight prior to the oceanic boundary and the accuracy of the external navigational facility should be taken into consideration when determining the advisability of updating the aircraft's navigation system. For example, an NDB would not be considered satisfactory for the purpose, unless care is taken to establish an accurate position overhead the facility.

The navigation system which has performed most accurately since departure should be selected for autocoupling.

In view of the importance of following the correct track in oceanic airspace, some operators advise that at this stage of the flight the third pilot or equivalent crewmember should check the clearance waypoints which have been inserted into the CDU, using source information such as the track message, when applicable.

Oceanic Boundary Position Report

Just prior to the oceanic boundary, and indeed, just before any waypoint, the present position coordinates should be monitored, recorded and verified, and the coordinates for the next waypoint monitored and verified. Thus, when the CDU alert light indicates, the crew should get ready to note and record the aircraft's present position on the **master document**. This should be verified against the current effective clearance on the master document. The waypoint number on the master document should be annotated with the appropriate symbol to indicate that it has in fact been verified.

Reaching an Oceanic Waypoint

As soon as the waypoint alert light illuminates, the following checks should be carried out:

1. Check the POS coordinates for each navigation system against the cleared route in the master document.

2. Check the next two waypoints in each navigation system against the master document.

3. When overhead the waypoint, check the distance to the next waypoint, confirm that the aircraft turns in the correct direction and takes up a new heading and track appropriate to the leg to the next waypoint.

4. Before transmitting the position report to ATC, verify the waypoint coordinates against the master document and those in the steering CDU.

5. After the ATC position report has been sent, the POS of the aircraft should be plotted (approximately 10 minutes after the waypoint and midway between waypoints to confirm correct tracking).

6. At this stage, the crew should be particularly alert in maintaining SELCAL watch for possible ATC follow-up to the position report.

Routine Monitoring

It is important to remember that there are a number of ways in which the autopilot may unobtrusively become disconnected from the command mode, therefore regular checks of correct engagement should be made.

Although it is common practice to display DIS/TIME, it is recommended that the navigation system coupled to the autopilot should display the present position coordinates throughout the flight. If these are then plotted on the master chart at approximately 20-minute intervals, they will provide confirmation at regular intervals that the aircraft is tracking in accordance with its ATC clearance. Distance-to-go information should be available on the instrument panel as previously mentioned, while the waypoint alert light provides a reminder of the imminence of the waypoint.

If, as an alternative, position check and verification is being made both at each waypoint and 10 minutes after each waypoint, then an additional plot 20 minutes later may perhaps be considered counter-productive as a normal routine. Even so there may be circumstances (e.g., when the flight is down to one system only) that justify the procedure.

The navigation system not being used to steer the aircraft should display cross-track distance (XTK) and track angle error (TKE). These should be monitored, with XTK being displayed on the HSI where feasible.

Where there is a discrepancy between the information provided by two navigation systems, the procedures detailed in the system operating handbook under the heading "Method of determining which system is faulty" should be applied.

Approaching Landfall

When the aircraft is approaching the first landfall navaid, it should acquire the appropriate inbound radial as soon as the flight crew is confident that the landfall navaid is providing reliable navigation information. The aircraft should then be flown to track, by means of radio navigation, overhead the facility which thus becomes the primary navigational guidance after leaving the oceanic area (e.g., for "direct" clearance overland). Consideration should be given to updating the navigation system overhead the landfall fix, using the appropriate procedures from a checklist.

Monitoring During Distractions from Routine

Training and drills should ensure that minor emergencies or interruptions to normal routine are not allowed to distract the crew to the extent that the navigation system is mishandled.

If during flight the autopilot is disconnected (e.g., because of turbulence), care must be taken when the A/P is re-engaged to ensure that the correct procedure is followed. If the system in use sets a specific value for the boundary of automatic capture, the cross-track indications should be monitored to ensure recapture of the programmed flight path.

Avoiding Confusion Between Magnetic and True

To cover all navigation requirements, some airlines now produce flight plans giving both magnetic and/or true tracks (courses). However, especially if crews are changing to a new system, there is a risk that at some stage (e.g., partial system failure, reclearances, etc.), confusion may arise in selecting the correct values. Operators should therefore devise drills which

will reduce this risk, as well as ensuring that the subject is covered during training.

Crews who decide to check or update their long-range navigation systems by reference to VORs should remember that in the Canadian Northern Control Area, VORs are not aligned with reference to magnetic north.

Navigation in the Area of Compass Unreliability

Note: Full coverage of this subject, including the provision of runway headings in grid is beyond the scope of this document. The following should therefore be considered as general guidance only.

In the above area, basic INS operation requires no special procedures, but most operators feel it is desirable to retain an independent heading reference in case INS failure occurs. There are various possible ways of doing this, dependent on the instrumentation fix.

See the discussion in Chapter 4 for a better understanding of navigation in areas of compass unreliability.

Altimetry becomes very important during descent.

The **transition level**, or **transition altitude**, the altitude where the altimeter setting changes from **QNE** (altimeter setting 29.92" or 1013 millibars or hectopascals) to **QNH**, varies considerably throughout the world. Transition altitude over Paris, France is 4,000 feet; in the U.S. it is 18,000 feet; and in the NAT it is 6,000 feet. The pilot must be alert for this difference, consulting approach charts and ATIS broadcasts (in some areas) for this information.

Some locations give altimeter settings as both **QNH** (altimeter reads field elevation at touchdown) and as **QFE** (altimeter reads height above touchdown point, or zero at touchdown).

QNH and QFE confusion can easily get the pilot in lots of trouble. A good example of this was related in the AAIB Bulletin from the U.K. CAA: The pilot of an aircraft en route from Teesside Airport to Leeds/Bradford received the landing information from Radar Approach Control which included the QFE of 983 mb. The pilot requested confirmation and the controller repeated both the QNH 1008 and QFE as 983. The controller then cleared the aircraft to "descend to 3,500 feet on the QNH." The pilot read the clearance back as "descend to 300 feet on 998." This was not noticed by the controller who later recleared the aircraft to 1,900 feet on the QFE of 983. After the pilot's confirmation of arrival at 1,900 feet, another clearance was issued for "further descent at 5 DME with the procedure, contact tower 120.3." The pilot read back only the frequency, then called the tower and received permission to continue and subsequently, permission to land. This was not acknowledged nor was any further contact with the aircraft established. The aircraft was found in trees near a ridge less than two miles from and nearly aligned with the runway. The altimeter sub scale (Kollsman window) was set to the QNH value, causing the aircraft to be flying 15 mb or 445 ft. lower than the pilot thought he was. The QNH-QFE confusion and improper readback technique were cited as contributing to the accident.

Note: One Bar (or 1,000 mb) of pressure is equal to 0.98692 Atmospheres or 0.98692 x 29.92 = 29.53 in. Hg. Since, as pilots, we know that 1" Hg equals about 1,000 feet of altitude, then it can be calculated that there are about 34 mb pressure change per 1,000 feet of altitude.

North Atlantic Procedures— An Example Flight

Sample Trip: FLT 894 IAD-CDG-GVA, a real flight as described by Captain W. Van Wormer. Refer to Figure 8-3 for the computer printout, and Figure 8-4 for the route chart.

Route Planning

To file the flight plan we need the proposed ETD, just as in a domestic flight plan. In addition we need "EET" for the significant points en route. (**Estimated Enroute Time**—the estimated elapsed time after T/O).

Why the change in the international flight plan to EET from ETA? Probably because it is easier to update the flight plan if there is a delay in the takeoff time (a common problem).

The estimate for the MNPSA boundary is extremely important because the aircraft will leave the radar environment and have to rely on **the Mach Number Technique**. For the nonradar portion of the flight, the aircraft will hold a specific assigned Mach number.

Now the crew must verify, by plotting the route assigned on charts, that the computer flight plan agrees with the real world. Make sure that there are no gaps in the route!

The track message must be checked against the flight plan also, especially since the track message creates routing which changes twice daily. There will never be charts of the tracks, so the crew must build its own chart for the flight. This plotting chart will be unique to this flight and may become the master flight deck document.

After the routing is charted, occasionally a new routing is issued after departure. Then the entire oceanic chart must be reworked on the pilot's lap clipboard, making it a pretty good idea to plot all active tracks on the chart before departure. A reroute on the tracks may also generate a new European routing, just to add to the crew's in-flight workload.

Track Planning

A crew doing flight planning may contact the Oceanic Planner at each region if concern exists as to whether a planned flight is likely to be one that fits with their traffic flow. When flight planning across a track (for example: going from northern Europe to the Caribbean crosses east-west tracks), the probability of getting a desirable clearance may be in question. This may be discussed with the Oceanic Planner in the region where the route crosses tracks. The Oceanic planner can look at track loading estimates and predict the probability of getting a track-crossing clearance at a particular al-

Aircraft:	Boeing 767	Empty Weight	178,000
		Payload	44,000
		Landing Weight	237,900
		Burn, lbs.	63,200
		Fuel Burn in U.S. Gallons	10,533
		Taxi Weight	301,100
Route:	Nautical Ground Miles	3,423	Average Wind PO86
	Nautical Air Miles	2,860	
	Total Air Time	06:33	
	Flight Level 330 for the first portion, climb as weight decreases, final cruise altitude 370		
Domestic Routing:	SWANN V268 BROSS DIRECT ODD J42 RBV J62 ACK DIRECT BRADD NA83 YYT		
International Routing:	Track Y		
European Routing:	UH111 CAN MERUE TRANSITION CDG		

Figure 8-3. Computer printout for sample trip Flight 894 IAD-CDG-GVA

Figure 8-4. Plotted arcs showing 2-hour, single-engine 767 distances to rim alternates of EGCC, BIKF and CYJT

titude and time. If the crew is not utilizing an international flight service provider (agent), phone numbers for oceanic planners may be available from the ATC facility when the flight plan is filed.

PRMS—Preferred Route Message

Before NAT tracks are "built" every 12 hours, the major service users (airlines and others) send a PRM to Gander and Shanwich by AFTN message to advise them (the service providers) of what routings would be optimum for the service users (considering wind aloft, etc.).

Preflight

Now with the route checked, the fuel checked, accuracy and gross error checks planned (*see* Chapter 16), and the flight plan verified, the preflight can begin. Because the aircraft is about to fly 2,000 NM over water, the preflight is different than it is for a domestic flight. On the 767, each alternate flight instrument source is checked. The ADFs are checked because many northern Canadian airways are NDB airways. In Europe, the ADF is still a common enroute navaid. Worldwide, the NDB system is still in common use. The engine oil is serviced to a higher level than for a domestic flight. Also, the minimum equipment list is different for an international flight. There are some differences between eastbound and westbound flight MELs (APU required eastbound). The oxygen system pressure is required to be higher for an international flight leg.

The reason for all of these differences is the longer distances between airports to be used for enroute alternates, and the fact that the weather on the North Atlantic is hard to predict.

ETOPS Planning

Since the 767 has only two engines we will operate under the EROPS system of rules ("Engines Running Or Pilots Swimming"). The latest version of these rules is called ETOPS, which is found in Advisory Circular 121-42A, "Extended Range Operations with Two Engine Airplanes."

This means that, for normal operation the flight must be within a specified distance from a **suitable airport** at all times. The flight must also be within a specified distance from an **adequate airport** at all times. (**Adequate** for the aircraft, **suitable** WX for operations—AC 121-42A also specifies the criteria for adequate and suitable airports.) This rule is imposed only on two-engine aircraft, not on the three- and four-engine aircraft. Those crews are not even required to carry approach plates for the enroute alternate airports. With the present reliability level of jet engines, engine failure is a rare occurrence. A more likely reason to divert is a system problem (pressurization, fire, smoke, passenger medical etc.).

This particular flight has three "rim" alternates specified by the dispatcher. They are Stephanville (CYJT), Keflavik (BIKF), and Manchester (EGCC) (*see* Figure 8-4). In the event an engine failure occurs, the crew is obligated to go directly to the closest **rim alternate**. The three chosen alternates allow flight along track "Y" without ever being beyond 825 NM of a suitable alternate. The distance 825 NM is significant. It is the distance the 767 can fly in still air in 120 minutes on one engine.

This 120-minute time is only allowed for operators who can show an acceptable engine failure rate. All of the engine shutdowns are reported to the FAA in order to establish an engine shutdown rate. All diversions are also recorded and a detailed report submitted.

In the initial stages of operation for a new airline or a new aircraft type, the FAA will allow only a 60-minute diversion time (single engine). With service experience, and a good record, an application is made to extend the time to 90 and 120 minutes, and finally 180 minutes. With the 180-minute rule in effect, the Pacific becomes a two-engine aircraft area. Looking at the effect on the Atlantic operation, 120-minute rule allows the entire track system to be used. If only the 90-minute rule is in effect, only the more northern tracks are available.

Takeoff and Enroute Alternates

Now the crew should review the enroute alternates. First, they look at the need for a takeoff alternate. The takeoff alternate is necessary if the weather is below landing limits at the takeoff airport, in which case the weather at one or more airports within 350 NM must have landing limits. If the engine fails on takeoff the crew is obligated to proceed to the selected takeoff alternate. (Nearest in point of time) For this flight, the crew needs to consider the weather at BWI, PHL, ACY, PIT, EWR, JKF, CLE, and BDL.

My technique is to list the possible alternates in order of distance. Start at the first alternate and check the weather, keep going out in distance until a suitable alternate is found. What is needed is a **suitable airport**.

This means checking NOTAMs, weather forecasts, and using all available information to make the decision (check WX trend and amended FCST, as well).

In selecting an alternate, both en route and for destination, consider the number and type of approaches, weather forecast at time of arrival, NOTAMs, FDC NOTAMs, and passenger handling. Enroute diversions may be caused by a passenger medical emergency. How should the captain determine the best alternate in point of time for this problem? Note that the regulations do not address this problem. Both time and available medical facilities must be considered. However, in the case of an in-flight fire, the crew should be looking to be on the ground as soon as possible. Airport facilities would be nice to have, but any runway long enough to land on would be adequate. After landing, in the case of fire, the crew should keep in mind that the direction the aircraft is parked, with reference to the wind, may partially determine the extent of injuries.

With METAR and TAF reports, what direction is the wind given, true or magnetic? No problem—true is the correct answer. Don't forget variation: in the Canadian Maritimes, the variation is between 22° and 28° west, and goes above 80° in other parts of the north. This area is also noted for poor weather and one can expect to see problems with maximum crosswind component. Also, with reference to single-engine operation, with a diversion due to engine failure, chances are 50/50 that the dead engine will be on the upwind side. In that case, would you like to change your definition of the term, "**critical engine**"? Remember also that the maximum crosswind was demonstrated by a test pilot on a dry runway. This will probably not be our case.

Loading the Nav Systems

Now, the crew is ready to go to the airplane and load the Nav system. The first step is to load the present position. Remember, all of the operational problems in this area have been due to pilot error (finger trouble). If the pilot tells the computer it is in a specific location, it will believe him (dutiful and dumb). But once the computer is airborne and starts to search for VOR/DME stations to update its position, our credibility is lost. If the computer cannot find the stations it has loaded in its database (which is essentially a computer map of the world), it is programmed to assume that the computer has failed. In this case, the computer shuts down ("if you lie to me, I won't play"). On the 767, it is not possible to restart an IRS (Internal Reference System) in flight. The aircraft must land to tell the IRS where it is! The passenger announcement for this unscheduled landing may be a real PR classic!

The routing is loaded next. All of the airports for this flight with their SIDs and STARs are in the database. Also, all of the high altitude airways, the VOR and NDB stations are stored, along with most of the five-letter identifier intersections. Two pilots must always be involved in the route loading. Each oceanic waypoint (Wpt) must be created (lat/lon) and loaded in the computer. A typical waypoint would be 56° North, 30° West. To load this into the computer, the format must be N56W030. Note that, for this particular computer system, the letter "N" must precede, and that "W030" is the only format the computer understands for longitude. The longitude must have three digits, probably to decrease the chance of finger trouble error. Only two digits are needed for degrees of latitude.

As the computer loads the Wpt we created, it assigns a waypoint number. Waypoint 1 may not be the first pilot-created waypoint. If the departure had a waypoint created by the computer, it may have been assigned Waypoint 1. This would cause the computer to assign the name Waypoint 2 to the first "hand-made" waypoint. Each time a waypoint is created, the leg distance must be checked against the flight plan distance. This is one of the gross error checks discussed later in Chapter 16, and it has been shown to be very effective to alert the crew to a position error.

From Launch to Coast-Out Point

Finally, we are out of the gate and under way! The computer agrees with the world and we have been cleared on course. One of the duties in operating a computer Nav system, is to verify the system accuracy. Flight over a known geographic point, checking the computer position against the charted position will be all that is necessary. We need to use something outside the aircraft to check the computer. Never use any portion of the computer to check itself. That would be too much like writing your own fitness report! VOR, DME and ADF may be used as outside sources to make an **accuracy check** (*see* also the discussion in Chapter 16).

The finished check must be logged on the plotting chart along with the time. *Always log the time for everything!* It is a fact that all the pilot has to defend decisions made on any flight is the flight log and operations manuals. If an error should creep in, the crew must find it as soon as possible and correct it. Normal operating procedures have been established to give the crew all the rope they need to make a safety net, or a noose—your choice!

In MNPS Airspace

Next, prior to entry into MNPS airspace, the crew must make a **gross error check**. This is done by showing on the **master document** plotting chart (Figure 8-4) that the aircraft is going as cleared to the first waypoint. All available methods must be used to assure that the aircraft is going as cleared. In addition, notice in Figure 8-4 that the crew has complied with the requirement to update the ETA for each next waypoint after giving a position report ETA and conducted another gross error check, as described earlier on Page 168 (items 1.–6. under "Reaching an Oceanic Waypoint"). A glance at this master document indicates the flight must be somewhere between 24°W and waypoint 4 (20°W), because the gross error checks for waypoints 4 and 5 have not yet been made.

As the aircraft gets into the MNPS airspace, the crew again confirms the position and plots it on the plotting chart. This is typically done at a point 2° longitude and again at 5° longitude beyond the last waypoint. At these points, the crew checks the estimate for and heading to the next waypoint, comparing them with the readouts from the IRS (**gross error check**). These plotting exercises verify that the aircraft is flying the cleared routing.

Considering the fact that the aircraft is in a nonradar environment for most of the oceanic portion of the flight, good position estimates and a constant Mach speed are very important.

All position reports are done on the HF radio, or by VHF or UHF transmissions to a satellite, and will continue to be until **ADS** becomes a reality—**Automatic Dependent Surveillance**, where the aircraft's position and other data are sent every few seconds by digital data transfer through a satellite to the ground controller. If there is significant sunspot activity, HF communications are not easy. Besides the normal background noise on HF, crews must expect to have difficulty finding a "blank space" to transmit in. Most of the traffic will be trying to use the same frequencies. When the oceanic clearance is given, it includes a primary HF frequency and a secondary frequency. Even this may not be enough. At times, the only way to do this may be a relay on the VHF to another aircraft who will transmit the position report on HF or VHF to the oceanic control center.

In-Flight Emergencies

On this portion of the flight, we are as isolated as it is possible to get in today's environment! If any deviation from the planned flight is necessary, there will be a delay to get an amended clearance. Take the example of an ngine failure: we need to go direct to the rim alternate now, if it is still suitable. Where does the crew go to get updated weather information? Back to the HF! The name of the continuous weather broadcast is **VOLMET**. The listings will show the station transmitting and the time (Reference each hour, i.e., H + 15) of the broadcast for the station concerned. Only one problem: if the crew misses the report, or a part of it, it may be 30 minutes or more before the report is transmitted again. Therefore, it is important that the VOLMET reports for the rim alternates be kept updated continuously while in flight.

VOLMETs give METARs, TAFs, and SIGMETs. Shannon VOLMET is synthesized and continuous. New York and Gander are human voices, thirty minutes each on common frequencies, alternating. One of these stations, notably New York, may miss their update, in which case nothing is heard. It is a good idea to keep updated about the WX at alternates in case this happens. Alternatively, WX is available from the oceanic controller.

Let's assume an engine failure. Below are the considerations in order of action.

1. Secure the engine.

2. Turn off course (we probably can't hold altitude).

3. Broadcast a Mayday on 121.5 (tells other ACFT of the problem).

4. Maintain drift-down airspeed/Mach number.

5. At 30 NM off course, turn parallel to the track until a constant altitude can be maintained.

6. Maintain an altitude not in use in the tracks and fly direc to the rim alternate.

7. Advise ATC as soon as possible and get an amended clearance!

8. Coordinate the crew for the arrival—plan a "pocket" alternate. (A **pocket alternate** is a second-level alternate, planned for in case the alternate becomes unsuitable.)

Would you agree that pre-planning for this possibility is the only way to assure success in this maneuver? No doubt for me!

Nearing the Coast-In Point

Now let us assume that there were no problems and the aircraft is approaching the European gateway (coast-in point). This will usually be within range of a VOR/DME. The crew will tune the VOR manually and watch the computer update our position, if it is necessary. On a typical trip, after flying over 2,000 NM on computed information, the update in position will be less than ¼ NM! Most of the time an update will be .1 NM, or no change at all.

Approaching the European side of the ocean, a new airways clearance will be issued. Watch the ATC grammar and format. For instance, "Cleared Standard Routing." What does this mean to a pilot on his first trip? Also note that the charts show the "Center" boundary lines; over here they are called "FIRs" (Flight Information Regions). These regions are usually country boundaries. Watch for the speech accent problems, and if in doubt, ask.

Arrival

Upon arrival, especially at Paris (CDG), the ATIS can be hopeless! First the report is read in French, followed by English. When receiving the altimeter setting, look out: it is in millibars or hectopascals, not inches! They also give **QFE** for each runway in operation and **QNH**! Some operators use QFE (Altimeter reads zero at touchdown) while most operators are looking for the QNH (Altimeter reads field elevation, MSL, on landing). The sequence of the report is also different from the U.S. format. Practice is the only way to handle this problem. Never feel that a partially understood clearance can be flown. Always clarify.

Watch the wording on the approach clearance. "Turn right heading 050 report established" may mean turn to intercept the final approach course, which is 050°. On one recent flight, this clearance was a clearance to intercept the final approach course. In the U.S., we would assume the same wording to be understood as "Report established on the heading 050"!

The landing was perfect and all the passengers clapped! Probably because they were glad to have the flight over. Now the crew must deal with customs and immigration…do you have a French Visa…or do you plan to sleep in the airplane and not go "ashore"?

9: Flying in Europe

Flying the European continent has some differences from other international flight. This chapter begins by describing the system, then describes an actual flight. It was prepared by Alberto Bernabeo, Ph.D., who is an aerospace engineer as well as an active charter and corporate pilot, rated in the BE 300 and 1900, C-500 and 550, and the DO 328.

European Air Traffic Flow Management

Organization and Procedures

It is the task of the Central Flow Management Unit (CFMU), administered by **EUROCONTROL**, to operate the Real Time Management of the flow of air traffic throughout the area of the member states of the European Civil Aviation Conference (ECAC). Its goal is to optimize the use of airspace, thus minimizing departure delays.

This system is entirely automated. It receives and processes all flight plans and repetitive flight plans submitted by aircraft operators departing from any airport in the world and operating into, over, or out of the CFMU area of responsibility. Through its computer program it will also assign takeoff slots whenever capacity of the European Air Traffic Services so requires, due to causes such as enroute restrictions, excessive traffic, destination airport capacity, etc. The EUROCONTROL countries are shown in Figure 9-1. (*See also the sidebar, Page 179, listing common acronyms used in European flight operations.*)

Used efficiently, the Central Flow Management Unit can be of great assistance to smaller airline operators and corporate crews, since slots are allocated strictly on a "first come first served" basis, with no priority given to a B747 from a major carrier over a corporate jet or turboprop. However, it is important that pilots must be fully familiar with the idiosyncrasies of the system and have a proactive approach to filing flight plans, and following through on slot requests.

All this means that, presently, flying in Europe requires a good knowledge of the Air Traffic Flow Management (ATFM) and its phases.[1] They are:

1. *The Strategic Phase,* defined as a period more than two days before the day of operation. Strategic activities include the coordination and promulgation by the CFMU of strategic routing schemes that are based upon strategic demand forecasts. Aircraft Operators (AO) are responsible for ensuring that flight plans are filed in accordance with any strategic routing scheme in force. Specific operating procedures governing a particular strategic routing scheme are published with the scheme.

2. *The Pre-Tactical Phase,* which is two days before the day of operation. During this phase, the ATFM plan for the day of operation is devised. The plan may include temporary adjustments to strategic routing schemes, the opening of Off-Load Routes (OLRs) and the initiation of re-routes for individual flights or particular groups of flights. Details of the plan will be published the day before the day of operation via the **ATFM Notification Message (ANM)** and/or as required, by the **ATFM Information Message (AIM)**.

3. *The Tactical Phase,* which is the day of operation. ATFM plans are executed, and where required, slots are allocated.

Flight Plan Filing Requirements

ATFM messages do not directly change or modify a flight plan. Certain ATFM messages do, however, require action by the AO to modify the flight plan. For example, any agreed change to the routing of a flight shall result in a subsequent modification of the flight plan initiated by the AO.

[1] ATFM Users Manual; EUROCONTROL Doc., 18 May 1995.

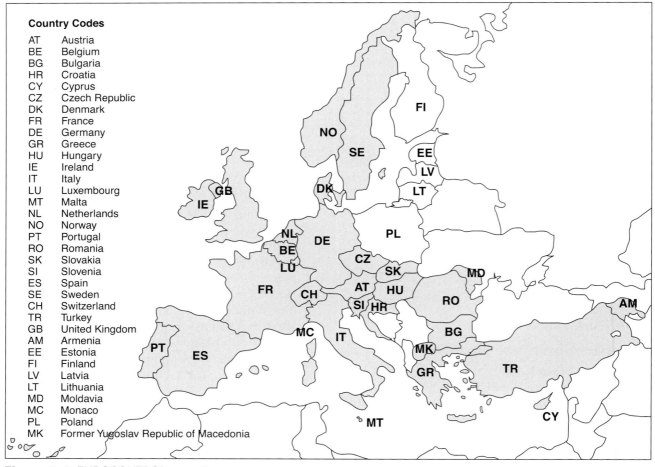

Figure 9-1. EUROCONTROL countries

Country Codes

AT	Austria
BE	Belgium
BG	Bulgaria
HR	Croatia
CY	Cyprus
CZ	Czech Republic
DK	Denmark
FR	France
DE	Germany
GR	Greece
HU	Hungary
IE	Ireland
IT	Italy
LU	Luxembourg
MT	Malta
NL	Netherlands
NO	Norway
PT	Portugal
RO	Romania
SK	Slovakia
SI	Slovenia
ES	Spain
SE	Sweden
CH	Switzerland
TR	Turkey
GB	United Kingdom
AM	Armenia
EE	Estonia
FI	Finland
LV	Latvia
LT	Lithuania
MD	Moldavia
MC	Monaco
PL	Poland
MK	Former Yugoslav Republic of Macedonia

No update of the flight plan is required to take account of delays received in a slot message. The CFMU slot allocation process for an individual flight is initiated by the filing of a flight plan. As in the U.S., filing a flight plan is therefore the first action required of an AO.

The primary ATFM rule for flight plan filing as defined in ICAO Doc. 7030 is:

"For flights likely to be subject to ATFM measures, AOs shall submit Flight Plans at least 3 hours before Estimated-Off-Block Time (EOBT)."

Every effort will be made by the CFMU to treat all flight plans in the same way. However, due to the impracticality of re-allocating a large number of departure slots at a late period, flight plans filed within three hours of EOBT may of necessity be dealt with out of sequence. This may result in such flights being more heavily penalized than flights with flight plans filed at least three hours ahead of EOBT.

The Slot Allocation Process

The slot allocation procedures are those applicable to all flights subject to ATFM departing from within a certain CFMU area, and can be extended to flights departing from FIRs immediately adjacent to the CFMU area that are planning to enter the CFMU area.

The slot allocation and slot modification process relies on an exchange of ATFM Messages between the AO, the CFMU and ATC units.

The Computer Assisted Slot Allocation (CASA) system extracts all the flights bound for a flow-controlled zone, and sequences them in the order they would have arrived at the restricted zone in the absence of any restriction. It then places the flights in slots, realizing an arrival rate in the zone requested by the restriction.

Acronyms

ATFM .... Air Traffic Flow Management

AIM .... ATFM Information Message

AMC .... Airspace Management Cell

ANM .... ATFM Notification Message

AO .... Aircraft Operators

ATM .... Air Traffic Management

ATC .... Air Traffic Control

AUPs .... Airspace Use Plans

CASA .... Computer Assisted Slot Allocation

CDRs.................. Conditional Routes

CFMU .... Central Flow Management Unit

CIS .... Cooperative Independent
Surveillance

CISINC .... Cooperative Independent
Surveillance Integrating Naviga-
tion and Communication

CNS .... Communications, Navigation and
Surveillance

CRAM.................. Conditional Route Availability
Message

ECAC .... European Civil Aviation
Conference

EOBT .... Estimated Off-Block Time

E.U. .... European Union

EUROCONTROL ... European Organisation for the
Safety of Air Navigation

FUA .... Flexible Use of Airspace

JAA...................... Joint Aviation Authorities

JAR .... Joint Aviation Requirements

NAA .... National Aviation Authorities

OLRs .... Off-Load Routes

TSAs .... Temporary Segregated Areas

On this basis, the optimum takeoff time for the flight is recalculated. It is this information, Calculated Take-Off Time (CTOT), which identifies the slot transmitted to the Aircraft Operators concerned, and to the control tower at the aerodrome of departure.

The Flexible Use of Airspace Concept Within Europe— Conditional Routes

In 1990 the European Civil Aviation Conference (ECAC) adopted an enroute strategy and European Air Traffic Control Harmonization and Integration Program. One of the most important objectives of this program is the introduction of the Flexible Use of Airspace (FUA) developed by civil and military representatives of Aircraft Operators.

The fundamental concept of the FUA is that the airspace should no longer be designated as either civil or military airspace, but should be considered as one continuum and used flexibly on a day to day basis.

The FUA concept is based on non-permanent ATS routes called **Conditional Routes (CDRs)**, **Temporary Segregated Areas (TSAs)**, and **Airspace Management Cells (AMC)** which are Manageable Restrictive or Danger Areas. Conditional Routes complement the permanent ATS route network and are divided into three categories:

1. CDR1—a permanently plannable CDR during the times published in the Enroute section of the Jeppesen Airway Manual. This route will be planned in the same way as a permanent ATS route during the times of availability.[2]

2. CDR2—a non-permanent plannable CDR. This route will be flight planned in accordance with conditions published daily in the Conditional Route Availability Message (CRAM) only.

3. CDR3—not plannable CDR. This route is usable on ATS instructions only.

TSAs and AMCs are airspaces of pre-defined dimensions within which activities require the reservation of airspace for the exclusive use of specific users during a determined period of time. The planned activity and conditions will be published daily in the national Airspace Use Plans (AUPs). The Airspace Use Plans will be published before 1400 UTC to cover the 24-hour period between 0600 UTC the following day to 0600 UTC the day after.

---

[2] Jeppesen Manuals.

New Trends and Developments

Communications in Advance, navigation and surveillance (CNS)[3] are the main functions needed for efficient air traffic management.

The proposed architecture to perform these functions, especially for areas not covered by ground stations, is based on low-elevation orbit satellites (the so called **ATM-Star** — Air Traffic Management constellation). The constellation is designed to supply the surveillance and data link capabilities of advanced secondary surveillance radar (SSR Mode S) worldwide, by means of space-based SSR. Mode S interrogators with phased array antennas will implement a Cooperative Independent Surveillance (CIS) as well as allow satellite communication and (by means of a GPS-compatible system) navigation function. Such a concept is called CISINC (Cooperative Independent Surveillance Integrating Navigation and Communication). Besides carrying definite improvements to ATM, CISINC would greatly facilitate the solution of legal, institutional and operational aspects for a medium-far-term CNS implementation (about 2005).

The CISINC design considers all traffic densities and all phases of flight: en route, terminal area, non-precision approach (excluding the CAT I, II and III landing that require ad hoc ground-based facilities). Its expected performance exceeds the ICAO specifications and recommendations. The CISINC utilizes a constellation of all identical low-orbit satellites and presents operational, technical and institutional advantages over "hybrid" systems using the present navigation and communication satellites at geostationary or high orbits.

A Few Words About Joint Aviation Authorities (JAA)[4]

The Civil Aviation Authorities of certain European countries[5] have agreed upon common comprehensive and detailed aviation requirements, referred to as the Joint Aviation Requirements (JARs). JAR will minimize Type Certification problems on joint ventures, facilitate the export and import of aviation products, make it easier for maintenance carried out in one European country to be accepted by the Civil Aviation Authority in another European country, and regulate commercial air transport operations.

The JARs are recognized by the Civil Aviation Authorities of participating countries as an acceptable basis for showing compliance with their national airworthiness codes.

At present, the JAA is simply a federation of National Aviation Authorities (NAA) with no legal authority to implement or enforce safety regulations. Its principal responsibility up to now has been to draft uniform Joint Aviation Requirements to replace individual European national standards. The JAA has adopted 21 JARs, most recently JAR-21, regarding certification procedures for aircraft, products and related parts, and JAR-FCL Parts 1 and 3 dealing with flight crew licensing.

ICAO Annex 6 has been selected as the law that provides the basic structure of JAR-OPS, (the JAR for Air Operator Certificate). The content of Annex 6 has been added to where necessary by making use of existing applicable European and U.S. regulations.

Future development of the requirements of JAR-OPS (issued the 22nd of May, 1995) will be in accordance with the JAA's Notice of Proposed Amendment (NPA) procedures. These procedures allow for the amendment of JAR-OPS to be proposed by the Civil Aviation Authority of any of the participating countries and by any organization represented on the Joint Steering Assembly.

JAA membership has grown to 27 nations in the last years, and the JAA is being solicited by more countries beyond Europe's borders for technical assistance and cooperation, including Russia, China and Canada.

---

[3] ICAO; "Aeronautical Mobile Communication Panel (AMCP)"; Third Meeting, Montreal, 7-22 April 1994.

[4] Joint Aviation Requirements; JAR-OPS 1: Commercial Air Transportation (Aeroplanes); Civil Aviation Authority, 22 May 1995.

[5] Austria, Belgium, Cyprus, Denmark, Finland, France, Germany, Greece, Iceland, Ireland, Italy, Luxembourg, Malta, Monaco, Netherlands, Norway, Poland, Portugal, Slovenia, Spain, Sweden, Switzerland and United Kingdom.

Hints for Flying in Europe

Even though flying through European States since the creation of the European Union (E.U.) is quite similar to flying throughout the U.S. (i.e., virtually there are no boundaries), pilots must consider the registration of their aircraft and the origin of their pilot certificates. Below are some important considerations to note:

1. Flying an N-registered airplane requires a U.S. pilot license. No pilot is allowed to fly an N-registered aircraft unless he or she is U.S.-licensed.

2. In some places the operator (pilot) is required to show evidence of the kind of operation being conducted in order to obtain duty-free fuel; otherwise the crew may expect to pay as much as $5 per gallon of JET A1. Remember that some countries' Customs want you to go to their office and fill the appropriate form (to be then submitted to the fueling company). You may even have to take a ride to reach their office, which may be miles from your parking position. Always call in advance to be certain about customs office hours. Many refueling companies have their normal duty hours; if fuel is needed outside of office hours, the crew is expected to pay a off-duty fee both for the fueling company and/or for customs (in some places it can be up to $100 for a Citation).

   Before attempting a landing, call and ask if they accept credit cards—some companies want cash and it could be embarrassing to land short of fuel in a place where one cannot buy any!

3. If a pilot wishes to rent an aircraft registered in any country within the E.U., he or she will need the pilot license of the country of registration in order to fly it solo.

4. Be prepared to pay landing and takeoff fees (even parking fees) at most European airports. An airplane such as a Citation may pay as much as $500 inclusive of handling (sometimes, this barely means somebody gives assistance in the parking of your aircraft) and a one-day parking fee!

5. VFR at night is forbidden in most European countries. Be sure to check airport operating hours before attempting to land where no IFR procedure is in use. Also, double-check the phone numbers found in the Airport Directory section of Jeppesen Manuals; sometimes they are not updated.

6. When filing an IFR flight plan in Europe, the pilot needs to receive an acknowledgement from the main control center in Brussels. Sometimes, due to congestion, it can take several hours before an answer is available. And if the flight plan filed doesn't fit the airway system (many airways are one-way airways) it will be rejected. Eventually, when the flight is airborne, some controllers will allow an aircraft to short-cut (go direct), but this may happen only in the air and not through the computer system. So, be prepared to file a new flight plan if the first one is rejected.

   Remember that the air traffic control system doesn't allow off-route flight plans; it simply will reject them. If you don't want delays or have to stay awake the whole night for an answer (which can be negative), follow strictly the published routes. Be alert that during certain seasons, the control system may have Conditional Routes (CDRs—*see* Page 179) in use, and pilots are expected to follow them in order to expedite the traffic flow.

7. Many airports have strict noise abatement rules and may be closed at night. When flying at night and planning to land in certain European countries, or during foggy periods of the year (which happens often during wintertime throughout Europe and the Eastern countries), be prepared to go to the alternate. The destination airport may be closed for any number of reasons, such as for emergency purposes.

Flying Within the European Control System: An Example Flight

Now that you know the system don't be afraid to use it. There are many interesting places to visit while you are here. To help solidify the knowledge of the system presented above, you will find in the pages following, a real flight as described by Captain R. Alberto Bernabeo. (*See* Figure 9-2.)

Example Flight

I-JESO, a Cessna Citation, flying the route: **LIPE-EDDM-LKPR-LRBS-LIML.**

Route Planning

This is an early departure from Bologna, Italy (LIPE) for one of our customers in Modena (the country of Ferrari, Maserati and Lamborghini).

Our ETD is 07:30; we filed the flight plan the night before through ATC (Air Traffic Control) in Bologna. Two hours before our ETD, we need to call again to the ATC in Bologna, to make sure our flight plan has been acknowledged by EUROCONTROL in Brussels, and that there is no airway slot requirement. If there is one, we want to be sure that it fits our customer's schedule. If it does not, we need to call EUROCONTROL directly in order to get a slot as close as possible to our ETD.

When flying through Europe as an executive operator (corporate or air taxi), it becomes apparent that the new system is not as flexible as it should be. Even if we try to comply with the procedures, we need to use some tricks. For example, my suggestion is to file two separate flight plans; one with the registration number of the aircraft, *and the other using the three-letter ICAO company code with an ETD half an hour later.* The reason is intuitive: if your customer is late, or if the first flight plan is lost, or an unacceptable route is given on the earlier flight plan, go with the second one—*but remember to cancel the flight plan that is not used,* in order that other pilots may fit their flight plan into the system.

Since it's Saturday and the holiday season has already gone, not too much traffic is in the air and we may leave LIPE as planned. As it turns out, there's no arrival slot requirement at München.

Figure 9-2. The Italian Citation I-JESO, on the ramp at Milan, along with aircraft from Portugal and Germany. (*See* Figure 1-4 on Page 12 for aircraft registration country identifiers.)

The Flight

Flying over the Alps with the sun shining is wonderful; however, weather in EDDM leaves no time for appreciation of beauty, since there's fog on the ground. Our Citation II is CAT II-certified, and as we review the procedure we decide upon EDDF for our alternate, just in case we need it.

(Weather has really changed on this side of the Alps; this reminds me of a few years ago when we had to fly at night from Mälmo, in Sweden, back to Bologna and it was foggy all over Europe, with many airports closing their operations at 10 P.M.… But that's another story!) Our landing in EDDM was completed with success and our passengers applauded, since they had a busy schedule.

Weather will improve later today, so for our next departure we consider Oberpfaffenhoffen as our alternate only if both runways at EDDM should close; otherwise we plan to fly to Prague (LKPR) directly. Again we file a flight plan through the ATC in EDDM, and ask both for an airport slot and an airway slot. Today we are lucky again and we don't have any slot, but still the operator asks us to double-check two hours before our ETD (this is common practice).

The night before we sent a fax to a handling facility at LKPR asking for ground transportation. The airport in Prague, which is quite new, has two separate gates for general aviation and for airlines, but many times you will be parked miles from the main facilities. Therefore, coordinate in advance what you need (fuel, transportation, catering, etc.). Those at the handling facility know their job and they are very helpful, even if you have to arrange your own accommodation while in Prague. They accept major credit cards and you may find little difference in handling facilities, compared to other European countries.

Keep in mind that at this airport you may get a weather briefing with digits in meters and kilometers per hour!

The Next Day

After a night in the very nice city of Prague, we are ready to fly to LRBS (Bucharest, Romania). The procedure is the same as it was in EDDM and in LIPE, so after reviewing the route and making sure there's no slot, we are ready to fly again. Arrival in Bucharest requires a little bit of flexibility in understanding ATC communications, but other than that everything is as usual.

When on the ground they ask for a visa, and if you don't have one, you need only to pay about $30 cash at the Immigration office. This visa is valid only for one entry, so if you foresee multiple entries into the country, ask for a different kind.

The procedure to file the flight plan is as usual, and you will probably find helpful operators for this task. However, other types of communication may prove difficult here. If you have to call your operation center, for example, in Italy, your mobile phone may be inoperative and it may be some time before you have a chance to call directly. Be prepared and know your passenger's plans exactly, so that you don't lose each other in countries where it's difficult to communicate.

If you have to fly in the area during wintertime, you should be aware that some airports here are not equipped for snow removal, and it may require plowing through snow to get to the runway!

Today, weather is not of concern and since our customers arrive at the airport right on time; after passing through customs, we are ready to fly again and complete our mission.

10: International Weather

Aviation Weather Information

The acquisition and interpretation of weather information is an essential part of the preflight planning process. The successful outcome, especially of international flight, is predicated on the decisions a pilot makes with regard to the weather. Weather planning influences all aspects of flight including fuel requirements, alternative plans of action if the original cannot be completed, and safety. It is clear that competent decisions are based on the availability of adequate weather data and the ability to interpret it.

Pilots operating in the United States have little difficulty obtaining weather information. The Federal Aviation Administration (FAA), in conjunction with the National Weather Service (NWS) and private vendors, have developed a well organized method for the collection, transmission and dissemination of meteorological data. Weather information is readily accessible to pilots via telephone, VHF communications radio, personal computer, or walk-in briefing. A pilot operating outside of the United States, however, may find the search for preflight weather a frustrating experience. Although guidelines have been set by the International Civil Aviation Organization (ICAO) and the World Meteorological Organization (WMO), each member nation is free to develop its own system of dissemination. Often the systems are not well documented, and it is left to the pilot to discover reliable briefing sources.

Although the dissemination of information may be somewhat disorganized, the structure and format of the message has been agreed upon. Meteorological code has been standardized by the ICAO and WMO and is generally accepted by most member nations. Information concerning the dissemination and interpretation of international weather products is published in ICAO's *Annex 3 to the Convention on International Civil Aviation*, and Volume I of the WMO's Manual on Codes. The purpose of this chapter is to introduce this international meteorological code and the method by which weather information is disseminated throughout the world. North America (U.S. and Canada) have moved toward full adaptation of the ICAO/WMO format, with only a few differences remaining. Presently, surface reports of U.S. stations sent outside the U.S. are sent as WMO format METARs and TAFs. The present WMO decoding formats for METARs and TAFs are presented in Figures 10-3 and 10-4 at the end of the chapter.

Meteorological Code

The purpose of meteorological code is to permit the efficient transmission of large quantities of information. In the decades prior to high speed computers, meteorological information needed to be coded in an effort to reduce the number of characters transmitted by communications circuitry. The analog transfer of information was slow and the transmittal time could be reduced by reducing the size of each message. The introduction of digital signal processing reduced transmittal time, but the amount of information now handled by communication circuits has grown exponentially. It appears meteorological code is here to stay.

Although meteorological code is somewhat difficult to learn, it does have the advantage of objectivity. Each character or group of characters have a specific meaning. Coded information is unambiguous. It is a precise description of conditions that exist or that are expected to exist at some future time.

Coded meteorological reports are used to describe current or forecasted conditions. They may be made by special observers, pilots, or forecasters. A few selected reports are detailed in the following sections.

International Surface Reports (METAR)

General

Surface observations describe the state of the atmosphere as viewed by an individual at the surface of the earth. They included parameters such as surface wind, temperature and dew point, sky cover and cloud height, and weather. Surface observations are produced by specially certified individuals who have passed a course of study designed to standardize their observation method.

While the method of observing is essentially the same, there exists two different methods to code surface weather information.

Synoptic code is a numeric code used by meteorologists to transfer information from meteorological stations to mainframe computers. The computers decipher the information and plot charts with minimal human intervention. Synoptic code is difficult to interpret and has little value to the aviator.

The **meteorological aviation report (METAR)** code was developed in the 1960s and is now used worldwide. It is designed strictly for use by pilots and issued hourly by meteorological stations. METAR (pronounced mee-tar) became the standard in the United States in 1996, replacing the surface airway (SA) format of the 1940s. Rather than cover a full description of METAR encoding, an overview of this format will be provided, *noting that there are some differences between the U.S. and international formats*. Although the U.S. differences from the international format are given, it must be emphasized that pilots may expect variations from the international format *in any country*.

Reporting Type, Time and Reporting Station

The type of report depends upon weather conditions at the reporting station. A **METAR** is a routine report and is issued hourly. A special (**SPECI**) report is issued anytime weather conditions meet predetermined criteria. These criteria are established by the Meteorological Authority of each member country but are generally based on changes in wind direction, wind speed, visibility, runway visual range, precipitation or ceiling. Frequently the time of the report is omitted, but it must be reported if the observation time is more than 10 minutes from the routine observations time. All times are with reference to UTC. The reporting station is dis-

tinguished by the international **four-letter identifier**. The first one or two letters represent the country code, and the last two or three represent the observing station. (*See* Figure 1-5, "ICAO identifiers for international airports.")

Wind

The wind group follows the station identifier and is coded by a five-digit number. The first three numbers represent the wind direction in degrees true north and the last two numbers indicate the magnitude. Winds in excess of 99 knots use three numbers. An abbreviation immediately follows the wind speed to define the measured units. Wind speed can be measured in knots (KT), meters per second (MPS) or kilometers per hour (KMH). The reported wind is a ten minute average and if the conditions exceed the average by more than 10 knots, the maximum speed is reported as a gust and is appended to the wind group by a solidus (/) and the magnitude of the gust. The wind direction is coded as variable (VRB) if the direction is not steady or if the wind speed is 3 knots or less (6 knots, in the U.S.).

Visibility

Visibility reported in the U.S. METAR code differs from the international standard. International METARs report minimum surface horizontal visibility which is defined as the minimum visibility in any direction. Prevailing visibility is given in the U.S. reports and is defined as the greatest distance objects can be seen and identified throughout at least 180 degrees of the horizon circle. International METAR visibility has the potential of being consistently lower than U.S. visibility. METAR visibility is reported in meters (vs. statute miles in the U.S.) in various increments. A visibility greater than 10 kilometers is coded as 9999. Conversion from meters to statute miles is painless if one remembers that 100 m is equivalent to $\frac{1}{16}$ mile and a KM is about 0.6 mile.

Runway Visual Range

Some airports with **transmissometers** have the ability to report **runway visual range** (RVR). It is defined as the distance a pilot can see surface markings or lights along the approach end of an instrument runway. The letter "R" precedes the four number group representing the RVR value in meters (feet, U.S.). If the RVR is different for two or more runways at a particular airport, the code specifies the runway at which the RVR was measured.

Present Weather

A combination of descriptors and observed weather abbreviations are used to indicate the type of weather occurring at the reporting station. Lists of these are given below in Figures 10-1 and 10-2.

MI	shallow
BC	patches
PR	partial
DR	low drifting
BL	blowing
SH	shower(s)
TS	thunderstorm
FZ	freezing (supercooled)
RE	recent

Figure 10-1. Weather descriptors

DZ	drizzle
RA	rain
SN	snow
SG	snow grains
IC	ice crystals (diamond dust)
PE	ice pellets
GR	hail
GS	small hail and/or snow pellets
BR	mist
FG	fog
FU	smoke
VA	volcanic ash
DU	widespread dust
SA	sand
HZ	haze
PO	dust/sand whirls (dust devils)
SQ	squall
FC	funnel cloud(s) (tornado or waterspout)
SS	sandstorm
DS	duststorm

Intensities

–	light
no indicator	moderate
+	heavy

Figure 10-2. Weather abbreviations

Clouds

The coverage and height of cloud layers is coded as a set of letters and followed by three numbers. Certain limitations exist on the reporting of cloud layers, but it is sufficient to say that a maximum of four cloud layer groups may be reported. (All layers are reported in the U.S.) The cloud amount is represented by the following abbreviations:

FEW .... 1 or 2 **oktas** (eighths)

SCT .... 3 or 4 oktas

BKN .... 5 to 7 oktas

OVC .... 8 oktas

The letters VV (vertical visibility) indicate that the sky is totally obscured. Two special cloud types may also be reported: CB for cumulonimbus, and TCU for towering cumulus with significant vertical extent. Cloud base height in hundreds of feet above ground level follows the cloud amount or type. Ceilings are not explicitly indicated by any special symbology. A ceiling is considered either the lowest layer of clouds that cover ⅝ or more of the sky, or an obscuration.

The contractions CAVOK or SKC may replace visibility and cloud groups if certain conditions are met. **CAVOK** means horizontal surface visibility is 10 km or greater, no clouds are observed below 5,000 feet or below the highest minimum sector altitude (whichever is higher) and there is no cumulonimbus, precipitation, sandstorm, dust storm, shallow fog or low drifting dust, sand or snow. If there are no clouds and the term CAVOK is not appropriate, the term **SKC** will be used, meaning the sky is clear.

Temperature and Dew Point

Temperature and dew point are reported in degrees Celsius and are separated by a solidus. A negative temperature is preceded by the letter "M."

Altimeter Setting

The altimeter setting is the next four digit group and is reported in either inches of mercury (A) or hectopascals (Q). One hectopascal is equivalent to one millibar.

Trend Forecast

(Not used in U.S.)

Expected changes from current conditions are sometimes included in a trend forecast. The trend forecast is generally appended to the end of a METAR if significant changes are expected. The forecasts are valid for two hours and are preceded by the contractions BECMG (becoming) or TEMPO (temporary change). The text of the forecast uses METAR format and may include wind, visibility, weather or clouds. No significant change in the weather is coded as NO SIG.

Remarks

Supplemental information may be appended to the end of a METAR. The addition of remarks is at the discretion of the meteorological station providing the observation and is used to amplify significant conditions or warn pilots of operational hazards. Remarks warning pilots of low level wind shear, braking action on the runway, or hazardous weather not occurring at the time of the observation are a few examples.

Examples:

METAR EGLL 2300 21015KT 8000 RASH SCT012 BKN020 10/08 Q1011

Decoded: Routine observation for London Heathrow (EGLL), 2300 UTC, wind 210 degrees at 15 knots, visibility 8,000 m (5 statute miles), moderate rain showers, $3/8$-$4/8$ cloud cover with bases at 1,200 feet AGL, $5/8$-$7/8$ cloud cover with bases at 2,000 feet, temperature 10°C, dew point 8°C, altimeter setting 1011 mb.

SPECI LFPO 0625 VRB01MPS 0200 RVR 0400 FG VV003 NO SIG

Decoded: Special observation for Paris Orly (LFPO), 0625 UTC, wind variable at 1 meter per second (2 knots), visibility 200 m ($1/8$ statute miles), runway visual range 400 m, fog, sky obscured, vertical visibility 300 feet, no significant change is forecast in the weather conditions.

METAR OERK 1700 33025/G36KT 4800 SA SCT1000 27/08 Q1030 TEMPO 2400

Decoded: Routine observation for Riyadh, Saudi Arabia, 1700 UTC, wind 330 at 25 knots, gusting to 36 knots, visibility 4,800 m (3 statute miles), sandstorm, $3/8$-$4/8$ cloud cover with bases at 10,000 feet AGL, temperature 27°C, dew point 8°C, altimeter setting 1030 millibars, temporary visibility change in next two hours to 2,400 m ($1\frac{1}{2}$ statute miles).

Airborne Reports

Airborne observations made by flight crews provide in situ descriptions of weather conditions. Although they are subjective in nature by design, airborne reports provide the only source of real time information on cloud tops, icing, turbulence, wind, and wind shear.

Two methods of reporting in-flight conditions exist internationally. The United States and Canada use a format of pilot reports (PIREP) that is different from the ICAO-endorsed **aircraft reports** (**AIREP**).

Aircraft observations are classified as either routine (ARP) or special (ARS). Routine reports are provided by aircraft to supplement the limited meteorological information available over sparsely populated regions of the world. The reports are made at selected air traffic control reporting points or at specific time intervals. Special aircraft reports are made when an aircraft encounters severe turbulence, severe icing, volcanic ash, or any weather phenomena that may affect the safety of aircraft operations.

AIREPs use blocks of alpha-numeric characters to code flight information. The data follow a standard sequence starting with the type of report and followed by the flight identifier, latitude and longitude, UTC time, flight level, temperature in Celsius degrees, wind, and concluding remarks. The following examples illustrate the ease with which AIREPs are decoded.

ARP DAL71 3156N06811W 1727 F310 MS40 250/ 40KT

Decoded: Routine aircraft report, Delta Air Lines Flight 71, 31° 56' North latitude, 68° 11' West longitude, time 17:27 UTC, flight level 310, temperature -40°C, wind 250° at 40 knots.

ARS KAL007 5918NI7145W 2019 F380 MS55 280/ 115KT TB SVR CAT

Decoded: Special aircraft report, Korean Air Lines Flight 007, 59°18' North latitude, 171°45' West longitude, time 2019 UTC, flight level 380, temperature -55°C, wind 280° at 115 knots, experienced severe clear air turbulence.

Forecasts (TAFs)

Terminal Forecasts

Forecasts for specific terminal locations are essential for safe air commerce. Flight crews must have precise weather information at their destination for their planned arrival time to decide if the flight can be completed safely. Weather forecasts dictate the selection of alternate plans of action if a landing at the destination becomes impossible.

Terminal forecasts are specifically designed for aviation use and include important aeronautical parameters such as cloud cover, visibility, significant weather and wind. Groups of letters and numbers are used to represent forecast weather conditions. They may be valid for a period of time at least 9 hours in length but no more than 24 hours, and are updated frequently or amended if the previous forecast is found to be in error. The coding is similar to METARs and is known as **terminal aerodrome forecast** (TAF) code.

A **TAF** always starts with the four-letter ICAO station identifier and four numbers which represent the valid forecast period in UTC. The first two numbers represent the beginning of the forecast period and the last two represent the end of the forecast period.

Forecast weather conditions can be categorized as **prevailing** or **variable**. Prevailing conditions imply the forecast weather is expected for a majority of the period while variable conditions represent deviations from the norm. Changes in prevailing conditions are preceded by the contractions BECMG (becoming) or FM (from) indicating the type of change along with the expected time of change. Variable conditions are preceded by the contractions TEMPO (temporary) or INTER (intermittent) and show short term changes from the prevailing conditions. Occasionally, the contraction PROB will be used to indicate the probability of the weather event.

Forecast weather conditions are coded in alphanumeric character blocks that are similar to those used in METAR reports. The order of the information is the same, with wind followed by visibility, weather and cloud cover. If one or more weather elements are missing from one time period to the next, those elements are expected to remain the same.

CAVOK and SKC may be used and have the same meanings as in METAR reports. NSC (no significant clouds) is used when forecast conditions are operationally insignificant, and NSW is used when significant weather is not expected. The U.S. does not use the terms CAVOK, NSC or NSW in forecasts.

Hazard groups may be appended to the terminal forecast to indicate the potential for icing or turbulence. Each hazard group consists of a block of six numbers indicating the type of hazard (icing "6" or turbulence "5"), the intensity, base of lowest layer and thickness of layer.

The following examples demonstrate the sequence of terminal aerodrome forecasts.

LFBD 0312 VRB05KT CAVOK TEMPO 0307 0300 FG VV008 BECMG 0708 3000 BR OVC006 BECMG 0810 VRB05 CAVOK

Terminal aerodrome forecast for Bordeaux, France, valid from 0300 UTC to 1200 UTC. Prevailing conditions from 0300 UTC to 0700 UTC: Wind variable at 5 knots, CAVOK (*see* definition of CAVOK under "Clouds," Page 187). Variations from prevailing conditions indicate a temporary change between 0300 UTC and 0700 UTC to visibility 300 m ($\frac{3}{16}$ statute miles) with fog and an obscured sky, vertical visibility 800 feet.

Gradual change to new prevailing conditions between 0700 UTC and 0800 UTC to visibility 3,000 m ($1\frac{7}{8}$ statute miles) with mist, overcast cloud coverage with bases 600 feet AGL.

Gradual change to new prevailing conditions between 0800 UTC and 1000 UTC to winds variable at 5 knots and CAVOK.

```
KRDR 1717 13009KT 3200 -SN BR BKN007
OVC015 620078 FM 08 10007KT 1600 -SN BR
VV004 BECMG 1415 02008KT 3200 -SN BR
OVC015
```

Terminal aerodrome forecast for Grand Forks Air Force Base, ND, valid from 1700 UTC to 1700 UTC.

Prevailing conditions between 1700 UTC and 0800 UTC: Wind 130 at 9 knots, visibility 3,200 m (2 statute miles), light snow and mist, broken cloud coverage with bases 700 feet AGL, overcast cloud coverage with bases 1,500 feet AGL. Light icing expected from 700 feet AGL to 8,700 feet AGL. Note: the icing code (620078) is not found in most ICAO METAR documentation but is used extensively in USAF METARs.

Rapid change to new prevailing conditions at 0800 UTC: Wind 100 at 7 knots, visibility 1,600 m (1 statute mile), light snow and mist, sky obscured, vertical visibility 400 feet.

Gradual change to new prevailing conditions between 1400 UTC and 1500 UTC: Wind 020 at 8 knots, visibility 3,200 m, light snow and mist, overcast cloud cover with bases 1,500 feet AGL.

VOLMETs

The **VOLMET** is a transcribed HF radio broadcast of selected METARs, designed to keep crews updated on weather developments at locations which may be flight plan or ETOPS alternates. Although typically sent on long-distance HF radio, a few VHF stations also transmit transcribed VOLMETs.

A selected listing of VOLMET broadcasts is available on the front panel of the AT (H/L) 1 and 2 and P(H/L) 3 and 4 charts. A complete listing of VOLMET frequencies is available in the Meteorology section of the Jeppesen manual. VOLMET HF and VHF weather broadcasts are normally used to obtain desired weather information. Request for updated weather information from Berna Radio (Atlantic) or ARINC (Pacific) can be made but there are cost considerations.

ICAO Annex 3— Meteorological Services for International Air Navigation

This annex deals with the ICAO recommended meteorological system. It also sets the standard for meteorological reports and forecasts that are used in international airspace. It contains information about the network of international weather stations, weather reports, and weather forecasts.

Definitions

Aerodrome Meteorological Office. An office at an aerodrome designed to provide international meteorological services.

Aeronautical Meteorological Station. A station that makes observations and reports for international meteorological purposes.

Aircraft Observation. A weather report made by an aircraft in flight, like a PIREP.

Control Area. Airspace which is controlled airspace.

Runway Visual Range. The farthest distance a pilot on the center line of a runway can see a light or runway marking further down the runway.

World Area Forecast System and Meteorological Offices

ICAO has developed a system known as the World Area Forecast System. This is a structure in which weather information is processed and communicated between various types of weather offices around the world. These weather offices are arranged in a hierarchical order. From highest to lowest level, the offices are the World Area Forecast Centers, the Regional Area Forecast Centers, Meteorological Offices, and Meteorological Watch Offices.

The World Area Forecast Centers are the meteorological centers that first analyze weather data. These centers are concerned with weather phenomena on a very large scale. Things such as global forecasts, upper-air analyses, and upper-air winds aloft data are what these centers handle. They then distribute this information to Regional Area Forecast Centers.

Regional Area Forecast Centers are the next offices in the hierarchy. These offices receive data from the World Area Forecast Center and process it to a more specific, aviation-related degree. The regional center makes detailed and specific forecasts and charts in a standardized, plain language format that is easily read by pilots. It should be noted that the world and regional forecast offices are only found in a few countries which agree to run them.

Every contracting state should establish the next type of office, however, the Meteorological Office. This office collects observations and prepares its own local forecasts. The office can specialize in local weather services and forecasts. Participation in the World Area Forecast System, and coordination with the other two offices, is encouraged to whatever extent possible.

The final type of office in the ICAO system is the Meteorological Watch Office. This is an office that is required of any contracting state that has accepted the responsibility of providing ATC enroute services. These offices are in charge of weather that may be significant to air traffic control. They are concerned with such things as the monitoring the actual weather as compared to forecasts, and issuing SIGMETs.

Each contracting state is responsible for establishing meteorological stations at international airports. The stations may encompass whatever services the state deems necessary for air navigation. The format of the information distributed for international operations should conform with the ICAO-approved formats. In addition, the instruments and procedures used in the observations should be in accordance with the World Meteorological Organization.

AERODROME ACTUAL WEATHER – METAR AND SPECI DECODE

WORLD METEOROLOGICAL ORGANIZATION

SUPPLEMENTARY INFORMATION

WIND SHEAR — WS RWYD$_R$D$_R$

	Replaced when all runways are affected by wind shear by: WS ALLRWY
Runway designator – for parallel runways, may have **LL, L, C, R** or **RR** appended. (**L**=left; **C**=centre; **R**=right)	
RUNWAY	
Wind **S**hear	

RECENT WEATHER — REw'w'

Recent weather since previous report

Indicator of RECent weather.

PRESSURE — QP$_H$P$_H$P$_H$P$_H$

QNH in whole hectopascals rounded down to nearest hectopascal or inches, tenths and hundredths of an inch depending on indicator

Indicator of **QNH** in hectopascals. If Q=**A** then QNH is in inches.

TEMP AND DEW POINT — T'T'/T'$_d$T'$_d$

Dew-point temperature in whole degrees Celsius (if below 0°C preceded by **M**)

Temperature in whole degrees Celsius (if below 0°C preceded by **M**)

CAVOK

Ceiling And Visibility OK. **Replaces** visibility RVR, present weather and cloud if: 1) Visibility is 10 km or more.
2) No cumulonimbus cloud and no cloud below 1500 metres (5000 ft) or below the highest minimum sector altitude whichever is greater, and
3) No significant weather (see table)

CLOUDS — N$_s$N$_s$N$_s$h$_s$h$_s$h$_s$(cc)

	Replaced when sky is obscured and information on vertical visibility is available by:	VVh$_s$h$_s$h$_s$	Replaced when there are no clouds and CAVOK is not appropriate by:	SKC SKy Clear
Cloud type - only **CB** (Cumulonimbus) or **TCU** (Towering cumulus) indicated		Vertical visibility in units of 30 metres (100 feet) /// = Vertical visibility unavailable		
Height of base of clouds in units of 30 metres (100ft)				
Cloud amount: **FEW** - FEW (1-2 oktas) **SCT** - SCaTtered (3-4 oktas) **BKN** - BroKeN (5-7 oktas) **OVC** - OVerCast (8 oktas)		Indicator of **V**ertical **V**isibility		

PRESENT WEATHER — w'w'

Present weather. See Table.

RUNWAY VISUAL RANGE — RD$_R$D$_R$/V$_R$V$_R$V$_R$V$_R$R$_t$

	Replaced when there are significant variations in RVR by:	R$_t$D$_R$D$_R$/V$_R$V$_R$V$_R$V$_R$V$_R$V$_R$V$_R$V$_R$R$_t$
RVR tendency over past ten minutes. **U**=upward; **D**=downward; **N**=no distinct change. **Omitted** if impossible to determine		RVR tendency
Runway Visual Range in metres (10 minute mean) P1500= more than 1500 metres, M0050= less than 50 metres		Runway visual range in metres (one minute mean maximum over last ten minutes)
		Indicator of significant **V**ariation
Runway designator – for parallel runways may have **LL, L, C, R** or **RR** appended. (**L**=left; **C**=centre; **R**=right)		Runway visual range in metres (one minute mean minimum over last ten minutes)
Indicator of RVR		Runway designator –for parallel runways may have **LL, L, C, R** or **RR**
		Indicator of RVR.

VISIBILITY — VVVD$_v$

	Followed when min. vis. < 1500 metres and max. vis. > 5000 metres by:	V$_x$V$_x$V$_x$V$_x$ D$_v$
Direction of lowest visibility (eight points of compass) where required		Direction of maximum visibility (eight points of compass)
Minimum horizontal visibility in metres 9999 = 10 km or more		Maximum horizontal visibility in metres. 9999 = 10 km. or more.

SURFACE WIND — dddff**G**f$_m$f$_m$ KMH or KT or MPS

	00000=calm	Followed when there is a variation in wind direction of 60° or more and wind speed >3 KT by:	d$_n$d$_n$d$_n$**V**d$_x$d$_x$d$_x$
Wind speed units used			Other extreme direction of wind (measured clockwise)
Maximum wind speed (gust) - if necessary			Indicator of **V**ariability
Indicator of **G**ust - if necessary			Extreme direction of wind
Mean wind speed. (ten minute mean or since discontinuity)			
Mean wind direction in degrees true rounded off to nearest ten degrees (**VRB** = VARIABLE)			

IDENTIFICATION

(AUTO)	Fully automated observation
YYGGgg**Z**	Indicator of UTC
	In individual messages, day of the month and time of observation in hours and minutes UTC. In bulletins, time of observation in bulletin header instead.
CCCC	ICAO four-letter location indicator
METAR or SPECI	**METAR** - Aviation routine weather report **SPECI** - Aviation selected special weather report

January 1996

Abbreviated decode of METAR and SPECI
For details of codes see
WMO Manual on Codes,
WMO Publication No. 306

Figure 10-3. World Meteorological Organization (WMO) METAR decoding format (Part 1)

AERODROME ACTUAL WEATHER – METAR AND SPECI DECODE CONTINUED

w'w' – SIGNIFICANT PRESENT, FORECAST AND RECENT WEATHER

QUALIFIER		WEATHER PHENOMENA		
INTENSITY OR PROXIMITY (1)	DESCRIPTOR (2)	PRECIPITATION (3)	OBSCURATION (4)	OTHER (5)
- Light Moderate (no qualifier) + Heavy or well developed in the case of PO and FC VC in the vicinity	MI Shallow BC Patches PR Partial - covering part of the aerodrome DR Low drifting BL Blowing SH Shower(s) TS Thunderstorm FZ Freezing (supercooled)	DZ Drizzle RA Rain SN Snow SG Snow grains IC Ice Crystals (diamond dust) PE Ice pellets GR Hail GS Small hail and/or snow pellets	BR Mist FG Fog FU Smoke VA Volcanic ash DU Widespread dust SA Sand HZ Haze	PO Dust/sand whirls (dust devils) SQ Squalls FC Funnel cloud(s) (tornado or water spout) SS Sandstorm DS Duststorm

NOTES:

1. The w'w' groups are constructed by considering columns 1 to 5 in the table above in sequence, that is intensity, followed by description, followed by weather phenomena. An example could be: **+SHRA** (heavy shower(s) of rain).
2. A precipitation combination has dominant type first.
3. **DR** (low drifting) less than two metres above ground, **BL** (blowing) two metres or more above ground.
4. **GR** used when hailstone diameter 5 mm or more. When less than 5 mm, **GS** used.
5. **BR** - visibility at least 1000 metres but not more than 5000. **FG** - visibility less than 1000 metres.
6. **VC** - within 8 km of the aerodrome perimeter, but not at the aerodrome.

TREND FORECAST
TWO HOURS FROM TIME OF OBSERVATION

CHANGE INDICATOR TTTTT or NOSIG	**BECMG = BECOMING** or **TEMPO = TEMPORARY** } see over for definitions **NOSIG = NO SIGNIFICANT CHANGE**	
CHANGE AND TIME TTGGgg	Associated time group in hours and minutes UTC	
	Can be **AT** or **FM** = FROM or **TL** = TILL	
FORECAST WIND dddff Gfmfm KMH or KT or MPS	Wind speed units	
	Forecast maximum wind speed (gust)	00000 = calm
	Indicator of **G**ust	
	Forecast wind speed	
	Forecast wind direction in degrees true, rounded to nearest ten degrees (**VRB** = VARIABLE)	
FORECAST VISIBILITY VVVV	Forecast surface visibility in metres 9999=10 km or more	
FORECAST WEATHER w'w'	Forecast significant weather. See Table.	Replaced when significant weather ends by: NSW Nil Significant Weather
FORECAST CLOUD NsNsNshshshs(cc)	Cloud type - only **CB**	Replaced when sky expected to be obscured and vertical visibility forecasts are undertaken by: VVhshshs Indicator of Vertical Visibility / Vertical visibility in units of 30 metres (100 feet)
	Forecast height of base of cloud	Replaced when a change to clear sky forecast by: SKC SKy Clear
	Forecast cloud amount	Replaced when no **CB** and no cloud below 1500 m (5000 ft) or highest minimum sector altitude whichever is greater, are forecast and **CAVOK** or **SKC** are not appropriate by: NSC Nil Significant Cloud
CAVOK	**Replaces** visibility, weather and cloud if these are forecast to be OK (see earlier definition)	
RMK	Information included by national decision but not disseminated internationally	

Figure 10-3. World Meteorological Organization (WMO) METAR decoding format (Part 2)

AERODROME FORECAST – TAF DECODE

$N_sN_sN_sh_sh_sh_s(CC)$ — FORECAST CLOUD AMOUNT AND HEIGHT

Cloud type - only **CB** (cumulonimbus)

Height of base of cloud in units of 30 metres (100 feet)

Cloud amount:
- **FEW** - FEW (1-2 oktas)
- **SCT** - SCaTtered (3-4 oktas)
- **BKN** - BroKeN (5-7 oktas)
- **OVC** - OVerCast (8 oktas)

Replaced when sky is expected to be obscured and information on vertical visibility is available by:

$VVh_sh_sh_s$ — Vertical visibility in units of 30 metres (100 feet)

Indicator of **V**ertical **V**isibility

Replaced when clear sky is forecast by:

SKC — **SK**y Clear

Replaced if agreed **regionally**, when no CB and no cloud below 1500 m. (5000 ft) or below the highest minimum sector altitude, whichever is greater are forecast and CAVOK and SKC are not appropriate by:

NSC — **N**il **S**ignificant **C**loud

w'w' — FORECAST SIGNIFICANT WEATHER

Forecast significant weather (see table on other side)

Replaced when significant weather phenomenon forecast to end by:

NSW — **N**il **S**ignificant **W**eather

VVVV — FORECAST VISIBILITY

Minimum horizontal visibility in metres

9999 = 10 km or more

dddffGf_mf_mKT or KMH or MPS — FORECAST SURFACE WIND

Wind speed units used

Maximum wind speed (gust)

Indicator of **G**ust

Mean wind speed

Mean wind direction in degrees true rounded to nearest ten degrees. (**VRB** = **V**A**R**IA**B**LE)

00000=calm

IDENTIFICATION

$Y_1Y_1G_1G_1G_2G_2$ — Y_1Y_1 day of month, beginning G_1G_1 and ending G_2G_2 in hours UTC

(YYGGgg**Z**) — Indicator of UTC

Date and time of origin of forecast in UTC

CCCC — ICAO four-letter location indicator

TAF — TAF - Aerodrome Forecast

Abbreviated decode of TAF
For details of codes see
WMO Manual on Codes,
WMO Publication No. 306

Figure 10-4. World Meteorological Organization (WMO) TAF decoding format (Part 1)

AERODROME FORECAST – TAF DECODE CONTINUED

BY REGIONAL AGREEMENT — FORECAST TEMPERATURE (TT$_F$T$_F$ /G$_F$G$_F$Z)

- Indicator of UTC
- Time UTC to which forecast temperature refers
- Forecast temperature at G$_e$G$_e$. Temperatures below 0°C preceded by **M**
- Indicator of forecast Temperature

SIGNIFICANT CHANGES IN FORECAST CONDITIONS INDICATED BY:

TIME	GGG$_e$G$_e$	Beginning GG and end G$_e$G$_e$ of forecast period in hours UTC
CHANGE	TTTTT	Type of significant change: **BECMG** -**BEC**o**M**in**G**, used where changes are expected to reach or pass through specified values at a regular or irregular rate. **TEMPO** - **TEMPO**rary fluctuations of less than one hour and in aggregate less than half the period indicated by GGG$_e$G$_e$
TIME	GGG$_e$G$_e$	Beginning GG and end G$_e$G$_e$ of forecast period in hours UTC
PROBABILITY	PROBC$_2$C$_2$	Only 30 or 40 used, indicating 30% or 40%
	PROBability	

Probability is used to indicate the probability of occurence of:
a) an alternative element or elements
b) temporary fluctuations

OR

if one set of weather conditions is expected to change more or less completely to a different set of conditions, thus indicating the beginning of another self-contained part of the forecast, by:

TTGGgg

This takes the form **FM**GGgg where **FM** is the abbreviation for 'FroM' and GGgg is the time in hours and minutes UTC. All forecast conditions before this group are superseded by conditions indicated after the group.

BY REGIONAL AGREEMENT

FORECAST TURBULENCE (5B$_h$$_Bh_Bt_L$)
- Thickness of layer (thousands of feet) with code figure 0 = up to top of clouds
- Base of layer of turbulence in units of 30 metres (100 feet)
- Type of turbulence (see below)
- Indicator of forecast turbulence

FORECAST ICING (6I$_c$h$_i$h$_i$t$_L$)
- Thickness of layer (thousands of feet) with code figure 0 = up to top of clouds
- Base of layer of icing in units of 30 metres (100 feet)
- Type of icing (see below)
- Indicator of forecast icing

CAVOK

Ceiling **A**nd **V**isibility **OK**. **Replaces** visibility, weather and cloud if:
1) Visibility is forecast to be 10 km or more
2) No cumulonimbus cloud and no other cloud forecast below 1500 metres (5000 ft) or below the highest minimum sector altitude whichever is greater, and
3) No significant weather forecast (see Table overleaf)

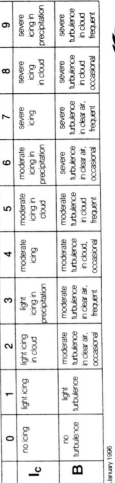

	0	1	2	3	4	5	6	7	8	9
I$_c$	no icing	light icing	light icing in cloud	light icing in precipitation	moderate icing	moderate icing in cloud	moderate icing in precipitation	severe icing	severe icing in cloud	severe icing in precipitation
B	no turbulence	light turbulence	moderate turbulence in clear air, occasional	moderate turbulence in clear air, frequent	moderate turbulence in cloud, occasional	moderate turbulence in cloud frequent	severe turbulence in clear air, occasional	severe turbulence in clear air, frequent	severe turbulence in cloud occasional	severe turbulence in cloud frequent

January 1996

Figure 10-4. World Meteorological Organization (WMO) TAF decoding format (Part 2)

11: Inertial Navigation

An Introduction to Inertial Navigation

The modern Inertial Navigation System (INS) is the only *self-contained* single source for all navigation data. After being supplied with initial position information, it is capable of continuously updating accurate displays of position, ground speed, attitude, and heading (Figure 11-1). In addition, INS provides guidance or steering information for the autopilot and flight instruments. In order to understand an inertial navigation system, one must consider the definition of "inertia" and the basic laws of motion as described by Newton over 300 years ago.

Inertia is a property of matter best described by Newton's first law of motion, which says *"A body con-tinues in a state of rest, or uniform motion in a straight line, unless acted upon by unequal external forces."*

Newton's second law of motion states *"The acceleration of a body is directly proportional to the sum of the forces acting on the body."*

Newton's third law of motion states *"For every action, there is an equal and opposite reaction."*

With these laws, we can mechanize a device able to detect minute changes in acceleration and velocity, an ability necessary to the development of an inertial system. Newton's second law states that the acceleration (that is, rate of change of velocity) is directly proportional to the force acting on the body. Velocity and distance are computed from sensed acceleration by the application of basic calculus. The relationship between

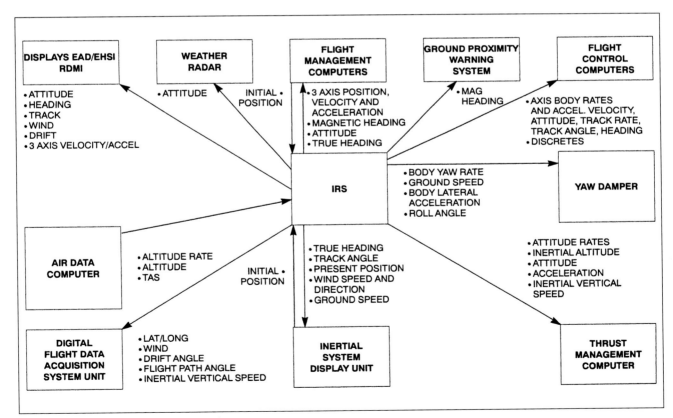

Figure 11-1. Initial position information

acceleration, velocity, and displacement are shown in Figure 11-2. Note that velocity changes whenever acceleration exists and remains constant when acceleration is zero.

The basic measuring instrument of the inertial navigation system is the accelerometer. Two accelerometers are mounted in the mechanical, gyro-stabilized platform, inertial system. One will measure the aircraft's acceleration in the North-South directions, and the other will measure the aircraft's acceleration in the East-West directions. The accelerometer is a pendulous device. When the aircraft accelerates, the pendulum, due to inertia, swings away from its null position. A signal pickoff device tells how far the pendulum is off the null position. The signal from the pickoff device is sent to an amplifier, and current from the amplifier is sent back into the accelerometer to the torque motor. The torque motor restores the pendulum back to its null position (Figure 11-3).

The acceleration signal from the amplifier is also sent to an integrator, which is a time-multiplication device. Acceleration, which is in feet-per-second squared, is multiplied by time resulting in velocity (feet per second) (Figure 11-4). The product (velocity) is then sent through a second integrator (again, a time multiplier). The input of feet per second is multiplied by time

resulting in a distance (feet or miles). Thus, a running total of distance traveled North-South and East-West is kept. For example, it can be computed that the aircraft has traveled 221 miles in a northerly direction from time of takeoff (Figure 11-5).

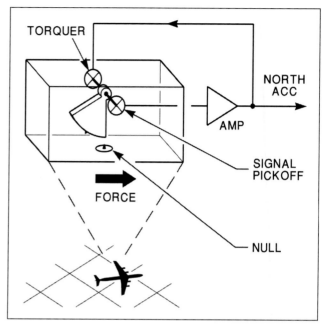

Figure 11-3. Accelerometer function

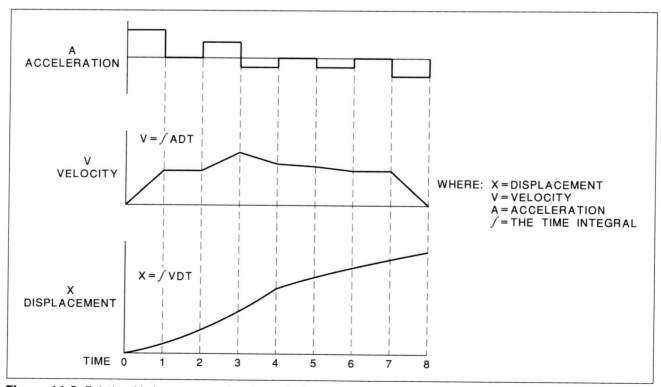

Figure 11-2. Relationship between acceleration, velocity, and displacement

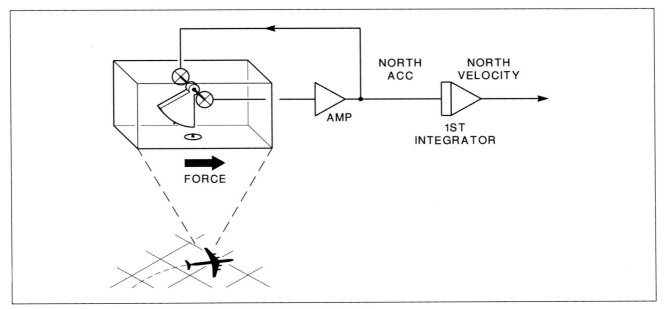

Figure 11-4. Acceleration integrated produces velocity information.

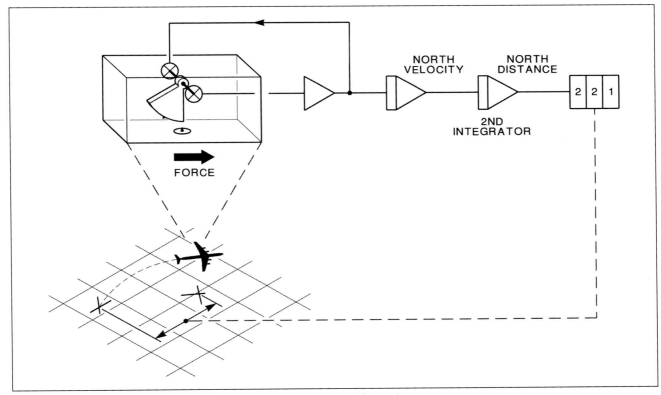

Figure 11-5. Acceleration integrated twice produces distance information.

The computer associated with the inertial system knows the latitude and the longitude of the departure point and calculates that the aircraft has traveled so far in a North-South direction and so far in an East-West direction. It now becomes simple for a digital computer to continuously compute the instantaneous **present position** of the aircraft.

If an accelerometer is hard-mounted to the aircraft, the accelerometer's output is affected by the attitude of the aircraft. In Figure 11-6, the aircraft is shown in a nose up attitude during takeoff. This pitch angle makes the pendulum swing off the null position due to gravity. The accelerometer would output an erroneous signal, which would result in computation of an erroneous velocity and distance traveled. Therefore, a false acceleration problem is caused by pitch angles other than zero (level flight). The solution to this problem is to keep the accelerometer level at all times.

To keep the accelerometer level, it is mounted on a gimbal assembly, commonly referred to as the **platform**. The platform is a mechanical device which allows the aircraft to go through any attitude change while maintaining the accelerometers in a level attitude, and with constant orientation with respect to north. The inner element of the platform where the accelerometers are mounted also mounts the gyroscopes used to stabilize the platform. The gyros provide signals to servo motors, which control the attitude and orientation of the platform gimbals (Figure 11-7).

Figure 11-8 shows how the gyro is used to control the level of the platform. The gyro and accelerometer are mounted on a common gimbal. While this gimbal tips from the level position, the spin axis of the gyro remains fixed. The case of the gyro moves with the gimbal, and the amount of movement is detected by a signal pickoff in the gyro. That signal is then amplified and sent to a gimbal drive motor, which restores the gimbal back to a level position. In this example, the accelerometer is "going along for the ride." Since the accelerometer is being kept level, it does not sense a component of gravity. Thus, the accelerometer senses only true horizontal accelerations of the aircraft. This discussion illustrates a single axis platform. In reality, movement occurs in three axes of the platform, pitch, roll, and yaw.

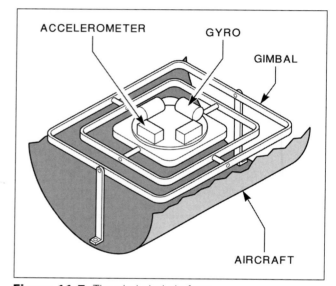

Figure 11-7. The gimbaled platform

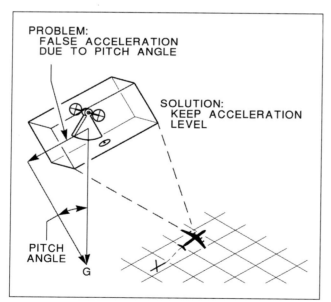

Figure 11-6. False acceleration information as the result of pitch angle

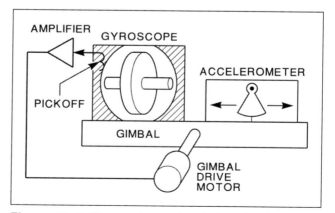

Figure 11-8. The gyro keeps the platform level.

The gyro-stabilized platform described above remains fixed in space, but the aircraft is not operating in space. It is operating on a sphere which is rotating. In order to keep the accelerometers level with respect to the earth, so that they sense acceleration of the aircraft in a horizontal direction only, some compensation must be made. Take the example of looking down at the earth from a point in space over the North Pole. At noon, the platform is leveled so that the accelerometers sense only horizontal accelerations. Now, as the earth rotates, the platform would maintain the same orientation in space; however, from an earth vantage point, the platform would appear to tip over every 24 hours (Figure 11-9).

To compensate for this apparent **tipping**, the platform is forced to tilt in proportion to the earth's rate. From the space vantage point, the platform appears to

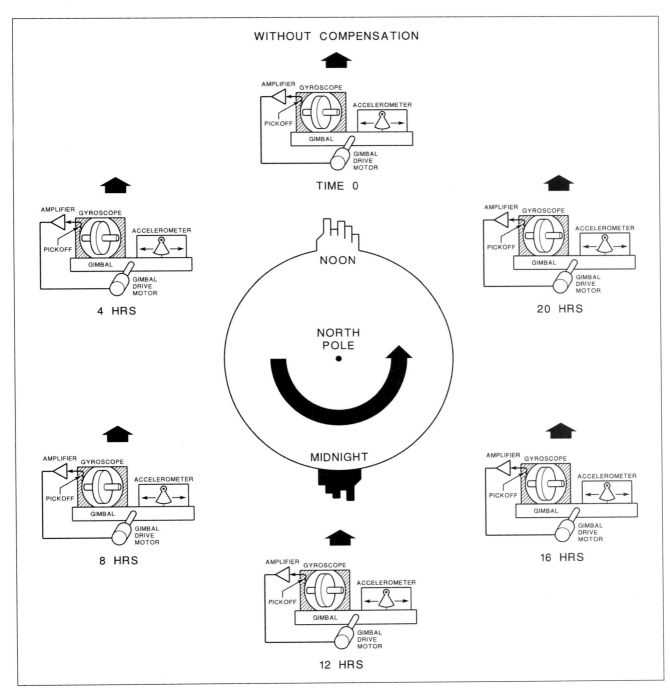

Figure 11-9. Apparent platform tipping due to rotation of the earth

tip over every 24 hours, while from an earth vantage point, it remains fixed and level as required for proper operation (Figure 11-10).

The required earth-rate compensation is a function of latitude, since what is being compensated for is the horizontal component of the earth rate. At the equator, this value is 15.04° per hour, and with travel north or south of the equator, it reduces until it becomes zero at the poles.

Inertial navigation depends on the integration of acceleration to obtain velocity and distance. In any integration process, the initial conditions must be known, which, in this case, are velocity and position.

The accuracy to which the navigation problem is solved depends greatly upon the accuracy of the initial conditions. Therefore, system alignment is of paramount importance.

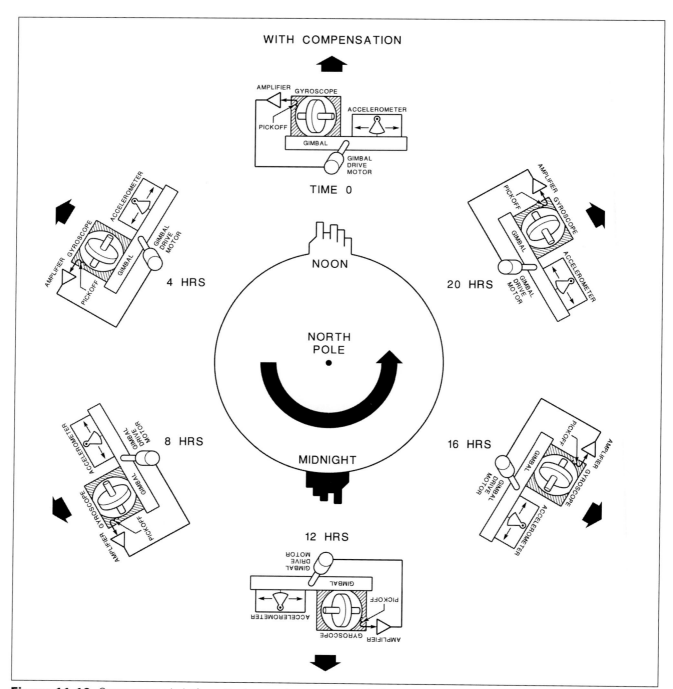

Figure 11-10. Compensated platform tipping resolves apparent platform tipping problems.

The initial latitude and longitude that are entered into the inertial system must be as accurate as possible. Inserting the coordinates of the airport of departure is not good enough, for improved performance the latitude and longitude of the departure gate or ramp location is much more desirable.

Principles of Strapdown Inertial Navigation

Introduction

For descriptive purposes, we are showing Honeywell's LASEREF II Inertial Navigation System. Though highly advanced, inertial systems show enough commonalty that the labels and terms are generic enough to apply to many different systems that are encountered.

What is a Laser-Gyro?

The strapdown laser-gyro **IRS** (Inertial Reference System) is a system that provides the following aircraft flight information without the need for gimbals, bearings, torque motors, or other moving parts:

1. Primary aircraft attitude in pitch and roll
2. Magnetic and true heading
3. Body linear accelerations
   a. Longitudinal
   b. Lateral
   c. Normal
4. Body angular rates
   a. Pitch
   b. Roll
   c. Yaw
5. Inertial velocity
   a. North-South, East-West
   b. Ground speed
   c. Track angle
   d. Vertical rate
6. Navigation position
   a. Latitude
   b. Longitude
   c. Inertial altitude

7. Wind data
   a. Wind speed
   b. Wind angle
   c. Drift angle
8. Calculated data
   a. Flight path angle and acceleration
   b. Along track and cross track acceleration
   c. Inertial pitch and roll rate
   d. Vertical acceleration and potential vertical speed.

The **strapdown laser-gyro system** utilizes inertial sensors that are fixed relative to the structure. These sensors consist of three or more ring laser gyros and three or more accelerometers. These sensors, coupled with high-speed microprocessors, allow the laser-gyro system to maintain a stable platform reference mathematically rather than mechanically. This results in a significant increase in accuracy and reliability over older, gimbaled stabilized platforms.

The laser-gyro system replaces, with respect to conventional stabilizing devices (Figure 11-11 on the next page):

1. Vertical gyro
2. Directional gyro
3. Flux valve and compensator
4. Rate gyros
5. Accelerometers.

System Description

The laser-gyro system includes components that may be configured into a single-, dual- or triple-IRS installation. In a strapdown inertial reference system (IRS), the gyros and accelerometers are mounted solidly to the system chassis, which is in turn mounted solidly to the airframe of the aircraft. Unlike earlier INS's with spinning gyros stabilizing a platform, there are no gimbals to keep the sensors level with the surface of the earth. The accelerometers are mounted such that the input axis of one accelerometer is always aligned with the longitudinal aircraft aids, one with the lateral aids, and one with the vertical axis. Likewise, the gyros are mounted such that one gyro senses rate of roll, one senses rate of pitch, and the other senses rate of yaw.

The **accelerometer** produces an output that is proportional to the acceleration applied along the sensor's input axis. The **microprocessor** integrates the accelera-

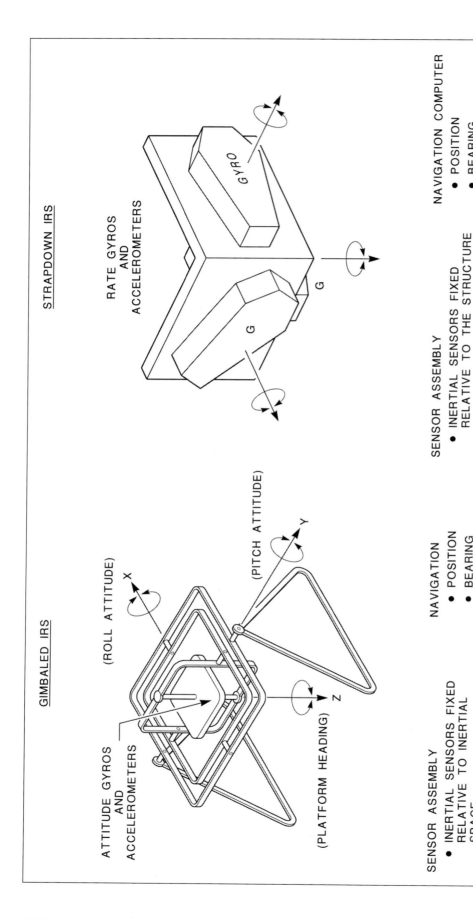

Figure 11-11. Functional comparison of strapdown and gimbaled IRS's

tion signal to calculate velocity. Integration is a function that can be viewed as a multiplication by time. For example, a vehicle accelerating at 3 feet per second squared would be traveling at a velocity of 30 feet per second after 10 seconds have passed. Note that acceleration was simply multiplied by time to get velocity. The microprocessor also integrates the calculated velocity to determine distance. For example, a vehicle traveling at a velocity of 30 feet per second for ten seconds will have changed position by 300 feet. Velocity was simply multiplied by time to determine distance traveled.

Although acceleration is used to calculate velocity and position, it is meaningless to the system without additional information. For example, consider an accelerometer strapped down to the longitudinal axis of the aircraft and measuring a forward acceleration. Is the aircraft acceleration north, south, east, west, up, or down? In order to navigate over the surface of the earth, the system's computer must know how this aircraft acceleration is related to the earth's surface. Because accelerations are measured by accelerometers that are mounted to the lateral, longitudinal, and vertical axes of the aircraft, the IRS must know the relationship of each of these axes to the surface of the earth. The laser gyros in a strapdown system make the measurements necessary to describe this relationship in terms of pitch, roll, and heading angles. These angles are calculated from the angular rates measured by the gyros through an integration similar to the manner in which velocity is calculated from measured acceleration. For example, suppose a gyro measures a yaw rate of 3° per second for 30 seconds. Through integration, the microprocessor calculates that the heading has changed by 90° after 30 seconds.

Given the knowledge of pitch, roll, and heading that the gyros provide, the microprocessor resolves the acceleration signals into earth-related accelerations, and then performs the horizontal and vertical navigation calculations. This can be illustrated with the following examples:

1. Suppose the gyro signals have been integrated to indicate that the aircraft's heading is 45° and the pitch and roll are both zero. The only acceleration measured has been in the longitudinal axis, and it has been integrated into a velocity of 500 MPH. After flying at a constant heading and attitude for one hour, the microprocessor has integrated the velocity to determine that the aircraft has flown to a latitude and longitude that is 500 miles northeast

of the original location. In doing so, the inertial reference system has used the acceleration signals in conjunction with the gyro signals to calculate the present position.

2. Consider an inertial reference unit with sensors measuring a heading of 90°, a pitch of 10°, a 0° roll angle, and only a longitudinal acceleration. The pitch angle indicates that the longitudinal acceleration is partially upward and partially eastward. The microprocessor uses the pitch angle to accurately separate the acceleration into upward and eastward components. The vertical portion of the acceleration is integrated to get vertical velocity which, in turn, is integrated to get altitude. The eastward portion of the acceleration is integrated to get east velocity which, in turn, is integrated to get the new east position or longitude.

Under the normal flight conditions, all six sensors sense motion simultaneously and continuously, thereby entailing calculations that are substantially more complex than shown in the previous examples. A powerful, high-speed microprocessor is required in the IRS in order to rapidly and accurately handle this additional complexity.

In addition to the basic strapdown concepts that have been discussed, there are some additional details that must be considered in order to navigate with respect to the earth's surface. These special considerations are necessitated by the earth's gravity, rotation, and shape. A **strapdown IRS** compensates for these special effects with the microprocessor's software, as described below.

Gravity

Vertical velocity and altitude are calculated using the acceleration that is measured perpendicular to the earth's surface. However, an inertial accelerometer cannot distinguish between gravitational force and actual aircraft acceleration. Consequently, any accelerometer that is not perfectly parallel to the earth's surface will measure a component of the earth's gravity in addition to the true aircraft acceleration. Therefore, the IRS's microprocessor must subtract the estimated local gravity from the measured vertical acceleration signal. This prevents the system from interpreting gravitational force as upward aircraft acceleration.

Earth's Rotation

As discussed previously, the purpose of the gyro is to measure rotational motion of the aircraft with respect to the earth. However, the laser gyro in a strapdown configuration inherently measures movement of the aircraft with respect to space. Another way of looking at this is that the gyros measure the motion of the aircraft with respect to the earth plus the motion of the earth with respect to inertial space. The earth rotates with respect to inertial space at a rate of one rotation per 24 hours as it spins from west to east on its own axis, plus one rotation per year as it revolves around the sun. The sum of these two rates is approximately equivalent to an angular rate of 15.04° per hour. The microprocessor compensates for this rate by subtracting this value, which is stored in memory, from the signal measured by whichever gyro or gyros are pointed eastward. Without this "earth rate" compensation, an IRS operating at the equator would mistakenly think that it is upside-down after 12 hours of navigation. At other places on the earth, the system would develop proportional errors in pitch, roll and heading.

Earth's Spherical Shape

The major effect imposed by the earth's spherical shape is somewhat similar to that caused by the earth's rotation. As an aircraft travels across the surface of the earth, its path becomes an arc due to the shape of the earth. Consequently, the gyros (particularly the pitch axis gyro) measure a rotational rate because traveling in a curved path always involves rotation. This rate, called the **transport rate**, does not describe rotational motion of the aircraft with respect to the earth's surface. Therefore, the IRS must calculate how much transport rate is occurring and being measured by the gyros, and subtract that value from the measurements.

Geometry can be used to visualize how the transport rate is calculated. It is well-known that the circumference of a circular path is equal to 2 x π x the radius of the circle. It is also well-known that the total angle bounded by a circle is 360° or 2 x π radians. The relationship between the circle's angle in radians and the circle's circumference is then 2 x π / (2 x π x the radius of the circle), or 1/the radius of the circle. Using this relationship, the angle that a body has rotated can be calculated, given the distance traveled. By dividing the distance (circumference) by time, and by also dividing the angle by time, the relationship can be extended to relate tangential (non-vertical) velocity to angular rate. When applied to inertial navigation, the result is that the angular transport rate is equal to the aircraft's horizontal velocity divided by the earth's radius plus the aircraft's altitude (which, in most cases, is insignificant). The microprocessor performs this calculation using an estimate of the earth's radius, and then subtracts the resultant transport rate from the gyro's measurements. This method of compensating for the transport rate is known as **Schuler tuning**. Transport rate compensation is essential to provide accurate navigation. For example, without this compensation, an IRS that flies from some position to a point on the other side of the earth would incorrectly report that it is upside-down when it arrives.

There are many other effects that are compensated for in commercial inertial reference systems, and even more in systems used in military applications. These effects have not been considered in this book because they get very complicated as higher precision is required, yet do not appreciably increase understanding of strapdown navigation principles.

Modes of Operation

Alignment

Purpose

During alignment the inertial reference system determines the local vertical, the direction of true north and the aircraft's latitude.

Gyrocompass Process

Inside the inertial reference unit, the three gyros sense angular rate of the airplane while it is stationary on the ramp. Since the plane is stationary during alignment, the angular rate is caused by the earth's rotation. The IRU computer uses this angular rate to determine the latitude.

Initial Latitude

During the alignment period, the **Inertial Reference Unit** (IRU) computer has determined true north by sensing the direction of the earth's rotation. The magnitude of the earth's rotation allows the IRU computer to accurately estimate latitude of the initial present position. This calculated latitude is compared with the latitude entered by the operator during initialization (Figure 11-12).

Note: In order to continue this explanation, an example is used: the Honeywell LASEREF. The reader must keep in mind that although the internal process is similar in all INS/IRS's, differences do exist between units of different manufacturers and even from model-to-model from one manufacturer.

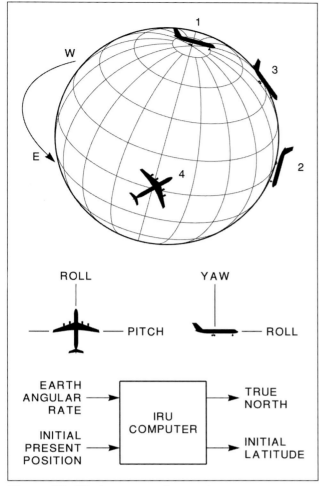

Figure 11-12. Laser gyro alignment

Alignment Mode

For the IRU to enter ALIGN mode, the Mode Select switch is set to ALIGN or NAV position. (It is preferable to set the switch to NAV.) During ALIGN, the system software performs a vertical leveling and determines aircraft true heading and latitude. The leveling operation brings the pitch-and-roll attitudes within 1° of accuracy (course leveling), followed by fine leveling and heading determination. Initial latitude and longitude data must be entered by manually entering the actual present position via the Inertial System Display Unit, or by entering it into the Flight Management System.

Upon ALIGN completion, the IRS will enter NAV mode automatically if the Mode Select switch was set to NAV during align. If the Mode Select switch was set to ALIGN, the system will remain in align until the pilot selects NAV mode. There is a disadvantage in leaving the switch in ALIGN, in that the IRS remains vulnerable to upset by excessive motion as long as the system remains in ALIGN mode.

Alignment Time

The IRU completes alignment in a minimum of 2.5 minutes at the equator and a maximum of 10 minutes at 70° latitude. During alignment, the ALIGN annunciator is lit.

High-Latitude Alignment

1. Under normal circumstances, alignment should be initiated only within the latitudes of 70° North to 70° South.

2. If necessary, alignment above 70° may be attempted; however, system navigation performance accuracies may be degraded to an extent that will prevent NAV mode engagement.

3. To improve navigation performance from high-latitude alignments, the alignment time can be increased beyond the normal 10 minutes by leaving the MSU mode select switch in the ALIGN position for an additional period of time before switching to the NAV position. However, only slight improvement is achieved after more than 15 minutes with the mode select switch in the ALIGN position.

Alignment Requirements

1. The aircraft must be stationary during the align mode. If the aircraft is moved, power must be cycled off for a minimum of three seconds before the align mode can be reestablished.

2. During alignment, the aircraft must remain stationary. If the IRU detects excessive aircraft motion, the ALIGN annunciator flashes and the FAULT annunciator lights. If this occurs, the MSU mode select switch must be set to OFF for a minimum of 3 seconds and then set back to ALIGN or NAV to restart alignment.

   Note: Normal passenger-loading activities and wind gusts will not disturb alignment.

3. If the pilot does not enter present position within the normal alignment time, the MSU ALIGN annunciator flashes, and the IRU will not enter the NAV mode until it receives a valid input of present position.

Continued

4. The pilot may update the current latitude and longitude entry any number of times without delaying alignment as long as the IRU has not entered the NAV mode. Each successive latitude and/or longitude entry writes over the previous entry. Only the latest entry is used for navigation.

Alignment Tests

The IRU conducts a **reasonableness test** and a system performance test on the position that the pilot has entered.

1. Reasonableness Test

   a. The IRU conducts a reasonableness test on latitude and longitude immediately after each has been entered.

   b. The IRU compares the entered latitude and longitude with the latitude and longitude stored at the last power down. If the entered position does not agree within a given limit of the stored position, the entered latitude or longitude fails the test, and the MSU ALIGN annunciator flashes.

   c. The IRU will accept additional latitude and longitude entries, although each entry must also pass or override the reasonableness test. To override the test, the new entry must be identical to the last entry. For example, if N47324 was entered and failed the test, then N47324 must be entered again to override the test. If a new entry passes or overrides the reasonableness test, the flashing MSU ALIGN annunciator will go steady.

   d. A correct latitude and/or longitude entry may fail the reasonableness test if a new IRU has been installed or if the aircraft has been moved to a different location without operating the IRU. In this case, identical coordinates should be entered twice to override the test.

2. System Performance Test

   a. At the end of alignment, the entered latitude must pass a **system performance test**. This test requires that the latitude entered by the pilot be within a given limit of the latitude computed by the IRU. If the entered latitude passes this test, alignment is completed.

   b. A flashing ALIGN annunciator at this time indicates that the entered latitude has failed the system performance test. IRU will not enter the NAV mode until the entered latitude passes the test.

   c. Additional latitude entries are still allowed until the test is passed. However, new latitude entries must also pass the reasonableness test. If two consecutive, identical latitudes are entered and the system performance test fails, the flashing ALIGN annunciator goes steady, and the FAULT annunciator lights.

   d. One entry of the correct latitude passes the test, turns the FAULT and ALIGN annunciators off, and allows entry into the NAV mode.

Mode Select Unit (MSU)

See Figure 11-13 below, and Figure 11-14 at right.

1. The triple-channel MSU provides mode selection, status indication, and test initiation for three IRUs.

2. The six-annunciator MSU provides mode selection, status indication, and test initiation for one IRU.

Inertial System Display Unit (ISDU)

The ISDU selects data from any one of three IRUs for display and provides initial position or heading data to the IRUs. Operator inputs to the ISDU provide position data to the IRU and select navigational data for display. (*See* Figure 11-15 at right and Figure 11-16 on Page 210.) The ISDU contains:

1. Keyboard

2. Display

3. System display (SYS DSPL) switch

4. Display select (DSPL SEL) switch

5. Dimmer knob

The keyboard is used to enter latitude and longitude in the alignment mode or magnetic heading in the attitude mode. The ISDU then sends the entered data simultaneously to all IRUs in multiple-channel installations.

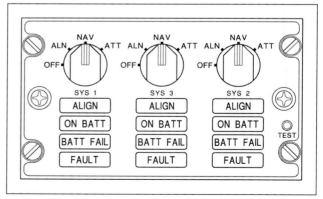

Figure 11-13. Triple-channel MSU

Inertial Reference Unit (IRU)

The IRU is the main electronic assembly of the IRS. The IRU contains an inertial sensor assembly, microprocessors, power supplies, and aircraft electronics interfaces. (*See* Figure 11-17, Page 211.)

Accelerometers and laser gyros in the inertial sensor assembly measure accelerations and angular rates of the aircraft.

The IRU microprocessors perform computations required for:

1. Primary attitude
2. Present position
3. Inertial velocity vectors
4. Magnetic and true north reference
5. Sensor systematic error compensation

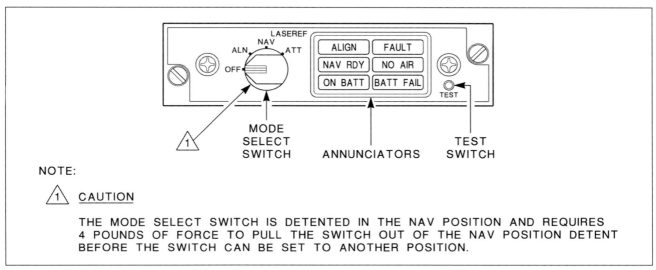

Figure 11-14. Six-annunciator MSU

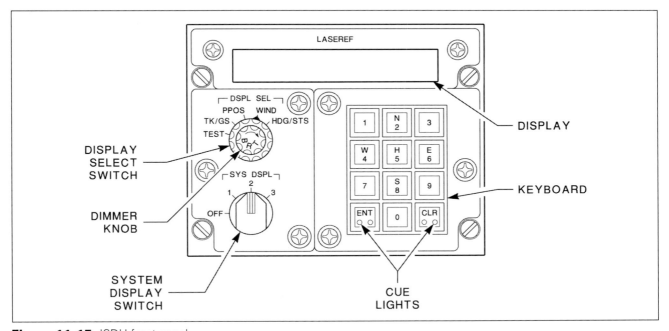

Figure 11-15. ISDU front panel

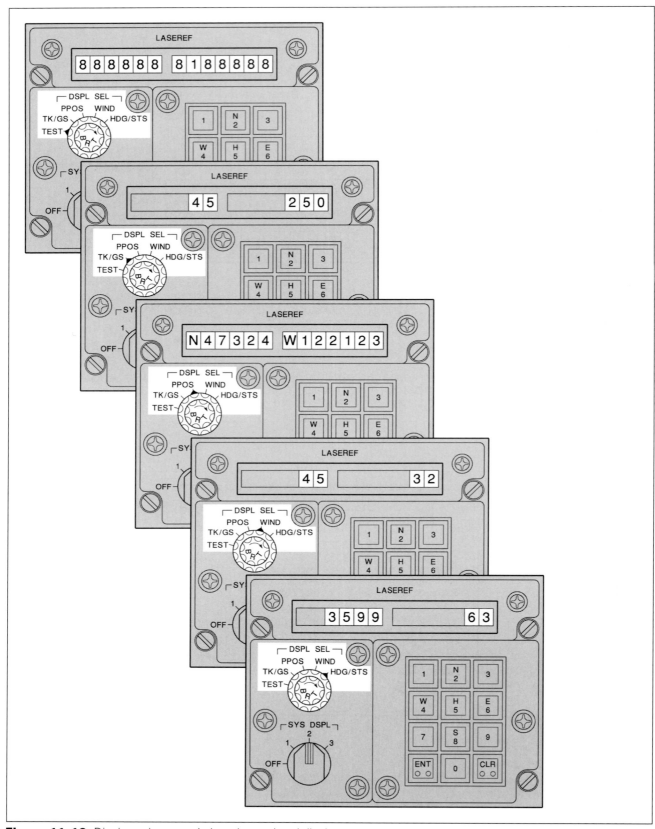

Figure 11-16. Display selector switch and associated displays

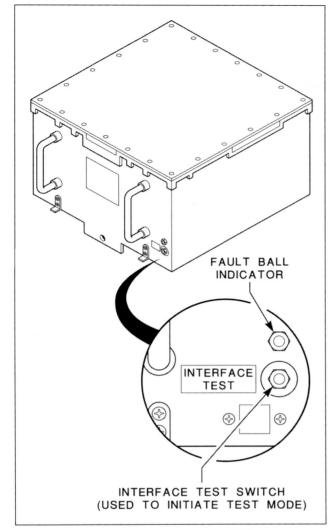

Figure 11-17. Inertial Reference Unit (IRU)

FAULT BALL
INDICATOR

INTERFACE
TEST

INTERFACE TEST SWITCH
(USED TO INITIATE TEST MODE)

Theory of Operation

Accelerometer Principle of Operation

The basic principles of an inertial accelerometer have not changed over the past several years. Pendulous accelerometers have exhibited very good performance and reliability at an acceptable cost, so new technology has not been applied to accelerometer designs.

Inertial accelerometers contain a pendulum that tends to swing off its null position when it is exposed to an acceleration or deceleration. A pick-off device is positioned so that it can measure the size of the swing, and generate an electrical signal proportional to the swing. This signal is amplified proportionately into a current which is used to torque the pendulum back to the null position. The net result of this control loop is that the pendulum remains in the null position, and a current has been generated proportional to the acceleration that the accelerometer is experiencing. This current is the output of the accelerometer.

Unlike the inherently digital output of a laser gyro, the current output of the accelerometer is an analog signal. The current is converted into a voltage, which in turn is converted into a digital signal by a high-precision analog-to-digital (A/D) converter. This digital signal is supplied to a microprocessor, which uses this acceleration measurement in the navigation computations, integrating that measurement once over time to give velocity. Velocity is then integrated once more over time to find distance traveled.

Triple-Axis Navigation Computation

As long as the airplane flies in only one direction, one accelerometer is sufficient to determine distance traveled from the starting position. Since the airplane may fly in any direction, three accelerometers mounted to sense acceleration 90° apart are required (*see* Figure 11-18 on next page).

The three accelerometers are stationary relative to the airplane frame. To determine how much acceleration is causing horizontal movement on the earth, the outputs of the accelerometers have to be compensated by the IRU computer, taking into account the airplane attitude, earth curvature, and rotation.

The compensated outputs from the accelerometers are vectorially added to determine the actual direction of travel and the amount of travel horizontally. In general, the accelerometers are not oriented north-south and east-west, but their output signals can be related

The power supplies receive AC and DC power from the aircraft or backup battery, supply power to the IRS, and provide switching to primary AC, primary DC, or back-up battery power.

The aircraft electronic interfaces convert Aeronautical Radio Incorporated (ARINC) and Avionics Standard Communication Bus (ASCB) inputs for use by the IRS. The electronic interfaces also provide IRS outputs in ARINC and ASCB formats for use by the associated aircraft equipment.

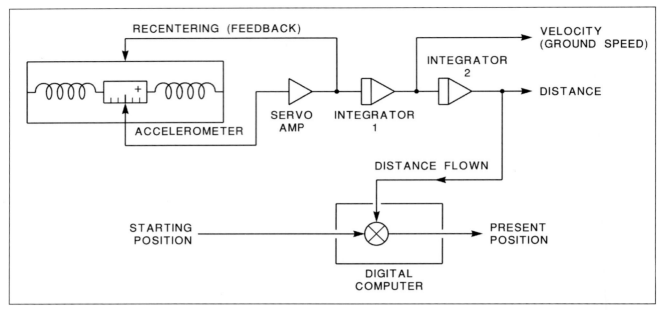

Figure 11-18. IRS—single-axis navigation computation

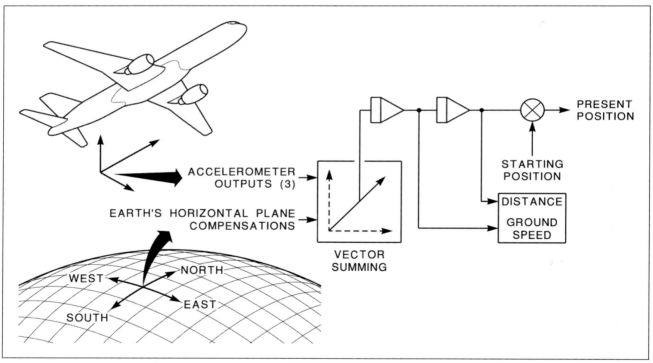

Figure 11-19. Triple-axis navigation computation

to a north-east coordinate system, and the present position can then be determined in terms of latitude and longitude (*see* Figure 11-19).

Laser Principle of Operation

In recent years, extensive applications have been found for lasers in many situations. Surgeons use lasers in eye surgery, tumor destruction and similar medical applications. Powerful lasers are used to cut or weld metal, while low-power lasers are used to communicate information. The laser gyro is among the most remarkable on this ever-growing list of laser uses. The laser gyro is a device that measures rotation by using the properties of two laser beams rotating in opposite directions inside a cavity. The principles of operation of an ordinary single-beam laser are described in the text that follows, and then expanded into a description of the double-beam laser gyro.

In a laser cavity, photons are emitted (or light is radiated) in all directions. However, only the light that radiates in a straight line between two or more mirrors is reinforced by repeated trips through the gain medium. This repeated amplification of the light reflecting between the mirrors soon reaches saturation, and a steady-state oscillation results. This light oscillating between the mirrors is typically called a laser beam. To obtain useful laser light outside the laser cavity, a small percentage of the laser beam is allowed to pass through one of the mirrors.

A laser gyro operates much like an ordinary laser, but rather than just two mirrors it contains at least three so that the laser beams can travel around an enclosed area. Such a configuration allows the generation of two distinct laser beams occupying the same space. One beam travels in a clockwise direction and the other travels in a counterclockwise direction (as viewed from above or below the gyro). The operation of a laser gyro is founded on the effects rotational motion has on the two laser beams.

Laser Gyro Operation

Laser gyros are not gyros at all, but emulate a gyro because they sense angular rate of rotation about a single axis. As exemplified in the Honeywell design, they may be made of a triangular block of temperature-stable glass weighting a little more than 2 pounds. Very small tunnels are precisely drilled parallel to the perimeter of the triangle, and reflecting mirrors are placed in each corner. After evacuation of air, a small charge of helium-neon gas is inserted and sealed into

an aperture in the glass at the base of the triangle. When high voltage is run between the anodes and cathode of the triangle, the gas is ionized, and in the energy exchange process many of the atoms of the gas transmit light in the orange-pink part of the visible spectrum. This action is abetted by the "tuned cavity" effect of the physical dimensions of the light path inside the glass block. The randomly moving particles resonate at a single frequency resulting in a thin, high energy beam of coherent light traveling through the triangle of tunnels. The mirrors serve as both reflectors and optical filters, reflecting the light frequency for which they were designed and absorbing all others.

In this type of laser gyro, two beams of light are generated, each traveling around the cavity (in this case, a triangle) in opposite directions.

Laser Gyro Function

Since both contrarotating beams travel at the same constant speed (speed of light), it takes each the same exact time to complete the circuit. However, if the gyro were rotated on its axis, the path length of one beam would be shortened, while that for the other would be lengthened. Since, as explained, the laser beam adjusts its wavelength for the length of the path, the beam that traveled the shorter distance would rise in frequency (wavelength decreases), while the beam that traveled the longer distance to complete the circuit would encounter a frequency decrease.

This frequency difference between the two beams is directly proportional to the angular rate of rotation about the gyro's axis. This is the principle of the laser gyro, simply stated; thus, frequency difference becomes a measure of rotation rate. If the gyro doesn't move about its axis, both frequencies remain equal (since the path lengths of both beams are equal) indicating that the angular rate is zero.

For those who might find it hard to understand that the laser gyro turning about its axis shortens the path length for one beam and lengthens it for the other, here is another way to explain the phenomenon. Consider a particle of light, a photon, just leaving the cathode and traveling toward the mirror on the right-hand corner (Figure 11-20 on next page). If the gyro turns clockwise on its axis, the mirror would move closer to the photon that was on its way toward it. Hence the photon's path length is shortened in the distance from cathode to mirror, and in the entire distance around the triangular race. Remember the photon is traveling in inertial space; it is not fixed to the gyro. Thus, this one photon and the millions of its traveling companions

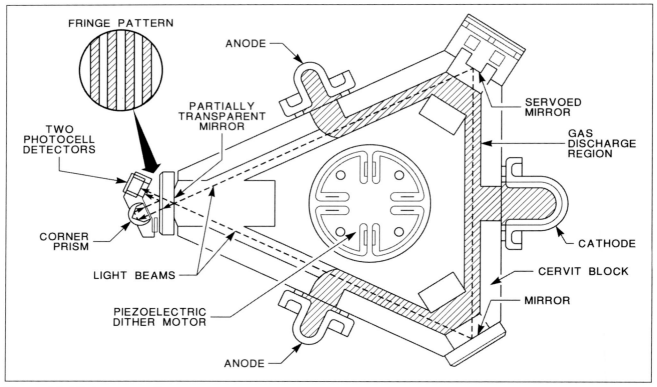

Figure 11-20. Laser gyro diagram

move around the circuit in a shorter time and in doing so they compress the waves in the laser beam and raise its frequency (number of cycles in a given time). Of course, the opposite happens to the photon traveling clockwise from the emitter because when the gyro turned clockwise about its axis, its mirror moved away from the clockwise-traveling photon, forcing it to travel further to reach the mirror and to complete the circuit.

Detecting the Difference

The difference in frequency in the laser gyro is measured by an optical detector that counts the fringes of the fringe pattern generated by the interference of the two light waves. Since the fringes are seen as pulses by the photocell, the detected frequency difference appears at the output of the detector in digital form, ready for immediate processing by the system's computer.

Note that there are two photocells (Figure 11-21). The function of one is to tell the direction in which the fringes are moving, which is an indication of the direction the gyro is rotating to the left or right.

As indicated in the more detailed diagram (Figure 11-20), the three corner mirrors are not identical. One is servoed so that it can make micro-

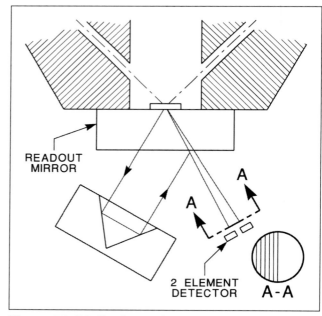

Figure 11-21. Readout optics

adjustments to keep the physical path always the same. Another (the one at the apex of the triangle in the diagram) permits a small amount of light to pass through so as to impinge on the photocell detectors. The prism, as shown in the figure, flips one beam around causing it to meet and interfere with the beam aimed directly at the photocells.

The interfering beams alternately cancel and reinforce each other, thus generating the fringe pattern.

The block of glass used for the Honeywell laser gyro is made from Cervit, a special glass, the physical dimensions of which remain constant over a wide temperature range (specified as -65° to +180°F).

To start the lasing action, 3,000 volts are applied across the anodes to the cathode. Although the laser beams in the laser gyro cannot be seen, a plasma is formed between the cathode and the two anodes that glows an orange-pink (the same part of the visible spectrum as the 6,328 Angstrom beams). This plasma can be seen.

In the center of the Cervit block is a device called a **dither motor**. This motor, which vibrates at 319 Hz, eliminates "laser lock," a hang-up that sometimes occurs in the deadband around the zero-rate point (zero rate of rotation).

Not Immune to Drift

As with spinning wheel gyros, a major source of error in a laser gyro is **random drift** (**precession**) and is caused by imperfect bearings and mass imbalances in spinning wheel gyros. Random drift in the laser types is caused by noise due almost exclusively to imperfect mirrors, including mirror coatings.

The other two errors associated with spinning mass gyrocompasses are also present: **real drift** and **changes in magnetic variation**. Both of these errors are predictable, and therefore can be compensated by the unit's computer. Of the three, only precession cannot be compensated for. It is suggested that the reader review the subject of gyro errors covered in detail in Chapter 4, Pages 55 – 57.

The Pilot's Perspective About INS Errors

The INS strongly exhibits error Type 2 (*see* Chapter 16 on errors) where the error *increases with time*. Modern inertial reference systems used in large aircraft are generally very accurate. It is not unusual to see errors of less than 0.5 miles after four hours of operation. However, these systems are also very expensive and relatively large.

As stand-alone systems, it is common to have two or three of these systems aboard, so that the crew may compare one against the other. As such, the IRS has the disadvantages of being large, expensive, exhibiting time-related errors; additionally, there are some other operational idiosyncrasies, such as not being able to initialize the system in flight, and not being able to manually correct position of some systems in flight.

Using recent technology, it is now possible to miniaturize IRS, to put one on a circuit board that will fit into a laptop computer. Accuracy is degraded, as compared to the large, expensive systems found on airliners. But this problem is mitigated by using GPS updates; the GPS is already miniaturized, making it possible to put a "GPS board" into the laptop also. This combination of IRS and GPS is a good one because, as the chapter on errors points out, the two systems together exhibit synergy—they compensate for each other's faults. If the author may be permitted a peek into the future, look for this combination of navigation systems to emerge as the next navigation system for general aviation aircraft.

12: LORAN-C

The LORAN-C System

Introduction

LORAN-C is a low frequency, pulsed, hyperbolic radio aid to navigation system, which operates in the 90-110 kHz frequency band. LORAN-C transmission may also be used for time dissemination, frequency reference purposes, and communication between transmitters for system control.

LORAN-C was developed to provide the U.S. Department of Defense with a radio navigation capability with longer range and much greater accuracy than its predecessor (LORAN-A). LORAN-C was selected as the federally provided radio navigation system for civil marine use in the United States coastal waters; the U.S. Coast Guard is responsible for system operation and maintenance in the United States and certain overseas locations (Figure 12-1).

The name LORAN is derived from the words LOng RAnge Navigation, which is an appropriate description of this hyperbolic system of electronic navigation. The electronic transmissions are transformed into LOPs (lines of position) over the surface of the earth and can either be plotted on LORAN charts or automatically deciphered by the computer portion of the modern LORAN receivers into a computed present position.

There has been publicity about shutting down the LORAN-C system, as early as the year 2000. When forecasting whether or not this will happen, consideration must be given to the fact that there are in excess of 100,000 aviation LORAN-C receivers in use today, not to mention over one million marine receivers. The decision to discontinue is a political one and therefore is not easy to predict when it will occur. LORAN-C is a very accurate navigation system that is relied upon by many users in various parts of the world. Thus, it continues to be a valuable international navigation tool.

Modern LORAN-C Aviation Receivers

A LORAN-C receiver is capable of determining a navigational fix with a great deal of accuracy. As amazing as this operation is, it falls short of what is required by aviation users. Pilots would still have a burdensome task of applying a known fix to manually computing heading, track, and ground speed. With the application of miniature computer processing and data storage, LORAN-C manufacturers have given the aviation community a user-friendly navigational system with almost unlimited amounts of information at the pilot's disposal.

By monitoring the fix generated by the LORAN-C receiver, a micro-processor can provide ground speed, heading, track, drift angle, wind speed and direction, and almost any other form of navigational information the manufacturer wants to generate. As convenient as the basic navigational information is, the data storage capability and its application to navigation is truly remarkable. Tens of thousands of waypoints and airports are programmed into the database. Simply requesting direct to any programmed VOR, NDB, intersection, or airport will generate a direct (great circle) shortest distance to the desired point. Information about airports, from runway lengths to frequencies for communication and navigation, is available from many of the LORAN-C navigational systems on the market today. The options and capabilities of what is available to install in even the smallest of aircraft is tremendous and is ever improving.

Theory of Operation

Since the speed of radio waves is virtually constant and quite accurately known, the time needed for a signal to travel a given distance can be determined with considerable accuracy. Therefore, the measurement of the time needed for a radio signal to travel between two points provides a measurement of distance between them. All points having the same difference in distance from two stationary points (called foci) lie along an open curve called a hyperbola. Actually, there are two

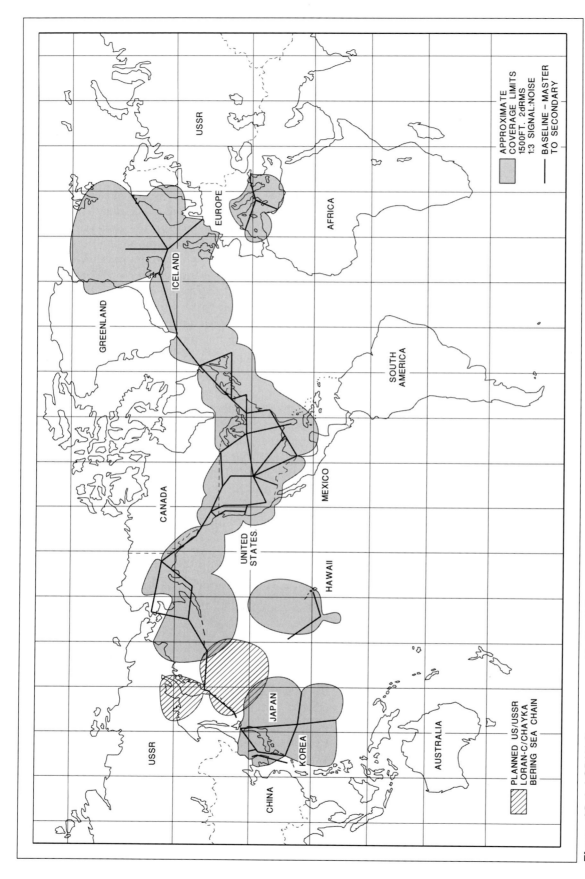

Figure 12-1. LORAN-C coverage provided by U.S.-operated or -provided LORAN-C stations

curves or parts to each hyperbola (Figure 12-2), each representing the same TD (time difference) but with the distance interchanged. Thus, the difference in the distances (200 NM) from the two stations is the same at points P1, P2, P3, and P4.

A LORAN-C user receiver measures the time difference between the master station signal and a secondary station (X) signal. This defines a hyperbolic line of position (Figure 12-3, Page 220). Measurement between the master signal and another secondary (Y) signal defines a second hyperbolic line of position. The receiver location is the intersection of the two LOPs. A third secondary station (Z) provides coverage for other receiver locations where one of the other secondaries does not provide good signals, closely spaced hyperbolas, nor good crossing angles.

The LORAN-C Chain

A **LORAN-C chain** is a group of LORAN-C transmitting stations having a common timing reference and located in the same general geographic area.

Chain Geometry

The relative location of stations in a typical chain is shown in Figure 12-4 on Page 220. A central station provides the chain timing reference and is called the **Mas-**

ter station. Other stations, called **Secondaries**, are identified by alphabetics. The minimum number of secondary stations is two, and although there is no defined maximum number of stations, six is the most that can reasonably be expected.

Base Line

A **Base Line** (BL) is the geodesic between any two stations. Its length is expressed in nautical miles, kilometers, or the time of travel in microseconds of a 100-kHz radio wave. The Base Line is approximately equivalent to the great circle between the two stations. A Base Line is identified by the alphabetic designators of the stations it connects.

Base Line Extension

The **Base Line Extension** is the extension of the geodesic beyond the stations. The master Base Line Extension extends beyond the master station and the secondary Base Line Extension beyond the secondary station.

Time Differences

Time difference is the time of arrival at the receiver of the radio wave from a secondary, minus the time of arrival of the radio wave from the master station.

Hyperbolic Line-of-Position

A **hyperbolic line-of-position** (LOP) is a line on the earth's surface having constant difference of geodesic distance from two transmitting stations and represents the difference in propagation time from the two stations. These LOPs may be overprinted on the charts for use in position fixing. On larger scale charts (1:100,000 or less), computed or observed time difference data may be used to correct LOPs for propagation velocity variations, in which case the LOPs will be called **time difference lines-of-position**. More modern, user-friendly receivers compute all this information internally and have done away with the LORAN plotting chart.

LOPs on charts are labeled with the chain identification, the secondary station, and the time difference in microseconds associated with the LOP. A chain identification 9930 indicates that particular chain's GRI (**group repetition interval**) is 99,300 microseconds. That time refers to the amount of time between the start and stop of the Master station transmission. Each chain can be identified by a particular GRI. For example,

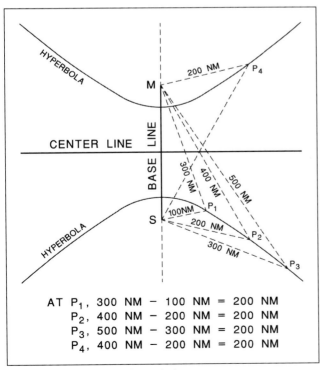

AT P₁, 300 NM − 100 NM = 200 NM
   P₂, 400 NM − 200 NM = 200 NM
   P₃, 500 NM − 300 NM = 200 NM
   P₄, 400 NM − 200 NM = 200 NM

Figure 12-2. LORAN hyperbolas

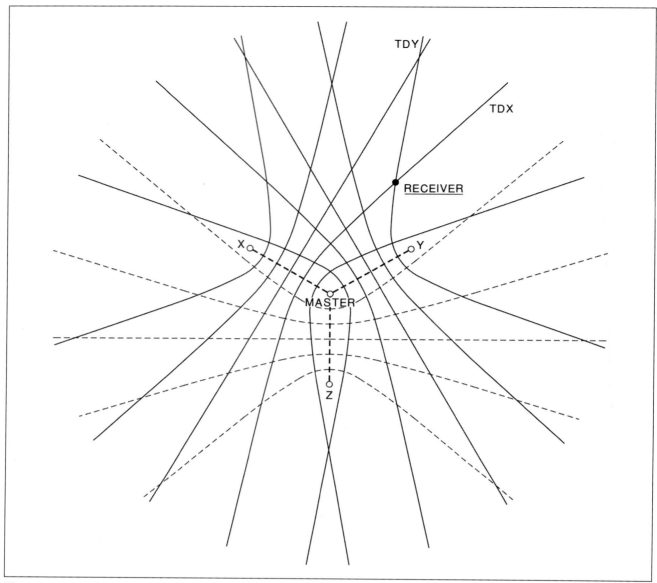

Figure 12-3. LORAN-C station chain showing hyperbolic lines of position

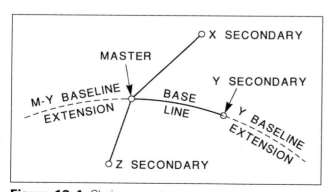

Figure 12-4. Chain geometry

9930-Y-494720 is the LOP in the chain 9930 associated with a station Y, with a secondary time difference of 49,720 microseconds. When it is clear which chain and secondary station are being used, time difference only may be shown, so as to avoid cluttering charts. Not all LOPs are plotted on charts. Usually, LOPs separated by multiples of 10 microseconds are shown so that the chart has lines spaced every 1-3 cm. For LOPs associated with time differences not shown, the navigator must interpolate between lines.

Gradient

Gradient is the vector rate of change of time difference with distance, in microseconds per kilometer, at a point on the surface of the earth. The vector direction is perpendicular to the LOP at that point in the direction of increasing time difference. The maximum magnitude of gradient is approximately 6.67 microseconds per kilometer which occurs on the base line. The gradient decreases off the base line to zero on the base line extension. Gradient is proportional to the sine of one half the angle subtended by the geodesics from the two transmitting stations at the point in question.

Fix

A **fix** is a statement of position expressed in any useful coordinate system, such as time difference coordinates, range and bearing coordinates, or in degrees of latitude and longitude. A fix is determined by the intersection of two or more LOPs.

Geometric Dilution of Precision

Geometric dilution of precision is a measure of the sensitivity of fix accuracy to errors in time difference measurement, expressed in meters per microsecond. As geometric dilution of precision increases in a given area, the impact of atmospheric noise, interference, and propagation vagaries increases. Figure 12-5 shows curves of constant geometric dilution of precision in the coverage area of a typical three station chain.

Geometric dilution of precision is a function of the gradient of each LOP, and the angle at which the LOPs cross. As crossing angles and/or gradient decreases, the geometric dilution of precision increases. Lines of constant geometric dilution of precision are lines on which accuracy of fix are expected to be equal.

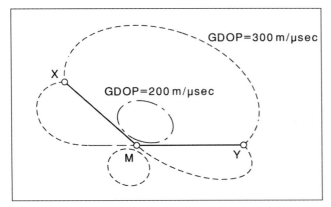

Figure 12-5. Curves of constant geometric dilution of precision

Chain Coverage Area

A chain's coverage is defined as the region where the geometric dilution of precision, transmitted power, estimated propagation unknowns, and predicted atmospheric noise will provide the indicated accuracy with the ground wave signal-to-noise ratio above a specified minimum 95% of the time over a period of a year.

For example, the advertised coverage of LORAN-C in the U.S. Coastal Confluence Zone is the region where the accuracy is one quarter of a nautical mile and where the signal to noise ratio is above 3 decibels. This region is plotted on a chart as the LORAN-C coverage area (*see* Figure 12-1 on Page 218).

Coverage areas for particular signal processing techniques, or "application coverage areas" may be different than the chain coverage areas. For example, a receiver which processes sky wave signals would operate over a much greater area than is indicated by the chain coverage area. System users operating on other than time differences would have an application coverage area extending beyond that shown on published charts. Operating in a range-range mode, using stations from different chains, or using secondaries without a master, are examples which alter the chain coverage area by virtue of application methods and crossing angles.

The Pulse

Each of the stations in the LORAN-C chains transmit pulses that have standard characteristics. The pulses consist of a 100-kHz carrier that rapidly increases in amplitude in a carefully controlled manner, and then decays at a specified rate forming an envelope of the signal (Figure 12-6 on the next page).

Signal Format

Each station in a chain repetitively transmits a series of closely spaced pulses called a pulse group at the group repetition interval of the chain (Figure 12-7). When the chain is synchronized to Universal Time, the master station also sets the time reference for the chain. Other stations of the chain are secondaries and transmit in turn after the master. Each secondary is delayed in time so that nowhere in the coverage area will signals from one station overlap another. The number of pulses in a group, pulse spacing in a group, carrier phase code of each pulse, time of transmission, the time between repetition of pulse groups from a station, and the delay of secondary station pulse groups with respect to the master signals, constitute the signal format.

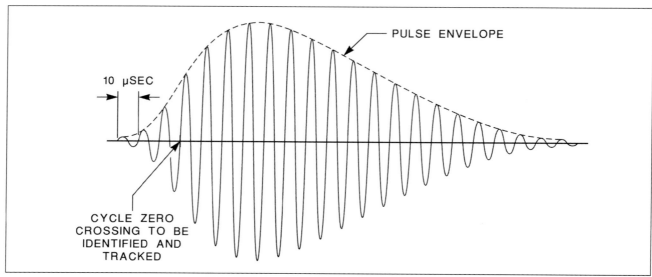

Figure 12-6. LORAN-C pulse detail

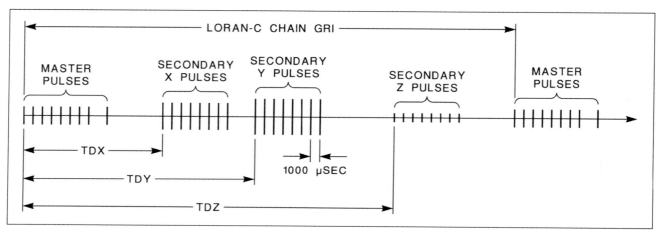

Figure 12-7. LORAN-C pulse pattern

Each station in a chain is assigned a signal format based on its function. The signal format is modified by "blinking" certain pulses to notify the user of faulty signal transmission. The signal format is also modified to accommodate a signal transmitter station to operate for two separate chains. This is accomplished by permitting transmission for one of the chains to take precedence over the other when the signal format calls for simultaneous transmissions in both chains. This function is called **blanking**. Signal format parameters, values and tolerances form part of this specification.

Communication

In addition to providing a navigation service, the LORAN-C transmissions can be used for the purpose of communications. For example, messages for system control may be sent from station to station within a chain by varying certain signal format parameters of the pulse. This can be accomplished without significant adverse effect on the processing of the navigation signals in receiving equipment.

Received Signal Characteristics

While the transmitted signal can be uniquely expressed and transmitting equipment built and adjusted to meet the specified criteria, the received pulse cannot enjoy this rigorous treatment. Vagaries in the earth's surface, atmosphere and ionosphere together with manmade radio noise and structures created by man, modify the transmitted pulses and add noise into the spectrum of frequencies to be received. These factors have to be considered when defining the area of coverage and the receiver design.

Coverage Area

The coverage area of a chain is usually defined in terms of signal strength and geometry of the transmitting stations with respect to each other, as they will support a specified position accuracy from a LORAN-C receiver having certain minimum performance characteristics. This specification defines coverage area as the term is applied on charts prepared by the U.S. National Ocean Survey and the U.S. Defense Mapping Agency, and in the LORAN-C implementation plan by the Coast Guard.

Propagation and Interference

The effects of the earth's shape, conductivity and permittivity, the atmosphere, the ionosphere, and natural and manmade noise modifies the LORAN-C pulse and alters components of the frequency spectrum that must be addressed in the receiver.

The path over which LORAN-C signals travel affects the range, the characteristics, and the reliability of time differences readings. Radio energy which travels along the surface of the earth is called the **ground wave**. The energy which is reflected from the ionosphere is called the **sky wave**.

A LORAN-C pulse which travels to the ionosphere and back travels a greater distance than one which follows the curvature of the earth. The additional distance it travels depends on the height of the reflecting layer, the number of hops it takes, and the distance of the receiver from the transmitter.

Modern aviation LORAN-C receivers use ground waves only, to determine their position. The exclusive use of the stronger ground wave signal will provide a useful range of up to 1,000 NM under ideal conditions, and 450-500 NM under average conditions. Receivers that use both sky and ground waves enjoy a maximum range out to 2,800 NM from a LORAN chain. There is an area between 1,000 and 1,400 NM where a receiver can have trouble distinguishing between sky and ground waves, so ambiguities may arise.

Static caused by a build-up of static electricity due to motion through a moist atmosphere can greatly diminish the maximum ranges as previously stated. This static usually causes interference with the received signal, and, when strong enough, can completely mask the LORAN-C signal. This (precipitation static noise) can be reduced by ensuring there is a proper ground and bond between the receiver antenna and the aircraft structure. The installation of static wicks on an aircraft is also a good precaution to avoid losing the reception of a LORAN-C signal due to static noise. **Signal-to-noise ratio** (SNR) is also an indirect function of distance from the station; the farther away, the lower the SNR. Therefore, the farther away, the less accurate the LORAN-C will be.

When a ground wave passes over land, its maximum range is reduced because of the attenuation properties of land. Large cities, mountainous regions, and thick ice also attenuate the LORAN-C signal and will reduce reception quality and range.

All of these factors combine to make LORAN-C navigation most accurate during clear weather, over water, and during daylight. Conversely, we can expect a reception and accuracy reduction in precipitation, over land, and at night.

Accuracy

LORAN-C is normally measured in two separate ways. The first measurement is referred to as **repeatable accuracy**. This refers to the system's ability to return to a specific previous position. The terrain and propagation errors unique to that particular location will be essentially the same upon return, and this effectively eliminates these factors as sources of error. While holding in position at the departure end of a runway, insert that position into the LORAN-C system. The accuracy of returning to that exact spot should be within 0.01 NM or about 60 feet.

The other LORAN-C measurement of accuracy is **absolute accuracy** (the ability to determine present position independently). This accuracy will vary from 0.1 NM to as much as 2.5 NM depending on distance from the station, geometry of the crossing angles, design choices made by the manufacturer, terrain and environmental conditions, and the signal-to-noise ratio.

Transmitter Blanking

At a double-rated station when the signals for both rates might overlap in time, the lower priority signal is blanked or suppressed. Priority is first given to a master signal if the station is a master on one of the rates, and second to the rate with the larger group repetition interval.

The priority blanking interval extends for one millisecond preceding the first pulse of the priority signal and one millisecond following the last pulse of the priority signal. Blanking is applied to individual pulses if they are of a lower priority and fall within the blanking interval.

LORAN-C Operations

Notes for Pilots

Initialization

Most LRNS (long range navigation systems) must be "initialized" upon start-up. The process requires certain procedures be performed by the user before the unit is ready for use. LORAN-C receivers are no exception.

The process requires that the unit be told where it is. Not precisely, like an INS system, but, for most sets, within 30-60 NM. Some sets also require the user to select the appropriate GRI (chain of stations) while others, once they know where they are, are able to automatically select the correct GRI.

First start-up often requires "setup" of various toggles, much like when installing a new software program in a personal computer. The user must decide what units of distance, time and even whether lat./lon. or TD lanes are to be displayed. This basic setup usually only needs to occur once, and most sets will remember where they were when shut off, so even that "tell me where I am" process is not required unless the aircraft is moved some distance with the set shut off.

Acquisition

After initialization, or if initialization is not needed, after startup, the set requires an interval of time to acquire each station of the chain and determine the appropriate cycle of each signal to identify. Typically, this interval is 1-5 minutes. When the initialization process is complete, the set begins tracking or displaying location information.

Warnings

Each set has its own way of warning the user if it is not able to operate normally because of problems such as weak signals/strong interference. Sixty-cycle AC is a fundamental frequency of which the 100-kHz LORAN-C signal is a harmonic, so proximity to power lines may render the LORAN-C receiver useless until the aircraft moves away from the interference source. Once moved, then the acquisition process can start, so expect a short wait after leaving the area of interference.

Other LORAN-C system problems such as transmitter problems (blink), poor signal geometry, or crossing baseline extensions should cause warnings to alert the user. Several years of use of these systems has caused me to become aware that I can often tell when the LORAN is struggling with a problem by watching the ground speed indication. An unstable ground speed reading often precedes a warning flag and also occurs without a warning flag. When that happens, if the unstable ground speed condition doesn't stabilize within a minute or so, I consider the LORAN position output to be suspect. Time for a gross error check! (*See* Chapter 16.)

Database

Modern LORAN-C receivers contain a powerful computer which may have a database capable of containing as little as a few user-entered waypoints, or as much as thousands of airport locations with extra useful information such as frequencies, altitudes, runways, services, etc., VORs, NDBs, and intersections — plus room for several hundred user-entered waypoints. Each set has its own procedures for accessing this information and programming the set to navigate to these locations. The user must learn the system by which the database is arranged and accessed.

LORAN Navigation Terminology

Many of the terms used in LORAN navigation have been around for a long time, used in marine and air navigation for many years. There are a few new terms, many of which have been covered in the preceding pages. Here are a few terms that every pilot should know. Caution! Each manufacturer of LRNS's takes some liberties in defining these terms, so pilots must read the operating manuals to be sure the manufacturers' use of these terms is in agreement with the pilot's. All of these terms are in use by one or more present day LRNS.

BRG .... **Bearing.** The direction (magnetic or true) from present position to the active "to" waypoint.

CDI .... **Course deviation indicator.** Indicates the direction an aircraft should fly to return to the selected course.

CMG .... **Course made good.** Bearing from "from" waypoint. (*See* TRK.)

CTS .... **Course to steer.** Computed optimum course to steer to reduce cross track error and stay on course.

DTK .... **Desired track.** The track that is desired to be flown. It is usually a course, or line representing the great circle path, from one waypoint to a second waypoint.

ETE .... **Estimated time en route.** Same as TTS, time to station. Time from present position to active "to" waypoint at present speed.

GS .... **Ground speed.** Caution: this may be the actual speed over the ground in whatever direction the aircraft is going, or it may be the speed at which the aircraft is closing with the "to" waypoint. One manufacturer defines GS as speed over the ground and uses VMG (velocity made good) as the closing speed with the active "to" waypoint.

RNG .... **Range.** Distance from present position to the active "to" waypoint.

TRK .... **Track.** Actual track being flown. Often the same as CMG.

XTD .... **Cross track distance.** The distance that the aircraft is off course.

Course Offsetting

Area navigation systems, including LORAN-C, have the capability to fly courses that are parallel to existing airways, which some pilots like to do to avoid traffic on the airways. Offsets are also useful to avoid hazardous weather, restricted areas, high density traffic areas, hazardous terrain areas, etc. When the area to be avoided has been, some sets can be switched back to normal navigation mode. Those sets not having an offset feature can easily be used for the same purpose using the XTD feature.

Historical Notes and the Future of LORAN-C

May 14, 1991 was a historic day for LORAN-C. That was the day the **Mid-Continent Gap** was closed by the activation of the NOCUS (North Central U.S.) and SOCUS (South Central U.S.) chains, providing coverage from coast to coast, and from northern Mexico into central Canada, to north of Thompson, Manitoba.

LORAN-C has been used in the radiosonde weather balloon program, providing improved accuracy in plotting wind and other weather data. It has assisted many technical programs such as wild animal counts, and surveys to accurately know location information. Lobster and crab fishermen have long used this system, especially its repeatable accuracy feature, to return exactly to the location of their traps in the water.

LORAN-C was utilized in the Desert Shield and Desert Storm operations as well as the Iran-Iraq War, using the Saudi-Arabian chain, to provide very accurate positioning. While the advent of GPS and slowed the development of new features for the LORAN system, it remains today a well-used system, with good potential to serve as an independent backup system for GPS, for some time to come. The dilemma for general aviation pilots will be whether to remove the LORAN-C receiver from their aircraft panels in order to install another GPS, or to keep this highly accurate, proven navigation system; as it is truly completely independent from GPS, and the potential for a failure of the GPS system, although remote, does exist.

13: Global Positioning System

As the reader will conclude after reading this chapter, GPS is a very complex system. Serious study is required in order to not be counted in the ranks of those pilots who use long range navigation systems (LRNS) blindly, without a clue as to how the system works or the extent and nature of the limitations of the system.

The authors have condensed the material on this subject as much as possible without losing the important aspects and details necessary to a proper understanding of this amazing, highly accurate, world-wide system. Therefore, we cannot apologize for the amount and complexity of the information in this chapter; we can only wish you happy hunting!

The planned Future Air Navigation System (*see* Chapter 18) expects that the GPS will evolve into GNSS (the Global Navigation Satellite System). This will be the key feature of the world's future navigation system, which will be accurate enough to support enroute and nonprecision approach needs. Along with DGPS (described in this chapter, Page 255), this system will meet precision approach needs of the world's air fleet, as well as provide efficient (direct) traffic control. Therefore, pilots need to understand the system.

GPS System Overview

General System Description

The Global Positioning System (GPS) is a space-based radio positioning system which provides suitably equipped users with highly accurate position, velocity, and time data. This service provides globally, continuously, and under all weather conditions to users at or near the surface of the earth. GPS receivers operate passively, thus allowing an unlimited number of simultaneous users. The GPS has features which can deny accurate service to unauthorized users, prevent **spoofing** (the deliberate transmissions of incorrect GPS information), and reduce receiver susceptibility to jamming.

The GPS comprises three major segments: space, control, and user (Figure 13-1). The **space segment** consists of a constellation of GPS satellites in semi-synchronous orbits around the earth. Each satellite broadcasts radio-frequency ranging codes and a navigation data message.

The **control segment** consists of a Master Control Station and a number of monitor stations located on the ground around the world. The Master Control Station is responsible for tracking, monitoring, and updating data messages.

The **user segment** consists of a variety of radio navigation receivers specifically designed to receive, decode, and process the GPS satellite ranging codes and navigation data messages.

The **ranging codes** broadcast by the satellites enable a GPS receiver to measure the transit time of the signals and thereby determine the range between a satellite and the user. The **navigation data message** enables a receiver to calculate the position of each satellite at the time of transmission of the signal. Four satellites are normally required to be simultaneously "in view" of the receiver for three-dimensional (3-D) positioning purposes. This allows the user **3-D position coordinates** (x, y, and z or latitude, longitude, and altitude) and the user clock offset to be calculated from the satellite range and position data (part of the navigation data message). Treating the user clock offset as an unknown eliminates the requirement for users to be equipped with precision clocks. Less than four satellites can be used if the user altitude or system time is precisely known. Presently, user altitude input will permit the use of these satellites with many, but not all receivers.

Program Management

Operation of the control and space segments is managed by the USAF Space Command, Second Space Wing, Satellite Control Squadron at Falcon AFB, Colorado. Satellite control operations were transferred from the prototype Master Control Station at Vandenberg AFB to the Satellite Control Squadron at Falcon AFB in 1986. The Satellite Control Squadron continues to assume additional operating responsibility as each new GPS satellite becomes operational. The develop-

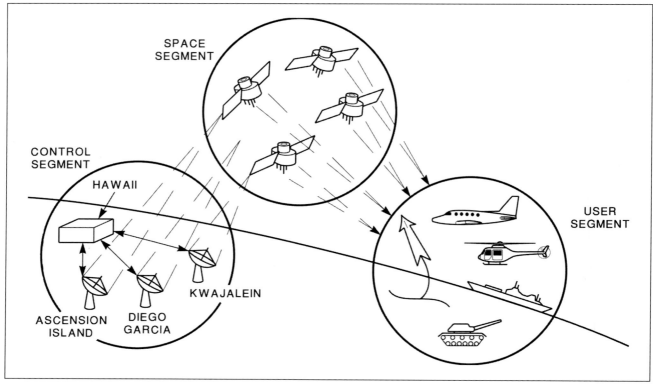

Figure 13-1. GPS major segments

ment organizations of the Joint Program Office completed turnover of all Master Control Station operation and control activities to the Satellite Control Squadron during 1990.

System Technical Description

Space Segment

The GPS space segment consists of 21 operational satellites. To ensure system availability, three additional satellites are in orbit as functioning spares. The satellites are placed in six orbital planes with three or four operational satellites in each plane. The satellite orbital planes has an inclination relative to the equator of 55° and the orbit height is about 10,200 km (Figure 13-2). The satellites complete an orbit in approximately 12 hours.

An observer on the ground will observe the same satellite ground track each day; however, the satellite becomes visible four minutes earlier each day due to a four minute per day difference between the satellite orbit time and the rotation of the earth. A satellite whose orbit passed over the observer's head would be visible for about six hours before setting. The time of visibility would increase with observer's altitude. The satellites are positioned such that a minimum of five satellites are normally observable by a user anywhere on earth. The satellites transmit on two frequencies:

L1 = 1575.42 MHz, and

L2 = 1227.6 MHz.

The satellites transmit their signals using spread spectrum techniques, employing two different spreading functions: a 1.023 MHz **coarse/acquisition code** of L1 only and a 10.23 MHz precision code on both L1 and L2. The minimum signal power for the different signals at a GPS receiver antenna is shown in Figure 13-3.

Both precision code and coarse/acquisition code enable a receiver to determine the range between the satellite and the user. Superimposed on both the precision code and the coarse/acquisition code is the navigation message, containing satellite **ephemeris data** (or, accurate orbit data), atmospheric propagation correction data, and satellite clock-bias information.

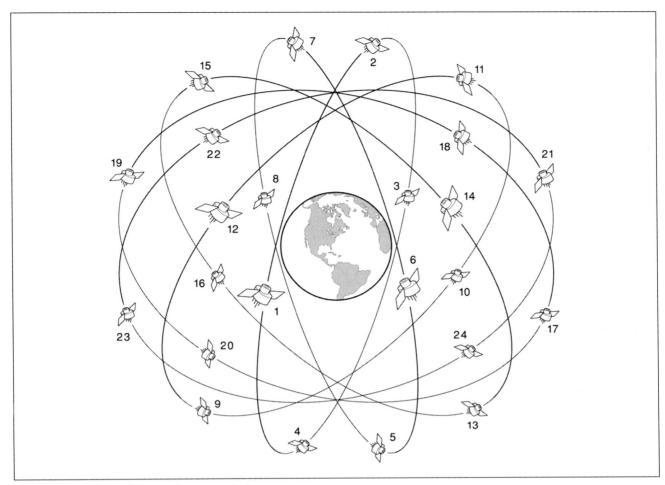

Figure 13-2. Operation satellite constellation

L$_1$	L$_2$
C/A = -160 dBW P = -163 dBW	P = -166 dBW

Figure 13-3. Power levels for received GPS signals

Control Segment

The control segment consists of one Master Control Station at Falcon AFB in Colorado Springs, Colorado, plus monitor stations at the Master Control Station, Hawaii, Kwajalein, Diego Garcia, and Ascension (Figure 13-4). All monitor stations except Hawaii and Falcon are also equipped with ground antennas for communications with the GPS satellites (Figure 13-5— *see* Pages 230; 231). The monitor stations passively track all GPS satellites in view, collecting ranging data from each satellite. This information is passed on to the Master Control Station where the satellite ephemeris

and clock parameters are estimated and predicted. The Master Control Station periodically uploads the ephemeris and clock data to each satellite for retransmission in the **navigation data message**.

User Segment

The user segment consists of a variety of military and civilian GPS receivers specifically designed to receive, decode, and process the GPS satellite signals. They include stand-alone receiver sets, as well as equipment integrated with or embedded into other systems. These receivers serve a variety of user applications including navigation, positioning, time transfer, surveying, and attitude reference. Consequently, GPS receivers for different applications can vary significantly in design and function.

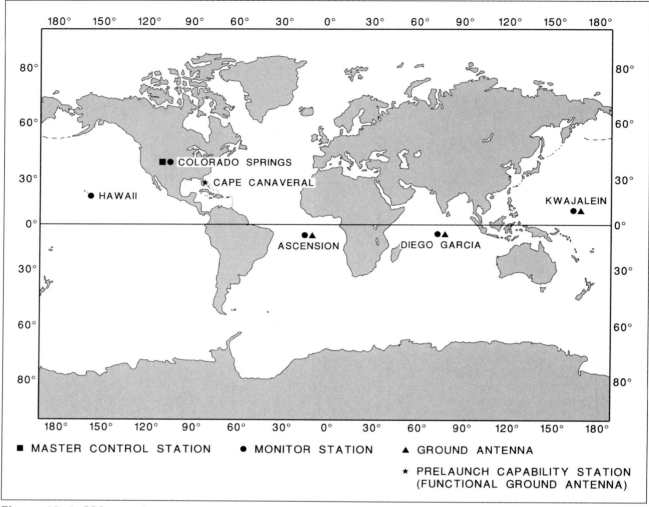

Figure 13-4. GPS control segment

- ■ MASTER CONTROL STATION
- ● MONITOR STATION
- ▲ GROUND ANTENNA
- ★ PRELAUNCH CAPABILITY STATION
  (FUNCTIONAL GROUND ANTENNA)

System Performance

Levels of Service

Two levels of navigation are provided by the GPS: the **Precise Positioning Service** and the **Standard Positioning Service**. The Precise Positioning Service is a highly accurate positioning, velocity, and timing service which is made available only to authorized users — principally, the military. The Standard Positioning Service is a less accurate positioning and timing service which is available to all GPS users.

Precise Positioning Service

The Precise Positioning Service is specified to provide 16 m Spherical Error Probable (3-D, 50%) positioning accuracy and 100 nanosecond (one sigma) Universal Coordinated Time (UTC) time transfer accuracy to authorized users.

This is approximately equal to 30 m (3-D, 95%) and 197 nanoseconds (95%). Precise Positioning Service receivers can achieve 0.2 m per second 3-D velocity accuracy, but this is somewhat dependent on receiver design. The Precise Positioning Service is primarily intended for military purposes. Authorization to use the Precise Positioning Service is determined by the U.S. Department of Defense, based on U.S. defense requirements and international commitments. Authorized users of the Precise Positioning Service include U.S. military users, NATO military users, and other selected military and civilian users such as the Australian Defense Forces and the U.S. Defense Mapping Agency.

Access to the Precise Positioning Service is controlled by two features using cryptographic techniques. A selective availability feature is used to reduce the GPS position, velocity, and time accuracy available

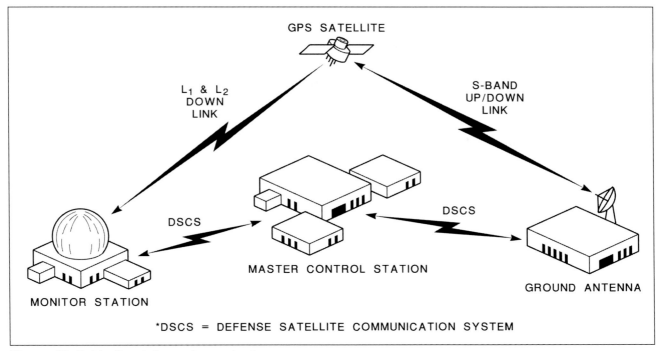

Figure 13-5. Monitor station and ground antenna

to unauthorized users. Selective availability operates by introducing controlled errors into the satellite signals. The U.S. Department of Defense has stated that in peacetime the effects of selective availability will be controlled to provide 100 m (95%) horizontal accuracy for Standard Positioning Service users.

System accuracy degradations can be increased if it is necessary to do so; for example, to deny accuracy to a potential enemy in time of crisis or war. An anti-spoofing feature is invoked at random times without warning by the U.S. to negate potential **spoofing** (hostile imitation) of Precise Positioning Service signals. The technique alters the precision code cryptographically into a code denoted as the Encrypted Precision Code (the coarse/acquisition code remains unaffected). Encryption keys and techniques are provided to Precise Positioning Service users which allow them to remove the effects of selective availability and anti-spoofing, thereby attaining the maximum available accuracy of GPS. Precise Positioning Service capable receivers that do not have the proper encryption keys installed will be subject to the accuracy degradations of selective availability and will be unable to track the Encrypted Precision Code.

Precise Positioning Service can use either the Encrypted Precision Code or coarse/acquisition code, or both. Maximum GPS accuracy is obtained using the Encrypted Precision Code on both L1 and L2. The dif-

ference in propagation delay between the two frequencies is used to calculate ionospheric corrections. Encrypted Precision Code capable receivers commonly use the coarse/acquisition code to initially acquire GPS satellites and determine the approximate Encrypted Precision Code phase.

Some Encrypted Precision Code receivers are able to directly acquire the Encrypted Precision Code by using a precise clock, instead of the coarse/acquisition code, to predict the Encrypted Precision Code phase. Some Precise Positioning Service receivers use only the coarse/acquisition code. Coarse/acquisition code-only receivers must use an **ionospheric model** to calculate ionospheric corrections (to correct for the signal bending that takes place as the satellite's message passes into and through the ionosphere), since the coarse/acquisition code is broadcast only on L1 and dual frequency delay measurements are therefore not available. This will typically result in less positioning accuracy (approximately 65 m, 3-D accuracy, 95%) than dual frequency Encrypted Precision Code receivers.

Standard Positioning Service
The Standard Positioning Service is specified to provide 100 m (95%) horizontal positioning accuracy to any GPS user during peacetime. This is approximately equal to 156 m 3-D (95%). Standard Positioning Service receivers can achieve approximately 337 nanosecond

(95%) UTC time transfer accuracy. The Standard Positioning Service is primarily intended for civilian purposes, although it has many peacetime military uses as well. The Standard Positioning Service horizontal accuracy includes the peacetime degradation of selective availability error source. The selective availability position error distribution resembles a Gaussian distribution with a long-term mean of zero. The Standard Positioning Service peacetime velocity degradation due to selective availability is classified.

The anti-spoofing feature denies Standard Positioning Service users access to the Encrypted Precision Code. Therefore, the Standard Positioning Service user cannot rely on the Encrypted Precision Code to measure the propagation delays of L1 and L2 and calculate ionospheric corrections. The coarse/acquisition code is unaffected by anti-spoofing, but is broadcast only on L1. Consequently, the typical Standard Positioning Service receiver uses only the coarse/acquisition code, and must use an ionospheric model to calculate the corrections. This is a less accurate technique than measuring dual frequency propagation delays. The Standard Positioning Service accuracy specification includes this ionospheric modeling error.

Standard Positioning Service Precise Code receivers and Precise Positioning Service Encrypted Precise Code receivers that do not have the proper encryption keys installed will typically operate as Standard Positioning Service dual-frequency Precise Code receivers, and revert to coarse/acquisition code (signal frequency) when unable to track the Precise Code. Nonmilitary aviation GPS receivers are of this type.

Navigation Using GPS

The ranging codes broadcast by the satellites enable a GPS receiver to measure the transit time of the signals and thereby determine the distance between a satellite and the user. The navigation data messages enable a receiver to calculate the position of each satellite at the time of transmission of the signal. From this information, the user position coordinates and the user clock offset can be calculated using simultaneous equations. Four satellites are normally required to be simultaneously "in view" of the receiver for three-dimensional positioning purposes.

GPS Satellite Signals

Precision Code

The precision code is a 267-day long code sequence, and each of the GPS satellites is assigned a unique one-week segment of this code. The precision code bit rate is 10.23 MHz. Each satellite has a 7-day-long portion that restarts every Saturday and Sunday at midnight. The precision code is normally transmitted on both L1 and L2, and it is protected against **spoofing** by encryption of the precision code.

Coarse/Acquisition Code

The **coarse/acquisition code** consists of a 1,023-bit code with a clock rate of 1.023 MHz; hence, it takes only one millisecond to run through the whole code. A different coarse/acquisition code is assigned to each GPS satellite and is chosen from a set of codes called "Gold codes." The coarse/acquisition code will normally be transmitted on L1 only, but it can also be transmitted on L2 instead of the precision code. The coarse/acquisition code is available to all users of GPS. The coarse/acquisition code is used by precision code users to assist the receiver in reducing the time to acquire the longer precision code. A coarse/acquisition code-only receiver is less complex and usually less expensive than a precision-code GPS receiver.

The Navigation Message

The **navigation message** is superimposed on both the precision code and coarse/acquisition code with a data rate of 50 bits per second. The navigation message contains 25 data frames, each frame consisting of 1,500 bits. Each frame is divided into five subframes of 300 bits each (Figure 13-6). It will therefore take 30 seconds to receive one data frame and 12.5 minutes to receive all 25 data frames. Subframes 1, 2, and 3 repeat the same 900 bits of data on all 25 frames. This allows the receiver to obtain critical navigation message data within 30 seconds.

The data in the navigation message is normally valid for a 4-hour period. The navigation message contains GPS system time of transmission; a hand-over word for the transition from coarse/acquisition code to precision code tracking; ephemeris and clock data for the particular satellites being tracked; and almanac data for all the satellite vehicles in the constellation. Additionally, it contains information such as satellite health, coefficients for ionospheric delay model for coarse/acquisition code users, and coefficients to calculate Universal Coordinated Time.

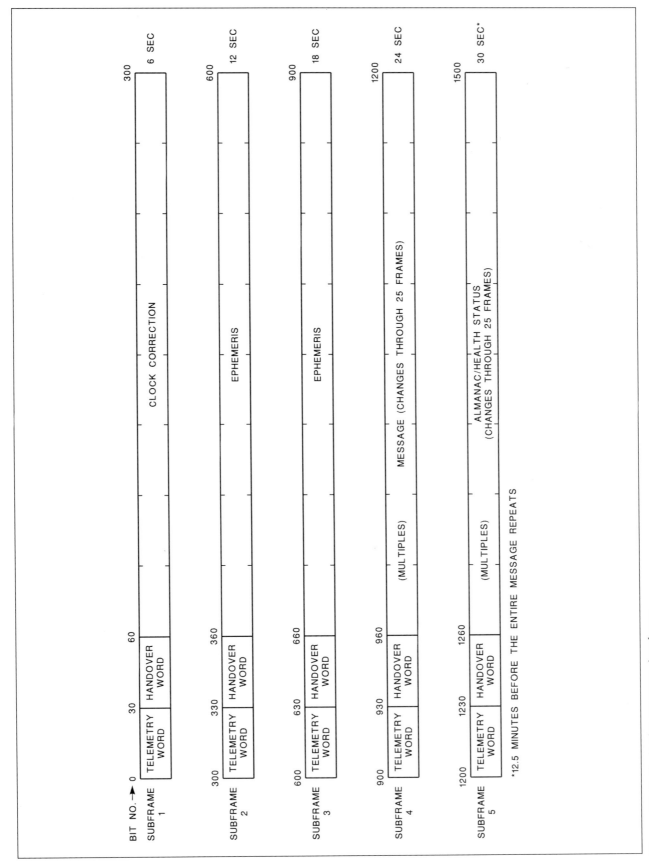

Figure 13-6. Navigation message data frame

Satellite Signal Modulation

The GPS satellites use a type of signal modulation called the bi-phase shift keying of the carrier. The bi-phase shift keying technique reverses the carrier phase when the digital pseudo-random noise code changes from zero to one or from one to zero (Figure 13-7).

The very long sequence of ones and zeros which constitute the coarse/acquisition and precision codes are called **pseudo-random noise codes** since, to a casual observer, the ones and zeros appear to occur in a random fashion. The resulting frequency spectrum for the carrier, due to the bi-phase shift keying, equals 20 MHz for the precision code and 2 MHz for the coarse/acquisition code (Figure 13-8).

The carrier frequency is suppressed. In actuality, the coarse/acquisition and precision codes generated are precisely predictable, relative to the start time of the code sequence. The user's receiver can therefore replicate the same code as the satellite. The amount the user receiver must offset its code generator to match the incoming code from the satellite is directly proportional to the range between the GPS receiver antenna and the satellite. Phase shifting of the carrier results in

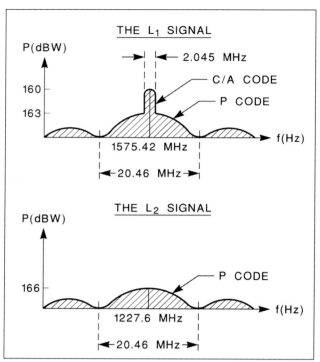

Figure 13-8. GPS signal frequency spectrum

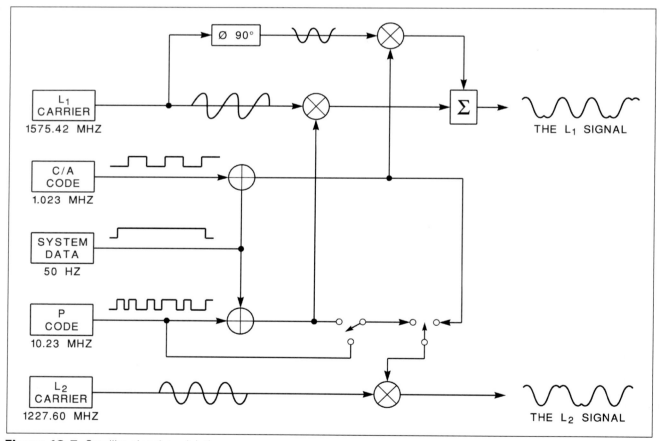

Figure 13-7. Satellite signal modulation

a spreading of carrier power between ±10.23 MHz of center frequency due to the precision code bi-phase shift keying, and ±1.023 MHz due to the coarse/acquisition code bi-phase shift keying. The resulting waveform (Figure 13-8) is equivalent to that of a carrier spread by a regular square wave function with precision code and coarse/acquisition code modulation (clipping) rates. When the spread spectrum signal is received at the GPS receiver, the signal power is below the thermal (background) noise level. When the satellite signal is multiplied with the GPS receiver-generated precision codes and coarse/acquisition codes, the satellite signal will be collapsed into the original carrier frequency band. Signal power is then again concentrated into a very narrow frequency band and is well above the thermal noise level (Figure 13-9).

GPS Receiver Operation

In order for the GPS receiver to navigate, it has to acquire and track satellite signals to make pseudorange and **delta range** (velocity) measurements, and collect the navigation message data. The measurement

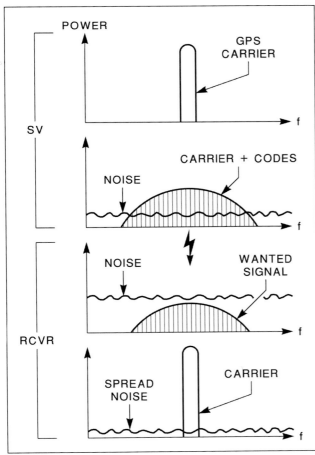

Figure 13-9. Spread spectrum used in GPS

is termed **pseudorange** because the clock offset of a GPS receiver introduces a bias to the true range of the satellite.

Satellite Signal Acquisition

The received satellite signal level near the Earth is actually less than the background noise level. Correlation techniques are used by the GPS receiver to obtain the navigation signals (Figure 13-9). A typical satellite tracking sequence begins with the receiver determining which satellites are visible for it to track. Satellite visibility is based on the user-entered predictions of present Position, Velocity, and Time (PVT), and on stored satellite almanac information residing in the receiver's computer. If no stored satellite almanac information exists or only a very poor estimate of position and time is available, the receiver must "search the sky," attempting to randomly locate and lock onto any satellite in view. If the receiver can estimate satellite visibility, it will target a satellite to track. When one satellite is being tracked, the receiver can demodulate the navigation message and read the almanac information about all the other satellites in the constellation.

A carrier tracking loop is used to track the carrier frequency while a code tracking loop is used to track the coarse/acquisition and precision code signals. The two tracking loops have to work together in an interactive process, aiding each other, in order to acquire and track the satellite signals. This process typically takes 15-60 minutes of tracking one satellite, but this is only necessary to initialize the receiver, a one-time process.

Carrier Tracking

The receiver's carrier tracking loop will locally generate an L1 carrier frequency which differs from the received carrier signal, due to a Doppler offset of the carrier frequency. This Doppler offset is proportional to the relative velocity along the line of sight between the satellite and the GPS receiver, plus a bias residual in the receiver frequency standard. In order for the carrier tracking loop to track the incoming carrier signal, the incoming satellite signal has to be code-correlated such that the carrier signal becomes visible again (Figure 13-9). This is done by the code tracking loop. The carrier tracking loop will adjust the frequency of the receiver generated carrier until it matches the incoming carrier frequency, thereby determining the relative velocity between the GPS receiver and the satellite being tracked. The GPS receiver uses the relative velocity to four satellites being tracked to determine the velocity of the GPS receiver Earth-Centered-Earth-Fixed coordinates (the receiver's velocity with respect to the Earth). The velocity output of the carrier tracking loop is used to aid the code tracking loop (Figure 13-10).

Code Tracking

The code tracking loop is used to make pseudorange measurements between the GPS satellites and the GPS receivers. The receiver's code tracking loop will generate a replica of the targeted satellite's coarse/acquisition code with estimated ranging delay. This replica is a spread-spectrum signal which has a center frequency (representing the suppressed carrier) and sidebands (created by modulating the carrier with precision code and/or coarse/acquisition code). In order to match up the received signal with the internally-generated replica, two things must be done: the center frequency of the replica must be adjusted to be the same as the center frequency of the received signal, and the phase of the replica code must be lined up with the phase of the received signal code.

The center frequency is set by using the Doppler-estimated output of the carrier tracking loop. The deviation of the code phase from the received code to the reference code is directly proportional to the pseudorange between the GPS receiver and the satellite. In general, prior to tracking, the signal generated in the code tracking loop will not correlate with the received satellite signal, due to the time delay for the satellite signal to reach the receiver, the receiver's clock bias error. The receiver will therefore slew the code loop-generated coarse/acquisition code through its millisecond search window to obtain coarse/acquisition code tracking.

Data Demodulation

Once the carrier tracking loop and the code tracking loop have locked onto the received signal and the coarse/acquisition code is stripped from the carrier, the 50 bits per second navigation message can be demodulated by performing bit synchronization and data detection on the carrier. The navigation message contains the satellite ephemeris and other relevant information allowing accurate pseudorange calculation.

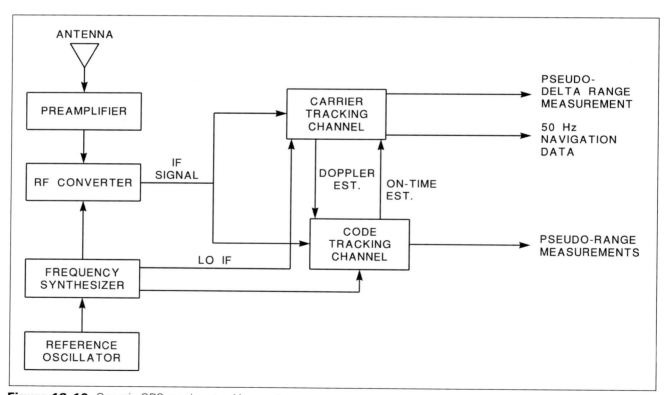

Figure 13-10. Generic GPS receiver tracking system

Precision Code Signal Acquisition

The coarse/acquisition code repeats every millisecond allowing for a minimal receiver search window. The precision code repeats every seven days requiring that the approximate precision code phase be known in order to obtain signal lock-on. The hand-over word contained in the navigation message (Figure 13-6) provides the precision code phase information. A precision code receiver utilizes the hand-over word and the coarse/acquisition-code-derived pseudorange to minimize the precision code search window requirements.

Direct Precision Code Acquisition

A precision code receiver can also attempt to acquire precision code directly, without first acquiring the coarse/acquisition code. This requires a good knowledge of the receiver position and a very good knowledge of GPS time. An external atomic clock is usually required to perform direct precision code acquisition (*see* "Time Aiding" below, Page 253).

Navigation

When the receiver has acquired the satellite signals from four GPS satellites, achieved carrier and code tracking, and has read the navigation message, the GPS receiver is ready to start navigating. The GPS receiver normally updates its pseudoranges and relative velocities once every second. The next step is to calculate the GPS receiver position, receiver velocity, and GPS system time. The GPS receiver must know GPS system time very accurately, because the satellite signals contain the time-of-transmission from the satellite in GPS time. Therefore, the GPS receiver must also use GPS system time as the reference for measuring time-of-arrival of the satellite signals. The difference in time between the signal leaving the satellite and arriving at the GPS receiver antenna is directly proportional to the range between the satellite and the GPS receiver. Therefore it is of the utmost importance that the same time reference is used by both the GPS satellites and GPS receiver.

However, the GPS receiver is not required to have a high accuracy clock such as an atomic time standard. Instead, a crystal oscillator is used, and the GPS receiver corrects its offset from GPS system time by making four pseudorange measurements. The GPS receiver can use the four pseudoranges to solve four simultaneous equations with four unknowns (*see* Figure 13-11 on Page 238). When the four equations are solved, the GPS receiver has estimates of its position and GPS system time.

The GPS receiver velocity is calculated using the same types of equations, using relative velocities instead of pseudoranges. GPS receivers perform most calculations using an Earth-Centered-Earth-Fixed coordinate system. They then convert to an Earth model defined by the World Geodetic System 1984. The World Geodetic System 1984 is a very precise model that provides a common grid system for transformations into other coordinate systems or map datums.

Types of GPS Receivers and Their Applications

GPS Receiver Architectures

There are basically three types of GPS receiver architectures used to perform satellite tracking: sequential tracking receivers, continuous tracking receivers, and multiplex receivers.

Sequential Receivers

A **sequential GPS receiver** tracks the necessary satellites by typically using one or two hardware channels. The set will track one satellite at a time, time-tag the measurements, and combine them when all four satellite pseudoranges have been measured. These receivers are among the cheapest available, but they cannot operate under high dynamics, and they have the slowest time-to-first-fix performance.

One-Channel Sequential Receivers

A one-channel sequential receiver makes four pseudorange measurements on both the L1 and L2 frequencies in order to determine a position and compensate for ionospheric delay. The navigation message from each of the satellites must also be read to obtain ephemeris data. To determine an initial position, the receiver must perform the following operations:

1. Coarse/acquisition code search for a space vehicle,
2. Coarse/acquisition code/carrier center,
3. Data bit sync,
4. Frame sync and Z-count,
5. Hand-over word, precision code carrier center, and
6. Data demodulation and ionospheric measurements.

Once these operations are complete for one space vehicle, the receiver must perform then again for three other space vehicles. The four pseudorange measurements must be propagated to the same reference time

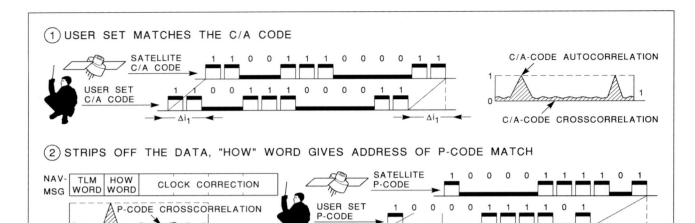

① USER SET MATCHES THE C/A CODE

SATELLITE C/A CODE   1 1 0 0 1 1 1 0 0 0 0 1 1

USER SET C/A CODE   1 1 0 0 1 1 1 0 0 0 0 1 1
Δi_1 ← ← → Δi_1 ←

C/A-CODE AUTOCORRELATION
C/A-CODE CROSSCORRELATION

② STRIPS OFF THE DATA, "HOW" WORD GIVES ADDRESS OF P-CODE MATCH

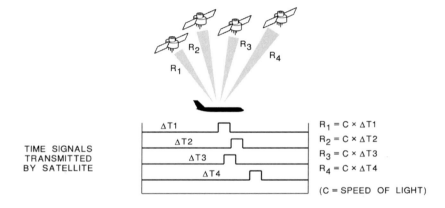

NAV-MSG	TLM WORD	HOW WORD	CLOCK CORRECTION

P-CODE CROSSCORRELATION
P-CODE AUTOCORRELATION

SATELLITE P-CODE   1 0 0 0 0 1 1 1 1 0 1

USER SET P-CODE   1 0 0 0 0 1 1 1 0 1
Δi_1 → ← → Δi_1 ←

③ USER OBTAINS PSEUDO RANGE MEASUREMENTS (R_1, R_2, R_3, R_4) TO 4 SATELLITES

R_2 R_3
R_1 R_4

TIME SIGNALS TRANSMITTED BY SATELLITE

$\Delta T1$
$\Delta T2$
$\Delta T3$
$\Delta T4$

$R_1 = C \times \Delta T1$
$R_2 = C \times \Delta T2$
$R_3 = C \times \Delta T3$
$R_4 = C \times \Delta T4$

(C = SPEED OF LIGHT)

④ USER SET PERFORMS THE NAV SOLUTION FOR POSITION

PSEUDO RANGES:

$R_1 = C\Delta t_1$

$R_2 = C\Delta t_2$

$R_3 = C\Delta t_3$

$R_4 = C\Delta t_4$

POSITION EQUATIONS:

$(X_1 - U_X)^2 + (Y_1 - U_Y)^2 + (Z_1 - U_Z)^2 = (R_1 - C_B)^2$

$(X_2 - U_X)^2 + (Y_2 - U_Y)^2 + (Z_2 - U_Z)^2 = (R_2 - C_B)^2$

$(X_3 - U_X)^2 + (Y_3 - U_Y)^2 + (Z_3 - U_Z)^2 = (R_3 - C_B)^2$

$(X_4 - U_X)^2 + (Y_4 - U_Y)^2 + (Z_4 - U_Z)^2 = (R_4 - C_B)^2$

R_i = PSEUDO RANGE (i = 1,2,3,4)

θ PSEUDO RANGE INCLUDES ACTUAL DISTANCE BETWEEN SATELLITE AND USER PLUS SV CLOCK BIAS, USER CLOCK BIAS, ATMOSPHERIC DELAYS, AND RECEIVER NOISE.

θ SV CLOCK BIAS AND ATMOSPHERIC DELAYS ARE COMPENSATED FOR BY INCORPORATION OF DETERMINISTIC CORRECTIONS PRIOR TO INCLUSION INTO NAV SOLUTION.

X_i, Y_i, Z_i = SATELLITE POSITION (i = 1,2,3,4)

• SATELLITE POSITION BRAODCAST IN NAVIGATION 50 Hz MESSAGE.

RECEIVER SOLVES FOR:

• U_X, U_Y, U_Z = USER POSITION

• C_B = USER CLOCK BIAS

Figure 13-11. Navigation using GPS

before a navigation solution is generated. Any movement of the host vehicle during the time the receiver collects the four pseudoranges will reduce the accuracy of the position, velocity, and time calculations in the receiver. One-channel sequential receivers are limited to low-dynamic or stationary applications.

Two-Channel Sequential Receivers

Two-channel sequential receivers have been developed for use on medium-dynamic vehicles such as helicopters. During initial power-up, each channel operates like a one-channel sequential receiver. After four space vehicles have been acquired, one channel is dedicated to navigation (pseudorange measurements, carrier tracking, etc.) while the other channel reads the navigation message from each satellite. Both channels are also used to perform dual frequency measurements to compensate for ionospheric delay and to measure differential channel delay. Two-channel sequential receivers decrease the time it takes to start navigating by better than one minute when compared to one-channel sequential receivers.

Continuous Receivers

A continuous tracking receiver must have at least four hardware channels to track four satellites simultaneously. Both four-channel and five-channel receivers are available. Due to their greater complexity, these receivers are the most expensive but offer the best performance and versatility. Both types of receivers track four satellites continuously. The five-channel receiver uses the fifth channel to read the navigation message of the next satellite to be used when the receiver changes the satellite selections. It also uses the fifth channel in conjunction with each of the other four channels to perform dual frequency measurements as well as differential channel delay measurements. Individual, dedicated tracking channels enable the receivers to maintain accuracy under high dynamics, provide the best anti-jamming performance, and have the lowest time-to-first-fix. This type of receiver is best suited for high-dynamic vehicles such as fighter aircraft, vehicles requiring low time-to-first-fix such as submarines, and any user requiring good anti-jamming performance.

Multiplex Receivers

A multiplex receiver switches at a fast rate (typically 50 Hz) between the satellites being tracked, continuously collecting sampled data to maintain two to eight signal processing algorithms in software. In addition, the 50 Hz navigation message data is read continuously from all the satellites. For a multiplex receiver tracking four satellites, this results in eight pseudochannels that deliver twenty observables continuously.

The observables are:

1. Four L1 code phases
2. Four L2 code phases
3. Four L1 carrier phases
4. Four L2 carrier phases
5. Four navigation messages.

From these 20 parameters, the four pseudoranges, four delta ranges (carrier frequency rate-of-change measurement), and the ionospheric delay can be derived.

In single-channel multiplex receivers the hardware channel is time-shared and only one code generator and one carrier synthesizer is required to track the satellites in precision code on both L1 and L2 frequencies. Inter-channel biases and inter-channel phase drift errors are eliminated because only one hardware channel is used. However, a multiplex receiver's measured carrier-to-noise ratio for any satellite signal will be about 4 to 8 decibels below that of a continuous tracking receiver, because the multiplex receiver only tracks each satellite a fraction of the time, and therefore cannot detect all the available spread spectrum signal power.

"All-In-View" Receivers

Traditionally, GPS receivers choose the four satellites of those available that give the best geometry to perform a position fix. However, in situations where one or more of the satellites are temporarily obscured from the antenna's view, the receiver will have to acquire additional satellite signals to generate a continuous position, velocity, and time solution. The position, velocity, and time solution degrades until the new satellites are acquired. One solution is to have a receiver which uses all available satellites in view to generate a solution.

The inherent advantage of this receiver is that if it is tracking six or seven space vehicles and a satellite becomes obscured, the receiver will continue to provide a position, velocity, and time solution with little, if any, degradation. The disadvantage to this type of receiver is the increased hardware, weight, power consumption, and cost if the design uses separate channels for each satellite it tracks. If the receiver does not dedicate one hardware channel per satellite, then the receiver must use some sort of continual reacquisition strategy.

Time-To-First-Fix

Time-to-first-fix is a measure of the elapsed time required for a receiver to acquire the satellite signals and navigation data, and calculate the first position solution. U.S. Department Of Defense source material may refer to time-to-first-fix-1 and time-to-first-fix-2. Time-to-first-fix-1 is based on coarse/acquisition code acquisition with hand over to precision code tracking. Time-to-first-fix-2 is based on direct precision code acquisition. Time-to-first-fix is also a function of the initial receiver state as well as receiver design. The following paragraphs describe the acquisition process in more detail.

Cold Start-Up

When a GPS receiver is initially turned on, time must be allowed for the receiver crystal oscillator to warm up and stabilize at its normal operating temperature. In a GPS receiver, it typically takes up to six minutes to complete this process. If the receiver is provided with a stand-by mode which keeps the oscillator warm, this contribution to time-to-first-fix can be avoided.

Almanac Collection

The first time a receiver is operated, it must perform an interactive search for the first satellite signal unless it can be loaded with a recent satellite constellation almanac, the approximate time and the approximate receiver location. The almanac gives the approximate orbit for each satellite, and it is valid for extended periods (up to 180 days). The almanac is used to predict satellite visibility and estimate the pseudorange to a satellite, thereby narrowing the search window for a ranging code. Once the first satellite signal is acquired, a current almanac can be obtained from the navigation message. It takes 12.5 to 30 minutes to collect a complete almanac after initial acquisition. An almanac can be obtained from any GPS satellite. Most modern receivers can update the almanac periodically and store

the most recent almanac and receiver position in protected memory. A clock can also be kept operating when the receiver is off or in stand-by mode, so as to minimize initial acquisition time for the next start-up.

Ephemerides Collection

Ephemeris data (accurate orbit data) forms part of the 50-Hz navigation message transmitted from the GPS satellites. Ephemeris must be collected from each satellite being tracked, unlike almanac data which can be obtained for the whole constellation from a single satellite. Ephemeris information is normally valid for four hours from the time of transmission, and a receiver can normally store up to eight sets of ephemeris data in its memory. Acquisition and reacquisition times for a receiver will vary, depending on whether valid ephemeris data is already available to the receiver. When testing acquisition time, it is necessary to specify whether a valid set of ephemerides is resident or not within the receiver. Depending on the navigation message collection scheme employed in a particular receiver, it can take between 30 seconds and 3 minutes to collect the ephemeris information.

Time-To-First-Fix Requirements

Figure 13-12 is a decision chart for determining time-to-first-fix requirements for different receiver designs, for the various initial conditions described above, including time-to-first-fix-1 and time-to-first-fix-2 code acquisition strategies. The time-to-first-fix values are based on 90% accuracy requirements appearing in ICD-GPS-200.[1]

Satellite Reacquisition

Satellite reacquisition assumes a temporary loss of a satellite signal due to masking or similar loss of satellite visibility. ICD-GPS-200 specified satellite reacquisition time is 10 seconds. Vehicle dynamics and elapsed time from loss of the signal are important in determining the accuracy of the receiver position estimate, as is the presence of GPS aids, such as an INS.

---

[1] ICD-GPS-200; NavStar GPS Space Segment/Navigation User Interfaces Specifications, by ARINC Research Corp., 1993.

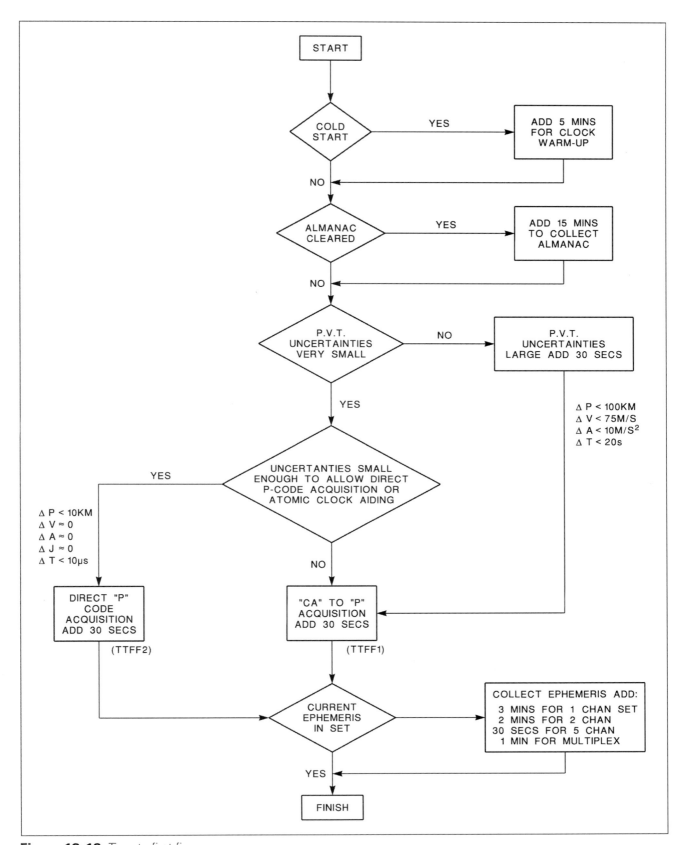

Figure 13-12. Time-to-first-fix

GPS Specification and Design Issues

System Availability

System availability is defined by the U.S. as the probability of having 21 operational satellites on orbit. GPS program specifications require that a system availability of at least 98% be maintained once the full GPS constellation becomes operational. The analysis that is conducted to verify meeting the 98% requirement uses inputs of launch vehicle reliability, satellite reliability with time, satellite wear-out, and launch call-up time. The analysis is probabilistic, based on Monte Carlo theory. There are three potential courses of action for a satellite launch and replenishment strategy: launch-on-anticipation-of-failure, launch-on-failure, and launch-on-schedule.

All these options have strong and weak points. With a launch-on-anticipation strategy, if a failure is anticipated in a specific orbital plane, a subsequent launch may be misdirected if the real failure occurs in a different plane. Launch-on-failure would require more on-orbit spares, since anticipated launch capability with essentially full queues at the launch pads would result in unacceptable launch delays and satellite outages. Launch-on-schedule, if used too rigidly, could result in either too few or too many satellites on orbit. As satellites grow old, they do exhibit symptoms that allow a failure to be anticipated (e.g., clocks, reaction wheels, battery power). The most attractive policy appears to be a modified launch-on-schedule with plane selection based on failure anticipation. This could result in having more than three effective spares in orbit, which would minimize the problem of launching into the wrong plane.

There will be other times when satellites are not available; for example, during satellite orbit adjustments, switching clocks or the ion pump on cesium clocks. These can be predicted and scheduled by the control segment: so advance notice will be given. There may also be unpredictable failures which can cause temporary loss of satellite availability. For both predictable and unpredictable events, the impact on users will be from very small to none. Ground and sea users should always have ample satellites for navigation.

Based on the 98% system availability requirement, these is no doubt that the U.S. Space Command has every intention of maintaining a minimum constellation of 21 GPS satellites. The experience with Block 1 satellites, and the current policy to maintain spares on orbit (most probably active) with further spares on the ground, indicates that the 98% availability figures will be maintained or exceeded. Space Command expects that if a system availability problem should ever occur, it is likely to be a single event lasting from a few weeks to a few months, due to an interruption in satellite launches, a delay in satellite procurement, or similar problem.

Positioning Availability

No formal definition of positioning availability has been documented, but it is generally accepted that positioning availability is the probability of the user having a position solution with a position **dilution of precision** of six or less. For simplicity, occurrences of positioning unavailability will be referred to here as an **outage** (Figure 13-13). Positioning availability, as measured at the user antenna, can be affected by the local conditions such as physical obstructions, vehicle maneuvering and aspect, jamming, or basic receiver design.

Positioning availability therefore cannot be categorized as a system requirement or specification (Figure 13-14). For purposes of this discussion, the assumption is made that local conditions are favorable and that the satellite signals are only limited by a default mask angle in the receiver. Positioning availability under these benign conditions is often referred to as satellite coverage.

Positioning availability is determined by system availability; however, there is no direct mathematical relationship between the two. Positioning availability is defined by the orbits of the active satellites, not just their total quantity. The orbits determine the geometric relationships between the satellites and the user, which the user measures as position **dilution of precision**. Since the geometric relationships continuously change as the satellites move round their orbits, so does the user's value of position dilution of precision (Figure 13-15 on Page 244). Similarly, position dilution of precision will also vary depending on the user location (Figure 13-16 on Page 244). Therefore, since navigation availability is defined with respect to position dilution of precision, it will also vary with the satellite orbital period and depend on the user's location.

A fully operational constellation (21 satellites plus 3 active spares) provides virtually continuous worldwide positioning availability. Figure 13-17 (Page 245) shows the cumulative outage pattern for the 21 plus 3 constellation over a 24-hour period. Only four outages occur for less than three minutes, each affecting a very small percentage of the earth, and position dilution of precision does not exceed 11.

There is a four-fold symmetry to the pattern of outages. One outage occurs approximately every six hours, shifted 90° east in longitude from the previous outage, and to the opposite hemisphere at the equivalent latitude. This symmetry occurs because the orbital planes are symmetrical about the equator, and because the satellites complete two orbits for each rotation of the earth. The outages will reappear above the same earth locations each day because the satellite ground tracks repeat. Each outage will appear approximately four minutes earlier each day because the satellites actually complete two orbits in 23 hours and 56 minutes, rather than 24 hours.

Continued on Page 246

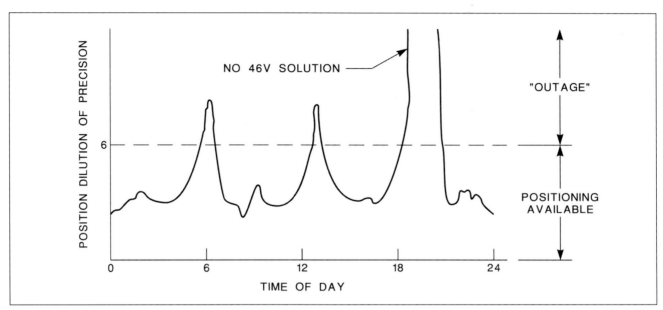

Figure 13-13. Definition of positioning availability

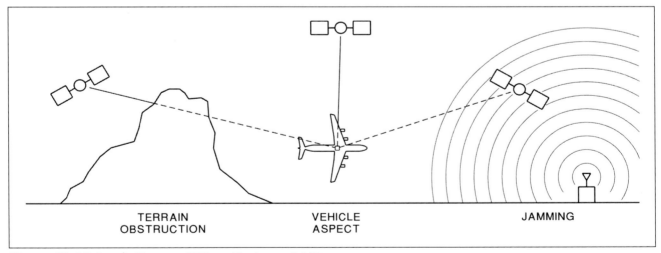

Figure 13-14. Local effects on GPS positioning availability

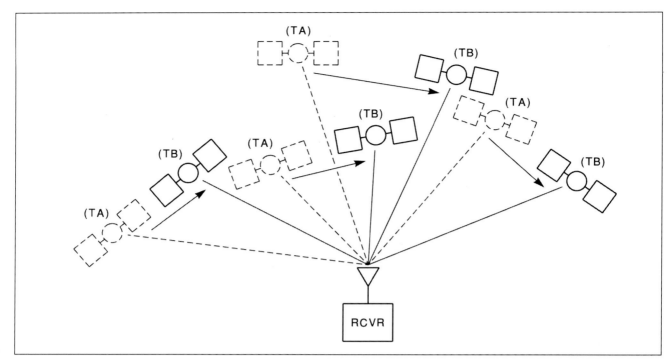

Figure 13-15. Position dilution of precision variation with time

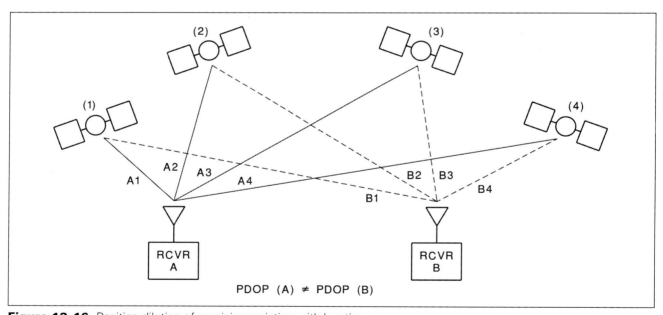

Figure 13-16. Position dilution of precision variation with location

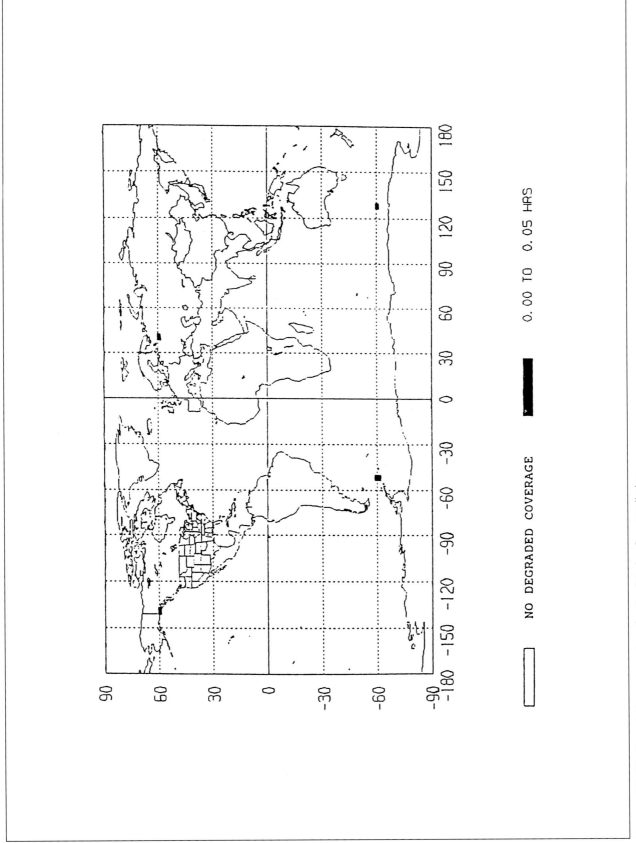

Figure 13-17. Cumulative outage time for the 21 plus 3 constellation

NO DEGRADED COVERAGE ▮ 0.00 TO 0.05 HRS

Continued from Page 243

Any satellite failure (or vacancy) from the full constellation of 24 satellites will result in outages. In general, the number of outages, and/or individual duration, and/or area affected will increase with each additional failure (vacancy) from the constellation. Figures 13-18 to 13-20 (on Pages 247 – 250) are samples of cumulative outage patterns for the 21 plus 3 constellation with one, two, and three failures (vacancies).

At any specific time during the day, the areas affected by individual outages will be much smaller than the cumulative areas shown in these figures. This is because of the four-fold symmetry described above, and because the individual outages are distributed intermittently over each six-hour interval. Different satellite failures or combinations of failures can produce different patterns and sequences of outages, since the arrangement of satellites in the constellation is not symmetrical. A particular pattern of outages will repeat as long as the number and arrangement of satellites remains the same. At any specific time, individual outages may be distributed randomly around the globe, although the overall pattern and sequence will exhibit the four-fold symmetry and daily periodicity mentioned above. The individual outages can persist for a few minutes, or up to a few hours in the worst cases.

The failure conditions presented in Figures 13-18 through 13-20 are typical, and chosen neither as best nor worst cases. Minor rephasing of satellites within the 21 plus 3 constellation can sometimes improve a "worst case" failure condition to one that approaches a "best case." This is an emergency technique the control segment could employ to alleviate a particularly severe outage condition if a replacement satellite was not readily available. Accelerated consumption of satellite fuel and other complexities prevent this technique from being used routinely. Figure 13-21 shows the cumulative outage pattern for an optimally phased constellation of 21 active satellites—and is an example of the "best case" that can be achieved with only 21 satellites. (This would require a major rephasing of the 21 plus 3 constellation and is presented as an upper limit of 21 satellite performance, rather than as a practical alternative to launching replacement satellites.) Maintaining a 98% probability of having 21 or more satellites available has been chosen by the U.S. as the best balance between system cost and long-term positioning performance.

The most effective method of determining positioning availability and dilution of precision distributions for the GPS constellation is by computer simulation. **Hypothetical almanacs** can be used to investigate the satellite orbits, and to predict the various failure scenarios that can be investigated. If the current almanac broadcast in the navigation message is used, a prediction for the current GPS constellation can be generated. The GPS System Effectiveness Model was developed for the GPS Joint Program Office and has been distributed to each NATO nation. The Version Three series of the System Effectiveness Model predicts dilution of precision (and estimated position accuracies) as a function of time for a single user-selected location, and is designed to run on IBM compatible personal computers. Note that the dilution of precision distribution over a single location repeats over the 23-hour, 56-minute period of the satellite ground tracks, resulting in a plot that might resemble Figure 13-13 (Page 243). Programs that perform similar calculations are also available commercially to help pilot/navigation predict GPS system usefulness.

A global average of positioning availability can also be calculated to assess the overall effectiveness of a particular constellation, or the overall severity of a particular failure condition. The four-fold symmetry of the outage patterns can be exploited to perform this calculation over a six-hour period rather than over 24 hours. This global average is termed the **constellation value**. This is also a measure of the average availability that users will see if they are randomly distributed round the globe.

As it operates, the GPS constellation will be in a continuous cycle of **satellite end-of-life failures** and corresponding replacements. It is expected that three to four satellites will reach end-of-life each year, based on experience with the Block I satellites and design improvements to the Block II satellites. This means that the global outage patterns and corresponding constellation value will probably change every few months as satellite failures and launches occur. As long as the U.S. can maintain 21 or more satellites on orbit, the constellation value should remain between 98% and 100% (*see* Figure 13-22 on Page 251). During the worst case three-satellite-failure condition, the worst location in the world may experience as low as 86% average positioning availability over a 24-hour period, while the best location may experience 100% availability.

Continued on Page 251

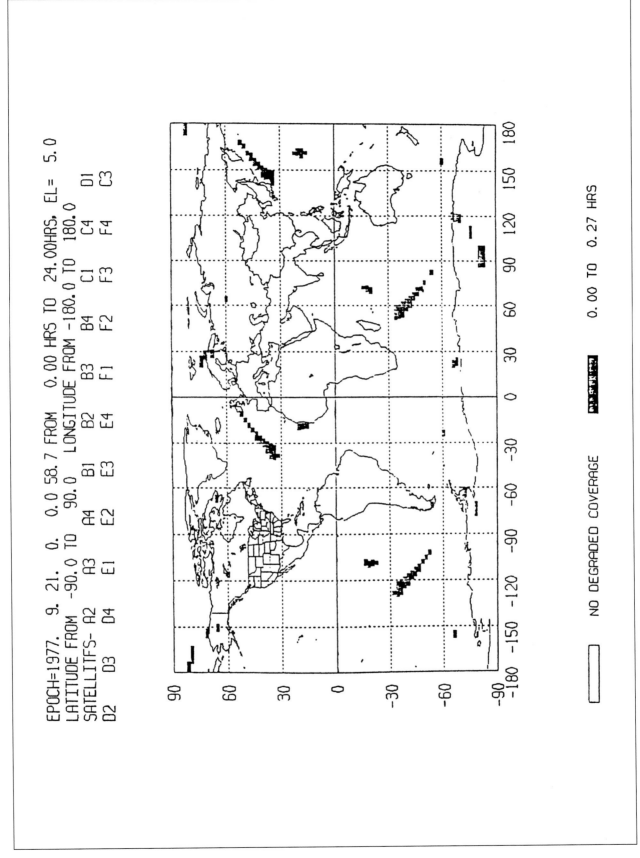

Figure 13-18. Cumulative outage time for the 21 plus 3 constellation with one satellite failure

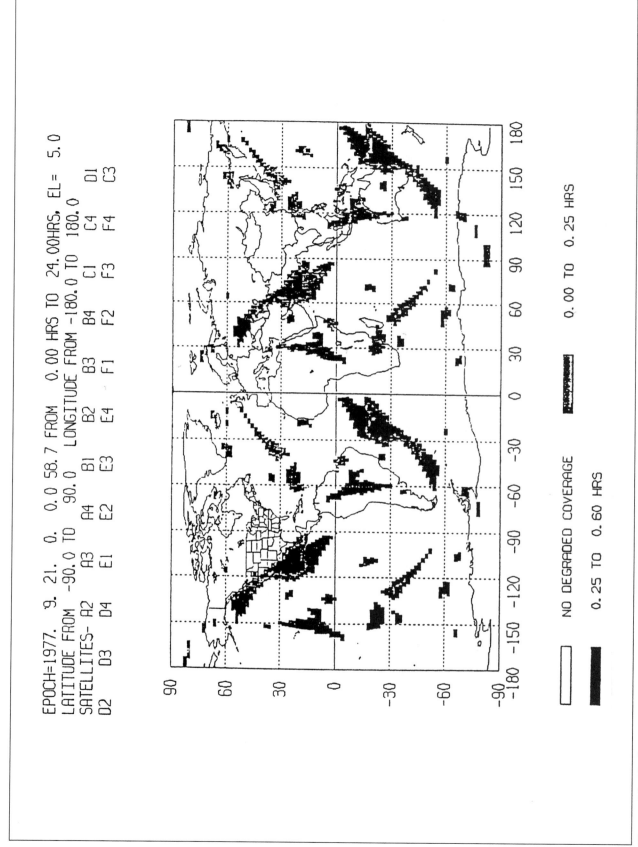

Figure 13-19. Cumulative outage time for the 21 plus 3 constellation with two satellite failures

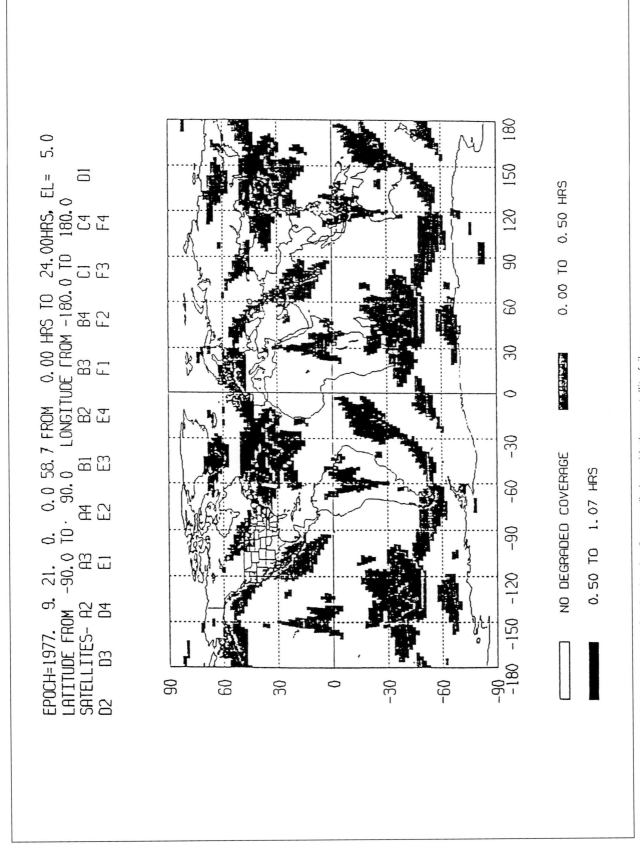

EPOCH=1977. 9. 21. 0. 0.0 58.7 FROM 0.00 HRS TO 24.00HRS, EL= 5.0
LATITUDE FROM -90.0 TO 90.0 LONGITUDE FROM -180.0 TO 180.0
SATELLITES- A2 A3 A4 B1 B2 B3 B4 C1 C4 D1
D2 D3 D4 E1 E2 E3 E4 F1 F2 F3 F4

NO DEGRADED COVERAGE   0.00 TO 0.50 HRS

0.50 TO 1.07 HRS

Figure 13-20. Cumulative outage time for the 21 plus 3 constellation with three satellite failures

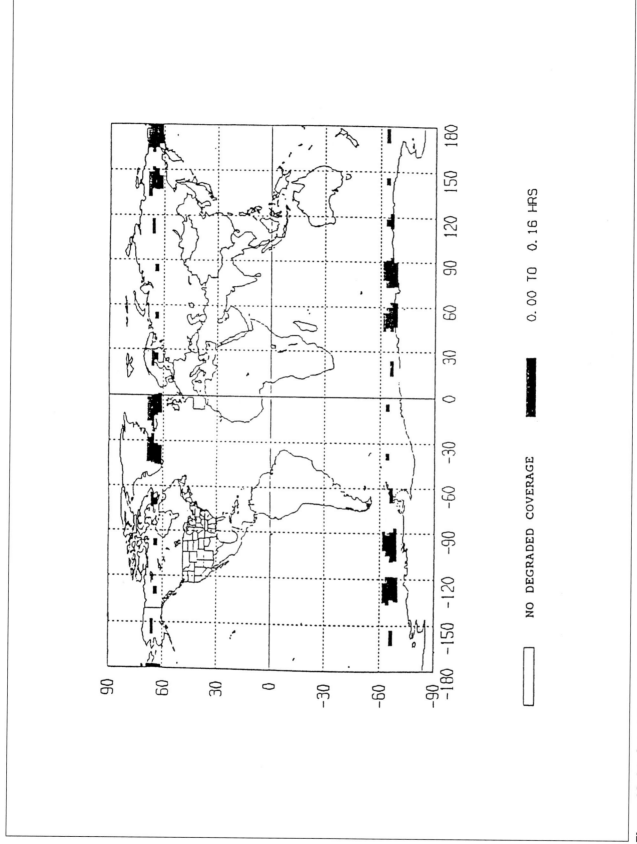

Figure 13-21. Cumulative outage time for an optimally phased 21-satellite constellation

No. of Vacancies	Best C.V.	Average C.V.	Worst C.V.
1	1.0000	.9999	.9997
2	1.0000	.9993	.9961
3	.9998	.9969	.9769
4	.9997	.9905	.9475

Figure 13-22. Robustness of the 21 + 3 constellation

Continued from Page 246

Dependability of the GPS system can only be anticipated, due to its short history. We know that other satellites have been made dysfunctional because of receiving high levels of high-energy radiation from the sun, receiving hits from meteorites and 'space trash' and there may be times in the future when GPS signals will be jammed.

For example, a note was distributed by Avweb's "Avflash" on January 12, 1998, to the effect that jamming could become a problem—quoting an article in *New Scientist* that a Russian company was offering "...a 4-watt GPS/GLONASS jammer for less than $4,000 at the September Moscow Air Show...The company claims it could stop civilian aircraft from locking onto GPS signals over a 200 km radius." *New Scientist* quoted an FAA spokesman saying that the agency is aware of the problem, but has no plans to reduce its future reliance on GPS.

Satellite Selection Criteria

Introduction

The criteria used for satellite selection is a very important factor in GPS receiver design. Different receivers perform satellite selection using different algorithms. The important satellite criteria to be considered include:

1. Health
2. Geometric dilution of precision
3. User range accuracy
4. Elevation angle
5. Availability of external aids.

Satellite Health

The navigation message contains satellite health information for all the satellites in the GPS satellite constellation. Each satellite broadcasts health summaries for all (up to 32) GPS satellites. Each summary consists of one bit indicating the health of the navigation message and five bits indicating the health of the satellite signals. A satellite should never be used in a navigation solution if its navigation message is indicated to be unhealthy. If the navigation message health is good, the five-bit signal status message should be compared against valid operating modes for the receiver to determine if the satellite can be used. For example, a precision code receiver could use a satellite broadcasting L1 only, if an **ionospheric model** can be used instead of dual frequency measurements to make the ionospheric corrections.

The navigation message also contains a health message in Subframe 1 which indicates the health of the broadcasting satellite. Since the data in Subframes 4 and 5 are updated less frequently than Subframe 1, Subframe 1 may be used to indicate short-term health problems or may be updated before subframes four and five. Therefore, after a satellite is acquired, the health data in Subframe 1 should also be checked to determine if the satellite can be used.

Geometric Dilution of Precision

Geometric dilution of precision is an important factor in determining the accuracy of the position (or time) solution. The combination of satellites which gives the lowest dilution of precision value will provide the most accurate solution, assuming that all satellites have the same pseudorange error. Depending on the user mission, best **position dilution of precision, horizontal dilution of precision**, or **time dilution of precision** can be used as a satellite selection criterion.

User Range Accuracy

Each satellite broadcasts a **user range accuracy** value in Subframe 1 of the navigation message. User range accuracy is a prediction of the pseudorange accuracy obtainable from the satellite signal in space. User range accuracy is based on recent historical data and is therefore most accurate immediately following an upload.

It does not include the **user equipment error**, and therefore does not include ionospheric compensation error if the ionospheric model is used instead of dual frequency measurements. These additional errors should be added to user range accuracy for the best estimate of pseudorange accuracy, especially if the receiver is capable of performing dual frequency measurements on some satellites. User range accuracy can be used in conjunction with dilution of precision to choose the best combination of satellites when the satellites have significantly different pseudorange errors. This is done by using user range accuracy as a weighting factor in the covariance matrix for user position and clock bias errors. Since user range accuracy is a prediction, it is not a guarantee of range accuracy; however, it can be used to help deselect satellites with known large pseudorange errors.

Satellite Elevation Angle

Selecting satellites by computing a minimum dilution of precision will usually de-select satellites at low elevation angles (angle between sighting to the horizon and sighting to the satellite, or the height of the satellite above the horizon). Since signals from satellites at low elevation angles must travel a longer distance through the ionosphere and troposphere than signals from satellites from high elevation angles, signals from low elevation satellites will incur greater pseudorange error due to ionospheric and tropospheric delay (*see* Page 257). Many receivers will not use signals below a specified elevation angle (masking angle) which is typically set at some angle between 5 and 15 degrees. On some receivers, the masking angle can be set by the user. Rejection of low angle satellites also helps to reduce multipath problems.

External Aids

When an external aid is available to the GPS receiver, it can be incorporated into the satellite selection algorithm. It can be incorporated as a fixed mode of operation, an optional mode of operation when only three satellites are visible, or it can be treated as an additional "satellite" to be selected when the best combination of satellites includes the aid. Decision logic for the first two cases is relatively simple. If the aid is treated as an additional satellite, the expected error and geometry must be modeled and included in the satellite selection algorithm. For example, mean sea level aiding can be considered to be equivalent to a satellite at the center of the earth with a user equivalent range error on the order of a typical satellite (6 to 7 m). Other aiding

schemes can be more complex, depending on the complexity of the integration, error model, and equivalent geometry. Barometric altimeter aiding should be treated with extra caution. Barometric altimeters are excellent devices for measuring pressure altitude, but **pressure altitude** can vary widely and non-linearly from geometric altitude.

The resulting vertical errors are difficult to predict and model since the errors depend on meteorological conditions and vehicle dynamics.

Figure of Merit

A **figure of merit** is an indicator of receiver positioning or time accuracy which may be displayed to the operator or communicated to an integrated system. A figure of merit may be either a qualitative or quantitative measure, depending on the accuracy and integrity of the data used to calculate the figure of merit. In general, a figure of merit is not suitable for making integrity decisions where safety of life is concerned.

However, a qualitative figure of merit may be perfectly suitable for integrity decisions regarding unmanned missions.

The U.S. Department Of Defense's use of receivers are good examples of statistical figures based on the following criteria:

1. GPS receiver state (e.g., carrier tracking, code tracking, acquisition);

2. Carrier-to-noise ratio (signal-to-noise ratio);

3. Satellite geometry (dilution of precision value);

4. Satellite range accuracy (user range accuracy value);

5. Ionospheric measurement or modeling error;

6. Receiver aiding used;

7. Kalman filter error estimates.

The U.S. Department Of Defense receiver presents the resultant figure of merit as a numerical value from 1 to 9, where "1" indicates the best navigation performance. A time figure of merit is also available to indicate the quality of the precise time information available from the GPS receiver via the precision time and time interval interface.

Aiding Capabilities for a GPS Receiver

Types of Aiding

Aiding a GPS receiver is done by incorporating inputs from an external sensor or source, and can be performed to accomplish the following:

1. Facilitate acquisition of initial satellite track.

2. Propagate the navigation solution to position in the Host Vehicle other than the GPS antenna.

3. Replace a satellite measurement in case of limited visibility or bad satellite geometry.

4. Maintain satellite track by increasing the tolerance of the GPS receiver to interference, jamming, or high host vehicle dynamics.

The interface options to provide aiding information to a GPS receiver are the separate interfaces (control display unit, data loader, INS/Attitude Heading Reference System, precise time and time interval, and altimeter), or the 1553 multiplex bus which links the receiver to other systems. Aiding information can also be stored in the receiver memory. Figure 13-23 illustrates these options. It should be noted that these are options; not all GPS receivers presently have the capabilities described.

Aiding During Acquisition of Initial Track

Position and Velocity Aiding

When a GPS receiver is first initialized for operation, approximate position and velocity of the receiver are required to minimize satellite acquisition time. The accuracy requirement of the U.S. Department of Defense program for position is d km of actual receiver location, and for velocity is d m/s of actual receiver velocity, to ensure that satellite acquisition is within specifications.

Acceleration aiding is normally not provided to a GPS receiver per se. Instead, velocity aiding data are supplied at a sufficiently high data rate (8 Hz or more) such that the rate of change of velocity (i.e., acceleration) is available for receiver aiding.

Time Aiding

Time aiding can be used during the initialization process, similar to position and velocity data. The time accuracy requirement is seconds relative to Universal Coordinated Time. This is to ensure satellite acquisition time is within specifications.

Time aiding, if sufficiently accurate, can also be used to enable a direct precision code acquisition without first acquiring the coarse/acquisition code. This

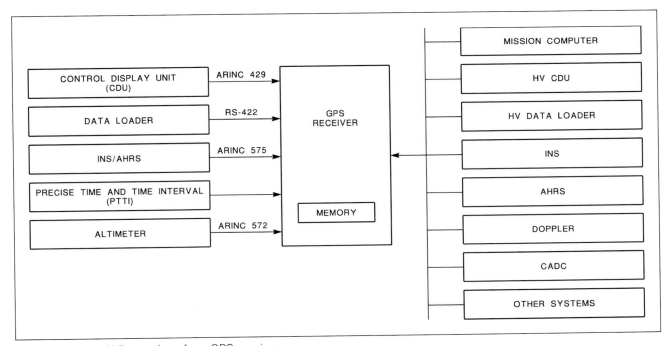

Figure 13-23. Aiding options for a GPS receiver

type of time aiding is relevant to host vehicles such as submarines, in which minimum exposure time of the GPS antenna on the ocean surface is of prime importance. An atomic time standard is necessary to enable direct precision code acquisition.

Almanac Data

Normal satellite acquisition requires the availability of a current satellite almanac, stored in the receiver memory. If there are no significant changes in the satellite constellation, then the almanac is valid for several weeks. For a very old almanac (180 days) or for a cold start of the receiver, new almanac information has to be provided (via control display unit or data loader).

If no stored or valid satellite almanac data are available, the GPS receiver to searches the sky attempting to locate and lock onto any satellite in view. Depending on the receiver search strategy and on the actual satellite constellation, this process may take 15-60 minutes. When one satellite is being tracked, the receiver can download and read the almanac information about all the other satellites in the constellation.

Time-to-First-Fix

Dependent on the type of integration (position, velocity, and time), aiding data is supplied to the GPS receiver during the initialization process as follows:

1. Manually by the operator via the GPS control display unit or host vehicle control display unit;

2. Automatically from INS/Attitude Heading Reference System, precision time and time interval or the host vehicle mission computer;

3. Default by using the shut-down values stored in the receiver memory.

Initial acquisition performance can be expressed by the time-to-first-fix. The **time-to-first-fix** is defined in ICD-GPS-200 as "the elapsed time from the initial command on a set that has been turned on for longer than five minutes to the subsequent display/output of present position and time." For a high dynamic aircraft, the U.S. Department of Defense has time-to-first-fix requirements of 90, 60, and 45 seconds for the different entry methods above. For a submarine, small time-to-first-fixes of several seconds are required. These times presume the availability of current satellite almanac information in the receiver.

Aiding to Replace a Satellite Measurement

During normal receiver operations, four satellite measurements are required inputs to solve the equations for position (U_X, U_Y, and U_Z) and clock offset (t). In case of limited satellite visibility or poor satellite geometry, one or more of the four satellite inputs may be replaced by inputs from an external aiding source.

When the GPS receiver is shipborne, has barometric altimeter aiding, or is stationary with known height, only three satellites are needed. Additional aiding by a precise clock can supplement the measurements in a two-satellite situation.

Clock Aiding

A GPS receiver uses its own internal clock or a more accurate external clock as time reference. If only three (instead of four) satellites are available, then the GPS receiver can assume that its time reference is correct (t = known), and treat the three available satellite range measurements as actual ranges instead of pseudoranges.

If the GPS receiver clock or the external clock can be monitored during a previous period in which the receiver navigates with four satellites, then the clock frequency, phase bias, and drift can be calculated. The resulting corrections for clock errors can be used to provide very accurate GPS time during a satellite outage and an accurate GPS position can be maintained for several minutes.

If the reference clock has not been monitored previously, then the GPS position accuracy will deteriorate rapidly during a satellite outage.

The method of using a clock instead of a satellite is not recommended as a permanent solution, but rather to help the GPS receiver operate during short periods when only a limited set of satellites are available. A GPS receiver should be capable of receiving (and providing) precise time via a dedicated precise time and time interval interface, or via the 1553 bus.

Altitude Aiding

As with the clock discussed in the previous paragraph, an airborne GPS receiver can use a barometric altimeter as aiding to replace a satellite measurement. Long-term altimeter errors are calibrated during periods of four-satellite operation. Subsequently, when less than four satellites are being tracked, the calibrated baroaltimeter data is used as a known U_Z value in the four unknowns of U_X, U_Y, U_Z, and t. An accurate GPS position can be maintained for 10 to 15 minutes, a good length of time where aircraft operations are considered.

Aiding to Maintain Satellite Track

Inputs from an INS or Doppler radar can be used by a GPS receiver to improve the quality of the GPS navigation solution under normal conditions or to increase the tolerance of the receiver to interference, jamming, or high dynamics.

In normal receiver operation, the code and carrier tracking loops are in lock. An INS or Doppler radar navigation solution may be input to the receiver, but this is only used in the computation of the foreground solution. The **foreground solution** is an interpolated navigation solution, a sort of "dead reckoning" solution, available at a higher rate (e.g., 10 Hz) than the **primary background solution** which is computed every time a new set of GPS measurements is available (usually at 1 Hz). Another benefit of aiding when the receiver is operating under normal conditions is calibration of errors of the INS or the Doppler radar. INS or Doppler radar are not used to aid either code or carrier tracking loop during normal conditions.

Differential GPS

Introduction

In 1983, the Radio Technical Commission for Maritime Service established a special committee to develop recommendations on standards for the broadcast of differential corrections to users of GPS, and to define the data format to be used between the reference station and the user. The committee recognized that **Differential GPS (DGPS)** has potential for users outside the marine environment, and Radio Technical Commission for Maritime Service SC-104. Therefore, they expanded their Terms of Reference to include the Radio Technical Commission for Aeronautics and other similar bodies, thereby ensuring that the standards and recommendations did not restrict differential operation to marine usage.

This overview of the techniques employed will outline some fundamental issues of Differential GPS, which should be considered by any military or civilian user who weighs the need for a positioning system that can give accuracies better than the precise positioning service, using standard positioning service equipment.

Why is a Differential GPS service needed? Its primary aim is to determine and then correct errors that are biases in the GPS system. Differential operation of the GPS system offers the possibility of accuracies of 5 to 20 m for dynamic navigation applications such as precision approaches (Figure 13-24 on next page), and better than 3 m for stationary applications using code-phase measurements.

Differential GPS Concept

The concept of Differential GPS is to operate a GPS receiver at a known location that has been previously surveyed. This stationary receiver must track all satellites in view in order to compute their differential pseudorange corrections. These corrections are generated by comparison of the measurements taken by the receiver with those based on the true receiver position. The receiver is part of the reference station, located in an area where higher accuracy is required. It is important to perform integrity management to ensure that the transmitted output data corrections are valid. The resultant valid corrections for each satellite in view are formatted in a standardized protocol and modulated onto the broadcast radio signal. Differential GPS derives its potential from the fact that the measurement errors are highly correlated between users located in local area. The pseudorange corrections are received by the user receiver and incorporated into the navigation solution to correct the observed satellite pseudorange measurement, thereby improving the position accuracy.

DGPS Implementation Types

Depending on the type of the information being transmitted, there are several options for the implementation of Differential GPS. The normal implementation method is to transmit the pseudorange corrections of each satellite in view. In this case, the user receiver needs to apply the received measurement corrections to achieve the improved accuracy available from differential GPS.

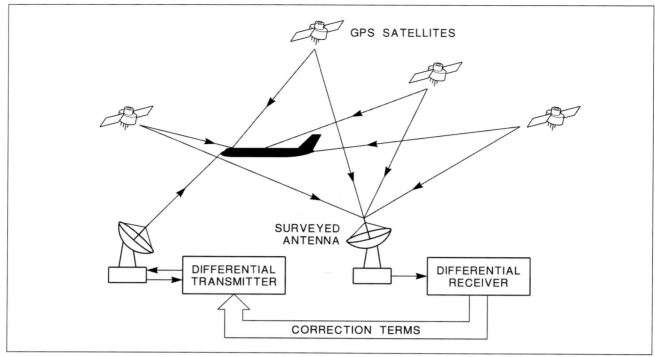

Figure 13-24. Principles of Differential GPS

The alternative is to transmit position corrections, such as latitude, longitude, and altitude, and apply them to the user navigation solution in the same frame. Though this approach looks easier to implement than the above method, the problem is that the position solution errors are dependent on which satellites are used. Since, in general, the reference station receiver has knowledge of which satellites might be in use by the user receiver, it must compute and transmit position corrections for all possible combinations of satellites.

The third option is called the translator method. Here, the user tracks the GPS signal, does not compute a navigation solution, but simply transfers the satellite signals to a communication frequency which is retransmitted to the ground (downlink). A GPS receiver on the ground receives this translated frequency and computes a GPS solution for the particular user. A separate conventional reference station provides the differential corrections to be applied to the previous solution.

The fourth method uses dynamic phase tracking to establish a relative phase position of the GPS carrier including the integer ambiguity. Absolute carrier lock must be maintained during the receiver movement, by avoiding cycle slips. This is a mobile version of the geodetic survey technique using the phase observable of GPS. This method is normally called kinematic phase differential GPS.

Depending on the type of data link used, differential GPS can also be implemented in various ways. In the uplink option, the differential corrections are sent from the reference station to the users as previously described. A downlink option is also possible, and in this case the differential solution is only calculated on the ground. This is the typical case for test range applications for precise vehicle surveillance. Another possibility is to use so-called "pseudolites," in which a GPS signal and code generator broadcast the differential corrections over an L-band signal (same frequency as received by the GPS receiver); therefore, a separate data link system is not required. However, the reference station becomes more complex.

Finally, if real time differential accuracy is not required, then the information generated at the reference station and by the user can be recorded for post-mission processing. This eliminates the need for a data link system.

GPS Error Sources

The major sources of error are:

1. **Selective Availability Errors.** Within the satellite, it is possible for the Master Control Station of the operational system to create two levels of accuracy. Intentional actual degradations are applied to the GPS navigation signals to create a lower level of accuracy. First, the ephemeris (location) parameters can be changed to give an apparent shift of satellite position. Secondly, the satellite frequency can be "dithered," thereby introducing errors in the coded signals. Authorized users of the GPS precise positioning service (i.e., those sets which include the precise positioning service security module and selective availability interface) will have the necessary crypto-keys to remove these artificially-induced errors entirely. Sets designed with purely the coarse/acquisition code (standard positioning service) will not be able to remove these errors, and they may need to be accounted for through a differential technique.

2. Ionospheric Delays. **Ionospheric signal propagation delay** errors can vary from 20 to 30 m by day, to 3 to 6 m at night. This is a particular problem with a single frequency user (i.e., a single frequency coarse/acquisition code set). Dual frequency receivers can correct for ionospheric delays with a residual error of some 2 m. The satellite navigation message contains correction coefficients for the single frequency user to reduce the ionospheric delay by approximately 50%, provided the appropriate algorithm is used.

3. **Tropospheric Delay Error.** This signal propagation delay is caused by the lower atmosphere. Such a delay will obviously be maximized for low altitude satellites. This error's magnitude is up to 3 m. It should be noted here that many receivers also employ algorithms to minimize this tropospheric delay.

4. **Ephemeris Errors.** These are differences between the actual satellite location and the position predicted by satellite orbital data. Normally, these errors will be less than 3 m.

5. **Satellite Clock Errors.** These are differences between actual satellite GPS time and that predicted by satellite data. The policy adopted by the U.S. is to apply selective availability to all Block II satellites as soon as practicable after launch. Selective availability will not be activated on the Block I satellites. However, a position solution only needs one Block II satellite to realize the application of

the nominal 100-meter effect. Without the appropriate software or S/M module in the precise positioning service set and the associated crypto-keys, even military users in peacetime will identify an error of up to 100 m.

Standard positioning service receivers will always suffer a position error. Differential GPS can correct for these errors and induced biases in the following manner:

1. Satellite Clock Errors. These are completely compensated, as long as both reference and user receivers employ the same satellite data.

2. Ephemeris Errors. Unless these are quite large (for example, 10 m or more), they are similarly compensated.

3. Selective Availability Errors. These affect the timing of the signals' location of the space vehicle and are compensated by Differential GPS.

4. Ionospheric and Tropospheric Delays. For users near the reference station, the respective signal paths to the satellites are close enough together that the compensation is almost complete. As the user-reference station separation is increased, the different ionospheric and tropospheric paths to the satellites can be far enough apart that the ionospheric delay is no longer consistent. Thus, a system can be provided that allows for the errors generated by the satellite itself or by its propagation path.

The basic concept of differential GPS is similar to that employed in differential LORAN-C, and the translocation mode using TRANSIT. The principle of the system is to place a receiver at a known, surveyed-in point.

This receiver will compute satellite pseudorange correction data, which can then be broadcast to users in the same geographical area (*see* Figure 13-24 at left). The pseudorange corrections are incorporated into the navigation solution of the user's GPS receiver to correct the observed satellite pseudorange measurements, thereby improving positioning accuracy. Another possible method is to let the reference station compare its GPS-measured position with its surveyed position, then broadcast the difference as a lat./lon. position correction to other users. This method is not preferred since the reference station and the user may be using a different satellite configuration.

The correlation of the errors experienced at the reference station and at the user location is dependent on the distance between them, but they are normally highly correlated for a user within 350 km of the reference station. Figure 13-25 shows the error budget for a precise positioning service Differential GPS system. It should be noted that all common error sources, such as the space and control segments, are eliminated in a differential system.

Atmospheric errors can be eliminated if the user is close to the reference station, but if they are more than 250 km apart, the user will obtain better results using correction models for ionospheric and tropospheric delay. Figure 13-25 shows how the reference station receiver noise and multipath errors are added to the dfferential corrections and become part of the user's error budget. 250 km is a reasonable division between near and far.

GPS as an Attitude Reference System

A vehicle's spatial angular orientation in three dimensions is frequently determined using an INS. However, an INS is expensive and its accuracy degrades with respect to time. A GPS receiver with two or more antennas has the capability to be used for 3-D angular reference.

Simulations and studies indicate that it may be cheaper and more accurate to use GPS for attitude reference than to use INS. Also, GPS attitude accuracy will not degrade with time. Combining GPS and INS for attitude reference would give the user the best of both worlds. First of all, the GPS will give very precise angular measurements under normal conditions and could provide updates to the INS, both for the wander error in the gyros and the platform tilt error. Secondly, if the GPS receiver is jammed, the INS would still provide position, velocity, and attitude. It could also be used to initialize the GPS receiver when the jamming is over.

Concept of Operation

There are two basic concepts of operation for using GPS as an attitude reference system: single and double differencing, and interferometry.

Both methods are based on calculating the difference in measurements of GPS signals at two separate antenna locations to determine the angle between the antenna baseline and the line of sight to a satellite (see Figure 13-26). The first method uses pseudorange or delta range measurements (differencing) and the second method uses carrier phase comparison (interferometry).

Single and Double Differencing

Single and double differencing compares pseudorange or delta range measurements from the same satellites) at two antenna locations.

Segment Source	Error	95% Confidence Level, Meters		
		95%	Differential Mode	
			Near	Far
Space	Clock and Nav Subsystem Stability	6.5	0	0
	Predictibility of SV Perturbations	2.0	0	0
	Other	1.0	0	0
Control	Ephermeris Prediction Model Implementation	8.2	0	0
	Other	1.8	0	0
User (P-code)	Iono Delay Compensation	4.5	0	4.5
	Tropo Delay Compensation	3.9	0	3.9
	RCVR Noise and Resolution	2.9	3.9	3.9
	Multipath	2.4	3.1	3.1
	Other	1.0	1.0	1.0
Predicted Total Error		13.0	5.1	7.8

Figure 13-25. Precise positioning service Differential GPS error budget

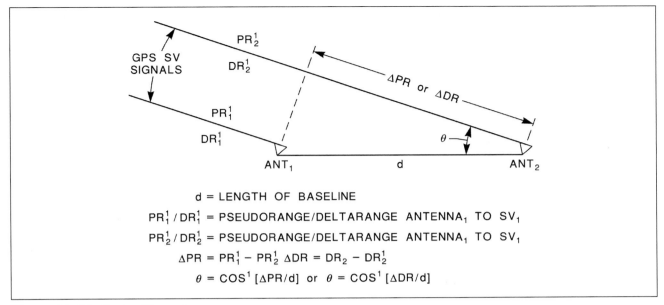

$d = $ LENGTH OF BASELINE

$PR_1^1 / DR_1^1 = $ PSEUDORANGE/DELTARANGE ANTENNA$_1$ TO SV$_1$

$PR_2^1 / DR_2^1 = $ PSEUDORANGE/DELTARANGE ANTENNA$_1$ TO SV$_1$

$\Delta PR = PR_1^1 - PR_2^1 \quad \Delta DR = DR_2 - DR_2^1$

$\theta = COS^1 [\Delta PR/d] \quad or \quad \theta = COS^1 [\Delta DR/d]$

Figure 13-26. Single differencing

Single Differencing

Computing the difference in pseudorange or delta range between two antennas is known as the single differencing of the original measurements. It is used to determine the angle between the baseline for the two antennas and the satellite (Figure 13-26). Differencing virtually eliminates the sensitivity of the antenna position errors to ephemeris, satellite clock, ionospheric, and tropospheric errors since they are common to both antenna positions.

Double Differencing

If the simultaneously obtained differenced pseudorange and delta range measurements are further differenced over two satellites, position error due to the receiver is eliminated (Figure 13-27 on next page). By using three antennas and the pseudorange and/or delta range difference between the three antenna locations, the attitude of the plane containing the three antennas can be determined.

Interferometry

A GPS interferometer measures the satellite carrier signal phase difference as it arrives at two different antenna locations. This is the same as single differencing; however, the accuracy of the measurements and therefore the accuracy of the attitude determination is much higher. The two antennas placed a distance (d) apart

will receive the carrier signal at a different time, therefore with a different phase (Figure 13-28, Page 261). The carrier wavelength ambiguity problem (determination of number of full cycles, (n)) can be solved by using INS information for initialization, use of multiple satellites to provide additional geometric information, use of precision code to reduce the possible number of carrier wavelengths, and jointly processing on L1 and L2 carrier signals by the interferometer.

The interferometry technique is recommended over the single or double differencing technique for better accuracy. The interferometry technique and delta range differencing requires that the receiver operate in state five (carrier and code tracking) while pseudorange differencing can be done in state three (code tracking only). A GPS attitude reference system should therefore be capable of using both techniques so that it can give maximum accuracy in state five, but also be able to track in state three.

Use of Interferometry for 3-D Attitude Reference System

3-D orientation requires at least three independent antennas to define a geometric plane. Four non-coplanar antennas could be used to define two planes and provide redundancy. Orientation solutions of the planes containing the antennas are related to the vehicle and therefore allow the orientation of the vehicle to be determined. The preferred method of operation is to get L1 and L2 frequency observations from four

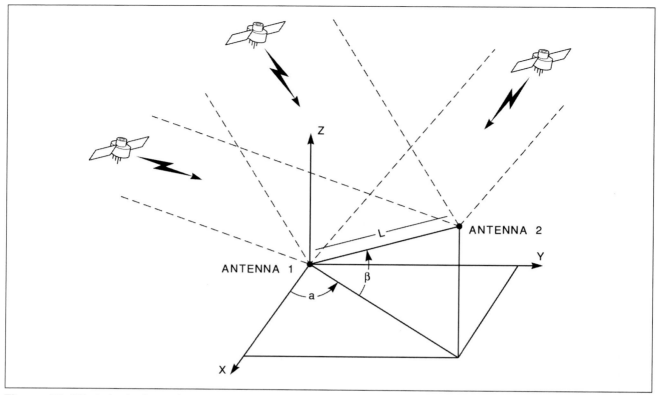

Figure 13-27. Attitude determination in three dimensions

satellites continuously. This would require one four-channel precision code receiver dedicated to each antenna. Optimum hardware for a 3-D attitude reference system is as follows:

1. Three antenna subsystems
2. Three GPS receivers
3. Data processing unit
4. External reference oscillator

A simpler alternative is to use one eight-channel precision code receiver and three antennas. Four channels would operate as a "sub-receiver" and would be dedicated to one "master" antenna. The sub-receiver and the master antenna read the navigation message, and provide position and velocity information for use when processing the signals from the other two antennas. This method can be used if the baselines between the antennas are sufficiently short to assume the position and velocity measurements are nearly the same for all three antenna locations. The two other antennas would only use two channels each to do carrier phase measurements on two of the four satellites that the "master" antenna was tracking. Which of the two satellites all three antennas would be tracking depends on the satellites' geometry relative to the antennas. In low dynamic platform cases, one multiplex receiver could replace the three four-channel receiver. The multiplex receiver would measure the carrier signal phase from four satellites on each antenna sequentially, dwelling for approximately 40 milliseconds on each antenna. All four satellites would thus be tracked by each antenna each 120 milliseconds. This technique requires that the measurement data is processed as if all satellite signals were received at the same time. Under high-host-vehicle dynamics, the INS-derived angular information may be better than GPS.

Use of Multiple Receivers and a Reference Oscillator

When multiple receivers are used for interferometry, it is recommended that a common external reference oscillator be used for all the receivers; otherwise, the oscillators in each receiver must be calibrated. A common frequency reference would improve the accuracy of attitude measurements because all phase measurements would be done using the same time reference, thereby eliminating "own clock errors."

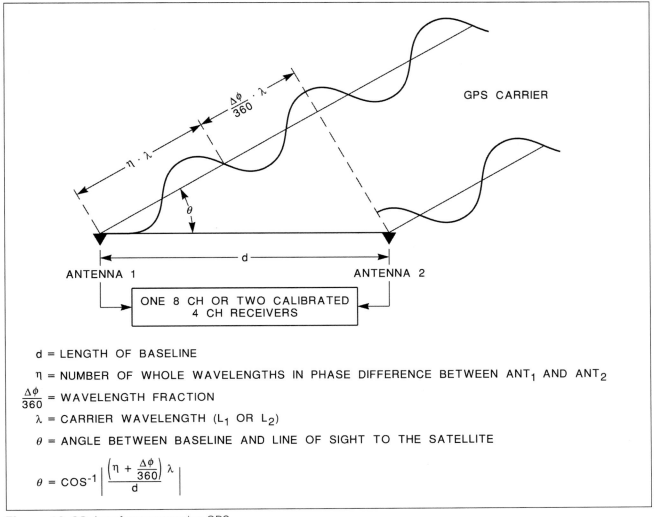

Figure 13-28. Interferometry using GPS

The diagram labels include:

d = LENGTH OF BASELINE

η = NUMBER OF WHOLE WAVELENGTHS IN PHASE DIFFERENCE BETWEEN ANT_1 AND ANT_2

$\frac{\Delta\phi}{360}$ = WAVELENGTH FRACTION

λ = CARRIER WAVELENGTH (L_1 OR L_2)

θ = ANGLE BETWEEN BASELINE AND LINE OF SIGHT TO THE SATELLITE

$$\theta = \cos^{-1}\left| \frac{\left(\eta + \frac{\Delta\phi}{360}\right)\lambda}{d} \right|$$

Error Sources and Degradation of Performance

The most dominant error sources for interferometry (in increasing order of importance) are as follows:

1. Absolute position uncertainty;

2. Position dilution of precision;

3. Antenna location;

4. Antenna position difference uncertainty in the body frame;

5. Measurement accuracy.

Absolute Position Uncertainty. Errors in knowledge of the absolute position of the primary antenna can cause an angular orientation error in the local-level frame with which attitude is referenced. This orienta-tion error transforms into an equivalent attitude error. Typical attitude errors of less than 0.03 minutes of arc can be expected.

Position Dilution of Precision. The attitude determi-nation accuracy is influenced by the satellite geometry the same way as position accuracy. Bad satellite geom-etry results in both bad position and attitude determi-nation accuracy.

Antenna Location. Antenna location errors are a mini-mum when the two position difference vectors are orthogonal. Simulation results indicate that acceptable performance can be obtained when the vectors inter-sect at an angle between 45° and 135°. The performance deteriorates rapidly outside this domain.

Antenna Position Difference Uncertainty in the Body Frame. Uncertainty of the difference vectors in body coordinates is a function of two primary factors: body flexure and errors inherited from the calibration process. Body flexure alters the relative position between antennas, hence causing errors.

Measurement Accuracy. The most significant factor influencing the feasibility of GPS attitude measurement is the accuracy of the range difference measurement. The error sources affecting accuracy are as follows:

1. Atmospheric delays which cause errors of less than one part in 100,000.

2. Multipath effects which can be quite significant, but are largely negated by proper antenna placement.

3. Phase difference measurement accuracy.

4. Transmission delay stability.

Very little is published about what accuracies can be expected when using GPS for attitude reference, but one manufacturer claims a heading accuracy of 0.3°, roll and pitch accuracy of 1°, updated at a 20-Hz rate with no practical speed limit, a maximum acceleration of 10 G, and a maximum angular velocity of 30° per second. The same manufacturer claims a heading accuracy of 0.05° within five minutes in a stationary mode. This performance is with a coarse/acquisition code receiver, using three antennas placed in a triangle, with a 57 cm baseline between the antennas. Generally, the measurement accuracy depends on baseline length and measurement time. Longer baselines and longer measurement times will usually improve the accuracy.

WAAS and LAAS

In order to implement DGPS for aviation, two systems have emerged. Wide Area Augmentation System (WAAS) and Local Area Augmentation System(s) (LAAS) are the means by which pilots will have most of the error removed from the present and future GPS systems. At this writing, both systems are in the developmental stages.

Wide Area Augmentation System (WAAS)

WAAS is a geographically expansive augmentation to the basic GPS service, designed to provide a quality of positioning information never before available to the aviation community. This augmentation of the GPS system will allow its use as a primary means of navigation for enroute travel and nonprecision approaches in the U.S., and will provide CAT I approach capability at some airports in the U.S.

WAAS is based on a network of approximately 35 ground reference stations located in the CONUS (conterminous U.S.)—*see* Figure 13-29. Each of these reference receivers is precisely surveyed, enabling each to determine any error in the GPS signals being received at its station. This error data is then passed to a master station computer which calculates correction algorithms and assesses the integrity of the entire GPS system. This data is then put into a message format and uplinked to a geostationary communications satellite which forwards the correction information to the aircraft's receiver. The aircraft's receiver then makes the needed adjustments to provide improved positioning accuracy. The communication satellites also act as GPS navigation satellites, thus adding to the number of satellites in the GPS constellation.

Local Area Augmentation System (LAAS)

LAAS, because it does not require any additional satellites, has the advantage of lower development costs and faster implementation. Its disadvantage is that an individual LAAS will only serve one location, in which there may be one or more airports, located within a limited distance, that can be served by one system.

LAAS will augment GPS to support Category I, II and III precision approach applications. LAAS is intended to replace the Instrument Landing System (ILS), complement the WAAS, and provide Category I capability at selected locations where the WAAS cannot. LAAS will provide a signal which can be used for area and surface navigation in and around the airport area.

LAAS consists of the equipment and software in three segments illustrated in Figure 13-30 (Page 264):

1. Space segment;

2. LAAS ground segment;

3. LAAS airborne user segment.

The space segment consists of the GPS and WAAS satellites which provide the ground and airborne segments with ranging signals and satellite ephemerides. The ground segment consists of a ground station (GS) and airport pseudolites (APLs). The precisely located GS determines the amount of position error inherent in the GPS and WAAS ranging signals, and passes the correction information via VHF data broadcast (VDB) to the user aircraft (airborne segment). The APL, be-

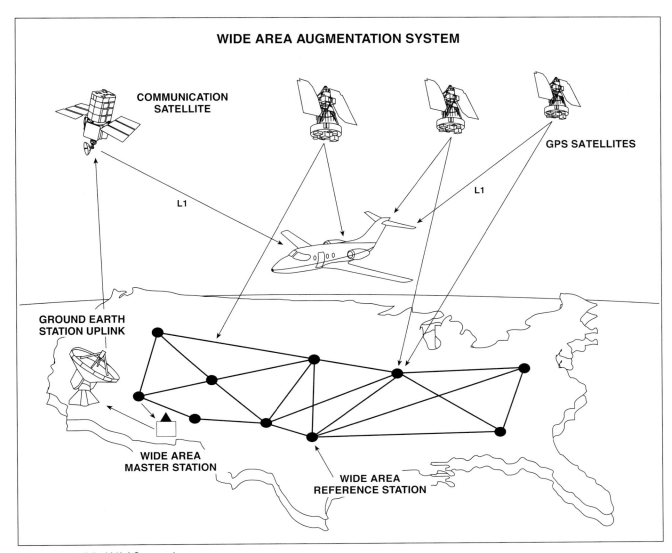

Figure 13-29. WAAS overview

ing precisely located from the GS, provides the GS an additional ranging source by which to more accurately determine errors, thus enhancing overall system availability and accuracy. The airborne segment applies the corrections to obtain a far more accurate determination of position. This data is then used to display deviation signals to the crew (left/right of course and glideslope displays), and sends those signals to drive the appropriate aircraft systems supporting a Category I, II, IIIa or IIIb precision approach.

Expected accuracy of the LAAS is shown in Figure 13-31 (Page 264) for the three approach categories. It shows 95% confidence errors in meters of deviation from centerline for both lateral and vertical dimensions. Deviation that activates the crew alarm and time to alarm activation are both shown. Although the values may be changed as the system develops, this gives some idea of the relative accuracy of the LAAS system.

In order to monitor developments with these two new systems, the reader may wish to monitor the FAA websites:

http://www.faa.gov/and/and700/and730/laas/spec/wholepgB.htm#opuse

http://www.faa.gov/waas/mainnav.htm

Additional information about the use of GPS and its related navigation systems are to be found in the chapters about Time (Chapter 15), Errors (Chapter 16) and FANS (Chapter 18).

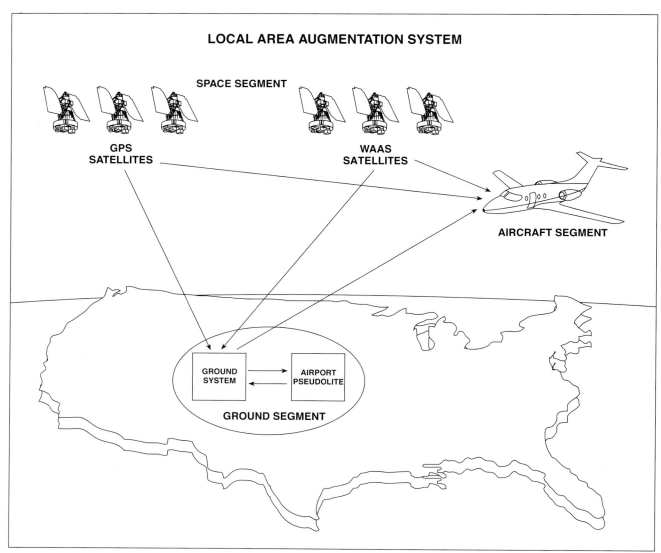

Figure 13-30. LAAS overview

Facility Performance Category	95% NSE Lateral[1]	95% NSE Vertical[1]	Alarm Limit[3]	Time to Alarm
I	9.0 m	4.4 m	10.2 m	6 s
II	6.9 m	2.0 m	5.3 m	1-2 s
III	6.1 m	2.0 m[2]	5.3 m	1-2 s

[1] The 95 percentile navigation system error (NSE) values for every approach are those required at the lowest HAT (height above threshold) for the intended operation, unless otherwise specified.
[2] Applies to 50' HAT.
[3] Applies to both vertical and lateral.

Figure 13-31. LAAS expected accuracy

14: Flight Management Systems

As a natural enhancement of the systems flying in today's new-generation aircraft, the Flight Management System (FMS) brings a wealth of total flight and performance management experience to any aircraft cockpit. Not only can it quickly define a desired route from the aircraft's current position to any point in the world, but the definition will be based on the operating characteristics of the aircraft. The modern FMS also features *user-friendly* operation, allowing the flight crew to perform aircraft management tasks in a straightforward, efficient manner.

FMS navigation provides highly accurate and automatic long-range capability by blending available inputs from both long-range and short-range sensors such as INS or IRS, GPS, VOR, and Scanning DME to develop an FMS position more accurate than any single sensor can provide. The FMS performs flight plan computations, displays the total picture on the **Electronic Flight Information System** (EFIS), and provides signals to the autopilot and autothrottle for automatic tracking.

The map displays on the HSI portion of the EFIS and on the center Multifunction Display (MFD) include the navigation waypoints with the actual curved-path transition for the active leg, along with airports and navaid position information. The maps can be used to provide a complete visual picture of the FMS flight plan. Should a pilot wish to insert a waypoint anywhere in the flight plan, the map display with a joystick-controlled designator symbol on the MFD greatly simplifies the procedure. The MFD also includes a unique **North-up** or **Relative-up** plan mode where the pilot can scroll through the entire fight plan. This allows the pilot to easily check the flight plan visually with a graphical display, rather than reviewing a list of waypoints, names, or lat./lon. positions.

Note: As of October 1997, there is an active internet website of value to those interested in FMS and other navigation issues. The website address is:

http://www.neosoft.com/~sky/bluecoat

System Description

Introduction

The Flight Management System, as an example of FMS, is designed as a **federated system**, where there are independent but interactive components but each component performs a system function. (*See* Figure 14-1.) The FMS is comprised of three basic components. The components of the system are the **Control Display Unit** (CDU), the **Series Navigation Computers**, and the **Performance Computer**. The key to the federated approach is to keep the navigation and performance functions as separate and independent as possible, and yet allow for their operation as an integrated system.

Some performance calculations, however, utilize navigation data and some navigation displays include performance data. The flight plan data and other joint-use information is shared between the navigation and performance computers on the Avionics Standard Communication Bus. This keeps the computers as independent as possible. It is a design feature to keep

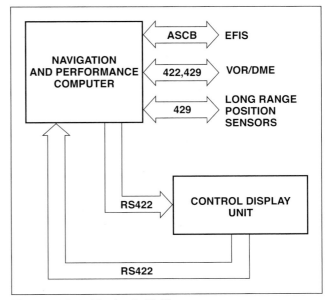

Figure 14-1. The basic FMS

aircraft variable data in the performance computer. The navigation computer is then able to be installed in any aircraft without changes in the software.

The **Control Display Unit** provides the primary means for pilot input to the system. It also provides output display for the navigation and performance computers. The CDU utilizes a full alphanumeric keyboard, with four line-selection keys on each side of the CRT. Seven function keys are provided to allow direct access to specific display pages. Annunciators are located in the top of the bezel to advise the pilot of the system's status. The CRT in the CDU has nine lines of text, 24 characters long. The top line of the CDU display is dedicated as a title line, and the bottom line is used for a scratchpad and the display of messages. A manual dimming knob is used for long-term dimming adjustments, while ambient light sensors are used for shorter-term display brightness adjustments under varying cloud/sunlight conditions.

The **Navigation Computer** is the component in the FMS which provides both lateral and vertical navigation guidance. It has two different sizes of internal navigation databases which are used for storage of way-points, navaids, routes, airports, and other NAV data. Both units can interface with five long-range sensors: three via ARINC 429 buses and two by ASCB buses. Each navigation computer can also connect to scanning DME and VOR receivers. The interface to the attitude heading reference, air data, MFD, EFIS, and autopilot is over the Avionics Standard Communications Bus (ASCB). Flight Plans are also transferred between Navigation computers over the ASCB, while the link to the CDU is over an RS-422 "private-line" interface. To provide high-accuracy long-range navigation, the navigation computer is designed to connect to INS or IRS, and GPS sensors plus VOR/DME. With links to the on-board navigation sensors, the navigation computer develops an FMS position based on a blend or mix of the sensors. The FMS does not directly display navigation maps on the CDU; however, the FMS is the source of map data for other cockpit displays such as EFIS.

The lateral navigation function of the FMS may be considered an area navigation system or RNAV. Its fundamental purpose is to provide navigation information relative to selected geographical points. Navigation management allows the pilot to define a route from the aircraft present position to any point in the world. The system will output advisory information and steering signals to allow the pilot or Automatic Flight Control System (AFCS) to guide the aircraft along the desired route. Routes are defined from the aircraft present position to a destination waypoint via a great circle route, or via a series of great circle legs defined by intermediate waypoints.

Navigation Management Functions

The navigation computer and CDU provide many varied navigation functions; *however, the primary function is to provide high accuracy long range lateral and vertical navigation*. To accomplish this function, the navigation computer connects to a variety of sensors. These sensors include VOR, DME, AHRS, IRS, INS, LORAN-C, and GPS receivers. The sensor inputs complement each other. For example, the Inertial Reference System (IRS) sensor has very good short-term accuracy, but has long-term drift. That error characteristic is complemented by the DME input which is not subject to drift error. By using a weighted average of the sensor inputs, the navigation computer can develop an FMS position which is as accurate as any single sensor under any given condition.

Another function of the navigation computer is *the ability to store and retrieve information on navaids, earth reference points such as airports, intersections, runways, and routes*. This storage area is referred to as the navigation database. The navaids, earth reference points, and published routes are subject to change and require updating every 28-56 days. The database memory is also used to store pilot-defined waypoints and pilot-defined routes; however, these are not updated. They reside in memory until changed by the operator.

Other functions of the navigation computer are *to provide guidance outputs to the autopilot and map display outputs to the EFIS*. To provide high accuracy navigation and guidance, the navigation computer must determine the optimum DME stations to tune based on the geometry between the stations, and other characteristics such as distance from the aircraft. A byproduct of the database is the capability to furnish map reference points near the aircraft's present position. The reference points can be both navaids and airports.

Since the navigation computer has outputs to automatically tune the NAV receivers, these outputs have been extended to provide keyboard control of other electronics, such as the ADF, VHF navigation and communications radios, and ATC transponders.

The guidance outputs vary with the axis and the flight profile. The roll axis is controlled directly by the navigation computer through a lateral steering signal. The pitch axis is controlled by sending airspeed, vertical speed, and altitude targets to the AFCS. The level-offs and transitions are controlled by the normal AFCS trip points. The turn anticipation is calculated within the navigation computer to prevent overshooting or undershooting the next course.

The following paragraphs give more details about the navigation functions.

Navigation Modes

The prime radio navigation inputs are VOR bearings and DME distance. This may be broken down into two categories: VOR/DME and multi-DME. Some DME receivers can be commanded to scan two or three channels, while others supply distance from a single channel (station). The navigation computer normally optimizes the present position calculation accuracy by utilizing DME distance data from at least two stations, versus VOR bearing and DME distance data from a single station, because the VOR bearing information is subject to errors which are greater than DME errors. Using multi-DME, a much more accurate position may be derived.

Two types of radio (VOR/DME) configurations are supported. First, the FMS will support a system with **single-channel DMEs**. In this system, both the onside VOR/DME and the cross-side DME are brought into the navigation computer. The second system configuration supported by the FMS is a **directed scanning DME**. In this configuration, multiple distances can be received from a single DME receiver. In this configuration, distances from three stations can be used for a precise position fix.

Long-range sensors are utilized in addition to VOR/DME or DME/DME inputs for overland flight. The IRS and GPS inputs are the navigation source inputs used when VOR/DME signals are not receivable. The navigation computer will automatically choose the best navigation combination (VOR/DME, IRS, GPS, AHRS) based on predefined priority. When using VOR/DME inputs, a blending of these inputs and IRS information occurs. This blending is done via complementary filtering. Filtering lessens the effects of error and noise in both the VOR/DME and IRS inputs, and thus provides a smooth and accurate position derivation. Airspeed information is used for blending in case the IRS inputs are not available.

The navigation computer provides automatic tuning of the aircraft VOR and DME receivers. Calculation of aircraft present position from VOR/DME information requires input of bearing and distance, and knowledge of the station coordinates. The database is periodically used by the navigation computer to find the coordinates and frequencies of the VORTAC and VOR/DME stations in the aircraft vicinity. When the desired VOR and DME stations are chosen, the frequency is output to the navigation receivers. Automatic receiver tuning is operationally transparent to the pilot other than a periodic change in the receiver's frequency display. Provision is included for remote tuning of receiver via the CDU, or manual tuning through the radio control heads.

For remote tuning via the CDU, the pilot can choose to enter the VHF navaid identifier or enter the frequency. The frequency of the entered station is found in the database and output to the navigation control heads.

For manual tuning via the radio control head, the navigation computer uses the frequency code from the receiver and compares it to the frequencies of stations in the aircraft vicinity. Frequency comparison allows the navigation computer to deduce what station is being tuned. A comparison of calculated bearing and distance to received bearing and distance is used to verify received information.

Database

An important part of the navigation computer is the navigation database, which contains information on navaids, airport, and airways. The database is integral to the navigation computer to allow quick access of the stored information. The database can be loaded with one of five regionalized databases. The data includes VOR, VORTAC, VOR/DME, ILS data, airport reference points, runway thresholds, high altitude airway intersections, airway routes, and SID/STAR procedures.

Database Applications

1. Flight Plan — The database is the source of waypoints used to create a flight plan. Complete flight plans or segments of routes such as SIDs and STARs are also accessible in the database for selection as the active flight plan or for modification of the currently selected active flight plan.

2. Position Fixing — Navaid position data from the database is used in the computation of radio position.

3. Local Navaids — The navaid portion of the data-base is the source of navaids available for autotuning. A list of fifty closest navaids is updated at a rate of once every two minutes while the aircraft is airborne.

4. Custom Data — Pilot-defined way-points and flight plans are stored in the custom portion of the database. A maximum of 100 flight plans and 200 waypoints may be entered.

5. Data Display — All navigation information related to navaids, waypoints, airports, runways, and airways is available for display on the CDU. Items copied into the custom data area from the standard database during the creation of a flight plan are not viewable in the custom data index, but appear only in the flight plan.

Database Configurations

Regional Types

The database is offered in the five coverages found in Figure 14-2.

Navaid Storage. Worldwide VHF navaids are included in all databases.

Airport/Runway Threshold. The data stored for airports include all airports with ICAO identifiers, and surfaced runways 4,000 feet or longer are included. (Runways 5,000 feet or longer are also included.) The runways associated with an airport can be included in an active flight plan as a waypoint using the Departure/Arrival pages.

SID/STAR Procedure Storage. From the stored data-bases, the approved standard instrument arrival or departure procedure for an airport can be accessed. The data is called up by first specifying the desired runway, procedure, and transition. The pilot can then link the SID or STAR with the active flight plan. The data includes the waypoint sequence, path type, waypoint

location, procedure specified navaids, airspeed, and altitude constraints. In addition to standard waypoints, SIDs and STARs may also include intercept and altitude defined points.

Airway Storage. In the regionalized databases, the high altitude airways can be accessed directly. The specification of a destination along a specific airway will automatically fill in all the navaids and intersections on the airway between the previous waypoint and the destination.

Note: Unnamed airway intersections are also included when airways are added to the flight plan. This is to permit changing airways at a point common to both airways.

Pilot-Defined Route Storage. Each flight plan is defined by a maximum of fifty waypoints. A maximum of twenty flight plans can be stored in the computer. Stored flight plans may be activated or linked to an existing active flight plan segment.

Pilot (User)-Defined Waypoint Storage. In addition to navaids and airports used for waypoint definition, the pilot may create a waypoint. Pilot-defined waypoints are entered by the pilot via the CDU. The pilot may define a waypoint by entering a latitude and longitude, by entering a bearing and distance from a defined waypoint, or by entering bearings from two defined waypoints. Two hundred pilot-defined waypoints may be stored in the nonvolatile database memory.

Guidance

Lateral Steering Output. In addition to the Electronic Horizontal Situation Indicator (EHSI) deviation output, a lateral steering signal is output to the AFCS. The AFCS will cause the aircraft to bank according to the lateral steering signal. The lateral steering signal is proportional to the calculated distance and angle deviations from the desired lateral course. Lateral steering mode is a desired track mode. The FMS steering command is bank angle and roll rate limited.

Vertical Deviation/Speed Target. In addition to providing a lateral steering signal, VNAV altitude, vertical speed, and speed targets are provided by the navigation computer. The vertical speed target is proportional to the calculated distance from the desired vertical path. VNAV allows the pilot to define waypoint altitudes and descent angles to waypoints, and command the AFCS to pitch the aircraft and fly the desired descent path. Speed targets are either calculated by the performance computer, or in the absence of a performance computer, input by pilot entry to the navigation computer.

Database Name	Area Covered
USA-CAN	U.S., Canada, Alaska
Europe	Europe
AFR-MES	Africa, Middle East
LAM-PAC	Latin/South America and Pacific
USA-EUR	Eastern U.S. and Europe (Primary Airports Only)

Figure 14-2. Examples of regional databases

Map Displays

The navigation computer provides guidance and map information to the pilot via the HSI, MFD, or navigation display. The navigation computer provides the NAV display positions of waypoints (lateral and vertical), closest navaids, and closest airport reference points as well as holding pattern information. The display includes the course line between the waypoints. When combined with weather radar on the map display, the waypoint and course line display will give the pilot a pictorial view of the waypoints with respect to the weather.

Miscellaneous Functions

Holding Patterns. The CDU allows holding patterns to be entered and automatically flown by the FMS and AFCS. After selecting the "hold prompt", the pilot may define the holding pattern at a waypoint by pushing the line-select key next to the desired waypoint. The holding pattern page now displays a standard holding pattern. The pilot can modify the pattern, make the holding active, or clear the entry. The FMS features automatic entry and exit of the holding pattern. Once the aircraft is in holding, the pilot initiates the exit from hold.

Radio Management. The FMS provides the pilot with the ability to tune aircraft radios via the CDU. Tunable radios can include:

1. Two VOR/DME receiver pairs
2. Three VHF communications radios
3. Two ADF receivers
4. Two MLS receivers
5. Two HF communication radios
6. Two ATC transponders

Cross Loading. Cross loading of flight plans between the two navigation computers, and thus CDUs, is provided either automatically or by pilot initiation.

Controls

Control Display Unit

The Control Display Unit (CDU), as shown in Figures 14-3 and 14-4, is the pilot interface with the Flight Management System. Its operation is designed to be simple and to minimize crew workload in all phases of flight. It serves as the pilot interface with the navigation and performance computers. The pilot may enter alphanumeric data into the system via the full alpha-numeric keyboard. This data appears in the scratch-pad to be "line selected" to the appropriate position on the display.

Architecture

The CDU consists of a keyboard, a CRT display, the electronics required to drive the CRT display, a microprocessor, power supplies, Programmable Read Only Memory (PROM), Random Access Memory (RAM), and Input/Output (I/O) buses to communicate with the navigation and performance computers. The keyboard consists of line-select keys, alphanumeric keys, and function keys. The line-select keys are positioned adjacent to the lines on the CRT that they operate on. Data may be selected to a line from the scratchpad or vice-versa through the use of the line-select keys.

Figure 14-3. Monochrome CDU with FLT plan

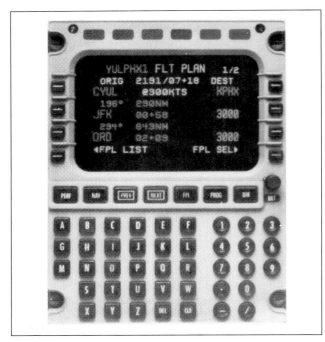

Figure 14-4. Color CDU with FLT plan

CRT

In the FMS described in this chapter, a monochrome CRT is used to display data on the CD-800 Control Display Unit and a color CRT is used on the CD-810 Control Display Unit. Both displays consist of nine lines with each line containing twenty-four characters. The first line is a title line and the ninth line is the "scratchpad."

Color Assignments

The use of colors on the CDU pages is designed to highlight important information. Color assignments are coordinated as much as possible with the EFIS/MFD.

The following general rules are used for assigning colors:

Vertical/Atmospheric .... Cyan (Blue)

Lateral .... Green

FROM Waypoint .... Yellow

TO Waypoint .... Magenta

Prompts & Titles .... White

Flight Plan Names .... Orange

Index Selections .... Green

Alphanumeric Keys

The control display unit provides a full alphanumeric keyboard to enable pilot inputs to the scratchpad of the CDU. A key is provided for each letter of the alphabet as well as each number, decimal, dash, and slash, as shown in the keyboard.

Scratchpad

The bottom line on the CRT is the scratchpad which provides a working area for the pilot to enter data and/or verify the data before line selecting it to the desired position. The scratchpad also provides **advisory** and **alerting messages** to be displayed to the pilot. Data is retained in the scratchpad throughout all mode and page changes.

Alphanumeric entries are made to the scratchpad via the keyboard. As each key is depressed, the character is displayed in the scratchpad. Information in the scratchpad does not affect the FMS until it is moved to a line on the display.

Line-Select Keys

There are four line-select keys on each side of the CRT display. Data may be selected to a line from the scratchpad or vice-versa through the use of the line select keys.

Direct Access Prompt/Mode Selects

The line-select keys are the most versatile keys on the CDU. When coupled with a CRT display unit, they are the most frequently used keys on a CDU. In the case of an index display, the line-select keys can be used to select sub-modes within the major modes. In displays other than index, the bottom line-select keys are primarily used for direct access to other modes in the FMS. This cuts the number of button pushes significantly, which minimizes pilot workload. The pilot may also access these modes via the main navigation and performance menus. The modes that are most likely to be accessed from the present page are displayed as prompts.

Transfer Line Data to Scratchpad

Data can be copied to the scratchpad through the use of a line-select key. Depressing a line-select key will transfer that information to the scratchpad if it is empty.

CRT Prompts

Once data has been entered into the scratchpad either via line selection or manual keyboard entry, it may be selected to any of the allowable line-select fields on a given page. This can be accomplished simply by depressing the key adjacent to the line in which you wish the scratchpad data to be inserted.

Paging

The number of pages in a particular mode or menu display are shown in the upper right hand corner of the display. The format is "AA/BB." "AA" signifies the number of the current page that is displayed. "BB" signifies the total number of pages that are available for viewing. Page changes are done by pressing the PREVIOUS and NEXT keys.

Function Keys

Clear Key (CLR)

This key has the following functions:

1. When a message to the pilot is present in the scratchpad, depressing the CLR key deletes that message.

2. When an entry beginning with an asterisk (*) or (#) is in the scratchpad, depressing CLR removes the entry.

3. When an alphanumeric entry resides in the scratchpad, one character is cleared from the scratchpad (from right to left) for each time the button is depressed.

4. When an alphanumeric entry resides in the scratchpad and the CLR key is held down, the first character is cleared. After approximately ½ second has elapsed, characters will be cleared for as long as the key is held down.

Delete Key (DEL)

The DEL key has one function. When there is no message in the scratchpad and the DEL key is depressed, "*DELETE*" will appear in the scratchpad. This may now be line-selected to delete waypoints and other items displayed to the CDU. When there is a message displayed, the delete operation is inhibited. "*DELETE*" is also used to return to default value after entries have been made.

Performance (PERF)

Depressing the PERF mode key enables the pilot to access the performance index. An example performance index page is shown in Figure 14-5. There are two different PERF INDEX pages depending on whether a performance computer is included as part of the system.

Navigation (NAV)

Depressing the NAV function key enables the pilot to access the NAV INDEX page. The pilot may select any of the sub-modes by depressing the line-select key. The navigation index pages are shown in Figure 14-6.

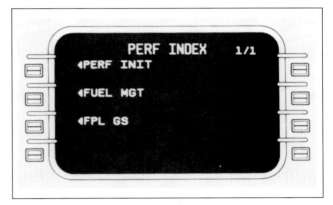

Figure 14-5. Performance Index

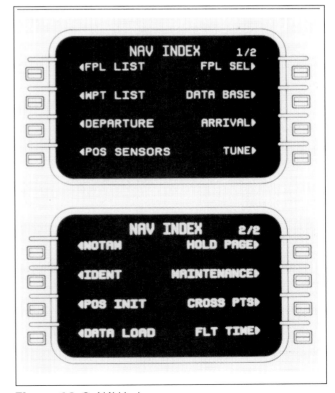

Figure 14-6. NAV Index

Flight Plan (FPL)

Pressing the FPL key displays the first page of the active flight plan. If there is no flight plan currently entered, the pilot may manually enter a flight plan, select a stored flight plan, load a flight plan from a disk, or create a stored flight plan. An example of this page is shown in Figure 14-7.

Progress (PROG)

Depressing the PROG key displays the first of the progress pages. The purpose of this mode is to show the current status of the flight. This first progress page displays the ETE, distance to, and fuel projection for the "to" waypoint and destination, the current NAV mode, the number of long range navs used, and the navaids that are currently tuned for radio updating. A typical progress page is shown in Figure 14-8.

Direct To/Intercept (DIR)

Depressing the DIR mode key displays the active flight plan with the DIRECT, HOLD, and INTERCEPT prompts as shown in Figure 14-9.

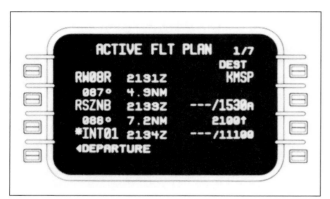

Figure 14-7. Active flight plan

Figure 14-8. Progress page

Annunciators

The six annunciators located at the top of the CDU keyboard panel operate independently from the CRT and keyboard. Illumination of the annunciators is initiated by the navigation or performance computer. The two colors used for annunciations are white and amber. White indicates an advisory type annunciation, and amber indicates an alerting type annunciation.

Display (DSPLY)

The DSPLY annunciator is an advisory type (white). This annunciator is illuminated when the CDU is displaying a page that is not relative to the current aircraft lateral or vertical flight path.

The DSPLY annunciator is illuminated in the following cases for the navigation computer only system while airborne:

1. When displaying a flight plan page other than page 1.

2. When displaying a stored flight plan page.

3. When displaying any of the review pages for SIDs and STARs.

4. When displaying the "CHANGE ACTIVE LEG" message.

5. When defining the "intercept" waypoint on the active leg.

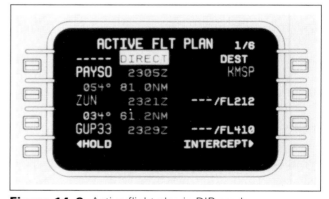

Figure 14-9. Active flight plan in DIR mode

Dead Reckoning (DR)

The DR annunciator is an alerting type (amber). This annunciator is illuminated when the FMS is navigating via the DR mode, which is defined to be the loss of radio updating and the loss of all position sensors.

1. This annunciator will illuminate when the FMS has been operating in the DR mode for longer than three minutes.

2. When the APRCH annunciator is illuminated and position updating from all sources is lost for more than 30 seconds, and the radio is not procedure tuned.

3. When the APRCH annunciator is illuminated and position updating from all sources is lost for more than 5 seconds, and the radio is procedure tuned.

Degraded (DGRAD)

The DGRAD annunciator is an alerting type (amber). This annunciator is illuminated when the FMS has entered a degraded navigation mode. The definition of "degraded" is when the FMS cannot guarantee the required accuracy for the present segment of flight. The following cases define when the annunciator will be illuminated.

1. When the aircraft is within the terminal area (50.8 NM) and the required accuracy cannot be guaranteed with the available position sensors.

2. When the aircraft is within the approach area (10 NM) and the required accuracy cannot be guaranteed with the available position sensors.

3. If a DGRAD annunciator condition exists when the DR annunciator is turned on, the DGRAD annunciator will be turned off.

Message (MSG)

The MSG annunciator is an advisory type (white). This annunciator is illuminated when the FMS is displaying a message in the scratchpad to the flight crew. The annunciator extinguishes after the message(s) have been cleared from the scratchpad.

Messages are displayed in the CDU scratchpad at various times. These messages are intended to inform or alert the pilot as to the system status. These messages are divided into two major groups: **advisory messages** and **alerting messages**. The alerting messages are higher priority messages than the advisory messages.

1. Advisory Messages—these consist of information that is helpful to the pilot, but does not require immediate attention or pilot action.

2. Alerting Messages—these consist of information that requires immediate attention and/or pilot action.

Messages are stacked for display in priority order in a first in/last out basis. In cases where there are multiple messages stacked, the message annunciator shall stay illuminated until all messages are cleared. Only one message may be cleared per key depression. In addition the, "CDU MESSAGE" discrete from the navigation computer is set.

Offset (OFFSET)

The OFFSET annunciator is an advisory type (white). This annunciator is illuminated when a lateral offset path has been entered into the FMS using the progress page. The annunciator extinguishes when the offset has been removed. If there is an offset when the APRCH annunciator is illuminated, the offset will be removed and the annunciator turned off.

Approach (APRCH)

The APRCH annunciator is an advisory type (white). This annunciator shall be illuminated when in approach mode. The HSI output sensitivity of lateral deviation is ramped to a higher sensitivity when the annunciator is illuminated. This annunciator will be illuminated under the following condition: the aircraft is within 10 NM of destination along the flight plan.

Brightness Control

Brightness control is provided for the CDU CRT display in order to maintain readability under dim light as well as direct sunlight shafting. This is accomplished in two ways:

1. *Manually by the brightness knob*—The brightness knob is provided to manually vary the intensity of the CRT display for a given ambient light level.

2. *Automatically by the photosensors*—The photosensors sense the ambient light and adjust the CRT brightness automatically to maintain the relative brightness set by the brightness knob.

Viewing Angle

All symbology is visible at a viewing angle of 45° from the sides, 15° from the top, and 30° from the bottom.

Navigation

The navigation functions of the system include accurate computations of aircraft position, ground speed, and altitude, navaid selection and tuning of the VOR and DME receiver, and use of MLS and ILS for position updates during approaches. Aircraft position is computed using data received from the radios (VOR and/or DME and/or GPS) and inertial systems. Although the Inertial Reference Systems (IRS's) output a ground speed, the navigation computer computes a more accurate ground speed (for IRS-equipped airplanes) by conditioning inertial velocity using radio inputs. For AHRS-equipped airplanes, the navigation computer calculates ground speed using inertial acceleration and radio inputs. Aircraft altitude is computed using available inertial and/or air data computer sensors.

The navigation computer selects frequencies for tuning the VOR and a directed scan DME, or two single channel DMEs. However, the NAV radios can be tuned by either the navigation computer supplied frequencies or a frequency transmitted by the VHF NAV control head. When in autotune, the VOR/DME is "listening" to the navigation computer for selection of the VOR frequency and as many as three DME frequencies. In the manual position, the VOR/DME is "listening" to the VHF NAV control head which can select a VOR and/or DME station for display on the RMI.

There are four position update modes that are a function of navaid and sensor availability: radio/inertial, inertial only, radio only, and dead reckoning. These modes indicate the primary method used by the navigation computer to compute aircraft position and ground speed. (*See* Figure 14-10.)

For IRS-equipped airplanes, the difference between the radio and inertial positions is filtered to compute a position error. This position error is then combined with inertial position and inertial velocities for computing radio/inertial position.

For Attitude Heading Reference System (AHRS)-equipped airplanes, the radio/inertial position is computed by using radio position in place of IRS position and position error. The radio position is then combined with the calculated inertial velocity for computing radio/inertial position.

Although radio tuning is done while on the ground, radio position is only computed while the aircraft is airborne for an IRS-equipped aircraft. For an AHRS-equipped aircraft, if valid VOR/DME or GPS data is being received on the ground, a radio position will be computed.

For an IRS-equipped airplane, the radio/inertial NAV mode is active when the following conditions are true:

1. Valid inertial position and velocity data are available.

2. A valid radio position is computed from either (1) at least two DMEs, (2) one VOR/DME pair or (3) a GPS sensor.

The IRS inertial-only NAV mode is active when at least one IRS is providing valid position and velocity data, and there is no valid radio position data. The inertial position is computed by combining the valid IRS positions. The inertial only mode is less accurate due to IRS drift.

For an AHRS equipped airplane, the radio/inertial NAV mode is active when the following conditions are true:

1. Valid acceleration and angular data are available.

2. A valid radio position is computed from either (1) at least two DMEs, (2) one VOR/DME pair, or (3) a GPS sensor.

The radio position and inertial acceleration are combined in the AHRS velocity filter to compute the north and east inertial ground speed components. These components are then combined with radio position in a complementary filter to compute the radio/inertial position.

With AHRS, the inertial-only NAV mode is active when at least one AHRS is providing valid acceleration and angular inputs, and there is no valid radio position data. The inertial-only mode is less accurate due to AHRS drift. In addition, if radio position is not computed within ten minutes of entering the AHRS inertial-only mode, the system reverts to dead reckoning.

The radio-only mode is active when there is no valid inertial data, and valid radio data is being received.

The dead reckoning mode is activated when the following conditions are true:

1. a. There are no IRS's in the normal mode, and there is at least one IRS in the Reversionary Attitude mode with the corresponding Set Heading bit.

    b. There is a valid mag heading input from an AHRS.

2. A radio position cannot be computed.

3. A valid true airspeed is available from the ADC.

A dead reckoning position is calculated from the last known aircraft position using the track and distance traveled along that track. IRS magnetic heading or AHRS heading, ADC true airspeed, and the last known wind are used to estimate aircraft ground speed and track.

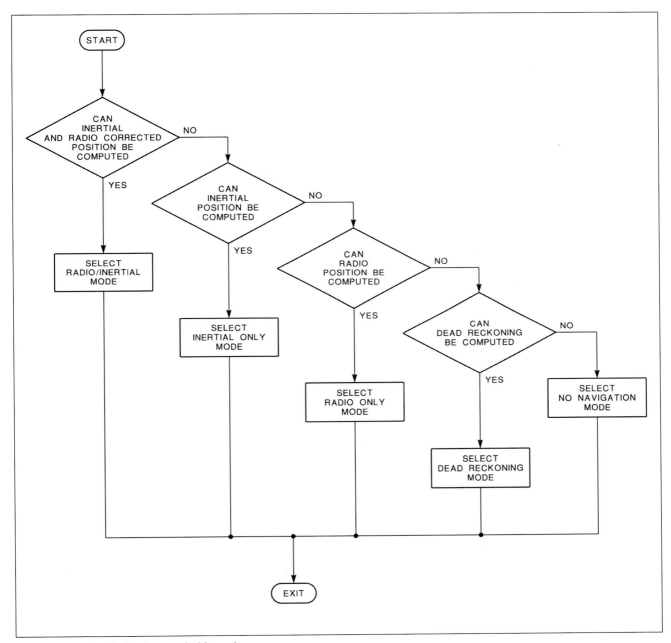

Figure 14-10. Navigation mode hierarchy

15: Time

A Concept of Vital Importance to Pilots

The dimension of time is vitally important to pilots. Schedules, ATC clearances, fuel planning, and navigation are just a few of the very important uses of time. For the navigator, distances traveled are a function of time. Fuel flow, climb rate, aircraft speed, vertical and horizontal distances, flight progress, aircraft maintenance schedules, and pilot age and experience are all quantifiable in units of time.

Until nearly 100 years ago, the rotation of the earth (or from the perspective of an observer on earth, the rotation of the stars) was considered to be the basis for an invariable time standard. In more recent years, man has determined that the earth's rotation is slowing and is variable because he has developed more sophisticated and accurate methods of measuring intervals of time by looking inward, to the vibrations and energy emissions of atoms and subatomic particles. Most of us wear "quartz" watches which count the vibrations of a small quartz crystal to establish the interval of time called the "second."

A study of the history of time measurement, development of time standards, and dissemination of time information gives the internationally traveling pilot a better appreciation of the complex concept of time. There are situations where understanding how other cultures view the concept of time may make the international traveler's dealings with other peoples easier (see the following section on the calendar).

Even today, we are in the midst of some important changes in the fields of time measurement and transmission of accurate time signals to all of us. For example, more of us still receive accurate time signals from the National Bureau of Standards (NBS) source by HF-SSB radio than from the atomic clock sources in GPS satellites—which also originate from NBS, but that is changing. The satellite signals are more accurate, already digitized for us and require a much smaller receiver/computer, which utilizes the time information for a myriad of tasks as well as displaying very accurate time. For pilots, GPS is rapidly becoming the time source in use (*see* Figure 15-1).

The importance of time to the pilot cannot be overstressed. As seen by the plot on the cover of this book (and in Figure 8-2), the pilot flying across the north Atlantic utilized time as one dimension in position determination, plotting and reporting (latitude, longitude, altitude, and *time!*). Time was also used by that pilot at each position reporting point and each 2° and 5° of longitude thereafter to accomplish a **gross error check** (*see* Chapter 16) on the navigation system in order to be sure, without relying on the navigation

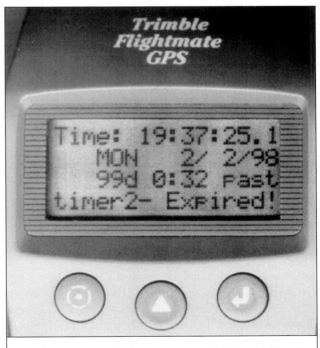

GPS receivers display very accurate time to $\frac{1}{10}$ of a second. Here it shows the time as 19:37:25.1 on Monday, February 2nd, 1998. This page also accesses the timer features.

Figure 15-1. Time from a GPS receiver

system, that the aircraft was indeed headed for the next designated waypoint while wending its way across the ocean.

In the following pages, the concepts and dimensions of time are explored in more detail to help the pilot expand his or her knowledge level about this very important dimension.

The Evolution of the Calendar

The Calendar of Romulus

Our present calendar represents an evolution from a series of Roman calendars, the first of which was instituted about 738 B.C. by King Romulus, founder of Rome. The complete calendar of Romulus consisted of ten months. It began on the date the vernal equinox was then celebrated (March 25th according to the present calendar) and ended about January 24th, making a year of 304 days. The balance of the 61 days to make up a year as we know it was not counted. This calendar is believed to have been patterned after the one followed in primitive areas in the north, where the deepest months of winter, being useless, were simply ignored. Most of the names of the months of the Romulus calendar have been perpetuated in the calendar of today. The first month of the Romulus calendar was named *Martius* after Mars, the god of war. The second month, *Aprilis,* was derived from the Latin *aperire,* meaning "to open," suggesting the period of budding leaves and opening flowers. The third month was *Maius,* after Maia, the goddess of growth. The fourth month was *Junius,* probably from *juvenis,* meaning "youth." The remaining six months were given numerical names: *Quintilis* (fifth), *Sextilis* (sixth), *Septembris* (seventh), *Octobris* (eighth), *Novembris* (ninth), and *Decembris* (tenth).

The Numa Calendar

Romulus was succeeded, around 713 B.C., by King Numa Pompilius who introduced a calendar based on lunar cycles. He added two new months to make a year of twelve months. The first of the two new months was named *Januarius,* after *Janus,* (guardian of the heavens and protector of gateways), suggesting the beginning, and was placed ahead of Martius. The second new month was called *Februarius,* named for *februalia,* meaning "repentance," a period when sacrifices were

to be made to the gods for offenses committed during the year. It was made the last month of the year and followed Decembris.

The calendar of King Numa continued the beginning of the new year at the vernal equinox. Even numbers were considered unlucky, so they arranged seven months of 29 days, four months of 31 days, and the leftover 28 days were given to Februarius which signaled the death of the year and not too lucky anyway. Isn't it interesting to note that the month of repentance was the shortest of all!

The year had 355 days. It was soon found that this ten-day shortage was making the vernal equinox ten days earlier year after year. To correct this, an extra month of 22 or 23 days, which was called *Mercedonius,* was introduced into the calendar every other year. This system did not fit well with the actual length of the solar year.

The Numa calendar had a life of something less than 300 years. In 450 B.C., the Council of Decemvirs, under Appius Claudius, reshuffled the months and placed the keeping of the calendar under the Pontifical College. It was at this time that Februarius was taken from the end of the calendar and placed between Januarius and Martius, making the year end with the month Decembris.

The Julian Calendar

Adopted from the Egyptians

Remember that there was no publication of this calendar. It was kept by the priests, who announced the time for celebrations and the time for the collection of taxes, interest, and rentals, providing the keepers with ample opportunity to realize profits by changing it. It is said that history repeats itself (I was thinking of our tax laws of today).

The number of days in the various months was changed at will until it no longer kept time with the seasons. The strong hand necessary to effect a drastic reform in the calendar appeared when Julius Caesar seized power in Rome and assumed the office of Pontifex Maximus. He thus became the leader of the state religion, in whose domain the calendar fell. The reform of the Roman calendar, ordered by Julius Caesar, was placed in the hands of the Alexandrian astronomer Sosigenes. In order to put the new calendar into effect, Caesar ordered a preliminary year of 445 days for the purpose of adjusting the calendar to the seasons. This has since become known as the "year of confusion." The calendar, as finally adopted, was essentially that of the Egyptian calendar then prevailing.

The Egyptians had observed a similar lunar calendar for close to 4,000 years with several differences. They began their year at about our July 19th, a date which signaled two important events: the rising of the dog star, Sirius (the Egyptian god Sothis), which appeared in the east just before dawn, and the annual flooding of the Nile, which covered the sand with rich silt and made possible the planting of grain, from which the wealth of the country came. At this time, the Egyptian months were 30 days long and the year covered 360 days. Over the years, the Egyptians found that a calendar based on lunar cycles caused the beginning of their new year and the flooding of the Nile to get out of date.

The average length of the lunar cycle is 29.53059 days. A lunar year of twelve lunations is about 354 days. From their study of the shadows of the obelisk, the Egyptians established the length of the solar year as 365¼ days. Around 238 B.C., five extra days were added to the end of the year, each a holiday. The practice of inserting extra days in leap years was also introduced. The story of how the Egyptians corrected their calendar is told by Plutarch, the historian, in approximately these words:

"When the sun-god, Ra, perceived that his wife, Nut, had been unfaithful to him, he declared with a curse that she should be delivered of the child in no month and no year! But the goddess had another lover, the god Thoth . . . and he, playing at draughts with the moon, won from her a seventy-second part of every day, and having compounded five whole days out of these parts, he added them to the Egyptian year of 360 days." (From "Adonis, Attis, Osiris," II, p. 6, in *The Golden Bough*, by Sir James George Frazer.)

This mythical story serves to show the underlying part that magic and religion played in the early development of time measurements.

The Julian calendar was based on the estimate of the year's length as 365¼ days. Caesar changed Quintilis, the seventh month, to *Julius* to suit himself. The months became Januarius, Martius, Maius, Julius, Septembris, and Novembris with 31 days each; and Aprilis, Junius, Sextilis, Octobris, and Decembris with 30 days each. Februarius was to have 29 days in common years, and 30 days in leap years or every fourth year. The new year started on January 1st instead of March 25th. The new Julian calendar went into effect in about 47 B.C.

With the death of Caesar, the Pontifical College, once more without effective leadership, again started tinkering with the calendar. For a period of 36 years, they made leap year every third year instead of every fourth, as the calendar had been planned.

The calendar was again reformed by Augustus Caesar in 8 B.C. It was brought into line by eliminating the leap years between 8 B.C. and A.D. 8. Then, following the precedent of Julius Caesar, Augustus also renamed a month in his honor. The old month Sextilis became *Augustus*. To avoid having bad luck associated with the even number of days assigned to this month, he added an extra day, taking it away from Februarius. Although radically changed by Augustus, the name *Julian* is customarily given to the calendar.

Another notable change took place in A.D. 532 when the Abbot of Rome, Dionysius Exiguus, participating in the then current tradition of acknowledging March as the month of Annunciation, named March 25th as the date of the conception of Christ, and further ordered that henceforth the year was to begin on that date which also determined the birthdate of Christ as December 25th. This was a radical change which was followed for over a thousand years. Dionysius is also credited with having begun the custom of counting historical periods B.C. (before Christ) and A.D. (*anno Domini*, the year of our Lord).

The Gregorian Calendar

In A.D. 532, when the Christian holidays were established, the calendar seemed to be well arranged. There was, however, a small error in the calculation of the actual length of the year. The calendar was based on the assumption that the year is 365.25 days long. Actually, the solar year is 365.2422 days, a difference of 0.0078 days in a year (one day in about 128 years). While the vernal equinox occurred on March 21st in A.D. 325, this celestial occurrence retreated to March 15th in A.D. 1093 and would have been occurring at Christmas before long except that the Council of Trent of 1582 authorized the Pope to correct this error. After consultation with many astronomers, Gregory XIII ordered that the day following Thursday, October 4, 1582, would be Friday, October 15, 1582. He changed the beginning of the year from March 25th to January 1st, as Numa had 2,295 years previously.

The change was not followed by England and the Colonies until 1752, by which time the old Augustan calendar had accumulated another day's error. So our country has no historical record between Wednesday,

September 2, 1752, and Thursday, September 14, 1752. Eleven days that just never happened! That is why the birthday of Washington, born February 1st on the old style calendar is today celebrated on the 22nd. Benjamin Franklin wrote in his Almanac to note the change necessary to begin the use of the new calendar:

"Be not astonished, nor look with scorn, dear reader, at such a deduction of days, nor regret as for the loss of so much time, but take this for your consolation, that your expenses will appear lighter and your mind be more at ease. And what an indulgence is here, for those who love their pillow to lie down in Peace on the second of this month and not perhaps awake till the morning of the fourteenth."

With the adoption of the new calendar, England and the Colonies, which had observed March 25th as New Year's Day, switched to our present January 1st.

The Gregorian calendar, which we now use, is not perfect, but is still an accurate timekeeper. Its error is calculated as 26 seconds per year which would add up to a whole day in 3,323 years!

The First Almanacs

In Europe, the calendar in published form (manuscript almanacs) can be traced back only to about the thirteenth century, but there is evidence that they existed much earlier in China. The first printed almanac known was that of the astronomer Purbach published in Vienna in 1457. General publication of calendars in the form of almanacs began in England around 1600. Most of the early almanacs, much like those of the present day, contained astrological information, home remedies for man and beast, weather prognostications, and advice for guidance of the reader in all matters of human life. In many early calendars, symbols were used for dates to make them readable to the illiterate. The first calendar published in the United States is believed to have been printed by William Bradford in Philadelphia in 1687. Benjamin Franklin began the publication of *Poor Richard's Almanac* in 1732, and it was continued for about twenty-five years.

The Greek Olympiads

A Form of Calendar

The Olympic games, which are held every four years, are a souvenir of the Greek method of chronology which was adopted around the third century B.C. The Olympiads (or 4-year periods) at that time were dated back to the restoration of the ancient games by Iphitus about 776 B.C. An Olympiad consisted of alternately

49 and 50 Greek months, because in order to adjust the calendar of twelve months, alternately of 29 and 30 days, it was necessary to introduce an extra month into every third year. Various adjustments had to be made in this scheme until the discovery of the Metonic cycle consisting of 235 lunations (19 years), mentioned also in connection with the dating of Easter. The Metonic cycle was used to make adjustments in the Greek system of chronology as long as the counting of Olympiads continued. When Dionysius Exiguus calculated the date of the birth of Christ, he placed it in the fourth year of the 194th Olympiad or the 753rd year from the founding of Rome. Astronomers of today seem to agree that he placed the date four years too late, but with the mixed-up chronology of the intervening three centuries and the absence of accurate written history, it still be seems a noteworthy achievement.

The Hebrew Calendar

The Hebrew calendar is now considered to have begun with the autumnal equinox (September 21st) in the year 3761 B.C., the date of the creation of the world according to the Book of Genesis of the Hebrew Scriptures. The letters A.M. (*anno mundi,* the year of creation) identify the Hebraic dates. The calendar is based on the cycles of the moon with six months of 29 days and six months of 30 days in the common year. Each day begins at sunset; each month begins at sunset on the day of the new moon (actually, the crescent moon). The important consideration is that solemn religious days must not fall on certain days prohibited by Mosaic and rabbinical laws. These are New Year's Day (Rosh Hashana). Passover (Pesach), the Day of Atonement (Yom Kippur), Feast of Lots (Purim), and Pentecost (Shabuoth).

To keep these religious festivals in order, an extra month of 29 days is added after Adar (called Veadar or second Adar) seven times in a cycle of 19 solar years. Veadar becomes the seventh month in the embolismic year which has 13 months. The Jewish years, thus, have variously 353, 354, 355, 383, 384, and 385 days, following a complicated system of rules almost beyond the comprehension of lay people. As with all calendars, which in early days were kept by priests for the use of priests in announcing the religious holidays, these complications are of little importance. The Jewish world still orders its religious life according to this calendar which calls the year 1960, A.M. 5721.

The French Revolutionary Decimal Calendar

Resistance to change was also a factor in acceptance of the Revolutionary calendar brought about by the National Convention of Revolutionary France. It was, in effect, a decimal calendar. The week of seven days was replaced by a ten-day week called a **decade**.

Three decades comprised a month. The days of each decade were given Latin numerical names. Each day was divided into ten hours, each hour into 100 minutes, each, minute into 100 seconds. The twelve 30-day months accounted for 360 days. The residual five or six added days were named in honor of the following and celebrated on the dates indicated:

Les Vertus .... (the virtues) .... September 17

Le Genie .... (the genius) .... September 18

Le Travail .... (the labor) .... September 19

L'Opinion .... (the opinion) ...... September 20

Les Recompenses ...... (the rewards) ...... September 21

The leap year days were called **Sans-culottides** and were dedicated to sports. The first month of the calendar was to begin at midnight between September 21st and 22nd, near the autumnal equinox.

The Revolutionary Convention enacted the new calendar into law April 7, 1795, and it had a life of thirteen years. Unfortunately for its success, one of the announced purposes of this calendar was to eliminate the grip and influence of the Catholic Church. Thus, it met with continuous resistance from Rome. Finally, with the ascension of Napoleon to the head of the government, he obtained the Pope's formal recognition of his personal authority over France and parts of conquered Europe, for which blessing he agreed to the death of the Revolutionary calendar and the rebirth of the Gregorian calendar with its Saints' days and church holidays.

The Soviet Russia Experiments in Calendar Changing

Another example is found in Soviet Russia where, in 1929, the Union of Soviet Socialist Republics replaced the Gregorian calendar with one of their own. The announced purpose, again, was to destroy the influence of the church. Each month was to consist of six weeks of five days. Each five-day week was to have four working days, the fifth to be a free day. As in the case of the calendar of Revolutionary France, the extra five days of the normal year and the six days of the leap year were declared holidays.

In 1932, the Soviet calendar was changed to twelve months with each month consisting of five weeks of six days' duration. The months were named according to the Gregorian calendar, but the days of the week were identified merely by numbers. On June 27, 1940, the Soviet Union, as a result of many protests, abandoned its effort to have its own calendar and readopted the Gregorian calendar.

In similar fashion, the Arab nations, which had followed the Mohammedan calendar, adopted the Gregorian calendar as their civil calendar, though reserving the Mohammedan calendar for religious use, as do the Jewish people.

The Julian Day of the Astronomers

The determination of the dates of past events is difficult, due to the chaotic chronology through the many calendars which have been used. For astronomical calculations, there is employed what is known as the **Julian period** with each period covering 7,980 years. The current Julian period began January 1st in the year 4713 B.C. The name of the period has nothing to do with Julius Caesar, but was applied in 1582 by its inventor, Joseph Scaliger, in honor of his father.

In using the Julian period, it is customary to indicate dates by the total number of days that have elapsed since the beginning of the period, no reference being made to the years at all. The **Julian day**, identified with the initials J.D., and is understood by all astronomers throughout the world. The system is especially useful for obtaining the interval in days between two observations, since the date of visibility of solar eclipses in various parts of the world can be readily estimated. Historic dates can also be determined with great accuracy if there is a recorded eclipse in the same era.

For the calculation of dates according to Julian days, astronomers have reference to a table which assigns a number to each year. To this is added a month number representing the accumulation of days to the end of the prior month, and finally, the date of the month. For example, the year number for 1965 is 2,438,761, representing the number of days since the beginning of the present Julian period (4713 B.C.). If the date were March 25, we would add 59, representing the number of days in the year to the end of February; then 25, the number of days which have accumulated in March. According to Julian days, March 25, 1965 is 2,438,845. This system appears to be a model for the time system used aboard the fictitious "Starship Enterprise" with its digital "star date."

Calendar Improvement

The Gregorian calendar is a patched-up, heavily massaged product involved with the whimsies of kings and dictators, which has grown out of the magic and religions of past times and conceived in a period of developing astronomical knowledge. Our present calendar, though reformed last within 400 years, is not keeping step with either our knowledge or social needs. The improvement of the calendar is a matter of international concern. The basic weakness is the lack of rational division of its components: the year, the half year, the quarter, the month, and the week.

The solar year does not contain an integral number of days, consequently the calendar never agrees with the solar year from year to year. Consisting of 365 or 366 days, it is not possible to divide the year into equal halves, quarters, and twelfths. The twelve divisions of the year are unequal. Months consist of 28, 29, 30, and 31 days, and any month can begin on any one of the seven days of the week. The calendar does not provide for an integral number of weeks. In common years, there are $52\frac{1}{7}$ weeks and in leap years, $52\frac{2}{7}$ weeks.

In order to achieve desired time standardization to eliminate wasteful recording and cumbersome calculations caused by the Gregorian calendar and to obtain comparative data relating to purchases, production, sales, costs, budgeting, labor turnover, overhead, and so forth, more than 20,000 firms in the United States alone have adopted a 13-month fiscal calendar. In the 13-month calendar, the months have 28 days, each month has 4 weeks, and each week is exactly like every other week, as shown by the following:

MON	TUE	WED	THU	FRI	SAT	SUN
1	2	3	4	5	6	7
8	9	10	11	12	13	14
15	16	17	18	19	20	21
22	23	24	25	26	27	28

Another proposal, called the **World Calendar**, provides uniformity of quarter-year periods. Both the 13-month fixed calendar and the World Calendar, which has been brought before the United Nations, appear to be superior to the Gregorian for practical modern use. Religious opposition and the natural resistance to change of the human mass is probably the greatest deterrent to calendar change.

Kinds of Time

The fact that many thousands of firms throughout the world are using the 13-month calendar for business purposes, while not interfering with the religious and other celebrations as dictated by the Gregorian calendar, suggests two calendars, one for religious and the other for civil use, as a means of effecting the change without incurring world-wide opposition.

Universal Time

It is apparent that, because there is not an integral number of days or months in the year, a rather ragged calendar results. As man improved his ability to measure time, it was noticed that the time of day as measured by a sundial could vary as much as fifteen minutes in February and November. This variation is caused by:

1. The earth doesn't travel around the sun in a circle, but in an ellipse. When the earth is nearer the sun (winter in the northern hemisphere), it travels faster in orbit than when it is farther away from the sun; and

2. The axis of the earth's rotation is tilted at an angle of about 23.5° with respect to the plane which contains the earth's orbit around the sun.

Because of this variation, the **mean solar day** was defined. This is an interval of time equal to the average length of all the individual solar days of the year.

Stellar or Sidereal Time

The solar day has long been recognized as the time between two "high noons." For an observer at any given point, the interval of time from when the sun is highest in the sky until that event happens the next day is the solar day. But, if the time interval were measured from the time a given star was highest in the sky until the next day when the event re-occurred, a different time (slightly shorter) would be found as compared to the solar day.

Why? Because the earth, during the time it is making one rotation about its axis, has moved some distance in its journey around the sun. Because the stars are so very far away from the earth that the tilt of the earth's axis and the elliptical orbit around the sun have a negligible effect, the net effect is that the mean solar day is about four minutes longer than the day determined from motion of the stars, called the **sidereal day**.

Unlike the solar day, the sidereal day does not vary in length from one time of the year to another, providing a more constant means for astronomers to measure time.

The Earth's Rotation and Universal Time

The earth does not rotate uniformly. Early clues to this were observed and documented as early as 1675 A.D. by English astronomer John Flamstead, and 1695 by Edmund Halley (of Halley's Comet fame), by observing that the moon and planets did not appear consistently at the same time each day, even when their respective orbits were considered.

The development of atomic timekeeping in the 1950s made it possible to more carefully study the irregularities of earth rotation, because time obtained from atomic clocks is far more uniform than earth time. These and other studies concluded that there are three main types of irregularities:

1. *The earth is gradually slowing down.* The length of the day is about 16 milliseconds (0.016 seconds) longer now than it was 1,000 years ago. It is believed that this slowing is largely due to frictional tidal effects of the moon on the earth's oceans.

2. *The positions of the north and south spin poles wander around by a few meters from one year to the next.* This is probably due to movement of water/ice mass to and from the earth's oceans and polar caps, and to rearrangements in the structure of the earth itself. Calculations show that this can cause discrepancies as large as 30 milliseconds.

3. *Regular and irregular fluctuations are superimposed on the slow decrease.* Largely due to mass redistributions on and near the surface of the earth, an example is the seasonal change in spin rate. During the northern hemisphere's winter, water evaporates from the ocean and accumulates as ice and snow on the high mountains. Just as the ice skater spinning on one toe spins faster with her mass concentrated near the spin axis (arms against the body) and slower with arms extended, so does the earth spin slower with some of its mass relocated to the mountain tops. What about the fact that it is summer in the southern hemisphere where ice has melted from the mountain tops? That may account for some of the relocation of the spin poles; but the fact is that the land area is far greater in the northern hemisphere, thus more mountains to accumulate ice answers the query.

All of these effects that conspire to make the earth a somewhat irregular clock have led to the development of three different scales of time that are called **Universal Time**, which has three levels of sophistication (accuracy):

1. UT0 is the scale generated by the mean solar day. Thus, UT0 corrects for the tilted earth moving around the sun in an elliptical orbit.

2. UT1 is UT0 corrected for the polar motion of the earth.

3. UT2 is UT1 corrected for the regular slowing down and speeding up of the earth in the spring and fall.

Each step from UT0 to UT2 produces a more uniform time scale.

Ephemeris Time

Time based upon the earth's rotation about its axis is irregular because, as just discussed, the earth's rotation is not regular. Also, because of this irregular rotation, mathematically predicted times of certain astronomical phenomena such as the orbits of the moon and the planets are not always in agreement with the observations of these celestial bodies. Unless we assume that the moon and all of the planets are acting in an unpredictable, but similar, fashion, we must accept the only alternative assumption—that the earth's rotation is not steady.

Since this assumption seems the more reasonable and has indeed been substantiated by other observations, it can be assumed that the astronomical events occur at the "correct" time and that we should tie our time scale to these events rather than to earth rotation. This was in fact done in 1956, and the time based on the occurrence of these astronomical events is called **Ephemeris Time**.

How Long is a Second?

The adoption of Ephemeris Time had an impact on the definition of the second, which is the basic unit for measuring time. Prior to 1956, the second was 1/86,400 of the mean solar day, since there are 86,400 seconds in a day. But we know that the second based on solar time is variable, so after 1956 and until 1967 the definition of the second was based upon Ephemeris Time. As a practical matter, it was decided that the Ephemeris second should closely approximate the mean solar second; and so the Ephemeris second was defined as very near the mean solar second for the tropical year

1900. (**Tropical year** is the technical name for our ordinary concept of the year and is discussed shortly in the section, "Length of the Year.")

Thus two clocks, one keeping Ephemeris Time (ET) and the other Universal Time (UT), would have been in close agreement in 1900. But because of the slowdown of the earth's rotation, UT was about 30 seconds behind ET by the middle of the century.

"Rubber" Seconds

Even with the refinements and corrections that had been made in UT, UT and atomic time (which is smooth and regular with extreme accuracy) will get out of step because of the irregular rotation of the earth. Thus, in the 1950s, a need persisted for a time scale that has the smoothness of atomic time, but that will stay in approximate step with UT.

Such a compromise scale was generated in 1958, when the definition of the second was based on atomic time but the time scale itself, called **Coordinated Universal Time** (UTC), was to stay in approximate step with UT2. UTC can be considered to be generally equivalent to the well known **Greenwich Mean Time** (GMT) or **Zulu Time** (Z). It was further decided that there would be the same number of seconds in each year.

But this is clearly impossible—unless the length of the second is changed periodically to reflect variations in the earth's rotation. This change was provided for and the "rubber second" came into being. Each year, beginning in 1958, the length of the second, relative to the atomic second, was altered slightly with the hope that the upcoming year would have the same number of seconds as the one just passed. But the rotation rate of the earth is not totally predictable, so there is no way to be certain in advance that the rubber second selected for a given year will be right for the year or years that follow.

In anticipation of this possibility, it was further agreed that whenever UTC and UT2 differed by more than 0.1 second, the UTC clock would be adjusted by 0.1 second to stay within the specified tolerance.

The Atomic Second and the Leap Second

After a few years the rubber-second system was considered to be a nuisance. All over the world, clocks had to be adjusted to run at differing rates. In 1967, the second was redefined in terms of the frequency of radiation of a cesium atom. Now, a **second** is defined as an interval of time during which the cesium atom oscillates 9,192,631,770 times.

To keep atomic time and earth time coordinated, the "leap second" was created in 1972. It is added or subtracted to keep UTC within 0.9 seconds of UT1 always, during the last minute of the year or of the month of June as determined by the Bureau International de l'Heure (BIH).

Length of the Year

Up to this point, we have defined the **year** as the time it takes for the earth to make one complete journey around the sun. But actually, there are two kinds of year. The first is the **sidereal year** which is the time it takes the earth to circle around the sun with reference to the stars, in the same sense that the sidereal day is the time required for one complete revolution of the earth around its aids with respect to the stars. We can visualize the sidereal year as the time it would take the earth to move from some point, around its orbit, and back to the starting point if we were watching this motion from a distant star. The length of the sidereal year is about 365.2564 mean solar days.

The other kind of year is the one we are used to in everyday life. It is the one that is broken up into the four seasons. This year is technically known as the **tropical year**, and its duration is about 365.2422 mean solar days or about 20 minutes shorter than the sidereal year. The reason the two years are different lengths is that the reference point in space for the tropical year moves slowly itself, relative to the stars. The reference point for the tropical year is the point in space called the vernal equinox, which moves slowly westward through the background of stars.

The Timekeepers

NBS and USNO

There are two organizations within the U.S. government primarily responsible for providing time and frequency information: the National Bureau of Standards (NBS) and the U.S. Naval Observatory (USNO).

As discussed above, the present UTC time scale has both an astronomical and an atomic component: The length of the second is determined by atomic observations, whereas the number of seconds in the year is determined by astronomical observations, adjusting by adding or subtracting leap seconds. The atomic component can be divided into two parts: one part related to accuracy and another related to stability.

Very roughly speaking, the USNO is responsible for the U.S. contribution to the astronomical part of

UTC, and NBS is responsible for the U.S. contribution to the accuracy part of the atomic component or length of the second. Both organizations provide input related to the stability part of the atomic component. The BIH in Paris accumulates this data from many laboratories and observatories all over the world and calculates "the time."

The NBS input is generated by a system of atomic clocks in laboratories in Boulder, Colorado. The system consists of a primary frequency standard, which is used to check the accuracy of a number of smaller, commercially-built secondary standards. The secondary standards run continuously and serve as a "flywheel" to perpetuate the system.

To carry out its responsibilities, the USNO makes observations at its main facility in Washington, D.C., as well as in Richmond, Florida. The observations are made using a special telescope designed to measure the time when a given star passes overhead. By measuring the time between successive overhead passages of the star, the earth's rotation can be monitored and thus UT can be derived.

The Bureau International de l'Heure

In an attempt to create a world time scale, some 70 nations of the world contribute data to the Bureau International de l'Heure (BIH) in Paris, France. The BIH is the international headquarters for keeping time. Its responsibility is to take the information provided by the contributing nations to construct an international atomic time scale (the TAI scale). Some nations provide only astronomical information, some only stability information, and others provide accuracy, stability and astronomical information. The time as determined by the BIH is just an average for all the various nations' time. It is also the responsibility of the BIH to determine when a leap second must be introduced.

From time to time, NBS and other national time keeping authorities make very exact comparisons of their clocks with the BIH clock. And with this clock as an agreed-upon standard, it is theoretically possible to keep all clocks in the world synchronized.

History of Time Broadcasts

During the early part of the 20th century with the development of radio, broadcasts of time information were initiated. In 1904, the U.S. Naval Observatory (USNO) experimentally broadcast time from Boston. By 1910, time signals were being broadcast from an antenna located on the Eiffel Tower in Paris. In 1912,

at an international meeting held in Paris, uniform standards for broadcasting time signals were discussed.

In March of 1923, the National Bureau of Standards (NBS) began broadcasting its own time signal. At first, there were only standard radio frequencies transmitted on a regularly announced schedule from short-wave station WWV, located originally in Washington D.C. One of the main uses of this signal was to allow radio stations to keep on their assigned frequencies, a difficult task during the early days of radio. In fact, one night in the 1920s, the dirigible *Shenandoah* became lost in a winter storm over the eastern seaboard, and it was necessary for the New York radio stations to suspend transmissions so that the airship's radio message could be detected. WWV was later moved outside Washington, D.C. to Beltsville, Maryland, and in 1966, to its present home at Fort Collins, Colorado, about 80 km north of Boulder where the NBS Time and Frequency Division is located.

A sister station, WWVH, was installed in Maui, Hawaii in 1948, to provide similar services in the Pacific area and western North America. In July 1971, WWVH was moved to a site near Kekaha on the island of Kauai, in the western part of the Hawaiian Island chain. The 35% increase in area coverage achieved by installation of new and better equipment extended service to include Alaska, Australia, New Zealand, and Southeast Asia.

Throughout the years, NBS has expanded and revised the services and format of its short-wave broadcasts to meet changing and more demanding needs. Today, signals are broadcast at several different frequencies in the short-wave band 24 hours a day. The signal format provides a number of different kinds of information such as standard musical pitch, standard time interval, a time signal both in the form of a voice announcement and a time code, information about radio wave propagation conditions, and even weather information about major storm conditions in the Atlantic and Pacific areas from WWV and WWVH respectively.

The broadcasts of WWV may also be heard via telephone by dialing (303) 499-7111 (Boulder, Colorado). The telephone user will hear the live broadcasts as received by radio in Boulder. Considering the instabilities and variable delays of propagation by radio and telephone combined, the listener should not expect accuracy of the telephone time signals to better than $\frac{1}{30}$ of a second.

NBS also broadcasts a signal at 60 kHz from radio station, also located in Fort Collins, in the form of a time code which is intended primarily for domestic uses. This station provides better quality frequency information because atmospheric propagation effects are relatively minor at 60 kHz. The time code is also better suited to applications where automatic equipment is utilized.

Standard Time Zones and Daylight-Saving Time

In the latter part of the 19th century, a traveler standing in a railroad station could set his pocket watch to any one of a number of clocks on the station wall; each clock indicated the "railroad time" for its own particular line. In some states, there were literally dozens of different "official" times, usually one for each major city, and on a cross-country railroad trip, the traveler would have to change his watch twenty times or so to stay in step with "railroad time." It was the railroads and their pressing need for accurate, uniform time, more than anything else, that led to the establishment of time zones and standard time.

One of the early advocates of uniform time was a Connecticut school teacher, Charles Ferdinand Dowd. Dowd lectured railroad officials and anyone else who would listen on the need for a standardized time system. Since the continental U.S. covers approximately 60° of longitude, Dowd proposed that the nation be divided into four zones, each 15° wide, which is the distance the sun travels in one hour. With the prodding of Dowd and others, the railroads adopted a plan in 1883 that provided for five time zones: four in the U.S. and a fifth covering the easternmost provinces of Canada.

The plan was placed in operation on November 18, 1883. There was a great deal of criticism. Some newspapers attacked the plan on the grounds that the railroads were "taking over the job of the sun," and said that, in fact, the whole world would be "at the mercy of railroad time." Farmers and others predicted all sorts of dire results from the production of less milk and fewer eggs to drastic changes in the climate and weather if "natural" time was interfered with. Local governments resented having their own time taken over by some outside authority. And so the idea of standard time and time zones did not gain popularity rapidly.

But toward the end of the second decade of the 20th century, the U.S. was deeply involved in a World War. On March 19, 1918, the U.S. Congress passed the Standard Time Act which authorized the Interstate Commerce Commission to establish standard time zones within the U.S. At the same time, the Act established "daylight-saving time" to save fuel and to promote other economies in a country at war.

The United States, excluding Alaska and Hawaii, is divided into four time zones. The boundary between zones zigzags back and forth in a generally north-south direction. Today, for the most part, the time-zone system is accepted with little thought, although people near the boundaries still complain and even gain boundary changes so that their cities and towns are not unnaturally separated from neighboring geographical regions where they do business.

The idea of "daylight-saving time" has roused the emotions of both supporters and critics, notably farmers, persons responsible for transportation and radio and television schedules, and persons in the evening entertainment business, and it continues to do so. Rules governing daylight-saving time have undergone considerable modification in recent years. Because of confusion caused by the fact that some cities or states chose to shift to daylight-saving time in summer and others did not, with even the dates for the shifts varying from one place to another, Congress ruled, in the Uniform Time Act of 1966, that the entire nation should use daylight-saving time from 2:00 a.m. on the last Sunday in April until 2:00 a.m. on the last Sunday in October. (Actually, "daylight-saving time" does not exist. There is only "standard time" which is advanced one hour in the summer months. "Daylight-saving time" has no legal definition, only a popular understanding.)

Any state that did not want to conform could, by legislative action, stay on standard time. Hawaii did so in 1967, Arizona in 1968 (although Indian reservations in Arizona, which are under Federal jurisdiction, use daylight-saving time), and Indiana in 1971. In a 1972 amendment of the Uniform Time Act, those states split by time zones may choose to keep standard time in one part of the state and daylight-saving time in the other. Indiana has taken advantage of this amendment so that only the western part of the state observes daylight-saving time.

When fuel and energy shortages became acute in 1974, it was suggested that a shift to daylight-saving time throughout the nation for the year around would help to conserve these resources. But when children in some northern areas had to start to school in the dark in winter months, and the energy savings during these months proved to be insignificant, year-round daylight-saving time was abandoned, and the shifts were returned to the dates originally stated by the 1966 Uniform Time Act.

In the long run, the important thing is that the changes be uniform and that they apply throughout the nation as nearly as possible. The whole world is divided into 24 standard time zones, each approximately 15° wide in longitude. The zero zone is centered on a line running north and south through Greenwich, England. The zones to the east of Greenwich have times later than Greenwich time, and the zones to the west have earlier times, with one hour difference for each zone (*see* Figure 15-2 on next page).

With this system, it is possible for a traveler to gain or lose a day when he crosses the International Date Line, which runs north and south through the middle of the Pacific Ocean, 180° around the world from Greenwich. A traveler crossing the line from east to west automatically advances a day, whereas one traveling in the opposite direction "loses" a day.

Both daylight-saving time and the date line have caused a great deal of consternation. Bankers worry about lost interest. Lawsuits have been argued and settled, often to no one's satisfaction, on the basis of whether or not a lapsed insurance policy covered substantial loss by fire; since the policy was issued on standard time and the fire in question had occurred during a period of standard instead of daylight-saving time, would it have been within the time still covered by the policy? The birth or death date affected by an individual's crossing the date line can have important bearing on anything from the child's qualifying for age requirements to enter kindergarten, to the death benefits to which the family of the deceased are entitled. The subject continues to be a lively issue, and probably will remain so.

How Pilots Know What Time It Is

Most of us regularly get a time check from a flight service station (FSS) or from Center (ATC) by voice. Their source can be traced back to the national time standard in Fort Collins (NBS) which is transmitted to these facilities by telephone or electronic code. However, with international flight carrying us out of VHF radio range of these facilities, other sources become necessary.

There are, throughout the world, special radio broadcasts of accurate time information. Most of these broadcasts are at frequencies outside the range of ordinary U.S. AM radio, so one needs a HF radio receiver to tune in the information. Many of these short-wave receivers are owned by radio and television stations, as well as by scientific laboratories in industry and government; and also by private citizens, such a boat owners, who need precise time information to navigate by the stars. Aircraft flying internationally and flying in remote regions of the world are likely to have HF receivers. Here is a list of transmitted time frequencies in North America and Hawaii:

WWV Boulder, CO kHz 2500, 5000, 10000, 15000, 20000
WWVH Hawaii   kHz 2500, 5000, 10000, 15000, 20000
CHU Ottawa   kHz 3330, 7335, 14670

Time checks received from controllers whose time information can be traced back to the nation's time standard and time signals received by HF radio were the two major sources of accurate time checks until very recently, when a new source became available. As mentioned at the beginning of this chapter, this new source is from the atomic clock sources in GPS satellites which also originate from NBS. The satellite signals are more accurate, already digitized for us, and require a much smaller receiver/computer which utilizes the time information for a myriad of tasks as well as displaying very accurate time. For pilots, GPS is becoming the source for accurate time (*see* Figure 15-1).

GPS is synchronized with UTC (Universal Coordinated Time), measured from the GPS zero-time-point of midnight January 5, 1980. However, because GPS time runs continuously, it cannot be as easily corrected for the leap seconds, and is at the time of this writing ahead of UTC by some part of a second. Mechanisms exist to adjust this time offset, and this is done periodically.

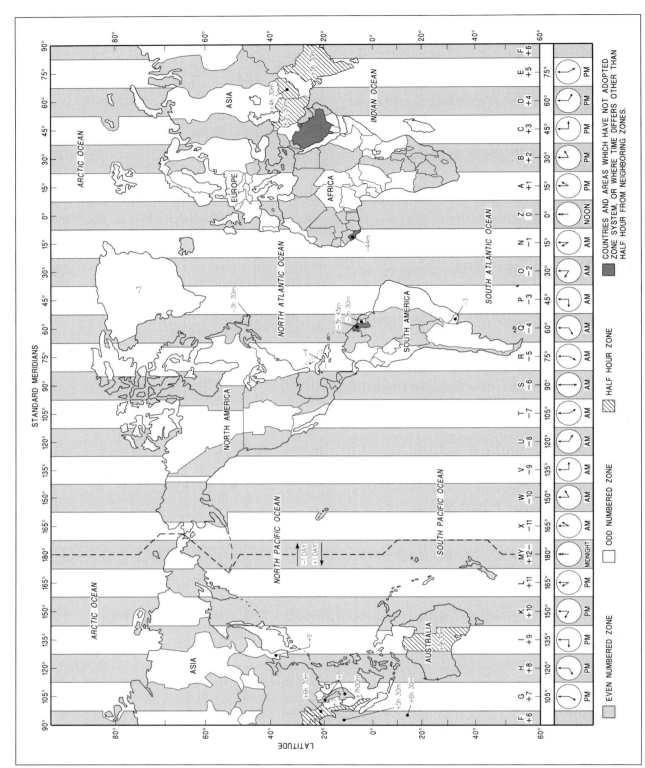

Figure 15-2. Standard time zones of the world

Where do the special broadcast stations go to find the time? Many nations maintain the time by using very accurate atomic clocks combined with astronomical observations which are constantly compared back to the international standards for time maintained by each country.

Time From the Sky

In celestial and satellite navigation, the position of the aircraft is determined by observing the celestial bodies or electronically determining the distance to the bodies. The apparent position of these bodies in respect to a point on the earth changes with time. Therefore, the determination of the position of the aircraft relies on exact timing of the observation.

Measuring Time

Today's navigator must think of time as being measured two ways: (1) in terms of Coordinated Universal time, which is readily available, used by most all of the world's society today, is a very consistent and steady time source; and (2) in terms of the rotation of the earth and the resulting apparent motions of the celestial bodies. Before getting into any further discussions of time, there is one basic term that must be understood. That term is **transit**. The time at which a celestial body passes the observer's *meridian* is divided by the earth's poles into halves. Notice in Figure 15-3 that the upper branch is that half which contains the observer's position. The lower branch is the opposite half. Every day, because of the earth's rotation, every celestial body *transits* the upper and lower branches of the observer's meridian.

As mentioned before, there are several kinds of time. The first presented here is solar time.

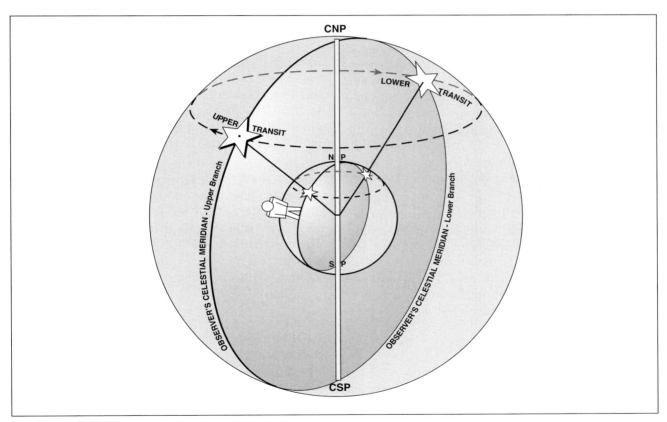

Figure 15-3. Transit is caused by the earth's rotation.

Apparent Solar Time

The sun as seen in the sky is called the true sun, and is also referred to as the apparent sun. Apparent solar time is based upon the movement of the sun as it crosses the sky. A sundial would accurately indicate apparent solar time. In this usage, apparent means "observed."

The use of apparent solar time is impractical because the apparent length of day varies throughout the year. A timepiece would have to operate at different speeds to indicate correct apparent time. However, apparent time accurately indicates upper and lower transit. Upper transit of the sun occurs at noon apparent time (usually called **local apparent noon** (LAN), the time when the sun reaches its greatest height in the sky) and lower transit occurs at 2400 apparent time. The difficulties utilizing apparent time led to the introduction of "mean time."

Mean Solar Time

A mean day is an artificial unit of constant length based on the average of all apparent solar days over a period of years. Time for a mean day is measured with reference to a fictitious body, the mean sun, so designed that its hour circle moves westward at a constant rate along the celestial equator. Time computed using the mean sun is called **mean solar time** and is nearly equal to the average apparent solar time. The coordinates of celestial bodies are tabulated in the Air Almanac with respect to mean solar time, making it the time of primary interest to the navigator.

The difference in length between the apparent day (based upon the **true sun**) and the mean day (based upon the **mean sun**) is never as much as a minute. The differences are cumulative, however, with the result that the imaginary *mean sun* is considered to precede or follow the *apparent sun* by approximately a quarter of an hour at certain times during the year.

Greenwich Mean Time (GMT) and Universal Coordinated Time (UTC)

GMT is especially important in celestial navigation since it is the time used for most celestial computation. Greenwich mean time is mean solar time measured from the lower branch of the Greenwich meridian westward through 360° to the upper branch of the hour circle passing through the mean sun (Figure 15-4). The mean sun transits the lower branch of the meridian of Greenwich at GMT 2400 (0000) each day and the upper branch at GMT 1200. The meridian at Greenwich

is the logical selection for this reference as it is the origin for the measurement of Greenwich hour angle and the reckoning of longitude. Consequently, celestial coordinates and other information are tabulated in almanacs with reference to GMT.

Greenwich mean time is not a convenient time for use in regulating everyday activities throughout the world. If all clocks were set to GMT, the time of occurrences at many places on the earth of such natural phenomena as sunrise, noon, and sunset would vary greatly from the time normally associated with these events. GMT has, in recent years, been redefined into UTC (Universal Coordinated Time). These two terms can be considered to be equivalent for practical purposes.

Local Mean Time (LMT)

Just as Greenwich mean time is mean solar time measured with reference to the meridian at Greenwich, so local mean time (LMT) is mean solar time measured with reference to the local meridian of an observer. LMT is measured from the lower branch of the observer's meridian westward through 360°, to the upper branch of the hour circle passing through the mean sun (Figure 15-4). The mean sun transits the lower branch of the meridian of an observer at LMT 0000 (2400) and the upper branch at LMT 1200. Note that if an observer were at the Greenwich meridian, GMT would also be the LMT of the observer.

LMT is not used to regulate everyone's activities because LMT, being based on the meridian of each observer, varies continuously with longitude. This disadvantage of LMT has led to the introduction of zone time as the basis for governing routine activities. The navigator uses LMT in the computation of local sunrise, sunset, twilight, moonrise, and moonset at various latitudes along a given meridian.

Relationship of Time and Longitude

It has been established that the mean sun travels at a constant rate. Consequently, the mean sun will make two successive transits of the same meridian in about 24 hours. Therefore, the mean sun travels an arc of 360° in 24 hours. The following relationship exists between time and arc.

Time	Arc
24 hours	360°
1 hour	15°
4 minutes	1°
1 minute	15 minutes
4 seconds	1 minute (1 NM on a great circle on the surface of the earth)

Local time is the time at one particular meridian. Since the sun cannot transit two meridians simultaneously, no two meridians have exactly the same local time. The difference in time between two meridians is the time of the sun's passage from one meridian to the other. This time is proportional to the angular distance between the two meridians. One hour is equivalent to 15.04° of arc.

If two meridians are 30° apart, their local time differs by two hours. The local time is later at the easternmost of the two meridians, since the sun crossed its lower branch first; thus the day is older there. These statements hold true whether referring to the apparent sun or the mean sun. Figure 15-5 (on the next page) demonstrates that the sun crossed the lower branch of the meridian of observer #1 at 60° east longitude four hours before it crossed the lower branch of the Greenwich meridian (60 divided by 15), and six hours before it crossed the lower branch of the meridian of observer #2 at 30° west longitude (90 divided by 15). Therefore, the local time at 60° east longitude is later by the respective amounts.

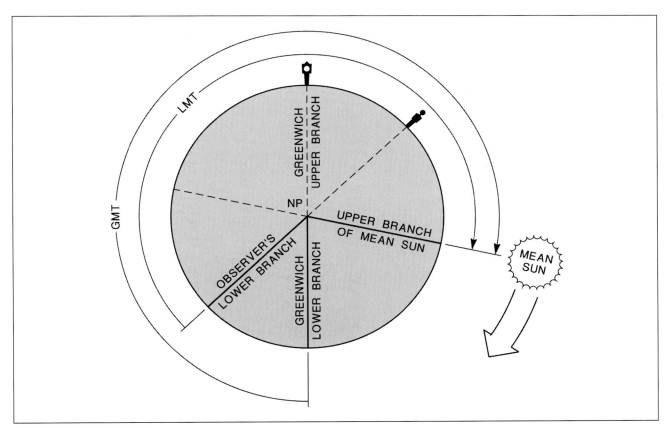

Figure 15-4. Measuring Greenwich Mean Time (GMT)

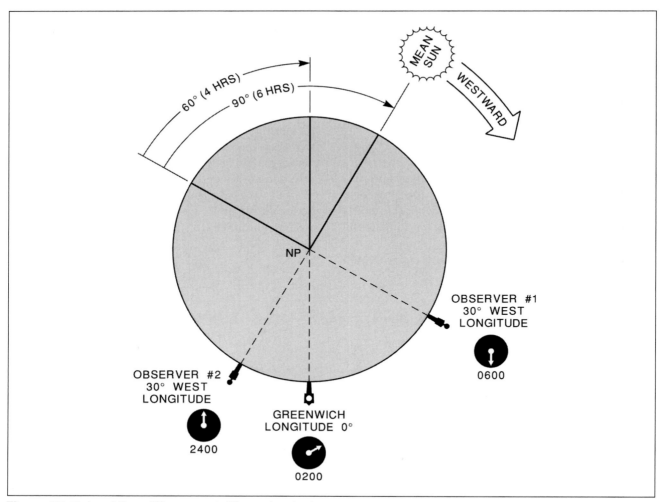

Figure 15-5. Local time differences at different longitudes

16: Navigation System Errors and Limitations

Risk Management

The role of the pilot in long-range operations is largely one of monitor and manager. It is mostly a supervisory function; to see to it that everything runs as previously planned and smoothly, making certain that the principal goal is achieved—getting from point A to point B speedily, economically, and as safely as possible.

This function can be broken down into tasks, one of which is to be certain that the aircraft follows the planned route. Accomplishment of this task involves subtasks that include selecting the appropriate navigation systems for use, proper initialization and use of those systems, and continuous monitoring of them for disfunction.

It is apparent that none of these subtasks can be accomplished unless the pilot has a good understanding of system function and its limitations. Beyond that, the pilot must be able to practice a form of risk management aimed at the early detection of errors and malfunctions.

The study of risk management teaches us that the first step in managing risk is to identify the risk. Just as a risk cannot be managed unless identified, a navigation system error cannot be corrected if the crew doesn't know it is there. Imagine being on a flight out over the North Atlantic one black night. The aircraft is on autopilot, its path being directed by a navigation system. How does the pilot know for sure that the aircraft is indeed being directed along its intended path?

That last question must be asked by the crew periodically and often during the flight in order to achieve early detection of navigation errors. To answer that question, the crew has in its "bag of tricks" the following:

- Knowledge of system limitations.
- The accuracy check, in its many forms.
- The gross error check, in its many forms.

- Procedures used to minimize errors.
- And finally, a high level of skill with the techniques of basic navigation, utilized to provide a cognitive or sometimes intuitive knowledge that "something is just not right."

Navigation System Limitations

Navigation systems can be classified by the dimension in which their inherent errors magnify. It helps to know the dimensional rate of increase of error in each system.

Type 1. Error increases with distance from station. VOR, DME, LOC, GS, ADF

Type 2. Error increases with time. DR, INS, IRS, Doppler

Type 3. Error not affected by time or distance, in which case *reliability* becomes the concern. Examples: Celestial (the navigator can't always see the celestial body), GPS (the system is new and therefore not yet fully trusted, the satellites aren't all in place yet, satellite failures occur occasionally), LORAN (stations go off the air occasionally).

Type 4. Signal quality decreases with distance from the station. Examples: all types of navigation systems except GPS and those not reliant on radio signals (Type 2 systems).

Type 5. Human error—the greatest error of all—deadly! (Korean Flight 007).

The pilot needs to understand the limitations of each navigation system in use. For example, the VOR system is known for the following errors:

Transmitter and Antenna Error: ±2.50°, ±1.25° for approach segment. Total error is typically less than 1°. This includes site and terrain error. If tests show errors greater than this, the station is NOTAM'd. If the errors are excessive, the system is automatically shut down.

Receiver/Antenna Error: Less than 4° up to 180° *legally,* depending on type of test used! (The 30-day test of 14 CFR Part 91.171, or its equivalent in Parts 121 and 135, could conceivably result in errors up to 180°.)

Typically, total error does not exceed 6°. A 6° error gives a cross-track error of 3 miles at 30 miles from the station or 6 miles if 60 miles from the station ("rule of sixty").

Each navigation system has its own unique inherent errors (Figure 16-1). Some of them are small, and some are large enough to, when active, make the system unusable. This text assumes the reader to be instrument qualified and therefore familiar with the inherent errors of the short-range navigation systems. Inherent errors in the long-range systems are discussed in the chapters that deal with each system, so let's move on to discuss the tools (other than system knowledge) available to crew members for use in avoiding or recording errors.

The Accuracy Check

The accuracy check is required after becoming airborne from the last airport before entering oceanic airspace. This check requires that the crew compare the position indicated on the long-range navigation system(s) (LRNS) in use to a position obtained either visually (landmark on the ground) or from a short-range navigation system (VOR overflight, DME-DME, VOR-DME, VOR-VOR, ADF-DME, ADF-VOR, or ADF-ADF) in order to determine the accuracy provided by the LRNS. Note that the examples of fixes obtained from short-range systems are given in order of decreasing accuracy and that conversion to lat./lon. is necessary—another source of error.

The accuracy check performed before entry into oceanic airspace must be logged, typically on the right hand panel of the plotting chart. Accuracy checks of any LRNS can be accomplished any time, anywhere a suitable comparative source exists.

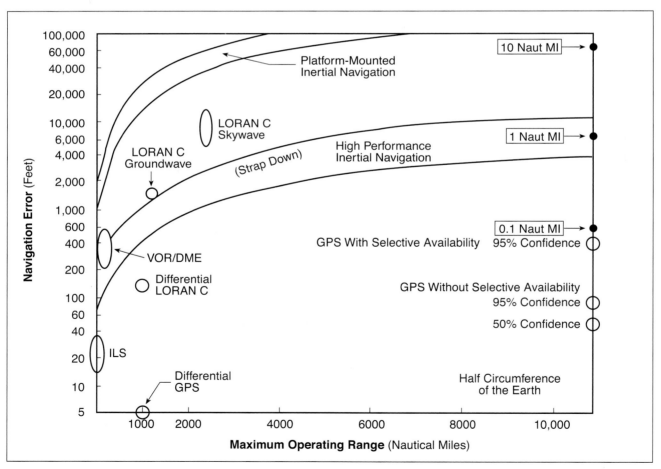

Figure 16-1. Comparison of navigational system typical errors

Another excellent way to accomplish the accuracy check is described in the last paragraph of the next section, which discusses the gross error check.

The Gross Error Check

The **gross error check** takes many forms. It is an extremely useful tool for every pilot using any type of electronic navigation system. Basically, it amounts to checking the system in question against another source of information.

A computer-generated flight plan can be checked for gross errors by plotting the route on a chart to see if distances and directions generated by the computer are correct. A LORAN system is checked in flight as the aircraft arrives at every waypoint by visually seeing if the aircraft is over the waypoint or checking the LORAN read-out against VOR-DME information. En route, the LORAN position can be checked against pilotage position if the ground can be seen and the terrain isn't featureless. When the aircraft arrives at a waypoint and the next waypoint is selected, the distance and bearing should be checked to be certain that it agrees with the distance/course for the next leg on the flight plan. This checks both the LORAN (or other LRNS) *and* the computer generated flight plan, doesn't it?

A fine example of the gross error check that is also a good and easy technique for use as an accuracy check is seen in Figure 16-2 on the next page. The trans-Atlantic flight depicted in Figure 16-2 (and on the book cover) shows the check done using the Cork VOR. The pilot has drawn the 180 degree TRUE radial on the chart, tuned in the Cork VOR with the OBS set at 188 degrees FROM (the 180 degree TRUE radial). When the VOR needle centers, the aircraft is true south of the VOR. The DME distance is noted. Since DME miles true north or south of the station convert directly to minutes of latitude, they can be subtracted (if south) from the published latitude of the VOR to obtain the aircraft's latitude. The aircraft's longitude will be the same as the VOR station's published longitude. These values of latitude and longitude can be compared with the lat./lon. reading from the LRNS in use, to provide either an accuracy check or a (quite accurate) gross error check.

Procedures Used to Minimize Errors

Gross error checks while flying transoceanic are a required procedure and are done with reference to short-range navigation systems if still within range, and if not in range, a plotting technique. As described in the MNPSA Operations Manual, and in Chapter 8 in the section on "Conducting the Flight in the MNSPA, On Reaching an Oceanic Waypoint" (on Page 168), the plotting technique consists of:

1. When the LRNS indicates the aircraft is at the waypoint, the waypoint is recorded and plotted. The distance and course, as reported by the LRNS, to the next waypoint is checked against the flight plan. Plotting the waypoint provides a visual check of the aircraft position reference the previously plotted flight plan/clearance course. Checking distance and course to the next waypoint checks LRNS function and proper crew entry of the coordinates of the next waypoint.

2. Within 10 minutes after the waypoint (usually a 2° change of longitude in fast aircraft), the aircraft's position is again plotted. This provides the crew a visual presentation on the chart of the aircraft's location reference the desired path so that errors can be detected and corrections made before the aircraft gets too far off course.

3. Halfway to the next waypoint (usually a 5° change of longitude), the aircraft's position is again plotted. Again, the crew can see if the aircraft is on course, and course and distance to the next waypoint can be easily checked (half of the flight plan distance from the last waypoint to the next waypoint).

Figure 8-4 on Page 171 shows examples of location plotting at approximately 2° and 5° after waypoints, indicating to the crew that the aircraft was indeed on the plotted track. No, the aircraft didn't crash just before waypoint number 4! A new clearance was received and a new plotting chart developed for the remainder of the flight. Note also the different symbology used for waypoints and gross error checkpoints, which is discussed below.

Continuous checks for waypoint insertion errors is another necessary procedure. (The next two paragraphs are paraphrased from the MNSPA Ops Manual).

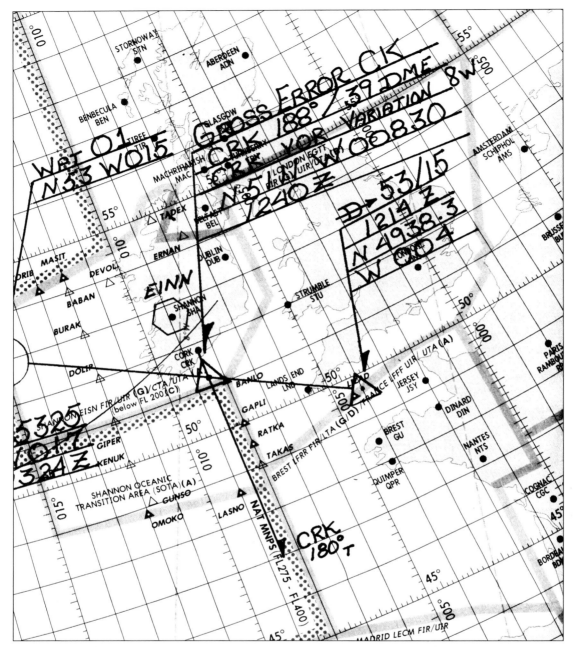

Figure 16-2. An accuracy check method using true north/south radials of a VOR which allows easy conversion to latitude/longitude.

"Experience has shown many of the INS/ONS tracking errors that occur result from failure to observe the principles of checking waypoints to be inserted against the ATC-assigned track, and of careful loading and cross-checking of onboard navigation systems. More detailed guidance on this subject is contained in Chapter 11 of this document [the MNSPA Ops Manual].

"Many of the navigation error occurrences detected by ATC oceanic exit radars are the product of one or both of these causes. It is therefore imperative that pilots double check each element of the oceanic clearance *on receipt, and at each waypoint,* since failure to do so may result in inadvertent deviation from assigned track resulting in possible collision hazard."

Additional Procedures for Error Detection

The aircraft navigation systems necessary for flying in the NAT MNPS Airspace are capable of a high standard of performance. In order to complement these, it is essential to have stringent routines of navigational cross-checking procedures. The following material offers guidance on the use of INS, GPS, and also on Inertial Reference Systems (IRS) and GPS when they are used to input navigation data to a Flight Management System (FMS).

There are various references below to "two pilots"; however, whenever a third crewmember is carried, that crewmember should be involved in all cross-check procedures to the greatest extent practical.

The Use of a Master Document

The navigation procedures must include the establishment of some form of **master working document** to be used on the flight deck. This document may be based upon the flight plan, navigation log or other suitable document which lists sequentially the waypoints defining the routes, the tracks and distances between each waypoint, and other information relevant to navigation along the cleared track. When mentioned subsequently in this text, this document will be referred to as the master document.

Misuse of the master document can result in gross navigation errors, and for this reason strict procedures regarding its use should be established. The MNPS OPS Manual recommends the following:

1. Only one master document shall be used on the flight deck.

2. Where appropriate, a waypoint numbering sequence should be established from the outset of the flight and entered on the master document. The identical numbering sequence should be used in storing waypoints in the navigation computers.

3. An appropriate symbology should be adopted to indicate the status of each waypoint listed on the master document. Following is a typical example routine:

    a. The waypoint number is entered against the relevant waypoint coordinates to indicate that the waypoint has been inserted in the navigation computers.

    b. The waypoint number is circled, to signify that insertion of the correct coordinates in the navigation computers has been double-checked independently by another crew member.

    c. The circled waypoint number is ticked to signify that the relevant track and distance information have been double-checked.

    d. The circled waypoint number is crossed out to signify that the aircraft has overflown the waypoint concerned.

All navigational information appearing on the master document must be checked against the best available prime source data. When an ATC track change is received or the ATC clearance is otherwise updated, it is recommended that a new master document is prepared for the changed portion of the flight. If the original master document is to be used, the old waypoints should be clearly crossed out and the new ones entered in their place.

Clearances

When ATC clearances or re-clearances are being obtained, headsets should be worn because the inferior clarity of loudspeakers has been known to result in mistakes. Two qualified crew members should monitor such clearances: one of them recording the clearance on the master document as it is received, and the other checking the receipt and read-back. All waypoint coordinates should be read back in detail. (Exception: wherever approved local procedures make this unnecessary, under the circumstances that the cleared track coincides with the filed ATC track. In this case, each detail must be cross-checked with the master document, and if appropriate, the track message.)

Any time the crew is operating in unfamiliar areas, especially foreign countries, and most especially in foreign-language-speaking countries, use only the phonetic use of the identifier (alpha, bravo, etc.) for any fix or intersection. Never attempt to use the pronunciation of the name of the fix or intersection when receiving or reading back clearances. If ATC uses the name, ask for the two-, three- or four-letter identifier, or ask for the phonetic spelling of the five-letter intersection (there are still some intersections in the world that are not five letters).

Position Plotting

It is very helpful for crews to use a simple plotting chart to provide themselves with a visual presentation of the intended route, which otherwise is defined only in terms of navigational coordinates. Merely plotting the intended route on such a chart may reveal errors and discrepancies in the navigational coordinates, which can then be corrected immediately before they reveal themselves in terms of a deviation from the ATC cleared route. As the flight progresses, plotting the aircraft's position on this chart will also serve the purpose of a navigation cross-check provided that the graticule is suitable.

As the flight progresses in oceanic airspace, plotting the aircraft's position on this chart will help to confirm (when it falls precisely on track) that the flight is proceeding in accordance with its clearance. But if the plotted position is laterally offset, it will be immediately apparent that the flight may be deviating unintentionally, and this possibility should be investigated at once.

It is recommended that a chart with an appropriate scale be used for plotting. Some company "Progress Charts" are too small. The AERAD NAT ½, Jeppesen AT (H/L) ½ are both useful compromises between scale and overall chart size, while the NOAA/FAA and Jeppesen North Atlantic Route/Plotting Chart has the advantage, for plotting purposes, of a 1° lat./lon. graticule.

Relief Crew Members

Flight crews conducting very long range operations may include an extra relief pilot. In such cases, it is necessary to ensure that the navigational procedures are such that the continuity of the operation is not interrupted, particularly in respect of the handling and treatment of the navigational information.

Preflight Procedures Aimed at Minimizing Error

System Alignment

The alignment of INS must be completed and the equipment switched to the NAV mode prior to releasing the parking brake at the ramp for push-back. This takes approximately 15 minutes, but can be longer. To ensure that there is adequate time for this, the first crewmember on the flight deck (often the crewmember responsible for the aircraft fueling) should place the system(s) in the align mode as soon as practicable. It is also recommended that the INS is realigned at the last transit stop before the oceanic segment.

The Initial Insertion of Latitude and Longitude

Early in the course of the pre-flight checking procedures, the aircraft's present position (POS) should be loaded (essential in the case of INS). This position must be checked against an authoritative prime reference source before insertion. Any latitude error in the initial position will introduce a systematic error into the calculations and cannot be removed in flight by updating the resulting erroneous indication of POS. Correct insertion of POS must therefore be checked before the ALIGN mode is selected, and the inserted POS must be recorded in the Flight Log or master document. Subsequently, silent checks of POS should be carried out independently by both pilots during an early stage of their pre-flight checks.

With regard to the insertion while on the ramp of the initial coordinates, the following points should be taken into account:

1. In the case of some INS systems, insertion errors exceeding about 1° of latitude will illuminate a malfunction light. It should be noted that very few systems provide protection against longitude insertion errors. (Remember that the INS system is itself capable, when stationary on the ground, of determining latitude—but not longitude; hence only latitude entry is checked.)

2. At all times but particularly in the vicinity of the equator or the prime meridian, care should be taken to ensure that the coordinates inserted are correct.

Loading of Initial Waypoints

The entry of waypoint data into the navigation systems must be a coordinated operation by two persons working in sequence and independently. One should key in and insert the data and subsequently, the other should recall it and confirm it against source information. It is not sufficient for one crewmember to merely observe another crew member inserting the data.

The ramp position of the aircraft, at least two additional waypoints, and if possible all the waypoints relevant to the flight, should be loaded while the aircraft is at the ramp. However, it is most important to ensure that the first enroute waypoint is inserted accurately, rather than to endeavor to load the maximum number of waypoints.

During flight, at least two current waypoints beyond the sector being navigated should be maintained in the CDU until the destination ramp coordinates are loaded. The two pilots should be responsible for loading, recalling and checking the accuracy of the inserted waypoints: one loading and the other recalling and checking them independently. Where remote loading of the units is possible, this permits one pilot to cross-check additionally that the data inserted by the other is accurate. In neither case should this process be permitted to engage the attention of both pilots simultaneously during the flight.

An alternative and acceptable procedure is for the two pilots silently and independently to load their own initial waypoints and then cross-check them. The pilot responsible for carrying out the verification should work from the CDU display to the master document rather than in the opposite direction. This may lessen the risk of "seeing what you expect to see" rather than what is actually displayed.

After the initial waypoints have been loaded, the initial track and AUTO track change should be selected.

Flight Plan Check

The purpose of this check is to ensure complete compatibility between the master document and the programming of the self-contained navigation systems.

1. DIS/TIME should be selected to check that the correct distance from the ramp position to the first waypoint is indicated. An appropriate allowance may have to be considered at this point since the great circle distance shown on the CDUs may be less than the flight plan, as a consequence of the additional mileage involved in ATC SIDs. However, if there is significant disagreement, POS and waypoint coordinates should be rechecked.

2. Select track change 1-2 and check the accuracy of the indicated distance against that listed in the master document.

3. Select DSRTK and check that the desired track indicated on the CDU is as listed in the master document. This track check will reveal any errors made in the latitude or longitude designators (e.g., north/south or east/west) of the aircraft's ramp position.

4. Similar checks should be carried out for subsequent pairs of waypoints and any discrepancies between the master document and the CDU indications checked for possible waypoint insertion errors. These checks can be coordinated between the two pilots checking against the information in the master document.

5. When each leg of the flight has been checked in this manner it should be annotated on the master document by means of a suitable symbology as previously suggested.

The above are examples, largely from the MNSPA OPS manual, of procedures designed to detect the errors often caused by "finger trouble," equipment operation, and data insertion errors caused by crewmembers or dispatchers. The reader will find many other in-flight procedures necessary for the detection of errors or omissions in the procedures section of Chapter 8 (on Pages 165 – 167).

Guarding Against Complacency—A Caution

Especially since 1977 when the MNPS rules were introduced, careful monitoring procedures have enabled the NAT Provider States to obtain a good indication, both of the frequency with which navigation errors occur, and their causes. Their frequency is low, and only one aircraft in many thousands is found to have a serious navigation error. Navigation systems are now so reliable that a typical crewmember could theoretically spend his complete career flying across the Atlantic without ever being more than 5 miles from cleared track. Not surprisingly, this may eventually lead, in some cases, to overconfidence.

Rare Causes of Errors

To begin with and to illustrate the surprising nature of things which can go wrong, here are examples of some extremely rare faults which have occurred:

- The lat./lon. coordinates displayed near the gate position at one international airport were wrong. (The crew used a source for lat./lon. information that was not a valid prime information source.)

- Because of a defective chip in one of the INS systems on an aircraft, although the correct forward latitude was inserted by the crew (51°), it subsequently "jumped" by 1° to 52°.

- The aircraft was equipped with an advanced system with all the coordinates of the waypoints of the intended route already on tape. The crew assumed that these coordinates were correct—but one was not.

- When crossing 40°W westbound, the Captain asked what coordinates he should insert for the 50°W waypoint and was told "48 50." He wrongly assumed this to mean 48°50'N at 50°00'W, and as a result deviated 50° from track.

- The flight crew had available to them the correct coordinates for their cleared track, but unfortunately the data which they inserted into the navigation computer was from the company flight plan, in which an error had been made.

More Common Causes of Errors

In the study by NAT provider states, the most common causes of gross errors, in approximate order of frequency, have been as follows:

- A mistake of 1° of latitude has been made in inserting a forward waypoint. There seems to be a greater tendency for this error to be made when a track, after locating through the same latitude at several waypoints (e.g., 57°N 50°W, 57°N 40°W, 57°N 30°W) changes by 1° (e.g., 56°N 20°W). Other circumstances which can lead to this mistake being made include getting a re-clearance in flight.

- The crew have been recleared by ATC or have asked for and obtained a re-clearance, but they have forgotten to reprogram the INS or ONS.

- The autopilot has been inadvertently left in the heading or de-coupled position after avoiding clouds, or left in the VOR position after leaving the last domestic airspace VOR. In some cases, the mistake has arisen during distraction caused by SELCAL or by some flight deck warning indication.

- An error has arisen in the ATC loop so that the controller and the crew have had different understandings of the clearance. In some cases, the pilot has heard not what was said but what was expected to be said.

Hints to Help Avoid Complacency

- Never relax or be casual with the cross-check procedure. This is especially important toward the end of a long night-flight.

- Avoid casual clearance procedures. A number of gross errors have been the result of a misunderstanding between pilot and controller as to the cleared route. Adhere strictly to proper phraseology and do not be tempted to clip or abbreviate details of waypoint coordinates.

- Make an independent check on the gate position. Do not assume that the gate coordinates are correct without cross-checking with another authoritative source. Normally, coordinates are given to the nearest tenth of a minute, so make sure that the display is not reading to the nearest hundredth or in minutes and seconds. If you are near the prime meridian, remember the increased risk of confusing east and west longitude coordinates.

- Before entering oceanic airspace, make a careful check of INS or ONS position when at or near the last radio facility or ground reference check (**accuracy check**).

- Do not assume that the aircraft is at a waypoint merely because the alert annunciator indicates. Cross-check by reading present position.

- Flight deck drills. There are some tasks on the flight deck which can safely be delegated to one member of the crew, but navigation using automated systems is emphatically not one of them, and the captain should participate in all navigation cross-check procedures.

- Waypoint loading. Before departure, make a check that the following agree: computer flight plan, ICAO flight plan, track plotted on chart (from flight plan); and that the plotted track agrees with the appropriate track message. In flight, involve two different sources in the cross-checking. Do not be so hurried in loading waypoints that mistakes become likely, and always check waypoints against the current ATC clearance.

- Use a flight progress chart on the flight deck. It has been found that making periodic plots of position on a suitable chart, and comparing with current cleared track, greatly helps to pick up errors before getting too far from track.

- Make use of basic DR Navigation as a back-up. Outside of Polar Regions, provided that the magnetic course (track) is available on the flight log, a check against the magnetic heading being flown, plus or minus drift, is likely to indicate any gross tracking error.

The authors wish to acknowledge that significant quantities of information from the MNSPA Operations Manual (FAA) have been used to develop this chapter. The reader is encouraged to obtain a copy of this document. Chapters 11-13 of that document contain good advice for all pilots flying anywhere regarding techniques and procedures to detect and avoid navigation errors, especially when using LRNS's.

17: Celestial Concepts

Celestial Navigation

For several hundred years, celestial navigation has been a universal aid to dead reckoning. Because it is available most of the time and in all areas of the globe, it was the only means to upgrade a DR position. Independent of ground aids, celestial navigation cannot be jammed nor does it give off any signals, so it is considered to be an **independent navigation system**.

In its simplest form, the pilot can use the sun to determine direction. If the sun's true bearing is known from a portable computer or set of tables, the aircraft can be pointed at the sun and the gyrocompass set to the sun's true bearing (if flying a true course), or set after correcting for magnetic variation (*see* the discussion in Chapter 4 dealing with the shadow pin peloris, Page 57).

Each celestial observation yields one line of position (LOP). In the daytime when the sun may be the only visible celestial body, it may become necessary to use single LOPs as course lines or speed lines. An observation taken at LAN (local apparent noon, when the sun is highest in the sky at the observer's position) yields latitude directly (an East-West LOP). Observations taken well after sunrise and well before sunset (to eliminate the error caused by observing a celestial body close to the horizon) yield LOPs that are more North-South oriented. Usually, the morning or noon LOPs are advanced using the **running fix** technique to obtain a fix. At night, when numerous bodies are visible, LOPs obtained from the observation of two or more bodies may be crossed to establish a fix.

It is impossible to state, in so many miles, the accuracy expected from a celestial fix. Celestial accuracy depends on the navigator's skill, the type and accuracy of the equipment, and the prevailing weather conditions. In most cases, however, this author's experience indicates that an accuracy of less than two miles error can be expected for any given LOP. With the ever-increasing speeds and ranges of aircraft, celestial navigation has become more demanding of the navigator's

ability. It is important that the fix be plotted and used as quickly as possible. For these reasons—the need for skill and the development of inertial and GPS systems which require less navigator skill and effort—celestial navigation has become a less popular navigation method and probably will, for air navigation accomplished by hand, become obsolete.

However, if a pilot has an understanding of the concepts involved in finding position using celestial observations, he or she will gain a better understanding of the world we fly in and air navigation in general. So the following discussion is meant to develop that understanding of the concept, rather than make the reader into a celestial navigator, although the process itself is not difficult.

The navigator does not have to be an astronomer or mathematician to establish a celestial line of position. The ability to use a sextant is a matter of practice, and specially designed celestial tables have reduced the necessary computations to simple arithmetic.

A detailed understanding of navigational astronomy is not essential to establish an accurate celestial position because many simplifications have eliminated the need for the navigator to know the relationship of the Earth to the other heavenly bodies. However, celestial work and celestial lines of position will have more meaning if the navigator understands a few basics of celestial astronomy. Celestial astronomy includes the navigational bodies in the universe and their relative motions.

Although there are an infinite number of heavenly bodies in the universe, celestial navigation utilizes only 63 of them: 57 stars, 4 planets, the moon, and the sun. Venus, Jupiter, Mars, and Saturn are the four planets that are used in navigation.

Celestial Concepts

To facilitate the use of celestial navigation, certain assumptions have been established. These assumptions enable the navigator to obtain accurate lines of position without a detailed knowledge of celestial astronomy. A working knowledge of celestial and other concepts discussed in this text will enable the pilot to understand what is seen of the celestial bodies through the cockpit window, to develop the ability to intuitively sense when one or more of the LRNS's is leading the aircraft astray, and to know how to fall back on the basic navigation skills that have served navigators so well for centuries.

Assumption/Concept #1

The initial assumption of celestial navigation is that the Earth is a perfect sphere; that is, every point on the Earth's surface is equidistant from the center forming the **terrestrial sphere**.

Assumption/Concept #2

The terrestrial sphere is assumed to be the center of the universe. All other bodies, with the exception of the moon, are considered to be at an infinite distance from the terrestrial sphere.

Assumption/Concept #3

Celestial bodies, except for our moon, are located on the inside surface of a concentric sphere (the **celestial sphere**).

Assumption/Concept #4

Because the stars, planets, and the sun are considered to be located at an infinite distance from the Earth's center, it is assumed that any point on the Earth's surface approximates the center of the universe (Figure 17-1).

In the relatively short periods of time involved with celestial positioning, it can be assumed that all bodies located on the inside surface of the celestial sphere rotate at the same rate. In actuality, over periods of months or years, the planets move among the stars at varying rates.

Assumption/Concept #5

These *celestial concepts* of the universe are similar to the theory proposed by Ptolemy in 127 A.D. That is, the Earth is the center of the universe, and all bodies rotate about the Earth from East to West.

Establishing an artificial celestial sphere with an infinite radius simplifies computations for three reasons. First, since the terrestrial and celestial spheres are geometrically similar, every point on the celestial

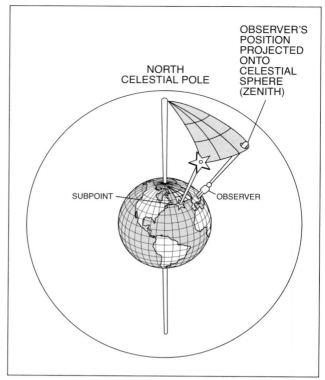

Figure 17-1. Points on a celestial sphere have the same relationship as their subpoints on Earth.

sphere has a corresponding point on the terrestrial sphere (**subpoint**), and conversely, every point on the terrestrial sphere corresponds to a point on the celestial sphere. By establishing concentric spheres, angular relationships remain constant.

Secondly, establishing an infinite radius leads to the assumption that a body's location on the celestial sphere will remain constant regardless of the observer's location. An infinite radius also means that all light rays from the celestial body arrive in parallel rays. This means that the angle will be the same whether viewed at the Earth's center, upon the surface, or at 35,000 feet in an aircraft.

Thirdly, all the relationships are valid for all bodies located on the celestial sphere. The moon, with its close proximity to the Earth, must be treated as a special case; but with certain corrections, the moon still provides an accurate LOP.

Because the celestial sphere and terrestrial sphere are concentric, every point on the terrestrial sphere has a corresponding point on the celestial sphere. Each sphere contains an equator, two poles, meridians, and parallels of latitude/declination. The relationships can be seen in Figures 17-1 and 17-2.

Assumption/Concept #6

Consistent with the celestial assumptions, neither the Earth nor the celestial meridians rotate. All celestial bodies located on the inside surface of the celestial sphere, with the exception of the moon, rotate at a constant rate of 15° per hour past the celestial meridians. The moon moves at approximately 14.5° per hour.

Two other relationships should be established. The observer on Earth has a point directly overhead on the celestial sphere called the **zenith**. A celestial body has a corresponding point on the terrestrial sphere directly below it which is referred to as the **subpoint** or geographic position. At the subpoint, the light rays from the body are perpendicular to the Earth's surface, and the body is located directly overhead.

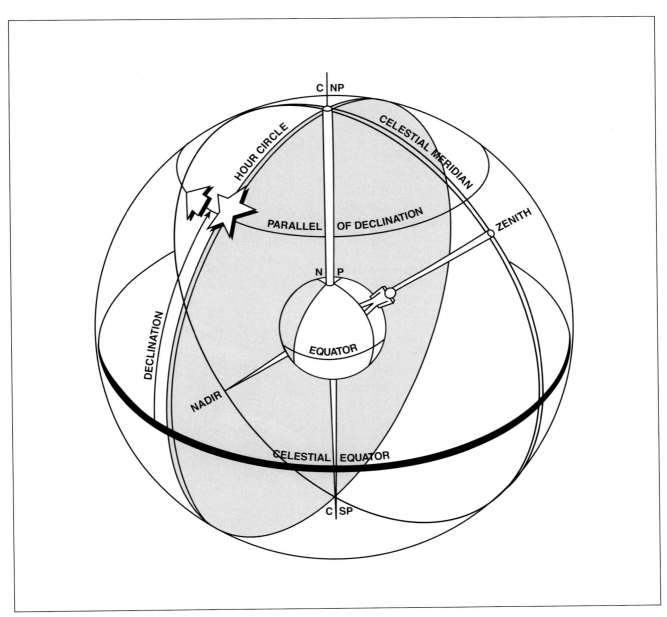

Figure 17-2. Elements of the celestial sphere

Motions of Celestial Bodies

All of the bodies in the universe have two types of motion: absolute and apparent. **Absolute motion** is measured relative to a fixed point. Because all bodies in the universe are in motion, it has been impossible to establish a definable point from which to reference absolute motion. **Apparent motion** is of more concern to the navigator. This is the motion of one celestial body as perceived by an observer on another body, which is also in motion. Since all apparent motion is relative, it is essential to establish the reference point for that motion. For example, the apparent motion of Venus would be different if observed from the Earth or from the sun.

Apparent Motion

The apparent motion of the celestial bodies as observed from Earth is a result of the combination of the Earth's rotation about the polar axis and its revolution about the sun. Rotation is the spinning of the Earth upon its axis, and it has the greatest effect on the apparent motion of bodies. It causes celestial bodies to appear to rise in the east, climb to a maximum height, then set in the west. All bodies appear to move along a daily circle or diurnal circle, which is approximately parallel to the plane of the equator.

The apparent effect of rotation varies with the latitude of the observer. At the equator, the bodies appear to rise and set perpendicular to the horizon. Each body is above the horizon for approximately 12 hours each day. At the North and South Poles, a different phenomenon occurs. The same group of stars is continually above the horizon; they neither rise nor set but move on a plane parallel to the equator. This characteristic explains the periods of extended daylight, twilight, and darkness at higher latitudes. Observers on the remainder of the Earth see a combination of these two extremes; that is, some bodies will rise and set, while others will continually remain above the horizon.

The greater the northerly **declination** (celestial latitude) of a body, the higher it appears in the heavens to an observer at the North Pole. **Polaris** has a declination of almost 90° and, therefore, will appear overhead at the north pole. Any body with a southern declination is not visible from the North Pole.

A **circumpolar** body appears to revolve about the pole and never set. If the angular distance of the body from the elevated pole (90° minus the body's declination) is less than the observer's latitude, the body is circumpolar. For example, the declination of Dubhe is 62° North. Therefore, it is located at an angle of 90° minus 62° from the North Pole or 28°. So, an observer located above 28° North will view Dubhe as circumpolar. Although Figure 17-3 uses the North Pole, the same characteristics can be observed from the South Pole.

If it were possible to stop the rotation of the Earth, the effect of the **Earth's revolution** on the apparent motion of celestial bodies would be more noticeable. The sun would appear to make one complete circle around the Earth each year. It would cover a 360° full circle in 365+ days, or move eastward at slightly less than 1° per day. The stars move at the same rate. This accounts for why different constellations are visible at different times of the year. Each evening the same star appears to set four minutes earlier.

After half a year, when the Earth has reached the opposite extreme of its orbit, its dark side is turned in the opposite direction in space and is facing a new field of stars. Hence, an observer at the equator will see an entirely different sky at midnight in June than the one which appeared at midnight in December. In fact, the stars seen at midnight in June are those which were above the horizon at midday in December, but were not visible because of the sun.

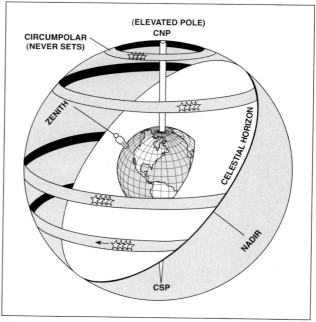

Figure 17-3. Some celestial bodies are circumpolar

Seasons

The annual variation of the sun's declination and the consequent change of the seasons are caused by the revolution of the Earth (Figure 17-4 on next page). If the **equinoctial** (celestial equator) coincided with the **ecliptic** (sun's apparent path on the celestial sphere), the sun would always be overhead at the equator, and its declination would always be zero, causing a perpetual **equinox**.

However, the Earth's axis is inclined to the plane of the Earth's orbit at an angle of about $66\frac{1}{2}°$; and the plane of the equator is inclined to it at an angle of about $23\frac{1}{2}°$. Throughout the year, the axis points in the same direction. That is, the axis of the Earth in one part of the orbit is essentially parallel to the axis of the Earth in any other part of the orbit (Figure 17-5 on Page 309). Thus, **equinox** occurs only twice a year, when the sun's subpoint crosses the equator.

In June, the north pole is inclined toward the sun and the south pole away from the sun, so that the sun is at a maximum distance from the plane of the equator. About June 21st – 23rd, at the **solstice**, the sun has its greatest northern declination. At this time in the northern hemisphere (**summer solstice**), the days are longest of any time during the year, and the nights are shortest, while in the southern hemisphere, the nights are longest and the days shortest. This is the beginning of summer for the northern hemisphere and of winter for the southern hemisphere. A half year later, the axis is still pointing in the same direction in space; but since the Earth is at the opposite extremity of its orbit and hence on the opposite side of the sun, the north pole is inclined away from the sun while the south pole is toward it. At the winter solstice, about December 21st – 23rd, the sun has its greatest southern declination. At that time in the northern hemisphere, days are shortest and nights longest, and winter is beginning to set in.

Halfway between the two solstices, the axis of the Earth is inclined neither toward nor away from the sun, and the sun is on the plane of the equators (celestial and terrestrial), causing **equinox** and defining **the first point of Aries** (*see* below, Page 310).

Celestial Coordinates

Celestial bodies and the observer's zenith may be positioned on the celestial sphere using a coordinate system similar to that of the Earth. Lines of latitude on Earth are projected onto the celestial sphere as parallels of **declination**. Lines of longitude establish the celestial meridians. A line extended from the observer's zenith, through the center of the Earth, will intersect the celestial sphere at the observer's **nadir**.

Celestial meridians are divided into two parts; the upper and the lower branch. The upper branch is the half of the celestial meridian divided at the poles containing the observer's zenith. The lower branch is the part remaining and contains the nadir. As a whole, the observer's celestial meridian is a great circle containing the zenith, the nadir, and the celestial poles (Figure 17-2 on Page 305).

A second great circle on the celestial sphere is the **hour circle**. An hour circle is a great circle containing the celestial body of interest and the celestial poles.

Unlike celestial meridians which remain stationary, hour circles (except for the moon) rotate at a standard rate of 15° per hour. Hour circles also contain upper and lower branches. The upper branch contains the body and is the half divided at the poles. The remaining half is the lower branch (Figure 17-2).

The location of any body on the celestial sphere can be described relative to the celestial equator and the Greenwich celestial meridian using declination and **Greenwich Hour Angle** (GHA).

Declination: The declination of a celestial body is the angular distance the body is north or south of the celestial equator measured along the hour circle. It ranges from 0 – 90° and corresponds to latitude.

Greenwich Hour Angle: The angular distance measured westward from the Greenwich celestial meridian to the upper branch of the hour circle. It has a range of 0 – 360°.

The Air Almanac lists the Greenwich Hour Angle and the declination of the sun, moon, four planets, and Aries. The latitude of the body's subpoint is derived from the declination. Longitude is derived from the GHA. Although GHA correlates to longitude, it is not exact. GHA is always measured westward from Greenwich celestial meridian, and longitude is measured in the shortest direction from the Greenwich meridian to the observer's meridian.

Continued on Page 310

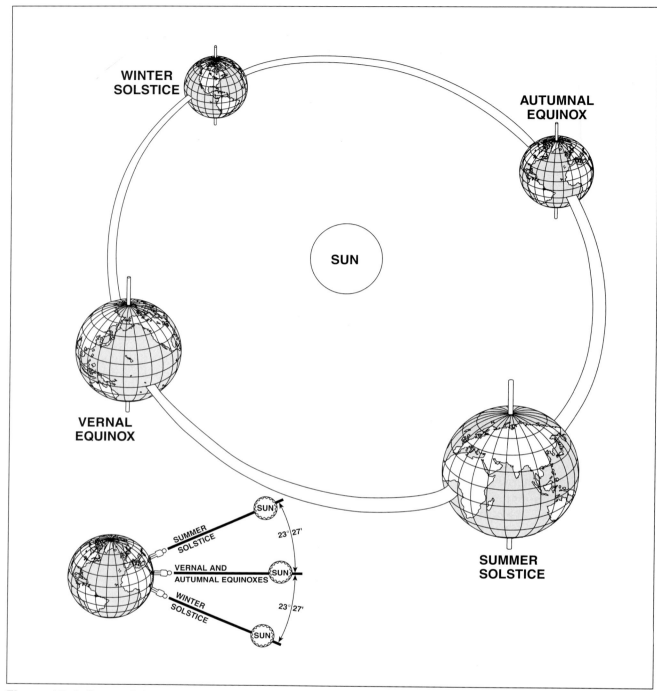

Figure 17-4. Seasonal changes of the earth's position

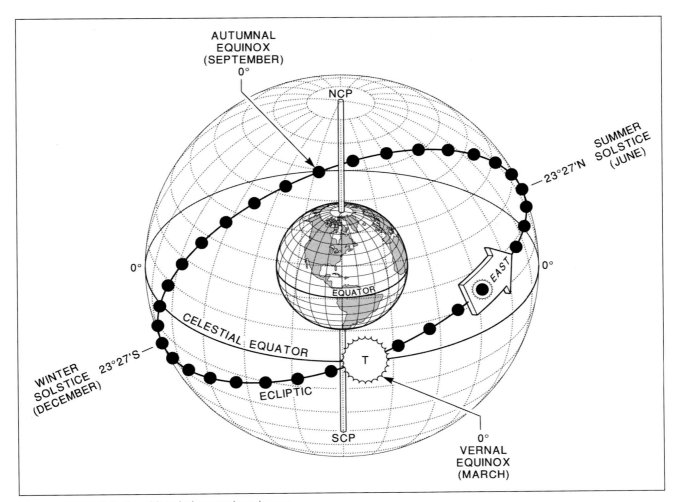

Figure 17-5. Ecliptic with solstices and equinoxes

The following are examples of converting the celestial coordinates of a body to the corresponding terrestrial coordinates of its subpoint. If the GHA is less than 180°, then the subpoint is in the western hemisphere and GHA = longitude. When the GHA is greater than 180°, the subpoint of the body is located in the eastern hemisphere and longitude = 360 – GHA. Again, declination and latitude equate (Figure 17-6).

Examples:

GHA = 135° – 00' ....Subpoint location: 135° – 00'W

Dec = S13° – 15' ....13° – 15'S

GHA = 290° – 00' ....Subpoint location: 70° – 00'E

Dec = N 110 – 32' ....11° – 32'N

In addition to Greenwich Hour Angle (Figure 17-7), there are two special hour angles used in celestial navigation. The first is **Local Hour Angle** (LHA). LHA is the angular displacement measured from the *observer's* celestial meridian clockwise to the hour circle of the body. LHA is computed by applying the local longitude to the GHA of the body (Figure 17-8). In the western hemisphere, LHA = GHA – W longitude, and in the eastern hemisphere, LHA = GHA + E longitude (Figure 17-9). When the LHA = 0, it means that the hour circle of the body is co-located with the upper branch of the celestial meridian of the observer, and the body is **in transit** (passing overhead, or, to the observer, the body has its highest altitude in the sky). An LHA = 180 puts the hour circle coincident with the lower branch of the celestial meridian of the observer.

The second special hour angle is the **sidereal hour angle** (SHA). SHA is used in conjunction with the first point of Aries. The **first point of Aries**, more commonly referred to as **Aries**, occurs on the celestial sphere where the sun's ecliptic crosses the celestial equator from South to North (Figure 17-5). Though not absolutely stationary relative to the stars, the first point of Aries changes so slowly that it may be thought of as a fixed point on the celestial equator for a period as

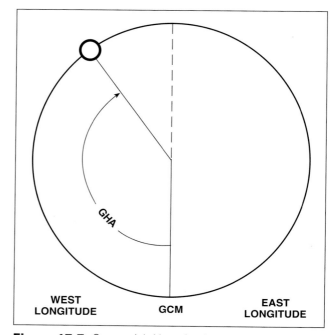

Figure 17-7. Greenwich Hour Angle

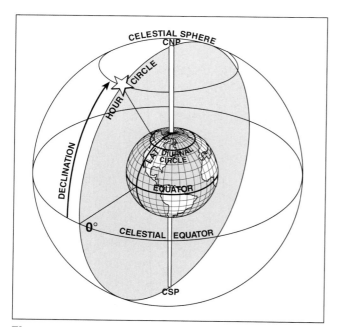

Figure 17-6. Declination of a body corresponds to a parallel of latitude.

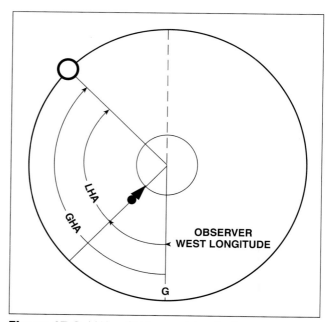

Figure 17-8. LHA = GHA – west longitude

long as one year. The SHA is the angular measurement from the hour circle of Aries to the hour circle of the star in question (Figure 17-10). Since both Aries and the stars are located on the celestial sphere, they move at the same rate and the SHA remains a constant figure for that year. The SHA and declination of any navigational star are listed in the Air Almanac.

The Celestial LOP

All of the celestial concepts and assumptions explained so far were done to help clarify the derivation of the celestial LOP. In a simplified explanation, the celestial LOP is a circle plotted with the center at the body's subpoint and having a radius equal to the distance from the observer to the subpoint. To accurately compute this distance and the direction to the subpoint of the body, the navigator must initially position the subpoint of the body, then measure the angular displacement of the body above the horizon. GHA and declination are used to position the body's subpoint, and the sextant is used to measure the angular displacement above the horizon. This is a quick explanation of the concepts involved in obtaining a celestial LOP.

After the celestial body and the observer's zenith are positioned on the celestial sphere, a sextant is used to measure the angle from the observer's horizon to the celestial body. The angular displacement as viewed through a sextant is the height observed, or H_O. H_O is measured along the vertical circle above the horizon.

The vertical circle is a great circle containing the observer's zenith, nadir, and celestial body, and its center is the center of the Earth. The altitude of a body is the same whether it is measured at the surface of the Earth from the visible horizon, or at the center of the Earth from the celestial horizon, or at the altitude of a high-flying aircraft from the artificial horizon; this is because the distance from observer to celestial body is considered to be infinite. The radius of the Earth is a very small distance compared to the distance to any of the stars. Thus, the error due to not measuring the H_O from the center of the Earth is very small (in the order of 0.15 NM for sun observations and far less for the stars).

The horizon most used by the air navigator is the bubble or artificial horizon. In the **bubble sextant** as in a carpenter's level, a bubble indicates the apparent vertical and horizontal. By means of the bubble, the navigator can level the sextant and establish a reference plane parallel to the plane of the celestial horizon. This plane is an artificial but very accurate horizon.

Observed Altitude

There is a definite relationship between the H_O of a body and the distance of the observer from the subpoint. When the body is directly overhead, the H_O is 90°, and the subpoint and the observer's position are co-located. When the H_O is 0°, the body is on the horizon, and the subpoint is 90° (5,400 NM) from the observer's position.

Figure 17-9. LHA = GHA + east longitude

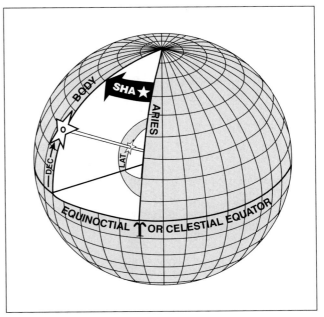

Figure 17-10. Sidereal Hour Angle

If the H_O is an angle between 0° and 90°, a circle of equal altitude forms a line of position on the surface of the Earth, on which the observer's position must be. All points on the circle of equal altitude are equidistant from the body's subpoint. The distance from the circle of equal altitude to the subpoint is called the **zenith distance**.

Basically, the angular zenith distance is equal to 90° minus the H_O, and is referred to as the **co-altitude**. The degrees are then converted to nautical miles by multiplying the number of degrees by 60 and adding in the odd minutes of arc.

Example:

$H_O = 37° 26'$

therefore,

Co-altitude = 90 – 37° 26' = 52° 34'

Zenith Distance = (52 × 60) + 34 = 3,154 NM

Zenith distance is the radius of the circle which becomes the celestial LOP. This circle is called the circle of equal altitude (Figure 17-11), as anyone located on it anywhere and viewing the celestial body at a common time will measure an identical H_O. This procedure determines the distance from the observer to the subpoint. The next consideration must be the direction from the observer to the body's subpoint.

True Azimuth

In celestial navigation, the direction of a body from an observer is called true azimuth (Zn). The true azimuth of a celestial body corresponds exactly to the true bearing of the subpoint from the observer. The **true azimuth** of a celestial body is the angle measured at the observer's position from true north clockwise through 360° to the great circle arc joining the observer's position with subpoint, as illustrated in Figure 17-12.

If the true azimuth of a body could be measured when its altitude is observed, a fix could be established. Unfortunately, however, there is no instrument in the aircraft which will measure true azimuth to the required accuracy. If a body is observed at an H_O of 40° and the Zn is measured incorrectly by 1°, the fix will be in error about 50 NM! With the instruments now in use, an accurate fix cannot be established by measuring the altitude and azimuth of a single body, except in the case of a very high body (85° – 90°), which decreases the error by decreasing the distance from observer to subpoint.

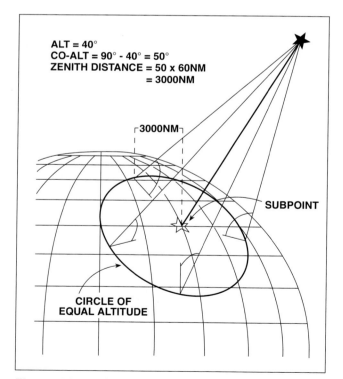

Figure 17-11. Construction of a circle of equal altitude

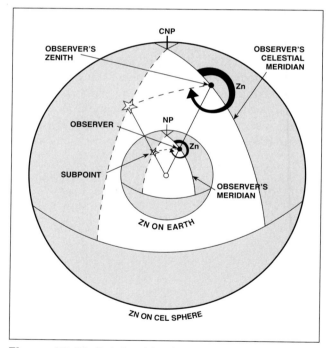

Figure 17-12. Relationship of Zn to an observer

The Celestial Fix

Since a fix cannot normally be obtained from a single body, LOPs from two or more bodies must be crossed. The fix position is the intersection of the LOPs. A celestial LOP is a circle; however, as shown in Figure 17-13, when two celestial LOPs are plotted, they intersect at two points, only one of which can be the observer's position. In practice, these two intersections usually are so far apart that dead reckoning removes all doubt as to which is the correct position.

Duration of Daylight

There are many times in a pilot's career when available light is a matter of concern. The time of sunset and sunrise determine whether flight time is logged as day or night. Adequate light to see for landing on unlighted fields or finding visual reference points extends beyond sunset and occurs before sunrise. A better knowledge of the terms should be useful.

Sunrise and **sunset** occur at the times when the upper limb (upper edge) of the sun is on the visible horizon. The time of these occurrences depends on the declination of the sun, and the latitude of the observer.

Unless the observer is located on a **standard meridian** (the Greenwich meridian and every meridian divisible by 15, such as 15°, 75°, 135°, etc.) tabulated sunrise/sunset values must also be corrected for longitude.

Since the sun appears to move 15° per hour or 4 minutes per degree, if it is overhead the Greenwich meridian at 12:04 p.m. (Greenwich time) on a given day, it will be overhead the 15°W meridian at 13:04 Greenwich time or 12:04 local time. An observer standing on the 90°W standard meridian would expect the sun to be overhead at 12:04 p.m. local time or 18:04 GMT. An observer standing on the airport at Omaha (longitude 95° 53.61W, which is 5° 53.6' west of the 90°W standard meridian) should expect **local apparent noon**—the sun's passage overhead (or, more correctly, when the sun's subpoint passes the same longitude)—to occur 5.8933° x 4 minutes/degree, or 23.57 minutes later, at 18:27:34. Since everyone rotates at the same rate on the Earth, sunrise, sunset, and twilight times are found the same way.

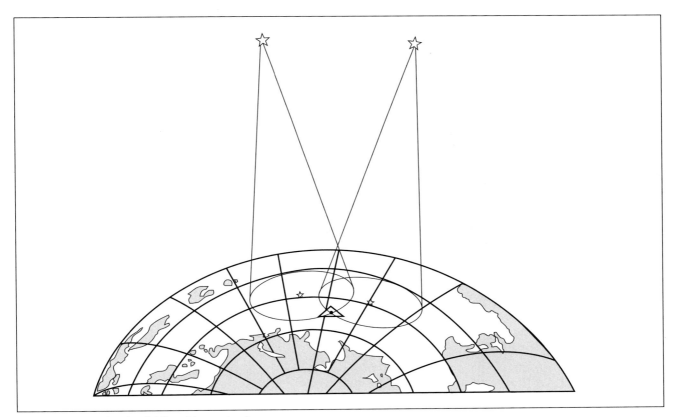

Figure 17-13. A celestial fix with two bodies

Twilight is the period of increasing darkness following sunset and decreasing darkness preceding sunrise that is useful to pilots who are using pilotage to find their way or landing on unlighted runways or waterways. The amount of available light during twilight varies with cloud cover (diminishes), ceiling (low ceiling diminishes) and ground cover (snow increases, dark colored ground diminishes).

The fact that there is any light at all while the sun is below the visible horizon is due to the presence in the atmosphere of dust, pollutant, and water particles. If these were not present, complete darkness would occur the moment the upper limb of the sun disappeared below the western horizon. Daylight would come with equal suddenness as the sun appeared on the eastern horizon. The presence of particulates in the atmosphere, often at very high altitudes, causes light from the sun to be scattered by refraction and reflection, and thus directed to the surface of the Earth when the sun is not directly shining on the surface. The brilliant colors in a sunset or sunrise are caused by selective absorption of certain light frequencies by the airborne particulates. Red and yellow are absorbed the least, hence their predominance in the twilight sky.

Various twilight values are defined based on ways the observer can evaluate the amount of light remaining. At about sunset, or sometimes shortly before, the brighter planets become visible. When the sun reaches a negative altitude of about $3°$, the brightest stars begin to appear. When the center of the sun is $6°$ below the celestial horizon, at the end of evening **civil twilight**, second-magnitude stars have appeared and useful light for pilots to see specific objects well enough to determine texture is gone. This is about the middle of that short period used by marine navigators to make sextant observations (when both celestial bodies and the ocean horizon are clearly visible).

When the center of the sun reaches $12°$ below the celestial horizon (the end of **nautical twilight**), the sky gives so little light, one gets the sense that darkness has really set in. When the center of the sun is $18°$ below the celestial horizon, light scattered from the highest levels of the atmosphere is negligible and complete darkness occurs. This is the end of **astronomical twilight**. Comparable periods of reduced illumination occur before sunrise.

The *Nautical Almanac* gives times of beginning and end of the various twilights (Figure 17-14). The *Air Almanac* gives the duration of civil twilight since it is of most use to pilots. Other tables of the rising and setting of the bodies are available. Using this data, the pilot must be alert to correct for differences in longitude and should choose locations of latitude comparable to the pilot's point of interest. Modern hand-held computers and some navigation systems will provide sunrise/sunset data for any selected location, freeing the pilot from the tasks of conversion from tables (*see* Figure 17-16).

If the time of sunrise or sunset is known, pilots can estimate the time of civil twilight without an almanac by using the table in Figure 17-15, which was derived from the June and December 21st pages of the almanac. As one can see, a value of thirty minutes for the period from sunset or sunrise to civil twilight provides an approximation but the relationship is really latitude dependent. Twilight lasts much longer near the poles than near the equator.

Altitude Effect

Perhaps the reader has noticed while flying at altitude that the sun may be visible while the ground beneath the aircraft is in shadow or even dark, so it is apparent that the observer's altitude above the ground delays the time of sunset and hurries the time of sunrise for the observer in the aircraft. Also, the duration of twilight rapidly diminishes as the height of the observer above the surface of the Earth increases. Calculating the times of sunset, sunrise and civil twilight at altitude is a somewhat complex task but can be done with the aid of the *Air Almanac*, explanation section, Item 14—*Corrections for height of observer*. Knowing the difference in time is of little practical value to the modern airman except perhaps in situations where seeing the sun helps the pilot navigate (determining the sun's true direction, etc.).

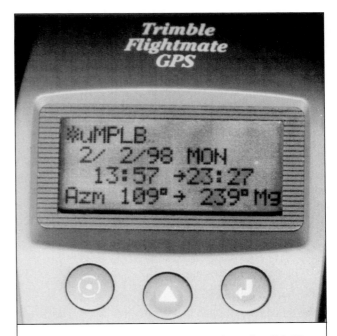

Lat.	Sunset	Twilight Civil	Twilight Nautical	Lat.	Twilight Civil	Twilight Nautical	Sunrise
°	h m	h m	h m	°	h m	h m	h m
N 72	■	13 03	15 33	N 72	08 27	10 57	■
N 70	■	14 05	15 53	N 70	08 07	09 55	■
68	■	14 40	16 09	68	07 51	09 20	■
66	13 25	15 05	16 22	66	07 38	08 55	10 36
64	14 07	15 25	16 33	64	07 27	08 35	09 53
62	14 35	15 41	16 43	62	07 17	08 19	09 25
60	14 57	15 55	16 51	60	07 09	08 06	09 04
N 58	15 14	16 06	16 59	N 58	07 01	07 54	08 46
56	15 29	16 16	17 06	56	06 55	07 44	08 31
54	15 42	16 26	17 12	54	06 49	07 35	08 19
52	15 53	16 34	17 17	52	06 43	07 27	08 08
50	16 03	16 41	17 23	50	06 38	07 19	07 58
45	16 23	16 57	17 34	45	06 26	07 03	07 37
N 40	16 40	17 11	17 45	N 40	06 15	06 50	07 20
35	16 54	17 23	17 54	35	06 06	06 38	07 06
30	17 07	17 33	18 03	30	05 57	06 27	06 54
20	17 28	17 52	18 19	20	05 41	06 08	06 32
N 10	17 46	18 09	18 36	N 10	05 25	05 51	06 14
0	18 04	18 26	18 53	0	05 08	05 34	05 56
S 10	18 21	18 45	19 12	S 10	04 49	05 16	05 39
20	18 40	19 05	19 34	20	04 26	04 55	05 20
30	19 02	19 30	20 03	30	03 57	04 30	04 58
35	19 15	19 45	20 22	35	03 38	04 15	04 45
40	19 30	20 03	20 45	40	03 15	03 57	04 30
45	19 48	20 26	21 16	45	02 44	03 34	04 12
S 50	20 11	20 56	22 01	S 50	01 59	03 04	03 49
52	20 22	21 11	22 29	52	01 31	02 49	03 38
54	20 34	21 29	23 15	54	00 44	02 31	03 26
56	20 48	21 51	///	56	///	02 09	03 12
58	21 05	22 21	///	58	///	01 39	02 55
S 60	21 26	23 11	///	S 60	///	00 49	02 34

Almanac values of sunrise, sunset, and twilights for Christmas day. Values are local time and must be adjusted for longitude for observers not on their standard meridian. The open box signifies that the sun is circumpolar (does not set), the dark box indicates that the sun does not rise, and the hash marks indicate that twilight lasts all night.

Figure 17-14. Almanac excerpt

Periods of morning and evening civil twilight for two dates (hr:min)

Latitude, Degrees	June 21 Period of Civil Twilight	December 21 Period of Civil Twilight
60	1:47	:58
50	:45	:38
40	:33	:31
30	:28	:26
20	:25	:24
10	:23	:23
0	:22	:23

Figure 17-15

This GPS receiver shows the time of sunrise (13:57 UTC) and sunset (23:27 UTC) on February 2nd, 1998, for user waypoint (u) Maple Bay (MPLB) near 50° north. Also shown is the sun's magnetic bearing at sunrise (109°) and sunset (239°). The sun's true or magnetic bearing at any time of any day, anywhere on Earth can also be shown (*see* Figure 4-14).

Figure 17-16. The Trimble Flightmate

Study Questions

1. Using Figure 17-14, find the time of sunset and sunrise on Christmas Day for:

   a. Your location. Compare it to a local source (newspaper, FSS, etc.) Quote the source.

   b. Salt Lake City airport

   c. Mexico City

   d. Churchill, Manitoba

   e. Pt. Barrow, AK

2. Also using Figure 17-14 and 17-15, find the times of civil twilight at Tufluk Lake airstrip (48° 45'N, 102° 30'W), to plan your time of departure and arrival. (You will need to interpolate for both latitude and longitude.) Give the answer in one of the local times and in Zulu time.

3. Celestial body Z has a GHA of 320°, declination of 0°. An observer is located at 47°N 97°W.

   a. Where is Z's subpoint at 00Z?

   b. When is Z (north of/south of/overhead) the observer?

   c. Approximately when will Z rise for the observer?

   d. What are the range of latitudes within which Z will be circumpolar for an observer?

   e. About where is Z's subpoint upon rising (see c.)?

   f. What time will Z be highest in the sky as viewed by an observer at Greenwich, England?

18: **The Future of Air Navigation**

FANS

In 1983, ICAO established the Special Committee on **Future Air Navigation Systems** (FANS). The FANS Committee's task was to develop the concept for the future Communications, Navigation and Surveillance/Air Traffic Management (CNS/ATM) system to take civil aviation into the twenty-first century. CNS/ATM was to provide for future growth in air transportation and eliminate the existing constraints. The Committee finalized its task in 1986 and recommended a concept based on satellites, data communications and automation, initially to augment and gradually replace existing systems. Before proceeding to the explanation of FANS, review the list of terms in Figure 18-1 (on the next page), as many of them are quite new to aviation and will likely constitute some of the future vernacular.

The Present Air Navigation System

ICAO (International Civil Aviation Organization) is the agency responsible for the safe and orderly growth of international civil aviation (including the CNS/ATM system) through establishing global standards for aircraft and ground systems. This organization (which was described in Chapter 1) is a specialized agency of the United Nations comprising the majority of countries that operate international civil aviation as signatories (Contracting States) to the Chicago Convention on International Civil Aviation.

International air traffic is channeled along specified air routes, and each air route is part of a network of air routes within a Flight Information Region (FIR). Today's Air Navigation System (ANS), through ICAO and its Contracting States, provides Air Traffic Service (ATS) within FIRs covering virtually all airspace in the world. The current airspace is divided into more than 200 FIRs of varying sizes.

Communications

Voice is the only method of air – ground communication used between the pilot and air traffic controller. Use of Very High Frequency (VHF) transceivers provides direct radio contact within the line-of-sight coverage between pilot and ATC. For communication over areas exceeding the range of VHF, High Frequency (HF) radios are used; however, HF voice communications require the assistance of a radio operator on the ground. On the ground, adjacent ATS units are linked by leased telephone lines providing direct-speech links between controllers. ATS units, other aeronautical authorities and some airlines are linked through the Aeronautical Fixed Telecommunication Network (AFTN), which provides character oriented and in some instances data communications in the form of aeronautical message switching.

Navigation

A good proportion of enroute navigation over land areas is provided by Non-Directional Beacons (NDB), with existing route structures covered by VHF Omni-directional Radio Range (VOR) and Distance Measuring Equipment (DME). These are not available world-wide because of geographic or economic constraints in many cases. Long-range navigation is provided by LORAN C, GPS or self-contained navigation systems such as Inertial Navigation Systems (INS).

Surveillance

The applied ATS procedures in a specific airspace are highly dependent on the available surveillance technique. Generally, primary and secondary radar coverage is provided in continental and coastal areas, and procedural voice reporting is used in oceanic and remote areas.

AAC .... Aeronautical Administrative
             Communications
ACARS .... Aircraft Communications Addressing &
             Reporting System
ACAS .... Airborne Collision Avoidance System
ACU .... Aerodrome Control Unit
ADF .... Automatic Direction-Finding Equipment
ADNS .... ARINC Data Network Service
ADS .... Automatic Dependent Surveillance
ADSP .... Automatic Dependent Surveillance Panel
AFS .... Aeronautical Fixed Service
AFTN .... Aeronautical Fixed Telecommunication
             Network
AL .... Alerting Service
AMCP .... Aeronautical Mobile Communications
             Panel
AMSS .... Aeronautical Mobile Satellite Service
ANC .... Air Navigation Commission
ANC .... Air Navigation Conference
ANP .... Air Navigation Plan
ANS .... Air Navigation System
AOC .... Aeronautical Operational Control
APC .... Aeronautical Passenger Communications
AR .... Arrival Route
ARINC .... Aeronautical Radio Inc.
ARTCC .... Air Route Traffic Control Centers
ASM .... Air Space Management
ATC .... Air Traffic Control
ATFM .... Air Traffic Flow Management
ATIS .... Automatic Terminal Information Service
ATM .... Air Traffic Management
ATN .... Aeronautical Telecommunication Network
ATNP .... Aeronautical Telecommunication
             Network Panel
ATS .... Air Traffic Service
AWOP .... All Weather Operations Panel
C/A .... Course Access
CAA .... Civil Aviation Administration
CBA .... Cost Benefit Analysis
CIDIN .... Common ICAO Data Interchange Network
CMA .... Central Monitoring Agency
CMU .... Communication Management Unit
CNS............. Communications, Navigation,
             and Surveillance
DC .... Departure Clearance
DGNSS .... Differential Global Navigation
             Satellite System
DME .... Distance Measuring Equipment
ETA .... Estimated Time of Arrival
FANS .... Future Air Navigation System
FDPS.......... Flight Data Processing System
FIR .... Flight Information Region
FIS .... Flight Information Service
FMS............ Frequency Management System
FMU .... Flow Management Unit
GES............ Ground Earth Station

GIC .... GNSS Integrity Channel
GLONASS ... Russian Federation Global Navigation
             Orbiting Satellite System
GNSS .... Global Navigation Satellite System
GNSSP........ Global Navigation Satellite System Panel
GPS .... Global Positioning System
HF .... High Frequency
IACSP .... International Aeronautical Communications
             Service Providers
IATA .... International Air Transport Association
ICAO .... International Civil Aviation Organization
ID .... Instrument Departure
ILS .... Instrument Landing System
IMA .... Integrated Modular Avionics
IMC............. Instrument Meteorological Conditions
INS .... Inertial Navigation System
IRS .... Inertial Reference System
ISO .... International Standards Organization
ITU .... International Telecommunications Union
LORAN .... Long Range Air Navigation System
MASPS........ Minimum Aircraft System Performance
             Specifications
MB .... Marker Beacon
MLS .... Microwave Landing System
MNPS .... Minimum Navigation Performance
             Specifications
MTN .... Mega Transport Network
NATS .... National Air Traffic Service
NDB............ Non-Directional Beacons
OSI .... Open System Interconnection
PDN .... Public Data Networks
RA .... Resolution Advisory
RAIM .... Receiver Autonomous
             Integrity Monitoring
RGCSP .... Review of the General Concept of
             Separation Panel
RNAV .... Area Navigation
RNP............ Required Navigation Performance
SARPs........ Standards and Recommended Practices
SATCOM ..... Satellite Communications
SICASP .... SSR Improvements and Collision
             Avoidance Systems Panel
SITA .... Société Internationale de
             Télécommunications Aéronautiques
SPS .... Standard Positioning Service
SSR .... Secondary Surveillance Radar
TA .... Traffic Advisory
TDMA .... Time Division Multiple Access
TLS............. Target Level of Safety
UTC .... Universal Coordinated Time
VDL .... VHF Digital Link
VHF .... Very High Frequency
VMC .... Visual Meteorological Conditions
VNAV.......... Vertical Navigation
VOR .... VHF Omni-Directional Radio Range
WGS .... World Geodetic System

Figure 18-1. List of acronyms

Air Traffic Services (ATS)

The purpose of ATS is to enable aircraft operators to meet their planned times of departure and arrival and adhere to their preferred flight profiles with minimum constraints and without compromising safety. To provide this service, ATS relies on the availability of a CNS system and ground ATC centers responsible for controlling the traffic.

The major shortcomings of the elements of the present ANS include the following:

Communications. The main shortcoming of the existing air-ground communications system is that the exchange of information between aircraft and ATC unit is mainly limited to voice only, and therefore is not readily usable by automated systems. It also means that the speed and volume at which information can be exchanged between pilot and ATC is limited by language differences, the need for re-transmissions due to adverse propagation conditions and interference from other stations. With increased aircraft movements, voice channels are becoming overloaded, resulting in a need for additional channel assignments. This introduces many frequency changes along a route, increasing pilot and controller communication workload.

Other shortcomings are related to the physical nature of radio wave propagation. Use of VHF radio between pilot and ATC is limited to a line-of-sight coverage. This physical limitation can be partly overcome through the use of extended VHF linked through fixed communication networks; however, it increases transfer delays and could become prohibitive from a maintenance costs viewpoint, due to the remote location of the ground installation. Once outside VHF coverage, communications must be conducted on HF radio which is subject to propagation anomalies, resulting in interference from other HF stations and fading. Because of these physical constraints, specially trained air-ground operators are used as a relay point between pilot and ATC.

For the aeronautical fixed ground data communications, the AFTN in many instances provides only a low-speed teletypewriter facility operating at the equivalent of 50 baud, with some message switching centers still operating manually. This slow data-handling rate delays the exchange of aeronautical information, e.g. flight plans, which reduces the efficiency of traffic service.

The Ground Communications Networks

Notwithstanding the importance of individual airline private networks, the major ground networks within the Aeronautical Telecommunications Network (ATN) are:

AFTN. The AFTN operates mainly between the ATS providers. It provides a telecommunications service between specified fixed points. Because many AFTN messages are required to be transmitted to a number of addressees, and because of economic factors, a method whereby circuits are physically connected to each other (to give a "through route" before a message is transmitted) is not normally practicable. The AFTN is accordingly organized around a system of relay stations. Messages are transmitted forward, circuit by circuit, by successive communications centers until they reach their destination.

ADNS. The backbone of the ARINC communication services is the ARINC Data Network Service (ADNS). This packet switch network has 13 nodes located in major U.S. cities and in London. In addition, there are connections to these network nodes from terminals and processors in many other countries. The network provides a communication interface between airlines, AFTN, Air Route Traffic Control Centers (ARTCC) and weather services. ADNS is also used to transport air-ground datalink messages and Aircraft Communications Addressing and Reporting System (ACARS). The network handles over 6 million messages per day related to air transportation.

SITA Network. SITA's world-wide telecommunications network is composed of switching centers interconnected by medium-to-high speed lines, including intercontinental circuits. The consolidated transmission capacity exceeds 20 megabits per second and the switching capacity exceeds 150 million data transactions and messages daily. The Data Transport Network (DTN) is currently the backbone for data transmission. The DTN is composed of 30 Data Switching and Interface Systems, which are meshed-packet switching nodes interconnected by 150 circuits.

Navigation. Transmissions from NDBs suffer from propagation problems similar to those of HF radio, and therefore they are limited in accuracy and coverage area. While VOR and DME transmissions are static-free (compared to an NDB), because they operate on line-of-sight range, siting problems due to mountainous terrain can limit the coverage of existing route structures. Because these navigation aids are terrestrial based, air routes are designed based on the location of these navigation aids; this reduces the availability of traffic routes and produces choke points.

Surveillance. Primary and secondary radar coverage is limited to continental and coastal areas with no coverage possible over oceanic areas and severe limitations for mountainous terrain and deserts.

Air Traffic Services. With its reliance on the CNS elements for its operation, the limitations of the existing ATS systems are in direct relation to the shortcomings of the CNS elements. The technical shortcomings can be summarized as:

- Propagation limitations
- Limitations of voice communications
- A lack of global coverage

The shortcomings result in a lack of real-time information on present position and short and long intent of the aircraft on certain parts of existing air-routes, which in turn requires the use of procedural methods of ATC. The use of procedural methods of ATC do not provide the most efficient flight profiles or system capacity, as in general, flights must be planned via intermediate waypoints rather than on the most direct routes. There is also a limited opportunity to make changes to the cleared flight profiles. This means the capabilities of modern airborne systems cannot be exploited fully and the provision of air traffic services is not always efficient and cost effective.

In addition, the lack of digital air-ground data interchange systems, and a lack of common standards and harmonization between different ATC units reduces the feasibility of automating the processing of ATS information. Because of this fragmented development of ATS, air traffic management systems, if they exist, cannot provide the most efficient use of airspace, and are limited to providing procedural (non-radar/ non-automated) ATC on certain parts of existing air routes throughout the world. Early implementation of interoperable ground automated functions is essential to overcome these shortcomings. This will enable the airspace users to fly their preferred flight trajectories with increased flexibility.

These shortcomings mean that the present system is incapable of making optimum use of ATC system capacity, available airspace and aircraft capability. The introduction of FANS CNS/ATM systems will provide global digital communications and improved navigation are essential to the evolution of the current system.

The shortcomings described are reflected in present day problems, such as:

- Schedule delays due to insufficient ATC capacity to meet the traffic demand in particular during peak hours.
- Differences in operating concepts and procedures and the lack of coordination between regions and FIRs causing increased workloads for both ATC and flight crew.
- ATFM which prevents matching available capacity with demand over the entire route, causing the need for flying holding patterns in the sectors with the highest capacity constraints.
- The inflexibility of fixed route structure systems preventing the most efficient use of airspace and most economical conduct of flight operations.
- The inability to expand to meet future traffic growth, in an evolutionary fashion.
- The inability to fully exploit the capabilities of advanced airborne equipment such as flight management systems.

The increasing operating costs of the present ATS system is associated with the need to increase capacity. Without advanced automation, increases in capacity can only be achieved by decreasing the size of existing control areas and increasing the number of controllers.

Unless there are improvements to the present system, international aviation can be expected to hHperience a continuing increase in airport and airspace congestion, which will become progressively worse as air traffic increases. This could result in higher operating costs and a stifling of the market for the aviation industry.

Need for Change

Recognizing the shortcomings and present day problems caused by the existing CNS/ATM system at the end of 1983, the ICAO-established Special Committee on Future Air Navigation Systems (FANS) was assigned to study, identify, and assess new concepts and new technologies in the field of air navigation, including satellite technology, and to make recommendations for the development of air navigation for international civil aviation over a period of twenty-five years. Membership of this committee was drawn from 22 ICAO Contracting States and International Organizations together with 10 others with observer status. The committee presented to the ICAO Council and the international aviation community a consolidated proposal for a future global air navigation system. The proposal concluded that the application of satellite technology was the only solution that would enable international civil aviation to overcome the shortcomings of the present CNS system and fulfill the needs and requirements of the foreseeable future on a global basis. In arriving at this concept of FANS, the committee was guided by the objectives a new CNS system should provide for:

• Global communications, navigation, and surveillance coverage from (very) low to (very) high altitudes, also embracing remote, off-shore and oceanic areas.

• Digital data interchange between the air-ground systems to fully exploit the automated capabilities of both.

• Navigation/approach service for runways and other landing areas which need not be equipped with precision landing aids.

The FANS I Committee completed its work on phase one of FANS in May 1988 and urgently recommended that the ICAO Council establish a new committee to advise on the overall monitoring, coordination of development and transition planning, in order to ensure that implementation of the future CNS system takes place on a global basis in a cost-effective manner, and in a balanced way between air navigation systems and geographical areas.

The Future Air Navigation System

The challenge for the Future Air Navigation System (FANS) is to meet the basic objective of the future ATM: "Accommodation of the users preferred flight trajectories." This requires the introduction of automation and adequate CNS tools to provide ATS with continuous information on aircraft position and intent.

Within this future system, the traditional segregation of CNS elements will be reduced due to technical advances and economical feasibility. However, in any ANS, the basic CNS/ATM functions will always remain. Figure 18-2 depicts the FANS as it is described below.

Communications

The aeronautical communications system, in the new CNS/ATM system, will extensively use digital modulation techniques to provide a high efficiency in information flow and optimum use of automation. While the need for voice communication will remain, the introduction of data communication enables the fast exchange of information between all parties connected to a single network while minimizing radio channel congestion.

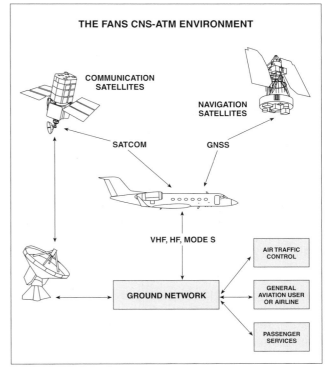

Figure 18-2. Future Air Navigation System (FANS)

The increasing use of data communications between aircraft and the various ground systems require a communication system that gives the user close control over the routing of data, and enables different computer systems to communicate with each other without need for human intervention. The system also has to support two-way pilot/controller data communications in addition to the present voice communications.

In computer data networking terminology, the infrastructure required to support the interconnection of automated systems is referred to as an **internet**. Simply stated, an internet comprises the interconnection of computers through subnetworks, using gateways or routers. This will allow the construction of a homogeneous virtual data network in an environment of administrative and technical diversity. Given the desire to interconnect an evolving and ever-widening variety of aircraft and ground-based computers, it is clear that the civil aviation community needs a global telecommunications network that will serve different user groups; i.e., Air Traffic Services (ATS), Aeronautical Operational Control (AOC), Aeronautical Administrative Communications (AAC), and Aeronautical Passenger Communications (APC). The design must provide for the incorporation of the different air – ground subnetworks and different ground – ground subnetworks, resulting in a common data transfer service.

The Air–Ground Communications Systems

The increasing interaction between the ground services and flying aircraft requires that the air-to-ground communication has sufficient capacity for the transfer of both voice and data. Following is a brief overview of the available/planned air-to-ground communication systems to be used:

Gatelink. The gatelink is a high speed, two-way data communication link between a parked aircraft and a ground-based communications system. The design is based on a data transfer of 100 megabits per second. The connection can be established either through an automatic connection using infrared beams across a free air gap, or through a manual connection using a ground connector.

HF. High Frequency radio (voice) may need to be retained initially to provide communication over the polar regions where geostationary satellites currently have no coverage. Employment of modern technology enables the unpredictable HF wave propagation to be overcome to a large extent. HF Packet Communication, highly developed and in use by amateur

radio operators to solve the problem of how to transmit error-free data for more than 20 years, is presently under development for datalink and is the subject of operational trials.

Satellite. Voice and data, using the Aeronautical Mobile Satellite Service (AMSS), will be the main new feature of future aeronautical communications systems. The use of communication satellites will provide global coverage and could support both high- and low-speed data links as well as high-quality voice links between aircraft and ground.

SSR Mode S. In addition to its use for surveillance, the Mode S option of SSR also makes available an air-ground datalink which could be used for ATS purposes in high-density airspace such as the U.S. and Europe. This system is further described in connection with "Surveillance" near the end of this chapter.

VHF. Very High Frequency radio (voice) will remain in use in many continental and terminal areas. However, increasing use will be made of VHF digital datalinks with data eventually being used more than voice.

Navigation

Notwithstanding the good performance of the present navigation systems, the ideal would be a single navigation system providing adequate navigation for all phases of flight under all meteorological conditions all over the world for all airspace users. This system still has to be invented; however, the new Global Navigation Satellite System (GNSS) applied within the RNAV/RNP (Area Navigation/Required Navigation Performance) concept is approaching this ideal. It provides the aircraft with the capabilities to fly through a predetermined four-dimensional "tunnel" from departure to landing.

GNSS

The **Global Navigation Satellite System (GNSS)** will be the key feature of the future navigation system and it will evolve to be a primary means of navigation. It will very likely be used in conjunction with simplified inertial navigation systems (INS), which are updated by GNSS but can function as a backup, stand-alone system in event of primary system failure. This combination will most likely eventually replace the current long-range and short-range navigation systems. The system will provide global coverage, and without additional ground-based augmentation, will be accurate enough to support enroute navigation and meet nonprecision, and probably (with some ground assistance) precision-type approach needs. *See* Chapter 13 for a description of this combined system as it is now, and as it is anticipated to be.

Precision Approach Aids

Investigations continue into whether or not GNSS can be used as a precision approach aid, and there is the growing acceptance that this is technically feasible. For navigation during the approach and landing phase, there are two basic candidates presently under consideration:

DGNSS. Differential GNSS is an augmentation to GNSS, the purpose of which is to determine position errors at one or more known locations and subsequently transmit derived information to other GNSS receivers, in order to enhance the accuracy of the position estimate. These errors can be introduced into the information transmitted by satellite, by propagation errors or by airborne receiver errors, and can in total exceed the permitted errors for some operations, such as precision approaches. Most of these error sources can be removed using a differential correction technique. A ground station determines the errors in the received signal by virtue of the fact that its actual position is fixed and known. It then broadcasts correction information to all parties in its vicinity. An airborne system, receiving and applying the differential correction data, can refine its position to a higher level of accuracy.

MLS. The Microwave Landing System (MLS) is a precision approach and landing guidance system which provides position information and various ground-to-air data. The position information is provided in a wide-coverage sector It is determined by an azimuth angle measurement, and elevation angle measurement and DME/P (Precision) for range (distance) measurement. Although this system has some valid features, it is this author's guess that MLS will not achieve wide acceptance.

Area Navigation

Area Navigation (RNAV) is a method of navigation which permits the aircraft to navigate along any desired flight path within the coverage of station-referenced navigation aids, or within the limits of the capability of self-contained aids, or a combination of these. Modern aircraft are being increasingly equipped with RNAV, as a separate system, or as a function in the Flight Management System (FMS). The RNAV function operates automatically and determines the aircraft position from one or more varieties of available navigation aids. Distances and along-track information is computed to provide estimated time to a selected point in space, together with a continuous indication of steering guidance.

RNAV operations permit flight in any airspace within prescribed accuracy tolerances, without the need to fly directly over ground-based navigation facilities. Within the RNP concept, RNAV only applies to the lateral navigation, although Vertical Navigation (VNAV) may also be implemented.

Required Navigation Performance (RNP)

The continued growth of aviation places demands on airspace capacity and emphasizes the need for optimum utilization of the available airspace. This, allied with the requirement for operational efficiency of each aircraft, has resulted in the need for aircraft to fly closer together; thus the need for RNP.

RNP as a concept applies to navigation performance within an airspace, and therefore affects both the airspace and the aircraft. RNP is intended to characterize achieved navigation accuracy. The RNP type is based on a navigation performance accuracy value which is expected to be achieved at least 95 percent of the time by the population of aircraft operating within the airspace. RNP can apply from takeoff to landing, with the different phases of flight requiring different RNP types. For example, an RNP type for takeoff and landing may be very stringent, whereas the RNP type for en route may be less demanding. The type of RNP required for a specific flight phase can be determined by the tunnel concept. This concept is already in practice, in the form of MNPS and RVSM.

The Tunnel Concept

The tunnel concept establishes airspace protection criteria based on the low likelihood that aircraft would unintentionally leave the tunnel. The requirement to keep the aircraft in the tunnel is of the RNP type, translated into **accuracy**, **integrity**, **continuity**, and **availability parameters**. These parameters constitute the probability that the aircraft will not leave the tunnel. Departure from the tunnel (assigned airspace) is called a "tunnel incident," and is the factor determining the separation between obstacles and other aircraft. In combination with other factors such as traffic density, flight phase and ability of the controller to detect and intervene, it determines whether the risk goal is met.

For example, for the approach phase, a tunnel incident for an individual aircraft requires that only one occurrence may take place once in a million approaches.

Surveillance

Surveillance is the basic tool the controller uses to monitor the maintenance of safe separation, manage the airspace efficiently, and to assist the pilot in navigating his aircraft safely. In addition, the pilot needs to be aware of proximate aircraft which may represent a collision risk. To fulfill this need, there will be three tools available: Airborne Collision Avoidance System (ACAS), Automatic Dependent Surveillance (ADS), and Secondary Surveillance Radar Mode S (SSR Mode S).

Airborne Collision Avoidance System (ACAS)

ACAS provides back-up to the air traffic services by alerting flight crew of potential collisions. The system is contained entirely onboard the aircraft and is not dependent on any ground-based system. ACAS equipment interrogates SSR transponders in its vicinity and receives transponder replies. By computer analysis of these replies, the ACAS equipment determines which of these aircraft represents potential collision hazards and provides appropriate advisory information to the flight crew to assure separation.

If proximate aircraft are considered to be a potential threat, the ACAS equipment can provide two classes of advisories. Resolution Advisories (RA) are generated to indicate maneuvers that are predicted to maintain or increase separation from threatening aircraft. Traffic Advisories (TA) are provided to indicate the positions of intruding aircraft that may later cause a potential threat.

The present ACAS system does not know the intent of the intruding aircraft. The advisories are generated if the calculated projected profile of the intruder aircraft indicates a potential conflict. The calculation is based on the last three or four interrogations of the proximate aircraft. As a result, ACAS is unaware of the altitude to which a climbing or descending aircraft is cleared and it is possible for RAs to be issued when an intruder is legally separated (per ATC requirements) from the ACAS aircraft.

Automatic Dependent Surveillance (ADS)

The future surveillance system will be characterized by the use of Automatic Dependent Surveillance. The purpose of ADS is to support automatic surveillance of appropriately equipped aircraft, with complete transparency to the controller and pilot regarding the communications mechanism.

ADS is a service for use by ATS in which aircraft automatically transmit via an air-ground data link, aircraft position and intent-related data derived from onboard navigation and position-fixing systems. The ADS service will be provided within an ADS base ATC system, comprising:

- **The airborne ADS function**—formatting the airborne data in ATC required surveillance information.

- **The air-ground data link**—transferring the data from the aircraft to the controlling ATC unit.

- **The ground-based Flight Data Processing System (FDPS)**—collecting and processing the received information to be presented to the controller and to probe for potential conflicts.

In addition, the pilot has the capability to initiate an emergency mode. In this mode, ADS reports will be transmitted at a high fixed rate to support ATC alerting procedures and to assist search and rescue operations. In the emergency mode, the basic ADS block will be transmitted with every report, while the ground vectors will be included in every fifth report.

The day may come when the ADS data is transmitted back up to the aircraft to display for the crew the entire picture of air traffic, and potential conflicts, for collision avoidance purposes. Since intent information will be available, many false conflict warnings will be avoided.

Secondary Radar Surveillance

Since its adoption by ICAO more than twenty years ago, the use of Secondary Surveillance Radar (SSR) for surveillance has spread throughout the world. As traffic increased and more aircraft were equipped with transponders during the 1970s, operation of the SSR system began to encounter saturation difficulties and the need to enhance SSR became imminent. The results of research have provided two methods to enhance SSR and to satisfy future automation requirements at least to the end of the century:

Monopulse. Without requiring modification of system design, the use of monopulse techniques in the ground radar can considerably improve the azimuth accuracy. Since fewer replies are needed to ensure decoding and satisfactory position measurement, this technique permits a reduction in the pulse repetition frequency of ground interrogators. Saturation of the SSR system due to traffic increases therefore may be postponed.

SSR Mode S. A technique using a unique address (the 24 bits ICAO address) for each aircraft, known as SSR Mode S, compatible with the existing SSR modes, has been developed to improve the aircraft identification and provide more aircraft position-related information. The airborne transponder will be required to support Modes A and C as well as Mode S interrogations. Because of the greatly expanded ability of the Mode S system, it may be possible for the aircraft to transmit and receive over this system, data transmissions such as clearances and requests for clearances, weather information, operational messages, and ADS functions.

Visionaries believe that this future system will have the capability to allow aircraft, even in crowded airspace, to fly direct, utilize the airspace efficiently and safely with reduced crew workload—anywhere in the world.

Epilogue

After completing the study of this chapter's subject, the future of air navigation, a pause to reflect may lead the reader to thoughts about the future of the pilots who navigate aircraft in the global system. Again, as mentioned at the beginning of Chapter 16 (Navigation System Errors and Limitations), it appears that the pilot is to become, more and more, a manager of systems. As manager of the navigation system, the human pilot must be capable of sitting in judgement of the navigation systems being used. To do that, he or she must be a navigator—able to understand and use basic navigation such as dead reckoning, as well as understand the errors involved with each system; moreover, how to detect and defeat, as well as avoid those errors. The authors wish you well in these endeavors.

Glossary of Terms

Terms not found in this section should be searched in the index as they are probably defined on the page(s) indicated by the index.

This glossary is divided into two parts: Part 1 covers terminology necessary to the art and science of navigation, and Part 2 is terminology necessary to international operations. (Note that some entries for international organizations include their internet/worldwide-web addresses.)

Part 1: Navigation Terminology

agonic line. A line on a chart joining points of no magnetic variation.

Air Almanac. A joint publication of the U.S. Naval Observatory and British Royal Observatory, covering a four-month period and containing tabulated values of the Greenwich hour angle and the declination of selected celestial bodies, plus additional celestial data used in navigation.

air distance (AD). Distance measured relative to the mass of air through which an aircraft passes; the no-wind distance flown in a given time (TAS x time). Also considers distance increase due to altitude above the earth's surface.

airplot (AP). A continuous plot of a graphic representation of true heading and air distance.

air position (AP). The no-wind position of an aircraft at a given time.

airspeed (AS). The speed of an aircraft relative to its surrounding air mass.

> **calibrated airspeed (CAS).** Indicated airspeed corrected for pitot-static installation errors, and/or the attitude of the aircraft.

> **equivalent airspeed (EAS).** Calibrated airspeed corrected for compressibility-of-air error.

> **indicated airspeed (IAS).** The uncorrected reading obtained from the airspeed indicator.

> **true airspeed (TAS).** Equivalent airspeed corrected for density altitude (variations in pressure and temperature).

airspeed indicator (ASI). An instrument that gives a measure of the rate of motion of an aircraft relative to the surrounding air.

air temperature.

> **basic air temperature (BAT).** Indicated air temperature corrected for the instrument error.

> **corrected mean temperature (CMT).** The average between the target temperature and the true air temperature of flight level.

> **indicated air temperature (IAT).** The uncorrected reading from the free air temperature gauge.

> **true air temperature.** Basic air temperature corrected for the temperature rise due to beat of compression and skin friction. Also known as outside air temperature (OAT).

> **static air temperature (SAT).** The temperature of the static air. Same as ambient temperature and true air temperature.

> **ram air temperature (RAT).** SAT plus temperature rise due to compressibility. Usually considered to be about 80% of TAT. Useful for computing jet engine performance (the temperature "seen" by the jet engine).

> **total air temperature (TAT).** The temperature actually sensed by the temperature probe (BAT). It is ambient temperature plus rise due to compressibility, plus rise due to skin friction.

airway. An air corridor established for the control of traffic and marked with radio navigation aids.

alter course (A/C). A change in course to a destination or a turning point.

alter heading (A/H). The change in heading to make good the intended course.

altimeter. A flight instrument that indicates the altitude above a given reference level or point. Altimeters generally are of two types: absolute and pressure. (*See also* **QNE, QFE, QNH**).

> **absolute altimeter.** The absolute or radar altimeter indicates the altitude above the terrain land or water directly below the aircraft. Operates on the principle of measuring the time for transmission and return of radio-frequency energy.

> **pressure altimeter.** The pressure altimeter uses an aneroid barometer to measure atmospheric pressure. The altimeter is calibrated to indicate feet of altitude above a selected datum plane, according to the ICAO standard atmosphere.

altimeter setting (ALT Set). Station pressure reduced to sea level, expressed in inches of mercury, millibars (MB) or hectopascals (HP). (1 MB = 1 HP). When this value is set into the Kollsman window of the altimeter, the instrument reading is indicated true altitude.

altitude. The vertical distance of a level, a point, or an object considered as a point, measured from a given surface.

> **absolute altitude.** The altitude above the terrain directly below the aircraft.

> **calibrated altitude.** Indicated altitude corrected for instrument and installation error.

> **celestial altitude.** Angular distance of a celestial body above the celestial horizon, measured along the vertical circle. *See* Chapter 17.

> **computed altitude (H_C).** A mathematical computation of the correct celestial altitude of a body at a specific geographic position, for a given date and time. This method helps navigators quickly find a specific celestial body.

> **density altitude pressure.** Altitude corrected for nonstandard temperature. Pressure and density altitudes are the same when conditions are standard (refer to standard atmosphere table). As the temperature rises above standard, the density of the air decreases; hence an increase in density altitude.

> **flight level.** A surface of constant atmospheric pressure related to the standard datum plane. In practice, a calibrated altitude maintained with a 29.92" Hg reference on the barometric scale.

> **indicated altitude.** Altitude displayed on the altimeter.

> **observed altitude (H_O).** The sextant altitude corrected for sextant and observation errors.

> **precomputed altitude (H_P).** Computed celestial altitude corrected for all known observational errors and adjusted to the time of the observed altitude.

> **pressure altitude.** The altitude above the standard datum plane. This standard datum plane is where the air pressure is 29.92 in. Hg (corrected to plus 15°C).

> **sextant altitude (H_S).** A celestial altitude measured with a sextant; the angle measured in a vertical plane between an artificial or sea horizon and a celestial body.

> **true altitude calibrated.** Altitude corrected for nonstandard atmospheric conditions. Actual height above mean sea level.

Aries, first point of. The point on the equinoctial where the sun moving along the ecliptic passes from south to north declination. Also known as vernal equinox.

assumed position (AP). The geographic position upon which a celestial solution is based.

astronomical triangle. A triangle on the celestial sphere bounded by the observer's celestial meridian, the vertical circle, and the hour circle through the body, which has as its vertices the elevated pole, the observer's zenith, and the body.

azimuth angle (Z). The interior angle of the astronomical triangle at the zenith measured from the observer's meridian to the vertical circle through the body.

azimuth stabilization. Orientation of the picture on a radarscope which places true north at the top of the scope.

azimuth, true (Zn). The angle at the zenith measured clockwise from true north to the vertical circle passing through the body.

base line. The line joining the master and slave LORAN stations.

base line extension. The extension of the base line through and beyond the master and slave LORAN stations.

beacon. A ground navigational light, radio, or radar transmitter used to provide aircraft in flight with a signal to serve as a reference for the determination of accurate bearings or positions.

beam width. The effective width in azimuth of radiation from an antenna.

beam width error. An azimuth distortion of a radar beam display caused by the width of the radar beam.

bearing. The horizontal angle at a given point, measured clockwise from a specific reference datum, to a second point. The direction of one point relative to another, as measured from a specific reference datum.

> **magnetic bearing (NM).** The horizontal angle at a given point, measured from magnetic north clockwise, to the great circle through the object or body and the given point.

> **relative bearing (RB).** The horizontal angle at the aircraft measured clockwise from the true heading of the aircraft, to the great circle containing the aircraft and the object or body.

> **true bearing (TB).** The horizontal angle at a given point measured from the true north clockwise, to the great circle passing through the point and the object or body.

Bellamy drift. The net drift angle of the aircraft calculated between any two pressure soundings.

celestial equator. The great circle formed by the intersection of the plane of the Earth's equator with the celestial sphere. Also known as the equinoctial.

celestial meridian. A great circle on the celestial sphere formed by the intersection of the celestial sphere and any plane passing through the North and South Poles. Any great circle on the celestial sphere which passes through the celestial poles.

celestial navigation. *See* **navigation aids, celestial.**

celestial observation errors (sextant).

> **acceleration error.** An error caused by deflection of the liquid in the bubble sextant's chamber due to any change in speed or direction of the aircraft during the observation.

> **Coriolis error.** The error introduced in a celestial observation taken in flight, resulting from the deflective force on the liquid in the bubble chamber caused by the path of the aircraft which adds to or subtracts from the rotation of the earth.

> **index error.** An error caused by the misalignment of the sighting mechanism of the sextant.

> **parallax error.** An error caused by the difference between a celestial body's altitude above an artificial or visible horizon, and above the celestial horizon. This error is introduced when a celestial body (sun, moon) is not at an infinite distance from the observer.

> **personal error.** Errors in celestial observations caused by sighting limitations of the observer (for example, "the shakes"), or visual interpretation variances by the observer in collimating the body during observations.

> **refraction error.** An error caused by the bending of light rays when passing through the various layers of the atmosphere.

> **refraction error.** An error caused by the bending of light rays when passing through the various layers of the atmosphere.

celestial poles. The points of intersection of the extension of the Earth's axis with the celestial sphere.

celestial sphere. An imaginary sphere of infinite radius whose center coincides with the center of the Earth, upon which all celestial bodies except Earth are imagined to be projected.

chart. A graphic representation of a section of the Earth's surface specifically designed for navigational purposes. A chart is sometimes incorrectly referred to as a map. Although a chart is usually specifically designed as a plotting medium for marine or aerial navigation, it may be devoid of cultural or topographical data. *See also* **map.**

check point. A geographical reference point used for checking the position of an aircraft in flight. As generally used, it is a well-defined reference point easily discernible from the air. Its exact position is known or plotted on the navigational chart, and was selected in preflight planning for this purpose.

circles. In celestial concepts and navigation:

> **circle of equal altitude.** A circle on the Earth which is the locus of all points equidistant from the subpoint of a celestial body. The altitude of a celestial body is the same measured from any point on the circle.

> **diurnal circle.** The daily apparent path of a body on the celestial sphere caused by the rotation of the Earth.

> **great circle.** Any circle on a sphere whose plane passes through the center of that sphere.

> **hour circle.** A great circle on the celestial sphere passing through the celestial poles and a given celestial body.

> **small circle.** Any circle on a sphere whose plane does not pass through the center of that sphere.

> **vertical circle.** A great circle that passes through the observer's zenith, nadir, and a body on the celestial sphere.

coast-in point. A point reached by an aircraft when flying from seaward, where land-based VHF navigation and communication signals can be received. Point of departure from NAT airspace.

coast-out point. A point reached by an aircraft when flying to seaward, where land-based VHF navigation and communication signals can no longer be received. Point of entry into NAT airspace.

co-altitude (co-alt). The small arc of a vertical circle, between the observer's position and the body (90°-altitude).

co-declination (co-dec). *See* **polar distance**.

co-latitude (co-lat). The small arc of the observer's celestial meridian, between the elevated pole and the body (90°-latitude).

collimation. The correct alignment of the images of the bubble of a sextant and the object being observed.

compass. An instrument which indicates direction measured clockwise from true north, magnetic north or grid north.

> **direct indicating.** A magnetic compass in which the dial, scale, or index is carried on the sensing element.

> **remote indicating.** A magnetic compass, the magnetic sensing unit of which is installed in an aircraft in a position as free as possible from causes of deviation. A transmitter system is included so that the compass indication can be read on a number of repeater dials suitably placed throughout the aircraft.

compass direction. The direction measured clockwise from a particular compass needle which is more often than not displaced from the magnetic meridian by local deviating magnetic fields.

compass rose. A graduated circle on an instrument, a map, chart or the ground, marked in degrees clockwise from 0° through 360° for use as a reference in measuring bearings and courses.

conformality. The characteristic of a chart projection that refers to how properly azimuth, land mass, shape, and accuracy of latitude and longitude are depicted. (*See* Pages 26 – 43 in Chapter 3.)

constellation. A recognizable group of stars by means of which individual stars may be identified.

contour lines. Lines drawn on maps and charts joining points of equal elevation; also, a line connecting points of equal altitude on a constant pressure chart.

controlled time of arrival. A method of arriving at a destination at a specified time by changing direction and/or speed of an aircraft.

control point. The position an aircraft must reach at a predetermined time.

coordinates.

> **celestial (1).** The equinoctial system involves the use of sidereal hour angle and declination to locate a point on the celestial sphere with reference to the first point of Aries and the equinoctial.

> **celestial (2).** The horizon system involves the use of azimuth and altitude to locate a point on the celestial sphere for an instant of time from a specific geographical position on the Earth.

> **celestial (3).** The Greenwich system involves the use of Greenwich hour angle and declination to locate a point on the celestial sphere with reference to the Greenwich meridian and the equinoctial for a given instant of time.

> **geographical.** The latitude and longitude system used to locate any given point on the surface of the Earth.

> **grid.** A system of coordinates in which the area concerned is divided into rectangles which are in turn subdivided, and in which the subdivisions or the dividing grid lines are designated by numbers and/or letters to serve as references in locating positions or small areas. Also, a rectangular grid or fictitious chart graticule which is oriented with grid north.

> **polar.** A system of coordinates used in locating a point by direction and distance from an origin.

> **rectangular.** A system of coordinates based on a rectangular grid; sometimes referred to as grid coordinates.

Coriolis error. *See* **celestial observation errors**.

Coriolis force. An apparent force due to the rotation of the Earth which causes a moving body to be deflected to the right in the northern hemisphere, and to the left in the southern hemisphere.

course. The direction of the intended path of an aircraft over the Earth; or, the direction of a line on a chart representing the intended aircraft path. Expressed as the angle measured from a specific reference datum clockwise from 0° through 360° to the line.

> **great-circle course.** The route between two points on the Earth's surface measured along the shorter segment of the circumference of the great circle between the two points. A great-circle course establishes the shortest distance over the surface of the Earth between any two terrestrial points.

> **grid course.** The horizontal angle measured clockwise from grid north to the course line. The course of an aircraft measured with reference to the north direction of a polar grid.

magnetic course (MC). The horizontal angle measured from the direction of magnetic north clockwise to a line representing the course of the aircraft. The aircraft course measured with reference to magnetic north.

true course (TC). The angle measured clockwise from true north to the line representing the intended path of the aircraft.

course line. A line of position which is parallel or approximately parallel to the track of the aircraft. A line of position used to check aircraft position relative to intended course.

crab. A correction of the aircraft heading into the wind to make good a given track; correction for wind drift.

cruise control. The operation of an aircraft to obtain the maximum efficiency on a particular mission (most miles per amount of fuel).

"D" sounding. The difference between pressure altitude and true altitude as determined at a given time in flight (true altitude minus pressure altitude).

datum. Refers to a direction, level, or position from which angles, heights, depths, speeds, or distances are conventionally measured.

day, civil. The interval of time between two successive lower transits of a meridian by the mean (or civil) sun.

day, sidereal. The interval of time between two successive upper transits of a meridian by the first point of Aries (23 hours 56 minutes).

day, solar. The interval of time between two successive lower transits of a meridian by the true (apparent) sun.

dead reckoning. The directing of an aircraft and determining of its position by the application of direction and speed data to a previous position.

dead-reckoning (DR) position. The position of an aircraft determined for a given time by the application of direction and speed data only.

declination (dec). The angular distance to a body on the celestial sphere measured north or south through 90°, from the celestial equator along the hour circle of the body (comparable to latitude).

deviation (dev). Compass error caused by the magnetism within an aircraft; the angle measured from magnetic north eastward or westward to the direction of the Earth's lines of magnetic force as deflected by the aircraft's magnetism.

deviation correction. The correction applied to a compass reading to correct for deviation error. The numerical equivalent of deviation with the algebraic sign added to magnetic heading to obtain compass heading.

dip, celestial. The angle of depression of the visible sea horizon due to the elevation of the eye of the observer above the level of the sea.

dip, magnetic. The vertical displacement of the compass needle from the horizontal caused by the Earth's magnetic field.

diurnal circles. *See* circles.

dog leg. A route containing a major alteration of course (as opposed to a straight-line course.)

double drift (DD). A method of determining the wind by observing drift on an initial true heading and two other true headings flown in a specific pattern. Also called multiple drift.

drift. The rate of lateral displacement of the aircraft by the wind, generally expressed in degrees.

drift angle. The angle between true heading and track (or true course) expressed in degrees right or left, according to the way the aircraft has drifted.

drift correction (DC). Correction for drift, expressed in degrees (plus or minus), and applied to true course to obtain true heading.

driftmeter. An instrument used for measuring drift.

ecliptic. The great circle on the celestial sphere along which the apparent sun, by reason of the Earth's annual revolution, appears to move. The plane of the ecliptic is tilted to the plane of the equator at an angle of 23°27'.

effective air distance (EAD). The distance measured along the effective air path.

effective air path (EAP). A straight line on a navigation chart connecting two air positions, commonly used between the air positions of two pressure soundings to determine effective true airspeed (ETAS) between the two soundings.

effective true airspeed (ETAS). The effective air distance divided by the elapsed time between two pressure soundings.

Electronic Flight Information System (EFIS). Displays all flight, navigation, and weather radar information on two or three CRTs. Consists of displays, user controls, and data input interfaces to flight computer, radar and navigation systems.

elevated pole. The celestial pole on the same side of the equinoctial as the position of the observer.

ephemeris. Great circle path scribed on the celestial sphere by the passage of a celestial body or satellite. The path or predicted path of a satellite.

equal altitude. *See* **circles**.

equation of time. The amount of time by which the mean sun leads or lags behind the true sun at any instant. The difference between mean and apparent times expressed in units of solar time with the algebraic sign, so that when added to mean time it gives apparent time.

equator. The great circle on the Earth's surface equidistant from the poles. Latitude is measured north and south from the equator.

equinoctial. *See* **celestial equator**.

equinox, autumnal. The point on the equinoctial at which the sun, moving along the ecliptic, passes from north to south declination. This usually occurs on 20-23 September.

equinox, vernal. The point on the equinoctial at which the sun, moving along the ecliptic, passes from south to north declination. This usually occurs on 20-23 March.

ETE. Estimated time enroute. *See also* **EET** (in Glossary Part 2).

field-elevation pressure. The existing atmospheric pressure in inches of mercury at the elevation of the field. Also known as station pressure, ambient pressure.

fix. The geographic position of an aircraft for a specified time, established by navigational aids. The intersection of two LOPs.

flight plan. Predetermined information for the conduct of a flight. The portion of a flight log prepared before the mission.

georef. An international code reference system for reporting geographic position (similar to rectangular coordinates).

geostrophic wind. The mathematically calculated wind which theoretically blows parallel to the contour lines, in which only pressure-gradient force and Coriolis force are considered.

gradient wind. Generally accepted as the actual wind above the friction level, influenced by Coriolis force, pressure gradient, and centrifugal force.

graticule. A system of vertical and horizontal lines that is used to divide a drawing, picture, etc., into smaller sections. On a chart, the graticule consists of the latitude and longitude lines.

Greenwich meridian. The prime meridian which passes through Greenwich, England, and from which longitude is measured east or west.

grid navigation. A method of navigation using a grid overlay for direction determination.

grivation (griv). The angle between grid north and magnetic north at any point.

ground plot. A graphic representation of track and ground speed.

ground range. The horizontal distance from the subpoint of the aircraft to an object on the ground.

ground return. The reflection from the terrain as displayed on a CRT.

ground speed (GS). The actual speed of an aircraft relative to the Earth's surface.

ground wave. A radio wave propagated over the surface of the Earth which tends to parallel the Earth's surface.

heading. The angular direction of the longitudinal axis of an aircraft measured clockwise from a reference point.

> **compass heading (CH).** The reading taken directly from the compass.

> **grid heading (GH).** The heading of an aircraft with reference to grid north.

> **magnetic heading (MH).** The heading of an aircraft with reference to magnetic north.

> **true heading (TH).** The heading of an aircraft with reference to true north.

heat of compression error. The error caused by the increase in the indication of the free air temperature gauge, due to air compression.

hertz (Hz). The standard unit notation for measure of frequency in cycles per second; i.e., 60 cycles per second is 60 Hz.

homing. A technique of arriving over a destination by keeping the aircraft headed toward that point by reference to radio, LORAN, radar, or similar devices.

horizon. In celestial navigation:

> **bubble horizon.** An artificial horizon parallel to the celestial horizon, established by means of a bubble level.

> **celestial horizon.** The great circle on the celestial sphere formed by the intersection of a plane passing through the center of the Earth which is parallel to the plane tangent to the Earth at the observer's position.

visible horizon. The circle around the observer where Earth and sky appear to meet. Also called natural horizon or sea horizon.

hour angle. In measurement of celestial coordinates:

Greenwich hour angle (GHA). The angular distance measured from the upper branch of the Greenwich meridian westward through 360°, to the upper branch of the hour circle passing through a body.

local hour angle (LHA). The angular distance measured from the upper branch of the observer's meridian westward through 360°, to the upper branch of the hour circle passing through a body.

sidereal hour angle (SHA). The angular distance measured from the upper branch of the hour circle of the first point of Aries westward through 360°, to the upper branch of the hour circle passing through a body.

hour circle. *See* **circle**.

IFIM. International Flight Information Manual, a document published by the FAA, which is a resource for information about visas and passports, national security, North Atlantic routes and entry airports and requirements for each country in the world.

index error. *See* **celestial observation error**.

inherent distortion. The distortion of the display of a received radar signal caused by the design characteristics of a particular radar set.

initial point (IP). A preselected geographical position used as a reference for the beginning of a run on a target.

intercept, celestial. The difference in minutes of arc between an observed altitude of a celestial body and its computed altitude for the same time. This difference is measured as a distance in nautical miles from the plotting position along the azimuth of the body, to determine the point through which to plot the line of position.

international date line. The anti-meridian of Greenwich, modified to avoid island groups and land masses. In crossing this anti-meridian there is a change of local date.

isobar. A line joining points of equal pressure.

isogonic line (isogonal). A line drawn on a chart joining points of equal magnetic variation.

isogriv. A line drawn on a chart joining points of equal grivation.

isotach. A line drawn on a chart joining points of equal wind speed.

isotherm. A line drawn on a chart joining points of equal temperature.

knots (k). Nautical miles per hour.

landfall. The first point of land over which an aircraft crosses when flying from seaward; also, as used in celestial navigation, the procedure in which an aircraft is flown along a celestial line of position which passes through the destination.

lateral axis. An imaginary line running through the center of gravity of an aircraft, parallel to the straight line through both wing tips.

latitude (lat.). Angular distance measured north or south of the equator along a meridian, 0° through 90°.

line of constant bearing. A line or course with unchanging directional relationship between two moving objects.

line of position (LOP). A line containing all possible geographic positions of an observer at a given instant of time.

log. A written record of computed or observed flight data; generally applied to the written navigational record of a flight.

longitude (lon.). The angular distance east or west of the Greenwich meridian, measured in the plane of the equator or of a parallel from 0° to 180°.

longitudinal axis. An imaginary line running fore and aft through the center of gravity of an aircraft, from nose to tail of the aircraft.

LORAN. *See* **navigation aid**.

lubber line. A reference mark on a compass or other instrument representing the longitudinal axis of the aircraft.

Mach number. The ratio of the velocity of a body to that of sound in the medium in which the craft is moving.

magnetic direction. A direction measured clockwise from a magnetic meridian.

map. A planar depiction of the location of specific features but lacking accuracy and/or proper scalar relationships of geographic features that is found on a chart. Air and marine navigation is done with charts.

map reading. *See* **navigation aid**.

map symbols. Figures and designs used to represent topographical, cultural, and aeronautical features on a map or chart.

marker beacons. Radio beacons established at range stations, along airways, and at intermediate points between range stations to assist pilots and observers in fixing position.

marker beacons. (*continued*)

fan-type. A 75-MHz radio transmitter usually installed at strategic points along a radio range across the on-course signal. The signal is produced in a space shaped like a thick fan immediately above the transmitter. The signal may be received visually or aurally, depending on the receiver.

m-type. A low-powered, nondirectional radio station which transmits a characteristic signal once every few seconds. The range of the receiver is approximately 10 miles.

master station. The primary or control transmitter station, the signal of which triggers the transmitter of one or more other stations. Also a transmitter station, the signals of which are used by other stations as a basis for synchronizing transmissions.

mean sea level (MSL). The average level of the sea, used to compute barometric pressure.

mean sun. An imaginary sun traveling around the equinoctial at the average annual rate of the true sun.

meridional part. A unit of measurement equal to 1 minute of longitude at the equator.

minimum flight path. A path which affords the shortest possible time en route, obtained by using maximum assistance from the winds.

most probable position (MPP). The computed position of an aircraft determined by comparing a DR position and an LOP, or a fix of doubtful accuracy determined for the same time, in which relative weights are given to the estimated probable errors of each.

nadir. The point on the celestial sphere directly beneath the observer's position.

nautical mile (NM). A unit of distance used in navigation, approximately 6,080 feet; the mean length of 1 minute of longitude on the equator; approximately 1 minute of latitude; 1.15 statute miles.

navigation aid. Any means of obtaining a fix or LOP as an aid to dead reckoning.

celestial. The determination of position by reference to celestial bodies.

consol/consolan. A rotating radio-signal system used for long-range bearings (nearly obsolete).

LORAN. *See* Chapter 12.

map reading. The determination of position by identification of landmarks with their representations on a map or chart.

pilotage. The process of determination of position by identification of landmarks with their representations on a map or chart.

pressure differential. The determination of the average drift, or the crosswind component of the wind effect on the aircraft for a given period, by taking "D" soundings and applying the formula:

$$Zn = K\,(D_2 - D_1)\,/\,ETAS$$

where —

Zn = cross wind component

K = Coriolis constant

ETAS = effective true airspeed

D_1 and D_2 = values of the pressure soundings

radar. The determination of position by obtaining information from a radar indicator.

radio. The determination of position by the use of radio facilities.

north, compass. The direction indicated by the north-seeking end of a compass needle.

north, grid (GN). An arbitrarily selected direction of a rectangular grid. In grid navigation, the direction of the 180° geographical meridian from the pole is almost universally used as standard grid north.

north, magnetic (MN). The direction towards the north magnetic pole from an observer's position.

north, true (TN). The direction from an observer's position to the geographical North Pole. The north direction of any geographical meridian.

paralax error. *See* **celestial observation errors**.

personal error. *See* **celestial observation errors**.

pitch. Movement of an aircraft around the lateral axis.

pitot. A cylindrical tube with an open end, pointed upstream; used in measuring impact pressure, particularly in an airspeed indicator.

pitot-static tube. A parallel or coaxial combination of a pitot and static tube. The difference between the impact pressure and the static pressure is dynamic pressure, a function of the velocity of flow past the tube; this may be used to indicate airspeed of an aircraft in flight.

polar distance. Angular distance from a celestial pole or the arc of an hour circle between the celestial pole and a point on the celestial sphere. It is measured along an hour circle and may vary from 0° to 180°, since either pole may be used as the origin of measurement. It is usually considered the complement of declination, though it may be either 90° − declination, or 90° + declination, depending upon the pole used.

precession.

> **apparent.** The apparent deflection of the gyro axis, relative to the Earth, due to the rotating effect of the Earth and not due to any applied forces.

> **induced (real).** The movement of the aids of a spinning gyro when a force is applied, usually due to friction in the gimbal bearings. The gyro precesses 90° from the point of applied pressure in the direction of rotation.

> **of the equinox.** The average yearly apparent movement of the first point of Aries to the west.

precomputed curve. A graphical representation of the azimuth and/or altitude of a celestial body plotted against time for a given assumed position (or positions), and which is computed for subsequent use for celestial observations. Used in celestial navigation for the determination of position, or to check a sextant.

pressure altitude variation (PAV). The pressure difference, in feet, between mean sea level and the standard datum plane.

pressure line of position (PLOP). A line of position computed by the application of pressure pattern principles. Specifically, a line parallel to the effective air path and Zn distance from the air position for a given time. *See* **navigation aid.**

projection (chart, map). A process of mathematically constructing a representation of the surface of the Earth on a flat plane.

QFE. A "Q" signal (originating from the "Q" signals used with teletype and Morse code) indicating an altimeter setting that causes the altimeter to read zero feet elevation at the elevation of the landing point, regardless of the altitude of the airport. For example, if the altimeter setting is 30.10 inches at an airport where the field elevation is 1,000 feet, setting 29.10" in the Kollsman window would cause the altimeter to read zero when the aircraft lands. 30.10" would be the QNH setting.

QNE. An altimeter setting of 29.92", causing the altimeter to read pressure altitude. Used at higher altitudes where terrain clearance is not an issue, to ensure that all aircraft are operating with the same altimeter setting.

QNH. Altimeter setting to correct for nonstandard pressure, to cause the altimeter to read a close approximation of true altitude for terrain clearance.

quadrantal error. The error in a radio direction indicator (ADF) introduced by the bending of radio waves by electrical currents, and the structural metal in the aircraft. It may also refer to magnetic-compass errors resulting from the same causes.

radio compass (ADF). A radio receiver equipped with a rotatable loop antenna, used to measure the bearing to a radio transmitter.

radio frequency (RF). Any frequency of electrical energy above the audio range capable of being radiated into space.

radio navigation. *See* **navigation aid.**

radius of action. The maximum distance that an aircraft can fly from its base before returning to the same or alternate base and still have a designated margin of fuel.

radome. A bubble-type cover for a radar antenna.

range control. The operation of an aircraft to obtain the optimum flying time.

range, maximum. The maximum distance a given aircraft can cover under given conditions by flying at the economical speed and altitude at all stages of the flight.

revolution (of the Earth). The Earth's elliptical path about the sun which determines the length of the year and causes the seasons.

rhumb line. A line on the surface of a sphere which makes equal oblique angles with all meridians. A loxodromic curve.

rotation (of the Earth). The spinning of the Earth from the west to the east on its own axis which determines the days.

running fix. A fix determined from a series of lines of position, based on the same object or body and resolved for a common time.

semidiameter (SD). The value in minutes of arc of the radius of the sun or the moon.

sextant. An optical instrument normally containing a two-power telescope with a 15° field of vision. It also contains a series of prisms geared to an altitude scale permitting altitude measurement of a celestial body from -10° below the horizon to 92° above the horizon.

sky waves. A radio signal reflected one or more times from the ionosphere, capable of long distance communication from one location on or near the earth to another. Not capable of traveling through the ionosphere to outer space. Not dependable for navigation purposes.

slant range. Measurement of range along the line of sight.

slave station. The station of a network which is controlled or triggered by the signal from the master station.

solstice. Those points on the ecliptic where the sun reaches its greatest northern or southern declination. Also, the times when these phenomena occur.

    summer. The point on the ecliptic at which the sun reaches its greatest declination having the same name as the latitude.

    winter. The point on the ecliptic at which the sun reaches its greatest declination having the opposite name as the latitude.

speed line. A line of position that intersects the track at an angle great enough to be used as an aid in determining ground speed.

standard lapse rate.

    temperature. A temperature decrease of approximately 2° Celsius or 3.5°F for each 1,000-foot increase in altitude.

    pressure. A decrease in pressure of approximately 1 in. Hg for each 1,000 feet.

star magnitude. A measure of the relative apparent brightness of stars.

statute mile. 5,280 feet, or .867 NM.

subpoint. The point on the Earth's surface directly beneath an object or celestial body.

sun line. A line of position obtained by computation based on observation of the altitude of the sun for a specific time.

time. *See also* Chapter 15.

    apparent time. Time measured with reference to the true sun. The interval which has elapsed since the last lower transit of a given meridian by the true sun.

    Greenwich apparent time (GAT). Local time at the Greenwich meridian measured by reference to the true sun. The angle measured at the pole or along the equator or equinoctial (and converted to time), from the lower branch of the Greenwich meridian westward through 360°, to the upper branch of the hour circle passing through the true (apparent) sun.

    Greenwich mean time (GMT). Local time at the Greenwich meridian measured by reference to the mean sun. The angle measured at the pole or along the equator or equinoctial (and converted to time), from the lower branch of the Greenwich meridian westward through 360°, to the upper branch of the hour circle through the mean sun.

    Greenwich sidereal time (GST). Local sidereal time at Greenwich. Equivalent to the Greenwich hour angle of Aries converted to time.

    local apparent time (LAT). Local time at the observer's meridian measured by reference to the true sun. The angle measured at the pole or along the equator or equinoctial (and converted to time), from the lower branch of the observer's meridian westward through 360°, to the upper branch of the hour-circle passing through the true (apparent) sun.

    local mean time (LMT). Local time at the observer's meridian measured by reference to the mean sun. The angle measured at the pole or along the equator or equinoctial (and converted to time), from the lower branch of the observer's meridian westward through 360°, to the upper branch of the hour circle through the mean (or average) sun.

    local sidereal time (LST). Local time at the observer's meridian measured by reference to the first point of Aries. Equivalent to the local hour angle of Aries converted to time.

    mean time. Time measured by reference to the mean sun.

    sidereal time. Time measured by reference to the upper branch of the first point of Aries.

    standard time. An arbitrary time, usually fixed by the local mean time of the central meridian of the time zone.

    zone time. The time used through a 15° band of longitude. The time is based on the local mean time for the center meridian of the zone.

    Z or Zulu Time. An expression indicating Greenwich mean time. Usually expressed in four numerals (0001 through 2400).

time zone. A band on the Earth approximately 15° of longitude wide, the central meridian of each zone generally being 15° or a multiple, removed from the Greenwich meridian so that the standard time of successive zones differs by one hour.

temperature. *See* **air temperature**.

track (Tr). The actual path of an aircraft over the surface of the Earth, or its graphic representation; also called track made good.

transmissometer. An instrument system that measures the transmissibility, or passage, of light through the atmosphere, and manually or automatically transmits the data measured.

twilight. That period of day, after sunset or before sunrise, when the observer receives sunlight reflected from the atmosphere. *See* end of Chapter 17 for a full discussion.

astronomical twilight. The period ending in the evening and beginning in the morning, when the sun reaches 18° below the horizon.

civil twilight. The period ending in the evening and beginning in the morning, when the sun reaches 6° below the horizon.

nautical twilight. The period ending in the evening and beginning in the morning, when the sun reaches 12° below the horizon.

variation (var). The angle difference at a given point between true north and magnetic north, expressed as the number of degrees to which magnetic north is displaced east or west from true north. The angle to be added algebraically to true directions to obtain magnetic directions.

wind. Moving air, especially a mass of air having a common direction or motion. The term is generally limited to air moving horizontally or nearly so; vertical streams of air are usually called currents. *See also* **geostrophic** and **gradient wind.**

wind direction and force. The direction from which, and the rate at which, the wind blows.

wind direction and velocity (W/V). Wind direction and speed. Wind direction is the direction from which the wind is blowing expressed as an angle measured clockwise from true north. Wind speed is generally expressed in nautical miles or statute miles per hour. In countries using the metric system, v is expressed in KM/HR.

year, apparent solar. The period of time between two successive passages of the mean sun through the first point of Aries. It has a mean value of 365 days, 05 hours, 48.75 minutes. This period contains one complete cycle of the seasons and is less than the sidereal year, owing to the precession of the equinoxes.

year, sidereal. The period of time between two successive passages of the sun across a fixed position among the stars. Its value is constant, and equal to 366 days 06 hours 09 minutes, a true measure of the Earth's period of orbital revolution.

zenith. The point on the celestial sphere directly above the observer's position.

zenith distance (ZD). The angular distance from the observer's position to any point on the celestial sphere, measured along the vertical circle passing through the point. It is equivalent to co-altitude, but when applied to a body's subpoint and the observer's position on the Earth, it is expressed in nautical miles.

Zn (Pressure Pattern Displacement). In pressure-pattern flying, the displacement in nautical miles at right angles to the effective airpath, due to the crosswind component of the geostrophic wind.

Part 2:
International Operations
Terminology

aerial work. An aircraft operation in which an aircraft is used for specialized services such as agriculture, construction, photography, surveying, observation and patrol, search and rescue, aerial advertisement, etc.

aerodrome. A defined area on land or water (including any buildings, installations, and equipment) intended to be used either wholly or in part for the arrival, departure, and surface movement of aircraft.

aerodrome operating minima. The limits of usability of an aerodrome for either takeoff or landing, usually expressed in terms of visibility or runway visual range, decision altitude/height (DA/H), or minimum descent altitude/height (MDA/H) and cloud conditions.

Aeronautical Information Publication (AIP). Publication issued by or with the authority of a state, containing aeronautical information of a lasting character essential to air navigation.

Aeronautical Radio, Inc. (ARINC). A corporation largely owned by a group of airlines, and licensed as an aeronautical station. ARINC is contracted by the VA to provide communications support for air traffic control and meteorological services in portions of international (usually oceanic) airspace.

Aeronautical Telecommunications Station (ATS). An aeronautical station that forms part of a radio telephone network by providing air/ground communications and flight information service as an integral part of air traffic services. Aeronautical Telecommunications Stations are also known as International Flight Service Stations, Aeronautical Radio, or aeradio stations depending on the state providing the service.

aircraft equipment. Articles, other than stores and spare parts of a removable nature, for use on board an aircraft during flight, including first-aid and survival equipment.

airline. As provided in Article 96 of the Convention, any air transport enterprise offering or operating a scheduled international air service.

airline and operators' documents. Air waybills/consignment notes, passenger tickets and boarding passes, bank and agent settlement plan documents, excess baggage tickets, miscellaneous charges orders (M.C.O.), damage and irregularity reports, baggage and cargo labels, timetables, and weight and balance documents, for use by airlines and operators.

air route traffic control center (ARTCC). A facility established to provide air traffic control service to aircraft operating on IFR flight plans within controlled airspace, principally during the enroute phase of flight. When equipment capabilities and controller workload permit, certain advisory/assistance services may be provided to VCR aircraft. An ARTCC is the U. S. equivalent of an area control center (ACC).

air traffic services (ATS). A generic term meaning variously, flight information service, alerting service, air traffic advisory service, air traffic control service, area control service, approach control service, or airport control service.

area control center (ACC). An ICAO term for an air traffic control facility primarily responsible for providing ATC services to IFR aircraft in controlled areas under its jurisdiction. An ACC is the international equivalent of an air route traffic control center (ARTCC).

area navigation (RNAV). LORAN-C, INS, GPS, etc.; a method of navigation which permits aircraft operation on any desired flight path within the coverage of station-referenced navigation aids, or within the limits of the capability of a self-contained navigation system, or a combination of these.

authorized agent. A responsible person who represents an operator and who is authorized by or on behalf of that operator, to act on all formalities connected with the entry and clearance of the operator's aircraft, crew, passengers, cargo, mail, baggage, or stores.

baggage. Personal property of passengers or crew carried on an aircraft by agreement with the operator.

cargo. Any property carried on an aircraft other than mail, stores, and accompanied or mishandled baggage.

control area (CTA). A controlled airspace extending upwards from a specified limit above the earth.

crewmember. A person assigned by an operator to duty on an aircraft during flight time.

dangerous goods. Articles or substances capable of posing significant risk to health, safety or property when transported by air.

direct transit area. A special area established in connection with an international airport, approved by the public authorities concerned and under their direct supervision, for accommodation of traffic which is pausing briefly in its passage through the contracting state.

direct transit arrangements. Special arrangements approved by the public authorities concerned by which traffic, pausing briefly in its passage through the contracting state, may remain under their direct control.

disembarkation. The leaving of an aircraft after a landing, except by crew or passengers continuing on the next stage of the same through-flight.

disinsecting. The operation in which measures are taken to kill the insect vectors of human disease present in aircraft and in containers (*International Health Regulations* (1969), Third Annotated Edition (1983), Part I, Article 1).

EET. Estimated elapsed time. Similar to **ETE** but used as EET in ICAO flight plans, European operations, and by pilots who fly internationally.

embarkation. The boarding of an aircraft for the purpose of commencing a flight, except by such crew or passengers as have embarked on a previous stage of the same through-flight.

EUROCONTROL. Title of the organization of European countries that administer the CFMU (Central Flow Management Unit), which is in charge of operating the flow of air traffic throughout the area of the member states of ECAC (*see* Pages 182 – 183 of Chapter 9). *See also* http://www.eurocontrol.be

flight crewmember. A licensed crew member charged with duties essential to the operation of an aircraft during flight time.

flight information center (FIC). A unit established to provide flight information service and alerting service in a specified geographic area.

flight information region (FIR). An airspace of defined dimensions within which flight information service and alerting services are provided.

flight information service. Provided for the purpose of giving advice and information useful for the safe and efficient conduct of flights.

flight level (FL). A plane of constant atmospheric pressure which is related to a specific pressure datum (i.e., standard pressure—29.92" Hg or 1,013 HP), and is separated from other such surfaces by specific pressure intervals. Each is stated in three digits that represent hundreds of feet (i.e., FL060 = 6,000 feet).

flight time. The total time from the moment an aircraft first moves under its own power for the purpose of taking off until the moment it comes to rest at the end of the flight.

Note: Flight time as here defined is synonymous with the term "block to block" time or "chock to chock" time in general usage, which is measured from the time the aircraft moves from the loading point until it stops at the unloading point.

free airport. An international airport at which, provided they remain within a designated area until removal by air to a point outside the territory of the state, crew, passengers, baggage, cargo, mail, and stores may be disembarked or unladen, may remain and may be trans-shipped, without being subjected to any customs charges or duties and to any examination, except for aviation security or for appropriate narcotics control measures.

free zone. An area where merchandise, whether of domestic or foreign origin, may be admitted, deposited, stored, packed, exhibited, sold, processed or manufactured, and from which such merchandise may be removed to a point outside the territory of the state without being subjected to customs duties, internal consumer taxes or to inspection except for aviation security or for appropriate narcotics control measures. Merchandise of domestic origin admitted into a free zone may be deemed to be exported. When removed from a free zone into the territory of the state, the merchandise is subjected to customs and other required entry procedures.

general aviation operation. An aircraft operation other than a commercial air transport operation or an aerial work operation.

ground equipment. Articles of a specialized nature for use in the maintenance, repair, and servicing of an aircraft on the ground, including testing equipment and cargo- and passenger-handling equipment.

hectopascals (HP). A metric system reference of pressure, significant in that one HP is equivalent to one millibar. Used to set altimeters in countries using the metric system.

high frequency communications (HF). Radio frequencies between 3 and 30 MHz used for air/ground voice and cw communications in overseas operations. HF is required for all IFR operations in controlled airspace when out of the range of VHF communications. If in doubt as to the VHF coverage along the intended route of flight, the aircraft should be equipped with HF.

inadmissible person. A person who is or will be refused admission to a state by its authorities.

infected area. Defined on epidemiological principles by the health administration reporting the disease in its country and need not correspond to administrative boundaries. It is that part of its territory which, because of population characteristics, density, and mobility and/or vector and animal reservoir potential, could support transmission of the reported disease (*International Health Regulations* (1969), Third Annotated Edition (1983), Part I, Article 1). A list of infected areas notified by health administrations is published in the World Health Organization's Weekly Epidemiological Record.

international airport. Any airport designated by the contracting state in whose territory it is situated as an airport of entry and departure for international air traffic, where the formalities incident to customs, immigration, public health, animal and plant quarantine and similar procedures are carried out.

International Air Transport Association (IATA). The international trade association of the airline industry, based in Montreal, Quebec. (*See* http://www.iata.org)

International Civil Aviation Organization (ICAO). A specialized agency of the United Nations whose objective is to develop the principles and techniques of international air navigation, and to foster planning and development of international civil air transport. (*See* http://www.cam.net/~icao)

international general aviation (IGA). All international civil aviation operations other than scheduled air services and nonscheduled air transport operations for remuneration or hire.

lading. The placing of cargo, mail, baggage or stores on board an aircraft to be carried on a flight, except such cargo, mail, baggage, or stores as have been laden on a previous stage of the same through-flight.

light aircraft. Aircraft with a maximum takeoff weight of 12,500 lbs or less.

mail. Dispatches of correspondence and other objects tendered by and intended for delivery to postal administrations.

minimum navigation performance specifications (MNPS). A specified set of minimum navigation performance standards which aircraft must meet in order to operate in MNPS-designated airspace. In addition, aircraft must be certified by their State of Registry for MNPS operation. The objective of MNPS is to ensure the safe separation of aircraft and to derive maximum benefits generally through reduced separation standards, from the improvement in accuracy of navigation equipment developed in recent years.

minimum navigation performance specification airspace (MNPSA). The portion of the NAT airspace between FL280 and FL420, extending between latitude 27°N and the North Pole; bounded in the east by the eastern boundaries of control areas Santa Maria Oceanic, Shanwick Oceanic, and Reykjavik, and in the west by the western boundary of CTA Reykjavik, the western boundary of CTA Gander Oceanic, and the western boundary of CTA New York Oceanic; excluding the area west of 60°W and south of 38°30'N.

mishandled baggage. Baggage involuntarily, or inadvertently, separated from passengers or crew.

narcotics control. Measures to control the illicit movement of narcotics and psychotropic substances by air.

oceanic area control center (OAC). Any area control center (ACC) with jurisdiction over oceanic airspace for the purpose of providing air traffic services. Responsibility for the provisions of ATS is delegated to various countries based primarily upon geographic proximity and the availability of the required resources.

oceanic airspace. Airspace over the high seas, for which ICAO delegates responsibility for the provision of ATS to various countries.

operator. A person, organization, or enterprise engaged in or offering to engage in an aircraft operation.

pilot-in-command. The pilot responsible for the operation and safety of the aircraft during flight time.

public authorities. The agencies or officials of a contracting state responsible for the application and enforcement of the particular laws and regulations of that state which relate to any aspect of these standards and recommended practices.

reduced vertical separation minimum (RSVM) airspace. That which has been designated by international agreement as airspace in which air traffic control separates aircraft by a minimum of 1,000 feet vertically. In 1998, applies only to airspace over the North Atlantic between the altitudes of FL290 and FL410.

security equipment. Devices of a specialized nature for use, individually or as part of a system, in the prevention or detection of acts of unlawful interference with civil aviation and its facilities.

spare parts. Articles of a repair or replacement nature for incorporation in an aircraft, including engines and propellers.

state of registry. A contracting state on whose register the aircraft is entered.

stores. Articles of a readily consumable nature for use or sale on board an aircraft during flight, including commissary supplies.

temporary visitor (visitor). Any person who disembarks and enters the territory of a contracting state other than that in which that person normally resides; remains there lawfully as prescribed by that contracting state for legitimate non-immigrant purposes, such as touring, recreation, sports, health, family reasons, study, religious pilgrimages, or business; and does not take up any gainful occupation during his stay in the territory visited.

through-flight. A particular operation of aircraft, identified by the operator by the use throughout of the same symbol, from point of origin via any intermediate points to point of destination.

unaccompanied baggage. Baggage that is transported as cargo and may or may not be carried on the same aircraft with the person to whom it belongs.

unclaimed baggage. Baggage that arrives at an airport and is not picked up or claimed by a passenger.

unidentified baggage. Baggage at an airport with or without a baggage tag, which is not picked up by or identified with a passenger.

unlading. The removal of cargo, mail, baggage, or stores from an aircraft after a landing, except cargo, mail, baggage, or stores continuing on the next stage of the same through-flight.

very high frequency (VHF). The frequency band between 30 and 300 MHz. Portions of this band, 108 to 118 MHz, are used for certain NAVAIDs, while 118 to 136 MHz are used for civil air/ground voice communications.

visitor. *See* **temporary visitor**.

Appendix

Readings in International Etiquette and Customs

Newsletter of the Global Institute of Languages and Culture.
Barnett Bank Center, 300 S. Pine Island Road, Ste.239, Plantation FL 33324. Phone: 305-424-1461. Worldwide web address: http://www.globalin@gate.net

Culturgrams. (157 countries)
At Brigham Young University, Phone: 800-528-6279. Worldwide web address: http://www.byu.edu culturgrams

Business and Social Etiquette with Disabled People: A Guide to Getting Along with Persons Who Have Impairments of Mobility, Vision, Hearing, or Speech.
Chalda Maloff and Susan Macduff Wood; foreword by Mel Tillis. Springfield, IL: C.C. Thomas, 1988. LCC# HV3011.M23 1988

Going International: How to Make Friends and Deal Effectively in the Global Marketplace.
Lennie Copeland and Lewis Griggs. New York: Random House, 1985. (First edition.) Includes bibliographical references and index. LCC# HD62.4. C66 1984

The Little Black Book of Business Etiquette.
Michael C. Thomsett. New York: AMACOM, 1991. (Little black book series.) LCC# HF5389.T48 1991

"Pardon Me, Your Manners Are Showing!": Professional Etiquette, Protocol & Diplomacy.
Bruce Gjovik. Grand Forks, ND: Center for Innovation and Business Development, University of North Dakota, 1992. LCC# BJ1853.G54 1992

When in Rome… : a Business Guide to Cultures & Customs in 12 European Nations.
John Mole. New York: American Management Association, 1991. LCC# HD70.EG M65 1991

For blank **ICAO Flight Plan form** which can be photocopied for practice and study, see the next page.

FLIGHT PLAN
Plan de vol

PRIORITY
Priorité

ADDRESSEE(S)
Destinataire(s)

<<≡FF →

<<≡

FILING TIME
Heurs de dépôt

ORIGINATOR
Expéditeur

→

<<≡

SPECIFIC IDENTIFICATION OF ADDRESSEE(S) AND/OR ORIGINATOR
Identification précise du(des) destinataire(s) et/ou de l'expéditeur

3 MESSAGE TYPE
Type de message

7 AIRCRAFT IDENTIFICATION
Identification de l'aéronet

8 FLIGHT RULES
Règles de voi

TYPE OF FLIGHT
Type de voi

<<≡(FPL

<<≡

9 NUMBER
Nombre

TYPE OF AIRCRAFT
Type d'aéronet

WAKE TURBULENCE CAT.
Cat. de turbulence de sillage

10 EQUIPMENT
Équipement

/

/

<<≡

13 DEPARTURE AERODROME
Aérodrome de départ

TIME
Heurs

<<≡

15 CRUISING SPEED
Vitesse croisière

LEVEL
Niveau

ROUTE
Route

→

<<≡

16 DESTINATION AERODROME
Aérodrome de destination

TOTAL EET
Durée totale estimée

HR.   MIN.

ALTN AERODROME
Aérodrome de dégagement

2ND. ALTN AERODROME
2ème aérodrome de dégagement

→

→

<<≡

18 OTHER INFORMATION
Renseignements autre

)<<≡

SUPPLEMENTARY INFORMATION (NOT TO BE TRANSMITTED IN FPL MESSAGES)
Renseignements complémentaives (À NE PAS TRANSMETTRE DANS LES MESSAGES DE PLAN DE VOL DÉPOSÉ)

19 ENDURANCE
Autonomie

HR.   MIN.

PERSONS ON BOARD
Personnes á bord

EMERGENCY RADIO
Radio de secours

— E /

→ P /

UHF   VHF   ELBA

→ R / U V E

SURVIVAL EQUIPMENT / Équipement de survie

JACKETS / Gilet de sauvetage

POLAR
Polaire

DESERT
Désert

MARITIME
Maritime

JUNGLE
Jungle

LIGHT
Lampes

FLUORES
Fluores

UHF   VHF

→ S / P D M J

→ J / L F U V

DINGHIES / Canots

NUMBER
Nombre

CAPACITY
Capacite

COVER
Couverture

COLOUR
Couleur

→ D / → → C →

<<≡

AIRCRAFT COLOUR AND MARKINGS
Couleur et marques de l'aeronet

A /

REMARKS
Remarques

→ N /

<<≡

PILOT-IN-COMMAND
Pilote commandant de bord

C /

)<<≡

FILED BY / Depose par

SPACE RESERVED FOR ADDITIONAL REQUIREMENTS
Espace reserve a ces fins supplementaires

Index